V&R Academic

Studia Aarhusiana Neotestamentica (SANt)

Edited by
Eve-Marie Becker, Ole Davidsen, Jan Dochhorn,
Kasper Bro Larsen and Nils Arne Pedersen

Volume 3

Kasper Bro Larsen (ed.)

The Gospel of John as Genre Mosaic

Vandenhoeck & Ruprecht

Bibliographic information published by the Deutsche Nationalbibliothek
The Deutsche Nationalbibliothek lists this publication in the Deutsche Nationalbibliografie; detailed bibliographic data available online: http://dnb.dnb.de.

ISSN 2364-2165
ISBN 978-3-525-53619-3

You can find alternative editions of this book and additional material on our Website: www.v-r.de

Typesetting by Konrad Triltsch GmbH, Ochsenfurt
Printed and bound by Hubert & Co GmbH & Co. KG, Robert-Bosch-Breite 6, 37079 Göttingen

Printed on aging-resistant paper.

Contents

Abbreviations

AB	Anchor Bible
AcBib	Academia Biblica
AGWB	Arbeiten zur Geschichte und Wirkung der Bibel
AnBib	Analecta biblica
ANRW	*Aufstieg und Niedergang der römischen Welt: Geschichte und Kultur Roms im Spiegel der neueren Forschung.* Edited by H. Temporini and W. Haase. Berlin: Walter de Gruyter, 1972–
ASH	Ancient Society and History
ATANT	Abhandlungen zur Theologie des Alten und Neuen Testaments
BBB	Bonner biblische Beiträge
BDR	*Friedrich Blass, Albert Debrunner, and Friedrich Rehkopf.* Grammatik des neutestamentlichen Griechisch. 16. ed. Göttingen: Vandenhoeck & Ruprecht, 1984
BETL	Bibliotheca ephemeridum theologicarum lovaniensium
BHHB	Baylor Handbook on the Hebrew Bible
Bib	Biblica
BibInt	*Biblical Interpretation*
BIS	Biblical Interpretation Series
BJRL	*Bulletin of the John Rylands University Library of Manchester*
BNTC	Black's New Testament Commentaries
BRLJ	Brill Reference Library of Judaism
BRS	The Biblical Resource Series
BTB	*Biblical Theology Bulletin*
BThS	Biblisch Theologische Studien
BTS	Biblical Tools and Studies
BZ	*Biblische Zeitschrift*
BZAW	Beihefte zur Zeitschrift für die alttestamentliche Wissenschaft
BZNW	Beihefte zur Zeitschrift für die neutestamentliche Wissenschaft
CBC	Cambridge Bible Commentary

CBQ	*Catholic Biblical Quarterly*
CNT	Commentaire du Nouveau Testament
ConBNT	Coniectanea Biblica: New Testament Series
ConBOT	Coniectanea Biblica: Old Testament Series
CRINT	Compendia Rerum Iudaicarum ad Novum Testamentum
DNP	*Der neue Pauly: Enzyklopädie der Antike.* Edited by H. Cancik and H. Schneider. Stuttgart: J. B. Metzler, 1996–2003
DSD	*Dead Sea Discoveries*
EvT	*Evangelische Theologie*
ExpTim	*Expository Times*
FCNTECW	Feminist Companion to the New Testament and Early Christian Writings
FRLANT	Forschungen zur Religion und Literatur des Alten und Neuen Testaments
HbS	Herders biblische Studien
HDR	Harvard Dissertations in Religion
HNT	Handbuch zum Neuen Testament
HThKNT	Herders theologischer Kommentar zum Neuen Testament
HTR	*Harvard Theological Review*
IBC	Interpretation: A Bible Commentary for Teaching and Preaching
ICC	International Critical Commentary
ITQ	*Irish Theological Quarterly*
JBL	*Journal of Biblical Literature*
JETS	*Journal of the Evangelical Theological Society*
JJS	*Journal of Jewish Studies*
JSJSup	Journal for the Study of Judaism Supplement Series
JSNT	*Journal for the Study of the New Testament*
JSNTSup	Journal for the Study of the New Testament: Supplement Series
JSOTSup	Journal for the Study of the Old Testament: Supplement Series
JTS	*Journal of Theological Studies*
KEK	Kritisch-exegetischer Kommentar über das Neue Testament (Meyer-Kommentar)
LCL	Loeb Classical Library
LEC	Library of Early Christianity
LNTS	The Library of New Testament Studies
LS	*Louvain Studies*
LXX	Alfred Rahlfs, ed. *Septuaginta: Id est vetus testamentum graec iuxta lxx interpretes.* 2 vols. Stuttgart: Priviligierte Württembergische Bibelanstalt, 1935

NA[28]	*Nestle-Aland: Novum Testamentum Graece*. Edited by the Institute for New Testament Textual Research, Münster. 28th revised edition. Stuttgart: Deutsche Bibelgesellschaft, 2012
NASB	New American Standard Bible
NCB	New Century Bible
NHS	Nag Hammadi and Manichaean Studies
NovT	*Novum Testamentum*
NovTSup	Supplements to Novum Testamentum
NRSV	*The HarperCollins Study Bible: New Revised Standard Version*. Edited by Wayne A. Meeks. New York: HarperCollins, 1993
NTAbh	Neutestamentliche Abhandlungen
NTGr	Neue Theologische Grundrisse
NTL	The New Testament Library
NTS	*New Testament Studies*
NTTS	New Testament Tools and Studies
OBO	Orbis Biblicus et Orientalis
ÖTK	Ökumenischer Taschenbuch-Kommentar
OTL	Old Testament Library
PNTC	Pelican New Testament Commentaries
PRSt	*Perspectives in Religious Studies*
QD	Quaestiones Disputatae
RAC	*Reallexikon für Antike und Christentum*. Edited by Theodor Klauser et al. Stuttgart: Hiersemann, 1950–
RNT	Regensburger Neues Testament
RPP	*Religion Past and Present: Encyclopedia of Theology and Religion*. Edited by Hans Dieter Betz et al. 14 vols. Leiden: Brill, 2007–2013
SA	Studia Anselmiana
SBB	Stuttgarter biblische Beiträge
SBLDS	Society of Biblical Literature Dissertation Series
SBLMS	Society of Biblical Literature Monograph Series
SBLSBS	Society of Biblical Literature Sources for Biblical Study
SBLSymS	Society of Biblical Literature Symposium Series
SBS	Stuttgarter Bibelstudien
SDSS	Studies in Dead Sea Scrolls & Related Literature
SemeiaSt	Semeia Studies
Sémiotique	*Sémiotique: Dictionnaire raisonné de la théorie du langage*. Edited by Algirdas Julien Greimas and Joseph Courtés. Langue, Linguistique, Communication. Paris: Hachette, 1979
SNTA	Studiorum Novi Testamenti Auxilia
SNTSMS	Society for New Testament Studies Monograph Series
SNTSU	Studien zum Neuen Testament und seiner Umwelt

SP	Sacra Pagina
SQAW	Schriften und Quellen der alten Welt
STAC	Studien und Texte zu Antike und Christentum
TBT	*The Bible Today*
TDNT	*Theological Dictionary of the New Testament.* Edited by Gerhard Kittel and Gerhard Friedrich. Translated by Geoffrey W. Bromiley. 10 vols. Grand Rapids: Eerdmans, 1964–76
THKNT	Theologischer Handkommentar zum Neuen Testament
TQ	*Theologische Quartalschrift*
TS	*Theological Studies*
TSAJ	Texte und Studien zum antiken Judentum
TZ	*Theologische Zeitschrift*
UTB	Uni-Taschenbücher
VC	*Vigiliae Christianae*
WBC	Word Biblical Commentary
WGRW	Writings from the Greco-Roman World
WUNT	Wissenschaftliche Untersuchungen zum Neuen Testament
ZBK	Zürcher Bibelkommentare
ZKT	*Zeitschrift für katholische Theologie*
ZNT	*Zeitschrift für Neues Testament*
ZNW	*Zeitschrift für die neutestamentliche Wissenschaft und die Kunde der älteren Kirche*
ZTK	*Zeitschrift für Theologie und Kirche*

Preface

The present volume is a study of the Fourth Gospel in light of ancient and modern genre theories and practices. The core of the book consists of a selection of papers from the conference *The Gospel of John as Genre Mosaic*, which took place at Aarhus University (Denmark) on 23–26 June 2014. In addition, a number of other international Johannine scholars with a special interest in John and genre have agreed to contribute to the book. The editor expresses his sincere gratitude to all contributors—and not only as a matter of complying with generic conventions!

The conference commenced exactly one year ago on the Eve of St. John—the Baptist, that is—with a keynote lecture by Professor Harold W. Attridge (Yale University) and a beautiful celebration of Midsummer with bonfires at the wooden boats marina in Aarhus. As the organizer of the conference, I wish to thank all conference participants for stimulating papers and inspiring discussions during the following days. A word of thanks is also extended to the conference assistants Anne Pedersen and Gitte Grønning Munk, who made it possible for the rest of us to focus on what we came for: scholarship. Further information on the conference is available on the website of the *Research Unit in New Testament Studies* at Aarhus University (http://nt.au.dk).

The conference was generously sponsored by the *Danish Council for Independent Research* (FKK), the research program *Christianity and Theology in Culture and Society*, and the *School of Culture and Society* at Aarhus University. The present publication was made possible by a substantial grant from the *Aarhus University Research Foundation* (AUFF). I wish to thank all the benefactors who made the project possible.

Finally, a word of appreciation is due to Copy Editor Moritz Reissing and Dr. Elke Liebig at Vandenhoeck & Ruprecht publishers in Göttingen for a smooth and professional publication process.

Kasper Bro Larsen — Aarhus, the Eve of St. John, 2015

Kasper Bro Larsen

Introduction: The Gospel of John as Genre Mosaic

1. John and Genre: From Form Criticism to Genre Criticism

In recent decades Johannine scholarship has developed an increasing interest in how the Fourth Gospel interacts with literary conventions of genre and form in its ancient Jewish and Greco-Roman context. A new exegetical genre criticism has emerged, which is not so much focused on the early formation of the Jesus tradition, nor on generic classification, but on how genre perspectives permit new insights on the Gospel in terms of ideology, theology, and social location. This interest in generic conventions and transformations regards the Johannine Gospel as a whole (for instance, *bios*,[1] drama,[2] historiographical writing,[3] and novel)[4] as well as the various generic parts that contribute to the Gospel, for

1 References in the present and the following footnotes identify conspicuous and recent examples of studies engaging in different aspects of John and genre. On John's Gospel (and the gospels) as *bios*, see Clyde Weber Votaw, *The Gospels and Contemporary Biographies in the Greco-Roman World* (Philadelphia: Fortress, 1970); Christopher H. Talbert, *What Is a Gospel? The Genre of the Canonical Gospels* (Philadelphia: Fortress, 1971); David E. Aune, *The New Testament in its Literary Environment*, LEC (Philadelphia: Westminster, 1987), 46–76; and Richard A. Burridge, *What Are the Gospels? A Comparison with Graeco-Roman Biography*, SNTSMS 70 (Cambridge: Cambridge University Press, 1992).

2 Jo-Ann A. Brant, *Dialogue and Drama: Elements of Greek Tragedy in the Fourth Gospel* (Peabody: Hendrickson, 2004); George L. Parsenios, *Departure and Consolation: The Johannine Farewell Discourses in Light of Greco-Roman Literature*, NovTSup 117 (Leiden: Brill, 2005); and idem, *Rhetoric and Drama in the Johannine Lawsuit Motif*, WUNT 258 (Tübingen: Mohr Siebeck, 2010).

3 Richard Bauckham, "Historiographical Characteristics of the Gospel of John," *NTS* 53 (2007): 17–36; idem, *The Testimony of the Beloved Disciple: Narrative, History, and Theology in the Gospel of John* (Grand Rapids: Baker Academic, 2007).

4 Lawrence M. Wills, *Quest of the Historical Gospel: Mark, John and the Origins of the Gospel Genre* (London: Routledge, 1997); Jo-Ann A. Brant, "Divine Birth and Apparent Parents: The Plot of the Fourth Gospel," in *Ancient Fiction and Early Christian Narrative*, ed. Ronald F. Hock, J. Bradley Chance, and Judith Perkins, SBLSymS 6 (Atlanta: Scholars, 1998), 199–211.

example, prologue,[5] dialogue,[6] riddle,[7] betrothal type-scene,[8] miracle narrative,[9] homiletic midrash,[10] forensic oratory,[11] parable,[12] farewell discourse,[13] symposium,[14] *consolationes*,[15] prayer,[16] *ultima verba*,[17] and recognition scene.[18]

5 The secondary literature is immense. Among recent contributions that discuss genre questions are Daniel Boyarin, "The Gospel of the *Memra:* Jewish Binitarianism and the Prologue to John," *HTR* 94 (2001): 243–84 and Matthew Gordley, "The Johannine Prologue and Jewish Didactic Hymn Traditions: A New Case for Reading the Prologue as a Hymn," *JBL* 128 (2009): 781–802.

6 C. H. Dodd, "The Dialogue Form in the Gospels," *BJRL* 37 (1954): 54–67; Paul N. Anderson, "Bakhtin's Dialogism and the Corrective Rhetoric of the Johannine Misunderstanding Dialogue: Exposing Seven Crises in the Johannine Situation," in *Bakhtin and Genre Theory in Biblical Studies*, ed. Roland Boer, SemeiaSt 63 (Leiden: Brill, 2008), 133–59; Johnson Thomaskutty, *Dialogue in the Book of Signs: A Polyvalent Analysis of John 1:19–12:50*, BIS 136 (Leiden: Brill, 2015).

7 Herbert Leroy, *Rätsel und Missverständnis: Ein Beitrag zur Formgeschichte des Johannesevangeliums*, BBB 30 (Bonn: Hanstein, 1968); Tom Thatcher, *The Riddles of Jesus in John: A Study in Tradition and Folklore*, SBLMS 53 (Atlanta: SBL, 2000).

8 P. Joseph Cahill, "Narrative Art in John IV," *Religious Studies Bulletin* 2 (1982): 41–48; Lyle Eslinger, "The Wooing of the Woman at the Well: Jesus, the Reader and Reader-Response Criticism," *Literature and Theology* 1 (1987): 167–83.

9 Ruben Zimmermann, ed., *Kompendium der frühchristlichen Wundererzählungen: Band 1. Die Wunder Jesu* (Gütersloh: Gütersloher Verlagshaus, 2013), 659–777.

10 Peder Borgen. *Bread from Heaven: An Exegetical Study of the Concept of Manna in the Gospel of John and the Writings of Philo.* NovTSup 10. Leiden: Brill, 1965.

11 Harold W. Attridge, "Argumentation in John 5," in *Rhetorical Argumentation in Biblical Texts: Essays from the Lund 2000 Conference*, ed. A. Eriksson, Th. H. Olbricht, and W. Übelacker, Emory Studies in Early Christianity 8 (Harrisburg: Trinity, 2002), 188–99.

12 Ruben Zimmermann, "Are there Parables in John? It is Time to Revisit the Question," *Journal for the Study of the Historical Jesus* 9 (2011): 243–76.

13 Fernando F. Segovia has a fine discussion of the genre of the discourse in idem, *The Farewell of the Word: The Johannine Call to Abide* (Minneapolis: Fortress, 1991), 1–58. For a more recent generic approaches, see Parsenios, *Departure and Consolation*; John Carlson Stube, *A Graeco-Roman Rhetorical Reading of the Farewell Discourse*, LNTS 309 (London: T&T Clark, 2006); Kasper Bro Larsen, "At sige ret farvel: Jesus' afskedstale i genrehistorisk belysning (Joh 13–17)," in *Hvad er sandhed: Nye læsninger af Johannesevangeliet*, ed. Gitte Buch-Hansen and Christina Petterson (Frederiksberg: Alfa, 2009), 85–102; and Ruth Sheridan, "John's Gospel and Modern Genre Theory: The Farewell Discourse (John 13–17) as a Test Case." *ITQ* 75 (2010): 287–299.

14 Harold W. Attridge, "Plato, Plutarch, and John: Three Symposia about Love," in *Beyond the Gnostic Gospels: Studies Building on the Work of Elaine Pagels*, ed. Edward Iricinschi et al., STAC 82 (Tübingen: Mohr Siebeck, 2013), 367–78.

15 Manfred Lang, "Johanneische Abschiedsreden und Senecas Konsolationsliteratur: Wie konnte ein Römer Joh 13,31–17,26 lesen?" in *Kontexte des Johannesevangeliums: Das vierte Evangelium in religions- und traditionsgeschichtlicher Perspektive*, ed. Jörg Frey and Udo Schnelle, WUNT 175 (Tübingen: Mohr Siebeck, 2004), 365–412; Parsenios, *Departure and Consolation.*

16 Carsten Claussen, "Das Gebet in Joh 17 im Kontext von Gebeten aus zeitgenössischen Pseudepigraphen," in Frey and Schnelle, *Kontexte des Johannesevangeliums*, 205–232.

17 Michael Theobald, "Der Tod Jesu im Spiegel seiner 'letzten Worte' vom Kreuz," *TQ* 190 (2010):

Of special inspiration to scholarship during the last decade—and to the present volume—was Harold W. Attridge's presidential address delivered at the 2001 Annual Meeting of the Society of Biblical Literature in Denver, Colorado. Attridge introduced the concept of "genre bending" to Johannine scholarship and raised the following question: "Why does the Fourth Gospel exhibit so much interest in playing with generic conventions, extending them, undercutting them, twisting traditional elements into new and curious shapes, making literary forms do things that did not come naturally to them?"[19]

The present book contains a range of different attempts to discuss and meet the challenge formulated by Attridge. Of course, Attridge was not the first to discuss genre issues in relation to the Fourth Gospel; since the late 1960s such issues have in fact gradually ascended the priority list of Johannine scholarship. But even in the mid-1990s Mark W. G. Stibbe could describe the question of genre as "a surprising 'gap' in Johannine research."[20] Stibbe did not explain *why* the "gap" was surprising—and in fact it is only so to a certain degree. It is of course remarkable that form criticism (*Formgeschichte*) to such a great extent bypassed the Gospel of John during large parts of the 20th century, given the fact that it was a well-established generic method in gospel research.[21] However, the reason for Johannine studies to overlook this gap is not very unexpected since it (as several other tendencies in then-current scholarship) had to do with the extensive influence of Rudolf Bultmann. It is telling that Bultmann's and Dibelius's classic works of form criticism focused on the *Synoptic* Gospels, which they regarded as folkloristic "Kleinliteratur" formed by collective use of traditions. In contrast to the synoptics, John's Gospel was taken to be a carefully crafted work produced by a more skillful mind in regard to both theology and literary artistry, and thus as an individual genius more independent of generic and formal constrains.[22] This

1-31; Kasper Bro Larsen, "*Famous Last Words:* Jesu ord på korset i evangeliernes sammenhæng," *Kritisk Forum for Praktisk Teologi* 111 (2008): 3–11.

18 R. Alan Culpepper, *The Gospel and Letters of John* (Nashville: Abingdon, 1998), 72–86; idem, "Cognition in John: The Johannine Signs as Recognition Scenes," *PRSt* 35 (2008): 251–260; Kasper Bro Larsen, *Recognizing the Stranger: Recognition Scenes in the Gospel of John*, BIS 93 (Leiden: Brill, 2008).

19 Harold W. Attridge, "Genre Bending in the Fourth Gospel," *JBL* 121 (2002): 20.

20 Mark W. G. Stibbe, *John's Gospel* (London: Routledge, 1994), 54. Stibbe, one of the pioneers in narrative exegesis of the Fourth Gospel, attempted to fill the gap by reading John's Gospel in relation to Northrop Frye's theory of four generic archetypes.

21 A useful survey of pre-1980 scholarship on the literary forms in John, leading to a similar conclusion as Stibbe, is presented in Johannes Beutler, "Literarische Gattungen im Johannesevangelium: Ein Forschungsbericht 1919–1980," *ANRW* II 25.3:2506–68. See also the research historical part of Jörg Frey's article in this book, where he touches upon Klaus Berger's rhetorical *neue Formgeschichte* as a later German development (as presented in, for instance, Klaus Berger, *Formgeschichte des Neuen Testaments* [Heidelberg: Quelle & Meyer, 1984], 9–24 and *Einführung in die Formgeschichte*, UTB 1444 [Tübingen: Francke, 1987], 13–18).

22 Dibelius was more explicit than Bultmann concerning their common tendency of contrasting

notion probably lies behind Bultmann's remarkable shift in method from his work on the Synoptic Gospels (form criticism, German: *Formgeschichte*) to his commentary on John (source criticism, German: *Literarkritik*).[23] Whereas form criticism suited the socio-literary study of collective traditions, source criticism (and history of religions) was considered a better method of capturing John's unique theological reception and transformation of existing sources. And since gospel literature as such was understood sui generis, it does not come as a surprise that Johannine scholars for decades regarded questions of form and genre as leading to a dead end as expressed in the following statement by Siegfried Schulz: "Aufs Ganze gesehen stellt die Formgeschichte im Joh-Ev einen toten Zweig dar."[24]

Today the scholarly situation is obviously very different from that of the Bultmann paradigm. Historical exegesis has made the linguistic turn.[25] This certainly affects the way scholars think of genre. Attridge's abovementioned formulations concerning "genre bending" and "playing with generic conventions" disclose an implicit concept of genre that has changed radically since form criticism: from a romanticist or idealistic understanding of genre as restraints and shackles on authorial creativity to a poststructuralist concept of genre as the very laboratory of the literary and theological imagination. (The latter concept is characteristic of this book). Despite these differences in genre theory, however, there are also points of agreement across paradigms. Bultmann and Attridge (and exegetical scholarship in general) agree that John's Gospel represents a particularly creative take on tradition. In the context of scholarship after the linguistic turn, genre criticism has become an important exegetical tool to understand that Johannine take. Genre, in other words, is not only a means of comparing John with other contemporary texts in order to establish similarities, but it is first and foremost a window into the distinctiveness of John's Gospel in terms of theology, ideology, and literary artistry.

---

the collective, formal "Kleinliteratur" of the Synoptic Gospels to John's individual literary art; see Martin Dibelius, *Die Formgeschichte des Evangeliums*, 6th ed. (Tübingen: Mohr Siebeck, 1971; [1st ed.: 1919]), 1–2. On the Synoptic Gospels as "Kleinliteratur," see ibid. and Rudolf Bultmann, *Die Geschichte der synoptischen Tradition*, 7th ed., FRLANT 29 (Göttingen: Vandenhoeck & Ruprecht, 1967 [1st ed.: 1921]), 5.

23 Idem, *Das Evangelium des Johannes*, KEK (Göttingen: Vandenhoeck & Ruprecht, 1941). Bultmann's veneration for John as a theological thinker also becomes evident from the prominent place John held in comparison to the other evangelists in Bultmann's opus on New Testament theology (idem, *Theologie des Neuen Testaments*, Neue Theologische Grundrisse [Tübingen: Mohr Siebeck, 1953]; see, for example, 360).

24 Idem, *Untersuchungen zur Menschensohn-Christologie im Johannesevangelium: Zugleich ein Beitrag zur Methodengeschichte der Auslegung des 4. Evangeliums* (Göttingen: Vandenhoeck & Ruprecht, 1957), 76; cf. 75.

25 Elizabeth A. Clark, *History, Theory, Text: Historians and the Linguistic Turn* (Cambridge: Harvard University Press, 2004).

2. A Mosaic of Tiles: Tiles in the Mosaic

The Gospel of John is a genre mosaic, and the present volume investigates the range of that metaphor. As a mosaic, the Gospel consists of tiles that are known, depending on the terminology we use, as primary/simple genres (Bakhtin), literary forms (*Gattungen*), micro-genres, or type-scenes (Alter). Several examples of such primary/simple genres have been given above, for instance, prologue (John 1:1–18), forensic oratory (John 5; 8), and prayer (John 17). These tiles can be observed closely in isolation, compared with other similar tiles in other works, and have their history reconstructed, but in the context of the composition the tiles are first and foremost contributors to the overall picture—an overall picture which is also on a larger scale related to genre, namely, secondary/complex genres (Bakhtin) or macro-genres such as, for example, *bios*, novel, and tragedy) A crucial exegetical question thus becomes how the tiles and the whole composition interrelate, a question that was made essential to genre theory by Mikhail M. Bakhtin in his discussion of the relation between primary/simple and secondary/complex speech genres.[26] How does the primary/simple genre contribute to and function in the text as a whole, and how does the whole color the primary/simple genre and its traditional ideologies and functions? Questions of this sort are addressed in different ways in this book as scholars discuss the relation between the parts and the whole of the Gospel. The purpose of the contributions is to illustrate how genre critical approaches contribute to an exegetical understanding of John's Gospel.

The generic approaches to Biblical texts in this book generally involve both a historical and a literary dimension as authors work with the Gospel as literature in a historical context. In terms of the literary dimension, however, generic approaches must be differentiated from the "autonomous" literary readings of texts in exegesis inspired by, for instance, New Criticism and structuralist narratology. According to genre critical approaches no text is an island. Texts make sense by relating to other texts in a process of imitation, mimicry, and transformation; and this interrelation over time establishes literary habits and conventions of genre—that are at the same time modified every time they are being used. When we study genre in texts, we are undertaking a comparative task by investigating how texts evoke general conventions of form, content, and function. Genre criticism is thus a "dialogic" (Bakhtin) and an "intertextual" (Kristeva) endeavor, yet not any kind of intertextual enterprise. Some precision may be gained from Gérard Genette's division of intertextuality or transtextuality (which

26 Mikhail M. Bakhtin, "The Problem of Speech Genres," in *Speech Genres and Other Late Essays*, ed. Caryl Emerson and Michael Holquist (Austin: University of Texas Press, 1986), 60–102 (62). See also Sheridan, "John's Gospel and Modern Genre Theory."

is his rather idiosyncratic term to describe the phenomenon) into five different types of which only the fifth has to do with genre: (1) paratextuality, which appears when a given text is attended or surrounded by other texts (for example titles, footnotes, back cover texts); (2) intertextuality proper, which appears when a text contains other texts (for example citations and allusions); (3) metatextuality, which is when a text is about another text (for example commentary and sermon); (4) hypertextuality, where a given text (the hypertext) is grafted upon another text (the hypotext) from which it derives (for example reproductions, fan fiction, rewritten Scripture, the synoptic tradition, and apocryphal gospels); and, finally, (5) architextuality, which relates to conventions of genre and mode established by already existing texts. According to Genette, architextuality (and thus genre) is the most implicit of the types since works (or parts thereof) do not always explicitly declare their generic quality. However, it is just as important as the other types since it to a considerable degree determines the expectations and thus the reception of the reader.[27]

The contributors to the present volume have not been asked to declare allegiance to a particular or a shared genre theory, but there seems to be agreement that genre becomes exegetically stimulating when it is less about taxonomic classification and more about how texts communicate and establish room for interpretation. On this point, exegesis seems to be on par with the main genre theoretical contributions of the 1970s and 1980s.[28] Moreover, there is agreement that "genre bending"—and "genre blending" for that matter—is not only a phenomenon of modern literature but certainly, as is argued in Attridge's contribution to the book, was intrinsic to the production of meaning in ancient Jewish and Greco-Roman literature. John's Gospel, in other words, presupposes a competent author (or authors) and readers socialized into contemporary habits of writing and reading—whether or not we are dealing with conscious use.

27 Gérard Genette, *Palimpsests: Literature in the Second Degree*, trans. Channa Newman and Claude Doubinsky, Stages 8 (Lincoln: University of Nebraska Press, 1997), 1–10. The five types are not mutually exclusive, but are textual strategies that may appear together in a given text. The examples given in parenthesis are partly my own. Genette seems to be paraphrasing Todorov's famous understanding of genre as "models of writing" for authors and "horizons of expectation" for readers (Tzvetan Todorov, "The Origin of Genres," *New Literary History* 8 [1976]: 163).

28 Alastair Fowler, *Kinds of Literature: An Introduction to the Theory of Genres and Modes* (Oxford: Clarendon, 1982), 37 and Carol A. Newsom, "Spying Out the Land: A Report from Genology," in *Seeking Out the Wisdom of the Ancients: Essays Offered to Honor Michael V. Fox on the Occasion of His Sixty-Fifth Birthday*, ed. Ronald L. Troxel et al. (Winona Lake: Eisenbrauns, 2005), 437–50.

3. The Present Volume: Presentation of Contributions[29]

3.1 The Gospel of John and Genre Theory

The contributions to the book are arranged in three main parts. The first main part, "The Gospel of John and Genre Theory," contains two articles discussing the Gospel in relation to both ancient and modern genre theory. Harold W. Attridge, professor at Yale University and Yale Divinity School, Connecticut (USA), opens the volume by asking how "genre matters" in the Gospel of John. Attridge advances his concept of "genre bending" from the 2002 article and argues, as already mentioned, that playful, artistic, and transformative genre practices are not only a modern phenomenon but were common in classical Antiquity as well as in the Hellenistic and Roman periods. John writes in continuance of the Synoptics; but unlike Luke, who created a historicizing gospel, John bends his narrative in the direction of drama (with prologue, irony, "delayed exit," recognition scenes, and identification/catharsis). This generic transformation serves the same purpose as the riddling and symbolic dimensions of the Gospel, which Attridge describes as a narratival "arabesque": to facilitate a transformative encounter between the reader and the risen Christ.

Sune Auken, scholar of literature from the University of Copenhagen (Denmark) and head of its research group in genre studies, introduces recent trends and tenets in genre studies with particular focus on North American rhetorical genre studies (RGS). Whereas *literary* genre studies had its heyday in the 1970s and 80s, genre studies has become a much broader field dealing with habitual and programmed action in everyday language and practice. Genres are "social action" (Carolyn Miller)—an idea that should not strike exegetes as totally alien, given the legacy of form criticism in biblical studies. Auken draws particular attention to concepts such as "genre chain" and "uptake" as potentially fruitful for literary and exegetical study. In the final part of his article, Auken presents a tentative reading of the arrest and the trial before Pilate (John 18–19) in light of these analytical concepts.

3.2 The Mosaic as a Whole

The second main part of the book deals with "The Mosaic as a Whole." As the title indicates, the articles in this part relate genre questions to the *entire* Gospel, discussing questions concerning secondary/complex genre. The approaches

29 In the whole book, Bible quotations in English are from the New Revised Standard Version (NRSV) where nothing else is stated.

range, as far as the editor is concerned, from articles with emic foci on historical genres (Conway, Persenios, and Brant) to those with etic emphases on theoretical genres (Petersen and Davidsen). In the first contribution, Colleen M. Conway, professor of religious studies at Seton Hall University, New Jersey (USA), discusses how Johannine gender ideology relates to the question of the Gospel's genre. Conway approaches the Gospel from various generic perspectives (*bios*, romance, and drama), claiming that the text does not "belong" to a specific genre but simultaneously "participates in" (Derrida) and evokes different contemporary genres. As regards the role of female characters in the Gospel, they are (as in the *bioi*) the narrator's instrument for staging the masculine self-mastery of Jesus. This is a matter of fact even when he appears in the presence of women who speak or act in erotic ways (as in the romances). Female characters confirm the narrative's patriarchal world-view, but nevertheless, in some instances, they represent a socio-cultural "otherness" (as in the dramas), out of which they lend voice to the evangelist's controversial theological ideas.

George L. Parsenios, associate professor at Princeton Theological Seminary, New Jersey (USA), examines the relationship between *diēgēsis* ("narration") and *mimēsis* ("imitation") in the Gospel, i.e., the two modes of discourse famously discussed by Plato in the *Republic.* Parsenios draws attention to examples in ancient narrative (for example, in Thucydides) where the narrator in the course of diegetic narrative becomes unexpectedly absent or silent. When the narrator withdraws, the characters in the story-world are left to interact without the narrator's guiding comments. This creates a mimetic or dramatic effect. In John, such features are particularly present in ch. 1, where Parsenios finds a parallel to the *stichomythia* of ancient tragedy (alternating lines spoken by alternating characters), and in chs. 3 and 14. John's Gospel is thus a narrative that, time and again, lapses into drama.

Anders Klostergaard Petersen, professor of the study of religion at Aarhus University (Denmark), seeks to determine the distinct character of the Fourth Gospel vis-à-vis the Synoptic Gospels in terms of genre and mode. In discussion with previous attempts like Ernst Käsemann's "naïve docetism" and Kasper Bro Larsen's "narrative docetism," Petersen advocates for "generic docetism" as a proper description of the Johannine gospel. In John, narrative development is reduced to a minimum, and the voice of Jesus in the story-world and of the implied author on the discourse level, respectively, have become so unison that the Gospel virtually ceases to be a narrative (in the narratological sense, with reference to Genette and Greimas). By means of the Johannine miracle stories as primary examples, Petersen argues that in John's Gospel the discourse (enunciation) has in fact appropriated the story-world (enunciate). John thus undermines the "narrative Christology" of the Synoptic Gospels in order to present a "discursive Christology."

Ole Davidsen, associate professor at Aarhus University (Denmark), discusses the Gospel of John in light of universal and cross-cultural genres of narrative. Taking Aristotle to be an "early narratologist" (in the *Poetics*), Davidsen understands the Gospel as *mythos* and further specifies: It is a religious narrative ("fiction") with a propositional truth-claim ("history"). Davidsen then applies Patrick Colm Hogan's cognitive anthropological theory of the existence of three cross-culturally dominant and prototypical narrative genres in human culture: the heroic tragicomedy, the sacrificial tragicomedy, and the romantic tragicomedy. In Davidsen's reading, John's plot is a blend of all three genres since Jesus acts as heroic protagonist competing for power ("the Lord"), as sacrificial scapegoat ("the Lamb"), and as philial or romantic companion ("the Lover"). According to Davidsen, the Gospel's participation in these universal genres may even help to explain the Gospel's cross-cultural and cross-historical success.

In the final contribution to the first main part of the book, Jo-Ann A. Brant, professor of Bible, religion, and philosophy at Goshen College, Indiana (USA), brings John's Gospel into conversation with the ancient novels. Brant neither claims that the Gospel *is* a novel nor that it is directly dependent on them—most novels are later than the Gospel—but they share propensities that throw light on John's particular way of narrating the gospel. Brant focuses on two points: The novels have, in contrast to epic, a "Menippean" tendency toward satire or parody, a tendency which is also present in the Johannine bending of generic conventions and synoptic traditions. The second point relates to novelized time, where Brant observes that the novels and John's Gospel share a more complex use of time (subjectivity, layers of time) than is generally custom in the biographies. According to Brant, it is thus reasonable to talk of elements of "novelization" (Bakhtin) in the Fourth Gospel.

3.3 Tiles in the Mosaic

The third and final main part of the book is also the largest. It contains a number of case studies of "Tiles in the Mosaic," i.e., various primary/simple genres or literary forms ("Gattungen") that contribute to the larger Gospel text. Contributions focus on specific genres and pericopes—from "exegetical narrative" and *peristaseis* in the prologue to the final recognition type-scenes in chs. 20–21—but they also discuss how these individual parts relate and contribute to the Gospel as a whole.

In the first case study, Ruth Sheridan, research fellow at Charles Sturt University, New South Wales (Australia), presents a reading of the Johannine prologue, not as a didactic hymn, but in continuation of and critical evaluation of Peter Borgen's and Daniel Boyarin's interpretation of the prologue as homiletic midrash. Sheridan understands the prologue as an "exegetical narrative" (Joshua Levinson) of Genesis and Exodus. The prologue retells the biblical story and encourages the reader to hold together in dialogue the interpreted Biblical narrative (the Genesis and Exodus narratives) and the interpreting Christological narrative (the Johannine Jesus narrative). According to Sheridan, however, the dialogue between the narratives ultimately serves a monologic rhetorical purpose in John's textual community vis-à-vis its opponents.

The second case study is also on the prologue. Douglas Estes, assistant professor at South University, South Carolina (USA), discusses the prologue in light of conventions of beginning in ancient narrative. According to Estes, the prologue is carefully crafted in accordance with the so-called *peristaseis (circumstantiae)* discussed in ancient rhetoric since Hermagoras of Temnos in the mid-2nd century BCE: *who*, *what*, *when*, *where*, *why*, *in what way*, and *by what means* (*quis*, *quid*, *quando*, *ubi*, *cur*, *quem ad modum*, and *quibus adminiculis*). According to Estes, John approaches and guides the implied reader from the very outset of his Gospel by answering these basic questions—in order to elaborate on them in the course of the subsequent narrative.

In his article, Jörg Frey, professor at University of Zurich (Switzerland), turns toward miracle stories. He argues that John has transformed miracle stories into *sēmeia* narratives in light of the Gospel's overall purpose of communicating, from a post-Easter perspective, a "significant" deep-level narrative about Jesus and his salvific works. In the course of his argument, Frey offers a research-historical survey of the "miracle narratives" genre in Johannine scholarship, and presents a reading of the first prototypical sign (the wedding at Cana, 2:1–11), the paradigmatic healing of the man born blind (9:1–41), the signs of John 20, as well as a discussion of how the cross (i. e., the death and resurrection of Jesus) plays the role of ultimate sign or the designatum of all other signs. The *sēmeia* narratives are, according to Frey, exemplary narratives of the Johannine gospel narrative in its totality.

Tyler Smith, doctoral candidate at Yale University, presents a theoretical discussion of the concept of type-scene, which was introduced to Biblical studies by Robert Alter in *The Art of Biblical Narrative* (1981). Smith discusses the concept in relation to John 4 ("betrothal type-scene") and develops a critique of the "list-of-features" and "family-resemblance" approaches to type-scenes found in Alter and subsequent Johannine scholarship. Looking to research in the cognitive sciences on the construction of categories in general, Smith suggests prototype theory as more helpful and precise way of talking about the type-scene in John 4. According to Smith, prototype theory better captures the way type-scenes function for primary audiences and allows for degrees of participation in a given type-scene (more or less resemblance with the prototype), avoiding the binary logic of earlier standard approaches (either participation or not). Smith argues that Genesis 29 (Jacob and Rachel) is the best prototype for a primary readership in a genre-oriented reading of John 4.

In his article, David Svärd, doctoral candidate at Lund University (Sweden), offers a reading of the anointing of Jesus (John 12:1–8) in light of royal anointing scenes in the Hebrew Bible and the Septuagint. Svärd reconstructs the pattern of the type-scene with its ten recurrent generic elements—this would probably qualify as a list-of-features approach in the terminology of the previous author—and contends that the fourth evangelist employed and twisted this pattern in order to substantiate his presentation of Jesus as the royal Messiah. John bends the genre and thus indicates how Jesus' kingship differs from that of predecessors such as Saul, David, and Jehu. Mary of Bethany's anointing of Jesus depicts him as a spiritual temple and as the bridegroom Messiah who is about to display a new kind of authority in his death and resurrection.

Eve-Marie Becker, professor at Aarhus University (Denmark), asks how the Fourth Gospel revises early Christian historiography. Her answer to the question takes the form of a reading of the footwashing scene in John 13:1–20. Becker understands the scene as a Johannine attempt at establishing a so-called "counter memory" (Foucault) that not only omits, but also suppresses and substitutes previous memories, in this case particularly the Lukan memory of the Last Supper. Whereas Luke represents an institutional approach to history-writing, John writes exemplary history (*hypodeigma*). John's Gospel thus embodies a certain kind of historiography that attacks and subverts existing memories in the mnemonic culture of early Christianity.

In his contribution, Troels Engberg-Pedersen, professor at the University of Copenhagen, argues that the unity, structure, and coherence of the farewell discourse in John 13:31–17:26 becomes clear when seen through a particular generic lens: *paraklēsis.* Engberg-Pedersen describes the text as a farewell discourse that engages in *paraklēsis* taken in the double sense also known from Paul: (1) "comfort encouragement" concerning the disciples' understanding in the presence and (2) "exhortation encouragement" concerning the disciples' behavior in the future. In the rhetorical *propositio* of the speech (13:31–35), both aspects are introduced and the speech subsequently alternates between the two: 13:36–14:31 (comfort encouragement), 15:1–16:15 (exhortation encouragement), 16:16–33 (comfort encouragement), and finally 17:1–26 (exhortation encouragement). It is the Spirit-Paraclete that holds the different aspects and time horizons of Johannine *paraklēsis* together.

Ruben Zimmermann, professor at Johannes Gutenberg University in Mainz (Germany) and research associate at the University of the Free State, Bloemfontein (South Africa), investigates one of the Gospel's most overlooked parables, the parable of the woman in labor in John 16:21. In the course of the article, Zimmermann expresses criticism of the general neglect of parables in Johannine scholarship since Jülicher, presents a definition of the parable as a generic family of necessary and optional elements, argues that John 16:21 complies with the definition, situates the parable's metaphorical language in the textual and cultural context, and finally offers a catalogue of open interpretations of the parable (for instance, christological, feminist, and anthropological interpretations)—in compliance with the nature of the parable genre.

The volume's final paper, by Kasper Bro Larsen, associate professor at Aarhus University (Denmark), seeks to demonstrate how the recognition type-scenes (*anagnōriseis*) of the Gospel tend to have a reciprocal structure comparable to so-called "double recognition" in Aristotle and ancient narrative and drama. When Jesus identifies human characters (for example, Nathanael, the Samaritan woman, and Mary Magdalene), they recognize him. The pervasive Johannine language of reciprocity and mutuality, in other words, not only contains *ontological* and *ethical* dimensions, but also a *cognitive* dimension: "I know my own, so my own know me" (10:14, Larsen's translation). This "covenantal epistemology" of divine action and human *re*action, well-known from biblical tradition and central to the Gospel's understanding of God and human beings, is played out and dramatized in the Johannine recognition scenes.

This introductory chapter has presented the general research questions and the content of the present book. As mentioned, it is the purpose of the book to show how genre critical approaches, in all their variety, contribute to Johannine studies. Genre critical approaches provide a map of literary, ideological, and theological possibilities that were available to John—and identify the particular paths he chose to follow. However, this book does not close the longstanding "gap" of form and genre criticism in Johannine scholarship; on the contrary, it serves as an invitation to further research and conversation on John and genre. The epilogue statement in John 21:25 is not very optimistic on behalf of the world's ability to contain all the books that could be written on the Johannine Jesus. But hopefully the world is able to contain the present book—and other books that may appear—on the ever-fascinating Johannine genre mosaic.

Part I: The Gospel of John and Genre Theory

Harold W. Attridge

The Gospel of John: Genre Matters?

1. Introduction

At the beginning of the century I suggested that one of the most important features of the art of the Fourth Gospel was its creative use of a wide variety of formal features, from the shape of the text as a whole to the fashioning of each of its many parts.[1] I labeled the phenomenon "genre bending," a title that elicited various responses. The most interesting were the colleagues who congratulated me on my engagement with the theory of gender bending (which may also be involved, as Colleen Conway's article in this collection will argue)! Nonetheless, the effort found some resonance in scholarship on the Gospel, as this volume attests.

In the intervening years there has been a good deal of attention to the relevance of genre to the interpretation of ancient texts. This interest crosses various disciplinary boundaries and is found among classicists, students of Second Temple Jewish literature, as well as students of early Christianity. The scholarly conversation has introduced useful clarifications and suggested considerations relevant to the investigation of the significance of literary genres. It will be useful to highlight a few important contributions.

On the classical side, Joseph Farrell contributed an important article, "Classical Genre in Theory and Practice," in 2003.[2] In many ways classical Greek literature provided the kind of paradigm of genre theory and practice that lurked in the minds of most modern scholars when they took up the question of genre. That model referred to the practices of ancient Athenian dramatists, whose works had to conform to an institutionalized set of expectations if their works were to be performed. Genres thus apparently constituted fixed ideals governing the pro-

1 "Genre Bending in the Fourth Gospel," *JBL* 121 (2002): 3–21, repr. in *Essays on John and Hebrews*, WUNT 264 (Tübingen: Mohr Siebeck, 2010), 31–45.

2 Joseph Farrell, "Classical Genre in Theory and Practice," *New Literary History* 34 (2003): 383–408.

duction of literature. That understanding of what genres were and how they worked was explicitly articulated by ancient theorists, particularly Aristotle, and his theoretical perspective continued to be passed along through antiquity and on into the modern period. Farrell points out, however, that the archetypical paradigms did *not* in fact govern the ways in which ancient authors actually worked, not in the classical period and certainly not in the Hellenistic and Roman periods. As he puts it:

> With time one finds an ever greater sense of adventure until, by the Hellenistic and Roman periods, it comes to seem that testing and even violating generic boundaries was not merely an inevitable and accidental consequence of writing in any genre, but an important aspect of the poet's craft.[3]

One can frame this observation within a grand narrative of decadence and decline, lamenting the loss of classical purity in the Hellenistic and Roman ages, or one can celebrate the creativity that generated new literary forms, such as the novel, a product of the Hellenistic world not recognized by its contemporaries. Or one can celebrate the subtle ironies of literary artists such as Horace who can theorize about the purity of genres and how they ought not be mixed within the context of a didactic poem, the *Ars Poetica,* that does that very thing. In the world of Hellenistic and Roman literature, as Jacques Derrida long ago noted, genres were mixed, or, if you will, "bent" on a fairly regular basis.[4] The phenomenon that we see at work in the Gospel of John is not unique or at all unusual. It may be the way that creative literary figures always work; it was certainly the way they did so in the first century.

But how exactly does the insight derived from the recognition of the fluidity and ironic play on generic expectations observed in high-level "classical" literature apply to the case of the Fourth Gospel? Are there recognized "genres" within which the evangelist is working? There is certainly nothing like the classical canon of institutionally guided formal literary types, but what level of formality is there in the evangelist's environment, or are "genres" only in the eye of the beholder?

Framing the question in that way suggests the same analytical space in which students of the literature of Second Temple Judaism find themselves. Many of them have long adopted a kind of pragmatic approach to the question of genre. While there is nothing in Hebrew or Aramaic like Aristotle's *Poetics* or Horace's *Ars Poetica*, there are observable commonalities in Jewish literary products of the Second Temple period. While Israelite genres were not institutionalized or theorized in the same way that Greek and Roman genres were, those who produced

3 Ibid., 388.

4 Jacques Derrida, "La loi du genre / The Law of Genre," *Glyph* 7 (1980): 176–232.

Jewish literature followed examples and engaged in mimetic plays. One prominent example of a scholar wrestling with this issue is my colleague at Yale, Hindy Najman, who treats the issue in a recent essay in a Festschrift for Eileen Schuller.[5]

Prof. Najman notes the fact that some theoreticians, such as Bakhtin[6] and Todorov[7] posit the inevitability of genres, as patterns in the way that human beings speak and write. Genres develop, whether or not they are formally recognized as such. One might think of them as simply the constructs of readers,[8] rather than models that somehow guide the formation of literary works. If they are only that, then modifications of or departures from some kind of accepted norms or expected behaviors are less helpful for analyzing the rhetoric of a given text. Prof. Najman, along with other scholars working on the literature of Second Temple Judaism such as Carol Newsom[9] and Ben Wright,[10] wants to preserve some "objective" character to the generic form. That is, they do want to allow for the possibility of something like the play on generic expectations that we find in Greek poets or in Horace, without positing a theoretically fixed, though practically fluid, set of generic norms. What will then count as the equivalent of a classical genre? Prof. Najman suggests an "idealized cognitive model," inspired by Wittgenstein's frequently cited "family resemblance" explanation of universals. Thus a genre in her realm would be a paradigm of some sort that is "conventionalized, though not institutionalized" as were classical genres. This kind of model allows scholars to posit not simply an etic theory of genre, i. e., a theory from the point of view of our observations of ancient literary behavior, but also an emic theory, i. e., one based on the understanding of the ancients whom we are observing.[11]

5 Hindy Najman, "The Idea of Biblical Genre: From Discourse to Constellation," in *Prayer and Poetry in the Dead Sea Scrolls and Related Literature: Essays in Honor of Eileen Schuller on the Occasion of Her 65th Birthday*, ed. Jeremy Penner, Ken M. Penner, and Cecilia Wassen (Leiden: Brill, 2012), 307–322.

6 M. M. Bakhtin, *Speech Genres and Other Late Essays*, trans. V. W. McGee (Austin: University of Texas Press, 1986).

7 T. Todorov, "The Origin of Genres," *New Literary History* 8 (1976): 159–70.

8 See Adena Rosmarin, *The Power of Genre* (Minneapolis: University of Minnesota Press, 1985).

9 Carol Newsom, "Pairing Research Questions and Theories of Genre: A Case Study of the Hodayot," *DSD* 17 (2010): 437–50, eadem, "Spying Out the Land: A Report from Genology," in *Seeking Out the Wisdom of the Ancients*, ed. R. Troxel, K. Friebel, and D. Margy (Winona Lake: Eisenbrauns, 2005), 437–450.

10 Benjamin Wright, "Joining the Club: A Suggestion about Genre in Jewish Texts," *DSD* 17 (2010): 288–313; R. Williamson, "Pesher: A Cognitive Model of the Genre," *DSD* 17 (2010): 307–331.

11 For an example of precisely this distinction at work, see George J. Brooke, "Reading, Searching and Blessing: A Functional Approach to the Genres of Scriptural Interpretation in the יחד," in *The Temple in Text and Tradition: A Festschrift in Honour of Robert Hayward*, ed. R. Timothy McLay (London: Bloomsbury, 2015), 140–56.

In sum, even when there are not established and putatively normative genres at play, there may well be literary models with some expected features with which authors of a particular work may be interacting, in much the same way as classical poets and Hellenistic novelists interacted with the genres that supposedly governed their literary worlds.

Other examples could easily be cited that illustrate the "bending" or conflation of genres. One example may prove relevant to our consideration of the Gospel of John. This comes from the realm of historiography, where actual "genres" may not have been as rigidly defined as in classical poetry, but where there were definitely recognized models or ideal types that, at least in theory, defined the kind of history writing that one might do.[12] One of these ideal types was the work of Thucydides, writing about contemporary political and military events, testing one's eyewitness sources, and striving for accuracy in reporting the facts of historical events, while of course making allowances for some creativity in reporting speeches. That model of critical historiography was maintained in the Hellenistic period by Polybius in his account of the rise of Roman hegemony over the eastern Mediterranean. The model was later maintained as an ideal in the work of the satirist Lucian, whose work *How to write History* criticized the imperialistic historiography that reported on the Parthian war of 162–165 CE.

Another model, ultimately derived from Herodotus, explored not contemporary political and military affairs, but the larger scope of the history and culture. That model found echoes in the early Imperial period in the works of Diodorus Siculus, whose *Bibliotheca Historica* presented an amalgam of ancient myths and legends, and Dionysius of Halicarnassus, whose twenty-volume *Roman Antiquities*, offered a Greek alternative to the Latin celebration of Rome's past in Livy.

That there were such ideal models is recognized by the Jewish historian Josephus, who shapes the programmatic statements of his *Jewish War* to conform to the Thucydidean-Polybian model and in his preface says that this is pretty much the only way to write history. The same historian, some twenty years later, produced his *Jewish Antiquities*, clearly modeled on the work of Dionysius of Halicarnassus. That there were different sub-genres of historiographical writing is evident. That their generic models had certain expectations was also clear. Polybius is particularly interesting in this regard, defining the kind of history that he was practicing over against a despised other, tragic drama. Criticizing his contemporary Phylarchus, Polybius writes:

12 The suggestions in this paragraph were first formulated in H. W. Attridge, *The Interpretation of Biblical History in the* Antiquitates Judaicae *of Flavius Josephus*, HDR 7 (Missoula: Scholars, 1976), and idem, "Historiography" and "Josephus and His Works," in *Jewish Writings of the Second Temple*, ed. Michael E. Stone, CRINT 2.2 (Philadelphia: Fortress, 1984), 157–232.

> The object of tragedy [i. e., the kind of thing that, according to Polybius, Phylarchus was up to] is not the same as that of history, but quite the opposite. The tragic poet should thrill and charm his audience for the moment by the verisimilitude of the words he puts in his characters mouths, but it is the task of the historian to instruct. (Polybius, *Hist.* 2.56 [Paton, LCL])

What we see in these cases is a discourse about history as a genre, rather like the discourse about poetic genres that Farrell describes. Authors felt free not only to write things in different sub-genres, as Josephus did, but also to "bend" or "tweak" the generic models to which they paid formal allegiance. Both Polybius, and in his footsteps, Josephus, admit to doing just that, when they introduce into their critical histories of political and military events touches of the "tragic," lamenting the fate of the peoples who fell to the imperial power of Rome. As Farrell noted of poetry, historical "genres" also could be subject to transformation even when they were being celebrated and affirmed. From all that we see about the role of and discourses about "genre" in the first century, we should probably expect that any creative author would be engaged in "bending" whatever genre was on the horizon. The key task for a contemporary reader is, as it were, to trace the arc of the bending.

2. The Genre of the Gospel of John

With this glance at genre theory in the background, it is appropriate to turn to the Gospel of John, beginning at the macro-level, that is, the level of the Gospel as a whole. Does it make any sense to worry about its genre? Does "genre" matter?

One way to pursue that question is to follow the lead of the many scholars who have worried about the genre of the gospels generally. The question is usually framed in terms of the possible relations between our gospels and some forms of Hellenistic literature, particularly biographies. Some scholars, such as Richard Burridge, note the similarities and argue that all the gospels are in some sense "bioi."[13] Others want to nuance that judgment and see particular gospels displaying features of other known literary types. In the case of Mark, Michael Vines finds connections with Jewish novels;[14] Adela Collins with apocalyptic mani-

13 Richard Burridge, *What are the Gospels: A Comparison with Greco-Roman Biography*, 2nd rev. ed. (Grand Rapids: Eerdmans, 2004); idem, "Genres of the Old and New Testaments: Gospels," in *The Oxford Handbook of Biblical Studies*, ed. John Rogerson and Judith M. Lieu (Oxford: Oxford University Press, 2006), 432–44. Most recently on the complexity of the genre in general, see Thomas Hägg, *The Art of Biography in Antiquity* (Cambridge: Cambridge University Press, 2012).

14 Michael E. Vines, *Problem of Markan Genre: The Gospel of Mark and the Jewish Novel*, AcBib 3 (Leiden: Brill, 2002).

festos, and I'm sure there are others.[15] The situation resembles the generic fluidity and creativity that Farrell highlighted. At the very least, one might suppose that if evangelists in general somehow modeled their proclamations of Jesus on ancient *bioi*, other literary elements were at work. Such reliance on a variety of generic conventions is certainly the case with our evangelist.

Is it possible to be more precise about what was going on with the genre bending of this Gospel? It may be helpful to keep in mind the suggestion about genre made by Hindy Najman that authors could work with an "idealized cognitive model." In the case of the Fourth Gospel, the "idealized cognitive model" is first and foremost not an abstraction. It is, instead, the literary tradition represented by the Synoptic Gospels themselves, a narrative of Jesus that is, as famously defined by Martin Kähler, "a passion narrative with an extended introduction."[16] It seems likely that the evangelist, while working within that framework, "tweaked" it in at least two major ways. In doing so, he drew on the resources of other well known "idealized cognitive models." Moreover, he drew on them precisely in the way that Farrell describes the poets and literary figures of classical, Hellenistic, and Roman traditions, did, by setting up conceptual dichotomies, defining what they were up to as "not X but Y." The evangelist's tweaking of his "generic" model used two complementary versions of such a dichotomy.

This proposal about John's genre bending at the macro level is founded on a judgment about a perennial source-critical issue, the relationship of the Gospel to the Synoptics. It is not necessary to review here the details of a long and complex debate, but I will just mention a few key points. John is clearly not dependent on any of the gospels in the ways that Matthew and Luke, in the usual two-source theory, are dependent on Mark. John probably has other sources and insofar as the evangelist rewrites anything from the Synoptics he does so with a sovereign freedom. Yet, with many scholars, from C. K. Barrett and Frans Neirynck on, there is abundant evidence that John did indeed know the Synoptics.[17] Partic-

15 Adela Yarbro Collins, *Is Mark's Gospel a Life of Jesus? The Question of Genre* (Milwaukee: Marquette University Press, 1990); eadem, *Mark: A Commentary*, Hermeneia (Minneapolis: Fortress, 2007), 15–44.

16 For a reflection on the application of Kähler's summary, coined for the Gospel of Mark, to John, see Raymond Collins, *Studies on the Fourth Gospel* (Louvain: Peeters; Grand Rapids: Eerdmans, 1990), 87–88.

17 On the general history of the issue, see Dwight Moody Smith, *John Among the Gospels: The Relationship in Twentieth-Century Research* (Minneapolis: Fortress, 1992). For reviews of the more recent scholarly debate, see Michael Labahn and Manfred Lang, "Johannes und die Synoptiker: Positionen und Impulse seit 1990," in *Kontexte des Johannesevangeliums: Das vierte Evangelium in religions- und traditionsgeschichtlicher Perspektive*, ed. Jörg Frey and Udo Schnelle, WUNT 175 (Tübingen: Mohr Siebeck, 2004), 443–516; Roland Bergmeier, "Die Bedeutung der Synoptiker für das johanneische Zeugnisthema: Mit einem Anhang zum Perfekt-Gebrauch im vierten Evangelium," *NTS* 52 (2006): 458–83.

ularly telling are the connections in the Passion and resurrection narratives. Decisive is the connection between John and Luke in the appearance stories, where the two appearance accounts of John 20:19–29 are clearly built on pieces of the one Easter appearance story of Luke 24:6–43, which the evangelist has deconstructed and recomposed, a technique he uses elsewhere.[18] It is highly likely that the evangelist knows Mark and Luke, and may well know Matthew.[19] There are things that he finds attractive in these texts, the mysterious qualities of Mark, and some of the encounters described by Luke, but he is not satisfied that any of the earlier narratives about Jesus does what it ought to do.

So, what is the evangelist's generic strategy in writing his Gospel? If he is using as models Mark and Luke (and possibly Matthew), why does he choose to go down a different path, to tell the story of the public activity, death, and resurrection of Jesus in a different key? The characteristics that suggest a different generic affiliation for the Gospel from either of its most clearly defined predecessors might well say something important about the point of its narrative rhetoric.

The evangelist apparently does what Farrell suggested classical genre benders regularly did, defining the Y that they were writing as a non X. The X that the fourth evangelist had most in his sights was most likely the Gospel of Luke. The third Gospel is, to be sure, a complex literary work, but it is a work with literary pretentions, as well as a rather simple and straightforward narrative style. The literary pretentions, moreover, at least gesture toward the generic ideals of historiography briefly discussed earlier. Scholars have debated both the significance and seriousness of Luke's gesture, and it is not necessary to resolve those debates about Luke here. The language of Luke's prefaces is not quite up to the level of sophisticated historiography, as Loveday Alexander has noted.[20] What Luke does within the narrative of the Gospel, and, if he is indeed the author of Acts,[21] what

18 See esp. Manfred Lang, *Johannes und die Synoptiker: Eine redaktionsgeschichtliche Analyse von Joh 18–20 vor dem markinischen und lukanischen Hintergrund*, FRLANT 182 (Göttingen: Vandenhoeck & Ruprecht, 1999).

19 Among recent commentators who take seriously the likelihood that the Fourth Evangelist knew the Synoptics, see especially, Hartwig Thyen, *Das Johannesevangelium*, HNT 6 (Tübingen: Mohr Siebeck, 2005). See also his earlier "Johannes und die Synoptiker: Auf der Suche nach einem neuen Paradigma zur Beschreibung ihrer Beziehungen anhand von Beobachtungen an Passions-und Ostererzählungen," in *John and the Synoptics*, ed. Adelbert Denaux, BETL 101 (Leuven: Leuven University Press, 1992), 81–108.

20 Loveday Alexander, *The Preface to Luke's Gospel: Literary Convention and Social Context in Luke 1.1–4 and Acts 1.1*, SNTSMS 78 (Cambridge: Cambridge University Press, 1993), and more recently, eadem, *Acts in Its Ancient Literary Context: A Classicist Looks at the Acts of the Apostles*, LNTS 298 (Edinburgh: T & T Clark, 2005).

21 Mikeal Parsons and Richard I. Pervo, *Rethinking the Unity of Luke and Acts* (Minneapolis: Fortress, 1993), and, for another perspective, Andrew F. Gregory and C. Kavin Rowe, *Re-*

he does there, is not exactly the work of critical historiography,[22] although the historical value of the Lukan two-volume set continues to have its defenders.[23] However critical one may be of the result, it is hard to ignore the gesture toward serious historiography in the claim to "set down an orderly account (διήγησις) of the events that have been fulfilled among us" (Luke 1:1). The language of Luke's preface finds corroboration in the efforts to synchronize the story of Jesus with imperial and local history (Luke 1:5; 2:1–2; 3:1–2). Whatever it may in fact be doing, Luke-Acts presents itself as a serious attempt to tell a historical tale accurately. And serious historians, as noted above, ought not be writers of drama.

So, what does John do in presenting his story of Jesus? Just the opposite of what Luke does! No, he says, "I am not going to offer you a simply historicizing account; historical recollection is not where you encounter God. I am going to offer you a dramatic encounter with the Divine Word itself; through my words you will be brought face to face with One who will change your life!" The evangelist, in other words, chooses to write something that both Plato and Aristotle had long since defined as the opposite of a διήγησις.[24]

3. Objectifying Narrative or Dramatic Encounter

Many scholars often use the adjective "dramatic" in speaking about John, and some, such as Ben Witherington[25] and Jo-Ann Brant,[26] have tried to make a more serious case for the relevance of the genre.[27] While much more could be said

thinking the Unity and the Reception of Luke and Acts (Columbia SC: University of Columbia Press, 2010).

22 See especially, Richard I. Pervo, *Profit with Delight: The Literary Genre of the Acts of the Apostles* (Philadelphia: Fortress, 1987), and *Acts*, Hermeneia (Minneapolis: Fortress, 2009). Not all have been persuaded by Pervo's analysis of Acts in the light of ancient romance, see, e.g., Craig Keener, *Acts: An Exegetical Commentary* (Grand Rapids: Baker, 2012), 1:62–83.

23 See, e.g., Colin Hemer, *The Book of Acts in the Setting of Hellenistic History*, WUNT 49 (Tübingen: Mohr, 1989), and the nuanced treatment by Keener, *Acts*, 1:166–220, ("Approaching Acts as a Historical Source").

24 See Plato, *Rep.* 392D, who frames the distinction between "narrative" (διήγησις) and "imitation" (μιμήσις). Aristotle classifies tragedy, with epic poetry, as a mode of "imitation" (*Poet.* 1 [1447a15]), and argues that a tragedy works δρώντων καὶ οὐ δι' ἀπαγγελίας (*Poet.* 6 [1449b27]), which I. Bywater usefully translates as "in a dramatic, not a narrative form," in Jonathan Barnes, *The Complete Works of Aristotle: The Revised Oxford Translation*, Bollingen Series 71.1–2 (Princeton: Princeton University Press, 1984), 2:2320.

25 Ben Witherington III, *John's Wisdom: A Commentary on the Fourth Gospel* (Louisville: Westminster John Knox, 1995), 4–5 labels it a "dramatic biography." He lists as dramatic elements: initial hymn, irony, magnitude of main character, dualisms, crescendo effect, self contained nature of certain scenes, rhetoric at key points, only three on stage, surprising revelations.

about the topic (and for example George Parsenios' article in this collection will contribute to that conversation), it is worthwhile to highlight four elements of the Gospel that bend this narrative in the direction of drama. The first is the Prologue, with its cadenced celebration of the divine Word made flesh. This introduction to the Gospel is unlike anything in Mark or Matthew. It has a parallel in Luke's prefaces. But, apart from the similarity in the general function of introducing their respective works, those Lukan prefaces are markedly different from John's Prologue. They are a prosaic, and somewhat apologetic, appeal to the reader, quite similar to what one finds in works of historiography[28] and in specialized technical manuals.[29] John's Prologue, with its quasi-poetic form, hints at many of the themes that will appear in the Gospel's symbolic and thematic worlds: the contrast between light and darkness, the relationship between Father and Son, the stark juxtaposition of those who accept the Word and those who do not, the contrast between what Jesus offers and what Moses provided, the emphasis on the presence of the Word in Flesh and the resultant experience of seeing and understanding that flows from encounter with that Word. The Prologue as we have it is not an afterthought, not a secondary and casual addition to the Gospel. It belongs where it sits, at the beginning of the complex Gospel in its final form. In that position it functions as does the "hypothesis" of a Greek drama, the prefatory passage that tells the audience what they will encounter in the acts that follow. Unlike any of the other Gospels, the Fourth Gospel begins as a drama. Whether to think of it as a tragedy or a comedy or something in between is open to discussion, but that its opening is dramatic (in many senses of that word) is clear. If one wants to understand the narrative rhetoric of the Gospel it is important to attend to the drama of the Gospel.

The second major dramatic feature has received considerable attention in recent decades, the irony that pervades the narrative.[30] Irony, in fact, comes in

26 Jo-Ann A. Brant, *Dialogue and Drama: Elements of Greek Tragedy in the Fourth Gospel* (Peabody: Hendrickson, 2004).

27 See also Mark Stibbe, *John as Storyteller: Narrative Criticism and the Fourth Gospel*, SNTSMS 73 (Cambridge: Cambridge University Press, 1992), and idem, *The Gospel of John as Literature: An Anthology of Twentieth-Century Perspectives*, NTTS 17 (Leiden; New York; Köln: Brill, 1993); G. Rochais, "Jean 7: Une construction littéraire dramatique, à la manière d'un scenario," *NTS* 39 (1993): 355–78.

28 See H. W. Attridge, *The Interpretation of Biblical History*, "Historiography," and "Josephus and His Works." More recently see John Marincola, *Authority and Tradition in Ancient Historiography* (Cambridge: Cambridge University Press, 1997), and Roberto Nicolai, *La storiografia nell' educazione antica*, Biblioteca di materiali e discussioni per l'analisi dei testi classici 10 (Pisa: Giardini, 1992).

29 As argued by Loveday Alexander. See n. 20 above.

30 See Paul D. Duke, *Irony in the Fourth Gospel* (Atlanta: John Knox Press, 1985), and Gail O'Day, *Revelation in the Fourth Gospel: Narrative Mode and Theological Claim* (Philadelphia: Fortress, 1986).

many forms in the Gospel, but the first and most obvious bit is what is usually called "dramatic" irony. Irony in general is the linguistic act of saying one thing and meaning another. Dramatic irony is the kind of irony that occurs "on stage," when a character says something that is very true but he or she does not realize it, while the audience does. Or a character may deny the truth of something that the audience knows to be true. The dramatist and his audience in effect share a secret of which the characters in the drama are unaware, the kind of irony most familiar from Euripides' *Bacchae.*[31]

The characters who interact with Jesus in the pages of the Fourth Gospel bear a strong resemblance to Pentheus in the *Bacchae.* They resist the presence of the divine in their midst; they deny truths that the audience knows, in statements such as the comment of Nicodemus, "How can anyone be born after having grown old" (3:4), implying that he understands Jesus's *anothen* to mean born "again." Or they articulate a truth that they do not grasp (5:18), as does the crowd in Jerusalem who think that Jesus is "making himself equal to God," or again, the Judeans who display the truth of their situation (7:27), saying "when the Messiah comes no one will know where he is from." The incredulous question of the crowds, in 7:35: "Does he intend to go to the Dispersion among the Greeks?" points to something that begins to happen in chapter 12. Perhaps the most famous of these bits of irony is the statement of Caiaphas (11:50): "It is better for you to have one man to die for the people."

In addition to the "dramatic irony" of the narrative, another irony governs the very structure of the Gospel's climax. The ironic claim, familiar to anyone who has read the Gospel even once, is that in being "lifted up" (Greek, ὑψόω), that is, on the shameful tree of the cross, Jesus is "lifted up in glory" (Greek, δοξάζω), a mysterious glory that is alluring and compelling. This element of the Gospel's narrative rhetoric deserves further comment. For the moment it is sufficient to note that irony is not a casual literary device embellishing the pervasive dramatic encounters, it is a conceptual device at the heart of the dramatic narrative.

So far this paper has explored ways in which the Fourth Gospel displays technical dramatic features. Both the Prologue as "hypothesis" and the pervasive irony are very much at home in dramas. A third, relatively minor element surfaces in an unexpected place, and in fact solves a problem that many modern readers have felt with the text, the device of the "delayed exit." This is a feature of the last supper discourses pointed out by a participant in this collection, George Parsenios.[32]

31 As pointed out long ago by George W. MacRae, "Theology and Irony in the Fourth Gospel," in *The Word in the World: Essays in Honour of F. L. Moriarty*, ed. Richard J. Clifford and George W. MacRae (Cambridge: Weston College, 1973), 83–96, repr. in Stibbe, *Literature*, 103–113.

32 George Parsenios, *Departure and Consolation: The Johannine Farewell Discourses in Light of Greco-Roman Literature*, NovTSup 117 (Leiden: Brill, 2005).

The conversation that takes place in the last supper seems to reach a conclusion at the end of chapter 14. Jesus has given an example of loving service by washing the feet of his disciples. He has given the "new commandment" to love, and he has promised the sending of the Paraclete. At the end of the chapter he tells his disciples that it is time to get up and go. The movement to Gethsemane in chapter 18 seems to follow quite naturally on this injunction. Instead of that smooth connection, however, Jesus talks for another three chapters, telling the "parable" of the vine and the branches. He repeats the promise of the Paraclete, warns his disciples of the world's hatred, and finally offers a prayer for the sanctification of the disciples through the name that he has given them. All of this is material important for the ultimate claims made by the Gospel, but is it just an afterthought or secondary addition? Whatever its place in the history of the Gospel's composition, it is finally the function of this block of material that deserves our attention. That function is precisely analogous to a phenomenon frequently encountered in ancient drama, both Greek and Roman, the "delayed exit" of a major character from the stage.

Such delayed exits usually take place when a leading character is on the verge of death, which, according to the conventions of ancient theatre, will take place offstage. With death or departure imminent, the character will gesture toward that conclusion, but then pause and go on for some time, often offering reflections on the significance of the coming separation.[33] What happens in John 15–17 is of a piece with that technique.

Recognizing the point of Parsenios' analysis is not meant to suggest that ancient drama is the only literary genre with significant parallels to the last supper discourses in the Fourth Gospel. Our creative author here and elsewhere combines features of a wide variety of literary types, including "testaments" of patriarchs about to depart in which they admonish their offspring and predict the future, or philosophical or rhetorical messages of consolation regarding death, and even symposia, or supper discourses, which focus on such important topics as love. Elements of all of these genres are at work in John 13–17.[34] The point here is that dramatic devices are part of the mix.

33 For examples, see the delay of Cassandra in Aeschylus, *Agamemnon*, 1290–1331; Sophocles, *Philoctetes*, 1402–15; Sophocles, *Antigone*, 883–930; Euripides, *Trojan Women*, 294–461. I am grateful to George Parsenios for the references.

34 See H. W. Attridge, "Plato, Plutarch, and John: Three Symposia about Love," in *Beyond the Gnostic Gospels: Studies Building on the Work of Elaine Pagels*, ed. Edward Iricinschi et al., STAC 82 (Tübingen: Mohr Siebeck, 2013), 367–78. Important analyses of the Farewell Discourse include: Johannes Beutler, *Do not be Afraid: The First Farewell Discourse in John's Gospel*, New Testament Studies in Contextual Exegesis 6 (Frankfurt am Main: Peter Lang, 2011) and idem, *Habt Keine Angst: Die erste Johanneische Abschiedsrede (Joh 14)*, SBS 116 (Stuttgart: Katholisches Bibelwerk, 1984); Fernando Segovia, *The Farewell of the Word: The*

One fourth and final dramatic device merits attention as a deliberate bending of a narrative form away from another recognized "genre." As suggested in passing, the Fourth Gospel can be construed as a series of dramatic encounters or interactions between Jesus and his various interlocutors, some positive, some negative. A device that appears in several of these encounters is another standard part of the dramatist's toolkit, the recognition scene. This device, and its importance for the Fourth Gospel has been creatively explored by Kasper Bro Larsen.[35] Three brief examples, familiar to any reader of the Gospel, will suffice to make the point. The Samaritan Woman in John 4 through her dialogue with Jesus comes to recognize that he might indeed be the Messiah. However tentative, she experiences a moment of recognition, of what the Greeks would call *anagnorisis.* Mary Magdalene, weeping at the entrance to the empty tomb and wondering what has become of the body of Jesus, recognizes, at the sound of his voice calling her name, that her beloved Lord is there, present with her. She too, at that verbal signal, reminiscent of the sheep and their shepherd (10:27), experiences a moment of *anagnorisis.* Thomas, the famous doubter, comes to faith through another, very tangible sign, the wounded body of the resurrected one. His confrontation with that reality enables him to confess his *anagnorisis* in the famous outcry, "My Lord and My God!" (John 20:28).

This paper has been arguing that the Fourth Gospel is an example of a particularly "dramatic" configuration of a narrative of an individual's life and death. But why, one might ask, is such an adaptation important? Why does this genre bending exercise matter? The basic response is that the evangelist is concerned above all to ensure that the reader/hearer of his text has the possibility of an encounter with the Resurrected Christ himself. Our evangelist may have feared that a reduction of the resurrected Christ to the object of historical testimony was not going to effect that transformative encounter. Relying on the tools of historiography, however properly they may have been used, was not going to accomplish the goal of engaging the reader/hearer with the living Christ. What might do so?

Part of the answer was a vivid "drama" illustrating encounters between Christ and various types of questioning, needy souls. But that move, in itself, was not enough. It was eminently possible that a dramatized roster of encounters could easily be historicized and vacated of its allure to foster a "true encounter" with the resurrected Christ. So the dramatic form needed to be tweaked further and our evangelist did so, poking yet another stick into the eye of antiquarians like Luke

Johannine Call to Abide (Minneapolis: Fortress, 1991); D. François Tolmie, *Jesus' Farewell to the Disciples: John 13:1–17:26 in Narratological Perspective*, BIS 12 (Leiden: Brill, 1995).

35 Kasper Bro Larsen, *Recognizing the Stranger: Recognition Scenes in the Gospel of John*, BIS 93 (Leiden: Brill, 2008).

or perhaps even early collectors of "historical" tradition such as Papias. As many contemporary critics have suggested, our evangelist makes a great deal of the category of "eyewitness," thereby calling on the long tradition from Thucydides through Polybius and Josephus to Lucian, all of whom celebrated the importance of reliable eye-witnesses.[36] Yes, our evangelist knows that historiographical tradition and exploits it, but to what end? At the heart of the appeal to an eyewitness in ancient legal transactions requiring such testimony is that the identity of the eyewitness be known.[37] It is hardly the case that the identity of the Beloved Disciple is a known commodity. No, it is possible to be more definite about that point: the Gospel systematically prevents anyone who wants to know who the Beloved Disciple, eyewitness extraordinaire, really is. The Gospel summons the reader back into the text, perhaps searching for the identity of the anonymous eyewitness,[38] only to encounter the One who bears witness to the Truth. When the reader sees Him, that reader becomes the reliable eyewitness.[39]

The trope on the figure of the Beloved Disciple accomplishes two dramatic ends. By inviting its "quest" it engages the reader in the possibility of a dramatic encounter that will result in his or her own *anagnorisis* of the significance of Jesus. It also thereby puts the reader in the position of the ideal disciple that the Beloved Disciple also represents. It effects, that is, the kind of "identification" that Aristotle identified as a feature of drama,[40] not with the protagonist perhaps, but with one as close to the protagonist as any ordinary mortal is likely to get.

So, to summarize the results so far: The way in which the whole story of Jesus' ministry, death and resurrection was framed mattered greatly to the evangelist. This article also argues that, in contrast to the "idealized conventional type" of similar narration, i. e., a historicizing gospel such as Luke's, our evangelist framed

36 On the importance of eyewitness testimony in general see Samuel Byrskog, *Story as History—History as Story: The Gospel Tradition in the Context of Ancient Oral History*, WUNT 2.106 (Tübingen: Mohr Siebeck, 2000).

37 See Howard M. Jackson, "Ancient Self-Referential Conventions and Their Implications for the Authorship and Integrity of the Gospel of John," *JTS* 50 (1999): 1–34.

38 On the role of anonymity, see David R. Beck, "The Narrative Function of Anonymity in Fourth Gospel Characterization," *Semeia* 53 (1993): 143–58, and idem, *The Discipleship Paradigm: Readers and Anonymous Characters in the Fourth Gospel*, BIS 27 (Leiden: Brill, 1997). On the general phenomenon of anonymity, see Adele Reinhartz, "Anonymity and Character in the Books of Samuel," *Semeia* 63 (1993): 117–42, and *Why Ask My Name? Anonymity and Identity in Biblical Narrative* (New York: Oxford University Press, 1998).

39 For my reflections on this process, see "The Restless Quest for the Beloved Disciple," in *Early Christian Voices: In Texts, Traditions, and Symbols. Essays in Honor of François Bovon*, ed. David H. Warren, Ann Graham Brock, and David W. Pao, BIS 66 (Leiden: Brill, 2003), 71–80, repr. in *Essays*, 20–30.

40 For Aristotle, the aim of tragedy is "catharsis" of pity and fear in the audience (*Poet.* 6 [1449b28]) achieved primarily through a well-designed plot, but also through characters who were morally attractive and realistic (*Poet.* 15 [1454a16–1454b14]).

his account in a significantly different way, a way that suggested how his account was supposed to work. For him, and for those of us who now read his work, genre matters.

4. Transparent Narrative or a Riddling Arabesque

This reflection on the genre of the Fourth Gospel began with the observation that, like much other literature of the period, the evangelist is playing with, or "bending" genres. The ideal type that he is working with is a distillation of other narratives about Jesus, particularly the Gospel of Luke, which he bends, first, in the direction of drama. Another important feature of this gospel is an attempt to bend the genre of historicizing narrative in a different direction from what it took in the other gospels on the first-century market.

Despite its deceptively simple Greek, the Fourth Gospel is a text filled with tensions, in Christology, eschatology, soteriology, and who knows what else. In the past these have often been explained on the basis of theories of source and redaction. With the literary turn in Johannine scholarship of the last decades many Johannine scholars have reconsidered the role of such tensions and have tried to find explanations of their function within the text. Perhaps the most prominent of those explanations is that the text is deliberately involved in creating "riddles."[41]

The phenomenon of paradoxes or riddles used as a literary device is, of course, not unique to the Gospel. Riddles are part of the educational technique of the angel in 4 Ezra, leading the seer to deeper insight into the mysteries of divine justice.[42] Bentley Layton has identified riddling as a key element in the baffling aretalogical form of the *Thunder, the Perfect Intellect* (NHC VI,2).[43] Riddling language is also identified, perhaps with a bit of irony, as a psychagogic technique in a Hermetic tractate that has occasionally been adduced as an instructive parallel to at least part of the Fourth Gospel, *Corpus Hermeticum* XIII.[44] This

41 Herbert Leroy, *Rätsel und Missverständnis: Ein Beitrag zur Formgeschichte des Johannesevangeliums*, BBB 30 (Bonn: Hanstein, 1968); Tom Thatcher, *The Riddles of Jesus in John: A Study in Tradition and Folklore*, SBLMS 53 (Atlanta: SBL, 2000); idem, "Riddles, Repetitions, and the Literary Unity of the Johannine Discourses," in *Repetitions and Variations in the Fourth Gospel: Style, Text, Interpretation*, ed. Gilbert van Belle, Michael Labahn, and Petrus Maritz, BETL 223 (Leuven: Peeters, 2009), 357–77; Paul Anderson, *The Riddles of the Fourth Gospel* (Minneapolis: Fortress, 2011).

42 See, e.g., 4 Ezra 4:5–7, 50; 5:36.

43 Bentley Layton, *The Gnostic Scriptures* (Garden City: Doubleday, 1983), 77–78, also noted by Pheme Perkins, *Gnosticism and the New Testament* (Minneapolis: Fortress, 1993), 132–34.

44 See C. H. Dodd, *The Interpretation of the Fourth Gospel* (Cambridge: Cambridge University

dialogue about rebirth (παλιγγενεσία) features Hermes instructing a befuddled Tat, who bears an uncanny resemblance to Nicodemus in John 3. After a series of exchanges that leaves him baffled, the pupil tells Hermes: "You tell me a riddle [αἴνιγμα], father; you do not speak as a father to a son."[45]

Concerned about the use of the category by Gnostic Christians, Church Fathers also wrestled the notion of the educational value of riddles and paradoxes. Clement of Alexandria did so extensively in *Stromata* 5.[46] Origen, in his *Commentary on John* 2.10, immediately after dealing with the theoretical issue of divine sovereignty and human responsibility in the soteriological process, calls attention to the importance of paradoxical language. He does not draw the connection made in this essay, and the illustration of "paradox" that he uses comes from the well-known list of Stoic examples of sayings about who is truly wise. Yet the basic point is clear, paradoxical statements can play a significant educational role.[47]

Another feature of the gospel, connected with its "riddling" quality, is the way in which it plays with a theme over a series of chapters. The treatment of many

---

Press, 1953), and more recently, in M. Eugene Boring, Klaus Berger and Carsten Colpe, eds., *Hellenistic Commentary to the New Testament* (Nashville: Abingdon, 1995), # 384, pp. 254–55.

45 The whole context is worth citing. The pupil, Tat, asks, "But after you talked with me coming down from the mountain, I became your suppliant and asked to learn the discourse on being born again since, of all the discourses, this one alone I do not know. … I do not know what sort of womb mankind is born from, O Trismegistus, nor from what kind of seed." [*Hermes*] "My child, [the womb] is the wisdom of understanding in silence, and the seed is the true good." [*Tat*] "Who sows the seed, father? I am entirely at a loss." [*Hermes*] "The will of god, my child." [*Tat*] "And whence comes the begotten, father? He does not share in my essence." [*Hermes*] "The begotten will be of a different kind, a god and child of god, the all in all, composed entirely of the powers." [*Tat*] "You tell me a riddle, father; you do not speak as a father to a son." [*Hermes*] "Such lineage cannot be taught, my child, but god reminds you of it when he wishes." Translation from Brian Copenhaver, *Hermetica: The Corpus Hermeticum and the Latin Asclepius in a New English Translation* (Cambridge, New York: Cambridge University Press, 1992), cited in Boring et al., *Hellenistic Commentary*, 254.

46 On this see Gedalyahu A. Stroumsa, *Esoteric Traditions and the Roots of Christian Mysticism* (Leiden, Boston: Brill, 2005), esp. ch. 6: "Mosaic Riddles: Esoteric Trends in Patristic Hermeneutics," 91–108.

47 Origen, *Comm. Jo.* 2.10 (112–13): "The Greeks have certain apothegms, called paradoxes, in which the wisdom of their sages is presented at its highest, and some proof, or what appears to be proof, is given. Thus it is said that the wise man alone, and that every wise man, is a priest, because the wise man alone and every wise man possesses knowledge as to the service of God. Again, that the wise man alone and that every wise man is free and has received from the divine law authority to do what he himself is minded to do, and this authority they call lawful power of decision. Why should we say more about these so-called paradoxes? Much discussion is devoted to them, and they call for a comparison of the sense of Scripture with the doctrine thus conveyed. so that we may be in a position to determine where religious doctrine agrees with them and where it differs from them." Trans. Allan Menzies in *The Ante-Nicene Fathers.* Edited by Alexander Roberts and James Donaldson (New York: Christian Literature Company, 1896), 9:332.

significant theoretical issues is not exhausted in a single pericope, and there is not, as in some of the Synoptics, a simple repetition of a particular point.[48] No, some themes develop over the course of the narrative. The phenomenon has been noted by several recent Johannine scholars, who have usually pursued one of the many thematic strands.[49]

It is also important to recognize how these sometimes meandering strands of reflection interact with one another. One might think of this phenomenon as the Johannine "arabesque," not the dance routine, but the pattern of interwoven vines found in some ancient and much medieval art, such as the apse of San Clemente in Rome. The literary phenomenon is appropriate for a text that may have originally been designed for meditative reflection in the context of a "study group" of Christians. The Gospel, in other words, facilitates an encounter with the resurrected Christ,[50] but in a context where theoretical issues arising from that encounter are matters of concern. The text offers suggestions about how those theoretical uses are to be resolved, but does not offer an argument that definitively resolves them. It is not, therefore, a work of systematic or philosophical theology, although it displays acquaintance with theories that philosophers or speculative theologians might pursue.[51] While it does not argue a case, it does lead readers to consider the complexity of certain issues and thus serves as a kind of psychagogic program,[52] always keeping the theoretical questions sub-

48 So "weeping and gnashing of teeth" in Matthew; or "give alms" in Luke, neither of which, of course, has a riddling quality.

49 See, e.g., Wayne Meeks, "The Man From Heaven in Johannine Sectarianism," *JBL* 91 (1972): 44–72, repr. in *Interpretations of the Fourth Gospel*, ed. John Ashton (London: SPCK; Philadelphia: Fortress, 1986), 141–73, and in idem, *In Search of the Early Christians* (New Haven: Yale University Press, 2002), 64, commenting on "the elucidation of themes by progressive repetition"; Jörg Frey, "Love-Relations in the Fourth Gospel: Establishing a Semantic Network," in van Belle et al., *Repetitions*, 171–98; Ruben Zimmermann, "Metaphoric Networks as Hermeneutic Keys in the Gospel of John: Using the Example of the Mission Imagery," in van Belle et al., *Repetitions*, 381–402; and on "glory," Nicole Chibici-Revneanu, *Die Herrlichkeit des Verherrlichten*, WUNT 2/231 (Tübingen: Mohr Siebeck, 2007), esp. 325–30.

50 For another text that tries to stimulate such an encounter, note the prominent theme of seeking and finding in the *Gospel of Thomas*, on which see H. W. Attridge, "'Seeking' and 'Asking' in Q, Thomas and John," in *From Quest to Q: Festschrift James M. Robinson*, ed. Jon Ma. Asgeirsson, Kristin de Troyer, and Marvin W. Meyer (Leuven: University Press; Peeters, 2000), 295–302.

51 See H. W. Attridge, "An Emotional Jesus and Stoic Traditions," in *Stoicism in Early Christianity*, ed. Tuomas Rasimus, Troels Engberg-Pedersen, and Ismo Dunderberg (Peabody: Hendrickson, 2010), 77–92, repr. in idem, *Essays*, 122–36.

52 Johannine psychagogy needs further systematic study. For the term and an approach to the subject, see Clarence Glad, *Paul and Philodemus: Adaptability in Epicurean and Early Christian Psychagogy* (Leiden: Brill, 1995). A more theoretical approach to the subject is the recent monograph on the Gospel of Philip by Hugo Lundhaug, *Images of Rebirth: Cognitive Poetics and Transformational Psychology in the Gospel of Philip and the Exegesis on the Soul*, NHS 73 (Leiden: Brill, 2010).

ordinated to the effort to facilitate an encounter of the reader and the crucified and glorified Christ.

Various examples could illustrate the technique. The theme of judgment, for example, is an important strand of the Johannine "arabesque." The theme's tensions have long attracted attention.[53] They begin with the first declaration of John 2:17 that God did not send the Son to Judge the world. The notion is repeated several times: neither does the Father judge (5:22); "I [i. e., Jesus] judge no one" (8:15); " For I did not come to judge the world" (12:47). Alongside these affirmations is the equal insistence that judgment does take place, brought about by the action of Jesus: "The one who does not believe has already been judged" (2:18); "As I hear, I judge" (5:30); more provisionally perhaps: "And if I do judge ..." (8:16); "I have much to say about you and to judge" (8:26). These apparently contradictory affirmations about the theme find some degree of resolution at 12:48–49, when Jesus affirms: "The one who rejects me and does not receive my word has a judge; on the last day the word that I have spoken will serve as judge, for I have not spoken on my own, but the Father who sent me has himself given me a commandment about what to say and what to speak." The resolution implicit here is confirmed by Jesus in 16:11: the Paraclete, when he comes, will prosecute its case (ἐλέγξει) against the world, "about judgment, because the ruler of this world has been condemned."[54]

In short, judgment happens, but not in the manner of traditional eschatological or apocalyptic scenarios, such as that of Matt 25:31–46. Jesus brings judgment, but not as something that issues from the bench of a great assize. He proclaims the word given him by the Father. Reaction to that word, in the form of belief or rejection, determines the verdict.

Similar to, and intertwined with, the sequence about "judgment" is another strand of somewhat paradoxical reflection, on the relationship between divine sovereignty and human responsibility in the process of salvation. Some readers find here a rigidly determinist scheme; others find something that creates a space for human responsibility. Others are content to affirm that the Gospel, perhaps like other Jewish sources, holds that the two principles are compatible, although it

53 The classic treatment is Josef Blank, *Krisis: Untersuchungen zur johanneischen Christologie und Eschatologie* (Freiburg im Breisgau: Lambertus Verlag, 1964).

54 The language is clearly forensic, as is the title Paraclete, but determining its precise connotations here requires separate analysis. Some more recent studies include Michel Gourgues, "Le Paraclet, l'esprit de vérité: Deux désignations, deux functions," in *Theology and Christology in the Fourth Gospel: Essays by the Members of the SNTS Johannine Writings Seminar*, ed. Gilbert van Belle, Jan G. van der Watt, and P. Maritz, BETL 184 (Leuven: Leuven University Press, 2005), 83–108; David Pastorelli, *Le Paraclet dans le corpus johannique*, BZNW 142 (Berlin: de Gruyter, 2006); Lochlan Schelfer, "The Legal Precision of the Term 'παράκλητος'," *JSNT* 32 (2009): 131–50.

is unclear how that compatibility works.[55] Yet others relate the tensive principles to the Gospel's social circumstances. In evidence here is another riddle or paradox, leading an attentive reader through a process of reflection to at least a tentative resolution.

Since there is a detailed analysis of this strain of Johannine thinking published elsewhere, a brief summary will suffice here.[56] From chapter 3 on, John sets up a tension between two principles, that origins are determinative and that one can reset the point of origin and be "born *anothen.*" Feints in one direction or another push the reader along, wondering how the tension is to be resolved until, finally, in chapter 12, in combination with the resolution of the "judgment" theme, the reader learns that what one loves determines whether one will accept the opportunity to believe in the revealer or not. The evangelist winds up with an implied account of divine sovereignty and human responsibility not unlike that of classical Stoicism. The force of the divine will is massive, summoning one to belief, making belief possible and attractive, but at the end of the day it does not force a decision. There is room for the individual to assent to the call to believe or to reject that call. The latter move is simply "sin."

Deploying riddling concepts is one way that the evangelist bends the narrative genre of the tale of Jesus. It is probably part of the grounds for the term "theologian" that tradition will apply to him, but it is only one part of the "arabesque."

5. Decorations or Visual Pointers to a Central Truth

In addition to the Gospel's riddles, which usually revolve around some important faith claim, there is another thematic strand that is woven into the story of Jesus. It is part of the "arabesque," the intricate interweaving of themes that contribute to one another and to the complex mosaic of the Gospel. The strand is the complex array of visual images that run through the text, visual flowers, as it were, on the conceptual vines that form the tendrils of the arabesque. Johannine imagery has been much studied in recent decades,[57] and the Johannine treatment

55 So, e.g., Craig Keener, *The Gospel of John: A Commentary* (Peabody: Hendrickson, 2003), 1:571–74, discussing John 12:37–45

56 H. W. Attridge, "Divine Sovereignty and Human Responsibility in the Fourth Gospel," in *Revealed Wisdom: Studies in Apocalyptic in Honour of Christopher Rowland*, ed. John Ashton (Leiden: Brill, 2014), 183–199.

57 Among others, see Craig Koester, *Symbolism in the Fourth Gospel: Meaning, Mystery, Community*, 2nd ed. (Minneapolis: Fortress, 2003); Dorothy Lee, *Flesh and Glory: Symbolism, Gender, and Theology in the Gospel of John* (New York: Crossroad, 2002); Jörg Frey, Jan G. Van der Watt, and Ruben Zimmermann, eds., *Imagery in the Gospel of John: Terms, Forms, Themes and Theology of Figurative Language*, WUNT 200 (Tübingen: Mohr Siebeck, 2006).

of imagery, which works like cubist art, bears an interesting formal resemblance to his handling of generic characteristics.[58] Quite familiar are the ways in which life, light, shepherds, vines, blood and water, flow through the text in interwoven streams, pointing to and emanating from the central image of the cross, that ironic symbol with which this article began. If the riddles of the arabesque appeal to the mind, the images appeal to the senses, but they do the same kind of work as the whole of the dramatic enterprise: they facilitate an encounter with the living Christ.

6. Conclusion

Much remains to be said about the ways in which generic characteristics work in this fascinating gospel, as a whole and in its individual parts and pieces. This essay has attempted to take a more global approach, first by situating the gospel both within a contemporary theoretical perspective and within the context of ancient literary practice. There were indeed ideal genres of ancient literature, but even when they were explicitly theorized, as in the classical Greek and Roman traditions, they were regularly the subjects of literary play, sometimes quite ironic. Our evangelist was writing in an environment in which a certain kind of historicizing impulse was at work. Telling the story of Jesus' life, death and resurrection was seen to be a way of connecting people to the reality of his being. Our evangelist shared the rhetorical goal, but apparently thought that generic historicizing narrative was inadequate to do the job. The story of Jesus had to be reconceived along the lines of other types of symbolic production. Most importantly and most clearly, the story needed to be dramatized, to display and to invite transformative encounters with the Crucified and Resurrected Way, Truth, and Life. But a simple dramatized narrative was not enough either. It offered the possibility of one type of encounter, through identification of the reader with a character in the story, but that left other dimensions of experience without adequate support. The dramatic narrative was further bent toward a bit of conceptual artistry that would at the same time bedazzle and perplex, but ultimately transform the attentive reader.

58 H. W. Attridge, "The Cubist Principle in Johannine Imagery: John and the Reading of Images in Contemporary Platonism," in Jörg Frey et al., *Imagery in the Gospel of John*, 47–60; repr. in *Essays*, 79–92.

Sune Auken

Contemporary Genre Studies: An Interdisciplinary Conversation with Johannine Scholarship

In order to grasp the state of contemporary genre studies one must recognize that literary scholarship has long been out of vogue. Scholars of literature may have defined the subject for many years, but those days are long gone. From the mid-eighties onwards, literary genre studies has stalled, whereas linguistic, rhetorical, and didactic genre studies have flourished—the dominant subject in genre studies these days is, in fact, writing studies, with ethnographic and sociological subjects following close on its heels. There is still interesting work being done among literary scholars, and I will marginally touch upon some of it here, but compared to the cohesiveness and impact achieved in the other fields, literary genre studies has fallen behind.

However, much remains to be done. Whereas genre as a phenomenon is omnipresent in human culture, understanding and communication, genre studies is not as prolific. It is a specific and highly specialized scholarly endeavour that may be very well developed but is not universally known, or even well-known in academia. Thus, you may live, study, interact with, and even research genres throughout your life without ever giving a thought to the existence of a cohesive body of knowledge concerned with the subject. Consequently, not only do scholars often discuss questions of genre without knowing the state of the art in genre studies; they may make discoveries which have already been made in genre studies and proclaim them as breakthroughs (bad), or make new discoveries relevant to genre studies without news of these developments ever reaching genre studies (worse).

Thus, the purpose of this article is to contribute to the mediation between contemporary genre studies and scholars from other fields who work with genre; in casu: Biblical scholars working with the Gospel of John. So it will present some of the developments in current genre theory and suggest some ways in which these may be worked into the interpretative practices in literary and biblical studies. These remarks are of a general nature and not aimed immediately at John. In order to illustrate a few of the points, the article will also attempt a tentative reading of one passage from John. This reading is only included for illustration. It is clearly literary in character, and has no claim to profoundness or originality in biblical studies.

1. The Social Function of Genre

The defining moment in modern genre studies is the publication of Carolyn Miller's "Genre as Social Action" from 1984.[1] This article forms a watershed because, retrospectively, it marks the point when genre studies moved from being a primarily literary and aesthetic to a rhetorical, linguistic, didactic, and, broadly speaking, interdisciplinary endeavour. Also, it gives a distinct character to the direction genre studies has taken over the last thirty years. There are several theoretical positions formulated in contemporary genre studies, none of them literary—the description presented by Sunny Hyon in 1996 still seems to hold[2]—but I am going to focus mainly on North American Rhetorical Genre Studies, or RGS. It is the most influential of the different positions, and also the one that traces its descendance most directly to Miller.

"Genre as Social Action" is central within genre studies for presenting a rhetorical definition of genre which has later become fundamental not just in the rhetorical field, but within genre studies in general, its basic assumptions being rarely challenged. Later researchers have, however, applied, deepened, expanded, systematized, and clarified the basic tenets, adding knowledge and demonstrating just how powerful the original position was.[3]

Miller's rhetorical understanding of genre has had its most fundamental impact on genre studies on two points: Genres are seen as functional, and the de facto genres of everyday life have become the predominant subject in genre studies. Today, the functional perspective on genre is so dominant that it not only heuristically determines the work done with genre in Rhetorical Studies, but is seen as defining for what genre is: The number of times Miller's definition of

1 Carolyn Miller, "Genre as Social Action," *Quarterly Journal of Speech* 70 (1984): 151–167.

2 Sunny Hyon, "Genre in Three Traditions: Implications for ESL", *TESOL Quarterly* 4 (1996): 693–722. For more on the state of modern Genre Studies see also Anis Bawarshi and Mary Jo Reiff, *Genre. An Introduction to History, Theory, Research, and Pedagogy* (Fort Collins: Parlor Press, 2010), as well as Sune Auken, "Utterance and Function in Genre Studies: A Literary Perspective," in *Genre Theory in Information Studies*, ed. J. Andersen, Studies in Information 11 (Bingley: Emerald Group, 2015), 155–178; and Anne Smedegaard, "Genre and Writing Pedagogy", in *Genre and …*, ed. S. Auken, P. S. Lauridsen, and A. J. Rasmussen, Copenhagen Studies in Genre 2 (Copenhagen: Ekbatana, 2015), 21–55.

3 Notable for raising some criticism is Inger Askehave and John Swales, "Genre Identification and Communicative Purpose," *Applied Linguistics* 2 (2001): 195–212, and Amy Devitt, "Re-Fusing Form in Genre Study," in *Genres in the Internet*, ed. J. Giltrow and D. Stein (Philadelphia: John Benjamins, 2009), 27–48.

genre as "typified rhetorical actions based in recurrent situations" (159) is used in modern genre studies is staggering. At the same time, the subject matter of genre studies has shifted, and the analysis of the genres in use (everyday genres), has taken centre stage. The high rhetorical genres of oratory are pushed into the background, literary genres are all but gone, and with them also most of what was done in literary genre theory. In hindsight, this development is unsurprising. It allows genre researchers a wider field of study, enables active interaction with other fields of research and with society at large, and in effect gives genre studies a much more extensive impact than had hitherto been the case.

Genres arise to carry out certain social functions; they are typified answers to recurrent situations. Basically: You discover that in a given situation, acting in a particular way will achieve a particular social purpose, and so a pattern (genre) is established. If you need a job, you write an application; if you want soldiers to attack, you give out an order etc. etc. This means that the function determines the genre. Genres are ways to do things with *typified* words. They are social actions.

The point of this interest in the social function of everyday genres is that it allows genre studies to track the impact and the use of genre in our social life, in organisations, and in activity systems. It shows how our interactions form genres, how genres form our interactions, how we are socialized into generic patterns, and how we use genres to achieve our social purposes both on an individual and on an institutional level.[4] Almost everything of note that has happened in genre studies the last three decades is centred on this social and functional perspective —even in those branches of genre scholarship that do not trace their origin as directly to Miller as does RGS. So it is characteristic of contemporary genre studies that it moves the interest of the field in exactly the opposite direction of the literary genre approach, as it emphasizes the functions of genre, but not the actual utterances that are crucial to text based fields like literary or biblical studies.

4 The available literature on genre use in institutions is quite overwhelming. A very modest selection includes Amy Devitt, "Intertextuality in Tax Accounting: Generic, Referential and Functional," in *Dynamics of the Professions: Historical and Contemporary Studies in Writing in Professional Communities*, ed. C. Bazerman and J. Paradis (Madison: University of Wisconsin, 1991), 291–303; Charles Bazerman, "Systems of Genres," in *Genre and the New Rhetoric*, ed. A. Freedman and P. Medway (London: Taylor & Francis, 1994), 79–101; David R. Russel, "Re-thinking Genre in School and Society: An Activity Theory Analysis," *Written Communication* 4 (1997): 504–554; Natasha Artemeva, "Approaches to Learning Genres: A Bibliographical Essay," in *Rhetorical Genre Studies and Beyond*, ed. N. Artemeva and A. Freedman (Winnipeg: Inkshed, 2008), 9–99; and Jack Andersen, "Re-Describing Knowledge Organization : A Genre and Activity-Based View", in J. Andersen, *Genre Theory in Information Studies*, 13–42.

2. Five Basic Tenets of Genre Studies

Since literary genre studies has been slow to progress in the last three decades, working with the new understandings of genre put forth in RGS and its modern compatriots in genre studies is not a matter of individual choice. We need to understand what has happened within the field, even if we want to challenge its state of the art. Otherwise we may well be working with a concept called "genre," but unrelated to the meaning of the word in current scholarship. A refusal to deal with the new research situation thus means making ourselves redundant in genre studies.

However, if we want to engage with contemporary genre studies, we need some reasonably coherent understanding of its state of the art. Therefore, I shall, in the following pages, lay out five points that present the fundamental tenets of contemporary genre studies, and then four points that approximate some of the central interpretative consequences of those tenets (see section 3).

First: Genres are omnipresent in culture. What is usually treated as genres in literary theory is, in fact, a very special case of genre practice. Even a very broad (and nefariously vague) genre category like "the literary work" is just one specialized version of a genre. Genres are not just found in literature; genres are everywhere in culture. All our social interactions are guided by generic patterns (they are, so to speak, "genred");[5] our perception, categorization, and interpretation of cultural phenomena are informed by genres—and by our understanding of how genres work. Thus every extended use of language, and even the overwhelming majority of brief uses, oral or written, will be structured by genre. And genres are not even limited to language. There are genres in film, painting, dance, architecture—and even for that matter in tea, food, and handbags. The naming of the genre will always be in language, of course, but you do not need to know the name or any definition of a genre in order to use and understand it. Most research at the core of genre studies focuses on textual genres,[6] and, as mentioned, there is a close connection between genre studies and writing studies

5 Catherine Schryer, "Genre and Power. A Cronotopic Analysis," in *The Rhetoric and Ideology of Genre*, ed. R. Coe, L. Lingard, and T. Teslenko (Cresskill: Hampton, 2002), 95.

6 See for instance Dorothy A. Winsor, "Ordering Work. Blue-Collar Literacy and the Political Nature of Genre," *Written Communication* 17 (2000), 155–184; Anis Bawarshi, *Genre and the Invention of the Writer* (Logan: Utah State University Press, 2003); Vijay K. Bhatia, *Worlds of Written Discourse* (London: Continuum, 2004); Amy Devitt, *Writing Genres* (Carbondale: Southern Illinois University Press, 2004); and Anthony Paré, Doreen Starke-Meyerring and Lynn McAlpine, "The Dissertation as Multi-Genre: Many Readers, Many Readings," in *Genre in a Changing World*, ed. C. Bazerman, A. Bonini, and D. Figueiredo (Fort Collins: Parlor, 2009), 179–193; John Swales, *Research Genres* (Cambridge: Cambridge University Press, 2004).

that merits closer attention,[7] even if its textual focus may somewhat skew the perception of genre. Within this field, however, there is an expansive research effort covering texts from a wide array of genres. Moreover there is a detailed knowledge of the manifold different ways in which our communication and understanding is conditioned by genre.

Second: Genres owe a large part of their proliferation and strength in culture to a combination of regulation and innovation. Genres form comprehensible patterns that can be carried over from situation to situation and from utterance to utterance, and that can, if needed, act normatively in new situations. At the same time, however, genres are also extremely flexible. Every new usage of a genre adds to or subtracts from the genre, manipulates it, gives it a new meaning, a new focus, a new context, a new form, or a new content. This is true even for strongly normative genres like those of the juridical system: laws, directives, ministerial orders, sentences, etc. As the situation to be regulated by the law often varies from one instance to the next, the application of the genres of law have to be modified accordingly.[8]

The point is that genres are so prolific in human culture because they are not monolithic, but simultaneously firm and flexible. They can frame and control any given situation, while also leaving room for creative actions and uptakes by individual genre users. The most famous description of this in contemporary genre studies is Catherine F. Schryer's declaration that genres are stabilized for now, or stabilized enough to allow for understanding, action and coherent communication.[9] Amy Devitt, another of the captains of modern genre studies, has suggested against Schryer that "genres are not even stabilized for now, as they live and breathe through individual instances and interactions across and within genres."[10] Devitt's point is that each instance of genre use will always somehow modify the genre, and thus cannot be reduced to, or adequately described in terms of, the genre or genres involved. For the very same reason individual

7 Thus a number of the central texts on genre have been developed and published through the so-called Writing Across the Curriculum Clearinghouse (http://wac.colostate.edu/index.cfm).

8 Thus one of the fundamental tenets of Danish legal practice is the principle that one must not "sætte skøn under regel" (bind the assessment with rules), the point being that the use of a reasoned assessment by the person making the ruling is not only allowed but required, and that the individual traits of any given situation must not be neglected when deciding how a given legal rule applies to it.

9 Catharine Schryer, "Records as genre," *Written Communication* 10 (1993): 208. Cf. Catharine Schryer, "The Lab vs the Clinic," in A. Freedman and P. Medway, *Genre and the New Rhetoric*, 108.

10 Amy Devitt, "Re-fusing Form," 39.

genres, too, cannot be put on a simple formula. So, their organizing and categorizing functions aside, genres both regulate and liberate users.[11]

Third: Genres do not exist in isolation, but form larger patterns including other genres. Current genre studies has developed a nuanced vocabulary describing different levels and forms of relationships between genres: "genre set,"[12] "genre chain,"[13] "genre system,"[14] "genre repertoire,"[15] and "genre ecology,"[16] to name but a few central ones. Charting out the interrelationship and the hierarchies between genres, these concepts allow us to see how, for instance, organisations get things done through patternings of genre, and through distributions of genre sets on different roles within the system.

Within the general area of genre patterns, one concept in particular seems relevant for us: the concept of *uptake*, introduced in genre studies by Anne Freadman who has it from the language philosopher J. L. Austin's famous *How to Do Things With Words.*[17] It may probably be seen as putting Miller's concept of genre as social action into motion. Uptake dynamizes social action. Miller describes how genres are used for actions in concrete situations and sketches out some of the principles on a general level. Freadman describes this in a dynamic perspective, demonstrating how genres interact—and even to a certain extent: interlock—in actual communication. The point of the concept is that genres are seen as *uptakes*; reactions to other uses of genre. The use of a genre takes another genre use as "an invitation or a request",[18] and answers it. In the words of Graham Smart, "the appearance of a text in one genre invites a responding text in the

11 Bawarshi, *Genre and the Invention*; Devitt, *Writing Genres.*

12 Devitt, "Intertextuality," 340.

13 Swales, *Research Genres*, 18–20.

14 Bazerman, "Systems of Genres".

15 Wanda J. Orlikowski and JoAnne Yates, "Genre Repertoire: The Structure of Communicative Practices in Organizations," *Administrative Science Quarterly,* 39 (1994): 541.

16 Clay Spinuzzi and Mark Zachry, "Genre Ecologies: An Open-system Approach to Understanding and Constructing Documentation", *Journal of Computer Documentation* 24 (2000): 169.

17 John L. Austin, *How To Do Things With Words* (Oxford: Oxford University Press, 1976); Anne Freadman, "Anyone for Tennis?" in A. Freedman and P. Medway, *Genre and the New Rhetoric*, 43–66, Anne Freadman, "Uptake," in R. Coe et al., *The Rhetoric and Ideology of Genre*, 39–53. For more on uptake see Celia Roberts and Sirkant Sarangi, "Uptake of Discourse Research in Interprofessional Settings: Reporting from Medical Consultancy," *Applied Linguistics* 24 (2003): 338–359: Katja Thieme, "Uptake and Genre: The Canadian Reception of Suffrage Militancy," *Women's Studies International Forum* 29 (2006): 279–288; Kimberly K. Emmons, "Uptake and the Biomedical Subject," in C. Bazerman et al., *Genre in a Changing World*, 134–157; Tosh Tachino, "Theorizing Uptake and Knowledge Mobilization: A Case for Intermediary Genre," *Written Communication* 29 (2012): 455–476; and Heather Bastian, "Capturing Individual Uptake: Toward a Disruptive Research Methodology," *Composition Forum* 31 (2015): n.p.

18 Freadman, "Uptake," 40.

second genre."[19] This interchange is an uptake. The new use of a genre in turn acts as an invitation or request, too, and thus begets further uses of genre—in effect taking part in a social *perpetuum mobile*. This process itself defines the genre of the utterance in question, as texts "become identified as being of a certain genre in their interaction with other texts. When a text finds a respondent, the text's generic identity can be confirmed, but it can also be modified."[20] So our genre attributions are not singular; the genre of an utterance is not always fixed, and the utterer is not the sole proprietor of the genre of his or her utterance. Freadman emphasizes that the uptake is "bidirectional," it establishes a relationship between two uses of genre.[21] Utterances, therefore, can be taken up as different genres than intended, for instance an attempt at giving "advice" can be taken up as an "insult."

Thus, given the creative element involved in genre use, it is unsurprising that the uptake intended by the original genre user need not be the one actually taken. There are multiple possible uptakes to most if not all uses of genre, and inviting or requesting a certain kind of generic response is not the same as getting it. Some of the invitations made by a genre may not even be desired by the user, but inherent in the genre none the less. Thus, an "application" invites a "rejection" as well as an "acceptance."

Fourth: Most of our interpretation through genre is tacit and rarely understood as generic interpretation.[22] Growing up in a cultural context, or getting socialized into one, we acquire an extensive tacit, even unacknowledged, understanding of a wide field of genres connected to that culture. This happens through a complex process which does not necessarily entail that the norms and forms of the genres are made explicit. Thus Paré, Starke-Meyerring, and McAlpine describe how even highly experienced PhD supervisors are unable to explicate the generic norms of good scholarship they are trying to teach their PhD students: "[M]uch of the advice offered by supervisors comes from a deep discipline-specific, but inexpressible discourse knowledge. Although we are attempting to get colleagues to articulate the standards to which they hold their doctoral students, even the most experienced supervisors seem uncertain."[23] This does not mean that they do not understand or master these norms, but merely

19 Graham Smart, "A Central Bank's 'Communications Strategy': The Interplay of Activity, Discourse Genres, and Technology in a Time of Organizational Change," in *Writing Selves/Writing Societies*, ed. C. Bazerman and D. R. Russel (Fort Collins: The WAC Clearinghouse, 2003), 16.

20 Thieme, "Uptake and Genre," 280.

21 Freadman, "Uptake," 43.

22 See Devitt, *Writing Genres*; and Sune Auken, "Genre and Interpretation", in S. Auken et al., *Genre and …*, 154–183.

23 Paré et al., "Dissertation as Multi-Genre," 187.

that they have acquired them through exposure to the practice of other genre users, and from practicing them themselves, not by way of explicit genre teaching. So, most of our understanding of genres is learned through practice, and is tacit, even unrecognised, as genre knowledge. We are able to perform highly complex interpretative moves through genres without realizing that we are interpreting—much less that we are interpreting through genre.[24]

It is an interesting fact about this surprisingly advanced, tacit interpretation that even explicating the implied interpretations at play in any given use of genre is an independent analytical task. Consequently, generic interpretation may to a certain extent be considered as a form of re-interpretation: A conscious charting of what is already assumed as knowledge. In a similar vein, one of the hardest things in dealing with genres from a different culture—be it foreign, historical, or both—is to understand that which is implied in any given genre use.

Closely related to this point is the *fifth:* Our perception of genres tends to naturalize them; probably because it depends on tacit knowledge and instantaneous recognition and understanding, Since genres are habitual, they acquire an "illusion of normalcy";[25] they are "naturalized or 'just the way we do things around here',"[26] and they may even lead to what has been called a "cultural reproduction of ignorance,"[27] as misconceptions inherent in a genre is carried over from person to person without reflection. In acquiring competency in a genre system, we also integrate ourselves into genre hierarchies that are both places of power relations and carriers of ideology. This is, for instance, demonstrated in Dorothy Winsor's analysis of the work order in an engineering company,[28] in Anthony Paré's work on the genre use of social workers, and it is also present (outside RGS) in Peter Seitel's analysis of Haia folktales.[29]

This naturalization of genre begs the question whether teaching genre is a conservative measure whereby the teacher, knowingly or unknowingly, naturalizes existing ideologies and power structures to the students.[30] It may also act to preserve in other ways, as it may become a done thing: "The mere existence of

24 See the examples in Auken, "Genre and Interpretation."

25 Anthony Paré, "Genre and Identity: Individuals, Institutions, and Ideology," in R. Coe et al., *The Rhetoric and Ideology of Genre*, 61.

26 Schryer, "Genre and Power," 76.

27 Judy Z. Segal, "Breast Cancer Narratives as Public Rhetoric: Genre itself and the Maintainance of Ignorance," *Linguistics and the Human Sciences* 3 (2007), 4.

28 Winsor, "Ordering Work."

29 Peter Seitel, "Theorizing Genres—Interpreting Works," *New Literary History* 34 (2003): 275–297.

30 Amy Devitt, "Teaching Critical Genre Awareness," in C. Bazerman et al., *Genre in a Changing World*, 337–351.

an established genre may encourage its continued use."[31] Thus even when the practical effect of a genre has receded, the habit of using it may linger.

The implied power relations and ideologies of any given genre are not invisible in the genre; they are merely naturalized to the user. Analytically speaking, an interpretation of the ways in which any individual or group apply genre will reveal these implied structures and facilitate an understanding of what is considered to be given and what, by comparison, is subject to debate for the genre user(s). This point is similar to the implied knowledge discussed in point four above, but the fundamental difference is that whereas the tacit knowledge in a genre is, in fact, knowledge, the assumptions which are normalized in a genre can be both erroneous and oppressive—even self-oppressive to the genre user(s).

3. Consequences for Interpretation

So far, this presentation remains squarely within the scope of RGS. However, in a critical reading of a complex text such as the Gospel of John, my application of the concepts outlined above diverges from the movement's usual path. Notably, this does not make the reading oppositional to or polemical against RGS. Nor does it challenge the basic assumptions of the movement. It is, however, somewhat off the beaten tracks of RGS.

First: Literary works and other hyper-complex utterances, like a gospel, are specialized cases of genre use. Most of the genre uses surrounding us are less formally and thematically complicated, more dominated by a particular social or institutional function, more regulated, and more standardized. They still leave room for individual creativity, but to a lesser degree.[32] This means, obviously, that any generalization from literary genres to genres as such must be mindful of the difference. As so often before, we are dealing with a continuum, and simple literary genres are less complicated than complex rhetorical ones, but the point still warrants caution. The same caution also applies the other way around; thus, one cannot expect hyper-complex utterances to be adequately described by reference to the terminology of function-based genre studies. They will have advanced internal features that require a prolonged study of their individual formal and thematic traits.

However, the special place thus awarded to hyper-complex utterances does not entail independence from the humble genres analyzed by RGS, it simply shifts

31 Devitt, "Intertextuality," 340–41. See also Kathleen M. Jamieson, "Antecedent Genre as Rhetorical Constraint," *Quarterly Journal of Speech* 61 (1975): 406–415.

32 Cf. Mikhail Bakhtin, "The Problem of Speech Genres," in *Speech Genres and Other Late Essays*, ed. C. Emerson and M. Holquist (Austin: University of Texas Press, 1986), 64–65.

their function. The basic point of Bakhtin's famous distinction between primary and secondary speech genres still holds: Complex genres are built from simpler genres.[33] Therefore, in order to understand a complex genre, one must understand the many simple genres which constitute it. Thus, in working generically with the interpretation of a work we are both looking for the overall genre of the work in its entirety and for the embedded genres used to compile the work.

Second: All genres, not just the literary ones, are a combination of norms and creativity. There is less room for free expression when you are placing an order for a product than when you are writing a long poem. Yet, since even the de facto genres are only at best stabilized for now, it is unsurprising that genre norms do not determine every single trait of every utterance. Consequently, in studying the relationship between an utterance and its genre, we need to look for both stability and variation. They will vary to different degrees, in different ways, and you may call this variation a lot of things—like "genre bending" made famous in Johannine studies by Harold Attridge.[34] But if one frames the demonstration of how an utterance deviates from its genre as a kind of revolution against the confines of that genre, one simply has not understood what genre is.

This, incidentally, is a recurrent phenomenon in modern day art criticism. Since originality—and with it: unconventionality—is highly valued in the evaluation of the arts, one way of marking a work as outstanding is to describe it as something that breaks or escapes genre norms, or cannot be grasped in the terms of genre, awarding genre the role of the boring "garde" to which the work can be "avant." However, since genres are at best stabilized for now, using generic norms innovatively or against the grain is a common, everyday occurrence, and the perceived escape from generic norms is therefore less than surprising. Many of the interpretative moves made in demonstrating how this or that work of art breaks away from generic norms, are original, profound, and enlightening, but the discovery itself is old as the hills.

Third: One of the fundamental influences from Miller is her vested interest in the de facto genres. The ones she terms "humble". Her interest here is one of the

33 The primary weaknesses of the distinction are two-fold. First, the notion of the primary speech genre is ill defined. A primary speech genre is "simple" (Bakhtin, "Speech Genres," 61) and takes form "in unmediated speech communication" (62). However, of the genres, he mentions, "rejoinders in everyday dialogue" and "private letters," one is written. The article never addresses this apparent contradiction, and offers no further explanation. Second, the model is too simplistic; the actual dynamic of building complex utterances out of simpler utterances is a many layered, complex process, often allowing complex genres, themselves consisting of simpler genres, to be building blocks in even more complex genres. The insight which is expressed in the distinction, however, is valid: the fundamental realisation that simple genres are the building blocks of more complex genres, and that the character and function of the simple genres change when they are embedded in more complex genres.

34 Harold Attridge, "Genre Bending in the Fourth Gospel," *JBL* 121 (2002): 3–21.

most profound influences in modern genre studies, as it opens up the entire field of inquiry that defines contemporary genre research. Following her lead, genre scholars have studied tax accounting, conference paper proposals, engineer work orders, scientific papers, etc. Interest no longer rests with the literary genres, and only marginally with the high rhetorical ones. Literary or biblical scholars, obviously, cannot transform their material into de facto genres like those described by Miller. However, we can shift our field of attention to include the function of the de facto genres in the works we are treating. Even a text laden with high meaning, like John's Gospel, will incorporate numerous instances of much more ordinary genres than the high rhetorical speeches of Jesus. An RGS inspired approach would turn its attention to the more humble genres in the Gospel, the genres used not in the impressive pieces of oratory spread throughout the Gospel, but in the formally more mundane, or at least less aloof, exchanges between Jesus and his followers, Jesus and his opponents, or any other combination of people interacting throughout the Gospel.

Fourth: Taking up the interest of RGS in the functional, rhetorical or social aspects of genre, we might ask some of the same questions about the uses of genres within the frames of John's Gospel that Miller would ask of genres in social life. I have previously sketched out how such an approach might work in a study of fiction,[35] and the general technique of superimposing Miller's approach on the study of the action of literary works seems feasible in the study of the Fourth Gospel as well. Looking at the actual uses of genre in John, if approaching it from an RGS point of view, one would ask a particular set of questions. One would ask as to the rhetorical situation involved, the exigence addressed by the use of genre, the recurring patterns available to the genre users, how these users employ the patterns, and thus, for the social purposes achieved (or strived for) by the concrete uses of genre.

Such an approach would activate all of the systematic and dynamic aspects of contemporary genre studies, for instance, John Swales' concept of genre chains, Freadman's concept of uptake, and, in particular, the relationship between the two.[36] Freadman's concept has already been sketched out above, so at this point we need only to touch upon Swales'. He describes how genres are formed and, to a certain extent, formalized into chains in order for users to accomplish larger tasks. So, for instance, a part of the genre chain (or, more correctly, part of one of the genre chains) involved in arranging a scholarly conference is the one leading

35 Sune Auken, "Genre as Fictional Action," *Nordisk Tidsskrift for Informationsvidenskab og Kulturformidling,* 2/3 (2013): 19–28.

36 Swales, *Research Genres,* 18–20, Freadman, "Anyone for Tennis?" and "Uptake."

to the individual paper presentations. If successful, it runs approximately like this:[37]

Call for papers
paper proposal
Review meeting/interchange
Letter of acceptance
Paper draft from presenters
Letter from arrangers to participants with paper draft
Presentation
Discussion

The central difference compared to the concept of uptake is that a genre chain is formalized. Each genre, of course, is an uptake on the former, but one must move through the whole series in order to present one's paper correctly. Some of the steps are structurally optional, not all conferences require paper drafts to be submitted, and some of the steps can be short-circuited: One can (for whatever reason) refrain from sending one's paper draft for a conference which requires it, or one can talk for so long during the presentation that there is no room for discussion—or, alas, even longer if the session chair is unwilling to exert his or her mandate. But these short-circuits are shortcomings compared to the purpose of the genre chain. A successful fulfilment of the purpose of the genre chain requires that each step is completed in order.

Both concepts, uptake and genre chain, describe how genres relate to one another in a dynamic process, and both are necessary in order to describe the actual interchanges through genre. Seen from one angle, a genre chain is a formalized series of uptakes. Genre chains are bound; they move in a particular order, and relate to one another in a particular hierarchy. Uptakes can be more creative; an uptake can easily follow a chain, but it can also deviate from, turn, or twist the purpose of the chain. Also, it may be an uptake to insert one or more new genres into the process in an attempt to achieve a desired purpose. One may, for instance, attempt to use the genres "bribery" or "seduction" in order to be allowed to give a conference paper instead of following the chain described above. Creative uptakes of genre chains may be effective, and sometimes they can even trump the chains, but in many cases the given chain is by far the stronger, and creative uptakes of it are likely to fail.

This applies to everyday life. When moving into the literary field, however, we will expect to see genre chains and uptakes entering into a somewhat different relationship. As narrative texts tend to deal with exceptional social situations, they will contain exceptional uses of genre. Thus, we will find uptakes trumping chains on a regular basis. Accordingly, in interpretation we would, following

37 This is an abbreviated version of a similar chain drawn up by Swales himself.

Swales and Freadman, be looking for the interaction and even interlocking of genre chains and uptakes. In interpreting through genre, we will look at the ways in which different actors handle these uptakes, how they choose between them, interpret, shape, or even manipulate them in order to suit their own social and communicative needs.

4. RGS and Form Criticism

The central concepts of RGS connect it with an important scholarly tradition in biblical studies: form criticism. There is an obvious parallel between the concept of the "recurrent rhetorical situation" central in RGS and the crucial place of the *Sitz im Leben* of a genre fundamental to the understanding of the *Gattung* in form criticism.[38]

Given the limited contact between RGS and biblical studies, it should come as no surprise that little is written on the subject. In literary studies, the *Sitz im Leben* has been discussed by Hans Robert Jauss[39]—though without reference to RGS as Jauss writes years before Miller—and the connection between it and the recurrent rhetorical situation of RGS has been noted by Beata Agrell.[40] However, little seems to have been done beyond this, and nothing at the core of genre studies. The scope of the present article does not allow a deeper engagement with this question; a few notes comparing the two must suffice for now.

Apart from the obvious fact that form criticism typically has the ambition to assist in the reconstruction of the history of specific traditions and RGS has not, form criticism and RGS share a common understanding of the situatedness of genre. They both see genres as responses to social situations; that is, as ways to handle social needs and carry out social intentions. Thus, to understand a genre is, to a large extent, to understand the function it serves to its users, and the interpretation of any given genre therefore hovers between a rhetorical, an ethnographic, a historical, a literary, and a sociological approach.

However, the differences between the two approaches are quite obvious. I will, for now, touch on only two. The fundamental method of form criticism is a "linguistic textual analysis that may be applied both synchronically and dia-

38 For a more detailed discussion of form criticism see Klaus Koch, *The Growth of the Biblical Tradition: The Form-Critical Method* (London: Adam & Charles Black, 1969) and Martin J. Buss, *Biblical Form Criticism in its Context*, JSOTSup 274 (Sheffield: Sheffield Academic Press, 1999).

39 Hans Robert Jauss, "Theory of Genre and Medieval Literature," in *Toward an Aesthetic of Reception*, trans. Timothy Bahti (Brighton: The Harvester Press, 1982), 102–104. Jauss' translator renders "Sizt im Leben" as "Locus in Life" (103).

40 Beata Agrell, "Genre and Working Class Fiction," in S. Auken et al., *Genre and …*, 286–327.

cronically to texts in either written or oral form."[41] It identifies textual regularities and works from these to establish the social situation of the genre, so the understanding of the genre is largely deductive. There are very practical reasons for this. In the words of James Muilenburg,

> [p]erhaps more serious is the scepticism of all attempts to read a pericope in its historical context. The truth is that in a vast number of instances we are indeed left completely in the dark as to the occasion in which the words were spoken, and it is reasonable to assume that it was not of primary interest to the compilers of the traditions.[42]

Consequently, form criticism aims to understand the genres through their *Sitz im Leben*, but can only get to it through an understanding of the genre. This leads to what Sellin has termed "literaturwissenschaftliche Paläontologie der christlichen Urgeschichte"[43] and also brings the method dangerously close to circular reasoning.[44]

The RGS researchers' understanding of the social situation is more empirical. Their understanding of genre is emphatically not based on textual regularities, but on generic function.[45] Miller's original article is mostly theoretical. But the subsequent studies branching out of the theory and terminology within the movement, have been working with analysable uses of genres in context. Some of these have been historical,[46] but most are rhetorical, linguistic, ethnographic, or, if you will, ethno-rhetorical.[47] Thus the concepts employed to describe the patterns and uses of genre have been developed in the description of how genres work in actual settings.

---

41 Marwin A. Sweeney, "Form Criticism," in *To Each its Own Meaning: Biblical Criticisms and Their Application*, ed. S. L. McKenzie and S. R. Haynes (Louisville: Westminster John Knox, 1999), 58.

42 James Muilenburg, "Form Criticism and Beyond," *JBL* 88 (1969): 6.

43 Gerhard Sellin, "'Gattung' und 'Sitz im Leben' auf dem Hintergrund der Problematik von Mündlichkeit und Schriftlichkeit synoptischer Erzählungen," *EvT* 50 (1990): 312.

44 Bultmann's hermeneutic statement of the relationship as a circular move between the "forms of the literary tradition" and "the influences operating in the life of the community" (Rudolf Bultmann, *History of the Synoptic Tradition* [Peabody: Hendrickson, 1963], 5) is quite valid, insofar as there is alternative source material available for the understanding of the life of the community. However, when this is not the case or to the degree that this is not the case, the circle loses its hermeneutic character.

45 Cf. Auken, "Utterance and Function."

46 For instance Charles Bazerman, *Shaping Written Knowledge* (Madison: The University of Wisconsin Press, 1988); Bazerman, "Systems of Genres"; Freadman, "Uptake"; and Laura Skouvig, "Genres of War: Informing a City," in J. Andersen, *Genre Theory in Information Studies*, 133–154.

47 Thus Devitt, "Intertextuality"; Schryer, "Records as Genre"; Russel, Rethinking Genre"; Winsor, "Ordering Work"; Paré, "Genre and Identity"; Heather MacNeil, "What Finding Aids Do: Archival Description as Rhetorical Genre in Traditional and Web-Based Environments," *Archival Science Sciences* 12 (2012): 485–500, and numerous other works.

Second, being developed for the understanding of the Bible, the genres analysed by form criticism are parts of a larger utterance. The fundamental building blocks of form criticism are the "individual units of the tradition,"[48] i.e., the genres embedded in the biblical texts on the level of the pericopes, whereas the larger units are seen as built up from these genres. The primary material of form criticism is thus below the level of the individual utterance. In contrast the topics chosen in contemporary genre studies are almost always above the level of the individual utterance, and only rarely do scholars move into the embedded genres that make up an utterance. This is more a difference of approach than a scholarly disagreement, but it is consequential none the less.

Due to the aforementioned differences, and others with them, the actual analytical work carried out in form criticism is closer to what is being done by philologists and literary scholars than to RGS, and comparing it to the other scholarly methods in contemporary genre studies would probably show even more fundamental differences. Yet, the second of the major differences mentioned above could also be seen as an obvious point of connection: Just as the *Sitz im Leben* of form criticism resembles the rhetorical situation in RGS, so, too, do the former's generic "units" (*Gattungen*) bear resemblance[49] to the rhetorical genres of the latter. Furthermore, given the complexity of the Bible and the relative simplicity of most texts discussed by RGS, there will often be cases where the embedded genres discussed in form criticism are actually as complex as, or more complex than, the individual genres studied in RGS.

5. Reading John through Genre

In bringing the concepts of contemporary genre studies to the Gospel of John, we are—despite the above points of contact—by necessity translating and re-contextualizing a scholarly endeavour which has been developed in order to treat a different set of scholarly problems and which has at certain points been developed in opposition to literary genre studies. Therefore, the practice cannot be mainline RGS, but must develop new approaches that combine the scholarly insights of contemporary genre studies with those of other research traditions. What follows is a tentative attempt at applying such an approach.

One of the longer connected actions in John is the story of Jesus' capture, trial, and crucifixion (John 18–19). Here, we have a situation ripe with conflict, one in

48 Bultmann, *History of the Synoptic Tradition*, 3.

49 Resemblance is not identity, and an extensive comparative study of the different concepts would be required to unravel their precise relationship. However, the concepts are sufficiently related for the parallels drawn here.

which a number of different actors try to achieve their own distinct purpose: The central actors in the passage are for our purposes here Jesus himself, the priests, the *Ioudaioi*, the disciples, the soldiers, and Pilate.

The social actions attempted by these actors are diverse. Not only do they not align smoothly, they are not even clearly opposed, or moving in opposite directions. To confuse matters even further, the passage is generically undermarked. Throughout the passage most utterances are simply described as something somebody "says"—not "threatens", "asks", "replies" or the like. So, for instance, the uptake presented by a question and reacted to by the answer is rarely marked as such. Though the genres at play in the passage are actually quite diverse, the text is subdued in its characterization of them.

The most obvious attempts at social action carried out through the two chapters are the endeavours of the *Ioudaioi*—and through them the priests—to get Jesus crucified, and Pilate's attempts to avoid having to pass the judgement for capital punishment. The two sides, then, are basically fighting over a genre, the sentence, and each of them is manoeuvring in order to achieve a certain kind of sentence. The generically challenging part of the process is that the *Ioudaioi* are looking to achieve a certain social aim, namely the execution of Jesus, that can only be fulfilled by Pilate who, in turn, is unwilling to order the execution—and is even unwilling to pass any kind of judgement on Jesus whom he considers innocent. The genres used by the *Ioudaioi* are reasonably straightforward: Accusations, demands, and threats. The threats are marked generically by the raising of their voices and by the fear that their words invoke in Pilate (19:8).

Generically speaking, what the *Ioudaioi* are trying to do is to set a genre chain in motion in the Roman administration which includes such moves as arrest–accusation–interrogation–conviction–execution. The evidence is weak, at best, but the social situation is strong.

Pilate is less straightforward. Cornelis Bennema claims that "Pilate is probably the most complex character in the Johannine narrative,"[50] and even if this may be overstating the case, at least the prefect's use of genre is rather complex. This may have to do with the fact that his situation is more muddled and his motives are more ambiguous. He does not want to execute Jesus, but he does not have the strength of conviction to match that of the *Ioudaioi*, and he is scared that the situation might backfire.

This makes him weak, despite his position as ruler.[51] It also makes him a fascinating genre user. He reacts to a number of uptakes and, through both

50 Cornelis Bennema, *Encountering Jesus: Character Studies in the Gospel of John*, 2nd ed. (Minneapolis: Fortress Press, 2014), 337.

51 But see the alternate interpretations of Pilate in Bennema, *Encountering Jesus* and Andrew T. Lincoln, *Truth on Trial: The Lawsuit Motif in the Fourth Gospel* (Peabody: Hendrickson,

standardized and individualized generic responses, he invites a number of uptakes. But he rarely, if ever, receives the responses he desires—even if he sometimes receives the responses his uses of genre invite. In this sense, for instance, his attempt to use the genre of the pardon to solve the problem is defeated by the demand of the *Ioudaioi* that he should pardon Barabbas (18:39–40). Thus, the power of genre works against him: Though he finds Jesus innocent and, formally speaking, has the power to acquit him, Jesus ends up dead on the cross. In spite of his attempts to break the genre chain that leads to the execution, his uptakes are thwarted by the other actors.

Among these actors is, surprisingly, the accused man himself. Interestingly, from a point of view of genre as social action, Jesus himself seems to act very little. In fact, when first looking at this passage, I found that he was by far the dullest character, if understood as a genre user. On a closer look, however, he is in fact the most interesting one. Even during the initial arrest, Jesus conducts himself in discordance with the given genre. Jesus "takes charge of the situation by disclosing his own identity before anyone else is able to make a move."[52] The force dispatched to arrest him is absurdly large, including not just the guard force, but servants of the high priests and the Pharisees as well (18:3). Normally under circumstances such as these, resistance is futile. However, the prisoner does not even need to resist arrest; as soon as he identifies himself, the arresting forces stumble backwards and fall. Yet, despite the ease with which Jesus overpowers his would-be captors he still allows them to arrest him. He thus steps out of the given roles in the genre of the arrest. Rather than being the object of an arrest, he becomes the subject of it, and his apprehension is, effectively, more an event of his own making than something which is done to him.[53]

This turn of events continues in the trial scenes. The trial as genre determines the particular roles of its participants: One is attributed the role of the interrogator and judge,[54] while the other—presumably unwillingly—assumes that of the defendant. The latter has the most to gain or lose, but he is also the person whose role is most severely restricted: In the genre chain of the trial, he has only one genre available to him: the answer to a question. This may be a general and overarching genre; however, its constraints are clearly demarcated: The interrogator's questions limit the possibilities as to what direction the answer may

2000), both of whom depict Pilate as a shrewd politician who uses the situation to his advantage.

52 Kasper Bro Larsen, *Recognizing the Stranger: Recognition Scenes in the Gospel of John*, BIS 93 (Leiden: Brill, 2008), 168.

53 Larsen, *Recognizing the Stranger*, 169.

54 This double role of interrogator and judge is, of course, unusual by modern standard, but seems quite natural in the text.

take. This is a highly artificial situation, and it has every trait of what Paré describes as the "illusion of normalcy" in genres.

Jesus' replies, however, break the illusion of normalcy in the situation. Instead of replying as a person who is subject to another's authority and must justify himself to this other person, Jesus replies as a person of authority. In accordance with his role as a judge elsewhere in the Gospel (i. e., 5:22; 8:16; 9:39; and 12:29–31), Jesus "puts his judge on trial regarding the truth,"[55] and this governs his stance as participant in the trial genre. His uptakes on Pilate's questions are consistently unorthodox compared to the genre. He asks questions instead of answering, he also throws Pilate's questions back in his face and, at a certain point (19:10–11), he even denies his judge the power of judgement. Furthermore, the Gospel confirms this point through an ironic reversal. Inherent in Pilate's original question is an implied threat against Jesus: I have the power over your life, so you should comply with me, or you will be in danger. This threat is not just made by Pilate but is part and parcel of the interrogation as genre. The Gospel, however, proves Jesus right: He is executed despite Pilate's efforts, and thus his denial of Pilate's power to rule over life and death is confirmed.

Jesus talks as if Pilate is somehow at a disadvantage compared to him, and the prefect never gets what he desires from his prisoner. Accordingly, as a genre user Jesus does not comply with the role attributed to him by the genre and the rhetorical situation. He exhibits what might be termed "generic insubordination." According to what has previously been said in this article, it is unsurprising that he does not achieve the usual aim of the accused man in a trial: Acquittal.

However, the point remains that Jesus, as is well known, acts in accordance with a master plan beyond the comprehension of the other characters. He does not achieve social action in the usual sense through his genre use, but he achieves divine action instead. The master plan is clearly marked in the beginning of chapter 18 which details the arrest. It is also evident in Jesus' pre-knowledge of the entire process (18:5), his care to comply with his own prophecy (18:9), and in his explicit acceptance of the Father's cup (John 18:11). From this point of view, the other actors in the narrative are embedded in a divine, ironic structure.

From their own perspective, the other actors behave according to their own purposes, and thus, their success of failure can be measured according to a socially established understanding of success and failure: The *Ioudaioi* triumph, Pilate fails, and, from this perspective, Jesus pays the ultimate price for his inability to act in his own best interest. From another perspective, however, which

55 Lincoln, *Truth on Trial*, 129.

is the perspective of the Gospel, the exchange is a path to Jesus' ultimate success; namely, the fulfilment of his—at once earthly and divine—purpose.[56]

This is quite evident in the crucifixion scene, which is, in John, less a scene of torture than of triumph. Jesus reinterprets the genre of the execution by taking it into his own hand. His genre-given role as victim is to suffer and die, but he remains active throughout. He knows when the purpose is fulfilled, asks for a drink in order to fulfil yet another bit of scripture, not because he is thirsty, and then—actively—gives up the Spirit, as if by decision. Like Pilate and the *Ioudaioi*, the other actors in the scene play into the prophecies and thus help to fulfil them, even as they believe that they are acting independently. The stabbing of Jesus' dead body is one more confirmation of the divine purpose that has been carried out (19:34–36): "[T]he death of Jesus is more of a *triumphal exit* than a kathartic degradation."[57]

All of this points to yet another genre towards which Jesus displays a loyalty that explains his otherwise aberrant behaviour as a genre user. This genre is, of course, the prophecy. The prophecy, as it appears here (5–6 times in chapters 18 and 19), is an earthly manifestation of a divine plan, established long before the events described, and possessing a transcendent reality beyond anything imagined by the other actors in the narrative. Jesus complies completely with this genre. This leads him to transcend all other generic purposes in order to fulfil the prophecies and thereby complete the divine plan expressed in them. Jesus fails to use genre as social action because he sees beyond this function to genre as divine action.

6. Conclusion

As should be evident from the analysis above, it is a quite apt metaphor when the editor of the present volume names John a "genre mosaic." The social genres involved in the trial scene—as well as the hidden, but stronger, genre of prophecy—interact through chains and uptakes to form a larger whole: The story of the arrest, interrogation, and execution of Jesus. They are stones and patterns in a mosaic, and, obviously, the story in chapters 18 and 19 must be understood in the larger context of the whole Gospel, and thus is only one pattern, albeit a very important one, within the larger context of the genre mosaic which is the Gospel of John.

56 In accordance with the concept of the "third 'law'" described in Larsen, *Recognizing*, 179. Jesus is convicted as a criminal when the law of the *Ioudaioi* and the imperial law finally meet, but the conviction actually displays and fulfils his kinghood according to the divine law that Jesus himself follows. See also Lincoln, *Truth on Trial*, 123–138.

57 Mark W. G. Stibbe, *John as Storyteller: Narrative Criticism and the Fourth Gospel*, SNTSMS 73 (Cambridge: Cambridge University Press, 1990), 125.

The basic assumption that underpins the metaphor of the genre mosaic is well-known in genre research in much the same way as the idea of "genre bending" is a local expression of an established understanding in genre research. In general genre studies, the relationship between genres within a complex genre is usually expressed through Bakhtin's distinction between primary and secondary speech genres. In Bakhtin's formulation, the complex genres (or "secondary speech genres") arise as combinations of simpler genres (or "primary speech genres"). These simpler genres lose part of their original character when they are used as building blocks, but they also add meaning to the overarching, secondary genre—in keeping with the metaphor. The stones in the mosaic are seen less as individual stones than as parts of a mosaic, but their presence also constitutes the mosaic.

But although the underpinnings of the metaphor are known already, this does not make it any less relevant for the understanding of the Gospel. It poses a number of questions that are analytically relevant for the interpretation. What genres form the individual "stones" in the mosaic of the Gospel of John? How do these genres link up to form larger patterns? And how do these patterns in turn hinge upon one another to create the complete mosaic that is the Gospel of John? That these questions can be asked in relation to other texts as well does not render them any less relevant in the Johannine studies. In fact, the possibility of asking similar questions in relation to different texts opens up the possibility of comparative interpretations through genre.

Generic investigations in John need not be as literary in character, as the example given above. I read the gospel "as text" and only incidentally engage in contextual—or for that matter theological—subjects. This process can be carried out on a much deeper level, but given the state of contemporary genre studies even this would barely be scratching the surface. More directly functional perspectives will offer different challenges to an understanding of genre in the Gospel of John. The actual functionality of genres and genre patterns is frequently researched through interview techniques, and through different kinds of fieldwork, and even when this is not the case, the studies are strongly focused on a contextual interest in the actual use and significance of genres for the people who use them. Interviews and fieldwork are not terribly viable methods in historical biblical studies, and the questions which can be dealt with contextually will always be limited by the available source material. Accordingly, the approaches have to be different. But given the centrality of genre in human culture, understanding, and communication, there will be numerous points of connection—of which this brief article has touched upon but a very few.[58]

58 Aside from the editor of the present volume, whose insightful comments have been crucial for the article, I wish to thank Helle Bildsøe and Søren Holst, both from the University of Copenhagen, for their help with the present study.

Part II: The Mosaic as a Whole

Colleen M. Conway

John, Gender, and Genre: Revisiting the Woman Question after Masculinity Studies

1. Introduction

While scholars have given considerable attention to gender in the Gospel of John, in particular the role of female characters in the narrative, most of this work has not given explicit attention to genre.[1] The opposite is also true. Of the many studies that explore genre in the Gospel, few include extensive discussion of gender representations. The goal of this article is to bring gender into conversation with genre in John. Theoretically, I follow Carol Newsom's suggestion (who follows Derrida) to think of texts as *participating* in particular genres rather than belonging to them.[2] She urges us to think how texts are continually invoking different genres, "gesturing to them, playing in and out of them, and in so doing, continually changing them."[3] Along these lines, my interest here is not in as-

1 Early studies of women in the Gospel were motivated by an interest in the role of women in the contemporary church. Many of these studies considered the Gospel to be a reflection of a particular historical community with the implication that the gospel supported women leaders in the church. A second wave of interest in gender analysis emerged with the literary turn in gospel studies. In this case, focus shifted to the literary function of male and female characters in the narrative. More recently, the study of masculinity has added another dimension of gender analysis to the study of the Gospel. For a review of scholarship on women in John through the mid-90s, see Colleen M. Conway, *Men and Women in the Fourth Gospel: Gender and Johannine Characterization*, SBLDS 167 (Atlanta: Society of Biblical Literature, 1999), 18–36. For the study of masculinity in the Fourth Gospel and the gospels in general, see "'Behold the Man!' Masculine Christology and the Fourth Gospel," in *New Testament Masculinities*, ed. Stephen D. Moore and Janice Capel Anderson (Atlanta: Society of Biblical Literature, 2003); *Behold the Man: Jesus and Greco-Roman Masculinity* (Oxford; New York: Oxford University Press, 2008).

2 Jacques Derrida, "The Law of Genre," *Critical Inquiry* 7 (1980): 55–81. Derrida here presents a hypothesis which reads, in part, "Every text participates in one or several genres, yet such participation never amounts to belonging" (65).

3 Carol Newsom, "Spying out the Land: A Report from Genology," in *Bakhtin and Genre Theory in Biblical Studies*, ed. Roland Boer, SemeiaSt 63 (Leiden: Brill, 2008), 21. First published in Kelvin G. Friebel, Ronald L. Troxel, and Dennis R. Magary, eds. *Seeking out the Wisdom of the*

signing the Gospel of John to a particular genre, but rather in exploring what we learn if we understand the Gospel to be participating in or invoking different ancient genres—biography, tragedy, romance—in ways that contribute to the gender construction of its characters. In so doing, I adopt an approach to genre that moves away from a strictly classifying approach and toward a consideration of literary works in their socio-historical context. Just as, for example, a particular mode of characterization or choice of metaphors has ideological implications for an interpretation of a literary text, so too, does the text's generic aspects. As Simon Goldhill observes, "there is a socio-politics of genre, which has all too often been forgotten in formalist analyses of particular genres."[4] If one is interested in how gender ideologies function in writing, it becomes all the more crucial to consider the socio-political implications of genre.

In what follows, I first argue that considering gender in the Gospel alongside ancient biographies leads to such a strong picture of a manly/divine Jesus that it raises again the question of what purpose the female characters serve in the narrative. This is especially the case because the ancient biographies do not make a point of featuring women in the way the Gospel does. This leads to the second two parts of the discussion. When we consider the Gospel in light of other ancient genres a more complex picture of gender dynamics emerges. Because both Greek drama and the Greek novels feature women in prominent roles, paying attention to how gender functions in these genres presents new possibilities for reading the role of women in John.

2. John, Gender, and Ancient Biography

Since Richard Burridge's detailed comparison of the Gospels with Greco-Roman biographies, many New Testament scholars have accepted his view that the gospels are a form of ancient biography, including the Gospel of John.[5] Burridge's systematic work is very much the classifying sort, although he repeatedly emphasizes the flexible boundaries of genre. But whether one wants to designate the Gospel as a whole as "biography" is not as important as recognizing the ways

Ancients: Essays Offered to Honor Michael V. Fox on the Occasion of His Sixty-Fifth Birthday (Winona Lake: Eisenbrauns, 2005).

4 Simon Goldhill, "Genre," in *The Cambridge Companion to the Greek and Roman Novel*, ed. Tim Whitmarsh (Cambridge: Cambridge University Press, 2008), 186. Goldhill is here drawing on Stephen Heath, "The Politics of Genre," in *Debating World Literature*, ed. Christopher Prendergast (London: Verso, 2004).

5 Richard A. Burridge, *What Are the Gospels? A Comparison with Graeco-Roman Biography*, 2nd ed., The Biblical Resource Series (Grand Rapids: Eerdmans, 2004). This second edition of the original 1992 publication includes a chapter where Burridge discusses and responds to the largely positive reactions to his work.

it participates in this genre. For instance, the Gospel clearly displays the character of Jesus by means of his deeds and words. The same is true of ancient biographies, as Burridge shows in detail.[6]

The socio-political function of most of these biographies is quite obvious. As a genre "nestled between historiography and rhetorical encomium,"[7] the biography typically promoted particular men, along with the values and virtues that these men were purported to display. Insofar has the genre promoted individual male subjects, we would expect to find examples of extraordinary self-control, a preeminent marker of manliness. Such displays of self-control are indeed common to ancient biographies and are often communicated via anecdotes that highlight the subject's remarkable sexual restraint.[8] This tendency is already evident in one of the first examples of Greek biography, Xenophon's encomium of the Spartan king Agesilaus (ca. 360 BCE). In order to show Agesilaus's self-control, Xenophon relates a story about the king's sexual restraint. He tells how Agesilaus resisted the kiss of a young Persian man for whom he felt passionate love.

> And, as concerning the things of Aphrodite, his self-restraint surely deserves a tribute of admiration, if worthy of mention on no other ground. That he should keep at arms' length those whose intimacy he did not desire may be thought only human. But he loved Megabates, the handsome son of Spithridates, with all the intensity of an ardent nature. (Xenophon, *Agesilaus* 5.4 [Marchant and Bowersock, LCL; translation slightly modified by the author])

When Megabates wants to kiss the king, a customary show of respect, Agesilaus refuses the gesture "with much show of battle." When Megabates feels slighted, Agesilaus is troubled and wants to restore his favor. But when the Spartan king is asked again whether he will receive a kiss from Megabates, Agesilaus still refuses vehemently: "By the twin gods, no, not if I were straightway to become the fairest and strongest and fleetest man on earth" (Xenophon, *Ages.* 5.5). To build on this picture of self-restraint and further reinforce the masculine image of the king, Xenophon goes on to note that Agesilaus always slept either in a temple or in public so that he could be easily observed and never fall under suspicion. As for women in this biography, they are nearly absent apart from a brief mention of Agesilaus's sister.

Xenophon is not unique in devoting attention to masculine comportment by emphasizing sexual restraint. We see a similar tendency in a later example of

6 Ibid., 232.

7 Ibid., 259.

8 The opposite is also true. When the author's intent is to provide an unflattering portrayal of his subject, he often does so, at least in part, by highlighting the man's uncontrolled sexual passion.

biography, Philo of Alexandria's first century CE *Life of Moses*. In Philo's attempt to situate Moses among and above the Greek heroes, he suggests that Moses had a level of self-mastery that elevated him far above normal men.

> And [Moses] tamed, and appeased, and brought under due command every one of the other passions which are naturally and as far as they are themselves concerned frantic, and violent, and unmanageable ... For he never provided his stomach with any luxuries beyond those necessary tributes which nature has appointed to be paid to it, and as to the pleasures of the organs below the stomach he paid no attention to them at all, except as far as the object of having legitimate children was concerned. (Philo, *Mos.* 1.6.26–28 [Colson])

In Philo's *Life of Moses*, women are a part of the story, but they are primarily present to aid in the construction of Moses' heroic masculinity. For instance, Philo draws on Exodus 2:16–17, Moses' encounter with the Midianite girls at the well, to relate what "may seem a trifling affair" but in fact testifies to the "lofty spirit" of Moses. While the biblical account is briefly reported and contains no direct or indirect speech, in Philo's version, Moses slings gendered invective at the shepherds. He addresses them as "masses of long hair and lumps of flesh, not men ... who go daintily like girls." In contrast, he portrays himself as a champion. "I fight to succor these injured maidens," he warns the bully shepherds, "allied to a mighty arm which the rapacious may not see, but you shall feel its invisible power to wound if you do not change your ways" (*Mos.* 1.10.56 [Colson]). But while Moses is eager to address the shepherds, he does not speak with the women. The women speak only to their father of Moses' virtuous conduct.

One last example comes from a still later biography which, while offering a much different model of an ideal man than either the Spartan king or the Hebrew lawgiver still emphasizes the self-mastery of its subject. Philostratus's *Life of Apollonius*, paints a picture of a wandering holy man/philosopher who, in the case of sexual restraint, surpasses the teaching of Pythagoras, and the example of Sophocles.

> Now Pythagoras was praised for saying that a man should not approach any woman except his wife, but according to Apollonius Pythagoras had prescribed that for others, but he himself was not going to marry or even have sexual intercourse. In this he surpassed the famous saying of Sophocles, who claimed that he had escaped from a raging, wild master when he reached old age. Thanks to his virtue and self-mastery, Apollonius was not subject to it even as an adolescent, but despite his youth and physical strength he overcame and "mastered" its rage. (Philostratus, *Vit. Apoll.* 1.13 [Jones])

Philostratus's account of Apollonius works to reinforce the holy man's escape from the "wild master" of desire in part by allowing women only an insignificant role in the work. Although Apollonius has frequent dialogic exchanges with the people he meets on this travels, his dialogue partners, when not his trusty companion Damis, are typically kings and wise men. When women do appear, it is often for healing, as with the woman who brings her spirit-possessed son to the Indian sages (3.38), or the young bride whom the holy man restores to life (4.45). These types of appearances echo the healing stories of the Synoptic Gospels, but are nothing like the sort of conversations that the Johannine Jesus has with women in the Fourth Gospel. Apart from these healing accounts, Philostratus also depicts women as a threat to chastity. Apolloinus's Egyptian guide, Timasion reports how he left home after rejecting the sexual advances of his stepmother. Predictably, the young man's ability to maintain his chastity delights Apollonius who suggests that he and his companions "vote a crown to him for his continence" (6.3 [Jones]).

These three examples suggest that if the gospels are a type of ancient biography, they should feature the masculine virtues of their male subject, Jesus, particularly the demonstration of his self-control. On this point, the gospels differ from other biographies, in that there is no overt statement of Jesus' self-mastery, either from the character Jesus or from the narrator. But the narrative form of the gospels does *display* the self-control of Jesus, and this is especially the case with the Johannine Jesus. In the Gospel of John, Jesus demonstrates a self-mastery that is both unique among the canonical gospels and in keeping with the ideal manliness of other biographical subjects. One could read the Johannine Jesus's interaction with female characters as going one better than even Apollonius. While Apollonius apparently avoids much contact with women, Jesus exhibits self-control while situating himself in close conversations with women. Indeed, the scenes that feature Jesus in the company of individual women are quite suggestive of intimate and even erotic circumstances. For instance, the evocation of the betrothal type scene in John 4 is widely recognized, and I will say more of other potentially erotic allusions below. In any case, if we read strictly through the expectations of ancient *bios*, the prominence of the women in the narrative stands out as unusual. If the women function as they do in the examples above, they would function to reinforce Jesus's own remove from matters of the flesh, which according to him, is useless (6:63). But given the relative inattention to women in many of the ancient biographies, and their relative prominence in the Gospel, I suggest more can be learned by considering the gospel in relation to other ancient genres that do feature female characters. If we are no longer strictly classifying the Gospel as biography, but considering ways that the narrative participates and evokes multiple genres, we can bring both Greek novels and Greek drama into the conversation.

3. John, Gender, and the Greek Novels

Like the gospels, the Greek novels emerged in the first century CE as a new type of literature, building on and adapting earlier literary forms. Later Christian literature would eventually intersect closely with the ancient Greek and Roman novels. But already with the canonical gospels one can see ways in which they overlap with ancient Greek fiction.[9] New Testament scholars have focused especially on how the novels inform studies of the Gospels of Mark, and Luke-Acts, but the Gospel of John also shares elements with the novels. For instance, Jo-Ann Brant understands the Gospel to share the same basic narrative strategies and structures with the novels. Like the novels, the Gospel "offers an adventure of a hero in an alien world with the restoration of a child to his true parent and the fulfillment of love rather than its tragic demise at its end."[10] Meredith Warren has also worked on intersections between the Fourth Gospel and the Greek novels, seeing a link between questions of identity and divinity with respect to the Greek heroines and the Johannine Jesus.[11]

Most relevant here are the ways that the Greek novels offer glimpses into how ideas of gender and sexuality were adapting to the conditions of imperial rule. For instance, Eric Thurman suggests that the presentation in the novels of "valorized male suffering" along with the ambivalent male subject that this suffering constructs represent an ideological overlap between the gospel genre and the ancient novel.[12] Along this line, he traces the similarities between the Markan Jesus and Habrocomes, the hero from Xenophon's *An Ephesian Tale*, as they both undergo "divinely-fated suffering." As Thurman further details what he sees as the "excessive and even effeminized passivity" of these two male heroes, he offers a postcolonial interpretation of both the Greek novel and the Gospel. In so doing,

9 See Ronald F. Hock, J. Bradley Chance, Judith Perkins, eds., *Ancient Fiction and Early Christian Narrative*, SBLSymS 6 (Atlanta: Scholars Press, 1998); Christine M. Thomas, *The Acts of Peter, Gospel Literature, and the Ancient Novel: Rewriting the Past* (Oxford: Oxford University Press, 2003); Jo-Ann A. Brant, Charles W. Hedrick, Chris Shea, eds., *Ancient Fiction: The Matrix of Early Christian and Jewish Narrative*, SBLSymS 32 (Leiden; Boston: Brill, 2005).

10 Jo-Ann A. Brant, "Divine Birth and Apparent Parents: The Plot of the Fourth Gospel," in Ronald F. Hock et al., *Ancient Fiction and Early Christian Narrative*, 211. See also Brant's contribution in the present volume.

11 Meredith Warren, "Equal to God: Divine (Mis)Identification in the Greek Novels and the Gospel of John" (paper presented at the International Meeting of the Society of Biblical Literature, London 2011). Many thanks to Meredith for making her paper available to me. See also now Meredith Warren, *My Flesh Is Meat Indeed: A Nonsacramental Reading of John 6:51–58* (Minneapolis: Fortress, 2015).

12 Eric Thurman, "Novel Men: Masculinity and Empire in Mark's Gospel and Xenophon's *An Ephesian Tale*," in *Mapping Gender in Ancient Religious Discourses*, ed. Caroline Vander Stichele and Todd Penner (Leiden: Brill, 2007), 192.

he also provides a good example of the socio-political dimension of genre. According to Thurman, by submitting to imperial violence both Jesus and Habrocomes expose the "arbitrariness of empire."[13]

This reading of the Markan Jesus alongside Habrocomes also creates a useful comparison to the way the Johannine Jesus looks in relation to the male heroes of the novels. While Jesus is crucified in the Fourth Gospel, and in this sense is passive, he is by no means excessively passive. Rather, he appears much more active in the scenes leading up to and including his crucifixion, both in relation to the Markan Jesus as well as the male heroes in the Greek novels. The Johannine Jesus, after all, approaches the soldiers who come out to meet him. He is not silent before Pilate as is the Markan Jesus, but talks to Pilate about his kingdom, truth and power (18:33–38; 19:9–11). If Jesus does not initially respond to Pilate in their second exchange, it takes only two additional questions before he resumes the dialogue (19:9–11; cf. Mark 15:1–5). What Jesus then goes on to say portrays Pilate as little more than a puppet in the whole affair, whose only power over Jesus is what God permits him to have. And of course, the Johannine Jesus is even instrumental in his own death, determining its time, bowing his head and giving up his spirit (19:28–30).

Together, these narrative details transform what would be an effeminizing, passive death in the Gospel into something quite different. To be sure, the narrative does not offer the picture of a militant or imperial masculinity; but neither is the Johannine Jesus the "hapless hero" of the Greek novels, as David Konstan dubs the novels' male protagonists.[14] These men are undone by Eros, spending much of their time in displays of despondency, helplessness, passivity and weeping when separated from their object of desire. In contrast, while it is true that the Johannine Jesus weeps, this brief show of emotion (colored also by anger and agitation, 11:33–35, 38) is hardly comparable to the persistent pathos of the novels' male characters. In other words, reading the gender of the Johannine Jesus alongside that of the male heroes in the novels, once again brings us to the Gospel's emphasis on Jesus' manly self-control.

Still, even if Johannine Jesus does not assume the helpless position of the novelistic heroes, the Gospel resembles the Greek novel by giving a prominent role to individual female characters, and by featuring the theme of love as a driving force for the protagonists. In the novels, Eros is a capricious god, responsible for both the joys and sufferings of the characters. In the Gospel, love motivates the divine intervention in the world (and in this sense also the suffering and death of the hero). Still, there are also key differences between the workings

13 Ibid., 226.

14 David Konstan, *Sexual Symmetry: Love in the Ancient Novel and Related Genres* (Princeton: Princeton University Press, 1994), 15–30.

of love in each work. In the novels, Eros so afflicts the male and female protagonists with love-sickness that they are compelled to overcome extreme adversities to be together in marriage. In the Gospel, the role of erotic attraction between Jesus and the women is ambiguous at best.

This ambiguity is clearly seen in the differing conclusions of Sjef van Tilborg and Jo-Ann Brant, both of whom examine the theme of erotic love in the Gospel with respect to its use in the Greek novels. According to van Tilborg, the women in the Gospel resemble the women in the novels (mainly the minor characters in the sub-stories) insofar as they exhibit a degree of freedom of behavior, but differ in their lack of "sexual freedom." Compared to the women in the novels, Tilborg suggests that "eroticism is absent in the Johannine women."[15] In sharp contrast, Brant sees the narrative portrayals of the meetings between Jesus and the Samaritan woman (4:1–42) and Mary of Bethany (12:1–8) as erotically driven. According to Brant, the first scene "follows a standard scenario in classical romances: the suitor encounters obstacles to his goal; in this case, the woman spurns her suitor, he courts her, and she relents."[16] In the second scene, Mary's use of fragrant oil, her foot anointing/washing, and her unbound hair indicate the performance of a prenuptial ritual with Jesus as the intended husband. Thus, Brant argues, various generic intersections in the narrative create audience expectations of erotic encounters between these women and Jesus. She concludes that by virtue of the desire expressed by these women, "Jesus appears as a character capable of receiving as well as responding to human love."[17] One could easily expand Brant's argument about erotic allusions to John 20:1–18. This scene between Mary Magdalene and Jesus has often been noted for its intimacy and erotic undertones. Generically, it evokes the recognition scenes like those found in Greek epics and novels in which the woman suddenly recognizes her long lost lover/husband.[18] The scene also evokes the lovers in the Song of Songs, with Mary seeking Jesus, as the women does her lover in the Song of Songs.[19]

Both Van Tilborg and Brant base their interpretations on generic analogies with the Greek novels and in so doing both are helpful in illuminating gendered elements in the Gospel. On the one hand, Brant's use of the novels vis-à-vis the

15 Sjef Van Tilborg, *Imaginative Love in John*, BIS 2 (Leiden: Brill, 1993), 177.

16 Jo-Ann A. Brant, "Husband Hunting: Characterization and Narrative Art in the Gospel of John," *BibInt* 4 (1996): 215.

17 Ibid., 222.

18 Van Tilborg puts the scene in conversation with recognitions scenes in the novels of Chariton, Xenophon and Heliodorus (Van Tilborg, *Imaginative Love in John*, 203–06). See also Kasper Bro Larsen, *Recognizing the Stranger: Recognition Scenes in the Gospel of John*, BIS 93 (Leiden; Boston: Brill, 2008), 196–205. Larsen's detailed discussion of John 20:11–18 as a recognition scene does not discuss the erotic implications of the scene.

19 Ann Roberts Winsor, *A King Is Bound in the Tresses: Allusions to the Song of Songs in the Fourth Gospel* (New York: P. Lang, 1999).

Gospel adds to the impression, already created by biblical allusions, that the women in John are portrayed as erotically attracted to Jesus. In this sense, she shows that eroticism of the novels is not absent in the Gospel, at least with respect to the female characters. On the other hand, Van Tilborg is also correct in noticing an absence of eroticism in the scenes between Jesus and the women at least on the part of Jesus. He does not respond to the women with anything indicating erotic attraction. We thus appear to arrive at the same conclusion we did in reading gender construction in relation to the ancient biographies. Jesus is presented in the Fourth Gospel as completely removed from the forces of desire that might threaten his masculine self-mastery, even when he is in the presence of women that speak or act in suggestively erotic ways.

But what of the love that courses through the narrative of the Gospel? Van Tilborg does not ignore the theme (indeed his whole study is devoted to it), but he finds that the love expressed in the Gospel is linked more closely to other Greek models of love than to the figure of Eros in the novels, namely the relationship of the male teacher for his favorite male disciple, and the intimate friendship between male friends.[20] As Van Tilborg notes only the beloved disciple lies with his head resting on Jesus (13:23), and Jesus speaks of his love for others only in the context of his intimate circle of male friends (13:34; 14:31; 15:9, 12). He also directly links love with male friendship with the declaration that, "no one has a greater love than this, that one lays down his life for his friends [ὑπὲρ τῶν φίλων αὐτοῦ]," (15:13). Apart from this discussion of love for his disciples, Jesus more regularly refers to himself as the object of love (3:35; 8:42; 10:17; 14:14, 21, 23–24, 28; 15:9; 17:23–26). Looking beyond Jesus's direct references, the narrator reinforces Jesus's love for a particular male beloved disciple (13:23; 19:26), and beyond that mentions more generally love for "his own" (though again with the masculine plural τοὺς ἰδίους 13:1) The only specific reference to Jesus loving women concerns the sisters of Jesus' friend Lazarus (11:5).

These observations about what the Gospel says about Jesus and love links well with a passage from Plutarch cited by Van Tilborg. He quotes Plutarch as evidence of the ongoing idea of a Platonic love between male teacher and student from a text contemporaneous with the Gospel. But the passage also points to an important contrast between the Gospel and the Greek novels. Plutarch's defender of *paiderastia* (with whom he disagrees), suggests that the love of young male students rather than women is preferable "since it is not 'flashing with desire,' as Anacreon says of the love of maidens, or 'drenched with unguents, shining bright'. No its aspect is simple and unspoiled" (*Moralia* 751a).[21] So, too, one could

20 Van Tilborg, *Imaginative Love in John*, 77–81, 18–154.

21 See Van Tilborg, *Imaginative Love in John*, 84.

say, the Johannine Jesus loves, but his is not a love "flashing with desire." It is an asexual love that is in keeping with masculine self-mastery.

But if this is the case, it still takes us no further in our search for a generic explanation for why women are featured at all in the Gospel. Especially given the positive outcomes Jesus' encounters with women have with respect to the plot of the Gospel, it seems unlikely that the only point is to show Jesus as uninterested in erotic partnerships with women. For additional insight into the role of women in the gospel, I turn finally to the Gospel's generic gesturing toward Greek drama.

4. John, Gender, and Greek Drama

Several significant studies have established the ways that the author of the Gospel of John drew on the conventions of Greek drama to present his story of Jesus.[22] Here I will focus only on how the role of women and the feminine in ancient Greek drama might inform an understanding of gender in the Gospel. For this, the work of classicists Froma Zeitlin and Helen Foley are worth examining in some detail. Zeitlin explores the function of women in Greek tragedy with respect to the body, plot, theatrical space, and mimesis. In each case, she suggests that the female characters function as part of the larger dramatic project of exploring male selfhood. In terms of plot, which is perhaps most relevant to the narrative form of the Gospel, Zeitlin suggests that the female characters of Greek tragedy "play the role of catalysts, agents, instruments, blockers, spoilers, destroyers, sometimes helpers or saviors for the male characters" but never function as an end in themselves.[23] In the Gospel, too, the female characters are present in the narrative as catalysts or instruments for the revelation of Jesus' identity. This is true for the mother of Jesus, who initiates the first sign at Cana (2:1–11), and the Samaritan woman who brings her village to eventual belief in Jesus (4:1–39), and also for Martha whose conversation with Jesus includes a full confession of belief in him as "the Messiah, the Son of God, the one coming into the world" (11:27). But, as with the female characters in Greek tragedy, the women in the Gospel are no end in themselves, and the author finds ways to dampen whatever role they do have. Jesus puts off his mother with a terse comment (2:4), and the Samaritan woman is eventually told that her words are no longer relevant to the belief of the

22 George L. Parsenios, *Rhetoric and Drama in the Johannine Lawsuit Motif*, WUNT 258 (Tübingen: Mohr Siebeck, 2010); idem, *Departure and Consolation: The Johannine Farewell Discourses in Light of Greco-Roman Literature*, NovTSup 117 (Leiden; Boston: Brill, 2005); Jo-Ann A. Brant, *Dialogue and Drama: Elements of Greek Tragedy in the Fourth Gospel* (Peabody: Hendrickson, 2004).

23 Froma I. Zeitlin, *Playing the Other: Gender and Society in Classical Greek Literature* (Chicago: University of Chicago Press, 1996), 347.

Samaritan villagers (4:42). Even Martha is mildly rebuked by Jesus, "Didn't I tell you that if you believed you would see the glory of God" (11:40), even though Jesus never actually says this to Martha in their earlier conversation.[24]

Other observations that Zeitlin makes about the feminine in Greek theatre contrast with the Fourth Gospel. For example, with respect to the "somantics of the stage," Zeitlin points out that the audience for drama is most interested in the body in an unnatural state of *pathos*, one that has fallen from the ideal of strength and integrity, and reduced to a helpless or passive condition. It is at this moment of weakness, Zeitlin suggests, that the male is both acutely aware that he has a body, and that he sees himself as most like a woman.[25] This is a compelling image of the male body in tragedies, and one might be tempted to look immediately to the crucified body of Jesus in the Gospel for a parallel dynamic. Indeed, the Markan Jesus may present just this collapse of the masculine ideal. But there is little to suggest that the Johannine Jesus ever perceives himself as weakened or helpless, even when he is on the cross. From early in the Gospel, the narrator works to preclude a reading of weakness in Jesus by defining the crucifixion as being lifted up and glorified (3:13; 13:31–32; 17:1), as something that happens only because Jesus allows it to happen (10:17–18), and as an indication of Jesus' return to the Father where he will assume the privileged role he has had alongside God since before creation (13:1). If the Gospel audience is fascinated by the image of the crucifixion of Jesus, it may be more by the way the Johannine Jesus transforms this typically emasculating event into his own orchestrated affair (especially if they are familiar with the Markan passion narrative).

In this sense, the conclusion of the Gospel is more in keeping with Zeitlin's assertion that however tragedy may use women and the feminine to explore male self-hood, it "arrives at closures that generally reassert male, often paternal (or civic) structures of authority, but before that the work of the drama is to open up the masculine view of the universe."[26] I will return to the second part of this statement below. Here, I want to affirm the first part with respect to the Gospel. At an explicit level, there is strong reassertion of patriarchal authority as Jesus is returning to the Father, who Jesus claims is greater than he is (14:28). It is this paternal authority who placed all things in Jesus' hands and gave him authority over all flesh (3:35; 17:2). Their heavenly reunion is thus a reaffirmation of the reigning divine, masculine authority, which was never absent in the Gospel, but was temporarily manifest in the one sent to earth by the Father. On an earthly

24 Van Tilborg also notices this diminishment of the female characters, and adds it to the evidence for the evangelist's preference to show Jesus in male centered relationships (*Imaginative Love in John*, 169–208).

25 Eadem, *Playing the Other*, 350.

26 Ibid., 364. Here I differ from Brant who argues that the Gospel of John does not reassert masculine structures of authority. See *Dialogue and Drama*, 210.

level, masculine authority is also asserted at the crucifixion, albeit ironically, when Pilate insists to the Jews that Jesus' cross be labeled with a placard proclaiming in Greek, Latin, and Hebrew that he is king of the Jews (19:19–22). While Pilate means to insult the Jewish leaders by exerting his own authority and undercutting theirs, his action asserts the Gospel's message of Jesus/God's sovereign power.

More implicitly, Jesus undertakes a final action just before his death that expresses masculine power by way of the female. In 19:26–27, Jesus again addresses his mother as "woman" (see 2:4) as he hands her over to the beloved disciple. Precisely when Jesus is supposed to be dying, he asserts himself as a subject by taking control of his mother's situation and giving her to his beloved disciple. At one level, this resembles the type of exchange of women in the ancient world that strengthened the bond between men. Jesus is not simply an object (dying on the cross) but a masculine subject, engaged in the affairs of his household. In this sense, it runs counter to the Greek tragedies that frequently represent something that goes awry in this commerce in women.[27] All this is to say that whatever role the female characters have in the Gospel, it does not, in the end, subvert the narrative's patriarchal worldview.

Still, both Zeitlin and Foley suggest that in Greek tragedy, the presence of women subjects does, at least temporarily or partially, offer a way of viewing reality apart from this dominant masculine perspective. As noted above, Zeitlin refers to the work of the drama as that which opens up the masculine worldview. In a similar way, Foley suggests that Greek writers use female characters to think in a challenging fashion. As she puts it,

> When tragic poets choose to allow an entire action to turn on the moral decision of a woman or to show women taking or urging significant moral positions in a public context, they apparently make at least a partial break from a cultural ideal and use female characters to explore ambiguous and often dangerous moral frontiers.[28]

According to Foley, because women are always, ethically speaking, a marked category (unlike the unmarked male) they offer dramatic opportunities. Here Foley is discussing tragedy as a genre that is fascinated with "flawed, mistaken, and partially appropriate ethical behavior" as well as with "issues that the cultural system and the dominant morality sacrifice or devalue."[29] She contends that women in tragedy can take ethical positions, "that either prove to be superior to those of men in particular instances or appropriate but different from those of

27 See Victoria Wohl, *Intimate Commerce: Exchange, Gender, and Subjectivity in Greek Tragedy*. Austin: University of Texas Press, 1998.

28 Ibid., 116.

29 Ibid., 118.

men due to the constraints of their social role or status."[30] The Gospel does not deal with moral issues in the way the tragedies do, but it does introduce provocative christological and theological positions. Likewise, while the women in the Gospel nowhere achieve the type of moral agency that characters such as Sophocles's Antigone or Electra demonstrate, they do assert their voices in significant ways in theological discussions in the narrative. For this reason, considering how their "marked" identity may open up opportunities for the audience to consider challenging ideas appears to be a rich interpretive vein to tap. In what follows, I can only raise some tentative suggestions about an approach that might inform our reading of gender in the Gospel.

Many characters in the Gospel, both women and men, display flawed and mistaken understandings of Jesus and one could say that the whole Gospel deals with christological claims that the dominant cultural system devalues. This Gospel, unlike the Synoptics, makes explicit the challenge that belief in Jesus represents for both the Jewish and Roman power structures (11:48). Thus, while the author is urging belief in Jesus—the adoption of certain values and the rejection of others—there is an awareness that such belief means engaging dangerous ideas.

Acknowledging Jesus as the son sent by God, who is one with his divine Father, is potentially dangerous precisely because this acknowledgement challenges the existing masculine authorities (albeit by surpassing them with a higher masculinity authority). The agnostic relationship between Jesus and the Jews repeatedly makes this danger clear. The danger is also reflected in the references to being afraid of the Jews, in the expressed anxiety about being cast out of the synagogue (7:13; 9:22; 12:42; 19:38; 20:19), and in Peter's denial of his discipleship (19:17, 25, 27). So with Foley, we can ask whether the women in the Fourth Gospel play prominent roles in light of the new and potentially risky theological ideas the gospel writer wants the audience to explore. If so, it may be that the function of women in the Gospel is not simply to show positive female disciples (even if they can legitimately be read in this way), but to use female difference or "otherness" to convey the potentially risky difference the Gospel offers for believers.

So, for example, after dismissing Nicodemus, the Jewish male teacher who cannot comprehend the language of being begotten from above (3:10), the evangelist introduces a anonymous Samaritan woman to further explore the claims of Jesus. Their extended conversation is framed by objections to their encounter. The first protest is openly voiced by the woman: λέγει οὖν αὐτῷ ἡ γυνὴ ἡ Σαμαρῖτις· πῶς σὺ Ἰουδαῖος ὢν παρ' ἐμοῦ πεῖν αἰτεῖς γυναικὸς Σαμαρίτιδος οὔσης (4:9). The second is the unvoiced question of the male disciples who, until their abrupt return to Jesus, have been absent throughout the story. Their sup-

30 Ibid.

pressed questions τί ζητεῖς ἤ τί λαλεῖς μετ᾽ αὐτῆς (4:27) contrasts with the woman's boldness with Jesus throughout the encounter. It is the Samaritan woman who asks Jesus the challenging question, "Are you greater than our ancestor Jacob, who gave us the well, and with his sons and his flocks drank from it?" (4:12). And it is to this woman that Jesus plainly reveals his identity as the Messiah, something he does not do with Nicodemus, or any other male character (4:26). The woman then submits for consideration his claim: "He can't be the messiah can he?" (4:26, 29). Beyond her role in drawing out this revelation and then communicating it, there is little indication of interest in the woman as an individual character. If we follow Foley's suggestion for how women function in Greek tragedies, this woman may play a similar role. It may be precisely her already marked character as "other" that opens up the space for the audience to listen in on a risky and unconventional conversation, consider claims of the Johannine Jesus and eventually entertain the possibility that he is the savior of the world.

Something similar may be at work in the conversations with Martha and Mary (11:1–53). Although the male disciples play an active role before going to Bethany, and then purportedly accompany Jesus on what they understand to be a dangerous, even deadly trip (11:7–16), they disappear completely from the rest of the story. Instead, the female characters become the primary focus of the narrative, engaging in conversations with Jesus about their brother. The sense of risk is extended as Martha first goes alone to meet Jesus at an undisclosed location (11:20) and afterward secretly conveys to Mary that Jesus wants to see her (11:28). All of this, including Martha's full confession of belief in Jesus, precedes the sign that will be the catalyst for Jesus' death sentence (11:53). In this case, the author uses these female characters to enable the audience to share not just theologically risky ideas, but also physically dangerous space with Jesus. In this context, Martha's confession of belief again affirms the identity of Jesus (11:27). Mary, like the Samaritan woman, leads some of her people to belief in Jesus, even while some who follow her will betray him to his enemies (11:31, 45–46).

Along this line, one other observation of Foley's is suggestive. She notes, insofar as women in tragedy and epic are moral agents with a difference, they reveal in a positive sense important social and ethical alternatives and in a negative sense the social consequences of actions undertaken from a marginal, morally questionable, or socially resistant position.[31]

The gospel writer does not understand the actions of Martha and Mary to be morally questionable (in spite of the negative assessment of both by some commentators), but their expressions of faith in Jesus represent a theological

31 Ibid., 116.

alternative. Moreover, the secrecy with which they converse with Jesus highlights the seriousness of the social consequences associated with this belief.

The same logic is also applicable in the Gospel's final scene between a woman and Jesus. In chapter 20, only Mary Magdalene is privy to the sight of Jesus while he remains in a liminal state, that is, not yet ascended to the Father (20:17). Again, the garden scene does not represent a place of moral or ethical ambiguity. But Jesus's physical presence in the garden after his death and his assertion to Mary that he is ascending to his Father and his God represent another challenge for the audience to accept the radical claims that Jesus has been making about his identity throughout the narrative, the same claims that cost him his life. Yet again, whatever positive implication there is for Mary as the one who witnesses this resurrection appearance, and as the one who is commissioned to deliver Jesus' message to the male disciples, it is dissipated by her disappearance from the narrative. There is no further reference to Mary once the male disciples have gathered and have themselves experienced the risen Jesus. If we consider John 21 as part of the Johannine drama, then Mary's absence is reinforced. This final scene concerns only the fate of the male disciples, especially Peter and the disciple whom Jesus loved, precisely the two who were taken off stage so that Mary would witness the liminal Jesus on her own.

5. Conclusion

The present article represents a further development of the question I raised at the end of *Men and Women in the Fourth Gospel.* There I asked whether the evangelist used the female characters in the Gospel, together with the anonymous male characters (the man born blind, and the beloved disciple) in a way that challenged institutional authorities. Here I am suggesting that if we include a focus on the construction of masculinity and give attention to the various ancient genres in which the Fourth Gospel participates, the pictures changes. On the one hand, female characters are used to accentuate the male self-hood of Jesus. They evoke expectations of erotic encounters only to show Jesus as completely impervious to such concerns. On the other hand, the female characters may also function to "safely" push the edges of theological and social boundaries. These women let the audience experience the marginal position of a believer by way of figures that are already marked as other.[32] In a sense, by listening in on their conversations and accompanying them to dangerous places, the audience tries on this alternative role in a space outside of the dominant masculine worldview

32 Here the man born blind should also be included. As a man with a defect, he too represents a "moral agent with a difference" who can push the boundaries of acceptable theology.

that might more readily reject the Christological claims being presented. But as we have seen, these female figures do little to permanently undercut masculine structures of authority. The focus of the narrative continually returns to the masculine—the masculine Father and Son, and the community of male disciples, and in the end, especially Peter, and the disciple whom Jesus loved.

George L. Parsenios

The Silent Spaces between Narrative and Drama: *Mimesis* and *Diegesis* in the Fourth Gospel

1. Introduction

The canonical Gospels are generally viewed as a form of ancient biography.[1] Just how neatly John fits this category is clear when we compare John to Plutarch, who opens his *Life of Alexander* by explaining the difference between writing history and writing biographies (*Alex.* 1).[2] A historian describes everything a person ever did. A biographer is more selective. In the same way that a portrait painter focuses on a few key expressions in the face and eyes to depict the character of a given subject, while ignoring the rest of the body, so the biographer passes quickly over the bulk of a person's life, and shares only those special sayings and particular behaviors that reveal the person's character. The Gospel of John is selective in the same way when it closes by saying, "Now Jesus did many other signs in the presence of his disciples, which are not written in this book. But these are written so that you may come to believe that Jesus is the Messiah, the Son of God, and that through believing you may have life in his name" (20:30–31)." John tells us much about Jesus, but covers the rest in silence, echoing the silence of Plutarch.

A different kind of silence occupies us here—not the silence that defines John as a biography, but the silence that distances John from biography, as it distances John as well from any other type of prose narrative. In a handful of key places in the Fourth Gospel, the narrator's voice is absent where it would be expected. These moments of silence are small but significant. They assimilate John to drama. Ancient discussions that distinguish drama from other literary forms

1 The work most often associated with this position is Richard Burridge, *What are the Gospels: A Comparision with Greco-Roman Biography*, SNTSMS 70 (Cambridge: Cambridge University Press, 1992). For an evaluation of this consensus, see Loveday Alexander, "What is a Gospel?" in *The Cambridge Companion to the Gospels*, ed. Stephen Barton (Cambridge: Cambridge University Press, 2006), 13–33. See also the papers by Harold Attridge and Colleen Conway in the present volume. I also would like to thank Kasper Bro Larsen for helpful suggestions in the improvement of this paper.

2 This insight arose in a conversation with Rainer Hirsch-Luipold.

regularly include a discussion about the presence or absence of a narrator's voice (see below). As a text becomes more dramatic, its narrator becomes less obvious. This article will comment on the genre of John, therefore, by exploring not only what the text *in*cludes, but also what it *ex*cludes. The silent spaces speak to us about John and genre. The silent spaces locate John between narrative and drama.

2. John 1: Are You the Prophet?

The first example of the silent narrator is the very first scene in the Gospel, the scene where emissaries from Jerusalem interrogate John the Baptist. The passage is presented here with the introductory comments of the evangelist in italics, in order to emphasize the brief moment when the narrator temporarily recedes. The passage reads as follows:

> *He confessed and did not deny it, but confessed*, "I am not the Messiah."
> *And they asked him*, "What then? Are you Elijah?"
> *He said*, "I am not."
> "Are you the prophet?"
> *He answered*, "No."
> *Then they said to him*, "Who are you? (1:19–22)

Every question asked, and every answer given is introduced by a narrator's framing comment such as: "He confessed and did not deny it," or "and they asked him," or "he said." No such introductory comment introduces the question, "Are you the prophet." As soon as John answers, "I am not" to the previous line, the question "Are you the prophet?" comes rapidly—so rapidly that the narrator disappears, and for a brief moment, John and his interrogators are speaking directly to one another as though in a drama, with no intervention from the narrator. To be sure, this silence lasts only for a moment. It is a brief and small lacuna. But this momentary silence might tell us much about the dramatic character of the scene.

Thucydides shows the way forward. In two key places in Thucydides' *History*, the narrator's voice recedes into silence in the very same way that we see in John 1, and the silence is noted by both ancient and modern commentators. The two relevant passages are the Melian dialogue in book 5 and the report of the Ambraciot herald in book 3. The famous Melian dialogue (5.85–113) contains a series of dueling arguments delivered back and forth between the Athenians and the people of the island of Melos. The opening speeches of both sides are introduced by a narrator's comment such as "They said." Thereafter follows a purely mimetic, dramatic presentation. The first two speeches—that of the Athenians in

5.86 and that of the Melians at 5.87, are introduced with narrator's comments. But the next speeches, beginning with that of the Athenians at 5.88 and that of the Melians at 5.89, are spoken with no narrator's introduction. The first four speeches read as follows, with the narrator's comments in italics in order to emphasize the moment where the narrator recedes into silence after the first two:[3]

1. *The Athenian envoys accordingly spoke as follows:* "Since our proposals are not to be made before the assembly, your purpose being, as it seems, that the people may not hear from us once for all, in an uninterrupted speech, arguments that are seductive and untested, and so be deceived ..." (5.85).
2. *The commissioners of the Melians answered:* "The fairness of the proposal, that we shall at our leisure instruct one another, is not open to objection ..." (5.86).
3. "Well, if you have met to argue from suspicions about what may happen in the future, or for any other purpose than to consult for the safety of your city ..." (5.87).
4. "It is natural and pardonable for men in such a position as ours to resort to many arguments and many suppositions ..." (5.88).

Speeches 1 and 2 are introduced by narrator comments, but not speeches 3 and 4, and not all the subsequent speeches. As with John 1, the disappearance of the narrator underscores the urgency and immediacy of the debate. The Melian dialogue, of course, is massive in scale and extends over several pages of text (chapters 5.85 to 5.111). In terms of length, this debate is very different from the interrogation in John 1.

But this is not the first time that Thucydides writes like this. It is the most famous example, but there is another example which resembles even more closely what we find in John, at least in terms of scale. This other episode appears in book 3. After the Athenian general Demosthenes defeats a force consisting of both Spartans and Ambraciots in 426 BCE near the city of Olpae, the Ambraciots send a herald to request that they might recover their dead. The herald sees many times more dead Ambraciots than he expects, because he does not know that a relief force had been sent to his comrades from their home, and then had been utterly annihilated. Not only does Ambracia lose the soldiers killed in the first battle, but, unknown to the herald, they also lose an entire army of soldiers sent in relief. Thucydides tells us that, owing to this disaster, no other city in the entire war suffers so great a loss in proportion to its size in so short a time (3.113). The reported number of dead seems too large even to be believed. The ensuing

3 Translation from *Thucydides, History of the Peloponnesian War*, trans. C. F. Smith, vol. 3, LCL (Cambridge: Harvard University Press, 1921).

conversation takes the form of the Melian dialogue. The first several lines of the conversation are introduced with narrator's comments, but then suddenly and briefly, the text shifts to direct conversation. The text reads as follows:[4]

> *And someone asked him why he was amazed, and how many of his comrades had been slain, the questioner on his part supposing that the herald had come from the forces which had fought at Idomene.*
>
> *The herald answered,* "About two hundred."
>
> *The questioner said in reply,* "These arms, though, are clearly not those of two hundred men, but of more than a thousand."
>
> *And again the herald said,* "Then they are not the arms of our comrades in the battle."
>
> *The other answered,* "They are, if it was you who fought yesterday at Idomene."
>
> "But we did not fight with anyone yesterday; it was the day before yesterday, on the retreat."
>
> "It is certain that we fought yesterday with these men, who were coming to your aid from the city of the Ambraciots."
>
> *When the herald heard this and realized that the force which was coming to their relief from the city had perished, he lifted up his voice in lamentation and, stunned by the magnitude of the calamity before him, departed at once, forgetting his errand and making no request for the dead.* (3.113.1–6)

The passage receives regular notice from commentators, and Simon Hornblower suggests that this briefer passage might have been a trial effort for the Melian dialogue.[5] Regardless of how it relates to the debate in Melos, though, it definitely resembles the debate in John 1. At the very point where the narrator disappears in the Ambraciot dialogue, the herald exclaims with great urgency and speed: "But we did not fight with anyone yesterday … ." The response to his comment is also stated directly, with no narrator, and this exchange has the same rapid fire quality as the question, "Are you the prophet?" in John 1. No less than the Melian dialogue, this passage from Thucydides demonstrates a lapse into a dramatic discourse in the midst of a text that is not otherwise a poetic drama. A prose text becomes temporarily dramatic. Hornblower underscores the dramatic character of the scene of the Ambraciot herald by saying,

4 Translation slightly modified from *Thucydides, History of the Peloponnesian War*, trans. C. F. Smith, vol. 2, LCL (Cambridge: Harvard University Press, 1921).

5 Simon Hornblower, *Commentary on Thucydides* (Oxford: Oxford University Press, 1993), 3:219.

> This [chapter], exceptionally, contains some rapid dialogue (the Melian dialogue is the only other example of this in [Thucydides]). This is a tragic feature …[6]

Modern scholars like Hornblower are not alone in seeing here a dramatic device. Making precisely this point in regard to the Melian Dialogue, Dionysius of Halicarnassus writes:

> Thucydides begins by stating in his own person what each side said, but after maintaining this form of reported speech (διηγηματικόν) for only one exchange of argument, he dramatizes (δραματίζει) the rest of the dialogue and makes the characters speak for themselves. (*On the Character of Thucydides* 37 [Usher, LCL]).

In case there is any doubt about exactly what Dionysius means here by the term "dramatizes," he tells us later. At precisely the point where the narrator falls out of the dialogue, Dionysius writes:

> After this, [Thucydides] changes the style of the dialogue from narrative (διηγήματος) to dramatic (τὸ δραματικόν) … (*On the Character of Thucydides* 38 [Usher, LCL]).

As long as the narrator is introducing the speeches, Dionysius refers to the text as "diegetic." As soon as the narrator falls away and the characters speak directly to one another, he defines it as "dramatic." The terms *diēgema* and *dramatikon*, which are here translated as "narrative" and "dramatic," respectively, deserve further comment. The term diegetic/narrative reminds one of the famous passage in the *Republic*, where Plato discusses different types of literary production. He writes:

> So don't they achieve this either by a simple narrative (ἁπλῇ διηγήσει), or by means of imitation (μιμήσεως), or a combination of both (δι' ἀμφοτέρων)? … I think I can now make clear to you what I couldn't before, the fact that of poetry and storytelling: the one is done entirely by means of imitation, i. e., tragedy and comedy exactly as you say, and the other is the recital of the poet himself, and you would find it in particular, I suppose, in the dithyramb. Where it is a combination of the two, you would find it in the composition of epic poetry and in many other places, if you follow me." (Plato, *Republic* 392d, 394b–c [Emlyn-Jones and Preddy, LCL])

The distinguishing characteristic of the different forms is the presence or absence of a narrator's voice. This seems to be what Dionysius has in mind, even though Dionysius does not follow Plato's terminology. If he were using Plato's categories, he would refer to a shift from diegetic to mimetic, not diegetic to dramatic. The term *dramatikon* shows the influence of Aristotle's *Poetics* (1448a28–9). Aristotle also categorizes different forms of literature as Plato did, though with certain changes.[7] Aristotle introduces different terms into the discussion, and he also

6 Hornblower, *Thucydides*, 1:533.

7 For discussion of Platonic and Aristotelian terms, see Rene Nunlist, *The Ancient Critic at Work:*

uses some of Plato's terms in different ways. It is, likewise, a matter of debate whether he divided literature into two or three different forms. Regardless of these differences, ancient interpreters often blend the categories and language of Plato and Aristotle. Rene Nunlist cites Prolegomena to Hesiod's *Works and Days* from Alexandrian scholia. The text seems to use Plato's categories, but only to a point. The passage reads as follows:

> Note that all poetry consists of three types: the purely narrative, the dramatic and the mixed. The narrative is the one in which the poet alone appears to be speaking, as in the present case the poet Hesiod alone appears to be speaking throughout the poem. The dramatic, in which the poet never speaks, as we see in comedies and tragedies. The mixed, in which the poet both speaks [himself] and introduces speaking characters, as it is done in the *Iliad*.[8]

Plato's three categories are obvious here in general, but Plato's terms "diegetic," "mimetic" and "both" have become "diegematic," "dramatic" and "mixed." The texts serving as examples of the different forms are also changed, and yet, the texts are still distinguished by the presence or absence of a narrator's voice. Most important for our purposes, Plato's "mimetic" has become here "dramatic." When Dionysius, therefore, identifies the Melian dialogue as a δραματικόν episode, we can safely assume that he means δραματικόν to correspond to Platos *mimetic*, i. e., that the text has no narrator present.

And what Dionysius says about Thucydides applies with equal force to John. John does what Thucydides does, lapsing into drama. A key concern of the essays in this volume is to determine to what extent ancient discussions of genre are relevant to John. I think this is a place where we see that relevance.

The shape of John 1 can be even more tightly connected to dramatic forms by noting two realities. The first has to do with the debate or interrogation taking place in the scene. Not only do two parties address one another directly in John 1, as well as in Thucydides, but they do so in the form of debate and interrogation. In the Melian dialogue, the Athenians and Melians argue hotly with one another over whether or not might makes right. In the speech of the Ambraciot herald, the herald interrogates the Athenians to find out exactly what happened. In just the same manner, the people sent from the Pharisees interrogate John the Baptist. Such quick and fast interrogations are a hallmark of ancient drama, particularly in the case of *stichomythia*. Stichomythia is the device by which tragic characters speak to one another in alternating one-line exchanges. It is a form of rapid and forceful questioning. The following conversation between Electra and the Chorus in the *Libation Bearers* is a famous example of stichomythia:

Terms and Concepts of Literary Criticism in Greek Scholia (Cambridge: Cambridge University Press, 2009), 95–102.

8 Translation and discussion in Nunlist, *Ancient Critic*, 97–98.

Electra: I see cut here on the tomb a lock of hair.
Chorus: From some man? Or from a slim-waisted girl?
Electra: This is an obvious clue for anyone to judge.
Chorus: Let me, then, learn how so—older learning from younger.
Electra: There is no one but me who could have cut it.
Chorus: Indeed, the ones for whom it would be appropriate to cut their hair are enemies.
Electra: And, likewise, it appears to be so very similar to …
Chorus: … to which tresses? For, I want to learn this.
Electra: …to my hair it bears a close resemblance.
Chorus: It couldn't be a veiled gift from Orestes, could it?
Electra: It most definitely resembles his locks (168–78, my translation).

Notice the urgency of the conversation when the chorus interrupts Electra and asks, "to which tresses?" The one-line interrogations in stichomythia mimic trial debates in the Athenian law courts.[9] Defining this aspect of stichomythia, Rush Rehm writes: "The rapid exchange of alternative points of view also reflects the process by which Athenian juries reached their verdicts."[10] This same sense of urgency appears in the question, "Are you the prophet?" One pictures a prosecutor attacking a witness on the stand, and it cannot be casual that this section of the Gospel of John begins with the phrase "This is the testimony of John." John is not just answering questions. He is giving testimony, as though in a court of law. The question and answer format that resembles dramatic stichomythia is part and parcel of the legal character of the scene. The trial is, literally, given a dramatic shape.

The same relation between form and function, incidentally, appears in Thucydides. The dramatic shape of the dialogue reinforces the dramatic pathos in the case of the Ambraciot herald in book 3. When he writes on the various dialogical passages in Thucydides, Simon Hornblower states,

> There are only two pieces of real dialogue in Thucydides: the exchange between the Ambrakiot herald and his anonymous interlocutor (3.113, where the dialogue form is a

9 Jennifer Wise argues that this mode of communication arises at least partly from the move to written texts in tragedy, which explains why stichomythia does not occur in the oral world of epic poetry (*Dionysus Writes: The Invention of Theatre in Ancient Greece* [Ithaca: Cornell University Press, 2000], 94). After asserting this, however, she adds, "As a poetic mode of representing human speech, however, it owes an equal debt to the model of forensic speech," ibid, 138–140.

10 Rush Rehm, *Greek Tragic Theatre* (New York: Routledge, 1994), 63–64.

very effective way of bringing out the magnitude of the human catastrophe), and the famous Melian Dialogue (5.85–113).[11]

The dramatic form of the scene with the Ambraciot herald is connected to the dramatic quality of the pathos of the scene. The reader is put in the place of the tragic audience, witnessing an event of horror and great suffering. Whether in John or Thucydides, form and function closely cohere. Scenes of great drama are presented in a dramatic form.

One final connection between John 1 and the scene of the Ambraciot herald in Thucydides is possible. As was just said, the dramatic mode of presentation in Thucydides highlights an important scene which is rich in pathos and is dramatic in a variety of ways. Most important of all, the episode has been read as a recognition scene, which comes to its height of dramatic power when the herald realizes just how many dead lie on the field. As Donald Lateiner says in regard to the herald, "He sees, wonders, does not know, supposes, contradicts, suddenly comprehends, is stunned and groans, goes off in disregard of his mission and sacral duty."[12] And why is the herald so dramatic a figure? Lateiner again says, "For him, his people, and for us the readers of the History, the bodies remain unburied on the battlefield."[13] This is the key. This scene is a paradigmatic scene for Thucydides, and one that shows what the war will bring. Recognition scenes usually appear at the close of a drama, but Thucydides employs the form early in his work because the scene is paradigmatic. It is the lens through which to read the entire work, because this scene demonstrates the catastrophic human toll of the war.

A similar device of recognition operates in the opening scene of John's Gospel. As Kasper Bro Larsen has shown, this opening scene in John is a recognition type-scene, which places great emphasis on the question to John, "Are you the prophet?"[14] Establishing a connection between Jesus and the expected "prophet like Moses" is an essential christological question in the Gospel of John. One of the final lines of the prologue is "The Law came through Moses, but grace and truth came through Jesus Christ" (1:17). The Mosaic prophet category is immediately given attention in this opening question: are you the prophet? In his study on recognition scenes, Larsen has shown that the opening question in John 1, "Who are you?" is a typical opening line in recognitions, such as in Sophocles' *Electra* and Euripides' *Electra*. The similarity with the language of dramatic

11 Simon Hornblower, *Thucydides and Pindar: Historical Narrative and the World of Epinikian Poetry* (Oxford: Oxford University Press, 2006), 324.

12 Donald Lateiner, "Heralds and Corpses in Thucydides," *Classical World* 71 (1977): 101.

13 Lateiner, "Heralds and Corpses," 101.

14 See Kasper Bro Larsen, *Recognizing the Stranger: Recognition Scenes in the Gospel of John*, BIS 93 (Leiden: Brill, 2008), 92–102.

recognitions is very close. When those sent from Jerusalem ask John, σὺ τίς εἶ (1:19), they sound very much like Electra who asks, τίς δ' εἶ σὺ (Euripides, *Electra* 765), or, ἐκεῖνος εἶ σὺ (580).[15] Thus, the relationship between John 1 and the scene of the Ambraciot herald is close on several fronts. Both are paradigmatic for their respective works. Both follow the pattern of recognition scenes. And, most important for our purposes, both shift at a key point into a dramatic form of dialogue. This lapse into dramatic dialogue makes these scenes in Thucydides and John 1 stand in some ambiguous place between narrative and drama.

3. John 14: Rise, Let Us Be on Our Way

John 14 provides a similar moment. The voice of the Evangelist drops out of view in the midst of the Farewell Discourses. The situation is somewhat different, but the same silence appears. As chapter 14 draws to its conclusion, Jesus says,

> I will no longer talk much with you, for the ruler of this world is coming. He has no power over me; but I do as the Father has commanded me, so that the world may know that I love the Father. Rise, let us be on our way. (14:30–31)

The important phrase is the last one: "Rise, let us be on our way." The passage is important because Jesus is describing his own movements. This is a place where a narrator would generally say, "He got up and left." But not only does Jesus give his own stage directions. These directions also have no accompanying narrator's comment. A defining quality of dramatic technique is that a character must give his or her own stage directions. A scholion passed down as a comment on Aeschylus' *Eumenides* makes this clear. At line 29 of the *Eumenides*, the priestess says, "I take my seat upon my throne." A scholion for this verse teaches us something about the difference between a prose text and a drama. The scholion says,

> [The priestess] says this herself, since the work is a dramatic one [δραματική]. If, on the other hand, it had been a narrative one [διηγηματική}, the poet would have said, "Saying these things, she sat upon the throne." (my translation)[16]

The priestess has to explain her own stage directions, since, in a dramatic mode, there is no narrator to explain them for her. If the character does not speak the stage directions, then there are no stage directions. A distinctive characteristic of the dramatic mode, therefore, is the absence of a narrator. Jo-Ann Brant makes the point nicely, when she writes,

15 Larsen, *Recognition Scenes*, 93.

16 For this scholion, see *Scholia Graeca in Aeschylum quae exstant Omnia*, ed. O. L. Smith, 2 vols. (Leipzig: Teubner, 1976), 1.44.

> In Greek tragedy, no audience is left wondering, "Who was that masked man?" Without the aid of a narrator to give character sketches, characters ... speak about themselves and each other to give important details about their background and desires ...[17]

and also says,

> Onstage, an actor's identity depends totally upon linguistic or symbolic markers. If the audience does not know that a character has a particular identity, that character does not have that identity.[18]

What Brant says about the identity of a character applies with equal force, as we have just seen in the scholion to Aeschylus, to stage directions. If the characters do not describe their actions, no narrator is present to help them. Jesus speaks his own stage direction when he says, "Rise, let us be on our way." The narrator says nothing, until several chapters later, and then Jesus continues his discourse in the very next line by saying, "I am the true vine." The silence of the narrator on Jesus' actions here has puzzled interpreters from antiquity to the present, and has given rise to numerous explanatory theories. Some have even suggested that Jesus does depart the Supper and delivers his discourses while walking with his disciples.[19] But the text does not say this. Others assume that we have here some form of sloppy editing. I think we have a lapse into a more dramatic mode. Jesus explains his own stage directions, just like the priestess in the *Eumenides*, and just like every other character in a dramatic performance.

As with the case of the interrogation of the Baptist, the lapse of the narrator is not an isolated dramatic feature, but is part of a much larger turn to drama in the scene. The announcement of Jesus' exit is dramatic, in other words, for at least two reasons. First, this exit takes place during Jesus' final speech before his death, and tragic characters regularly deliver a speech before their death. Fiona Macintosh has labeled this final address the "Big Speech," and the speech of Jesus in the Farewell Discourses bears striking resemblance to the tragic "Big Speech."[20]

Second, Jesus announces his departure to march toward death, but does not actually go anywhere. He announces, "Arise, let us go forth," but he does not actually depart until three chapters later, and his departure resembles the delayed exit of tragic characters. Dramatic characters often announce an exit that they do not immediately take in order to isolate their last words before departure, and in order to abstract themselves from their immediate surroundings, thereby

17 Jo-Ann A. Brant, *Dialogue and Drama: Elements of Greek Tragedy in the Fourth Gospel* (Peabody: Hendrickson, 2004), 187.

18 Ibid, 186.

19 For discussion, see George Parsenios, *Departure and Consolation: The Johannine Farewell Discourses in Light of Greco-Roman Literature*, NovTSup 119 (Leiden: Brill, 2005), 37.

20 See George Parsenios, "'No Longer in the World' (John 17:11): The Transformation of the Tragic in the Fourth Gospel," *HTR* 98 (2005): 18.

speaking from a more objective and universal vantage point.[21] Jesus does the same. The effect of all these devices is intimately connected to his impending death. He already begins to abstract himself from the surrounding action, and already begins to speak to his disciples as the one who has returned to the Father. Thus, the fact that the narrator's voice recedes in this scene is part of a much larger turn to drama in the Farewell Discourses. The silence of the narrator, that is, places the text in a space somewhere between narrative and drama.

4. John 3: Jesus or the Baptist

A final example of the silent narrator appears in the contested and confusing case of John 3:31–36. The reader struggles to understand who speaks in these verses. The last mentioned speaker is John the Baptist, who is identified at 3:27, and his words clearly extend to 3:30, where he says, "He must increase, while I must decrease." Some interpreters believe, therefore, that the Baptist continues speaking in verses 3:31–36, which read as follows:

> The one who comes from above is above all; the one who is of the earth belongs to the earth and speaks about earthly things. The one who comes from heaven is above all. He testifies to what he has seen and heard, yet no one accepts his testimony. Whoever has accepted his testimony has certified this, that God is true. He whom God has sent speaks the words of God, for he gives the Spirit without measure. The Father loves the Son and has placed all things in his hands. Whoever believes in the Son has eternal life; whoever disobeys the Son will not see life, but must endure God's wrath.

If these are the words of the Baptist, then he is setting up a distinction between himself and Jesus, in order to explain why Jesus must increase, while the Baptist decreases. As Barrett writes in regard to 3:31, "[t]his verse carries on the thought of vv. 22–30—Jesus and John are now contrasted as 'He that is from above' and 'He that is of the earth' …."[22]

The gravest difficulty with such a reading is that the sentiments expressed in 3:31–36 sound exactly like the words of Jesus, not the Baptist. Brown writes, for example:

> An even stronger case can be made for Jesus as the speaker … . Amid all these theories it should be clearly observed that the discourses in vv. 31–36 resemble closely the style of speech attributed to Jesus in the Gospel, and in particular it has close parallels in Jesus' words to Nicodemus.[23]

---

21 Parsenios, *Departure and Consolation*, chapter 2.

22 C. K. Barrett, *The Gospel according to St. John: An Introduction with Commentary and Notes on the Greek Text* (London: SPCK, 1956), 187.

23 Raymond Brown, *The Gospel according to John*, AB 29 (New York: Doubleday, 1966), 1:159.

In this way of reading, Jesus resumes speaking, as he had been prior to the words of John, but the narrator gives no notice of the change. And that last matter is the key: If Jesus is here speaking, then the reason for the confusion among interpreters is the fact that the evangelist gives no notice of a shift back to Jesus. The narrator is silent—again. The precise dramatic purpose of the narrator's silence is in this case not so clear as it was in the others. But, like the episodes in John 1 and John 14 already discussed, this passage in John 3 has analogies in other texts where the narrator lapses into silence unexpectedly.

There are a handful of passages in the Iliad—7 to be exact—that turn our attention in the right direction. In these 7 cases, the text of Homer transitions from narrative to speech without a phase such as "He said" to mark the beginning of the speech. The scholiasts on Homer define these examples as a shift from *diegesis* to *mimesis*, meaning not merely a transition from narrative to speech, but rather a transition from a narrative with a narrator into a dramatic mode with no narrator.[24] Scholia are not finally decisive, of course, in interpretation. They need to be read critically. Simon Pulleyn strikes the right note when he says, "Although it would be naïve to suppose that scholia offer definitive answers to vexed questions simply by virtue of their antiquity, it cannot be denied that they reflect the intuitions of people who knew ancient Greek as a living language, and they often show sensitivity to literary matters."[25] With the right amount of caution, then, the scholia are helpful in showing us that an ancient commentator would notice the lack of a narrator's comment in a transition from a text with a narrator introducing speeches, to a more dramatic mode without the presence of a narrator. If John 3:31–36 is a speech of Jesus, then we have here a shift from one speaker to another without the intervening comment of a narrator. This marks a shift from a diegetic mode of representation to a more dramatic/mimetic one that does not rely on the intervention of a narrator. Once again, the silence of the narrator places a scene in the Gospel of John somewhere between narrative and drama.

5. Conclusion

Ancient readers and critics regularly recognized that the retreat of the narrator within a text would give that text a more dramatic character. The fact that the narrator's voice of the Evangelist is often silenced in the Gospel of John causes the biography of Jesus to seem much more like a drama, and the ancient comments of readers of Homer and Thucydides demonstrate how an ancient reader

24 See Nunlist, *Ancient Critic*, 106.
25 Simon Pulleyn, *Homer, Iliad 1* (Oxford: Oxford University Press, 2000), 50.

might have read these passages in John, how an ancient reader might have heard the silent spaces. These silent spaces place John between narrative and drama.

Anders Klostergaard Petersen

Generic Docetism: From the Synoptic Narrative Gospels to the Johannine Discursive Gospel

1. The Tension of John and the Question of Genre and Mode[1]

A mosaic is commonly conceived of as a harmonious composition consisting of an assemblage made of a variety of individual pieces, be they bits of glass, stone or other material. Traditionally, a mosaic comprises an iconic motif such as, for instance, a representation of a flower or a bird that is easily decoded by the viewer. In contemporary art, however, one may also come across mosaics that are far from harmonious and well-balanced. Frequently, they are characterised by being of a non-figurative kind and by demonstrating a tension, verging on an intense rivalry between the materials used. Sometimes they even exhibit a poignant employment of differences pertaining to the depth and height of the individual pieces of the mosaic. Whereas the traditional mosaic has a flat nature, modern mosaics often play with differences with respect to levels of height. In the contemporary cases, the lack of proportionality and the arresting disorderliness challenge the viewer and induce him or her to search for a meaning beyond the chaotic impression conveyed by the work of art.

As suggested by the title of this volume (*The Gospel of John as Genre Mosaic*), one may examine the Gospel of John as a compilation of different micro-genres, but such an approach, of course, begs the questions not only with respect to the over-all genre and, possibly, sub-genre of the text and its mode but also with regard to the relationship between the individual micro-genres employed by the Gospel.[2] Should John's Gospel be conceived of in terms of an eirenic and har-

1 I want to express my sincere thanks to Kasper Bro Larsen for a very thorough response to my paper. I have benefited considerably from his comments and suggestions for improvement.

2 For the distinction between mode, genre, and sub-genre, see Alisdair Fowler, *Kinds of Literature: An Introduction to the Theory of Genres and Modes* (Oxford: Oxford University Press, 1982), 56. Fowler operates with a tripartite differentiation that enables him to distinguish between mode, genre, and sub-genre. The sub-genre is conceived to add features to the genre and the mode to select or abstract from the genre proper. In the first case, we find a generic addition, whereas in the latter case we are confronted with generic subtraction. According to

monious composition or should it rather be understood on the basis of a rivalling relationship between different micro- and sub-genres used for particular purposes? And what does a stance on this question imply for the view of the over-all genre and the mode of the text? What are the implications if we also allow ourselves to include the question of John's rewriting of his predecessors in terms of genre and perhaps even more so in terms of mode?

In this essay, I shall not focus particularly on the use of the individual micro-genres of John's Gospel, that is, the mosaic pieces, and the relationship between them. Rather, I shall concentrate on the general nature of the mosaic and the genre and mode subscribed to, since I am inclined to think of John's text more in terms of a contemporary mosaic characterised by asymmetry and unevenness. In order not to be misunderstood, I shall emphasise the analogous nature of my comparison. I am not asserting that the Gospel of John by any means constitutes a modern text embodying fragmentation, paradoxes, and ruptures, and being voiced by an unreliable narrator as part of its textual strategy. On the contrary, I retain the ancient nature of John. It is not a piece of postmodern literature. In my reading, John is an unmistakably ancient text dating to the end of the first century or beginning of the second century, and should, therefore, within such an interpretation be historically interpreted in terms of a plausible reconstruction that aims to locate the text in this period and within a socio-cultural milieu to which the text may reasonably be allocated. What I do contend, however, by my analogy to the two types of mosaic is that John at the level of textual mode and genre exhibits a tension—a tension, that to the best of my knowledge has not been satisfactorily highlighted in previous scholarship. The friction originates in a conflict that stems from the Gospel's adherence to the scriptural, narrative *Vorlage* of the Synoptic Gospels,[3] on the one hand, and its endorsement and

Fowler, the sub-genre embodies the same external characteristics as those found in the genre, together with an additional specification of content. To this it adds "an obligatory part-repertoire of substantive rules, optional in kind (to which it is related, therefore, almost a sub-class)." Mode, conversely, "has few if any external rules, but evokes a historical kind through samples of its internal repertoire," Fowler, *Kinds of Literature*, 56. In this manner, sub-genre, genre, and mode may be thought of as a recurrent number of shared properties both with respect to content and to form. Cf. Tzvetan Todorov, "The Origin of Genres," *New Literary History* 8 (1976): 159–70 (162). For the use of these distinctions in the context of a study of early Christianity, see Anders Klostergaard Petersen, "The Diversity of Apologetics: From Genre to a Mode of Thinking," in *Critique and Apologetics: Jews, Christians, and Pagans in Antiquity* (ed. Anders-Christian Jakobsen, Jörg Ulrich and David Brakke: Frankfurt am Main: Peter Lang 2009), 15–41. Micro-genre, conversely, designates a particular generic element used in a particular text such as catalogues of virtues and vices, lists of sufferings, recognition scenes, etc.

3 Due to constraints of space, I shall not delve on the exact relationship between John and the Synoptic Gospels but talk about the previous tradition in general. It may well be that John primarily knew the Synoptic tradition via the traditions transmitted by Luke, whereby I do not say that John had the Gospel of Luke at his disposal. However, since I here focus on genre and

inculcation of a Christology that by its nature is of a discursive and non-narrative character, on the other hand. To put my point even more bluntly, I surmise that the Synoptic Gospels exhibit what may be dubbed a narrative Christology, whereas the Gospel of John in my view bears witness to what I shall designate a revelatory, discursive Christology. But we may take this difference one step further whereby the argument becomes noticeably more contentious.

To take a closer look at the genre and the question of mode pertinent to John will also bring us to the centre of discussion of some of the pivotal aspects pertaining to the fundamental message which the text wants to convey to its intended audience. Needless to say, in a short article like this I cannot provide an interpretation of the entire Gospel text. What I shall do, therefore, is of a more limited scope, and in line with the general aim of the volume. I will examine one particular micro-genre, that is, the miracle texts of the Gospel which in my view exemplify the tension I have indicated.[4] They are indicative of a collision of genres that springs from the christological disagreement between the Synoptic tradition and John's Gospel, and possibly reflects not only a different date of composition but also an origin in conspicuously different socio-historical settings.[5] The core of my argument is that John by virtue of the logic of his Christology is really abstaining from composing a narrative about Jesus. Yet, the narrative tradition of his predecessors was plausibly so strong that in terms of genre he had to follow in the wake of what they had initiated by creating some sort of Jesus biography as that familiar to us from the Synoptic Gospels. At the same time as he created his gospel biography of Jesus, he, I argue, came to undermine its narrative nature by means of a Christology that does not leave room for narrative development. This may, for instance, be seen on the basis of the miracle-stories. This argument may initially sound peculiar, but the underlying idea is that there is an intrinsic relationship between micro-genre, genre,

---

mode I can allow myself to bracket the question of the exact historical relationship between John and the Synoptic tradition. For the discussion of this question, see the classic re-opening of the modern debate in Percival Gardner-Smith, *Saint John and the Synoptic Gospels* (Cambridge, Cambridge University Press 1938). For more current literature on this field of problems, see Adelbert Denaux, ed., *John and the Synoptics* (Leuven: Leuven University Press; Peeters, 1992); James D.G. Dunn, "John and the Synoptics as a Theological Question," in *Exploring the Gospel of John. In Honor of D. Moody Smith*, ed. R. Alan Culpepper and C. Clifton Black (Louisville: Westminster John Knox, 1996), 301–313, as well as the recent standard commentaries.

4 See Jörg Frey's contribution in this volume for an over-view of the history of research on the miracle stories in John's Gospel.

5 By saying this, I do not presume that the Synoptic Gospels originated in the same socio-cultural milieu. On the contrary, each of the three Synoptic Gospels arose from individually very specific circumstances and in particular environments. Yet, in spite of notable differences pertaining to origin, I do suggest that the social circles in which they arose were closer to each other than to the circles behind the Gospel of John.

mode, and the over-all message of the text. In fact, it is the transition in meaning so evident when one compares John with the Synoptic Gospels that may account for the bending of genre and mode, verging on a rupture of both, in John vis-à-vis the previous tradition.

2. The Background for the Discussion

In his important work *Recognizing the Stranger: Recognition Scenes in the Gospel of John*, Kasper Bro Larsen makes the case that the central narrative structure of John should be interpreted in accordance with the ancient Graeco-Roman and Jewish recognition type-scene.[6] He asserts that "the recognition scene is a recurrent, generic vehicle in John, which serves to host and thematize central problems in the Gospel concerning the knowledge of God through Jesus, as well as the believers' access to Jesus in his physical presence and absence."[7] In the same vein, Larsen argues that the Johannine Christ should be conceived of in terms similar to the homecoming Odysseus: Larsen's paradigmatic example of ancient *anagnōrisis* literature.

Parallel to the dual nature of Odysseus, the earthly Christ of John's Gospel manifests himself in the external form of flesh (*sarx*) although his true nature is of a divine kind, that is, he is representative of the glory of the Father (*doxa*). Yet, Larsen is also keenly aware of the conspicuous difference between John's Christ and Odysseus. Contrary to Odysseus, who appears to people who have previously known him and who are, therefore, confronted with the challenge of being able to recognise him, Christ is a heavenly sojourner and stranger who has intervened in a world that he did not have any previous contact with.[8] In that sense, the recognition of Christ has a rather different nature. Larsen also underlines the concomitant difference with respect to the character of the recognition. In contrast to Odysseus, the Johannine *anagnōrisis* scenes focus on the social recognition of the thematic roles of Christ and not on his proper-name identity.

In my view, Larsen has made a persuasive case for how the inclusion of the ancient recognition type-scene may be advantageous for shedding light on a

6 The work was submitted in 2006 as a Ph.D. thesis at the University of Aarhus. Since I acted as chairman of the assessment committee, I had the pleasure of working intensely with Larsen's work. The thesis has since been published in a revised version, see Kasper Bro Larsen, *Recognizing the Stranger: Recognition Scenes in the Gospel of John*, BIS 93 (Leiden: Brill, 2008).

7 Larsen, *Recognizing the Stranger*, 219.

8 It is, of course, said that "Christ came to his own (εἰς τὰ ἴδια), and that his own (οἱ ἴδιοι) received him not" (1:11), but I read that statement as part of the rhetorical attempt to form an in-group that cannot but think of itself as necessarily belonging from pristine time to the Johannine Christ.

number of aspects in John's Gospel not satisfactorily illuminated by previous scholarship. This pertains not least to the structure of the *anagnōrisis* micro-genre which in Larsen's reconstruction is constituted by five fundamental elements:

> (1) the meeting which determines the economy of knowledge in the scene to follow; (2) the move of cognitive resistance, which contains expressions of doubt, requests for proof, suggestions of alternative identification, judicial investigation, or sheer rejection; (3) the display of the recognition token; (4) the moment of recognition; and (5) the move of attendant reaction and physical (re)union. The recognition scene seems to reflect an ideology where identity is conceived of as integration into a social body.[9]

I think there is much in John to substantiate the reading advocated by Larsen, but at the same time I have to acknowledge that I do not find the over-all interpretation convincing. I grant Larsen that ancient texts of *anagnōrisis* may advantageously be used to cast light on particular passages in the Johannine text that in terms of micro-genre share some of the same narrative features as the recognition type-scenes of Graeco-Roman literature. Although Larsen endorses the view that the *anagnōrisis*-nature of John's Gospel constitutes a type-scene at the level of the enunciate (story-world) but simultaneously may be used metaphorically to describe the basic content of John's discourse, I think that the latter by being anchored in ultimately a narrative micro-genre does not satisfactorily convey the "philosophical" character of John. By interpreting textual passages in this manner and in particular the entire Gospel text along these lines of *anagnōrisis*, I argue that a decisive element in John's staging of the scenes is not given due emphasis, that is, the focus on the cognitive component on the discourse level pertaining to the intended audience of the Gospel. By ultimately applying a theoretical model to John that comes from the narrow field of narratology, Larsen in my view underestimates the fact that the text is predominantly working with changing the mind of the intended audience.[10] To formulate my view rather crudely, I do not think that John's Gospel—unlike the Synoptic Gospels—is as interested in telling a story as it is focused on framing the mind-set of its intended audience.

I acknowledge that this may sound like a feigned distinction, since the telling of a story inevitably is also part of an act of persuasion. Nevertheless, I surmise that there is a differentiation between the two that hinges on whether one is engaged in creating a discourse or recounting a story. Although these reflections initially perhaps may sound peripheral to the discussion of John as a genre

9 Larsen, *Recognizing the Stranger*, 219–20.

10 See, however, Larsen's final chapter in *Recognizing the Stranger* on "The Reader as *Anagnōstēs*," which does attempt to pay remedy for what I think is an underestimation of the cognitive component on the discursive level.

mosaic, I believe that by focusing on the question of John's discursive elaboration of the inherited Gospel tradition we are actually touching upon a central element in the discussion of the genre of John. To epitomise the problem, the question is whether John, as in Larsen's reading, should be interpreted primarily in terms of narrative categories or, as I am inclined to think, in discursive terms. In order not to be misunderstood, let me specify that my purpose here is not to rehearse the old debate initiated by Käsemann on John's Gospel as exhibiting a form of docetism. Although I think that there was more than a kernel of truth in Käsemann's insight, I shall not have recourse to his manner of presenting the issue. The problem pertaining to his argument was that it was developed in narrow theological terms which I for various reasons want to distance myself from.[11] I am more interested in the problem exhibited by John's Gospel in terms of genre, mode, and type of persuasion. What I shall suggest is that John may be exhibiting a form of thinking that I—due to a lack of better terminology—for the time being shall designate "generic docetism." To formulate the point rather bluntly, my

11 Ernst Käsemann, *Jesu letzer Wille nach Johannes 17* (Tübingen: Mohr Siebeck 1966). In another work, Kasper Bro Larsen also takes up this question of "docetism" in a manner similar to the ideas I am espousing in this essay. Larsen, however, does not make the further suggestion that John's excessive "discursive" rewriting of the synoptic tradition ultimately undermines the narrative form of his generic predecessors. Interestingly enough, Larsen does neither point out that by shifting the focus of interest from the strictly narrative to the discursive components of John, he does to a certain extent take leave with his argument in *Recognizing the Stranger.* See Kasper Bro Larsen, "Narrative Docetism: Christology and Storytelling in the Gospel of John," in *The Gospel of John and Christian Theology*, ed. Richard Bauckham and Carl Mosser (Grand Rapids: Eerdmans, 2008), 346–355: "John did what Paul could not, would not, or simply did not: he shaped a high Christology within the literary frame of elaborate narrative. By telling the story of an omniscient divine being, he reached the limits of the logical possibilities given to any storyteller, since the tension of narrative normally comes from the limited knowledge and the perspective point of the narrated actors. John, however, does not compromise by lowering his high Christology for the sake of narrative dynamics and thus creates the effect of "narrative Docetism." But whereas the Gospel stands still as to Jesus' existence in the pragmatic dimension, it reveals its dynamics at the cognitive level. It is on this level that the Fourth Gospel struggles with its central epistemological question: how does one recognize a stranger?" (354–55). For a similar emphasis attributed to the cognitive dimension of John, see Jesper Tang Nielsen, *Die kognitive Dimension des Kreuzes: Zur Deutung des Todes Jesu im Johannesevangelium*, WUNT 2/263 (Tübingen: Mohr Siebeck 2009). Parallel to Larsen, Nielsen attributes significance to the cognitive aspect pertaining to Jesus' narrative development, but without fully acknowledging that John's Gospel is mostly working at the level of the enunciation or discourse rather than at the level of the enunciate or story-world, see Nielsen, *Kognitive Dimension*, 273: "Wenn er [sc. Jesus] nach der Inkarnation in die aristotelische Mitte der Erzählung bzw. in die Greimas'sche Phase der Performanz eintritt, ist es deshalb seine Aufgabe, die Menschen zu überzeugen, dass sein Status tatsächlich der des Geheimnisses und nicht derjenige der Lüge ist. So ist Jesu Tätigkeit an der kognitiven Dimension der Erzählung orientiert. Er muss, um seinen Befehl auszuführen, eine kognitive Reaktion hervorrufen, damit die Menschen erkennen, dass er Gott offenbart."

assertion is that John is only superficially and due to his reliance on his Synoptic predecessors employing the narrative form in order to have his distinctive mode of Christ-belief come through.[12]

3. Narrative and Discourse from a Semiotic Perspective

Needless to say, the categories of discourse and narrative are of a modern nature and are without firm grounding in the ancient textual world, although Aristotle in the *Poetics* did provide important insight into the character of narratives. In fact, the *Poetics* may be understood as a precursor to the perception that in a far more elaborate and formalised manner was developed among French semioticians in the 1960s.[13] I am using the terms discourse and narrative at an etic level of analysis, and I shall have recourse to the French tradition of semiotics that will serve as the theoretical springboard for my take on John's Gospel. Despite the fact that in recent years this tradition may have fallen slightly into oblivion, I think that there is still much to gain from this trajectory of scholarship, especially so in a context in which the focus is directed towards the interpretation of narrative texts and not least to the question of the relationship between texts of a narrative and discursive nature.

As already pointed out by Algirdas Julien Greimas and Joseph Courtés in their article on narrativity in their semiotic dictionary, Émile Benveniste should be credited for his differentiation between narrative discourses and other types of discourses.[14] Benveniste contrasted story with discourse firstly by placing emphasis on the personal category, i. e., that the positions "I" and "you" are intrinsic to discourse and congruently that the non-person is characteristic of narrative. Secondly, he placed emphasis on the particular distribution of verbal tenses as useful for a distinction between the two types of literature.[15] In continuity of

12 Something slightly similar has been argued by Geert Hallbäck in the emphasis he places on the undynamic narrative character of John. See idem, "The Gospel of John as Literature: Literary Readings of the Fourth Gospel," in *New Readings in John. Literary and Theological Perspective: Essays from the Scandinavian Conference on the Fourth Gospel in Århus 1997*, ed. Johannes Nissen and Sigfred Pedersen, JSNTSup 182 (Sheffield: Sheffield Academic Press 1999), 31–46.

13 See the use of Aristotle in Ole Davidsen, *The Narrative Jesus: A Semiotic Reading of Mark's Gospel* (Aarhus: Aarhus University Press, 1993), 12–13. Davidsen rightly contends that the narrative schema developed by Greimas "seems to be a reformulation of Aristotle's semiotic conception of the narrative's internal organization" (12).

14 Algirdas Julien Greimas and Joseph Courtés, "Narrativité," *Sémiotique* 247–250, 248.

15 It was the latter part that constituted the focus of Benveniste's examinations, see his seminal *Problèmes de linguisticque générale. Vol. 1* (Paris: Galimard 1966), 237–250, particularly 242.

Gérard Genette,[16] Greimas and Courtés proceeded to argue how the two forms of discourse, that is, narrative and discourse *sensu stricto*, rarely appear in pure form. Most often they are intertwined with each other as in cases when conversations slide into stories about different things or when correspondingly narratives include dialogical parts between the narrated figures. Greimas and Courtés, therefore, concurred with Genette that it may be advantageous to distinguish between narrative as the recounted story and discourse as the form through which a narrative is recounted. Additionally, they refined the distinction by differentiating between what they designate the enunciate, i. e., the recounted story, and the enunciation as the instance through which the exercise of the semiotic competence is taking place. They define the enunciation as: "D'un autre côté, si l'énonciation est le lieu d'exercise de la competence sémiotique, elle est en même temps l'instance de l'instauration du sujet (de l'énonciation)."[17] Furthermore, there is an additional nuancing that is important to bear in mind with respect to the enunciation. Greimas and Courtés are careful to underline that the genuine enunciation which by virtue of its mode of existence logically presupposes the enunciate is often conflated with the enunciated or recounted enunciation. However, the latter is as they emphasise an imitation or simulacrum of the enunciating performance within the discourse: the "I," the "here," and the "now" found in the enunciated discourse do not represent the subject, the time or the space of the enunciation.[18] Ultimately, however, they assign the discourse to the level of the enunciation and narrative to the level of the enunciate.[19]

4. Narrative and Discourse in John

Superficially speaking, there is no doubt about the over-all mode of John. From its beginning the Gospel presents itself as a narrative: "In the beginning was the Word, and the Word was with God, and the Word was God" (1:1); but needless to say there is an implicit act of enunciation taking place. The "I" underlying the enunciation is concealed just as the "you" to whom the message is directed is implicit: "[I tell you that] In the beginning was the Word …."

16 See, for instance, Gérard Genette, *Narrative Discourse Revisited* (Ithaca: Cornell University Press, 1988), 13–17.

17 See Algirdas Julien Greimas and Joseph Courtés, " Énonciation," *Sémiotique* 125–128.

18 See ibid., 128.

19 Germane to my considerations is also the fact that Courtés and Greimas with respect to the narrative underline how it may be of either a pragmatic or of a cognitive nature, but we need to be alert not to conflate this with what takes place at the discursive level of the enunciation, although the two may sometime come close to each other.

Unlike its predecessors, John does not specify his text in terms of a further characteristic of genre such as the ἀρχὴ τοῦ εὐαγγελίου of Mark 1:1, the βίβλος γενέσεως of Matt 1:1, or the διήγησις of Luke 1:1,[20] which all to a greater or lesser extent may be seen to resemble the contemporary Graeco-Roman biography.[21] The closest one comes to a specification of the purpose of John's Gospel and, thereby, the genre evoked by the work is the finale of John 20:30–31: "Now Jesus did many other signs in the presence of his disciples, which are not written in this book (Πολλὰ μὲν οὖν καὶ ἄλλα σημεῖα ἐποίησεν ὁ Ἰησοῦς). But these are written so that you may come to believe that Jesus is the Messiah, the Son of God, and that through believing you may have life in his name." Thereby, at its very conclusion the book instantiates itself as a work of persuasion that consists of two elements.[22] Firstly, it is a textual reproduction of those signs (σημεῖα) of Jesus which are held particularly pertinent for inducing the intended audience to acknowledge that Jesus is to be identified with the Christ, the Son of God. Needless to say, that of course points to the importance of those places in the work in which the term σημεῖον/α is used. Secondly, as a result of the πίστις of the intended audience, the group addressed will obtain eternal life. As is evident from these two statements of the purpose of John's Gospel, the emphasis is assigned to the aspired results of the book with respect to the intended audience. It may well be an account of the signs of Jesus before his disciples, but the ultimate concern of the presentation is to achieve the two goals at the level of the discourse. It may, of course, well be that ultimately something similar is at stake in the Synoptic Gospels, but that is just not the way these works present themselves. On the contrary, they are first and foremost meant to convey to their intended audience the story of Jesus so that it may not fall into oblivion which is the essential concern of any work of history writing in the ancient world, including the biographical genre.

This purpose of John, conversely, has already been pointed out in the prologue to the Gospel in which John the Baptist is pregnantly emphasised as: "He came as a witness to testify to the light, so that all might believe through him (ἵνα πάντες πιστεύσωσιν δι' αὐτοῦ)" (1:7). In continuity of 1:5, in which it was said that the light (i. e., Christ) shines in darkness, and that darkness did not comprehend it, 1:10 repeats the idea that Christ was in the world and that the world was made

20 By emphasising these three designations, I am not saying that they constituted institutionalised and, therefore, acknowledged genre categories in the world in which the respective texts came into existence. I am only making the argument that in terms of the texts in which they appear they do function as genre designators.

21 See the now classical discussions of this matter in Clyde Weber Votaw, *The Gospels and Contemporary Biographies in the Greco-Roman World* (Philadelphia: Fortress, 1970); Christopher H. Talbert, *What Is a Gospel? The Genre of the Canonical Gospels* (Philadelphia: Fortress, 1971); and Richard A. Burridge, *What Are the Gospels? A Comparison with Graeco-Roman Biography*, SNTSMS 70 (Cambridge: Cambridge University Press, 1992).

22 Like most scholars I take chapter 21 to be a later addition to John.

through him, but that the world did not acknowledge (ἔγνω) him. Although he came to his own (εἰς τὰ ἴδια), his own did not receive him (1:11). But as many, however, as did receive him, he gave the right to become children of God (1:12a–b). In accordance with the finale of the Gospel, this group is further characterised as those who believe in his name (τοῖς πιστεύουσιν εἰς τὸ ὄνομα αὐτοῦ, 1:12c), and who were born not of blood, not of the will of flesh, nor of the will of man, but of God (1:13). In this manner and fully compliant with the end of the Gospel, it is made patently clear that the work is not concerned with the narrative development of Jesus as such. Despite the fact that there will be no real narrative development in terms of the recounted main protagonist, the Gospel, however, could potentially remain a narrative although unfolded in the cognitive dimension primarily. In this manner, one could envision a narrative about how the group of people that did receive Jesus, came to be endowed with the right to become the children of God (cf. 1:12). Yet, as soon as we enter into the subsequent verses there is a remarkable shift from the level of the narrative or the enunciate to the level of the enunciation which, once again, underlines the tension I have spoken of.

In 1:14 the enunciator reveals himself by pointing to his own engagement in the creation of the discourse—in terms of an imitation of the enunciating performance of the discourse: "And the Word became flesh and lived among us (ἐν ἡμῖν), and we have seen (ἐθεασάμεθα) his glory, the glory as of a father's only son, full of grace and truth." Thereafter, a new transition or *de-engagement* takes place at which the text returns to the level of the enunciate:[23] "John bore witness of him and cried out, saying: "John testified to him and cried out, 'This was he of whom I said, 'He who comes after me ranks ahead of me because he was before me.''" (1:15). But rather than resuming the recounting of the story of how John the Baptist and Jesus came into contact with each other, there is an additional slide back or *engagement* to the level of the enunciation that is emphatically highlighted: "From his fullness we have all received (ἡμεῖς πάντες ἐλάβομεν), grace upon grace" (1:16).

In 1:17 there is a transition from the enunciation to the enunciate once again, but at this point it is unclear whether it is a return to the macro-story or a transition to a micro-story that further illuminates what has just been communicated at the discursive level. The use of the introductory particle ὅτι points to the latter option: "The law indeed was given through Moses; grace and truth came through Jesus Christ. No one has ever seen God. It is God the only Son, who is

23 For the technical terms of "shifting out" and "shifting in" (here preferably rendered *de-engagement* and *engagement*) to and from the enunciation and the enunciate, see the entries Algirdas Julien Greimas and Joseph Courtés, "Débrayage" and "Embrayage," *Sémiotique* 79–82, 119–121.

close to the Father's heart, who has made him known" (1:17–18). However, this uncertainty about exact reference, and the *de-engagements* and *engagements* between enunciate and enunciation, points in the direction that John's Gospel in contrast to the previous gospel tradition is not a straight-forward account of how Jesus became Christ. The intended audience of John does not constitute a group that did have or, perhaps, rather ought to have had direct access to acknowledging Jesus as Christ (cf. 1:11). On the contrary, the Gospel is directed to those who have received him and, thereby, have become the children of God, that is, those who believe in his name and have been born of God. In line with the concluding statement of the purpose of the Gospel, the point of John's Gospel is by virtue of a revelatory discourse to induce people into believing that Jesus is the Christ and, thus, the Son of God. The reward or gain of this belief is life in his name. Needless to say, there is a tension here which has also been a classical topic of discussion in Johannine exegesis. If the intended audience is conceived of already to have received Jesus, why write the Gospel? If, contrariwise, it is composed with an intended audience in mind that has not yet become children of God, how could they possibly make this choice if it has already been decided beforehand who the children of God are and who are excluded from this group? I think the best way to solve this tension is to conceive these statements in terms of essentialising metaphorical inculcations that serve to strengthen the awareness of the intended audience of "belongingness." By making the belongingness something that has already been decided from pristine time and, similarly, using a metaphor of birth, the choice of belongingness and the averse risk of falling out of this state of thinking is thereby considerably diminished, because the affiliation to God comes out as something cosmically inevitable, as sheer "natural" reality.[24] But let us resume the question of John as discourse or narrative.

One may undoubtedly argue with a firm basis in the text that John by means of a narrative, i. e., the enunciate or recounted story, strives to inculcate this sense of belongingness of the children of God in the minds of his intended audience. As previously indicated, I think such an assertion is superficially true, but I shall argue that John by his very peculiar manoeuvre comes close to undermining the narrative form that he has inherited from his predecessors. The continuous shiftings between enunciation and enunciate transforms John's Gospel from a narrative strictly speaking to something that comes close to a revelatory discourse in which the narrative is only adhered to due to the heavy load of the precedent tradition, hence my coinage "generic docetism." A prominent example

24 Cf. the over-all argument in a Pauline context in the two books by Caroline Johnson Hodge, *If Sons, Then Heirs. A Study of Kinship and Ethnicity in the Letters of Paul* (Oxford: Oxford University Press, 2007), and Denise Kimber Buell, *Why this New Race? Ethnic Reasoning in Early Christianity* (New York: Columbia University Press, 2005).

of this shift from the Synoptic Gospels to John may, I think, be seen in John's use of the miracle stories of Jesus.

5. The Discursive Embedment of the Miracle Stories in John

The argument that I pursue is that the miracle stories of John may be taken as paradigmatic of the transition from narrative to discursive Christology of which I have spoken, and that on the basis of them we should be able to observe the concomitant aspect that ultimately leads to an undermining of the narrative form of John's predecessors and, thereby, also of his own mold which only superficially comes out as a narrative.[25]

In John's Gospel there are seven miracle stories (2:1–11; 4:46–54; 5:1–47; 6:1–15; 6:16–71[59]; 9:1–10:21; 11:1–44), among which two of them are embedded in each other (chap. 6).[26] The two first miracle stories are singled out by an explicit sequence of signs which, however, is not taken up in the subsequent narrative.[27] The transformation of water into wine is emphatically underscored as: "Jesus did this, the first of his signs [ταύτην ἐποίησεν ἀρχὴν τῶν σημείων ὁ Ἰησοῦς], in Cana of Galilee, and revealed his glory [ἐφανέρωσεν τὴν δόξαν αὐτοῦ]; and his disciples believed in him" (2:11). The use of the verb φανεροῦν is, of course, also spectacular in light of the statement of John the Baptist in 1:31 that "I myself did not

25 For the most current discussion of miracle stories as an independent micro-genre despite Klaus Berger's criticism of the concept as a reflection of modern problems of coming to grips with a conspicuously different ancient understanding of reality, see Michael Labahn, *Jesus als Lebensspender: Untersuchungen zu einer Geschichte der johanneischen Tradition anhand ihrer Wundergeschichten*, BZNW 98 (Berlin; New York: De Gruyter 1998), 78–113. For Berger's understanding, see among Klaus Berger's several works on the topic, *Formgeschichte des Neuen Testaments* (Heidelberg: Quelle & Meyer, 1984), 305–307.

26 I acknowledge that most commentators in their singling out of three of these miracle stories delimit them to a considerably fewer verses than I do (e. g., especially the infirm person at the pool of Bethesda [5:1–9]; the walking over the Sea of Galilee [6:16–21]; the healing of the man born blind [9:1–7]). As I will argue, such a confinement of the miracle stories to fewer verses is due to the influence which the parallel narratives in the Synoptic Gospels have exerted on our understanding of them. In John, however, it is crucial also to include the subsequent speeches and dialogues as part of the miracle stories in order to understand what is at stake for this author in conveying these narratives.

27 There is a close relationship between the use of σημεῖα and miracle stories in John since it appears in the context of six of the seven miracle stories: 2:11; 4:54; 6:2, 14; 7:31; 9:16; 11:47 (with regard to the healing of the lame man in 5, however, only in the wider context of 6:2 and 7:31)—the exception is the epiphany on the sea). But the use of the term "sign" cannot be reduced to miracle stories as is evident from 20:30 in which it is employed as a general description of Jesus' works before his disciples and in a context of signs written down (for other uses of σημεῖον, see also 10:41). For discussion of σημεῖον in the Gospel of John, see Charles K. Barrett, *The Gospel According to St. John: An Introduction with Commentary and Notes on the Greek Text*, 2nd ed. (London: SPCK, 1978), 75–78.

know him; but I came baptising with water for this reason, that he might be revealed (ἵνα φανερωθῇ) to Israel" in addition to the prologue's emphasis on the relationship between the *logos* of God and light. In 1:4–5, the text states that God's *logos* was inhabited by life, and that this particular life was the light of humans, and that it shines in the darkness, and that the darkness did not comprehend it. John the Baptist is emphatically emphasised as not being the light despite the fact that he was sent to bear witness to the light (1:7–8). Further emphasis is attributed to the notion of light in 1:9 in which God's λόγος is depicted as the true light that illuminates every human. This metaphorical cluster is also reverberated in the subsequent description of the λόγος that became flesh and found dwelling with the de-engaged enunciator and his group, so that they were enabled to see "his glory, the glory as of the only begotten of the Father, full of grace and truth" (1:14). In this manner, the enunciator in the first miracle story of the Gospel establishes a close connection between the light and glory motifs of the prologue and the miracle in order to convey to the intended audience that the signs of Christ (σημεῖα Χριστοῦ)—to which by virtue of the occurrence of this term the miracles may be inferred to belong—need to be conceived of as a manifestation of Christ's glory.

The next miracle story is emphatically designated by the use of spatial markers and an explicit recalling of the essence of the first story to be understood along the lines of the previous one: "Then he came again to Cana in Galilee where he had changed the water into wine. Now there was a royal official whose son lay ill in Capernaum" (4:46). The healing is parallel to the first miracle by means of the similarly poignant importance assigned to the miracle as a sign: "Now this was the second sign (δεύτερον σημεῖον) that Jesus did after coming from Judea to Galilee" (4:54). From this point on, however, the numbering of the miracles disappears; but at the same time as this occurs there is an increase in the extent of the individual miracle stories. A number of the subsequent miracle narratives are all succeeded by a long closing speech the precise extent of which may be difficult to ascertain.[28] At this point, one may, of course, contravene against the interpretation I here present that it falters on the ground that even the discursive elements of the miracle stories are not only embedded but also subordinated to the narrative unfolding per se. True as this may be in terms of the formal level of analysis, one needs to consider the possibility that the extensive speeches of Jesus which complete the remaining miracle stories are a reduplication of the ennunciator's voice transposed to the central recounted figure.

28 The story about Lazarus marks an exception in this regard, since the speech here not only predates the resuscitation of Lazarus, but is composed of two distinct speeches. First, Jesus speaks to his disciples (11:9–14), and, secondly, he talks with Martha (11:21–27). For an appraisal of this, see R. Alan Culpepper, "Cognition in John: The Johannine Signs as Recognition Scenes," *PRSt* 35 (2008), 251–260.

If we proceed to the story of the healing of the lame person at the Pool of Bethesda, we see how the miracle story is intertwined with a dialogue of controversy pertaining to the observance of the Sabbath. Even more importantly, however, the conflict between Jesus and the Johannine stereotypically classified group of the *Ioudaioi* about the accurate observance of the Sabbath is succeeded by an extensive discourse on how the Son has been endowed with a commission by the Father (5:19–47).[29] The completion of this discourse is succeeded by two additional miracle stories (the multiplication of the bread and fish and the walking on the Sea of Galilee) that in turn are followed by another extensive speech of Jesus on the bread of life.

The extraordinary healing of the lame person is emphasised by virtue of the fact that he is described as having been ill for 38 years. Being lame, however, he has nobody to assist him in order that he may first reach the ritually efficacious water at the time when it is stirred up and, thereby, become healed. Jesus is portrayed as equipped with a counter-intuitive knowledge that enables him to acknowledge the duration of the man's disease despite the fact that he has not been informed about it. The staging of Jesus as a miracle worker is further highlighted by the depiction of him as an alternative and stronger source of ritual efficacy than the water that occasionally comes into motion. The charade character of the narrative is evident from the question posed by Jesus to the lame man: "Do you want to be made well?" Needless to say, this is a rather odd question given the man's strong wish to obtain healing. The theme of the subsequent discourse is intonated in the man's response to Jesus: "Sir, I have no one to put me into the pool when the water is stirred up; and while I am making my way, someone else steps down ahead of me" (5:7). As the intended audience is soon informed about, Jesus is exactly the prime person in cases of assistance needed.

The subsequent healing scene is brief, since Jesus only needs to utter a word in order to cure the lame person (5:8). Although the story was introduced by the temporal location of the event to a feast of the Jews (μετὰ ταῦτα ἦν ἑορτὴ Ἰουδαίων, 5:1), this theme is not taken up before 5:10, where it is said that, since it was Sabbath on that day, the Jews scolded the healed person by telling him: "It is the Sabbath; it is not lawful for you to carry your mat." The man attempts to escape

29 I shall emphasise that I understand John's Gospel to be just as "Jewish" as any other text belonging to the Christ-movement of the first two centuries. Since John arrogates the key symbol of true Israel for his own group also this text should be conceived of as a *totaliter et aliter* Jewish text which by use of the term "Jews" simply drives in a wedge between true and false Israel. On this whole question, see my essay "At the End of the Road: Reflections on a Popular Scholarly Metaphor," in *The Formation of the Early Church*, ed. Jostein Ådna (Tübingen: Mohr Siebeck, 2005), 45–72, 55–58, and the related essays in Adam H. Becker and Annette Yoshiko Reed eds., *The Ways that Never Parted: Jews and Christians in Late Antiquity and the Early Middle Ages*, TSAJ 95 (Tübingen: Mohr Siebeck, 2003).

responsibility for the action by blaming Jesus, whose identity he has not come to acknowledge, spatially expressed in the fact that Jesus because of the multitude has left the location of the Pool of Bethesda. When Jesus subsequently encounters the man in the temple, another symbol of an alternative source of divine power, Jesus inculcates the man by telling him not to sin again lest a worse thing come upon him (5:14). But this is exactly what the man does by telling to the *Ioudaioi* that Jesus is responsible for his cure. This, of course, is only a superficial identification of Jesus, because as the intended audience comes to learn through Jesus' subsequent discourse his true identity can only be revealed by appreciating and acknowledging his intimate relationship with God as the Father.

It soon becomes evident to the intended audience that the preceding healing story should be symbolically understood. It is a narrative unfolding of the crucial point that the Son can only work in indissoluble cooperation with the Father, and that the current deeds of Jesus are a token of the Father's and his continuous work (5:17–20). In fact, the healing of the lame man should be conceived of as a symbolic staging of the acts of vivification of both the Father and the Son (5:21). Contrary to the healed lame man, who did not acknowledge Jesus' true identity, the intended audience by their recognition of Jesus as the Son of the Father shall make—in the context of their cognitive act—a movement symbolically described as the transition from death to life or, in terms of the previous miracle, a movement from lameness to mobility (5:24–26). As is evident from this unfolding of the preceding miracle story, the whole emphasis of John's narrative is placed on the cognitive movement expected by the enunciator from the intended audience. They are the ones to whom the enunciator—concealing himself in the figure of Jesus—is directing his voice: Recognise and become alive by irreversibly leaving death behind. Needless to say, death in this context first and foremost is transposed to designate a particular state of thinking, i.e., the non-acknowledgement of Jesus as the revealer of the true God.

The particular status of Jesus is further elaborated by linking his identity to the previous identification of him by John the Baptist (1:15, 29–36). Although John the Baptist had the role of a burning and shining lamp the rays of which illuminated Jesus, he was subordinate to Jesus. But yet, the *Ioudaioi* only had evanescent pleasure in him. Similarly, despite the fact that the *Ioudaioi* had been scrutinising the Scriptures on the basis that they constituted a source of eternal life, they had never come to understand how the Scriptures bore witness to Jesus (5:40). And as if this was not enough, they had not understood Moses either, since Moses in fact bore testimony of Jesus as the Son of God (5:45–47). The discourse makes it patently clear that unlike the intended audience of the Gospel who shall acknowledge Jesus' true identity by undergoing a cognitive transition, the "Jews" will never come to do that. In order to formulate or to reveal the true identity of Jesus, we have seen how a miracle narrative is staged in such a manner that it provides the basic symbols which are then subsequently unfolded in a revelatory discourse by Jesus—acting as a reduplication of the voice of the enunciator.

The end of the discourse slides over into the next two miracle stories (the feeding of the five thousand and the walking on the sea) which are not only closely intertwined but are both succeeded by a speech by Jesus similar to what we have observed in the healing of the lame man. Although the healing of the lame person is partly related and may in my view be understood as a rather excessive rewriting of Mark 2:1–12,[30] it is indisputable that the next two miracle stories are representative of John's rewriting of an older Synoptic tradition.

The location is suddenly transposed from Jerusalem to the far shore of the Sea of Galilee. Similarly, the temporal placement of the next scenes is dated to the period immediately preceding Passover.[31] Be that as it may, once again the text focuses on what the true identity of Jesus implies. To formulate this, the text makes use of an intricate double play between discourse and narrative, between intended audience and recounted figures of the story. Together with his disciples, Jesus has withdrawn to a mountain despite the fact that a multitude attracted by his sign performances is following him. Jesus is again emphasised for his counter-intuitive abilities. He knows that he is capable of multiplying five loaves in order to feed the entire mass of people. Yet, Jesus, and thereby the enunciator, tests the level of Philip's and, therefore, also the intended audience's understanding of Jesus' true identity: "Where are we to buy bread for these people to eat?" (6:5). By virtue of their questions, both Philip and Andrew document that they are far from acknowledging the true identity of Jesus. In this manner, not only the *Ioudaioi* are representative of a false understanding of Jesus but also the multitude of appreciating seekers of Jesus as well as his disciples demonstrate a deficient acknowledgement of his true identity. As the genuine shepherd of Israel, Jesus not only feeds the five thousand people of the multitude but also symbolically provides food for all the twelve tribes of Israel (6:13). Despite this powerful sign, Jesus' identity is once again not acknowledged, since the multitude takes him to be the prophet of end time whom they can turn into their messianic king.

The subsequent miracle story with the walking on the Sea accentuates the problems of truly acknowledging Jesus' identity. The multitude realises that something eerie has taken place, since Jesus and his disciples are no longer where

30 Cf. Barrett, *Gospel According to St. John*, 249. For a more thorough discussion of the story's relationship to the Synoptics and to Mark in particular, see Raymond E. Brown, *The Gospel According to John (i–xii): Introduction, Translation, and Notes*, AB 29 (Garden City: Doubleday, 1966), 208 who nevertheless maintains that "the two stories are quite diverse."

31 For the discussion of the problems pertaining to this rather drastic shift in the narrative, see the relevant sections in the standard commentaries. See, for instance, Barrett, *Gospel According to St. John*, 23, 271; Brown, *Gospel According to John*, 206, 232.

they expect to find them but have apparently traversed the Sea. Yet, this makes them only even more eager to ask for new signs from Jesus. He, however, declines their demand by calling their attention to the *signifié* of the sign and not the *signifiant.* They have never understood that the miracles such as the multiplication of the bread were signs that referred to another reality which is the pivotal *raison d'être* of the sign. Jesus scolds them for solely focusing on ephemeral food and not on the food that will lead them to eternal life and which they can only be given by the Son of Man whom God has set his seal on (6:27). Confronted once again with the question what the multitude shall do in order to obtain food for eternal life, Jesus anew emphasises the intrinsic relationship between God and himself: "This is the work of God, that you believe [ἵνα πιστεύετε] in him whom he has sent" (6:29).

The ignorance of the multitude is further elaborated in the discourse which, obviously, serves to inform the intended audience about the true revelatory nature of Jesus and, thereby, also John's Gospel. The mass asks for a sign and refers to the manna their fathers had been given in the desert; but the whole point, of course, is that they have not only received bread and fish under fecundatory circumstances (the plentitude of the food as well as the fact that they were located in a place with much grass, 5:10, 13) but have also been given heavenly bread to which the sign refers, namely Jesus. This is made conspicuously clear in Jesus' self-proclamation that he is the bread of life (6:35) and the concomitant announcement of the correspondence between the will of the Father and that of Jesus (6:38–40). At this point, the *Ioudaioi* are introduced as a new character in the discourse which, thereby, develops into a dialogue of controversy between Jesus and the "Jews" (6:41–59).

The extension of the dialogue to include the "Jews" as well enables the author to emphatically underscore his understanding of Jesus as the true bread of life (ὁ ἄρτος τῆς ζωῆς, 6:48), and that this bread is a prerequisite for obtaining eternal life in the present as well as the life ever-after: "I am the living bread (ὁ ἄρτος ὁ ζῶν) that came down from heaven. Whoever eats of this bread will live forever; and the bread that I will give for the life of the world is my flesh" (6:51). The sacrificial and eucharistic allusions are difficult to ignore.[32] Jesus presents himself in third person as the Son of Man whose flesh one shall eat and whose blood one shall drink that he or she may obtain eternal life. In fact, the eucharistic celebrations of the intended audience have already endowed them with eternal life in their current situation, but, additionally, they shall also be bequeathed with eternal life at the last day (6:54). Cognitively, the intended audience is already efficiently experiencing the life which ultimately belongs to the ever-after. At the

32 Cf. Peder Borgen, *Bread from Heaven. An Exegetical Study of the Concept of Manna in the Gospel of John and the Writings of Philo*, NovTSup 10 (Leiden: Brill, 1965), 91–97, 186–192.

same time, in terms of physical completion, that life still pertains to the future when the intended audience shall undergo a complete physical transformation initiating them into a state of irreversibility and finality which they are excluded from falling out of.

In vein with the previous argument, the author once again has Jesus place emphasis on the innate relationship between Father and Son, since the living Father has sent Jesus and since Jesus lives in him. Therefore, he who eats Jesus as the living bread shall obtain the particular state of life that Jesus is enjoying, i.e., in union with the Father (6:57). Also in the wake of what we have already observed, the enunciator has Jesus accentuate that as the bread that has descended from heaven he is not identical with the previous forms of bread sent by God to the fathers of Israel, since that bread could not prevent them from dying. It is contrary with the bread provided by Jesus, since this bread does not have an ephemeral significance only. In fact, Jesus as the bread of life is endowing those who accept it with eternal life (6:58). Similar to the third miracle story (the healing of the lame person), the fourth and fifth miracle narratives find their meaning in a subsequent extensive monologue in which Jesus on behalf of the enunciator is unfolding his true identity: an identity he has had from eternity and which has not undergone any developments through the narrative. The Jesus of the Cana episode is the same as the Jesus multiplying bread and fish and crossing the Sea of Galilee.

The sixth and second-last miracle story concerns the healing of a man born blind. By now it should come as no surprise that the enunciator once again exploits the micro-genre of the miracle narrative to intonate his message of the true identity of Jesus, and that this takes place by means of a metaphor symbolising a cognitive dimension. The scene is now located in Jerusalem. Jesus coincidentally meets a person blind from birth on his way from the temple to escape the furious *Ioudaioi*, who have become outraged by his usurpation of the Abraham tradition (8:31–58) and, therefore, want to stone him. Confronted with the question from his disciples whether the man or his parents have sinned, since he is blind, Jesus underlines that his blindness should be conceived of as a sign indicative of the fact that God is working through Jesus (9:3). At the same time, the subsequent healing scene is interpreted as an anticipation of Jesus' future death. The actions of Jesus can only be done during daytime, that is, during his ministry which subsequent to his death cannot be continued (9:4–5). The day and night metaphor supplemented by the life and death of Jesus is further transposed to the state of the person born blind and through the story transferred to the level of realisation vs. non-realisation of Jesus' true identity.

As a powerful narrative elaboration of Jesus' self-proclamation to be the light of the world (9:5), Jesus cures the person by an act of contagious ritualised behaviour. He spits on the ground and makes out of the saliva mixed with soil a lump of clay which he conveys on the eyes of the blind. Subsequently, the man is told to go to the Pool of Siloam, the Hebrew meaning of which the enunciator informs his intended audience is "sent." In this manner, the enunciator establishes a close relationship between the mission of Jesus, that is, that he has been sent by God, and the act of healing. This leads to yet another discussion about the true identity of Jesus.

Similar to the lame person who handed Jesus over to his antagonists, the cured blind person gives Jesus away to his opponents. Neither the neighbours, nor the Pharisees or the *Ioudaioi*, which once again appears as a standard phrase for designating the group of people of Israel adversary to Jesus and reflecting an erroneous understanding of his identity, have acknowledged the true meaning of the sign. Some Pharisees claim that Jesus is not from God, since he does not observe the Sabbath, while others—pointing to the effect of the healing—argue that Jesus by virtue of the occurred signs (σημεῖα) cannot be a sinner (9:16). The result is that the "Jews" are depicted as entering into internal strife about the identity of Jesus. Next and once again the cured person is called upon. This time it is not the neighbours but the Pharisees who ask him for his understanding of Jesus. He responds by asserting that Jesus is a prophet (προφήτης, 9:17).

Far from being satisfied with this answer the *Ioudaioi* proceed to his parents to ask them about his identity. Out of fear for the *Ioudaioi*, the parents refrain from taking responsibility by recounting how their son is old enough to speak for himself. The healed person similarly desists from entering into discussion with the *Ioudaioi* but restricts himself to pointing out the actual effects of the healing. Again the enunciator has them challenge him by slightly rephrasing their question (9:26). Despairingly, the man underscores that he has already responded to the question and retorts their sham by asking them if they want to become disciples of Jesus. In a dialogue of controversy, they reproach him by emphasising their allegiance to Moses and their ignorance of Jesus' place of origin (τοῦτον δὲ οὐκ οἴδαμεν πόθεν ἐστίν, 9:29b). Contrary to their blindness, the blind man has come to see and, thereby, to understand. He retorts them that since Jesus has opened his eyes, the eyes of a sinner, he must come from God (9:30–33). Defeated by the logic of the argument, the reaction of the *Ioudaioi* consists in expelling the man for his audacity to teach them.

At this point, the enunciator has Jesus reenter the scene and confront the man subsequent to having learned about his expulsion. Jesus asks him if he believes in the Son of Man, and contrary to the *Ioudaioi* who are unwilling to learn the healed person pleads Jesus to reveal the Son of Man that he may believe in him (9:35–36). Jesus reveals himself and the man acknowledges him by testifying that he believes. As a consequence he is shown to worship him (προσεκύνησεν, 9:38). To sum up the morale of the healing miracle per se, the enunciator has Jesus proclaim that he has come for judgement into the world "so that those who do not see may see, and those who do see may become blind" (9:39). Finally, the Pharisees are shown to exhibit their own ignorance by asking Jesus about his view on their potential blindness. He mercilessly uncovers them as self-seekers of blindness: "If you were blind, you would not have sin. But now that you say, 'We see,' your sin remains" (9:41).

Similar to the three previous miracle stories, the present one is succeeded by an extensive discourse in which Jesus unfolds the meaning of the miracle by speaking of himself as the good shepherd (10:1–18, followed by a brief dialogue of controversy 10:19–21). The main point of the shepherd discourse is to stage Jesus as the true shepherd of Israel who, contrary to the Pharisees and the *Ioudaioi*, is concerned about his sheep, while they illegitimately have arrogated to themselves access to the fold of Israel. Parallel to the previous discourses that also highlighted the close relationship between the Father and the Son (cf. 5:19–30, 36–40; 6:36–40, 44, 46), the present one places emphasis on the innate bond between the Father and the Son (10:14–18). In the discourse, the enunciator also has Jesus anticipate his pending death: "And I lay down my life (καὶ τὴν ψυχήν μου τίθημι) for the sheep" (10:15, cf. 10:17). Additionally, Jesus predicts the future mission of the Christ-group to people outside a Jewish context (10:16).

Once again, we see how Jesus in the essential role of the revealer by means of a reduplicated discourse of the enunciator uncovers the true meaning of the sign performed and, thereby, of his own true identity.[33] This revelation can in principle only take place in the context of the speeches in which the enunciator is having Jesus reveal an identity that can only be disclosed by a heavenly agent who has been bequeathed with his particular status by the Father. Since the Father by virtue of his distance and principal inaccessibility cannot reveal the wisdom of heaven,[34] the enunciator has a recounted heavenly figure sent by the Father unveil this particular knowledge in the world of humans. This is the particular role of the speeches encircling the narratives of the miracles.

The last and climatic seventh miracle story concerns the resurrection of Lazarus. Similar to the majority of miracle narratives in John, this is a unique

33 Kasper Bro Larsen has rightly pointed out to me that this argument may be further supported by the inclusion of passages in John 1 and 3 in which Jesus by his talk appears to direct himself straightforwardly to the intended audience of John, which means it really becomes difficult to decide whether it is Jesus or the enunciator who is talking (see, for instance, 1:51; 3:11–21 (which slides into general formulations of the enunciator); 3:34–36. There is a similar ambiguity in the farewell discourses where Jesus in terms of temporality is sometimes located in what appears to be the temporal horizon of the enunciator, see, for instance, 13:15–17, 20, 34–35; 14:19–21; 15:18–19; 16:1–4, 33b.

34 See my essay "Wisdom as Cognition: Creating the Others in the Book of Mysteries and in 1 Cor 1 and 2," in *The Wisdom Texts from Qumran and the Development of Sapiential Thought*, ed. Charlotte Hempel, Armin Lange, and Hermann Lichtenberger, BETL 159 (Leuven: Leuven University Press; Peeters, 2002), 405–432, 407–409.

Johannine tradition (the only exception being the multiplication of bread and fish and the walking on the Sea of Galilee which we also find in the Synoptic Gospels). In the Johannine context, there is a close parallel between Jesus' resurrection of Lazarus and the subsequent passion story of Jesus that has its beginning in chapter 12. In this manner, the death and subsequent resurrection of Lazarus functions as a prefiguration of the death and resurrection of Jesus. In addition, the miracle story is a narrative unfolding and manifestation of what was said by Jesus in his speech on how he can only work in indissoluble cooperation with the Father (5:19–30). In 5:21, Jesus emphasised how the Father raises the dead and gives life to them just as the Son gives life to whom he will (cf. 5:24, 28–29).

The story opens by informing the audience about how Lazarus (a Greek transcription of Hebrew אלעזר meaning "God helps") was sick. In addition, the story is located in Bethany which is further specified as the village of Mary and Martha. The close relationship between the passion story of Jesus and the sickness of Lazarus is emphasised by a comment of the enunciator in which the audience—in anticipation of 12:3—is told that it was that Mary who anointed the Lord with fragrant oil and wiped his feet with her hair (11:2). The sisters send for help to Jesus saying to him that the one whom he loves is sick. The enunciator once again has Jesus speak in an ambiguous manner. Rather than being concerned about his friend, Jesus retorts by telling that the disease of Lazarus is not unto death but to the glory of God (ἀλλ' ὑπὲρ τῆς δόξης), so that the Son of God may be glorified through it (ἵνα δοξασθῇ … δι' αὐτῆς, 11:4). However, this response is subsequently negated by Jesus' action, since rather than leaving for Bethany he remains two additional days at his present and unspecified position (11:6). After a brief discussion with his disciples about the reasonableness of returning to Judea, where Jesus according to his disciples knows that he is likely to be stoned by the *Ioudaioi*, Jesus rebukes them by stating ambiguously and figuratively that he who walks in the day does not stumble, since he sees the light of the day (11:9).

Once again, the lack of understanding of Jesus' true identity among the disciples is pointed out. Jesus' desire to go to Lazarus in order to wake him up is once more emphatically highlighted by the enunciator as being misunderstood by the disciples. Rather than acknowledging that Jesus is talking about his proximate resurrection of Lazarus, the disciples take him to be speaking about Lazarus sleeping (11:13). However, the disciples' lack of understanding is partly and superficially understandable, since they are not partaking in the hidden knowledge that Jesus, by virtue of his origin in the divine world, is sharing. Given their close relationship to Jesus, they should, of course, have acknowledged that he was speaking about the death of Lazarus. At the time when Jesus arrives, Lazarus has already been in the tomb for four days—this information serves to make the subsequent miracle of Jesus appear even more spectacular (cf. 11:39).

Jesus is met by Martha, who in recognition of his special status acknowledges that had Jesus been there, Lazarus would not have died (this information contributes to re-focus the attention of the audience on the fact that Jesus deliberately remained at the distant place for another two days rather than hurrying to Bethany). At first, Martha acknowledges Jesus by confessing that despite this ("even now [καὶ νῦν]") she knows that "whatever you ask of God, God will grant you" (11:22). Again, the audience is confronted with a deliberately ambiguous response placed in the mouth of Jesus by the enunciator, since Jesus grants Martha that Lazarus will rise again (ἀναστήσεται, 11:23). Martha, however, misunderstands him by acknowledging that her brother will rise again in the resurrection on the last day, but that, of course, does not console her immediate grief over the loss of her brother. So, like all other persons in the recounted story of John's Gospel with the exception of Jesus, Martha does not exhibit a genuine true understanding of Jesus' identity. This, of course, is not particularly enigmatic, since by now we have come to see that the true understanding of Jesus can only be revealed by Jesus himself by virtue of his status as divine revealer acting on behalf of not only himself but also in direct congruence with God.

Similar to the previous speeches that complete several of the preceding miracle stories, but which here is reduced to a single verse, Jesus tells Martha that he is the resurrection and the life, and that he who believes in him, though he may die, shall live (11:25). This is exactly what will take place in the subsequent resurrection of Lazarus which thus functions as a narrative manifestation of Jesus' self-proclamation. In addition, Jesus asks Martha whether she believes in this, and she consents by confessing unequivocally that "Yes, Lord, I believe that you are the Christ, the Son of God, who is to come into this world" (11:27). Then follows a scene in which Jesus is approached by Mary, who has remained in the house of the three siblings, but who now—confronted by Martha—rises to meet him (11:28–37).

Parallel to the meeting with Martha, also Mary contends that if Jesus had been there, her brother would not have died. She weeps and so do the other *Ioudaioi*, which leads Jesus to take action and also to become emotionally affected himself: by groaning in the spirit (ἐνεβριμήσατο τῷ πνεύματι), becoming troubled (ἐτάραξεν ἑαυτὸν), and, subsequently, falling into tears (ἐδάκρυσεν, 11:33–35). Some of the *Ioudaioi*, however, react by questioning and challenging Jesus' identity once again: "Could not he who opened the eyes of the blind man have kept this man from dying?" (11:37). This reaction on the part of some of the *Ioudaioi* causes Jesus once again to become agitated (ἐμβριμώμενος, 11:38a) and go to the tomb. Martha reproaches Jesus when he commands them to take away the stone from the cave by pointing to the fact that Lazarus has already been placed there four days before and that the decomposition of his body has begun (11:39). Jesus reproves her by pointing to his previous statement that to the extent she believes, she shall also see the glory of God (ἡ δόξα τοῦ θεοῦ, 11:40; cf. 2:11; 11:4).

At this point, Jesus resurrects Lazarus by praying to God in a manner that confirms the innate relationship between the Father and him: "Father, I thank you for having heard me. I knew that you always hear me, but I have said this for the sake of the crowd standing here, so that they may believe that you sent me" (11:41c–42). Thereafter, he calls upon Lazarus, who comes out of the cave in his grave clothes (11:44). The miracle induces many of the *Ioudaioi* who had been with Mary to come to believe in him (ἐπίστευσαν εἰς αὐτον, 11:45). Others, however, secretly tell on him and report the event to the high priests and the Pharisees. Hereby, the transition to the subsequent story of the passion of Jesus is initiated. Caiaphas involuntarily, and as an example of the rhetorical and narrative device of tragic irony, comes to pronounce the truth that will determine the entire subsequent passion story. Confronted by a question of the chief priests and the Pharisees about what they shall do with Jesus, since this man performs many signs (πολλὰ ποιεῖ σημεῖα, 11:47), Caiaphas as chief priest of that year proclaims to the respondents: "You do not understand that it is better for you (συμφέρει ὑμῖν) to have one man die for the people (ὑπὲρ τοῦ λαοῦ) than to have the whole nation destroyed" (11:50). The enunciator is keen to point out the irony of the statement: "He did not say this on his own, but being high priest that year he prophesied that Jesus was about to die for the nation, and not for the nation only, but to gather into one the dispersed children of God" (11:51–52).

We shall leave Jesus and Lazarus at this point and turn towards the conclusion of this essay. What we have seen in this seventh miracle story confirms the impression we have formed on the basis of the previous miracle narratives. In the context of the Gospel of John, the whole emphasis in the miracle stories is placed on the relationship between a particular aspect pertaining to the true identity of Jesus which the miracle *per se* makes it possible to accentuate and the over-all revelation of John concerning Jesus' true identity.[35] By virtue of John's christological emphasis on Jesus as the exclusive revealer, this identity can only be revealed by Jesus himself. The miracle stories, therefore, find their fulfilment in self-speeches of Jesus in which he points out or reveals the precise relationship between the sign (the miracle) as the signifier and the signified, i.e., a dimension of Jesus' identity that induces the intended audience to acknowledge who Jesus

35 I realise that there are other ways of looking at the miracles in John, and that I place decisive emphasis on the miracles as signs that primarily serve to underline the almost tautological message of Jesus as the Son of God. For a different perspective that accentuates the miracle stories as conveyors of diverse symbolic meaning, see Craig Koester, *Symbolism in the Fourth Gospel: Meaning, Mystery, Community*, 2nd ed. (Minneapolis: Augsburg Fortress 2003).

really is. Although the resurrection of Lazarus does not conclude with an extensive speech subsequent to the miracle, we have noticed something similar at stake in the brief dialogue between Jesus and Martha, in which Jesus reveals his true identity as the resurrection and the life. Somehow, this is a very concise epitome of what we have observed in the other miracle narratives as well.

6. Conclusion

At the end of this essay, let me return to my introductory remarks. Although I have not yet come to the point of expressing in a satisfactorily nuanced manner the way I understand the relationship between narrative and discourse in John's Gospel, I think there is enough substantiation to invite others to share in these considerations. The core of the argument is that John by virtue of the logic of his Christology is really precluded from composing a narrative about Jesus. Yet, the narrative tradition of his predecessors was plausibly so strong that in terms of genre he had to follow in the wake of what they had initiated by creating some sort of Jesus biography as the one we well know from the Synoptic Gospels. At the same time as he created his gospel biography of Jesus, he, I argue, came to undermine its narrative nature by means of a Christology that does not leave room for narrative development.

Due to the constraints of this article and congruent with the framework of the over-all intention behind this volume, I have limited myself to examining a particular micro-genre of John's Gospel, i.e., the miracle stories. Yet, I also surmise that John's version of the miracle stories is a particularly suitable case for making the argument that I am pursuing: John's Gospel as a testimony of what I for want of a better term call generic docetism. I argue that John by virtue of tradition is dependent upon the narrative cloak of his predecessors, but the real core of his message cannot be of a narrative nature. The focus of the Fourth Gospel is placed on the relationship between enunciator and enunciatee, between gospel writer and audience. It is not a story about the narrative development of Jesus, how Jesus became Christ, since he already from the beginning of the Gospel has the status of a heavenly revealer fully in compliance with God, the Father. In fact, it would be detrimental to the christological logic of John's Gospel were Jesus capable of undergoing narrative development.

Jesus is a "rare bird" in this world. He is the heavenly revealer who has come to earth in order to reveal the truth of God, i.e., that Jesus is the Christ, the Son of God, and that they who believe in him shall have life by his name. The miracle stories of John's Gospel are meant to inculcate this message again and again on the intended audience of the Gospel by highlighting various aspects of the meaning and significance of being Jesus the Christ, the Son of God. In order to do that, John's miracle stories—in contrast to those of the Synoptic Gospels—do not so much focus on the miracle *per se*. The miracle story is reduced to a sign, figuratively speaking a *signifiant*, the *signifié* or reference of which is discursively spelled out in subsequent self-revelations of Jesus the revealer.[36] Initially I pointed to the difference between the classic mosaic and modern forms of mosaics, where differences between the individual parts are not only expressed in terms of contrasts on the mosaic surface but also by divergences in height. John's Gospel is odd in this regard. In my view it conveys an almost monotonous, self-affirmative, tautological message that Jesus Christ is the Son of God who is Jesus Christ the Son of God who comes from the Father and shall return to the Father who is the Father of the Son of God. It is a discursive riverrun "from swerve of shore … ." Yet, it is far from simple and harmonious when one juxtaposes it with the precedent gospel tradition. It sticks out in terms of both mosaic height and shrill colours by rewriting the previous tradition in such a manner that it comes close to abolishing the narrative development orchestrated by the previous tradition. John's Gospel preserves the narrative mode of the scriptural predecessors and it retains the genre of the antecedents' gospel format. In practice, however, John has splintered the flat mosaic by endowing it with height—a height dictated by a discursive vertical scale that nullifies narrative development at the horizontal scale.

I have throughout the essay been arguing that the micro-genre of the miracle stories is particularly apt for substantiating this line of argument. I have emphasised one reason, namely the point at which the Johannine miracle narratives depart from their synoptic predecessors; but there is another and very important reason for this emphasis assigned to the miracle stories. In the Synoptic Gospels it is very conspicuous that the conflict between Jesus and his "Jewish" opponents, especially the "Jewish" establishment, hinges on his confrontation with the Jerusalem temple (this being particularly prominent in Mark and Matthew). That is entirely different in the Gospel of John, in which the controversies are accentuated in the context of Jesus' miracles and not least the subsequent discursive unfolding of them in the self-speeches of Jesus.[37] Therefore, it makes perfect sense to place emphasis on an examination of the particular Johannine Christology in the context of the miracle stories.

Ultimately, what I have argued is that the continuous shiftings between enunciation and enunciate in John's Gospel transforms it from a narrative strictly speaking to something that comes close to a revelatory discourse in which the

36 The figurative aspect of this way of phrasing the problem stems from the fact that a sign cannot be identified with the *signifiant* as such. Any sign consists of both a *signifiant* and a *signifié*; but for the sake of perspicuity I drive in a wedge between the two by more or less conflating them with resp. sign and reference.

37 Cf. Geert Hallbäck, *Det Nye Testamente: En lærebog* (Copenhagen: Anis, 2010), 151.

narrative, due to the heavy load of the preceding tradition, is only superficially adhered to. In the context of both literary development and intellectual history, I think there is a direct line that proceeds from the Gospel of John to such later texts as, for instance, the *Evangelium Veritatis* of the later second-century Christ religion. But to appreciate this, it is pivotal to understand how the author of John reduplicates the role of the enunciator in the self-speeches put in the mouth of Jesus.

Ole Davidsen

The Lord, the Lamb, and the Lover: The Gospel of John as a Mixture of Spiritualized Narrative Genres

1. Introduction

In the *Poetics*, Aristotle succeeded in describing essential features of narrative literature with a general or even universal status, and his work continues to inspire storytelling as well as narrative theory.[1] As the Gospel of John is narrative literature, a story told in writing, we should therefore not be surprised if the *Poetics* shows itself to be relevant for the study of this gospel story too. On the contrary, it would be quite strange and irrational if John's Gospel had nothing to do with the fundamentals of narrative as described by Aristotle. I shall therefore use some of the relevant theory in the Poetics to analyze the Gospel of John concerning the question of narrative genre. I shall proceed in two steps.

First, I shall extract and operationalize some observations from the work itself. Then I shall introduce some elements of Patrick Colm Hogan's modern narrative theory, which to some extent is an elaboration of Aristotelian concepts. I use this approach although I do not think the author of John ever read the *Poetics.* He might have, of course, but it is of no relevance for this study if he did so or not. What Aristotle presents as a *normative* definition of the tragedy of his days, we can read as a *descriptive* disclosure of *prototypical* plot structures revealing some general features of the human mind's narrative competence. The narrative syntax and semantics of story are in some respects comparable to the grammar of language. We can use the language with or without conscious knowledge of its grammar. Likewise, we can tell stories with or without consciousness of narrative semiotics. As storyteller, the author of the Gospel certainly demonstrates a practical narrative competence, but he need not have had any theoretical consciousness of the narrative semiotics involved. Our theoretical knowledge of narrative semiotics, on the other hand, is very useful for practical exegesis. In fact,

1 Michael Tierno, *Aristotle's Poetics for Screenwriters: Storytelling Secrets from the Greatest Mind in Western Civilization* (New York: Hyperion, 2002), illustrates how the ancient Greek philosopher pointed out the fundamentals of storytelling, still valid for modern drama and film.

if certain basic narrative elements form the base of storytelling, the *exegetes* need to have conscious knowledge of them in order to understand the type of texts they are dealing with.The Gospel of John may fit into multiple genres, depending on our genre theory and focus. In this article, I shall use narrative theory in discussing the genre of the Fourth Gospel. Therefore, my focus will not be on the rhetorical function of the gospel discourse, but on how a mixture of types and elements of plot is forming the Gospel as a religious narrative.

2. Aristotle: An Early Narratologist

Aristotle's *Poetics* is about Greek tragedy, we would say, because contemporary tragedy was the main subject matter of his work. However, when Aristotle says, "Epic and tragedy have some components in common, while others are peculiar to tragedy" (1449b16–20 [Kenny]), we understand that the *Poetics* is dealing with basic elements of narrative literature that transcend the classification of genres like "tragedy" and "epic."[2] Though dealing with tragedy, much of what Aristotle says in the *Poetics* is relevant to the study of narrative literature in general, and I shall thus quote and comment on some of the most relevant passages.

Of relevance for our study is the fact that "tragedy" and "epic" have the primacy of plot in common, and the *Poetics* appears in this perspective as a general theory of story. When Aristotle says that "story is the foundation and as it were the soul of tragedy, while moral character is secondary" (1450a38–39 [Kenny]), he is simply recognizing that plot is the first principle in story, even when story is staged as drama. It is because of its narrative plot that "[t]ragedy is a representation not of persons but of action and life, and happiness and unhappiness consists in action. The point is action, not character: it is their moral status that gives people the character they have, but it is their actions that make them happy or unhappy" (1450a16–19 [Kenny]). Gen 2:4b–3:24, for convenience called the Adam story, demonstrates this point in an exemplary way. It is the actions of Adam, Eve, and the Serpent that establish their final unhappy life-conditions (compared to their previous happiness in Eden). Actions have consequences and establish the character's objective reality in the story-world.[3]

A representation that takes the form of narrative, says Aristotle, should, as in tragedy, "be constructed dramatically, that is, based on a single action that is

2 I have consulted the Greek text in Aristotle, *Poetics*, ed. and trans. Stephen Halliwell, LCL 199 (Cambridge: Harvard University Press, 1999), but quote from the new English translation in Aristotle, *Poetics*, trans. Anthony Kenny (Oxford: Oxford University Press, 2013).

3 It is important to notice that the characters' subjective perception of their state of being is often secondary also. The common narrative objectively defines the characters' state of being as good or bad fortune.

whole and entire and that has a beginning, a middle, and an end" (1459a16–19 [Kenny]). Stories with a complex action, those whose "change [*metabasis*] of fortune involves a reversal [*peripeteia*] or a discovery [*anagnōrisis*, recognition] or both" (1452a15–16 [Kenny]), are of particular interest. Reversal and discovery "should grow naturally out of the plot of the story, so that they come about, with necessity or probability, from the preceding events. There is a great difference between something happening *after* certain events and happening *because of* those events" (1452a11–22 [Kenny]). In the Adam story, we have reversal as well as discovery, and the expulsion from Eden is because of the transgression of the divine prohibition. What I call *narrative causality* (in opposition to natural laws as well as to social rules) is a decisive feature in storytelling. In the gospels, the resurrection of Jesus happens after his death on the cross, but it is only meaningful if it happens because of that event.

The poet, Aristotle further says, should be a maker of stories

> … in so far as it is representation [*mimēsis*] that makes him a poet, and representation is of actions. Even if it turns out that he is writing about historical events he is no less a poet for that, since nothing prevents such events being the kind of thing that would happen. It is in that respect that he deals with them as a poet. (1451b27–33 [Kenny])

This observation is perhaps the most important for our discussion of the genre of John's Gospel. The poet's job, Aristotle emphasizes,

> … is not relating what actually happened, but rather the kind of thing that *would* happen—that is to say, what is possible in terms of probability and necessity. The difference between a historian and a poet … is that the one relates what actually happened, and the other the kinds of events that would happen. For this reason poetry is more philosophical and more serious than history; poetry utters universal truths, history particular statements. The universal truths concern what befits a person of a certain kind to say or do in accordance with probability and necessity—and that is the aim of poetry, even if it makes use of proper names. (1451a36–1451b10)

More subject matters may be hiding behind these dense formulations, but the difference between relating fact (what actually happened in the history-world) and relating fiction (what might happen in the story-world) naturally comes to mind. However, that cannot be the point, since the poet writing about historical events is no less a poet for that. The real difference between history and poetry is that poetry utters universal truths, history particular statements.

Aristotle is trying to identify "the soul of narrative poetry," as it were, but what he has in mind is not quite clear. He senses, however, that poetry (narrative literature as creative and imaginative writing) differs from history even when it makes use of proper names (for example Jesus and Pilate). To proper names, we may add place names (for example Nazareth and Jerusalem) and time-markers (for example under Pilate and Tiberius, in principle identifiable according to some chronometrical calendrical system). Such *individual* markers for Person, Space, and Time (the PST coordinates) tend to give the representation a historical anchorage, though we may still be dealing with poetry (understood as man-made literature or literary art, since verse form is irrelevant for our study). If we wish to understand what kind of text we are dealing with, the first thing to recognize is that the author of the Gospel of John is a poet rather than a historian. Even if he to some extent is writing about historical events, he is no less a poet for that, since he deals with these events as a poet in order to utter universal truths, not historically particular statements. Explicitly religious literature, however, merges poetry and history, so below I shall take a closer look at the intricate relationship between poetry and history in John's Gospel.

In complex stories, the change of fortune involves reversal (*peripeteia*) and recognition/discovery (*anagnōrisis*). We have reversal from adversity (*dystychia*, misfortune) to prosperity (*eutychia*, fortune) or prosperity to adversity (1451a11–15). Reversal, I would add, is caused by a *pragmic* action (or process), while discovery is caused by a *cognitive* action (or process). Discovery is a cognitive change from ignorance to knowledge about the reality of the characters destined for good or bad fortune in consequence of some pragmic action (cf. 1452a30–32).

Now, disregarding any other use of "tragedy" and "comedy," "tragic" and "comic," I define a plot reversal from adversity to prosperity as comedy/comic, and a plot reversal from prosperity to adversity as tragedy/tragic. The Adam story is a tragedy (*dysangelion*) in this sense. A pragmic action, the transgression, implies a reversal from fortune to misfortune, which is discovered by the characters when their eyes are opened and they recognize the nature of their existential reality. The story about the tragic destiny of the first human beings is of interest to others because it does not tell a particular history, but presents a universal truth, since Adam and Eve perform as socially representative characters. The gospels, on the other hand, are comedies in the sense defined above. They are "good news" (*euangelion*) informing the audience about a change in their existential conditions: that a process of reversal from misfortune to fortune is taking place. In order to discover this change, a messenger (Jesus or his instructed co-workers, including the authors of the gospels) must inform people of it. The gospels, however, are complex stories, because Jesus is more than a cognitive messenger in words and deeds. He is also the socially representative person who, by giving his life, performs the principal pragmic action that causes the reversal.[4]

4 The sacrificial interpretation of Jesus' death has been a scandal to people since antiquity, but nowadays it is painful even to Christian believers. Exegetes and other interpreters are therefore looking for alternative readings, and find the Gospel of John convenient for such an endeavor,

3. Patrick Colm Hogan: A Contemporary Narratologist

Aristotle continues to inspire literary studies, and we can detect his influence in most narrative theory, or at least recognize a set of recurring narratological concerns. The works of A. J. Greimas and Claude Bremond form the basis of my own general understanding of narrativity, but works by Patrick Colm Hogan have inspired this particular study of genre, especially his book *The Mind and Its Stories: Narrative Universals and Human Emotion.*[5] As the title implies, the approach is a general cognitive anthropological perspective on narratology, with a special interest in emotion. The idea of literary universals brings many theoretical and philosophical questions into discussion, and Hogan deals with them in detail. Here I can only briefly present the principal aspects of his conclusive suggestions: that three narrative genres—the romantic, the heroic, and the sacrificial tragicomedy—dominate not all, but the most common stories across cultures.

Hogan's work is part of a general interest in *narrativity.* Early narratology saw narrativity as formal features of the figurative discourses that we call stories. Narrative semiotics (and other literary theories), however, have revealed the abstract forms of organization, i.e., the narrative structures governing production and reception of stories, which point beyond mere textual features. Thus, narrativity refers to a fundamental language and thought form. Tradition sometimes identifies narrativity with *mythos* in opposition to *logos,* but even non-figurative or rational discourses seem organized by narrative syntax and semantics. Stories give us privileged access to understanding narrative thinking

since the *cognitive* function dominates the account; cf. for example Jesper Tang Nielsen, *Die kognitive Dimension des Kreuzes: Zur Deutung des Todes Jesu im Johannesevangelium,* WUNT 2/263 (Tübingen: Mohr Siebeck, 2009). Maybe the author of John's Gospel was trying to deconstruct and reinterpret a common sacrificial understanding in early Christianity. The difficulty is, however, that the story of John's Gospel tends to lose intelligibility if there is no *pragmic* action causing the reversal from the world's misfortune to fortune. We have the same problem with the presupposed pre-story about the events or actions that caused the world's deficiency, the reversal from fortune to misfortune, and that explicate its need for salvation. The Gospel of Mark contains some manifest clues to its presupposed pre-story, cf. Ole Davidsen, "Adam–Christ Typology in Paul and Mark: Reflections on a *Tertium Comparationis,*" in *Mark and Paul. Comparative Essays Part II: For and Against Pauline Influence on Mark,* ed. Eve-Marie Becker, Troels Engberg-Pedersen, and Mogens Müller, BZNW 199 (Berlin: de Gruyter, 2014), 243–72. The Gospel of John, however, never reveals how this deficiency was established. The world is under Satan's rule, but the author never tells his audience why. The most obvious explanation would be that the pre-story is the Adam story, as presupposed knowledge in a double sense. The author and the implied audience not only know the Adam story, they are also familiar with the community's assenting reception and use of it.

5 (Cambridge: Cambridge University Press, 2003). Cf. also his books *Affective Narratology: The Emotional Structure of Stories* (Lincoln: University of Nebraska Press, 2011) and *Philosophical Approaches to the Study of Literature* (Gainesville: University of Florida Press, 2000).

as a basic function of the human mind. Hogan shares the idea that a limited number of standard narrative structures guide and organize our ideas about, evaluations of, and emotive responses to different phenomena.[6] Human thought, value, and feeling imply emplotment, i.e., narrativization.

"The prototypical narratives," in Hogan's terms, "have a telic structure including an agent, a goal, and a causal sequence connecting the agent's various actions with achievement or nonachievement of the goal" (*The Mind,* 205).[7] If for example we identify Jesus' goal as establishing God's kingdom under messianic leadership, then a gospel story should tell how and in what sense he achieved or did not achieve this goal. Whatever the hero Jesus says and does, we understand according to such a general telic sequence. It directs our search for meaning, even if we disagree with what his ultimate goal could be. We expect an initial situation (where the hero lacks a goal), a liminal or transitional phase (where he pursues his goal), and a final situation (where he has or has not achieved his goal). We can easily recognize the presence of Aristotle here, since the telic structure explains why the plot structure should have a beginning, a middle, and an end.

When the narrator shares the hero's values, the story leads the reader to share the hero's happiness when he succeeds and his sorrow when he fails. In the first case, I identify the plot structure as *comic,* in the second as *tragic* (as defined above). Comedy and tragedy, however, are not simply balanced but contrary formal terms. These narrative basic genres do not appear in simple form. Tragedy implies moments of happiness to be lost, just as comedy implies moments of sorrow to be overcome. Furthermore, a value perspective defines tragedy as the deficient mode of comedy. Tragedy moves us because it shatters our default hope for happiness, which is why I, following Hogan, use the overall complex term *tragicomedy* (or *tragicomic*) for the prototypical story (or plot structure). I identify the Gospel of John as a (quite complex) tragicomedy in this sense. Like the Synoptic Gospels, it is a narrative construal showing that an apparently *tragic* succession of events (culminating in the crucifixion of Jesus as failure) was actually a *tragicomic* succession of events (culminating in the resurrection of Jesus as success).[8] The Gospel of John, however, is not least a challenge because of its tendency to de-articulate the narrative plot structure. The post-resurrection perspective has infused the presentation intensively, and tends to blur any dis-

6 Hogan, *The Mind,* 5.

7 Hogan, *The Mind,* 205. A similar understanding is found in the French semiotic tradition; cf. for example Claude Bremond, *Logique du récit* (Paris: Éditions du Seuil, 1973).

8 For an early discussion of "tragedy," "comedy," and "tragicomedy" as relevant concepts for the study of the New Testament (with focus on Paul and Mark), see Dan O. Via, *Kerygma and Comedy in the New Testament: A Structuralist Approach to Hermeneutic* (Philadelphia: Fortress Press, 1975), especially 97–103.

tinction between existence and coming-into-existence, and between manifest tragic degradation and latent comic elevation (cf. 3:14).

The hero (as an individual and/or a representative character) is an agent striving to achieve enduring happiness, often idealized and spiritualized as everlasting. He or she imagines the goal to be the eliciting conditions for such happiness, or the means to the eliciting conditions for such happiness.[9] According to Hogan, the goal of the romantic tragicomedy is the union of lovers; in heroic tragicomedy, the goal is recognition and social dominance (often as restoration of kingship); and in sacrificial tragicomedy, it is reconciliation with the gods and the return of plenty. As regards the contents, one of these thematic narrative genres may dominate a given empirical text, but often elements from the other genres play into the main genre. The Gospel of John, I suggest, combines elements from all three of the prototypical narrative genres in a single story, and does it so pervasively that we may in fact talk of a mixture or blend of genres. The thematic roles "Lord," "Lamb," and "Lover" refer to the heroic, the sacrificial, and the romantic tragicomedy, respectively, although as modified forms of ordinary bravery, scapegoating, and affiliation.

4. The Question of Goal

According to John 20:31, the goal of the Gospel as proclaiming discourse is to have the addressees come to believe (or remain to believe) that Jesus is the Messiah, the Son of God, and that through this belief they may have life in his name. Belief in Jesus would qualify people's life already in this present world, but the ultimate goal is eternal life in another future world. This message is not different from the message given by Jesus in the story-world. It is evident that Jesus as an "influencer" is trying to call people into discipleship, to make them believe that he is the Messiah, the Son of God. Whether we focus on Jesus as teacher or prophet, he is evidently performing in a *cognitive* role as the enlightening Light.

The cognitive dimension of the discourse deals with the interpretation of its pragmic dimension (concerning actions and events). The pragmic dimension is the object of the cognitive dimension (concerning knowledge, belief, and truth). The pragmic dimension does not imply the cognitive dimension, but the cognitive dimension presupposes the pragmic dimension, even if only as a pretext for cognitive activity.[10] The pragmic dimension is the basis of any story and concerns

9 Hogan, *The Mind,* 221.

10 Cf. A. J. Greimas and J. Courtés, "Cognitif" and "Pragmatique," *Sémiotique* 40–42 and 288. To avoid confusion I use *pragmic* instead of *pragmatic.* Cf. also "Somatique," *Sémiotique* 358.

the preservation or change of a character's somatic being (life and life-conditions), either for the better or for the worse. Compared to the Synoptic Gospels, the cognitive dimension is more dominant in the Gospel of John. Nevertheless, we should keep the *intentionality* of the cognitive dimension in mind (it is always about things, properties, and states of affairs). In other words, Jesus' message and cognitive work must ultimately concern the audience's somatic being (even if spiritualized).

The main purpose for Jesus is stated rather clearly: God sends Jesus to save the world through him (3:17). Yet, the Gospel text does not state in a simple manner how Jesus saves the world, or what salvation implies for its beneficiaries. The reason for this obscurity has to do with at least two particular features: First, at the time when the story is written, Jesus has not yet fully accomplished his salvific project; and second, what he has accomplished is only recognizable to those who can discern hidden meaning by the methods of interpretation provided by Jesus. So people should come *to believe* that Jesus is "truly the Savior of the world" (4:42), that he has come to save the world, that he is in fact carrying the salvific program into effect, and that he has accomplished the critical part of it to a point of no return by his death and resurrection. The *telic* saying on the cross, "It is finished" (19:30; cf. τέλος: 13:1; τελειόω: 4:34; 5:36; 17:4; 19:28; τελέω: 19:28, 30), interprets the principal pragmic action in Jesus' overall salvific program. When Jesus gave his life, he performed an intentional act fulfilling the Father's command (cf. 10:17–18; 18:11).

5. The Gospel: A Mythical Narrative

The empirical text we call the Gospel of John is a written discourse presenting a story-world, and we easily and intuitively identify it as a narrative. Actually, it is a special kind of narrative. It is a religious narrative with some claim for historicity and truth. However, from a critical point of view, a view that circumvents the narrative's self-knowledge, we have a man-made myth disclosing how the author imagined the relationship between God, humankind, and the world. As mythical narrative art, the Gospel is neither totally fiction nor totally non-fiction, but rather mythicized history and historicized myth. Only a religious narrative can establish such a sophisticated blend. The problem is, however, that whatever the reader may find historically plausible has been captured by the poet and turned into story by imaginative writing. The author of the Fourth Gospel is a religious poet rather than a rational historian. The story is told not only from a post-resurrection perspective, but also from a post-historical perspective, from a literary narrative perspective. As Aristotle says, even if the poet is writing about historical events, he is no less a poet for that, since he deals with these events as a poet in order to utter universal truths, not historical, particular statements.

When it comes to religious literature like the gospels, however, the challenge is precisely their claim to historicity. Does this claim not deny the gospels' status as poetic literature? In a sense, it does; but from a critical point of view, the gospel story is still literature. A statement like "Jesus is the Son of God" is either true or false; but whether or not it is true or false, the meaning of the utterance's *propositional* content is the same. We can explain the basic meaning of the proposition whatever the statement's truth-value. The basic meaning of the utterance does not depend upon its truth-claim. Similarly, the narrative makes sense irrespective of its correspondence to external reality. The religious story makes sense whether its statements are historically true or false, fact or fiction. The propositional content remains the same and constitutes the narrative.

Even if the Gospel of John is semi-fiction rather than pure fiction, it is a piece of literary art. For want of a better term, we may initially call it *religious fiction*, because the narrative's propositional content is a blend of fictionalized history and historicized fiction. Unlike ordinary fiction, religious fiction is legendary. Both teller and listeners perceive the narrated actions and events to be possible, realistic or plausible within human history (not merely in the story-world). Legends claim to tell history, to tell about historical actions and events in the past. I, however, wish to emphasize the other side of the coin. Religious fiction comes close to etiological legends, which explain the present state of affairs by means of a narrative (cf. the Adam story). Religious fiction claims to have *a metonymical link* to the reader's actual world. Jesus is the Savior not only in the story-world, but in the reader's world also. Ordinary fiction preserves *a metaphorical distance* from the reader's actual world. The reader of ordinary fiction does not conflate the story-world with the real world (a person who goes to England to seek out the wardrobe that gives access to the world of Narnia has made a mistake). The reader of religious fiction, on the other hand, is supposed to do precisely this, and the story-world thus appears as a revelation of the reader's actual historical conditions.

I use the term "religious fiction" in order to emphasize the fictional quality of the religious narrative (which is a break with the narrative's own claim). Ordinary fiction does not claim to relate actual events. The historian, however, does so. Religious fiction is a blend, and I define it as *fiction with a historical truth-claim:* partly because historical material has been absorbed and used at will to fit the religious purpose of the story, and partly because the purpose of the religious story is to reveal the audience's actual, historical life-conditions. The definition is paradoxical but thereby fits the paradoxical religious narrative very well. Only after this detour, I shall identify religious narrative as *myth,* meaning an explanatory elucidation in narrative form of the actual state of affairs in life and in the world. In the story it is God who gives knowledge of the actual situation, either directly or through a messenger (a cognitive revelator), and prototypically this knowledge includes an explanation of how a socially representative character brought this situation about by a non-cognitive action, i. e., a pragmic action. As mentioned, the Adam story is exemplary. Knowledge is an important theme in this story, but its relevance is mainly that it reveals the causal connection between the protagonists' pragmic action (the transgression) and their actual conditions in a world of a particular nature (hard work, sexual reproduction, and death, all concerning their somatic being). The linkage between the narrative's discourse and the story is the tricky part. How the narrator comes to tell the story often remains a mystery. If asked, the answer will be that he was told directly by God, or by one of the characters in the story performing as observer or eyewitness. In order to make the historical claim convincing, however, the best thing would be to have the narrator himself performing as a witness in the story, as observer and/or participant. In John's Gospel, the eyewitness plays an important role, but it is questionable whether a critical perspective should take this claim at face value. The "we" in John 1:14 who has seen the glory of the Father's Son may have perceived the Son only in the narrative revelation of him. Any truth-claim could thus be a statement of belief up-raised to knowledge.

Despite its claim to historicity and truth, I read the Gospel of John as literature. I am not interested in the gospel text as a possible historical source concerning the narrated events, but regard it as a source that tells us how an ancient author understood the relationship between his God, humankind, and the world. The text is of course a piece of art from history, but it is part of the Gospel's literary quality that it transcends its historical setting of production and use. For various reasons, this narrative has been able to function for other people in other times and places. As literature, the gospel text has disengaged itself from its historical origin in a double sense. History became story; story became literature.

After this theoretical introduction, we may now take a closer look at John's Gospel as a mixture or blend of narrative genres. As the title suggests, I shall focus on Jesus in three genre-constituting thematic roles: as Lord, as Lamb, and as Lover.

5.1 The Lord

In numerous places in the text, Jesus is addressed and mentioned as *Lord* (κύριος). He is the leader of a religious group of followers, a movement, and a community of servants. The title designates a functional role. The Lord has the power and the authority to exercise dominion, to control, to command, and to rule. As a designation, this belongs to a series of other christological titles.

In John 1:35–51 the author presents a catalog (a mixture rather than a structure) of identifying epithets. They refer to different aspects of Jesus as a subject of being (qualifications) and a subject of doing (functions and tasks). With the exception of *Son of Joseph*, all may be relevant for the understanding of Jesus as Lord in his exercise of pragmic and/or cognitive power, but here I shall focus on Jesus as *Messiah/Christ* and as *King*. We find even more epithets and roles scattered in the text, for example *Word, Light*, and *Shepherd*, but important for my purpose is the (implicit and explicit) use of *Savior*. Jesus is sent by God in order to save the world (3:17), that is his goal, and he is indeed confessed as the Savior of the world (4:42). The tension between ideas of communitarian, nationwide, and worldwide lordship/kingship is obvious. Things become even more complex when world dominion is displaced from a political, earthly kingship to a cosmic, heavenly lordship. In order to to sort out (at least some important aspects of) this complex Christology, in this section I shall take my point of departure in Hogan's description of the heroic tragicomedy.

5.1.1 The Heroic Tragicomedy

The heroic tragicomedy recounts the story of the rightful leader of a society being displaced from rule or being prevented from assuming rule. The leader/king is absent, exiled, or imprisoned, and society suffers consequently. Internal rivalry, allied with external demonized forces, often an invading army, threatens the kingdom. The hero defeats these outside forces and combats the usurper and his followers before being restored to his proper place as king. The kingdom then prospers in peace and happiness.[11]

We have no difficulty in recognizing the prototypical messianic narrative in this narrative prototype (one could think of the Maccabean revolt against the Seleucid Empire or Pss. Sol. 17). It is about social and political power with both an individual and a collective component. An individual seeking deserved or legitimate dominance in society is prevented from achieving that dominance and may even be exiled from society. Eventually, however, the hero succeeds. The society as in-group defeats both the internal opposition and the external threat to the kingdom. Ultimately, the entire society may seek deserved or legitimate dominance over other societies (linked with totalizing imagery of world dominion). Striking similarities immediately suggest that the Gospel of John, although probably in an elaborate manner, is based on the heroic tragicomedy prototype.

In the story-world, Jesus reveals himself as the Messiah/Christ (John 4:25–26), and the gospel discourse is in itself a confession of Jesus as Christ (cf. 20:31),

11 Hogan, *The Mind*, 110–111.

presented as testimony to this fact. Jesus as Christ is the fulfillment of a promise and a hope for the coming Messiah. As such he is identified as the "one who is coming into the world" (ὁ ἐρχόμενος, 11:27; cf. 4:25; 6:14; further 7:27–42; 8:42; 12:13, and 18:37; the present progressive form of the saying covers the past situation, before Jesus' first coming, as well as the present situation, before Jesus' second coming). The Messiah is a power figure, the leader of a people, prototypically in the role of an anointed king, and we do indeed find Jesus presented as king. We meet, however, a complex characterization of the implied kingship. On one (denotative) level Jesus is (explicitly or implicitly) presented as "the king of Israel" (1:49; 12:13, 15) or as "the king of the Jews" (18:33, 39; 19:3, 12–15, 19, 21). On another (connotative) level, he declares himself to be king of a different kingdom, one that is not of this world (18:36). It is not easy to make sense of this ambiguity. Part of the explanation may be that we are facing a blend of several messianic stories.

5.1.2 The Messianic Stories

I suggest an identification of *four messianic stories:* (1) the Davidic messianic narrative, (2) the Jesuanic messianic narrative, (3) the messianic Christ narrative, and (4) the Johannine messianic Christ narrative.

The Davidic messianic narrative. The story of the Davidic messianic kingdom is a utopian myth. Legendary history is idealized, not only because the past is idealized, but also because this idealization is seen as a program to be fulfilled in the future according to divine prophecy and promise. In an absolute sense, God's prophecy will always come true in stories, since God by definition cannot but fulfill his promises. Unlike human promises, divine promises are immune to blocking circumstances or contra-actions. The divine promise is magical (causative). Once uttered, it determines a destined succession of events, which itself a causal process of destiny will inevitably become reality. Even if, for humans, the realization of the divine goal may seem deferred, it is only a matter of time until the divine decision finds itself realized by action, even if that action may take surprising and unexpected form. People who revert to this mythology would expect God to send a Davidic king in due time. Of course, the longing for such a savior king takes as a fact that society is suffering under illegitimate leadership.

The Jesuanic messianic narrative. Whether historical or not, the entry into Jerusalem is dramatically staged as the coming of a Davidic savior king leading his followers, including some senior disciples designated to be his co-leaders after the assumption of power. This (presumably unarmed) movement trusted in its magical (spiritual) power, linked to the supremacy and the will of God. Realizing the illusory nature of the project, however, Judas decided to save his own neck by delivering Jesus to the religious and political authorities. When Jesus is arrested, most of the other disciples run away. The Jesuanic messianic narrative is thus the story of a person who thought he was the God-chosen Messiah, the legitimate King of the Jews. Jesus believed himself to be capable of achieving power thanks to his words (proclamation of the kingdom's imminence), his somatic magical deeds (healings and exorcisms), his social sense of superior righteousness, and his political-religious symbolic actions (the entry into Jerusalem and the temple action). However, Jesus did not succeed. The story ends in the crucifixion, a clear sign of the movement's and its leader's self-delusion. The Jesuanic messianic story is thus the tragic story of a self-deceiving "wannabe" hero who, while not being a voluntary deceiver, involuntarily deceived the people. This narrative is close to how Jesus' opponents would tell the story.

The story of the coming Davidic king is a version of the myth of the return of the exiled king coming to defeat the usurper and to restore legitimate dominion over the nation. From the perspective of his allies, Jesus embodies and enacts this messianic role, probably in the history-world, but certainly in the story-world. The usurper may be a rival indigenous king or a foreign occupying power. It is the national perspective that is dominant here, and the Jesuanic story refers to a situation where Israel is under Roman control, in collaboration with local vassal kings and the political and priestly aristocracy. The temple action (2:13–22) and the entry into Jerusalem (12:12–19) are a challenge both to the religious and the political powers' legitimacy (in John, both actions are given a symbolic second-order interpretation). The picture of a civil war comes to mind (as when Herod the Great was appointed king by the Romans, but had to defeat what he considered illegitimate internal powers before he could become king). However, Jesus and his movement seem to be fighting an unarmed battle in the hope that omnipotence of thought, language (performative commands and prayer), and prophetic symbolic actions will move God to intervene and make their dreams come true. The establishment, however, regards Jesus as a false Messiah, a false pretender to the Israelite throne, and has him killed as such.

The first two narratives are about a historical, earthly kingdom. The Davidic king is a prototypical political king possessed with institutional power and military force. Idealizations saying that the kingdom will last forever do not contradict its historical, earthly quality. The Jesuanic king is a Davidic king, *except* for the means used to try to achieve power. The entry into Jerusalem with Jesus as a Davidic king leading his followers points to Jesus' self-knowledge as a hero who rightfully seeks the throne as king of Israel or as the King of the Jews. It remains quite unclear how such a pretender without an army might have imagined succeeding, but from Josephus we know of other religiously motivated socio-political movements that took action out of belief in mythological ideas about divine intervention rather than rational planning.[12] Despite the mythological ideas of the movement, the expectation was that Jesus would be "the one to redeem Israel" (Luke 24:21) and "restore the kingdom to Israel" (Acts 1:6) as an independent nation under God's rule in this world. However, Jesus is not able to convince the Jewish and Roman leaders that he is the legitimate King of the Jews. They execute him as a usurper, and that is the tragic end of this story. Much depends, of course, on the point of view, and the question is whether Jesus is an illegitimate or legitimate pretender to the throne, and if legitimate, whether he can conquer the usurper and *de facto* obtain the power of kingship. In a world where might is right and defines legal power, a pretender failing in his attempt to seize the throne is proved wrong. Jesus' execution denies him legitimacy. Only a divine Supreme Court might vindicate him and change the outcome.

The messianic Christ narrative. Once the idea of God's resurrection of Jesus has established itself, the tragic messianic narrative becomes a profound tragicomedy. The story of Jesus, his sayings, works, and fate, however, needs to be retold from a new perspective as a historicized Christ myth (cf. John 2:22). The resurrection confirms Jesus' claim to be the Messiah, but the rehabilitation is more than a question of postmortem honour. Normally a dead person is definitively out of action. Jesus' revival, however, brings him back into the fight. What seemed to be a settled matter is now a reopened case.

The resurrection of Jesus (possibly augmented, in John, as self-resurrection, cf. 10:18) differs from Jesus' resurrection of people before his own death. Jesus is not restored to his former mundane existence. He has not only been raised from death, but has been lifted up (from the earth, cf. John 12:32) and exalted to a higher position as Lord (John 20:28; cf. Phil 2:9–11). The ascension is a kind of exile for a period before returning for a new round of battle, this time definitely with more power. The absent king returns to establish God's kingdom, a kingdom under the leadership of the Messiah. It is hard to determine, however, whether tradition understands this idealized kingdom as earthly and historical or as heavenly and mythological/cosmological.

Even if the idea of God's restoration of the kingdom of David indicates that it is an *idealized* kingdom that is being pictured as everlasting, the kingdom is still an earthly and historical one (cf. the use of εἰς τὸν αἰῶνα, 4:14; 6:51; 12:34 et al.). This idea seems related to the horizontal idea of an old age being replaced by a new age via a liminal phase of transition. When the Messiah arrives, he will

12 Although he surprisingly neglects Mark 11:1–11, I refer to John Dominic Crossan's extensive survey and discussion of the relevant passages of Josephus's works in *The Historical Jesus: The Life of a Mediterranean Jewish Peasant* (New York: HarperCollins, 1992), 168–206. Gerd Theissen and Annette Merz give a shorter survey of Josephus' mention of messianic movements and prophetic oppositions in *Der historische Jesus: Ein Lehrbuch* (Göttingen: Vandenhoeck & Ruprecht 1997), 138–142.

initiate this transitional phase, and the final goal is seen as already/not yet realized. The eschatological idea of God's/the Messiah's final intervention for victory—including judgment and resurrection on the Last Day (cf. John 6:39, 40, 44, 54; 11:24; 12:48)—may, on the other hand, exemplify the idea of a vertical movement from earth to heaven (cf. John 3:13; 3:31; 6:38 et al.), from this world to another world, to a utopian place difficult to imagine in detail.[13] The displacement from a worldly to an other-worldly perspective I conceptualize as *spiritualization*, and by *spiritual* I understand something of a mystical, divine, unworldly/other-worldly, non-physical, and transcendental quality of being.

The Johannine messianic Christ narrative. This narrative is a semantic rewriting of the messianic Christ narrative, yet still containing substantial traces of the Davidic and the Jesuanic narratives. The exchange between Pilate and Jesus during the interrogation shows the author struggling with the problem of how to re-semanticize the role of king. As things have turned out, Jesus is evidently not a king in any ordinary political or national sense. The interrogation is played out as an examination of what Jesus' kingship might mean. To Pilate's question, "Are you the King of the Jews?" (18:33), Jesus at first answers evasively with a counter-question (like "Who says so?"), then immediately explains that his kingdom is not of this world (18:36). Since Jesus speaks of his kingdom (βασιλεία), Pilate infers that Jesus is a king (βασιλεύς) in some sense, and Jesus confirms this, saying that he was born and came to the world as a king (18:37). Nevertheless, it remains unclear what "king" means, since the question is no longer who is the legitimate king of Israel in a political or earthly sense. We may say that Jesus is the king of the world, but then in a universal or cosmological, rather than a particular or political sense. This is a clear kind of idealization and spiritualization of the kingdom (cf. 3:3, 5). When Pilate claims that he has the authority, the power, and the right to crucify Jesus and to release him (19:10), Jesus replies that Pilate would have no authority over him if it had not been given to him from above (19:11). Unwittingly Pilate is only playing a forced role in a tragicomic drama written, staged, and produced by God.

We may find the same tendency to refer to a higher justice in the messianic Christ narrative, but in John's Gospel, the idea of God's kingdom as a world-transcending reign seems more distinct than in the Synoptic Gospels. If focus were on Jesus as the King of the Jews, his return from exile would be in order to take control over the social forces and to redeem the nation and the people from political suppression and economic distress. The expected result would be the restoration of a Davidic kingdom, prospering in peace and harmony. According

13 Cf. 1 Thess 4:13–17; the idea of a thousand-year reign on earth, cf. Rev 20:4–6; 1 Cor 15:23–28, *before* God's end-time victory and some definitive cosmological transformation represents an alternative, intermediate version.

to John's Gospel, however, when Jesus returns, he comes as the world's creator, commanding cosmic forces in order to save humankind from a world of suffering and death. Social disorder is only the most visible symptom of a dysfunctional world, a sign of the world's bad quality, its deficient ontological nature as a condition and way of functioning. Here we are facing a personalization of nature. Forces of nature leading to hunger, sickness, and death are believed to be caused by sin. The world's character is believed to be the result of a violation of some divine rule by action. The kingdom to be restored is no longer a social structure in the world: it is now a cosmic structure, to be understood either as a reborn or recreated physical world or as a spiritual domain in heaven. In John, the idea of salvation may be that those who are reborn have qualified themselves to be removed from this earthly world into another heavenly world. They have been liberated from sin (8:31–36), and will later be liberated from the corruptible world that is doomed to destruction.

This turn to a theology of creation (and re-creation) determines the displacement from a particular and national kingship to a universal and cosmic lordship. In addition, we have a merging of the heroic and the sacrificial tragicomedy. Above all, the heroic act is the commanded, but voluntary sacrifice, somehow necessary for the salvation of the world. Next, the resurrected and elevated hero will return from exile in order to fulfill the instated action of salvation.

John's Gospel, however, gives us no clear picture of how the community understood the coming hero's eschatological programme. The apocalyptic idea of God's final intervention for definitive victory points to Jesus not as king, but as judge (cf. 5:22, 30; 8:16; 12:48). Although it is said more frequently that Jesus has not come to judge (3:17; 12:47 et al.) but to save the world, the idea of judgment is not totally absent (6:44). The meaning seems to be that Jesus did not come to condemn a world deserving of ultimate punishment but to save a world already doomed and as such otherwise definitively lost in an inexorable fate (a process of fatal destruction). Those who refuse to believe in Jesus as Christ are already judged, since belief in him (with whatever that may imply of a new way of living) is the *sine qua non* for a favorable verdict at the final judgment.[14]

14 The judgment may be staged as a legal process with accusation, verdict, and sanction; but the outcome of a fight for dominion may as well be seen as a sort of judgment (the verdict of history), in that the winner of the final battle is proving not only his power, but even his right. God comes to honour and dignity when the enemy is defeated. If God's final victory is certain and modalized as inevitable, it is evident that one's choice of side in this battle right away places one on the side of the winners or the losers. Judgment may refer to an idea of a postwar judicial purge, when the winner has re-established law and order after a period of fighting for dominion.

His resurrection, and the elevation it implies, raises Jesus to an even higher kingship. However, he leaves the battlefield and goes into voluntary exile in heaven. Before leaving, he secretly promises some loyal disciples that he will return—not, however, to restore the ideal earthly kingdom, but to gather his friends and bring them to another heavenly kingdom. The relationship between the savior king and his friends (the chosen ones, his own flock) is a social bonding. As we shall see, John's Gospel brings this social affection into focus and identifies it as a bond of love by including the genre of the romantic tragicomedy. First, however, I shall focus on Jesus as the Lamb of God.

5.2 The Lamb of God

In the first part of this section, I shall present the Gospel's interpretation of Jesus as the Lamb of God, an interpretation, which points to a sacrificial understanding of the death of Jesus. In the second part, I shall look at some implicit sacrificial theories, before discussing in the third part how this theme relates to a widespread narrative genre, the sacrificial tragicomedy.

5.2.1 Jesus as the Sacrificial Passover Lamb in John

According to John 19:14, Jesus is crucified on the day of preparation for the Passover, the day when the paschal lambs were slaughtered. It was forbidden to break any bone of the Passover lamb (Exod 12:46; Num 9:12), so when 19:33–36 emphasizes that not one bone of Jesus had been broken, an interpretation of him as a sacrificed paschal lamb seems implied. Even at the beginning of the story, however, John the Baptist points out Jesus with the words "Here is the Lamb of God who takes away the sin of the world!" (1:29; cf. 1:34). The identification of Jesus is related to his sacrificial death and to the effect of that death (the taking away of the sin of the world, as by a scapegoat). Jesus has come to take away the sin of the world by his sacrificial death—not John the Baptist by the baptismal ritual, his alternative to the temple's atonement rituals. John was not the Lamb of God: he was sent only to testify to that lamb (cf. 1:8, 20).

5.2.2 Sacrificial Ideas in John

It is notable that the Gospel text includes several implicit "sacrificial theories," all regarded as valid in some respect. Caiaphas's unintentional prophecy in 11:50 (it is better that one man dies for the people than that the whole nation perishes) points to one version of a scapegoat theory. In order to protect Jewish, limited self-governement, it is necessary to put down the insurrection against the Romans. Caiaphas regards Jesus as the leader of such an insurrection and thus as endangering the whole nation. The Romans may use this rebellion as a reason for crushing the nation. By giving up Jesus to the Romans, the people may be able to ward off the threatening danger. To sacrifice Jesus in order to save the people is to perform a social apotropaic sacrifice. The author, however, regards the High Priest as a prophet, unwittingly pronouncing a hidden truth: that Jesus was in fact meant to die for the people, according to God's plan. Yet this interpretation is only valid if taken in an even wider sense. Jesus dies not for his country alone, but for all people, and their suffering is not primarily caused by Roman suppression and destruction. People are suffering under the world's actual *ontological* state of affairs, a world functioning according to Satan's rule.[15] The political fight has turned into a cosmological fight, and the time has come to cast out the ruler of this world (12:31; the devil or Satan).[16]

The scapegoat theory (one individual must die in order for the community to be saved) may come in different versions. If the scapegoat himself is the one who has caused the danger, we have a kind of criminal story, and the offender is to be executed as violator of a divine law (as an evildoer; 18:30; cf. Sophocles, *Oedipus the King*). If the scapegoat, however, is innocent and sacrificed in place of the person(s) responsible for the threat to the community (as when Pilate sacrifices an apparently innocent Jesus instead of Barabbas), we have the suffering of the righteous. Moreover, we need to distinguish between an innocent victim who performs this role involuntarily and one who does it voluntarily. Jesus acts voluntarily. He is innocent or righteous not because he has done nothing, but because he is the *unjustly* rejected legitimate king. In any case, however, here we have a plain social theory of the scapegoat, needing no metaphysical or mythological backup.

The same is true with the version of a scapegoat theory involved when focus is on the relationship between Jesus and his disciples before his death. In Jerusalem, Jesus and all his followers are in danger of arrest and punishment

15 It is difficult to see how the author would explain the establishment of the actual world situation. We have either a dualistic point of view, seeing God and Satan as rival kings fighting for world domination, or a more monistic point of view, seeing Satan's rule as God's punishment because of humankind's sin. The understanding of Jesus' death as a conciliating sacrifice implies the idea of humankind's sin, possibly due to Satan's seduction. The author, however, neglects this question. His point of departure is the actual state of affairs. Compared to some ideal, the actual world is the victim (self-inflicted or unprovoked) of sin and death, and for some reason God has decided to save the world out of love for the world. Salvation of the world, however, is not possible without a sacrifice.

16 Satan may have been a cover name for the Romans and their domestic allies in earlier tradition, when hostile social forces were conceptualized by mythological and cosmological imagery. Later on, this mythological and cosmological imagery is taken literally. Christ is no longer a particular king fighting the Romans, but a universal lord of creation fighting Satan.

as insurrectionists. In the garden (18:1–11), Jesus voluntarily reveals his identity to the band of men in search of him, and proposes a deal. Since they are mainly seeking him, he suggests they let his disciples off (18:8). The author understands this favour as a significant example of how Jesus saves his followers by delivering himself into the hands of his opponents (18:9): the one gives his life in order that the many may live. Jesus does not hesitate to save his disciples. Instead of trying to save himself, he focuses on saving his companions. Love for the disciples may be part of his motivation, but the perspective is narrow: the disciples' salvation here means escaping death by preserving a mundane life.

Jesus as the good shepherd who lays down his life for the sheep (10:11, 15) has a wider perspective. This idea stands parallel to the generic statement in 15:13: "No one has greater love than this, to lay down one's life for one's friends." Here the flock of friends, however, consists of all Christ-confessors, and salvation ultimately points to eternal life. For love to have significant meaning, we must understand the self-sacrifice in these contexts differently than above. The idea of the self-sacrifice as an act of socially representative love depends on *two principles.*

The first of these is that the beneficiary, the one who is saved (due to an objectively established possibility), initially is the victim of an ongoing process of destruction—either through his or her own doing (or lack of it) as perpetrator or sinner, or because of some other person's or personified power's doing/activity. Two statements in the First Letter of John are of great help here: "Everyone who commits sin is a child of the devil; for the devil has been sinning from the beginning. The Son of God was revealed for this purpose, to destroy the works of the devil" (1 John 3:8); and: "he was revealed to take away sins" (1 John 3:5). Here, the devil as the ruler of this world is influencing the individual person as a subject of doing and a subject of being, the group dynamics of a social community, and/or this world as a whole (the world's ontological and material nature with its unavoidable corporeal defects like hunger, sickness, and death). The person, the community, and/or the world are the victims of evil forces.

The author never tells how this situation was established. People are like sheep fallen into a pit from where they are unable to escape by their own efforts. Why they got into this mess—by accident, because of ignorance, seduction or plain evil coercion—we do not know. Evidently, however, they are doomed. They can be saved only if someone appears with the strength and intention to pull them up. In other words, the sin of the world (as a destructive dynamic force seen as punishment and/or as qualifying for punishment) must be nullified. If the devil, in the last instance, is to blame, his works must be destroyed and he himself must be expelled from the world. On the one hand, we have the idea of the purging of the actual world (cf. 12:31); on the other, the wider idea that the actual world is the pit out of which one has to be saved—if eternal life is more than purified life in the actual world (12:32).

Here I leave out the issue of whether those born again of God—ideally speaking—have received a competence making them able not to sin. It is more important to notice that narratives tend to understand natural *processes* (like hunger, sickness, and death) as the result of a complex *action* referring to responsible subjects of doing. Processes threatening life and life-possibilities are perceived as an intentional agent's punishment of sinners (cf. the use of the Adam story in Paul).

The second principle is that the subject responsible for the saving action is acting voluntarily and is doing the beneficiary a favor. The Savior of the world (4:42) may be understood as an ally motivated by pity and mercy. Seeing the suffering of humankind, God is overwhelmed with pity for his beloved ones and gives (δίδωμι) his Son, so that whoever believes in him should not perish, but have eternal life (3:16). The idea that the world is doomed to perish because of the sin of humankind is downplayed (or at least concealed). The idea that the righteous God has a clear right to punish humankind for its sins is downplayed (or at least occulted) too. However, these ideas are not completely absent. Speaking of God's love may mean that he is tempering justice with mercy.

The interpretation very much depends on the question of humankind's responsibility for its actual situation. Is the sin a voluntary or involuntary action of which humankind is the responsible subject of doing and by which humankind becomes a victim? Alternatively, is humankind the (innocent) victim of external evil forces, personified as Satan or the Devil? The concept of sin is sufficiently vague to oscillate between guilt and fate. Anyway, God's intervention is a favor in the strict sense, since he is under no obligation to intervene. He acts from love, not in order to fulfill an obligation. It may still be a conundrum why God has to give his Son (as a mandatory sacrifice on the cross) rather than merely sending him (as an enlightening messenger), but even if the Father has commanded the Son to give his life, the Son himself must act out of love. He must be in full agreement with the Father and act voluntarily, so that no one is *taking* his life, but he himself is *giving* away his life (cf. 10:17–18). Here we have left behind the "sociological" understanding of Jesus' death. It is a sacrifice needed to stop the ongoing process of destruction (the works of the devil aimed at death) *and* to start a contra-process of restoration (the works of God, Jesus, and the Spirit) aiming at eternal life. The first step is to stop the diabolic process of death; the next step is to initiate the reverse, divine process of life. The saying in 5:24, "anyone who hears my word and believes him who sent me has eternal life, and does not come under judgment, but has passed from death to life," explains this modal *peripeteia.* The believer has passed from a fatal somatic process of death into a fatal somatic process of life, which is why eternal life is already certain, though not yet fully achieved.[17]

5.2.3 The Sacrificial Tragicomedy

According to Hogan, the goal of the sacrificial tragicomedy is a sort of bodily or physical happiness. In the prototypical plot, the human community has committed an ethical violation that offends the gods. This violation gives rise to a famine, and in order to remedy the situation the community has to make some sort of offering to the gods and/or send a messenger to ask for divine intervention. In response, the gods grant humans their food, and introduce ritual that will preserve their wellbeing.[18]

The focus on famine may surprise us, but famine and hunger are recurring themes in the Hebrew Bible. 2 Sam 21:1–10 is a good example. Here we have the story of a famine during the reign of King David, caused by a spell of drought, a lack of rain. The drought, on the other hand, is explained as God's punishment resulting from the bloodguilt on Saul's house. By delivering seven members of Saul's descendants to be killed, David atones for this sin against God on behalf of the nation, and shortly thereafter, the rain is pouring down from the sky. Again, God is sending the rain, so important for the fertility of land and crops, the people's somatic livelihood. In general, this story fits the prototypical sacrificial tragicomedy. The question is whether traces of this kind of plot are to be found in John's Gospel as well.

The first thing to notice is that famine and hunger refer to the fundamental fact that humans need to eat and drink in order to sustain life. It is a question of bodily or somatic subsistence. The following model presents a categorical presentation of the different principal levels concerning such somatic (physical) wellbeing:

17 The believer does not undergo a pragmic somatic transformation, but achieves the status as "heir" to eternal life, becomes a person who has achieved the right to access eternal life. This telic state of being, earlier modalized as possible, is now modalized as necessary (inevitable).

18 Hogan, *The Mind,* 187.

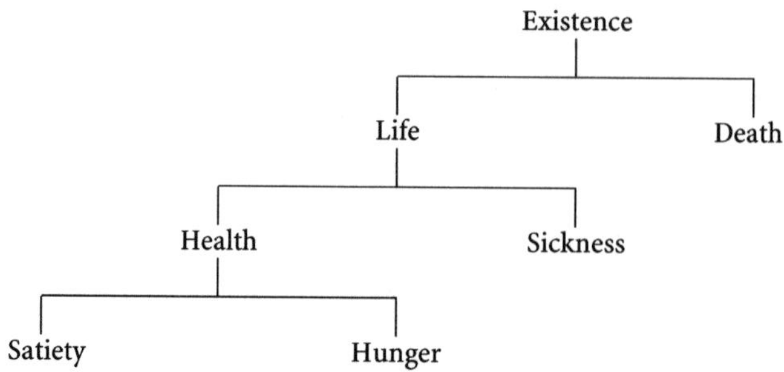

Here we have a hierarchical set of connected and embedded oppositions.[19] Hogan points to famine and hunger as the dominant theme in sacrificial tragicomedy, but that theme implies sickness and death (we do not die from instant hunger, but starvation may lead to sickness and sickness may lead to death). Therefore, we can expect to find prototypical stories about plagues of all different sorts, including sickness and death, seen as punishment for violation of given norms and requiring sacrifice in order to come to a halt.

Hunger and satiety. We find more examples of hunger and thirst in John's Gospel—though mostly with a symbolic or spiritual meaning pointing beyond the mundane somatic needs of the perishable body. At the meeting with a woman of Samaria (4:1–15), thirst for water is the dominant motif together with food (4:8, 31–35), even if used as the basis for metaphorical instruction about spiritual food and drink to sustain eternal life. In 6:1–15 Jesus acts as an extraordinary provider, this time of food for the five thousand. The feeding of the multitude solves a small-scale famine. When Jesus perceives that the crowd is intending to make him king, he withdraws (6:15). The text may play on the idea that one of a king's tasks is to secure food supplies for his subjects. The Johannine Jesus, however, is no political figure of this world. A king he may be, but his kingdom is not in this world (18:36). His task is therefore not to sustain actual life, but he gives food and drink for eternal life, as explained in 6:22–58. Lacking space for a closer look at this interesting text, I call attention only to the fact that it refers to a particular kind of famine, the lack of food during the Exodus, when God gave the people "bread out of heaven" in the form of manna. This miraculous food did prolong lives (postponing death), but it could not give eternal life (overcoming death). Furthermore, the text, in our view, evidently refers to some eucharistic ritual practiced in the community. The flesh of Jesus is the true food and his blood is the true drink (6:55). Finally, we have a story about lack of food and plenty of food in 21:1–14.

19 I formed this model in a study of miracle stories in Mark's Gospel, stories concerned with basic threats to human life; see Ole Davidsen, *The Narrative Jesus: A Semiotic Reading of Mark's Gospel* (Aarhus: Aarhus University Press, 1993), 61–82.

The overall picture presents Jesus as a provider, one who has come to satisfy people's hunger and quench their thirst in a figurative sense. It may be partly right to understand his food and drink as knowledge: food and drink for the mind. Knowledge, however, is always knowledge of something—eventually of persons' somatic being. The Gospel story is good news because it informs its addressees that their tragic being (or life-conditions) have been changed for the better (due to a comic pragmic *peripeteia,* which of course implies a corresponding cognitive *anagnōrisis* based on some sort of information). The initiated process of salvation is in progress, and it is possible to pass from a fatal process of death into a process of life, ultimately aiming at eternal life. All of this, however, has only become possible because of a sacrifice. The Eucharist provides ritual food and drink to preserve and sustain the subsistence (or mode of existence) of the reborn who is destined for eternal life.

Sickness and health. Here I must confine myself to some general observations. First, healing points to Jesus' extraordinary competence. As a counterintuitive action, a miracle, healing implies his participation in the Father's creative power. As sent and endowed by God, Jesus performs his life-protecting good works in order to display the works of God for the world. When people see the glory of God in these good works, the intention is that they will believe that Jesus has been sent by the Father, and that they will trust his message of salvation in the wider sense. Second, healing means restoration of mundane life to the sick, not the achievement of eternal life. Thus the challenge for the reader is to realize how healing as a restoration to mundane life relates to salvation from this world.

Life and death. While the resurrection of Lazarus (11:1–44) as a restoration to mundane life is possible before Jesus' death and resurrection, resurrection to eternal life is only possible after this sacrificial event. The effect of healing and mundane resurrection is only a temporary postponement of death. Yet, as signs, they anticipate the final goal, the overcoming of death by eternal life. The narrative thinking may eventually construe mundane life as an afterglow of former splendor, with resurrection to eternal life being seen from the point of view of hindsight as the restoration of humankind to a former mythological glorious state of being.

5.3 The Lover

The interpersonal relationship between Jesus and his disciples is a love relation characterized by mutual affection, attraction, and attachment as found in familiarity and friendship. Romantic desire, on the other hand, involves sexual practice, typically between a man and a woman. The romantic tragicomedy may therefore seem irrelevant in this case. It may, however, be important, once some modifications are taken into consideration.

First, we should recognize that it is difficult to define love, a complexity of emotions, categorically. Even friendship may involve some homoerotic or heteroerotic affections, even if they remain suppressed or sublimated and shown only in non-sexual physical contact, brotherly kisses and caresses (cf. 13:23). Second, romantic love is a striving not only for sexual union, but for lasting closeness and friendship in pursuit of mutual happiness. Therefore, we should not be surprised if romantic love and philial love share some common features. Philial love seems to be a sublimated (spiritualized) version of romantic love, and the community's ideal self-understanding seems to be that of an extended family or household, an intimate group of brothers (and sisters).[20]

5.3.1 The Romantic Tragicomedy

"The most common plot structure across different traditions," says Hogan, "is almost certainly romantic tragicomedy, the story of the union, separation, and ultimate reunion of lovers."[21] The two lovers cannot be united because of some conflict between their desire for personal happiness and the social structure, typically represented by the parents' resistance. The separation, frequently involving exile and imprisonment, often involves death or death imagery. In the end, the lovers are reunited, possibly only in the afterlife.

The temporal separation is assimilated with the prototype eliciting conditions for sorrow and images and metaphors of death. In romantic tragicomedy, however, this preceding sorrow only intensifies the final joy and happiness.[22]

---

20 In his article "Massenpsychologie und Ich-Analyse" from 1921, reprinted in *Fragen der Gesellschaft. Ursprunge der Religion*, Studienausgabe 9 (Frankfurt: S. Fischer, 1974), 61–134, Sigmund Freud has convincingly argued "dass es Libidobindungen sind, welche eine Masse charakterisieren" (95). We need not subscribe to the whole theory in order to accept that an in-group like the Johannine community is based on affective bindings and on the idea "dass ein Oberhaupt da ist … das alle Einzelnen der Masse mit der gleichen Liebe liebt" (89). What Freud says about the group in general and the Church in particular is no less true for the Johannine community: "Nicht ohne tiefen Grund wird die Gleichartigkeit der christlichen Gemeinde mit einer Familie heraufbeschworen und nennen sich die Gläubigen Brüder in Christo, das heißt Brüder durch die Liebe, die Christus für sie hat. Es ist nicht zu bezweifeln, dass die Bindung jedes Einzelnen an Christus auch die Ursache ihrer Bindung untereinander ist" (89; cf. John 13:14). According to Freud, the love drive has its source in sexual drives transformed into more tender feelings. He admits, however, that it hardly has any meaning to ask, "ob die Libido, welche die Massen zusammenhält, homosexueller oder heterosexueller Natur ist, denn sie ist nicht nach den Geschlechtern differenziert und sieht insbesondere von den Zielen der Genitalorganisation der Libido völlig ab" (131–32).

21 Hogan, *The Mind*, 101.

22 The romantic tragedy, on the other hand, like *Romeo and Juliet*, is a "truncated tragi-comedy" (*The Mind*, 103) since the protagonists were still striving for the comic goal of romantic union.

Sometimes the imagery of exile and imprisonment is used even if there is no literal exile or imprisonment because the narrative imagination may use prototypical cases of sorrow for social life outside their usual domains. Finally, the ultimate reunion of the lovers is seldom a simple resumption of the initial reunion. There are sacred or otherwise absolutized aspects to the reunion, as when the lovers are joined only after death, in heaven. Heaven imagery, however, may have a more figurative sense, since heavenly happiness is the prototypical metaphor for enduring happiness.

5.3.2 The Philial Tragicomedy

The Gospel of John may be distinct among early Christian writings for several reasons, but it seems justified to claim that the emphasis on the love relation between the Father and the Son and between the Son and his friends is the most dominant particularity. Here I shall focus on the love relation between Jesus and his disciples (cf. the use of φιλέω and φίλος).[23]

I identify the following sequence of movements in this relationship:

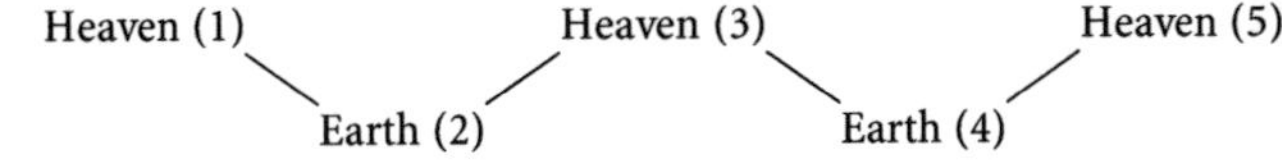

1–2: A realized first move from heaven to earth identified as Jesus' incarnation (cf. 6:38), arrival and presence.

2–3: A realized second move from earth to heaven identified as Jesus' ascension, his departure, and absence.

3–4: A future third move from heaven to earth identified as Jesus' *parousia*, his second coming and presence.

4–5: A future fourth move from earth to heaven identified as the final exodus, when Jesus leads his friends to the Father's house in heaven.

We have no difficulty seeing that this process schema deals with a story of union, separation, and reunion of lovers, though in several steps.

The first move initiates the process, the establishment of contact. I dare to say, the falling in (reciprocated) love. One does not fall intentionally, so falling in love is an unintentional event. That is no less true as regards the philial love for a leader. The love relation establishes itself by recognition in an event as un-

This suggests "that comedy is, indeed, the primary form, and tragedy operates as a shortened version of comedy" (104). This observation by Hogan is remarkable. It reveals a distinctive value-perspective of the narrative mind. In a theological interpretation, it points to the Creator's good intentions for life and happiness and claims that a tragic life story is only a tragicomic life story waiting to be finished.

23 John 3:29; 5:20; 11:3, 11, 36; 12:25; 15:13–15, 19; 16:27; 19:12; 20:2; 21:15–17.

predictable as the blowing wind (3:8). It simply happens. At the very moment, however, when this contingent event takes place, the partners find they have known each other before. The first union is a phenomenological experience of mutual recognition, of a reunion, as if the partners have been destined for each other in all eternity. The sheep follow the shepherd because they know his voice, his calling (cf. 10:2–4). It is this *retrospective* experience of predestination, which creates the social bond's stability and solidity. Any hindrance of this love relation would be an attack on a hidden, but divinely intended order, now revealed.

The reciprocal immanence formula ("to be in"/"to stay in") refers to a love relation both between the Father and the Son and between the Son and his beloved friends (17:23). It is said that the Father has loved the Son before the world was founded (17:24), and by analogy the same is the case with the Son's love for those given him by the Father (cf. 17:6). The love relationship between the Son and his disciples is also founded in eternity.

From another angle, the incarnation—primarily understood as the move from heaven to earth (if not simply as the appearance on stage)—is a return from a forced or deliberate exile. Satan, the usurper, is in charge, but the author never tells how this situation was established. The world is living in a kind of imprisonment or slavery. An unclear longing with a feeling of sorrow may be the basic emotion among people waiting for deliverance.

The second move concerns the separation of the lovers. The love between Jesus and the community is mutual, though the Gospel text focuses mostly on Jesus' love for his friends, like that of a shepherd for his sheep. The forthcoming death of Jesus directly prompts his farewell discourse. This is a comforting speech promising a new presence on earth after death, resurrection, and ascension to heaven. A lot of material in the Gospel text deals with the community's liminal situation as separated from its lover. The promise of the Paraclete's presence is a theme of its own. Here I shall focus on the Lover's promise to return to the community, his partners in love.

On one level of meaning, Jesus is driven into exile in an absolute sense because of his death. The separation of the lovers is definitive, and elicits sorrow in the partner left behind. If the story would have ended here, we would have a tragedy, since the goal for the lovers is to be together for all eternity. On another level, however, the resurrection and the ascension to heaven raise hope for reunion. The exile of Jesus may be forced by divine necessity, but it is nevertheless deliberate in nature, since he is believed to be in full control of the situation. He will return once more, this time, it is to be expected, for good and for the final victory over the enemy. The stories of Jesus' appearance after his death and resurrection but before the ascension to the Father (20:11–29; 21) depict a momentary reunion, anticipating the later final reunification.

The third move is a future event. The author of the Gospel text may be focusing on the liminal period of separation in an attempt to emphasize that the Lover may somehow be spiritually present even while bodily absent. A ritualized form of recollection of the Jesus story, actualizing past traditions' significance for the present, may explain the experience of such a presence. We should avoid, however, a one-sided focus on "realized eschatology." It will not work without the underlying expectation of a future reunion, of which the present experience of presence is only a transient foretaste, and which has to be evoked repeatedly. Presumably this is to be done in devotion orchestrated by a community leader embodying the absent Jesus (and the present Paraclete?), who as such will speak not in his own right, but as an interpreter saying only what Jesus—or the Spirit—commands him to say.

When Jesus returns, a reunion will take place. It is, however, quite unclear how the author conceives of what will happen. The Gospel text, at least, only gives hints as to his understanding. Here we should not overlook the fact that human imagination falls short when it tries to imagine what will happen in a world quite distinct from the world of mundane experience. In any case, the author might therefore only have been able to give a tentative suggestion.

Right before the separation, Jesus informs his disciples that, for a short while, they will see him no longer (16:5–22). At the same time, he promises that after yet another short interval they will see him again in reunion. Jesus is going to the Father—to heaven—but will return to the earth in the immediate future. The temporary separation of the lovers is a well-known element in the romantic tragicomedy. On Jesus' return, it is to be expected, the separation will not only be overcome, but the forces that parted the lovers in the first place will be defeated and possibly destroyed, since Jesus will have conquered the world (16:33). Time has now come to cast out the ruler of this world definitively (12:31), and we do find some judgment imagery in 5:24–30. The author, however, does not focus on Jesus as a returning king or judge, though such an idea seems to have been a part of the community's all-embracing mythology. The story of the Lover overrules, or at least overlays, the story of the Lord.

The fourth move is an integrated part of the Gospel story's plot. When Jesus comes, he does not come to stay in this world. Jesus is going away in order to prepare a place in heaven for his followers, and when he comes back again, he will take them to himself, so that where he is, they may also be (14:1–3). Jesus comes to embrace the loved ones and take them to their real homeland, to the house of the Father. Rather than a story of messianic victory and a subsequent judicial purge, we have a story of a lover who comes to liberate his loved ones from a suppressive structure (cf. 12:32). Here the perspective is turned around. It is not Jesus the Lord who is in exile, but, as prisoners in a foreign world, the loved ones require release by the Lover. Jesus, the hero, promises to return and rescue the loved ones and bring them home.[24] How this event will take place, the story never depicts in any detail.

6. Conclusion

The Gospel of John is a complex text, an intricate piece of religious literary art. Read as a whole it appears coherent, but at closer sight, it tends to break down into a collection of themes and plots full of tensions and loose ends that hint at a more extensive (and perhaps more intelligible) underlying theology of God, humankind, and the world. The text as it stands appears to be a narrative discourse that was revised and reworked several times by an author or redactor in order to emphasize a more symbolic or spiritual understanding of the related events.[25]

A focus on the question of genre may help us understand the character and composition of a text. I have identified the Gospel of John as a *myth,* a story of fictionalized history and historicized fiction. What we find to be historically plausible material (for example, Jesus' crucifixion), the religious poet has captivated and transformed into story by narrative emplotment. What we find to be historically impossible material (for example, Jesus' resurrection), the religious poet has integrated into a plot structure claimed to represent historical events. As religious story, the Gospel of John challenges the reader's intuitive conception of reality based on everyday experience (so that believing replaces knowledge). Historical scholarship is inherently a methodologically qualified understanding of such everyday experience, which is why there is an inevitable conflict between the Gospel text's self-knowledge and the historian's rational perspective. Philosophers and theologians may claim that a restricted historical perspective distorts reality since we have no absolute knowledge of reality. This controversy, however, does not really matter to the historian as historian, since the restricted rational perspective defines the historical approach. Historical scholarhip is not only the study of the past (history), but the study of the past based on a rational

24 Somehow, in likeness to a bridegroom bringing his bride, cf. 3:29, which, as mentioned by C. K. Barrett, may play on the idea of the church as the bride of Christ (idem, *The Gospel According to St John: An Introduction with Commentary and Notes on the Greek Text* [Cambridge: SPCK, 1978], 222–223).

25 Craig R. Koester points out that "[w]e can discern symbolic significance in images, events, or persons without undercutting their claims to historicity, and we can recognize that certain images, events, and people are historical without diminishing their symbolic value." (*Symbolism in the Fourth Gospel: Meaning, Mystery, Community* [Minneapolis: Fortress, 1995], 8). However, it seems more adequate to say that the Gospel narrative depicts a story-world in which a denotative level of meaning (with both historically plausible an implausible events) forms the basis for a connotative level of meaning.

understanding of the world's character (scholarhip). From a rational and historical perspective, the Gospel of John is a myth: religious poetry with a historical truth-claim.

I have furthermore examined the Gospel of John in order to see if its narrative relates to what Patrick Holm Cogan has claimed to be the cross-culturally dominant narrative genres, and my conclusion is positive. In order to eliminate a widespread misunderstanding of such an approach among historical-philological scholars, I began with Aristotle, showing that the fundamentals of narrative theory were formed even before the Gospel of John was written. Modern narrative theory is based on or is congenial with Aristotle's ideas of storytelling—which is why the objection that narrative analysis is anachronistic is simply wrong. Aristotle pointed to the primacy of emplotment of action leading either from happiness to unhappiness (tragic plot reversal) or from unhappiness to happiness (comic plot reversal). Hogan, seeing the tragic plot as a deficient comic plot, defines the prototypical plot structure as tragicomic, and points out three dominant prototypical stories on a more specific thematic level: the heroic, the sacrificial, and the romantic tragicomedy.

One can hardly deny that the Gospel of John is a tragicomedy, even if the hopeful joy from the good news is in want of final confirmation. The involvement of the specifications—sacrificial, heroic, and romantic—is evident to varying degrees, but all are present. Our order of presentation may cloud the order of presupposition defining their interrelatedness. Although the heroic plot does not imply the sacrificial plot, the latter presupposes the former. The sacrificial plot implies neither the romantic nor the philial plot, but, again, the latter presupposes the former. This order of presupposition probably corresponds to developmental stages in the formation of an accumulating, but reworked tradition over time.

The heroic tragicomedy of the rightful claimant seeking to assume legitimate dominance is perhaps the most fundamental prototype plot in John. Jesus is the fulfillment of the promise of a Davidic king sent by God to save a suffering nation from domestic and foreign enemies of the ideal kingdom of God. As Gerd Theissen has pointed out, the historical Jesus and his followers lived in a myth. Myth and history were combined right from the beginning.[26] The messianic narrative of Jesus as the legitimate king of the Jews may correspond to the self-understanding and actions of the historical Jesus. The crucifixion crushes this hope.

26 Theissen asserts "that everything suggests that neither a myth which was historicized at a secondary stage nor a history which was mythicized at a secondary state stood at the centre of primitive Christianity. At the beginning stood a unity in tension of both history and myth." See Gerd Theissen, *A Theory of Primitive Christian Religion* (London: SCM Press, 1999), 22–23.

The resurrection, on the other hand, is a contra-denial in the objective story-world. Jesus is the anointed Messiah, but now in a more ambiguous way. It is difficult to see whether the first Christ-confessors believed that this mythological figure would come to establish the worldly kingdom *of* heaven, or to take them out of a corruptible world to the kingdom *in* heaven. We have, however, early traditions where a displacement from social history to cosmic nature has taken place. The political Christ of history has been transformed into a cosmic Christ, and God's salvation becomes ultimately founded in a theology of creation, not in a theology of historical revelation. The revelation of this theology must necessarily take place in historical time, of course, but it reveals a secret about the end of the world of history.

It all seems to hinge on the interpretation of Jesus' death as self-sacrifice. On a denotative (manifest) level, his executioners take his life, but on a connotative (latent) level, Jesus gives his life as sacrifice. The sacrificial interpretation implies that society is suffering due to the violation of divine rules. God has punished society (or the world) because of the people's sin; and salvation, reconciliation, and return of plenty depend on the sacrifice. We have no explicit reference to such a primordial crime (for example to the Adam story in Genesis), but Satan is in charge. His rule may explain the social disaster, but again we find a displacement of conflict to an ontological and cosmological level. Nor does John's Gospel give us a clear picture of the eschatological events that are foreseen, but it shines through that a future eschatology was part of the community's belief-system. In the end, the Lord will return and take his friends with him to the Father's place in heaven.

The overall focus, however, is on the liminal period between Jesus' ascension and his final return. The Gospel text recounts past and future events, but the community's present situation of separation motivates the discourse. As myth, the narrative defines the community's identity and existential situation. It further functions as the (past) mythological ground for the community's (present) ritual practice and ethical ideals. Even if the heroic and the sacrificial plot are the more fundamental, they form the background of the discourse, whereas the romantic/philial plot forms its foreground.

Whereas the involvement of the prototypes of heroic and sacrificial tragicomedy is obvious, it is less evident that the romantic tragedy genre has informed John's Gospel. It is true that imagery of wedding (in Cana) and of romantic love do appear in the story (at the meeting at the well in John 4; perhaps also at the meeting at the tomb in John 20:11–18), but it is also a fact that this story line concerns non-sexual philial and familial love. So is it justifiable to include the romantic tragicomedy as a possible narrative source? I think so, if philial love is a spiritualized version of romantic love. The pattern of union, separation, and happy reunion that characterizes the romantic tragicomedy is evidently present in the Gospel story.[27] Moreover, the depiction of intense and intimate philial love in the Gospel of John leaves the impression of a non-sexual spiritualization of romantic love.

However, perhaps we should disregard the sexual connotation of romantic love all together and focus alone on the attachment part. Discussing Freud's concept of Eros, Hogan suggests that sexual desire and attachment function as two distinct systems and among some minor cross-cultural genres he points to certain attachment stories, mostly about separation and reunion of parent and child, less frequently about separation and reunion of friends.[28] Therefore, it is tempting to merely point to stories about friendship, but we are dealing with complex matters. Thus, it is evident that the parent-child relation between the Father and the Son plays a major role. It is less observable that this parent-child schema sometimes even colors Jesus' relation to his disciples as when he addresses them as children rather than as friends (cf. John 13:33, "Little children, I am with you only a little longer," and 14:18, "I will not leave you orphaned; I am coming to you").[29] It might therefore be more correct to assert that the text is overdetermined, because the narrative imagination may use features from more prototypical genres where attachment is involved. The interpersonal relationship between Jesus and his beloved disciples, characterized by mutual affection, attraction, and attachment, may be conceptualized as a relation soon between family members (parent and child), soon between friends, and soon between lovers.

According to Hogan, three narrative genres—the sacrificial, the heroic, and the romantic tragicomedy—dominate not all, but the most common stories across cultures. If so, these prototypical genres must point to basic cognitive predispositions for the way we tend to understand and interpret our human existence in a pre-philosophical and pre-scientific, i. e., a narrative, manner. As prototypes, these are open for specification and modification, displacement and spiritualization, without losing their impact on the production and perception of meaning. We can explain the Gospel of John as a mixture or blend of these narrative genres concerning existential challenges of our deepest concern. The combination and elaboration of these dominant narrative genres into a complex

27 For another example, see Homer's *Odyssey*, a narrative in other respects important for the study of John's Gospel, cf. Kasper Bro Larsen, *Recognizing the Stranger. Recognition Scenes in the Gospel of John*, BIS 93 (Leiden: Brill, 2008) and Hogan, *Affective*, 206.

28 Hogan, *Affective*, 17–18; 199–209.

29 For a different approach to the parent-child schema, see Jo-Ann A. Brant, "Divine Birth and Apparent Parents: The Plot of the Fourth Gospel," in *Ancient Fiction and Early Christian Narrative*, ed. Ronald F. Hock, J. Bradley Chance, and Judith Perkins, SBLSymS 6 (Atlanta: Scholars, 1998), 199–211.

and perplexing narrative myth may even explain the Gospel story's own cross-cultural success.

Jo-Ann A. Brant

John Among the Ancient Novels

1. Introduction

Few would deny the novelty of the Gospel of John; many have dismissed a generic relationship between John and the novel. In his 1977 publication *What is a Gospel?*, Charles H. Talbert sets aside consideration of the "romance" by pointing to them as accounts of the fictitious "experience and emotions of private individuals" that aim "at nothing more than outright entertainment" with "no desire to inform."[1] As the label romance—a term than in modern English connotes a frothy, little love story—has given way to the language of ancient novel, classicists and biblical scholars have become more willing to consider these narratives worthy of study.[2] Although Johannine scholarship no longer ignores the novels, their use has generally been limited to a source for understanding the socio-economic and religious world in which the Gospel was read.[3] To my

1 Charles H. Talbert, *What is a Gospel? The Genre of the Canonical Gospels* (Philadelphia: Fortress, 1977), 17. See, for example, Tobias Hägerland "John's Gospel: A Two-Level Drama?" *JSNT* 25 (2003): 313–14; Richard Bauckham, *The Testimony of the Beloved Disciple: Narrative, History and Theology in the Gospel of John* (Grand Rapids: Baker, 2007), 20. By the time Talbert publishes *Matthew* (Grand Rapids: Baker, 2010), the novels are well established in his bibliography.

2 The term romance was first adopted when it referred to verse or prose tales about times remote from the present such as the age of knights or tales of extravagant fiction. In the late 17th century, usage associated with what we think of as romance began to appear. The use of the term novel has become normative among English speaking classicists only since 1976 when B. P. Reardon sponsored the first of a series of meetings of the International Conference on the Ancient Novel.

3 For example, in his argument for understanding the Johannine concept of love within a familial context, Sjef van Tilborg draws from Achilles Tatius and Longus for a picture of familial love and sexual mores (*Imaginative Love in John*, BIS 2 [Leiden: Brill, 1993], 151, 204), and Willis Hedley Salier turns to Achilles Tatius, *Leucippe and Clitophon* 2.2 as a source for Dionysus legends (*The Rhetorical Impact of the Sēmeia in the Gospel of John*, WUNT 2/186 [Tübingen: Mohr Siebeck, 2004], 68). The earliest significant use of the novels, to my knowledge, appears in Craig A. Evans's 1982 article "Peter Warming Himself: The Problem of an

knowledge there has been no thorough attempt to argue that the Gospel belongs to the genre of the novel. Lawrence Wills perhaps comes closest by arguing that John is an aretalogical biography that exploits novelistic techniques comparable to those found in the biographical novel, *Life of Aesop*.[4] While I do not want to risk my credibility as a scholar by arguing that John is a novel, I will argue that serious consideration of John within the genre of the ancient novel is a worthwhile expenditure of intellectual capital. Under the influence of Mikhail Bakhtin, attention will be given to propensities the Gospel shares with the ancient novel that I catalogue under two headings: a tendency toward innovation through what might best be called Menippean parody and a tendency to represent events in what might be called novelized time.[5]

2. Defining a Genre

As various contributors to this volume have noted, defining genre is no easy matter. Aristotle wrote about the means of representation and the object of representation but not in terms of genre. He defined the essence of tragedy by identifying what he considered to be the best exemplar, Sophocles *Oedipus Tyrannus*. Under the influence of post-modern thought, we no longer take it for granted that genre can be defined in exclusive terms or by one set of necessary devices or ways of combining linguistic elements. As Jean-François Lyotard notes, "a text is always more than a genre allows, and this surplus is incorrigible for no genre can totally saturate all the phrases and the gaps in a text."[6] Marília P. Futre Pinheiro describes modern genre theory as "endowing genre with a non-normative, instrumental, and operative nature."[7] For example, Charles Bazerman calls them "frames for social action," "familiar places we go to create intelligible communicative action …, guide posts we use to explore the familiar."[8] Both John

Editorial Seam" (*JBL* 101 [1982]: 245–49) in which he argues that John is attempting to narrate simultaneous action using a technique also found in Achilles Tatius, *Leuc. Clit.* 2.2.1–2.12.1.

4 Lawrence M. Wills, *Quest of the Historical Gospel: Mark, John and the Origins of the Gospel Genre* (London: Routledge, 1997), 10–11, 24.

5 Ibid., 10–11, 49, 68. Wills distinguishes *Aesop* as satire from the gospels of Mark and John but links the satirical tone in the gospels' miracle stories to comparable patterns of evolution of genre.

6 Jean-François Lyotard, *The Differend: Phrases in Dispute*, trans. G. van den Abeele (Manchester: Manchester University Press, 1988), 94.

7 Marilia P. Futre Pinheiro, "The Genre of the Novel: A Theoretical Approach," in *A Companion to the Ancient Novel*, ed. Edmund P. Cueva and Shannon N. Byrne (London: Routledge, 2014), 202.

8 Charles Bazerman, "The Life of Genre, the Life in the Classroom" in *Genre and Writing: Issues, Arguments, Alternatives*, ed. Wendy Bishop and Hans Ostrom (Portsmouth: Boynton; Cook, 1997), 19.

and the novelists were seeking to create intelligible narratives by borrowing and adapting familiar forms. In doing so, they produced new and closely related forms, not so closely related to label them retrospectively as the same genre, but activating the potential within the literary antecedents from which they drew in similar ways that allow identification of common propensities.

Defining the genre of the novel is a slippery business. One might call the novel an episodic or extended fictional prose narrative until one reads Vikram Seth's *The Golden Gate* (1986), a novel composed from its front matter "Acknowledgements" to the end piece, "About the Author," in sonnets of iambic tetrameter. Mikhail Bakhtin contends that no such thing as a typical novel exists because the novel is still a "genre-in-the-making" with a history that begins with the ancient novels. Bakhtin prefers to describe the novel as not just a genre but as a force that he calls "novelization":

> The novel parodies other genres (precisely in their role as genres); it exposes the conventionality of their forms and their language; it squeezes out some genres and incorporates others into its own peculiar structure, reformulating and re-accentuating them.[9]

This force of "novelization" will inform my analysis, but I will limit my discussion to a small canon of novels all of which are extended prose narratives that tell a fictional story.

In four of the five Greek novels in the "traditional" canon of ancient novels (Chariton's *Chaereas and Callirhoe*, Xenophon of Ephesus' *An Ephesian Tale*, Achilles Tatius' *Leucippe and Clitophon*, and Heliodorus' *An Ethiopian Story*), a boy and girl from the elite class meet, fall in love, sometimes marry at the beginning of the story, are separated by various misfortunes such as shipwrecks and abductions by pirates, remain true to each other in love, reunite, and return home to live happily ever after. The fifth volume in the canon, Longus' *Daphnis and Chloe* differs insofar as the story includes restoration of the lovers' true identities as the children of an elite rather than pastoral class and ends with marriage.[10] The remaining members of the "established" canon are two Latin satirical novels: Petronius' *Satyricon* (the story of the escapades of a former gladiator and his former lover) and Apuleius' *The Golden Ass* (a picaresque novel that tells the story of Lucius a young man whose obsession with magic leads to his

---

9 "Epic and Novel" in *The Dialogic Imagination: Four Essays by M. M. Bakhtin*, ed. Michael Holquist, trans. Caryl Emerson and Michael Holquist (Austin: University of Texas Press, 1981), 5.

10 Parthenius of Nicaea (1st cent. BCE) compiled a collection of thirty-six epitomes of such love stories that he called *Erotica Pathemata* (*The Sorrows of Love*). The Emperor Julian, *Letters* 89.301b (ca. 363 CE), referred to fictions (πλάσματα) in historical guise (ἐν ἱστορίας εἴδει) as love stories that arouse passions (ἐρωτικὰς ὑποθέσεις).

accidental transformation into an ass). Many scholars have stretched this canon to include other Greek narratives such as Lucian's *A True Story* (about a journey to fanciful places) and Pseudo-Callisthenes' *Alexander Romance* (mythical exploits of Alexander the Great), and the *History of Apollonius, King of Tyre* (a hero's flight from persecution leading to marriage to a king's daughter) as well as early Jewish novellas, such as Tobit, Esther, Judith, and *Joseph and Aseneth*, and some early Christian narratives, such as the *Acts of Peter*. For the purpose of this chapter, I will limit my comparisons to the Greek novels. Since none of these novels can be proven to pre-date the Gospel of John, there can be no argument for literary dependence of the Gospel upon the novels; however, some have ventured to make a case for the dependence of the novels upon the gospels.[11]

3. Menippean Tendencies

The ancient novels, like contemporary biography and historiography, quote Homer as their scripture, but they distinguish themselves by a degree of playfulness.[12] Bakhtin goes so far as to say that the path from the epic to the novel passes through Menippean satire.[13] This tendency toward satire or parody manifests itself in very different ways from author to author. Achilles Tatius begins his novel with an ekphrasis of a painting, the abduction of Europa by Zeus, which the author as narrator is studying with pleasure. His diversion is interrupted when Clitophon, inspired by the aesthetic enjoyment of the synthesis of beauty and violence in the painting, tells his story of love and abduction casting Leucippe in the role of Europa.[14] The author continues to move freely from quasi-poetical diction and rhetorical flourishes to a plain style.[15]

11 Ewen Bowie, "Literary Milieux," in *The Cambridge Companion to the Greek and Roman Novel*, ed. Tim Whitmarsh (Cambridge: Cambridge University Press, 2008), 21–32, opens the door to some literary relationship by providing an early date for Chariton based upon comparison with various literary milieu: *Chaereas and Callirhoe* (31 BCE–50CE); *Leucippe and Clitophon* (50–160 CE), *Daphnis and Chloe* (160–220 CE); *An Ethiopian Story* (220–270 CE). The *Ephesian Tale* probably belongs to the mid-second century.

12 Bryan P. Reardon, *The Form of Greek Romance* (Princeton: Princeton University Press, 1995), 15; Massimo Fusillo, "Modern Critical Theories and the Ancient Novel," in *The Novel in the Ancient World*, ed. Gareth L. Schmeling (Leiden: Brill, 1996), 278.

13 Mikhail M. Bakhtin, "From the Prehistory of Novelistic Discourse," in idem, *The Dialogic Imagination*, 41–83 (esp. 60).

14 See Jennifer R. Ballengee, "Below the Belt: Looking into the of Adventure Time," in *The Bakhtin Circle and Ancient Narrative*, ed. Robert Bracht Branham (Groningen: Barkhuis, 2005), 144.

15 Karl Plepelits, "Achilles Tatius," in *The Novel in the Ancient World*, ed. Gareth Schmelling (Leiden: Brill, 1996), 399.

John displays a similar propensity to appropriate genre by maneuvering through humor and gliding from plain to grand prose. Harold W. Attridge aptly describes this blending and adaptation of dialogic discourse, type-scene, forensic discourse and oratory, homiletic midrash, *paroimia*, and consolatory forms as "genre bending."[16] The Gospel's first phrase, "In the beginning," tricks its audience into expecting a reading of Genesis. Wayne Meeks calls Jesus' conversation with Nicodemus a "virtual parody of a revelation discourse."[17] Werner Kelber calls Jesus' writing in the dirt "a parody of formal, literary writing and the permanence that comes with texts and words etched in stone."[18] By dipping bread and giving it to Judas, Jesus seems to parody the Eucharist by providing Satan's presence rather than his own. If John's genre is determined by its capacity to "novelize" other genres, it stands comfortably among the novels.

According to Bakhtin, the novel as a force pushes against both the constraints of previous literary norms as well as social norms. In the Synoptic Gospels, Jesus challenges norms in both his preaching and his actions. Without sermons on the nature of the reign of heaven, John is left with only narrative to capture Jesus' breaches of social propriety. The genre of the novel in this capacity is well suited to John's method. In the encounter with the Samaritan (John 4:1–26), in which many readers have noted the twist upon the woman at the well type-scene found in Genesis 24:10–61, 29:1–20, and Exodus 2:15b–21, Jesus crosses gender and ethnic boundaries.[19] Andrew E. Arterbury moves beyond the idea of the betrothal type-scene to examine the story as a "literary depiction of ancient hospitality" comparing John's appropriation of tropes associated with hospitality in Hebrew Bible and Second Temple Jewish literature to the appropriation of the tropes in hospitality stories from Homer in the ancient Greek novels.[20] His focus is more sociological than literary, but the example that he lifts up from Heliodorus illustrates what Bakhtin calls carnivalesque where in the novels serious aspects of class culture—prohibitions and limitations—give way to an excess of openness.[21] Nausikles, an Athenian, extends to Knemon, an Ethiopian, permanent friendship

16 Harold W. Attridge, "Genre Bending in the Fourth Gospel," *JBL* 121 (2002): 9–10.
17 Wayne Meeks, "The Man from Heaven in Johannine Sectarianism," *JBL* 19 (1972): 57.
18 Werner Kelber, *The Oral and the Written Gospel: The Hermeneutics of Speaking and Writing in the Synoptic Tradition, Mark, Paul, and Q*, 2nd ed. (Philadelphia: Fortress, 1997), 18.
19 E.g., Lyle Eslinger, "The Wooing of the Woman at the Well: Jesus, the Reader and Reader-Response Criticism," *Literature and Theology* 1 (1987): 167–183; reprint in *The Gospel of John as Literature: An Anthology of Twentieth-Century Perspectives*, ed. Mark W. G. Stibbe (Leiden: Brill, 1993) 165–182; Jerome H. Neyrey, "Jacob Traditions and the Interpretation of John 4:10–26," *CBQ* 41 (1979): 419–437.
20 Andrew E. Arterbury, "Breaking the Betrothal Bonds: Hospitality in John 4," *CBQ* 72 (2010): 63–83.
21 Idem, *Rabelais and his World*, trans. Hélène Iswolsky (Bloomington: Indiana University Press, 1984), 283.

by offering him his daughter, Nausiklea, with a magnificent dowry asking nothing in return simply because Knemon told him his story. Nausikles thereby unknowingly fulfills Nausiklea's secret desire for the sort of independence enjoyed by her Ethiopian friends (6.8). John's story also entertains unheard of hospitality and fulfillment of desires.

In a thorough study of the recognition scenes in the Greek tragedies, Homer's epics and the Greek novels, Kasper Bro Larsen constructs a model that he applies to recognition in the Gospel of John.[22] Features of this model that depend upon the novels tend to include more comedic aspects. For example, the topos of the "chase toward the locus of recognition" picked up in John 20 is present in Achilles Tatius (*Leuc. Clit.* 7.15–16) when Clitophon with Sostratos, his uncle and intended father-in–law, races toward Leucippe whom he had believed was dead. Clitophon's description contains elements comparable to the humor of Wile E. Coyote in pursuit of the Road Runner: "I jumped into the air, chains and all, and flew to the temple as if hurled from a catapult" (Achilles Tatius, *Leuc. Clit.* 7.15.3 [Winkler]). Larsen's examination of the action in the Gospel in conjunction with the novels tempers the tendency to view the race to the tomb as an indication of the priority of one disciple or form of discipleship over another giving way to the theme of non-recognition and humor. While John does not reduce episodes to ribald comedy, we can see that he follows the same tendency as the novels by incorporating the elements of disguise, signs and running from the recognition scenes in ways that add dramatic irony to the scenes in chapter 20.

Another aspect of the recognition scene is worth noting at this point, although I cannot fit it into this Menippean pattern. Larsen provides an extensive discussion of the similarity of the emphasis upon signs in both John and Greek literature as central to the act of recognition. The comparison pieces from Homer and the tragedies disappear when he comes to the discussion of the moment of Mary's recognition of Jesus at the sound of his voice speaking her name (20:16a). For this he turns to the novels.[23] As Silvia Montiglio notes, "The exploitation of the voice as the revealing sign of identity in a formal recognition scene seems to be unknown to classical Greek literature."[24] She attributes this avoidance in the tragedies and epics to the desire to prolong the act of recognition by avoiding the instant recognition facilitated by the voice. She attributes the novelists' interest in using the voice to enable recognition to two factors: first, to record vocal nuances and emotional effects, but more importantly, to endow the voice with strong

22 Idem, *Recognizing the Stranger: Recognition Scenes in the Gospel of John*, BIS 93 (Leiden: Brill, 2008), for example, 71, 89, 102, 126, 199, and 212.

23 Idem, *Recognizing the Stranger*, 201. Larsen cites: Chariton, *Chaer.* 8.1.8; Xenophon, *Eph.* 5.10.11; and Achilles Tatius, *Leuc. Clit.* 3.18.1.

24 Eadem, *Love and Providence: Recognition in the Ancient Novel* (Oxford University Press, 2012), 20.

erotic powers.[25] John the Baptist likens the joy that he feels to that of the friend of the bridegroom who rejoices at the bridegroom's voice (3:31). The dead rise at the sound of the Son of Man's voice (5:28; 11:43). The sheep follow the good shepherd because they know his voice (10:4). Mary recognizes the resurrected Jesus when he speaks her name (20:16). The epistemology of the Gospel of John is a topic to which scholars repeatedly turn, and the novels provide near contemporary narratives in which to examine this shift from sight to sound or voice (see John 6:30, 47; 12:44–50).

A significant and growing trend in Johannine scholarship is to turn to Greco-Roman rhetoric to understand the discourses as well as characterization in the Gospel of John. The aspect of rhetoric to which this study attends, once more borrowing language from Bakhtin, is the construction of the "speaking person" that is central to the novel.[26] One of the most noted aspects of the use of the arts of rhetoric in the novels is how it appears on the lips of characters not assumed to be educated. In Chariton's novel, first Chaereas mistakenly assumes that Callirhoe is dead; when he learns otherwise, he pursues her pirate captors, and when his ship sinks, Callirhoe assumes that he is dead. Her lament (Chariton, *Chaer.* 3.10.4–8) —an overstated echo of Andromache's lament of Hector in the *Iliad* (Homer, *Il.* 22.477–514; 24.725–745)—is filled with devices such as asyndeta, arrangement of word order so that the most forceful word falls at the end of the sentence (3.10.4 and 6), and successive pairs of verbs, one positive, the other negative (3.10.6) that lend force to brevity.[27] Konstantin Doulamis suggests what is significant in a speech like this is "Chariton's ability to balance pathos and irony by injecting a light ironic twist into scenes which would otherwise be taken as serious."[28] We can see a similar infusion of rhetorical sophistication in the speech of the formerly blind man that tempers the gravity of the action with a form of humor. The Pharisees' questions, designed to force the man to denounce Jesus, instead provoke him to speak with forceful rhetoric by using asyndeta (9:25), rhetorical question (9:27), exclamatio (9:30) and irrefutable logic that Jesus is a godly man (9:33). Among other things, the eloquence of the blind man portrays the lowly beggar besting the educated elite at their own game, leaving them recourse only to violence.

Saundra Schwartz sees the frequency of trials, both formal and informal, in the novel as feeding the hunger of their audiences for forensic rhetoric and legal

25 Ibid., 27–28.

26 Mikhail M. Bakhtin, "Discourse in the Novel," in idem, *The Dialogic Imagination*, 332–33.

27 Konstantin Doulamis, "Rhetoric and Irony in Chariton: A Case Study from *Callirhoe*," *Ancient Narrative* 1 (2000–2001): 61–62.

28 Ibid., 69.

complexities.[29] In the novels, rather than serving their ideal purpose by restoring order and vindicating the innocent, the procedures of the trials subvert a just ending and are aborted leaving order to be restored by a battle or through supernatural agency.[30] In her conclusion, she sets the playful construction of the novels' trials within a context in which people frequently find themselves subject to overlapping legal systems. The audience of the Gospel may have shared a similar appetite and context for appreciating the series of inquisitions culminating in Jesus' appearance before Pilate in which John highlights the tensions between official power and divine authority. Unlike the debates in the Synoptics about purity, divorce, and how to keep the Sabbath, John's arguments revolve around the rules of evidence and prosecution. Jesus contends that he fulfills the law of testimony (5:31) and that his accusers fail to receive testimony (5:41–47). He describes the Paraclete as a legal defender who will refute the arguments of the disciples' accusers (16:8–11). The scene in the praetorium returns repeatedly to Pilate's conclusion that he cannot find a charge to lay upon Jesus (18:38b; 19:4; 19:6) until the priests move from evading naming an offence (18:31) to citing a violation of Jewish law (19:27) and finally to offering an offence against Rome (19:12b). Before Pilate renders his verdict, Jesus' accusers become the ones who violate the core defining confession of their covenant with God (19:15). The novelists relish similar unfolding of legal technicalities and ironic reversals of guilt. Mithradites, accused of designing to seduce Dionysius' illegitimate wife Callirhoe, defends himself by questioning whether Dionysius is entitled to bring the charge if he cannot prove himself to be her legitimate husband (Chariton, *Chaer.* 5.6). To do so, Dionysius must sidestep the fact that he purchased Callirhoe as a slave and prove that Chaereas, Callirhoe's first and real husband, is indeed dead. Dionysius contends, "[W]hen Mithridates wants to commit adultery, he resuscitates the dead!" (Chariton, *Chaer.* 5.7.3–4 [Reardon]). Mithridates then argues that even if he were guilty of attempting to seduce her and even if Dionysius were her legal husband, he would raise a legal objection on the basis that no act of adultery took place (Chariton, *Chaer.* 5.7). In Heliodorus' novel, Charikleia interrupts her sacrifice claiming the right to lay a case before Sisimithres, the Ethiopian Ambassador in Egypt. Hydaspes, her father, who exposed her at birth and does not recognize her, argues against the legality first of a captive woman and then of a foreigner to bring a case (Heliodorus, *Aeth.* 10.10). When Charikleia identifies herself as a member of the royal house of Ethiopia, Hydaspes' daughter and Sisimithres' kin, Hydaspes counters that the girl is insane and tells lies (10.12). Charikleia then argues another point of law: "The law

29 Saundra Schwartz, "Clitophon the Moichos: Achilles Tatius and the Trial Scene in the Greek Novel," *Ancient Narrative* 1 (2000–2001): 94.
30 Ibid., 97.

may permit you, sire, to kill aliens, but neither law nor nature allows you, Father, to murder your own child!" (10.12 [Morgan]). Once again, we see a common impulse in gospel and novel to exploit rhetoric and legal complexities and employ irony in the representation of fidelity and love as heroic virtues. Through parody and by rewriting the rules of convention, the novels replace the Homeric heroes with ordinary citizens and the Gospel, with a crucified Messiah.

Significant research has been done on Christian storytelling from the second and third century and its close relationship to the novel at the forefront of which stands Judith Perkins' *Suffering Self: Pain and Narrative Representation in the Early Christian Era.*[31] In both the novels and these Christian narratives, enduring love for which one suffers becomes a heroic act. Central to the contentions of the Gospel of John stands Jesus' assertion that his death is the consummation of his joy (15:9–13): death becomes a happy ending. While multiple cultural forces are at work in this transformation of vulnerability to love and suffering into heroism, the creativity of the Gospel's author allows the transgression of boundaries and reinterpretation of reality critical to this development, an artistic sensibility shared with authors of the novels.

4. Novelized Time

The Gospel's fabula, the life of Jesus, leads many scholars to categorize the Gospel as a biography. Alicia Myers, in her discussion of the character of the narrator, makes a salient point in response to Charles Hedrick's contention that the narrator of the Gospel of John is comparable to that of Achilles Tatius:

> [W]hile Tatius may seek to craft 'believable' characters, he can create any ending he should so choose for them since they are fictional. The Fourth Evangelist, however, does not have that same freedom. Instead, for his *bios* to be persuasive, it must align with facts already known about the historical person of Jesus.[32]

If one describes the plot of the Gospel of John as beginning with origins, proceeding through a public life and ending with death, it looks very much like an ancient biography but this is a description of chronology not plot. Aspects of the Gospel's emplotment of events, subjective experience of time, layers of time, and

31 Judith Perkins, *Suffering Self: Pain and Narrative Representation in the Early Christian Era* (London: Routledge, 1995).

32 Eadem, *Characterizing Jesus: A Rhetorical Analysis on the Fourth Gospel's Use of Scripture in its Presentation of Jesus*, LNTS 458 (London: T&T Clark, 2012), 26 citing Charles W. Hedrick, "Authorial Presence and Narrator in John," in *Gospel Origins and Christian Beginnings*, ed. James E. Goehring et al. (Sonoma: Polebridge Press, 1990), 77–81.

unfolding present, push the description closer to that of the novel.[33] The novel is different from the biography, not because it is about a fictional person—the *Alexander Romance* proves this not to be true—but because it is freed from the tempo of historical time, the retrospective narrative of a life ended, a story already complete, to the time of experience, to the passage of time moving forward that is individual rather than historical.

If we consider the subjective experiences of the characters, the plot of the Gospel can be described as curiously similar to that of the ancient novels under consideration. In the novels, the ordeals through which the hero and heroine pass test their faith in each other and reaffirm their love. Current scholarship on the novels will not allow the distinction that the bios is a didactic work providing its audience with a model to imitate, while the novel serves to entertain. Although many readers of novels do seek pleasure from the novel, the description of that experience might better be characterized as an opportunity to inhabit an interpreted world, not the "raw" life we experience, where one can gain access to personal experiences that one might not have or might not want to have.[34] The novels encourage their readers to consider love as the basis for an enduring union between man and wife and to value the chastity of both wife and husband.[35] John's Gospel is also a story of love and fidelity. The disciples are first drawn to Jesus by appearances (2:11), their faith is challenged (6:60; 18:25–27) but in the end they reaffirm their love (21:15–17). Jesus, through his ordeal, proves his love for his loved ones. The Gospel's narrative attests to the values that Jesus and the narrator explicitly teach, abiding in love (John 15:4–10) and fidelity in the relationship to Jesus (20:31). This similarity of plot is not determined by genre, but it does invite the question of whether the way that time works in the novels and the gospels is inextricably linked to their ideals.

In the Gospel, competing understandings of time are central to the action and retrospective narratives invite the audience to relate to particular character's experiences. Jesus repeatedly makes statements like "My time has not yet come, but your time is always here … go to the festival yourself. I am not going to this

33 Philostratus' *Apollonius of Tyana* and the anonymous *Life of Aesop* could be cited as examples of biographies that refute this contention, but the former is a parody of the life of Pythagoras (and perhaps also Jesus' story) placing its status as a biography in doubt (see Tim Whitmarsh, "Philostratus," in *Time in Ancient Greek Literature*, ed. Irene J.F. de Jong and René Nünlist, Literature Studies in Ancient Greek Narrative 2 [Leiden: Brill, 2007], 413) and many classify the later as a type of novel (see Francisco R. Adrados, "The 'Life of Aesop' and the Origins of the Novel in Antiquity," *Quaderni urbinati di cultura classica* 1 [1979]: 93).

34 Martha Nussbaum, *Love's Knowledge: Essays on Philosophy and Literature* (London: Oxford University Press, 1992), 47–48.

35 See David Konstan and Ilaria Rameli, "The Novel and Christian Narrative," in *A Companion to the Ancient Novel*, ed. Edmund P. Cueva and Shannon N. Byrne (London: Routledge, 2014), 185.

festival for my time has not yet fully come" that refer to time as he experiences it (7:6; see also 7:33, 8:38; 9:4–5; 16:31–33). Characters in the novels, reflecting upon their experience of time, distinguish between the time that they must endure and a freedom from time's tyranny. Anthia laments the imminent death of Habrocomes:

> I am being taken away to Syria as a gift for Manto; soon I will be in the hands of the girl who envies me. But you are still in prison and dying miserably, with no one even to lay out your corpse. But I swear by our mutual guardian angel that I will still be yours as long as I live, and even if I have to die (Xenophon of Ephesus, *Ephes.* 2.7.4–5 [Anderson]).

While Jesus and Anthia are subject to the passage of time, both express a freedom from the limits of time. Bakhtin calls this psychological language with its "subjective palpability and duration" one of the novel's more original contributions insofar as it creates layers of time.[36] The love of the protagonists dwells in a leisurely moment of introspection, delay and repeated discourse, juxtaposed with the unrelenting forward progression of the narrative with its urgency and unpredictability, and played against the normal time of daily life from waiting at pools to be healed and begging by the side of the road to weddings and festivals.[37] Such layering constitutes the complexity of Johannine time that combines the urgency of eschatological fulfillment with the cycle of annual festivals and stretches of narrative and discourse with the pace of lived time.

In the novels, the personal experience of time is not linked to a historical chronology. Luke's Gospel is explicitly anchored in the history of the church as told in Acts. The commission to make disciples of all nations with which Matthew ends easily fits that gospel into the same history. John's Gospel strains to fit into the same history; its chronology of events in Jesus' ministry differs. John's Gospel moves at its own pace set by the movement of the sun (e.g., John 1:29, 35, 43; 2:1, 4; 4:6, 21–22, 40, 43, 52). The synchronization of Johannine time with the Jewish Sabbath and festivals gives it more concrete substance than what we find in the novels but it is similarly self-contained. The form of time in the Gospel, in part, supports a hypothesis that the Gospel was the property of a self-contained community whose story is untold by historians. The jump to the sectarian hypothesis may be begging the question of whether the evidence used to reconstruct

36 Mikhail M. Bakhtin, "The *Bildungsroman* and Its Significance in the History of Realism (Toward a Historical Typology of the Novel)" in *Speech Genres and Other Late Essays*, ed. Caryl Emerson and Michael Holquist, trans. Vern W. McGee (Austin: University of Texas Press, 1990), 15.

37 See Lawrence Kim, "Time," in *The Cambridge Companion to the Greek and Roman Novel*, ed. Tim Whitmarsh (Cambridge: Cambridge University Press, 2008), 157.

a historical context might be a feature of the literary form that John adopts to tell his story of Jesus.

Mikhail Bakhtin observes that the novel inserts into other genres "an indeterminacy, a certain semantic openendedness, a living contact with unfinished, still-evolving contemporary reality (the openended present)."[38] John adopts vivid language transforming a past event into an event unfolding before the reader's eyes. For example, his use of the historical present in the episodes at the Samaritan well (4:5–29), the footwashing (13:1–10) and Mary's discovery of the empty tomb (20:1–2) gives the impression that one is watching the action.[39] Heliodorus and Xenophon use the historical present with comparable effect providing immediacy and variations in pace (e.g. Heliodorus, *Aeth.* 4.4, Xenophon of Ephesus, *Ephes.* 3.9). A more thorough examination of the vivid quality of both novels and gospel might be warranted.

5. Conclusion

As Lawrence Wills notes at the beginning of his volume on the genre of John and Mark, modern readers are comfortable in thinking that the gospel is a genre.[40] Thinking of John's Gospel as a novel makes those who read it for devotional purposes extremely uncomfortable. For the academic reader, such discomfort may be an extremely useful reaction given that he or she seeks a heightened perception of the variations in the literary surface of the Gospel that point to patterns of significance. Johannine parody and complex representation of time comes into sharper relief when read in the company of the novel. Studying John among the ancient novels may in the end lead the examiner back to the conclusion that John stands more comfortably among the biographies but with a consciousness of the force of "novelization" apparent in its playful appropriation of various genres and its representation of time as a subjective experience.

38 Bakhtin, "Epic and Novel," 7.

39 Any discussion of the historic present in John should begin with Mavis M. Leung, "The Narrative Function and Verbal Aspect of the Historical Present in the Fourth Gospel," *JETS* 51 (2008): 703–20.

40 Wills, *Quest of the Historical Gospel*, 1.

Part III: Tiles in the Mosaic

Ruth Sheridan

John's Prologue as Exegetical Narrative

1. Introduction

In 1990 John Pryor asserted that debates about the prologue to John's Gospel (John 1:1–18) "seem to be never-ending."[1] Almost fifteen years later scholarly debates about John's prologue have only continued to proliferate. While Pryor isolated two features intrinsic to these debates—namely, the prologue's prehistory and its exegesis, as points of contention—one observes today a handful of issues routinely discussed in the scholarship over which there reigns little consensus. These issues are interrelated, and include: (a) the prologue's internal structure and style; (b) its possible *Sitz im Leben* in the so-called "Johannine community"; (c) the derivation of the term λόγος in its opening verses; and (d) its appropriate form or genre.

The interrelationship of these issues is evident in the scholarly tendency to assess the prologue's genre on the basis of judgments made about the first three of these points. For example, discussion of the literary influences upon John's λόγος concept often implies a one-to-one correspondence between the genre of those influences and the genre of the prologue.[2] Discussion of the possible *Sitz im*

1 John Pryor, "Jesus and Israel in the Fourth Gospel: John 1:11," *NovT* 32 (1990): 201. Another opening quip by a scholar lamenting the ability of anyone to say something new about the prologue of the Gospel can be found in R. Alan Culpepper, "The Pivot of John's Prologue," *NTS* 27 (1981): 1.

2 The literature on the "Logos" in the prologue is prohibitively extensive. General overviews of the manifold possibilities of literary "influences" can be found in Ed L. Miller, *Salvation-History in the Prologue of John: The Significance of John 1:3–4*, NovTSup 60 (Leiden: Brill, 1989). Claims range on either side of a (regrettably persistent) dichotomy: a Hellenistic (speculatively philosophical) Logos (see Henrik Pontoppidan Thyssen, "Philosophical Christology in the New Testament," *Numen* 53 (2006): 133–176) and a biblically "Jewish" Logos: (see Craig A. Evans, *Word and Glory: On the Exegetical and Theological Background of John's Prologue*, JSNTSup 89 [Sheffield: JSOT Press, 1993]; John Ashton, "The Transformation of Wisdom: A Study of the Prologue of John's Gospel," *NTS* 32 [1986]: 161–186). But the dichotomy is not exclusive; see e.g., Calum M. Carmicheal, *The Story of Creation: Its Origin and Interpretation in Philo and the Fourth Gospel* (Ithaca: Cornell University Press, 1996). Ne-

Leben of the prologue naturally carries generic assumptions with it: commonly, that the prologue is/was a "Logos-hymn" arising out of a cultic setting in the early church.[3] Finally, discussion of the prologue's stylistic, structural and rhetorical features relate to how its genre is understood.[4]

A minority of scholars has critiqued the notion that John's prologue is generically a hymn; they argue instead that the prologue is an expositional narrative akin to the Targumim.[5] Following this recent scholarly turn, this article will examine the narratival dimensions of the Gospel's prologue, arguing that the prologue presents itself as an "exegetical narrative" of Genesis and Exodus. John's prologue encourages a dialogic mode of reading that retells the biblical story of creation and revelation via a thoroughgoing Christocentric lens. Ap-

vertheless the supposed derivation of the "Logos" concept does determine which genres these scholars are willing to assign the prologue, and further discussion of this will follow below. Recently, some scholars have rejected all non-Johannine antecedents for the Logos concept, insisting on the Gospel itself as a source text: Ed L. Miller, "The Johannine Origins of the Johannine Logos," *JBL* 112 (1993): 445–457; Sean McDonough, *Christ as Creator: Origins of a New Testament Doctrine* (Oxford: Oxford University Press, 2010), 212–233.

3 Originally, see Rudolf Bultmann, *Das Evangelium des Johannes* (Göttingen, 1941), 1–5 (Eng. Trans.: idem, *The Gospel of John: A Commentary*, trans. G. R. Beasley-Murray et al. [Oxford: Blackwell, 1971], 13–14); followed by R. Schnackenburg, "Logos-hymnus und johanneischer Prolog," *BZ* 1 (1957): 69–109; Jürgen Becker, *Das Evangelium nach Johannes* (Gütersloh: Mohn, 1979), 1:67; Gérard Rochais, "La Formation du Prologue (Jn. 1:1–18)," *SE* 37 (1985): 7–9; Chr. Demke, "Der sogenannte Logos-Hymnus im Johannes-Prolog," *ZNW* 58 (1967): 45–68. I discuss the specific "Wisdom"-hymnic parallels in more depth in the essay below.

4 Particularly the prologue's versification, coupled with its rhetorical feature of "introducing" or prefacing the Gospel text, has led numerous scholars to refer to John 1:1–18 as an "overture" or "curtain-raiser", sometimes considered akin to the "hypotheses" in Greek drama. See Bultmann, *The Gospel of John*, 13; Barnabas Lindars, *The Gospel of John*, NCB (London: Oliphants, 1972), 81; George Beasley-Murray, *John*, WBC 36 (Waco: Word Books, 1987), 5; Mark Stibbe, *John* (Sheffield: Sheffield Academic Press, 1994), 22; F. F. Bruce, *The Gospel of John* (Grand Rapids: Eerdmans, 1994), 28. For the prologue as a "foyer" to the Gospel see Donald A. Carson, *The Gospel According to John* (Grand Rapids: Eerdmans, 1991), 111; for the prologue as a "preamble" see C. H. Dodd, *The Interpretation of the Fourth Gospel* (Cambridge: Cambridge University Press, 1953). Of course, it would be remiss to refrain from noting that the scholarly designation "prologue" is itself redolent with generic signification: the Greek verb προλέγειν means "to announce beforehand"; see Elizabeth Harris, *Prologue and Gospel: The Theology of the Fourth Evangelist*, JSNTSup 107, (Sheffield: Sheffield Academic Press, 1994), 12. The adopted designator "prologue" goes back, presumably, to Jerome: see John McHugh, *John 1–4*, ICC (London: T & T Clark, 2009), 5. Dissenting from the view of the prologue as a preface or overture are two notable scholars: Rudolf Schnackenburg, *The Gospel According to St. John*, trans. K. Smyth et al. (London: Burns & Oates, 1968), 1:221, and Ernst Käsemann, "The Structure and Purpose of the Prologue to John's Gospel," in idem, *New Testament Questions of Today* (London: SCM, 1968). The provisional, or analogical, status of the term "overture" is evident at least in that it describes the rhetorical features of the prologue—but thematic elements of the prologue induce other generic assessments (such as "hymn"; see n. 3 above, and discussion below).

5 The work of these scholars will be discussed in detail in the following sections of this essay.

proaching the prologue, the reader is invited to effectively hold two tales together —the biblical and the kerygmatic—and to weave together an integrated narrative by means of John's exegetical "play." I will lead into this by previewing the scholarly literature about the prologue's genre. After that, I will introduce the theoretical work of Joshua Levinson who has analyzed the aggadic midrashim as examples of the "exegetical narrative." Finally, I will turn to a close reading of John's prologue in this light, and draw some conclusions about the social function of the prologue's genre.

2. The Prologue as a Hymn: Developments and Critiques

Stylistically the text of John 1:1–18 differs from the rest of the Gospel (John 1:19–20:31). It is perhaps, most of all, the singular style of the prologue that has affected its generic assignation as a "hymn." The main debate relevant to this point has been whether the prologue's style constitutes "prose" or "poetry." The adjective "poetic" does tend to surface repeatedly in discussions of the prologue, inclining scholars to interpret the text as a poem-like hymn, with a distinct strophic arrangement. Thematic features also factor into this debate. The subject matter of the prologue is "elevated," dealing with mythic themes: the pre-existent Word (1:1–2), his appearance in, and rejection by the world (1:10–11), his incarnation (1:14), his unique status as the "only-begotten" of God (1:18), and so on. Those who classify the prologue's language and style as "poetic" duly ascribe to the text the genre of a "Logos-hymn."[6] The prologue (or its reconstructed hymnic predecessor) is, in this view, a hymn *about* Jesus-the-Logos, and a hymn *to* Jesus-the-Logos. As such, it is thought to correspond to other Christological hymns found in the New Testament (cf. Col. 1:15–20; Phil. 2:6–11; 1 Tim 3:16b–c; Heb 1:1–4).

Scholars perceive thematic parallels between John's prologue and Jewish wisdom hymnody, both biblical and apocryphal (cf. Prov. 8:1–36; Job 28:12–28; Sir 24:1–34; Bar 3:9–4:4; Wis 7:22–10:21). John's Logos is thought to be an adaptation of the quasi-hypostasized feminine figure called "Wisdom" (Σοφία), who is depicted as always present with God in the work of creation, or in other texts, seeking a home among the dwellers of the earth. John Ashton has argued that the prologue offers a meditation on the theme of Wisdom articulated as the conscious design of God, now functioning, in John's text, as a hymn to the victory of the incarnate Word.[7] On his reading, the once remote "plan" or "Wisdom" of

6 Schnackenburg, *The Gospel According to St. John*, 225.
7 John Ashton, "The Transformation of Wisdom: A Study of the Prologue of John's Gospel," *NTS* 32 (1986): 179.

God arrives at greater precision and accessibility as the fullness of revelation occurs in the incarnation.[8]

This identification of John's Logos with the figure of Wisdom in Hellenistic Jewish texts is a compelling thesis in the secondary literature.[9] A difference in the gender of the respective nouns denoting the Wisdom figures (Σοφία/Λόγος) has not deterred scholars from propounding this view. In a recent article, Matthew Gordley has forcefully reasserted the thesis that John's prologue obeys the conventions of the Wisdom-hymn genre of antiquity. But Gordley specifies the *didactic* hymn as the exact subspecies of genre to which John's prologue belongs.[10] Didactic hymnody is a subgenre, embedded in other primary genres, such as in the Psalms (cf. Pss 34:11; 78:1), the hymns and prayers at Qumran (4Q381 frag. 1, line 1 and 1QH[a] IX, 33–35) and other prophetic and wisdom texts (Isa 42:10–17; Prov 8:22–31; Sir 24:1–22).[11]

The one text that supremely exemplifies the standard features of the "didactic hymn" is, according to Gordley, Wisdom of Solomon 10. This apocryphal text contains a sweeping "review of history" that is brought within the parameters of a didactic purpose, with the figure of Wisdom acting as a saving power.[12] Gordley claims that John's prologue, as a didactic hymn, aims to present history in such a way that it speaks afresh to "situations facing the people of God in the present."[13] John's prologue is at once a "hymn" to the Logos, but more importantly, an historical review propounding the activity of the Word in the world. As a non-liturgical hymn combining all the standard *topoi* of ancient didactics, John's prologue was composed to address the Johannine community in their situation of crisis, as they struggled to hold onto belief in the incarnate Word.[14] Primarily in response to an earlier article by Daniel Boyarin (with which I will engage below), Gordley argues that not all hymns are liturgical, and that texts like Wis 10 and the Johannine prologue can blend hymnic style with narrative elements (i.e., a backward-looking historical review for instructional purposes in the present).

Gordley's reassertion of the validity of the hymn genre for categorizing John's prologue indicates that the "hymn-hypothesis" has had its share of detractors.[15]

8 Ashton, "The Transformation of Wisdom," 173.

9 Cf. Catherine Cory, "Wisdom's Rescue: A New Reading of the Tabernacles Discourse (John 7:1–8:59)," *JBL* 116 (1997): 95–116.

10 Matthew Gordley, "The Johannine Prologue and Jewish Didactic Hymn Traditions: A New Case for Reading the Prologue as a Hymn," *JBL* 128 (2009): 781–802.

11 Gordley, "The Johannine Prologue," 783.

12 Gordley, "The Johannine Prologue," 783.

13 Gordley, "The Johannine Prologue," 785–786.

14 Gordley, "The Johannine Prologue," 796.

15 Earlier critiques of the "hymn-hypothesis" include: C. K. Barrett, *The Gospel according to St John*, 2nd ed. (London: SPCK, 1978), 126–127, who calls it a "prose introduction"; F. F. Bruce, *The Gospel of John: Introduction, Exposition, Notes* (Grand Rapids: Eerdmans, 1994), 28; and

Boyarin's aforementioned article, to which Gordley responds, offers one such pointed critique.[16] Boyarin argues that the ostensible thematic parallels between the prologue and Jewish wisdom texts—which he does not dispute—have too frequently led scholars to the erroneous conclusion that the genre of the Johannine prologue is therefore also a (Wisdom) hymn.[17] On formal grounds, Boyarin finds this identification inaccurate: The Wisdom texts are "mostly in the first person and represent the speech of personified Wisdom herself or the object of her instruction."[18] Thus, Boyarin states, "the Wisdom aretalogy is indeed" the prologue's "theme, but not its *Gattung*."[19]

This distinction between the thematic core of the prologue and its genre is vital for Boyarin's argument. The main thematic feature of the prologue remains in place, i. e., the presentation of the Logos and his descent into history; but Boyarin invites us to read this theme in concert with the prologue's prosaic (rather than poetic) stylistic medium, and consequently, to interpret the prologue not as a hymn but as a kind of midrashic narrative. Boyarin is looking for, in his words, "an alternative form-critical proposal" that accepts the connections between the Wisdom hymns and the prologue without assuming a formal identity between them.[20] And along the lines of form criticism, Boyarin does propose an alternative *Sitz im Leben* for the Prologue: that of a "homiletical or preaching situation [derived from a synagogue setting], and not one of praise or adoration [i. e., to Jesus]." For Boyarin, the prologue is "a homiletic retelling of the beginning of Genesis, and therefore interpretative and narratival in its genre and not hymnic and cyclical, that is, liturgical."[21]

Such synagogue homilies would take a Torah text as its basis and extrapolate from it a network of (explicit or implicit) intertextual ideas woven from secondary texts in the Prophets or the Writings. These secondary texts were used to fill in and interpret the Torah text.[22] On this model, John's prologue would be using Genesis 1:1–5 as the primary Torah text (cf. John 1:1–5), and the "text that lies in the background as hermeneutic intertext is Prov 8:22–31," which is extrapolated in John 1:7–13.[23] Accordingly, Boyarin finds that John 1:1–13 "fits" the "form" of

---

C. H. Dodd, *Interpretation*, 272. See also C. H. Giblin, "Two Complementary Literary Structures in John 1:1–18," *JBL* 104 (1985): 87–103.

16 Daniel Boyarin, "The Gospel of the *Memra:* Jewish Binitarianism and the Prologue to John," *HTR* 94 (2001): 243–84.

17 Boyarin, "The Gospel of the *Memra*," 262.

18 Boyarin, "The Gospel of the *Memra*," 266.

19 Boyarin, "The Gospel of the *Memra*," 266.

20 Boyarin, "The Gospel of the *Memra*," 266.

21 Boyarin, "The Gospel of the *Memra*," 264.

22 Boyarin, "The Gospel of the *Memra*," 268–269.

23 Boyarin, "The Gospel of the *Memra*," 269.

the midrashic homily "almost perfectly."[24] This midrashic form was encapsulated particularly in an extant Targumic fragment called "On the Four Nights" (Tg. Neof. at Exod 3:12–14).[25]

The Targum fragment makes the *Memra* (the Aramaic for "Name," which Boyarin reads as an hypostasized figure) responsible for light and illumination in creation, conflating aspects of the creation account in Genesis with a comment on the saving power of the Memra/Name of God at the revelation to Moses in Exodus 3. Boyarin claims that the author of the Johannine prologue probably heard this poetic homily read in the synagogue and emulated its form.[26] The homily draws into its topic discussions of events in biblical history, such as when the divine name was revealed to Abraham, and on which of the "Four Nights" this took place. In like manner, the opening verses of John's prologue expound upon Genesis 1:1–5 and also substitute God's "speaking" in Gen 1:1–3 with a nominal term (the *Logos*). The Targums, moreover, invest the Memra with divine-like attributes, leading Boyarin to conclude that the *Memra* was thought of as a *deuteros theos*, not a "mere" divine title. John's (binitarian) Logos figure was derived from this tradition, and his prologue imitated the midrashic form of the Targums.

According to Boyarin's reading, then, John 1:1–15 offers a midrash on the first days of creation, relying on Gen 1:1–5 for its "controlling discourse"—but then this is

> ...elaborated into an extended narrative via the application to it, as a virtual hermeneutical key, of the well-established myth of Wisdom's frustration in her desire (and God's) that she find a home in the world, a frustration for which a new cure will be offered: God's extraordinary Incarnation of his son, the Logos.[27]

In Boyarin's view, vv. 7–13 of the prologue constitute "the specifically Johannine version" of that myth.[28] What is specific about vv. 7–13 is that these verses do not tell the story of *Jesus'* failure to be received in the narrative of his (incarnate) lifetime as detailed by the Gospel; rather, they narrate the rejection of the *Logos*

24 Boyarin, "The Gospel of the *Memra*," 268.

25 From Michael L. Klein, ed. and trans., *The Fragment-Targums of the Pentateuch according to Their Extant Sources*, AnBib (Rome: Biblical Institute Press, 1980), 2:47; cited in Boyarin, "The Gospel of the *Memra*," 259. Such connections or correspondences were earlier noted by Martin McNamara, "Logos of the Fourth Gospel and *Memra* of the Palestinian Targum: Ex 12:42," *ExpTim* 79 (1986) 115–117.

26 Boyarin, "The Gospel of the *Memra*," 259–260. Independently, Nicola Denzy has argued that the divine word/name motif operated in several Gnostic texts combining a midrash on Genesis; see Nicola Frances Denzey, "Genesis Traditions in Conflict? The Use of Some Exegetical Traditions in the *Trimorphic Protennoia* and the Johannine Prologue", *VC* 55 (2001): 20–44._

27 Boyarin, "The Gospel of the *Memra*," 271.

28 Boyarin, "The Gospel of the *Memra*," 274.

Asarkos, the pre-incarnate Word, or Wisdom, of God.[29] It is the appearance of the *Logos Ensarkos* (in v. 14) that provides the prologue's unique intuition and turning point: the Word was made flesh in order to attenuate this pattern of rejection and to effect the acceptance of God's Word/Wisdom among his people. The incarnation is presented as a "remedy"—as a necessary divine move to "save the many."[30]

In sum, on Boyarin's reading, John's prologue evinces a chronological *narrative* trajectory in a tripartite structure: it begins with a midrash on Genesis (in John 1:1–5) and follows (vv. 7–13) with an embedded narrative about the *Logos Asarkos.* The two texts about John the Baptist (vv. 6, 15) bracket this embedded narrative. The final part of the prologue is a "Christological conclusion" (vv. 16–18). It hints at the insufficiency of the revelation of the Torah, and the necessity of the *Logos Ensarkos* for the reception of the divine wisdom to be fully effectuated ("the law was given through Moses").[31] The *Logos Asarkos* came in the form of the Torah, but was not satisfactorily received; he appears now as the Logos incarnate in Jesus.

At this point, I will raise two points at which I differ from Boyarin, before further developing his fascinating insight that John's prologue can be read as the kind of "heightened narrative prose" we find in the Targumic forms of midrash.[32] First, for Boyarin to uphold his tripartite structural division of the prologue (and his concomitant assessment of the prologue's genre), he repeatedly insists that the "wisdom" motif operative in vv. 7–13 does not comment at all on the narrative of John's Gospel, i. e., that it does not proleptically allude to the rejection experienced by Jesus in his public ministry. As such, the prologue does not have a "recursive" structure, repeatedly referring to the same set of themes. Neither does it allude, even obliquely, to the incarnation before v. 14. However, I think that the incarnation *is* anticipated before v. 14 and that it is still possible to assert this and accept that the prologue is "narratival."[33]

The second point feeds into the first: If vv. 7–13 speak of the *Logos Asarkos*, and if the incarnation is only mentioned in v. 14 as a unique remedy for human obtuseness—as a more effective "teaching" method—then we are led to assess, in "narrative-empirical" terms, the degree to which the "remedy" of the incarnation was successful. The answer to that will then reflect back on the question of whether John means to present the incarnation in "remedial" terms at all. The Gospel shows us that the incarnation was not a spectacularly successful "remedy"

29 Boyarin, "The Gospel of the *Memra*," 273.

30 Boyarin, "The Gospel of the *Memra*," 279.

31 Cf. Boyarin, "The Gospel of the *Memra*," 279.

32 Cf. Boyarin, "The Gospel of the *Memra*," 279.

33 Similarly, see Peder Borgen, "Observations on the Targumic Character of the Prologue of John," *NTS* 16 (1969/70): 288–295. This will be developed in more detail below.

in this respect: The *Logos Ensarkos* was rejected by many of "the Jews," and came into conflict with many more of the authorities (cf. 2:13–20; 5:9b–18; 6:41–59; 7:1, 15–24, 32–36, 45–52; 8:12–26, 31–59; 9:13–41; 10:22–39; 11:45–57), whereas some accepted him and believed in his name (cf. 2:21–22; 4:28–30; 9:35–38; 11:27). But on the whole, Jesus faced the hatred of a dark world (15:18–19) and his life ended in betrayal and crucifixion (cf. 13:21–27; 18:40; 19:1–37). The resurrection appearances are selective (20:1–29); the universality of the *Logos Ensarkos*' revelation is an open question by the end of the Gospel, contingent for its success on the ongoing witness of the disciples and the Paraclete (15:26–27). In this light, I think vv. 7–13 of the prologue may well comment on the Gospel story rather than function exclusively as a "backstory" to it.[34]

This is not to deny Boyarin's astute observation that the prologue is a kind of exegetical narrative. But as an exegetical narrative, it looks both backward (to the biblical texts it exegetes) *and* forward (to the subsequent narrative of Jesus in the Gospel). It merges two narrative worlds, and oscillates between them. The literary achievement of the prologue is in making these worlds cohere so well.[35] In the following section I will introduce and develop Joshua Levinson's theoretical concept of the "exegetical narrative" before returning to assess the Johannine prologue in its light.

3. Theorizing the "Exegetical Narrative"

I take the term "exegetical narrative" from the recent, groundbreaking work of Joshua Levinson on the rabbinic midrashim.[36] Levinson finds a distinct genre present in, primarily, but not exclusively, the later (aggadic) midrashim, which he calls the "exegetical narrative"—a genre which was produced by, and which produces, a dialogic way of reading. The exegetical narrative is distinct for its "synergy of narrative and exegesis": "as exegesis, it creates new meanings from the biblical verses, and as narrative it represents those meanings by means of the biblical world."[37] As exegesis, the exegetical narrative "is subservient to the

34 Boyarin disputes Raymond E. Brown's position (*The Gospel according to John*, Anchor Bible 29a [New York: Doubleday, 1966], 29) that this notion of becoming "children of God" is consequent upon the incarnation and can only happen after it, at least in the evangelist's mind. In my view, Brown's position is considerably less counterintuitive than Boyarin's on this point.

35 Cf. Borgen: "it is … difficult to avoid the conclusion that not only v. 14 but also vv. 9 and 11 refer to the incarnation and not to different periods of redemptive history" (Borgen, "Observations," 289).

36 Joshua Levinson, "Dialogical Reading in the Rabbinic Exegetical Narrative," *Poetics Today* 25 (2004): 497–528.

37 Levinson, "Dialogical Reading," 498.

biblical world, but as a story in its own right, it creates a narrated world which is different from its biblical shadow."[38] Narrative and exegesis are two different means of persuasion, of course, so there is a certain dissonance involved. But this tension and dissonance is in fact constitutive of the genre's identity.[39]

Levinson argues that the rabbinic exegetical narrative invites us to read "two texts as one ... with and against each other."[40] As the reader shifts between the two texts, she "ensures that their old meanings now become potential sources for new ones."[41] A special kind of reader is created by this genre, one with a "dialogic consciousness, of being both inside and outside the text at the same time" because the reader "must follow two plots simultaneously."[42] Two stories consequently jostle side by side and inform each other. Or, as Levinson expresses it: "[E]xegesis and narrative, subordination and creativity are in continual tension ... the narrative created from the verses it claims to represent also reinterprets the verses that nurtured it, and the axis that joins these aspects is the reader."[43] Moreover, the reader "not only interprets the midrashic narrative against the background of the biblical story, but also reinterprets the biblical story against the background of the midrash."

The rabbinic exegetical narrative bases itself on the canonical biblical text. A canonical text carries a particular kind of authority and defines a particular "textual community." Levinson's idea of a "textual community" is appropriated from Brian Stock and it describes a "microsociety organized around the common understanding of a sacred script."[44] But that "common understanding" is forged through the retelling and reinterpretation of the canonical text: The self-definition of a textual community does not, perhaps cannot, rely on the simple preservation of, or adherence to, the text "as it is." Once more, Levinson phrases it well: "[I]t is precisely the canonical status of the text—that which acts as the foundation for its cultural legitimacy—that invites its constant transformation, violation and appropriation" by the community in question.[45]

There are different ways in which the exegetical narrative achieves its transformation of the canonical text. Relying on the theorist Lubomír Doležel and his concept of "literary transduction," Levinson claims that the rabbis achieved

38 Levinson, "Dialogical Reading," 498.

39 Levinson, "Dialogical Reading," 498.

40 Levinson, "Dialogical Reading," 524.

41 Wolfgang Iser, *Prospecting: From Reader Response to Literary Anthropology* (Baltimore: Johns Hopkins University Press, 1989), 237. Cited in Levinson, "Dialogical Reading," 524.

42 Levinson, "Dialogical Reading," 524.

43 Levinson, "Dialogical Reading," 501.

44 Brian Stock, *Listening for the Text: On the Uses of the Past* (Baltimore: Johns Hopkins University Press, 1990), 23.

45 Levinson, "Dialogical Reading," 499.

"transduction" of the biblical text via a process of literary expansion.[46] Expansions extend

> ... the scope of the protoworld, by filling its gaps, constructing a pre-history or post-history, and so on. The protoworld and the successor world are complementary. The protoworld is put into a new co-text, and the established structure is thus shifted.[47]

As Levinson understands it, the authors writing for their "textual communities" may also have had various motivations for employing literary "expansions." They might have perceived a deficiency in the original text, or alternately, have felt impelled to introduce their point of view between its lines because of a perceived lack of representation.[48]

The exegetical narrative forms its textual community in the process of retelling the canonical narrative upon which it rests. Much of literary theory has described how "the reader creates the text," but less attention has been paid, according to Levinson, to the dynamic ways in which "the text creates its reader."[49] So while the "rewriter" of a canonical text necessarily adopts a stance towards that text—admitting and/or challenging its authority, continuing or subverting its *telos*—there is also the socio-cultural need to shape a given "textual community" in light of that stance. To quote Levinson, "[o]ne may ask to whom the story belongs, who is given a central role, and who is moved behind the scenes in order to tell it."[50] The exegetical narrative revisions and recreates the original canonical text precisely to shape a new community and to make the story "belong" to them.

This involves launching from "what was said" in the biblical text to the "something new" that the exegetical narrative produces inside its own frame. Its exegetical discourse enables it to "breach" the canon. It must move from "A" to "B," like the biblical story. But it cannot do so directly, as this would constitute what Levinson calls "canonicity without breach" (i. e., it would exactly replicate the biblical tale rather than reinvent it). So the rewriter has two options: He can "interrupt this progress, creating obstacles that impede the development of the biblical script" or "he can suggest an alternate narrative trajectory so as almost to tell a different story, thus threatening to subvert the biblical telos."[51]

One way to instill an alternate narrative trajectory into the established story is to bring what theorists call a "virtual embedded narrative" (or disnarrated event) to the fore, actualizing it within the exegetical discourse. Every narrative thus

46 Lubomír Doležel, *Heterocosmica: Fiction and Possible Worlds* (Baltimore: Johns Hopkins University Press, 1998), 206.
47 Doležel, *Heterocosmica*, 207 (cited in Levinson, "Dialogical Reading," 499).
48 Levinson, "Dialogical Reading," 499.
49 Levinson, "Dialogical Reading," 502.
50 Levinson, "Dialogical Reading," 499.
51 Levinson, "Dialogical Reading," 504.

consists of an "actual" world but also a "virtual" world, i.e., the prevented/anticipated events. Levinson argues that the exegetical narrative "threatens to derail the biblical telos by making these virtual narratives actual."[52] On the other hand, the rewriter may keep the biblical conclusion in place, but create suspense by interposing unexpected stories between the lines, tricking the reader and leading her down false paths. In short, "the narrator can confirm the expectations of his readers or thwart them; he can create tension or surprise by manipulating and playing with the accepted and innovative meanings."[53]

4. John's Prologue as Exegetical Narrative

We can only cautiously propose that John's prologue is generically the kind of "exegetical narrative" found in the midrashim analyzed by Levinson. Qualifications must be added, lest anachronism results. Of course, John's prologue is not rabbinic midrash, but the "dialogic" mode of reading that the rabbinic exegetical narrative promotes is at work in a comparable way in John's prologue.

Levinson differentiates the rabbinic "exegetical narrative" from forms of "rewritten bible" (found in the Second Temple period) on the basis of a central criterion: the status of exegesis within the narrative.[54] The aggadic midrashim build one story on top of another by slicing the biblical text into commentary-like segments, filling out gaps and fashioning an authoritative narrative that supplements the original text. Alternatively, "rewritten bible" texts such as *Jubilees* are autonomous, non-commentary-like narratives that employ "paraphrasing expansions" rather than direct quotation; in other words, the "exegesis" in the "rewritten scripture" genre is implicit and allusive instead of explicit.[55]

Of course, this difference can be understood in light of Tzvetan Todorov's idea of genres as historically contingent, as evolutionary (growing out of former

52 Levinson, "Dialogical Reading," 505.

53 Levinson, "Dialogical Reading," 513.

54 Levinson, "Dialogic Reading," 500–501.

55 Another difference, of course, is that for the amoraim, the biblical stories (Torah) were assuredly "canonical." The rewritten scripture texts and John's Gospel (circa 90s CE) were presumably written before the "Old Testament" was officially deemed canonical. However, with respect to John's Gospel, it is evident that the "Old Testament" writings were "scriptural" for the Johannine community (cf. 20:8). It is worth clarifying that Levinson considers the aggadic midrashim to be more "self-conscious" than the "rewritten bible" genres because of the extent to which the former explicitly cites and comments upon the scriptural material. By contrast the "rewritten bible" genres (e.g., *Jubilees*) are extended narrative paraphrases of the text, with elaboration ("Dialogic Reading," 500–501). See Sidnie White Crawford, *Rewriting Scripture in Second Temple Times* (Grand Rapids: Eerdmans, 2008), for the choice of the term "rewritten scripture" over "rewritten bible" on the basis of the absence of canonical status.

genres) and as hierarchical, existing in a network of genre systems.[56] Modern genre theory understands genres to exist in a somewhat unstable relationship with texts, which accounts for the dynamic ways texts "skew" generic conventions.[57] No single composition can fully define a genre, and each text "performing" a genre ever so slightly alters the understanding of the class of literature to which it might be assigned. In a recent article, George Brooke has traced the diachronic development of ancient Jewish commentary genres; he suggests that from the second century BCE onwards, "rewritten bible" genres—or texts that aimed to represent authoritative traditions, from Chronicles through to *Jubilees* or the *Genesis Apocryphon*—gradually increased in amounts of lemmatized, explicit exegetical commentary.[58] Levinson's "exegetical narratives" in the aggadic midrashim would thus be on the latter end of this evolutionary spectrum.

From within this diachronic trajectory we can understand John's prologue as a sort of proto-exegetical narrative. Its covert exegetical dimensions and autonomous literary structure might place it closer on the spectrum to other Second Temple texts like *Jubilees.* John's prologue is likewise an autonomous narrative, paraphrasing the creation story in Genesis but launching directly—and without self-conscious commentary—into its own tale. In this regard it may be closer to the exegesis of selected "rewritten scripture" narratives than to the aggadic midrashim.

But although John's prologue differs from the rabbinic exegetical narrative in the degree to which it explicitly cites and comments upon scripture, it is analogous to the exegetical narrative in another way. Levinson raises a second criterion that differentiates the aggadic midrashim from the "rewritten scripture" genre: that of their respective "authoritative voices." Levinson suggests that the "rewritten scripture" genre anchors its interpretive authority in revelation, but that the rabbis anchor theirs in the "dignity of exegesis."[59] To follow Levinson's

56 Tzvetan Todorov, *The Fantastic: A Structural Approach to a Literary Genre*, trans. R. Howard (Ithaca: Cornell University Press, 1975), 6.

57 John Frow, *Genre* (London: Routledge, 2005), 1–3.

58 George J. Brooke, "Genre Theory, Rewritten Bible and Pesher," *DSD* 17 (2010): 361–386.

59 Levinson, "Dialogical Reading," 500–501. Of course, this claim can be disputed: Josephus' *Antiquities of the Jews* is considered to be a work of "rewritten scripture" but it is not hermeneutically anchored in the authority of revelation. It is worth noting that these generic categories ("rewritten bible/scripture," "midrash," "exegetical narrative") – and the criteria used to define and differentiate them – are etic categories, heuristic constructs created by scholars to categorize the material. There is little evidence that the ancient Jewish authors were consciously adopting set generic forms along the lines of these descriptive categories (perhaps with the exception of the *pesharim* at Qumran, which could nevertheless be defined as a technique of interpretation rather than a genre). For a solid discussion see, Timothy Lim, "The Origins and Emergence of Midrash in Relation to the Hebrew Scriptures," in *The*

claim here, John's prologue does not merely anchor its authority in revelation, but claims a whole new basis of revelation, even as it takes its starting point from a reinterpreted "beginning" present in Genesis 1. Like the rabbinic exegetical narrative, John's prologue restates the old in order to craft something new—and something radically new at that. Indeed, the prologue takes such leeway with the possibilities of exegesis to express something new that it ends up grounding definitive exegetical capability in the Word itself—in Jesus, as the only one that has "made God known" (ἐξηγήσατο; 1:18b). This is what Levinson would call "canonicity with breach" in the aggadic midrashim.[60] It also inclines me to suggest that the similarities between the rabbinic exegetical narrative and John's prologue should not be dismissed lightly, despite the risks of anachronism. Below, I explore the ways in which John's prologue fosters a dialogic mode of reading as it narrates the story of Jesus against the exegetical background of the biblical tale.

4.1 The Prologue and the Dialogic Mode of Reading

Like the "dialogic" mode of reading encouraged by the rabbinic exegetical narrative, John's prologue places two texts side-by-side, and requires the reader to interchange between the plots of two different stories. As we have seen, many scholars identify the biblical narrative of creation told in Gen 1:1–5 as the plot evoked by the opening lines of John's prologue. What is less recognized is that the prologue "exegetes" a narrative arc that extends from Genesis to Exodus, from the theme of creation to the theme of Sinaitic revelation and divine encounter.[61] In so doing, the prologue offers a Christocentric vision of "salvation-history." The reader interprets these two texts as one, moving between the concurrent contexts, challenging the meanings of the original biblical story and engendering radically new meanings from within the scope of the prologue's purview.

As the overview of the scholarly literature has already demonstrated, the verbal parallels between John 1:1–5 and Gen 1:1–5 are immediately detectable. Basically, the first verses of the prologue (1:1–5) retell the opening verses of Genesis using the exegetical technique of "expansion." John develops an alternative plotline that competes with the basic thrust of the primordial creation narrative, even as it employs that originating narrative as an interpretive basis. Peder Borgen's work has already touched on the nature of these paraphrasing

---

Midrash: An Encyclopedia of Biblical Interpretation in Formative Judaism, ed. Jacob Neusner and Alan J. Avery-Peck (Leiden: Brill, 2004), 595–612.

60 Levinson, "Dialogical Reading," 504.

61 But see M.-Emile Boismard, *Le prologue de saint Jean* (Paris: du Cerf, 1953) and Francis Moloney, *John*, SP 4 (Collegeville: Liturgical Press, 1998), 41.

expansions. John expands on the verbal forms in Gen 1 ("God said …") giving us the *hypostasized* noun, "the Word" who was with God from the beginning.[62] The prologue's retelling threatens to subvert the biblical telos, for the end and purpose for which the world was created is, according to John, to be found in what went on at/before creation: the presence of the Word with God, who later became incarnated in Jesus, and who was the singular agent of creation (John 1:1–3).

John's opening verses are a story of the success of the Word/Logos from the outset, and in this respect John steers the beginning of Genesis in a different direction. "Light" was contained in the Logos from the beginning, ready to illuminate humanity upon creation (1:3), and so the "darkness" has no temporal priority in John's tale. Unlike the tale in Gen 1:1–5, light did not illuminate the existing darkness, become distinct from it and become named. The light always was—it shines (φαίνει) in the darkness and the darkness has not overcome it (οὐ κατέλαβεν). That story of success is repeated in the more specific reference to the work of the Logos in the world in vv. 9 and 14.

But now the "darkness" takes on a moral valence even as it acts as the venue for the drama of the Word's entrance into the "world": "the true light that enlightens everyone was coming into the world" (v. 9). Because the reader is aware in advance that the "light" shines in the darkness (v. 5), the advent of the true light in the world in v. 9 must indicate the necessity of the "true light" entering a dark world. Verses 10–11 of the prologue depict a situation of "homelessness-at-home" so to speak; what looks like a familiar narrative trope of "homecoming"—the Word coming into his own—is imagined as a pathos-inflected moment of the hero's rejection; and the possibility of the darkness being victorious over the light surfaces for the first time. The Word had come into the world that was made through him (v. 10) but he remained unrecognized by the world (v. 10b). He came "to his own [home] and his own [people] received him not" (v. 11). This unexpected response from "his own" operates as a paradox, a plot "stunner" on two levels: that the Word could be *in* what came to be through him, and that "his own" could not know him.

Scholars are correct, therefore, to read v. 12 as the "pivot point" of John's prologue—the "redemptive" turning point that hints at the victory of the Word in the world when accepted by those who believed in his name.[63] Verse 12 thus also functions as recursive commentary on the inevitable victory of the light over darkness expounded in v. 5. After this "pivot point," comes the climactic statement about the incarnation of the Word in v. 14, and the intertextual register of the prologue's narrative arc subtly shifts from an exegetical play on the creation story in Genesis to an engagement with the narrative of the Exodus.

62 Borgen, "Observations," 289–293.

63 E.g., Culpepper, "The Pivot of John's Prologue."

What makes this Christocentric climax so compelling is that it does two things at once (again, reinforcing the dialogic mode of reading): It gives the creative Word of God an enfleshed existence in time, thus "fulfilling" that story, and simultaneously turns toward *another* story—that of the revelation in the wilderness. The verb ἐσκήνωσεν in v. 14 gives us our hint at this exegetical turn, particularly as it is associated with the visible "glory" of God: The Word "pitched his tent" among us, and we saw his glory (καὶ ἐσκήνωσεν ἐν ἡμῖν, καὶ ἐθεασάμεθα τὴν δόξαν αὐτοῦ). A play on Sir 24:8 (that of Wisdom "tenting" in Israel) could be present here.[64] But the verb σκηνόω could also evoke the Hebrew שׁכן, which is used in the Hebrew Bible to denote the dwelling of YHWH in Israel (Exod 25:8; 29:46; Zech 2:14).[65] Here, I will take a closer look at one of those texts, Exod 25:8 to further draw out these nuances.

Exod 25:1–31:17 is concerned with the building and functioning of the tabernacle, the portable sanctuary to house the ark and tablets. In 25:8 God instructs the people to make him a "sanctuary" (מקדשׁ) so that he can "indwell among them" (ושׁכנתי בתוכם) following the momentous revelation at Sinai. God does not dwell "in" the sanctuary but "among them." The literal meaning of שׁכן is "to rest": God's dwelling is in heaven, but he rests in the sanctuary, which represents the immanence of the "indwelling" God among his people. The rabbis would later use the word שׁכן to denote the "resting" of the divine glory (כבד) upon the tabernacle. Their interpretive traditions recognized that the act of fashioning sacred space itself recalled the divine act of creation from the following play of words: the building of the ark (ארון) was comparable to God's creation of light (אור) used to illuminate the universe; sacred space separates from the "profane" in like manner to God's initial separation of light and darkness at creation.[66] In antiquity it was not uncommon to find the intermixture of themes from Genesis and Exodus in new exegetical compositions, as both this rabbinic text and the Targum fragment discussed earlier in this article make clear.

Something similar is happening in vv. 10–14 of the prologue. The Word who "was God" (v. 2) comes to dwell "among" his own, but was *not* received by his own. Unlike Boyarin, I do not take this to refer to an embedded narrative about

64 So, Moloney, *John*, 39.

65 Cf. Don Seeman, "'Where is Sarah Your Wife?' Cultural Poetics of Gender and Nationhood in the Hebrew Bible," *HTR* 91 (1998): 125. Seeman explains that the "tent" image in Genesis is associated with interiority, women, and fecundity, but in Exodus, the same image is associated with divine revelation (e.g., Moses encounters YHWH in the Tent of Meeting as an interior space). I cite this finding to suggest that the emergence of the theme of "dwelling" or "en-tenting" in vv. 10–14 of the Prologue moves the reader subtly away from an interpretation of Genesis and towards a midrash on Exodus. Interestingly, the reference to birth and "seed" in v. 12 also alludes to fecundity of sorts.

66 Exodus Rabbah 33:4, in *Midrash Rabbah: Exodus*, ed. H. Freedman and Maurice Simon, trans. S. M. Lehrman (London: Soncino, 1939), 3:416–418.

the misadventures of the *Logos Asarkos*/Wisdom in the world of biblical history, at least to the exclusion of all other possibilities. Raymond Brown is correct to state that, in John's worldview, the ability to become "children of God" (1:12) is predicated solely on the reception of the incarnate Jesus (see note 34 above). Instead, vv. 10–14 elaborate on vv. 3–5 of the prologue, and are returned to once again in more specific detail in vv. 16–17. But the whole while, they are drawing on Exodus motifs of divine encounter.

The Word's rejection by his own does not prevent the "children of God" from "gazing upon" the Word's "glory," which manifests the Word's singular filial relationship with God. The glory "rested" among them, we might say, recalling the rabbinic interpretation of the Exodus instructions around the sanctuary, and the remnant "gazed upon it." For the prologue, the "resting" of the glory was an actual "indwelling" in human form unlike the Exodus narrative, which insisted that God could not be imaged or imagined in any actual sacred space. In the prologue, therefore, the "dwelling" of the Word is not just a symbolization of divine immanence. John insists that the enfleshed Word really *was* God in some sense and was with God in (and from) the beginning. But an additional "skew" is apprehended: The prologue looks back on the biblical texts but simultaneously sets up the forthcoming Gospel narrative (thus its "double-voiced discourse"), and while it leads the reader to believe that the "glory" was seen in Jesus, when the Gospel narrative plays out we find that this "gazing upon the glory" takes place at the cross (cf. 7:38–39; 8:28; 12:23, 32; 19:37). The retelling and foretelling of the prologue, in other words, keeps suspense alive by hinting at what turns out to be a surprise ending.

Boyarin is right to read v. 14 as a radical departure, and as the true beginnings of the Christian kerygma. This is substantiated by these short reflections about the "tenting" of God's presence, and the play on the Exodus themes noted. The prologue announces the "impossible" in terms of the ancient Jewish understanding of the divine; it narrates this "impossibility" in the process of exegesis. As Levinson would say, the "canon" is breached by a radically different plotline that subverts the biblical telos and introduces an unexpectedly new mode of revelation. Following in the footsteps of the biblical narrative, John does move from "A to B," from creation to revelation, as it were, but he does so in a way that fashions a revised meaning out of a familiar storyline.

The merging and mixing of texts and themes from Genesis and Exodus gives way, in vv. 15–18 of the prologue, to a more pronounced reflection on the consequences of the new Christian kerygma for the ongoing relevance of the Sinaitic revelation. The narrative arc that began in vv. 1–5 of the prologue with a midrash on Genesis 1 concludes with an exegetical comment on the supremacy of the incarnate Word vis-à-vis the whole direction of the Exodus narrative. John the Baptist is reintroduced in v. 15 and his laconic "witness" statement is cited in the prologue. The speech of this important character becomes part and parcel of the biblical story being interpreted, almost as if his witness about the *Logos* is on par with the scriptural record. There is no need to think of v. 15 as an inappropriate interpolation. John's witness specifies the pre-existent status of the incarnate word, now named as "son of the father." It also speaks of the Word's supremacy to John as a historical figure ("he who comes after me ranks ahead of me because he was before me"). The incarnate Word"s pre-existence and supreme rank reveals a "fullness" about him that others are now able to partake of—and so v. 16 follows on: "from his fullness we have all received grace upon grace [ἡμεῖς πάντες ἐλάβομεν καὶ χάριν ἀντὶ χάριτος]."

An alternative reading might be: "one grace in place of another." The explicative use of the conjunction ὅτι that opens v. 17 alerts the reader to how v. 16 is to be understood: "for, the law was given through Moses; grace and truth have come through Jesus Christ [ὅτι ὁ νόμος διὰ Μωϋσέως ἐδόθη, ἡ χάρις καὶ ἡ ἀλήθεια διὰ Ἰησοῦ Χριστοῦ ἐγένετο]." Of course much ink has been spilled over the apparent or genuine antithetical stance in v. 17, and whether or not the prologue intends its readership to view Moses and the gift he mediated (the Torah) as now replaced by Jesus and the gift (grace and truth) that he brings.[67] Boyarin's view on the matter is that there is no temporal supersession intended here, but simply the superior authority of clarity brought by the enfleshment of the teaching Word. Moses, indeed, "wrote of Jesus," according to the Gospel (5:44). However, it is difficult to deny the exclusivism of the final verse: "it is God the only Son, who is close to the Father's heart, who has made him known (literally, "exegeted" God: ἐξηγήσατο v. 18b)—and no one else can claim a like epiphany of the divine, no one else has seen God.

As desirable as it would be to suppose that John 1:16–18 does not imply the supersession of one reality (i.e., the gifts brought through Jesus) over another (i.e., the Torah mediated through Moses), I think that it is too optimistic to imagine that John means us to view both Moses and Jesus, both the Torah and Jesus' revelation of grace and truth, to be compatible, continuous, or not antithetically posed. For example, Francis Moloney tries to achieve an irenic reading by suggesting that the "former gift" of the law is now "perfected" in the gift of the truth occurring in Jesus.[68] But the language of "perfection" suggests, by its very nature, imperfection, i.e., a lacking of "fullness," an incompleteness pertaining to the former gift. Even if the new gift does not replace the former gift, Moloney's explanation implies that it at least makes good what the former was lacking. In the prologue's view, Moses' ascent of Mount Sinai did not qualify him as one who

67 For a summary discussion see Ruth Edwards, "ΧΑΡΙΝ ΑΝΤΙ ΧΑΡΙΤΟΣ (John 1:16): Grace and Law in the Johannine Prologue," *JSNT* 32 (1988): 3–15.

68 Moloney, *John*, 40.

"saw" God, even if Moses spoke with God "face to face," as the Torah's metaphorical expression of intimacy implies (Exod 33:11). The "only-begotten son, who is close to the Father's heart" has made God known (1:18).

This is a definitive "breach" of the biblical *telos.* It is at once an alternative plotline, an expansion on the Sinaitic narrative of revelation, and the actualization of an impossible-to-conceive "embedded narrative": the speaking Word in Gen 1:3 that brings light *became* the indwelling "glory" that filled the sanctuary; but the twist is that this glory was visible when the "Word became flesh," dwelt among the people in the person Jesus, who was "glorified" (1:14b) through his "lifting up" (cf. 12:23, 32) on the cross. It presents a version of events that supplants the original, even as it builds on the original narrative. As exegetical narrative, the Gospel's prologue has its own *telos*, but it cannot help relying on the *topoi* and direction of the narratives it exegetes. Paradoxically, replacement (or supersession) *requires* continuity, something to latch onto and subvert.

4.2 Formation of a Textual Community

This final section returns us to Brian Stock's notion of the "textual community." Stock conceived of the "textual community" as a group of people whose social activities centered around canonical or sacred texts; one literate interpreter made the text accessible to the community, and the members of the community discussed the meaning of the text, in the process fashioning their own distinct social identity.[69] Although Stock's concept emerges out of his study of literacy and "reading groups" in the Middle Ages, I think it also has some usefulness for describing the so-called "Johannine community." The exegetical narrative evokes and forms a new reading community, and John's prologue hints that its textual community was held together in a common structure of belief in the "name" of Jesus (1:12–13; cf. 1 John 1:2–4).

We could see the prologue as an explicative text that programmatically defines a communal identity in light of the biblical narrative, one that moreover, interprets the Gospel text that it prefaces. The prologue voices the authority of a group —what I would term, following literary theorist Uri Margolin the "we-voice" (e.g., "we have seen his glory," 1:14b) and it manages to create an implied reading position which real readers are invited to adopt as they imitate the faith per-

69 Steven Fraade has suggested that the Qumran community was a "study group" along these lines, but to my knowledge no one has used Stock's idea with reference to the Johannine community. See Fraade, "Interpretive Authority in the Studying Community at Qumran," *JJS* 44 (1993): 46–69.

spective of the "we-voice."[70] If they adopt this faith position, they become the "we," and are addressed as the "you" of 20:31 in the Gospel's conclusion. The prologue makes the story of creation and revelation belong to the textual community, the "we-voice" of belief; it gives Jesus, as *Logos Ensarkos*, a central role, with John (1:6, 15) functioning as the supreme witness on his behalf.

But in order to tell this story others are moved behind the scenes: The darkness that was unable to "overcome" the light (1:5) and "his own" in the world who did not recognize the Word (1:10–11). While these characters have a significant role in the prologue's tale, providing it with its moment of "plot frustration" and with character foils, they also nevertheless get truncated treatment. We do not know about their reasons for not receiving Jesus, we are simply informed that, by associative contrast, their inadequate response must have something to do with the fact that they were not "born of God" (cf. 1:13).

This "othering" function is what I have elsewhere called the "monologic" rhetoric of John's Gospel, following the theoretical work of Mikhail Bakhtin. That is, the legitimacy of the inner world and motivations of the characters that act as negative foils in the story are subsumed into the larger ideology of the narrator and his point of view.[71] This is why I have trouble wholly adopting Levinson's use of the term "dialogic" in his analysis of the rabbinic exegetical narrative, even though he does not purport to use the term in a Bakhtinian sense. The rabbinic texts are nevertheless genuinely more "open" to letting two worlds sit side-by-side (i. e., they are dialogic), whereas John's Gospel is not.

The prologue itself is progressively more monologic as it goes on: It speaks of Jesus' exclusive exegesis of the Father, of his exclusive intimacy with God, and of the reception of Jesus as the sole means of becoming "born of God" (1:12–18). To shape an exclusive textual community, invested with authority (ἐξουσία) to become "children of God" through their reception of Jesus (1:12–13), the prologue *does* have to shift other voices behind the scene. So, while technically the prologue promotes a dialogic way of reading by virtue of its performance of the exegetical narrative genre, it does not disguise its monologic rhetoric, which has a key role in creating the Gospel's ideal reader.[72]

---

70 On the "we-voice" in literature, see Uri Margolin, "Telling in the Plural: From Grammar to Ideology," *Poetics Today* 21 (2000): 591–618. I have developed Margolin's insights in relation to John's Gospel more extensively in Ruth Sheridan, "Identity, Alterity, and the Gospel of John," *BibInt* 22 (2014): 188–209.

71 Ruth Sheridan, "Issues in the Translation of *Hoi Ioudaioi* in the Fourth Gospel," *JBL* 132 (2013): 671–695. See Mikhail Bakhtin, *Problems of Dostoyevsky's Poetics*, ed. and trans. Caryl Emerson, Theory and History of Literature 8 (Minneapolis: University of Minnesota Press, 1984).

72 For more on the Gospel's creation of the ideal reader, see Ruth Sheridan, *Retelling Scripture: 'The Jews' and the Scriptural Citations in John 1:19–12:15*, BIS 110 (Leiden; Boston: Brill, 2012).

The rabbinic exegetical narrative, the "rewritten bible" genres, the "didactic hymn"—and, I think John's prologue—all bring the authoritative past into the present, contemporizing the authoritative text, maybe undermining, but always acknowledging, the authority of the canonical text. And they do so with "textual communities" ever in mind, shaping values and defining "others." This is clearly at work in John's articulate ethical dualism. John's prologue performs the exegetical narrative genre in a way that not only represents the biblical story, but also recasts it and reshapes it entirely around the story of Jesus as the ultimate and exclusive "exegete" of God (cf. 1:18). The incarnation is the core subject of the prologue's exegetical narrative, and is the event that enables Jesus himself to carry on and create God's story.

Douglas Estes

Rhetorical *Peristaseis* (Circumstances) in the Prologue of John

1. Introduction

Of all the segments of a text, the prologue—actually any prologue, beginning, opening or lead—is the most consequential for generic evaluation.[1] This is because many (if not most) texts identify (or at least give clues to) what the text aims to do in its opening, if not in the first couple of sentences. For example, a text beginning with the brief, mundane words, "once upon a time," triggers a reaction that alerts readers to what kind of text they are reading.[2] "Once upon a time" at the beginning of a text indicates the text is a fairy tale (of some sort) and not a manual of automobile maintenance. These few, simple words—warning the reader of the "genre" of the text—have a profound ability to shape the meaning of the text for the rest of the reading.[3] As a result, the first few sentences of a text

1 Francis M. Dunn, introduction to *Beginnings in Classical Literature*, ed. Francis M. Dunn and Thomas Cole, Yale Classical Studies 29 (Cambridge: Cambridge University Press, 1992), 9; Stephen Harrison, "Epic Extremities: The Openings and Closures of Books in Apuleius' *Metamorphoses*," in *The Ancient Novel and Beyond*, ed. Stelios Panayotakis, Maaike Zimmerman, and Wytse Keulen, Mnemosyne Supplements 241 (Leiden: Brill, 2003), 239; Loveday C. A. Alexander, *Acts in its Literary Context: A Classicist Looks at the Acts of the Apostles*, LNTS 289 (London: T&T Clark, 2005), 21; Richard A. Burridge, "The Genre of Acts—Revisited," in *Reading Acts Today: Essays in Honour of Loveday C. A. Alexander*, ed. Steve Walton, Thomas E. Phillips, Lloyd Keith Pietersen, and F. Scott Spencer, LNTS 427 (London: T&T Clark, 2011), 10; and cf. Anthony Davenport, *Medieval Narrative: An Introduction* (Oxford: Oxford University Press, 2004), 35–42; Gérard Genette, *Paratexts: Thresholds of Interpretation*, trans. Jane E. Lewin; Literature, Culture, Theory 20 (Cambridge: Cambridge University Press, 1997), 10–11, 163–67.

2 This assumes, of course, that the reader has some reading experience (a naïve, first-time reader would not know what type of literature "once upon a time" launches) and that the author is not trying to confuse, mislead or obfuscate the genre of the text with false clues in the opening. See for example, Jack Zipes, *Why Fairy Tales Stick: The Evolution and Relevance of a Genre* (New York: Routledge, 2006), xi.

3 Cf. Richard A. Burridge, *What are the Gospels? A Comparison with Graeco-Roman Biography*, 2nd ed. (Grand Rapids: Eerdmans, 2004), 109; and Sean A. Adams, *The Genre of Acts and Collected Biography*, SNTSMS 156 (Cambridge: Cambridge University Press, 2013), 48.

communicate more than just the literal written words; they are also generic cues that are "metacommunications, [or] aspects of the text which somehow stand out as being also, reflexively, *about* the text and how to use it."[4] These generic cues create a pathway for meaning for a text, thereby shaping and constraining its reading and interpretation.[5]

This is one reason the creation of prologues is so difficult, their interpretation so challenging, and their importance so great. The difficulty of creating a beginning—even merely starting to write—is a universal problem of writing. The beginning poses a unique problem in writing as it is the transition between the idea and the word; the initial crossing of that boundary causes some anguish for almost every writer. Once the writer has created the beginning, the rest of the text starts to flow a little better. If a writer can use a framework or outline to help launch their text, then so much the better.

Tradition holds that Plato reflected at great length to come up with the exact right words to open his *Republic*.[6] Likewise, ancient rhetorical practice placed significance on the opening words of a speech (Aristotle, *Rhetoric* 1414b). As one example of this significance, the statesman Demosthenes (384–322 BCE) created prologues for his orations, and they were compiled together by Callimachus (ca. 305–240 BCE). It is likely that Demosthenes wrote out multiple prologues to be used on different occasions, depending on the situation.[7] Similarly, readers often hear (perform) the opening of Genesis with epic overtones (Longinus, *On the Sublime* 9.9). Some notable examples of well-crafted openings from the ancient world include:

The First Tetralogy (Antiphon):
Ὁπόσα μὲν τῶν πραγμάτων ὑπὸ τῶν ἐπιτυχόντων ἐπιβουλεύεται …
When a crime is planned by an ordinary person … (Antiphon, *First Tetralogy* 115.1 [Maidment, LCL])

Jewish War (Josephus):
Ἐπειδὴ τὸν Ἰουδαίων πρὸς Ῥωμαίους πόλεμον συστάντα μέγιστον …
The war of the Jews against the Romans—the greatest not only … (Josephus, *J.W.* 1.1 [Thackeray, LCL])

4 John Frow, *Genre*, The New Critical Idiom (New York: Routledge, 2005), 115.

5 Frow, *Genre*, 6–12; and cf. Anna Marie Wasyl, *Genres Rediscovered: Studies in Latin Miniature Epic, Love Elegy, and Epigram of the Romano-Barbaric Age* (Kraków: Jagiellonian University Press, 2011), 40, 65, 139.

6 J. D. Denniston, *Greek Prose Style* (Oxford: Clarendon, 1952), 41.

7 Ian Worthington, introduction to *Prologues* in *Speeches 60 and 61, Prologues, Letters, by Demosthenes*, trans. Ian Worthington, Oratory of Classical Greece 10 (Austin: University of Texas Press, 2006), 57–58.

Tristia (Ovid):
Parve—nec invideo—sine me, liber, ibis in urbem …
Little book, you will go without me—and I grudge it not—to the city … (Ovid, *Tristia* 1.1 [Wheeler, LCL])

Hebrews 1:1–4:
Πολυμερῶς καὶ πολυτρόπως πάλαι ὁ θεὸς λαλήσας τοῖς πατράσιν …
In many places and ways, and throughout history God speaks to his people …

John 1:1–5:
Ἐν ἀρχῇ ἦν ὁ λόγος, καὶ ὁ λόγος ἦν πρὸς τὸν θεόν …
In the beginning was the Word, and the Word was with God …

Each of these examples betrays a craftsmanship and an attention to detail in how the writer launches the opening; none of these are haphazard or unintentional. Each example also shows the impact of the opening to define "the rest of the story," and some do it more successfully than others (cf. Aristotle, *Poet.* 1450b27–28). For example, in the *First Tetralogy*, not only does Antiphon alert his readers that he is discussing crime, he also uses his opening words to indicate what kind of text it is—a legal argument.[8] However, if a reader is not familiar with legal argumentation, then the generic clues would be less well understood. Thus, it is important for the writer to connect the generic indicators in the first few words with the expected and implied readership. Some of these examples are fiction, and rely on the dramatic; but non-fiction openings are actually more important than fiction openings because non-fiction openings require more information and more skill to hook the reader.[9]

In Greco-Roman rhetoric, the widely-accepted term for a prologue was προοίμιον, and in some cases πρόλογος, but the rhetorician Hermogenes (ca. 2nd century CE) refers to the lead as a κεφάλαιον, even though this term had wider currency in general language use and could refer to a title, heading or prefatory text (Hermogenes, *On the Invention of Arguments* 140). This is a result of the fluidity by which ancient writers understood titles, paratexts and leads in a technical sense—terms and concepts that are much more concrete in the modern, printing press world. Since many documents in the ancient world did not have titles, the first couple of sentences often defined for the reader what the text would be about (cf. Dionysius of Halicarnassus, *Antiquitates romanae* 1.1–2). A

8 A more experienced reader may recognize Antiphon's work as an *antilogiae*; see Michael Gagarin, *Antiphon the Athenian: Oratory, Law, and Justice in the Age of the Sophists* (Austin: University of Texas Press, 2002), 103.

9 Brian Richardson, "Narrative Beginnings," in *Narrative Beginnings: Theories and Practices*, ed. Brian Richardson (Lincoln: University of Nebraska Press, 2008), 8.

classic example is the first word of the κεφάλαιον of Genesis (בראשית), so well-recognized as a defining beginning that it acts as a title to the text itself.[10] Since these first couple of words or sentences perform a unique function, they set the tone for not just the prologue or introduction, but also the rest of the text. These types of beginnings serve as genre indicators for what will follow.

As with these examples, there is a rather obvious genre indicator at work in the first couple of sentences of the Fourth Gospel that gospel research has not considered—*peristaseis* (περιστάσεις). This genre indicator is, as I shall argue, the most notable formal feature of the prologue of John, and it points directly to the rhetorical purpose of the full gospel text. In using this indicator, coupled with the dramatic story of the Word, the fourth evangelist bent common rhetorical circumstances into a framework for the spiritually-rich beginning of the Gospel —in a similar way that Josephus, the writer of Genesis, the writer of Tobit, and so many others did before John.

2. Genre and Prologue

Relative to the importance of this issue, the genre of the Gospel of John has received relatively light attention in Johannine scholarship of the 20th century.[11] When this issue received attention, most of the focus was placed on the categorization of the Fourth Gospel over and against the Synoptic Gospels and other ancient parallels. One of the most influential of these discussions was Richard Burridge's argument that the four canonical gospels are best understood as forms of βίος,[12] thus taking a position against the previous generation's argument that the gospels are *sui generis*,[13] and moving back in the direction of a categorization that held for centuries before the modern era of biblical scholarship.[14] However, many of the attempts at discussing gospel genre seem to receive little traction.

10 Barry Bandstra, *Genesis 1–11: A Handbook on the Hebrew Text*, BHHB (Waco: Baylor University Press, 2008), 42.

11 This is unfortunate, as genre "is the most powerful explanatory tool available to the literary critic"; Adena Rosmarin, *The Power of Genre* (Minneapolis: University of Minnesota Press, 1985), 39; and also Adams, *Genre of Acts*, 1; and Justin Marc Smith, *Why βίος? On the Relationship Between Gospel Genre and Implied Audience*, LNTS 518 (London: Bloomsbury T&T Clark, 2015), 202.

12 Burridge, *What are the Gospels?*, 231.

13 For example, Rudolf Bultmann, "The Gospels (Form)," in *Twentieth Century Theology in the Making*, ed. Jaroslav Pelikan (London: Collins, 1969), 1:89.

14 For example, Craig S. Keener, *The Gospel of John: A Commentary* (Peabody: Hendrickson, 2003), 1:4.

Most likely this is due to the impasse represented by a group of texts that resist easy categorization, for reasons that include style, purpose, and context.[15]

Nonetheless, this approach to genre has some usefulness as categorization—if nothing else—allows us to see quite clearly what type of text the fourth evangelist did *not* create: he did not create a legal argument, nor a sayings collection, nor a chronicle, nor *progymnasmata*, but something intentionally and specifically focused on the life of Jesus.[16] In response to this impasse, Harold Attridge proposed a remedy, arguing that the evangelist bends a variety of genres to create a rather unique narrative.[17] Rather than treat the genre of the Fourth Gospel monolithically, Attridge also suggests it is possible to see the text of John as a patchwork of a variety of different "micro-genres" woven together to make the narrative of the Fourth Gospel.[18] As a result, while the Gospel as a whole may have an identifiable genre, the different parts of the Gospel are at times more reflective of their individual micro-genres. These micro-genres were then bent and blended by the creator of the Fourth Gospel into the sections of the text we have today. This technique of mixing genres existed long before John wrote,[19] grew in popularity in the first centuries CE, and became quite fashionable in many circles by the time of late antiquity (cf. Horace, *Ars poetica* 93–98).[20] In fact, rather than rigidly following clear generic lines, genre bending was perhaps in retrospect one of the key features of ancient Greek and Latin writing.[21]

---

15 Of course, good writing will always resist easy categorization, and will always find new ways to communicate (even in a Greco-Roman mimetic culture); cf. Harold W. Attridge, "Genre Bending in the Fourth Gospel," *JBL* 121 (2002): 21.

16 Udo Schnelle, *Antidocetic Christology in the Gospel of John: An Investigation of the Place of the Fourth Gospel in the Johannine School*, trans. Linda M. Maloney (Minneapolis: Fortress, 1992), 229; and also James D. G. Dunn, "Let John Be John: A Gospel for Its Time," in *The Gospel and the Gospels*, ed. Peter Stuhlmacher (Grand Rapids: Eerdmans, 1991), 322.

17 We should expect that the evangelist would do this, as it was true of ancient writers such as Callimachus and other contemporaneous Hellenistic writers such as Josephus; see for example, Annette Harder, introduction to *Aetia: Volume 1: Introduction, Text, and Translation*, by Callimachus, ed. Annette Harder (Oxford: Oxford University Press, 2012), 23; and Fausto Parente, "The Impotence of Titus, or Flavius Josephus's *Bellum Judaicum* as an Example of 'Pathetic' Historiography," in *Josephus and Jewish History in Flavian Rome and Beyond*, ed. Joseph Sievers and Gaia Lembi, JSJSup 104 (Leiden: Brill, 2005), 45. Not only is Callimachus known for bending genres, he bends several of them a great deal in the prologue to his *Aetia*, for example; see Callimachus, *Aet.* 1.1–40.

18 Attridge, "Genre Bending," 11.

19 For example, Aristophanes (ca. 450–385 BCE) mixed in various genre types for comedic effect; see Charles Platter, *Aristophanes and the Carnival of Genres*, Arethusa (Baltimore: Johns Hopkins University Press, 2007), 3. Similarly, Virgil (70–19 BCE) manipulated genres into his battle narratives in the *Aeneid*; see Andreola Rossi, *Contexts of War: Manipulation of Genre in Virgilian Battle Narrative* (Ann Arbor: University of Michigan Press, 2004), 2.

20 Wasyl, *Genres Rediscovered*, 7.

21 Joseph Farrell, "Classical Genre in Theory and Practice," *New Literary History* 34 (2003): 392–93.

Attridge's approach accords far better with recent developments in genre studies than the more traditional attempts at formal categorization. While discussion of genre began with the earliest Greek literary critics,[22] genre studies remained "stuck" in a categorical mindset up until the last few decades, where the rigidity of a formalist approach began to give way to a rhetorical approach.[23] Traditionally, one evaluated genre by creating analogies based on the form of the text in comparison with other texts;[24] but in the rhetorical approach, one seeks to focus "not on the substance or the form of discourse but on the action it is used to accomplish."[25] This does not mean that modern genre studies do not look at formal features within the text; rather, they consider those formal features as elements within the rhetorical act that the text seeks to perform. Thus, in order to consider the genre of the Fourth Gospel, we will be better served to ask *not* as much what form(s) the Gospel is closest to by way of categorical analogy, but *more so*, what forms the Gospel uses to shape its rhetorical goals. The same is therefore true of the prologue of John—a prologue that was created and mixed by its creator to be the opening to a gospel. In other words, John's prologue is the prologue to a text that has the rhetorical act of *gospel* (John 20:30–31), not to a text with the form of gospel (as it would later be categorized).[26]

Whether we prefer a traditional or modern approach to genre, one of the most important factors to consider is the genre indicators in (and the micro-genre of) the opening sentences of the text in determining the genre of the full text.[27] Yet, the study of how narratives begin is one of the most "critically neglected" in the theory of literature.[28] More work can be done in this area, and if we want to understand better the genre (and genre bending) and meaning of the Fourth Gospel, the best place to start is in its opening.

---

22 For example, the opening of Aristotle's *Poetics*, where he speaks of kinds (εἴδη); see Aristotle, *Poet.* 1447a1. This idea eventually evolved into classifications (σχήματα) in later centuries; see Leonardo Tarán and Dimitri Gutas, *Aristotle* Poetics: *Editio Maior of the Greek Text with Historical Introductions and Philological Commentaries*, Mnemosyne Supplements 338 (Leiden: Brill, 2012), 80–1. Similarly, Horace, *Ars* 92.

23 Northrop Frye, *Anatomy of Criticism: Four Essays* (Princeton: Princeton University Press, 1957), 13; and Amy J. Devitt, *Writing Genres*, Rhetorical Philosophy and Theory (Carbondale: Southern Illinois University Press, 2004), 1–2; and see also, Ruth Sheridan, "John's Gospel and Modern Genre Theory: The Farewell Discourse (John 13–17) as a Test Case," *ITQ* 75 (2010): 293–96.

24 Frye, *Anatomy of Criticism*, 95.

25 Carolyn R. Miller, "Genre as Social Action," *Quarterly Journal of Speech* 70 (1984): 151.

26 Even here, describing the rhetorical act of John as *gospel* is somewhat a blanket term for what might be better described as *writing-to-believe* (John 20:30–31) or *testifying-about-Jesus* (John 21:24).

27 Devitt, *Writing Genres*, 10.

28 Brian Richardson, editor's preface to *Narrative Beginnings: Theories and Practices* (Lincoln: University of Nebraska Press, 2008), vii.

3. Writing *Peristaseis* in a Prologue

The first principle of starting a narrative is that there need be some *intent* in the creation. Whatever this intent is, it shapes and defines the preliminary material that the writer will use. For a technical treatise such as Aristotle's *Sophistical Refutations*, or the Gospel of Mark, a clear statement is made by the writer to introduce the topic. For a letter such as any found in the New Testament, a salutation is used by the writer to welcome readers. However, for a narrative such as the Gospel of John, more robust strategies to introduce a story are available.

If a writer intends to write a story (a narrative), then the creation of that story requires some delineation. Who will the story be about? What will happen in the story? Where will the story take place? To resolve this, writers can use a prefabricated framework of *circumstances* to introduce their story in as clear a manner as possible. Schoolchildren in English-speaking countries of today learn from an early age that there are five *ws* that should be answered when defining the intent of the writing: *who*, *what*, *when*, *where*, and *why* (plus sometimes *how*, the honorary "w" word). In order to tell a story based on events, Western journalists follow much the same procedure to define the story and introduce it to their readers in the lead. These five *ws* are not a modern invention as they played an important role of topical delineation throughout Western thought. These circumstances constitute the foundation of the "elements of narration" (διηγήσεως στοιχεῖα; Theon, *Progymnasmata* 5), or a common framework for a writer to organize their thoughts and material into a meaningful narrative.[29]

The first person most credited with thinking about "the five *ws*" is the rhetor Hermagoras of Temnos (ca. mid-2nd century BCE). While his work on rhetoric is no longer extant, it was highly influential in the ancient world, with a notable impact on the thoughts of Cicero, Quintilian, and Hermogenes. Much of what we know about Hermagoras comes from the records of (Pseudo-)Augustine in his work, *On Rhetoric.* Hermagoras describes seven περιστάσεις (*circumstantiae*, circumstances) that in English we render as *who*, *what*, *when*, *where*, *why*, *in what way*, and *by what means* (*quis*, *quid*, *quando*, *ubi*, *cur*, *quem ad modum*, and *quibus adminiculis*) ([Pseudo-]Augustine, *Rhet.* 7–8).[30] These circumstances

29 Ruth Webb, *Ekphrasis, Imagination and Persuasion in Ancient Rhetorical Theory and Practice* (Surrey: Ashgate, 2009), 62–64; and Cristina Pepe, *The Genres of Rhetorical Speeches in Greek and Roman Antiquity*, International Studies in the History of Rhetoric 5 (Leiden: Brill, 2013), 293.

30 Whether five *ws* or seven *peristaseis*, the exact number of circumstances has varied in small ways over the last two millennia. Jonsen and Toulmin recount the story of the rediscovery of Aristotle in Europe, which caused some debate over the exact number of circumstances, given that Aristotle has one more circumstance than Cicero and Boethius. This debate even included Aquinas and affected ecclesiastical practice; see Jonsen and Toulmin, *The Abuse of Casuistry: A History of Moral Reasoning* (Berkeley: University of California Press, 1988), 133–

were an important part of rhetorical stasis theory, especially in relation to defining the limited question (ὑπόθεσις) and setting the parameters for the argument or case.[31] However, recent research reveals that Aristotle was proposing seven circumstances in his *Nicomachean Ethics* long before Hermagoras.[32] Unlike the rhetor Hermagoras, Aristotle approached these circumstances from a philosophical perspective, to better understand why events and actions occur (Aristotle, *Eth. nic.* 1111a3–8). Even before Aristotle, Herodotus starts his *Histories* very differently than Homer or earlier poets, with some details and circumstances cited in the opening sentences.[33] What this reveals is that circumstances are most likely part of a self-evident need for delineation that occurs when writing narratives, but then the formal idea of defining circumstances most likely started in the area of philosophical discussion (4th century BCE), and within two centuries moved into much more practical use as a characteristic of argumentation (2nd century BCE), only to further find a place in the Ciceronian corpus (1st century BCE),[34] complete the move to Latin via Quintilian (1st century CE), and become a staple of later works of narrative instruction including the *progymnasmata* (Theon, *Prog.* 5; Hermogenes, *Inv.* 140). This movement among notable cultural influencers meant that literate Greek-speakers by the late 1st century CE would understand the concept of limiting questions or the delineation of narrative events due to circumstance, even if they did not understand all the ins and outs of rhetorical and poetic theory.[35] Average Greek and Latin writers were aware of the seven circumstances in at least a general way by the time of the writing of the prologue of John (as I show below). Further, the seven circumstances in general are of such an untechnical nature that writers who knew nothing of rhetoric (presumably Homer) may still utilize them unconsciously,

34; and Thomas N. Tentler, *Sin and Confession on the Eve of the Reformation* (Princeton: Princeton University Press, 1977), 116–19.

31 For a discussion of this theory and how it developed into an important rhetorical tool in the medieval period, and up to present day, see Rita Copeland, *Rhetoric, Hermeneutics, and Translation in the Middle Ages: Academic Traditions and Vernacular Texts* (Cambridge: Cambridge University Press, 1991), 67.

32 Michael C. Sloan, "Aristotle's *Nicomachean Ethics* as the Original *Locus* for the *Septem Circumstantiae*," *Classical Philology* 105 (2010): 236; and cf. William M. A. Grimaldi, "The Sources of Rhetorical Argumentation by Enthymeme," in *Landmark Essays on Aristotelian Rhetoric*, ed. Richard Leo Enos and Lois Peters Agnew (Mahwah: Lawrence Erlbaum Associates, 1998), 126.

33 Simon Goldhill, *The Invention of Prose*, Greece & Rome: New Surveys in the Classics 32 (Oxford: Oxford University Press, 2002), 11.

34 Cicero gives a rough overview of the circumstances in his work on invention; see Cicero, *De inventione rhetorica* 1.21.29; and cf. 1.24.34–1.28.43.

35 For example, Sextus Empiricus (ca. 200 CE) makes a play on the idea of *peristaseis* to introduce the Fourth Mode of scepticism; see Julia Annas and Jonathan Barnes, *The Modes of Scepticism: Ancient Texts and Modern Interpretations* (Cambridge: Cambridge University Press, 1985), 82.

especially when writing narrative.[36] As a result, the circumstances were less a rigid rule and more of a guiding framework; writers could use some or all of the circumstances, and put them in any order seen fit to best tell their story.

Let's consider several examples. In the ancient world, using περιστάσεις (circumstances) to create the lead for the reader was a mildly common occurrence. This appears to be most true of ancient narratives, where ancient writers tended toward a number of common goals. First, we consider the role of *peristaseis* in the creation of the opening of the book of Tobit (ca. 2nd century BCE):

> This book tells the story of *Tobit* son of Tobiel son of Hananiel son of Aduel son of Gabael son of Raphael of the descendants of Asiel, of the tribe of Naphtali, who *in the days of King Shalmaneser of the Assyrians* was *taken into captivity* from *Thisbe*, which is to the south of Kedesh Naphtali in Upper Galilee, above Asher toward the west, and north of Phogor (Tobit 1:1–2; emphasis mine)

The περιστάσεις in the prologue of Tobit:

who	Tobit (1:1)
what	taken captive (1:2)
when	in the days of King Shalmaneser (1:2)
where	Thisbe (1:2)
why	—
in what way	—
by what means	—

In reading the prologue to Tobit, we see that the creator selected a truncated version of the seven circumstances. In the first two verses, the writer opens his narrative with details about the forthcoming story. The writer of Tobit quickly identifies four of the seven circumstances: *who*, *what*, *when*, and *where*—and reserves the *why* and *hows* for the reader to discover throughout the book.[37] Tobit's identification of the *peristaseis* is both clear and explicit. As a Hellenistic work, it is possible that the author of the book of Tobit was aware of *peristaseis* theory, but it is more likely that the circumstances arose from the general expectations that come with narrative prose writing. To put it another way: Letting the reader know the *who*, *what*, *when*, and *where* is self-evident to the creation of narrative by the time of the writing of Tobit. What makes the book of Tobit interesting (given its place in the history of literature) is its clear leading with four of the seven circumstances.

---

36 Which is perhaps one reason why Pseudo-Augustine does not want to give a definition of the circumstances, preferring to just give their partition as explanation enough for the average reader; see (Pseudo-)Augustine, *Rhet.* 7.

37 Cf. Robert J. Littman, *Tobit: The Book of Tobit in Codex Sinaiticus*, Septuagint Commentary Series (Leiden: Brill, 2008), 44.

We now move to two significant narratives from the same time period and in the same language as the prologue of the Fourth Gospel. First, the novel *Chaereas and Callirhoe*, written in a koine form of Greek probably in the early 1st century CE by Chariton,[38] is a narrative that opens with most of the circumstances in the first sentences:

> I, Chariton of Aphrodisias, clerk of the lawyer Athenagoras, am going to relate *a love story* which took place in *Syracuse. Hermocrates*, ruler of Syracuse, victor over the Athenians, had a daughter named *Callirhoe* ... suitors came pouring in ... But *Love wanted to make a match of his own* devising (Chariton, *Chaer.* 1.1 [Goold, LCL; emphasis mine])[39]

The περιστάσεις in the prologue of *Chaereas and Callirhoe:*

who	Callirhoe
what	a love story
when	(during the rule of) Hermocrates
where	Syracuse
why	Eros wanted to make a match of his own
in what way	—
by what means	—

When we consider Chariton's opening, we can immediately detect four of the seven circumstances: *who*, *what*, *where* and *why*. *When* is not as obvious to the modern reader, but the ancient reader would clearly have understood the *when* to be during the rule of Hermocrates (the reign of a ruler being an acceptable temporal marker for 1st century readers).[40] Thus, Chariton opens his story with five of the seven rhetorical circumstances. Like Tobit, Chariton makes his use of the *peristaseis* clear and explicit for his readers.

Even more so than Chariton, Josephus opens *The Jewish War*, an eyewitness account written in a more formal Greek around 75 CE, with a strong use of circumstances to set the details and expectations of his story for his readers in the prologue:

38 This date follows current scholarly consensus, and makes *Chaereas and Callirhoe* the oldest of the Greek novels; see Ronald F. Hock, "The Greek Novel," in *Greco-Roman Literature and the New Testament*, ed. David E. Aune, SBLSBS 21 (Atlanta: Scholars, 1988), 128.

39 Chariton's lead appears to follow or mimic the lead of Thucydides' *History of the Peloponnesian War* from the late 5th century BCE, which also leads with most of the circumstances; see Thucydides, *Hist.* 1.1.1; and cf. Stefan Tilg, *Chariton of Aphrodisias and the Invention of the Greek Love Novel* (Oxford: Oxford University, 2010), 157, 217–18.

40 Aristotle's use of the idea of "when" does not indicate an exact moment in time, as a modern reader may expect from a date, but instead a season of time in which the events may occur; see Sloan, "*Septem Circumstantiae*," 239.

> *The war of the Jews against the Romans* ... [previous accounts are flawed and nowhere there is] ... *historical accuracy.* In these circumstances, I—Josephus ... [eyewitness] ... propose to provide *the subjects of the Roman Empire* with *a narrative of the facts*, by *translating into Greek the account* ... (Josephus, *J.W.* 1.1 [Thackeray, LCL, emphasis mine])

The περιστάσεις in the prologue of *The Jewish War:*

who	the subjects of the Roman empire
what	the war of the Jews against the Romans
when	[autobiographical: the war and its aftermath]
where	[autobiographical: the war and its aftermath]
why	(for the sake of) historical accuracy
in what way	a narrative of the facts
by what means	translating into Greek my previous account

In Josephus' prologue,[41] the reader can spot most of the seven circumstances: *who*, *what*, *why*, *in what way* and *by what means.*[42] At first blush, *where* and *when* appear to be missing in Josephus. However, because Josephus begins with a first-person, eyewitness style, the *where* and *when* are understood implicitly as coming from his autobiographical point of view—meaning that the *where* and *when* are intended to be construed by the reader as the war and its immediate aftermath (recent history).[43] If we accept the implicitly stated situation at the beginning of *The Jewish War*, we have a narrative from the 1st century CE whose prologue is comprised of all seven circumstances. While Josephus' use of the circumstances are not as explicit as Tobit's or Chariton's, they are clear enough for his readers to frame the trajectory of the rest of the story.

Before turning to the Fourth Gospel, we should consider the role of *peristaseis* in the first three gospels. The Gospel of Matthew does not use circumstances in its prologue, with the Matthean writer choosing instead to set the direction for his work with a long and complex genealogy. In this way, Matthew follows a generic

41 For those who speak of the lead to Josephus as a prologue, see for example Daniel R. Schwartz, *Reading the First Century: On Reading Josephus and Studying Jewish History of the First Century*, WUNT 300 (Tübingen: Mohr Siebeck, 2013), 27; and Steve Mason, "Of Audience and Meaning: Reading Josephus' Bellum Judaicum in the Context of a Flavian Audience," in *Josephus and Jewish History in Flavian Rome and Beyond*, ed. Joseph Sievers and Gaia Lembi, JSJSup 104 (Leiden: Brill, 2005), 88–90.

42 Perhaps unwittingly, R. J. H. Shutt writes that "Josephus first explains the circumstances which led to the composition of the *Jewish War*"; see idem, *Studies in Josephus* (London: SPCK, 1961), 18.

43 Steve Mason offers a related take on the autobiographical point of view, or the *now* of the implied author, arguing English translations often mislead modern readers into thinking that Josephus speaks only in the historic past, whereas the actual text is "much livelier and more fluid," as Josephus is in the midst of a "vigorous debate with other [contemporaneous] writers"; see Mason, "Of Audience and Meaning," 88–89.

pattern that is found in Hebraic writing.[44] The gospel of Mark also does not use circumstances in its prologue, with the Markan writer instead choosing to open with a purpose statement that is in many ways more akin to a Greek treatise (Aristotle, *Eudemian Ethics* 1.1) or an OT oracle (Joel 1:1; Obad 1; Hab 1:1) than the other canonical gospels. In contrast to these two gospels, the Gospel of Luke follows closely with Josephus in a less explicit use of the *peristaseis* to frame its prologue:

> Inasmuch as many have undertaken to compile *an account of the things accomplished among us*, just as they were handed down to us by those who from the beginning were eyewitnesses and servants of the word, it seemed fitting for me as well, *having investigated everything carefully from the beginning, to write it out for you in consecutive order, most excellent Theophilus; so that you may know the exact truth about the things you have been taught* (Luke 1:1–4 [NASB]; emphasis mine)

The περιστάσεις in the prologue of Luke:

who	most excellent Theophilus
what	an account of the things accomplished among us
when	[autobiographical: completion of investigation]
where	[autobiographical: completion of investigation]
why	so that you may know the exact truth …
in what way	having investigated everything carefully …
by what means	to write it out for you in consecutive order

In Luke's gospel, the reader can spot five of the seven circumstances. At first blush, *where* and *when* appear to be missing in Luke, just as in Josephus. However, because Luke begins with a first-person, eyewitness style, the *where* and *when* are also understood implicitly as coming from his autobiographical point of view—meaning that the *where* and *when* are intended to be construed by the reader as the follow-up to his investigation (recent history). As a result, we have a second narrative from the 1st century CE whose prologue is comprised of all seven circumstances. In fact, if we consider the prologue of the *Jewish War* and the prologue of Luke through the lens of the *peristaseis*, they are similar in virtually every way.

Finding *peristaseis* in the Gospel of Luke is probably not surprising to the implied reader, given its historiographical tendencies. However, more like Tobit

44 See for example, Herbert W. Basser, *The Gospel of Matthew and Judaic Traditions: A Relevance-Based Commentary*, with Marsha B. Cohen, BRLJ 46 (Leiden: Brill, 2015), 29; Craig A. Evans, "'The Book of the Genesis of Jesus Christ': The Purpose of Matthew in Light of the Incipit," in *Biblical Interpretation in Early Christian Gospels: Vol 2, The Gospel of Matthew*, ed. Thomas R. Hatina, LNTS 310 (London: T&T Clark, 2008), 63–67; and Brian M. Nolan, *The Royal Son of God: The Christology of Matthew 1–2 in the Setting of the Gospel*, OBO 23 (Göttingen: Vandenhoeck & Ruprecht, 1979), 24–28.

and Chariton, than Josephus and Luke, the Fourth Gospel makes even more clear and explicit use of the *peristaseis* to frame its narrative than any of these previous examples.

4. The Peristaseis in the Johannine Prologue

In light of these examples, we now turn to the prologue of the Fourth Gospel. One part of the Gospel that most stands out as potentially representative of a micro-genre, and was created in a way that is indicative of genre bending, is the prologue. Consequently, the reader should expect the prologue of John to show evidence of a specific type of genre formation that is related to, but may also transcend, the basic character of βίος. The reader can also expect the prologue to be formed in such a way as to both introduce and then integrate (in some way) with the remainder of the Gospel.[45]

In traditional Johannine scholarship, the first section of the Gospel is widely held to be John 1:1–18, the "prologue." Yet, the text itself does not seem to be so obvious in this distinction. While there is consensus in modern scholarship that there is a plot shift at John 1:19, a similar (if not stronger) plot shift also occurs at John 1:6. In fact, P. J. Williams has recently shown that the reception history of the Fourth Gospel strongly favors that the first five verses are most likely the "real" prologue to the gospel text.[46] This is the reason that Augustine labelled John 1:1–5 as the "first chapter" of the book.[47] Therefore, the prologue in John 1:1–5 is the jewel in the crown of the beginning of John, and is the most important part of the longer introduction for discerning the genre of the rest of the Gospel.

In the prologue of the Fourth Gospel, all seven circumstances appear explicitly and in short order to introduce the reader to the narrative:

> *In the beginning* was the *Word*, and the Word was *with God*, and the Word was God. He was *in the beginning with God*. All things *came into being through him*, and *without him not one thing came into being*. What has come into being in him was *life*, and the life was *the light of all people*. And the light shines in the dark, and the dark has not overcome it (John 1:1–5; emphasis mine)

45 Of course, this view runs counter to those commentators who see John as a reworking of multiple sources, replete with seams, aporias, and awkward editorial transitions. This debate is far beyond the scope of this essay, but for just one discussion on the weakness of many of these arguments, see Douglas Estes, *The Temporal Mechanics of the Fourth Gospel: A Theory of Hermeneutical Relativity in the Gospel of John*, BIS 92 (Brill, 2008), 165–86.

46 P. J. Williams, "Not the Prologue of John." *JSNT* 33 (2011): 375–386.

47 As an ancient reader, Augustine's view of the segmentation of the text is quite important here; see Augustine, *Tractates on the Gospel of John* 2.1.

The περιστάσεις of the prologue of John:

who	the Word (1:1)
what	life (1:4)
when	at creation (1:1)
where	with God (1:1)
why	to be the light for all people (1:4)
in what way	came in to being (1:3)
by what means	through the Word (1:3)

That all seven circumstances are accounted for in the first several clauses of the Gospel is substantial evidence that the gospel writer created the lead around the seven circumstances with the intent of defining the story for the reader. Since the Gospel writer was in some way writing about Jesus (John 20:31), the writer tied each of these circumstances to his protagonist (akin to Tobit and *Chaereas and Callirhoe*). That is not all. To even more clearly demonstrate the structuring effect of the circumstances on the reader of the prologue, here is the clausal breakdown of the circumstances in the prologue, with an explicit structuring of the *peristaseis:*

Ἐν ἀρχῇ ἦν ὁ λόγος,	when
καὶ ὁ λόγος ἦν πρὸς τὸν θεόν,	where
καὶ θεὸς ἦν ὁ λόγος.	who
οὗτος ἦν ἐν ἀρχῇ πρὸς τὸν θεόν.	when, where
πάντα δι' αὐτοῦ ἐγένετο,	in what way
καὶ χωρὶς αὐτοῦ ἐγένετο οὐδὲ ἕν. ὃ γέγονεν	by what means
ἐν αὐτῷ ζωὴ ἦν,	what
καὶ ἡ ζωὴ ἦν τὸ φῶς τῶν ἀνθρώπων	why

When we display the first clauses of the prologue in accordance with their circumstances, the prose clauses line up in such a way as to create a stylistic pattern that reinforces each of the circumstances. Unlike Josephus and Luke, writers who meander through the circumstances with extraneous phrases and clauses, the fourth evangelist does less of this by setting up an intricately tight frame to lead his readers through the circumstances. First, there is the situation of the *when* and *where* (1:1a, 1:1b), followed by the important *who* (1:1c). Next, the evangelist restates the situation (1:2). Then the reader learns the *hows* of the story (1:3), followed by the acknowledgement of the *what* (1:4), and concludes with the all-important *why* (1:4). (Verse 5 develops the *why* with secondary *how* explanations). Because of the subject matter, readers commonly accept the fact that the *who* is the most important part of the Johannine lead. However, Aristotle noted that the *why* is the most distinct, and is in many ways the most important—which raises the question as to whether readers should emphasize the *why* of the prologue as much as the *who.*[48] If Aristotle is correct, perhaps modern interpreters should spend time emphasizing "to be the light for all people" almost as much as the "Word."

Based on this evidence, the *intent* of the opening of John is to define for the reader what the circumstances of the story will be in as clear means as possible. The gospel writer used a series of successive clauses to lead the reader carefully through each of the seven circumstances. This should not surprise us. As we have seen, delimiting and structuring the story through the use of *peristaseis* was a common feature of narrative prose in the ancient world, and common enough to have provided direction for the fourth evangelist.[49]

5. Implications of the *Peristaseis* in the Johannine Prologue

As Horace (65 BCE – 8 BCE) reminds us, one of the worst mistakes a writer can make is to put the wrong beginning at the head of their creative work (Horace, *Ars* 1–13). Unsurprisingly, ancient writers took extra steps to grab the attention of their readers while appropriately positioning the prologue in such a way as to lead readers deeper into the narrative world. In the case of the Fourth Gospel, the gospel writer turned to the basic *circumstances* of the story to be told to create a framework for setting up his story. In doing so, seven out of the seven περιστάσεις appear in tight succession in the opening sentences of the prologue. There are at least three exegetical implications for reading John in light of its circumstantial framework.

First, the fourth evangelist uses the *peristaseis* to help reveal the genre of the text. The presence of the circumstances is an indicator for the reader to expect a narrative or story, such as a biography or history or tall tale. Perhaps more importantly, John uses the *peristaseis* in the prologue to point out what the genre of the prologue and Gospel is *not:* The Gospel is not a meditation, a hymn, a legal argument, a letter, an oracle, or a sectarian tract. Instead, the *peristaseis* in the prologue reveal that the rest of the Gospel will be a story about a person in a certain time and place in which certain events happen for a certain reason (in other words, the "elements of narration").

Second, the fourth evangelist does not introduce the circumstances of the story in the way that his implied readers may expect; rather than starting at a point in Jesus' life (such as his birth), John starts before the beginning of the

48 Cf. Sloan, "*Septem Circumstantiae*," 240–41.

49 Both Hebrews 1:1–4 and Revelation 1:1–3 open with several of the circumstances grouped together at the very beginning, though they do not appear to have the same consistency or commitment to the circumstances as John's Gospel, *Chaereas and Callirhoe*, or *The Jewish War*.

world as in the book of Genesis. Thus, John bends the micro-genre of circumstances with that of mythic beginnings, creating a new type of prologue that is framed as both *peristaseis* and *archaiologia.* These opening lines take on a prosaic form, bent with a poetic feel, eminently suitable for introducing the remainder of the prose narrative of John, given his take on the divine identity of Jesus.[50] By blending these two generic types together, John signals to the reader that this story is not some mundane story, but is an epic tale in which creation erupts (ברא), and from this the λόγος traverses time and space, and descends from the Father.[51] There is no doubt the evangelist does this in part to grab the reader's interest.[52] This genre bending and blending is also quite interesting for the reader: The creative movement depicted in John 1:1–5 is not itself circumstantial, as it lies outside the ken of human understanding of the circumstances of time and space; yet John writes with the *peristaseis* to create the illusion of time and space to introduce the reader to a Word who is both divine and enfleshed (John 1:14).[53]

Third, the fourth evangelist uses the *peristaseis* in the prologue to not only introduce the topic but to set a framework for the rest of the text. These circumstances communicate preliminary details about the Word, but they metacommunicate to the reader that the rest of the story is going to be about the further adventures of the Word. The evangelist uses the *peristaseis* framework as a launch pad for the rest of the plot of the narrative.[54] In some ways, this is a literal launch—the reader starts with the information from each of the circumstances, and as the reading ensues, begins to follow the *who*, *what*, *when*, *where*, *why*, *in what way*, and *by what means* through the story world. These circumstances keep moving from the starting point as the reader moves; for example, the reader should not expect the same *when* and *where* in the rest of the narrative as the prologue; this is the natural progression of a plot. But the *when* and *where* of the prologue sets up the rest of the story by providing an "on-ramp" for the reader. In contrast, it is not uncommon for a prologue to use the *peristaseis* to launch the *who* (explicitly, if the *who* is the protagonist as in Tobit, *Chaereas and Callirhoe*, and John; and implicitly, if the *who* is the narrator as in Josephus and Luke). But as the story proceeds, the details about the *who* changes and grows, developing the character for the reader. In other ways, John's use of the *peristaseis* is a

50 Not unlike the "fusion of poetry and prose" found in Genesis 1; see Claus Westermann, *Genesis 1–11*, trans. John J. Scullion, CC (Minneapolis: Fortress, 1994), 90–1.

51 Estes, *Temporal Mechanics*, 226.

52 In return, it helps set up the rhetorical and dialectical dimensions of the Fourth Gospel; cf. Douglas Estes, *The Questions of Jesus in John: Logic, Rhetoric and Persuasive Discourse*, BIS 115 (Leiden: Brill, 2013), 166–71.

53 For experienced readers of John, the mixing of genres becomes ironic by reducing divine acts to mundane circumstances.

54 Which occurs along the arc of a temporal geodesic of creation (past), testimony (present), and glorification/disciples' journeys (future); see Estes, *Temporal Mechanics*, 224–26.

rhetorical launch—a launch that starts the reader within the framework of the *peristaseis* and *archaiologia* of the Word, pushing the reader to believe (John 20:30–31), so that the Word may be the light to all people (John 1:5).

Jörg Frey

From the *Sēmeia* Narratives to the Gospel as a Significant Narrative: On Genre-Bending in the Johannine Miracle Stories*

In his article "Genre Bending in the Fourth Gospel," Harold Attridge has suggested a new way of understanding literary genres in the Fourth Gospel, demonstrating the presence of "genre-bending" in John.[1] The idea is that in this Gospel literary genres are not simply used or adopted, but rather modified, twisted, or blended.[2] By his remarkable literary artistry, the evangelist develops a new literary technique, a language that goes beyond that of the earlier tradition or the Synoptic Gospels in order to communicate his message. While Attridge has demonstrated that these modifications chiefly appear in the discourses and dialogues in John and as his student George Parsenios has successfully applied this new paradigm in his interpretation of the Johannine farewell discourses,[3] the present article will focus on the *sēmeia* narratives of the Fourth Gospel. In the present article, we will inquire into the particular design of the Johannine miracle stories and their modification of traditional narrative patterns in order to establish a web of signification encompassing not only the Johannine *sēmeia* narratives, but also the Gospel as a whole. These observations are important both for understanding the literary genres in John and for reconstructing the epistemology and the narrative intentions of the Fourth Gospel.

---

* For numerous corrections and suggestions I am grateful to Dr. Anni Hentschel and to Jacob Cerone.

1 H. Attridge, "Genre Bending in the Fourth Gospel," *JBL* 121 (2002): 3–21; republished in *Essays on John and Hebrews*, WUNT 264 (Tübingen: Mohr Siebeck, 2010), 61–78.

2 Cf. G. Parsenios, *Departure and Consolation: The Johannine Farewell Discourses in Light of Greco-Roman Literature*, NovTSup 117 (Leiden, Boston: Brill, 2005), 10. Parsenios writes that "this 'bending' is the effect of blending various literary forms," and John "bends and twists the testament form" (ibid.).

3 In the farewell discourses of John 13–17, Parsenios shows various blendings between forms of the literary testament, the symposium, consolation literature, and elements of the ancient drama.

1. On Genres and Genre Research

The identification of literary genres and the comparison of aspects of genre is one of the most important and problematic methodological tools of NT research. Although there were already discussions on the rhetorical forms of speech in antiquity[4] and early Christian authors were involved in debates about the style of the New Testament,[5] and although the interest in the literary shape of the New Testament was later adopted by Humanists and humanistically educated Reformers,[6] the interest in particular literary genres of the New Testament was introduced only at the beginning of the 20th century classical form criticism ("Formgeschichte"),[7] as developed by the Classicist Eduard Norden[8] and the New Testament scholars Karl Ludwig Schmidt, Martin Dibelius, and Rudolf Bultmann.[9] The heralds of the new method were, however, only interested in the Synoptics where the observation of literary forms and their alleged oral pre-history was considered a tool to discover the earlier and earliest strata of the Jesus

4 Cf. Quintilian, *Inst.* 3.4.1–4 or also Cicero, *De or.* 2.11 ff., where it is discussed whether there are only the three "classical" genres of speech (symbouleutic, epideictic, dicanic), or many genres (e.g., for giving thanks, mourning, comfort).

5 Origen could reject the idea that the NT had a "barbarian" style with the argument that the lack of rhetorical bliss and persuasive artistry is a sign of its truth and Divinity (*Cels.* 1.62); Augustine, on the other hand, regarded the NT as a book of rhetorical examples (*Doctr. Chr.* 4); cf. M. Reiser, *Sprache und literarische Formen des Neuen Testaments*, UTB 2197 (Paderborn: Schöningh 2001), 31–32.

6 Cf. C. J. Classen, "Melanchthon's Rhetorical Interpretation of Biblical and Non-Biblical Texts," in idem, *Rhetorical Criticism of the New Testament*, WUNT 128 (Tübingen: Mohr Siebeck, 2000), 99–177.

7 The German term "Formgeschichte" is more appropriate to that approach since it was decidedly interested in the historical quest for earliest oral traditions, not just in distinguishing and describing genres.

8 Norden used the plural term "Formengeschichte" (cf. E. Norden, *Agnostos Theos: Untersuchungen zur Formengeschichte religiöser Rede* [Leipzig and Berlin: Teubner, 1913]). "Formgeschichte" was coined later by Martin Dibelius (see next footnote).

9 K. L. Schmidt, *Der Rahmen der Geschichte Jesu: Literarkritische Untersuchungen zur ältesten Jesusüberlieferung* (Berlin: Trowitzsch & Sohn, 1919); idem, "Formgeschichte," in *Die Religion in Geschichte und Gegenwart*, 2nd ed. (Tübingen: Mohr, 1928), 2:638–640; M. Dibelius, *Die Formgeschichte des Evangeliums* (Tübingen: Mohr, 1919; [6th ed., with additions by G. Iber; Tübingen: Mohr, 1971]); idem, *From Tradition to Gospel*, trans. Bertram Lee Woolf; Scribner Library (New York: Charles Scribner's Sons, n.d.); R. Bultmann, *Die Geschichte der synoptischen Tradition*, FRLANT 29 (Göttingen: Vandenhoeck & Ruprecht, 1921; [10th ed., with a postscript by G. Theißen; Göttingen: Vandenhoeck & Ruprecht, 1995]); idem, *The History of the Synoptic Tradition*, trans. John Marsh (New York: Harper & Row, 1963). On the backgrounds, see W. Baird, *History of New Testament Research: Volume Two: From Jonathan Edwards to Rudolf Bultmann* (Minneapolis: Fortress, 2003, 269–286), and F. Hahn, "Die Formgeschichte des Evangeliums: Voraussetzungen, Ausbau und Tragweite," in idem, *Zur Formgeschichte des Evangeliums*, Wege der Forschung 81 (Darmstadt: Wissenschaftliche Buchgesellschaft, 1985), 427–477.

tradition from the written gospels and sources. According to the critical consensus established around 1900,[10] the Fourth Gospel was generally considered a late stage of the development of the Jesus tradition or even a historically invalid theological allegory.[11] Accordingly, the "Formgeschichte," developed with regard to the Synoptics for the sake of historical Jesus research, was considered less fruitful for the interpretation of John,[12] and, in the classical works of "Formgeschichte," Johannine texts are only marginally discussed as they were thought to be late developments, legendary expansions, mixtures of the respective genres, or the result of a transfer of Hellenistic narratives into early Christian preaching.[13]A fruitful change in scholarship can be seen in the development of a new type of form criticism, inspired by modern linguistics and the consideration of ancient rhetoric. The *Neue Formgeschichte*, developed by Klaus Berger in the 1980s,[14] was conceptualized as a rejection of the ideological presuppositions of classical form criticism, its predominant interest in historical reconstruction of the "beginnings," and its "Romantic" understanding of literature idealizing the "pure" and simple forms.[15] Berger classifies the forms of NT literature according to the organizing patterns of ancient rhetoric, and the focus is on the textual elements that shape a single text rather than on the common elements that constitute a genre. In a more "nominalistic" understanding of genres, it is now considered that literary genres do not simply "exist" like a box in which a number texts can be put, but are defined according to various criteria and particular research interests.[16] For the present purpose, it is important that the new form criticism is interested in all texts of the NT (and beyond), including the Synoptics, John, and the other writings. This is made possible since the focus on the reconstruction of historical origins or the earliest tradition is abandoned.

10 Cf. J. Frey, *Die johanneische Eschatologie: Ihre Probleme im Spiegel der Forschung seit Reimarus*, WUNT 96 (Tübingen: Mohr, 1997), 38–39.

11 Thus A. Loisy, *Le quatrième évangile*, 2nd ed. (Paris: Picard, 1921), 75; see also A. Jülicher, *Einleitung in das Neue Testament*, 5/6th ed. (Tübingen: Mohr, 1906), 379.

12 J. Beutler, "Literarische Gattungen im Johannesevangelium: Ein Forschungsbericht 1919–1980," *ANRW* II 25.3: 2506–2568. Beutler writes, "daß die … ‚Formgeschichte' lange Zeit als wenig erfolgversprechend in der Johannesexegese angesehen wurde" (2508).

13 Cf. Beutler, "Gattungen," 2510–2513; on the discussion of the Johannine miracle stories, see Dibelius, *Formgeschichte* (6th ed.), 88–90; Bultmann, *Geschichte* (10th ed.), 242, 253.

14 Cf. his book-length "article": "Hellenistische Gattungen im Neuen Testament," *ANRW* II 25,2, 1031–1432, 1831–1885; K. Berger, *Formgeschichte des Neuen Testaments* (Heidelberg: Quelle & Meyer, 1984); idem, *Einführung in die Formgeschichte*, UTB 1444 (Tübingen: Francke, 1987); idem, *Formen und Gattungen im Neuen Testament*, UTB 2532 (Tübingen: Francke, 2005).

15 Cf. the contrasting comparison of old and new form criticism in Berger, *Einführung*, 241–261.

16 On the issue of "nominalism" and "realism" in genre research, cf. R. Zimmermann, "Frühchristliche Wundererzählungen: Eine Hinführung," in *Kompendium der frühchristlichen Wundererzählungen: Band 1: Die Wunder Jesu*, ed. R. Zimmermann (Gütersloh: Gütersloher Verlagshaus, 2013), 23–24.

This type of form criticism provides a theoretical concept for the interpretation of the individual design of particular texts within the context of the various genres of speech or literature. In this paradigm, the genre of Johannine texts and their literary design can be discussed more fruitfully; there is no need to presuppose any "original" and "pure" form, and even the modification or mixture of genres can be discussed without the negative evaluations of classical form criticism. This is particularly interesting for the Johannine miracle stories.

2. Miracle Stories as *Sēmeia* in John in the Scholarly Debate

But before focusing on these stories, we must briefly note the problems of the term miracle stories. As Berger rightly criticizes, this term, as used in Bultmann's pioneering history of the synoptic tradition,[17] does not denote a coherent genre but rather an ancient concept of reality from a modern perspective.[18] The term arises from a modern concept of nature and its laws, as Bultmann's basic distinction between healing miracles (which may be historically "possible") and miracles of nature (considered as "impossible") is quite obviously based on such presuppositions. In opposition to such philosophical views, Berger tries to keep within the literary description. Avoiding the label "miracle story," he can attribute the respective NT texts to a wide range of rhetorical genres.[19] Other scholars still use the term but with an awareness that they do not make up a real common genre.[20] This confirms the view that genres, as such, never "exist" but are actually defined. Albeit, we cannot ignore that ancient readers already had some kind of genre awareness.[21] The Fourth Gospel plays with such an awareness of genre by its particular use of the term σημεῖα, primarily in relation to six of the seven miracle stories.[22] It is no coincidence that, apart from John 20:30, this term is used precisely with regard to those narratives of Jesus' miraculous acts. Those

17 Cf. Bultmann, *Geschichte* (10th ed.), 223–260.

18 Berger, *Formgeschichte*, 305: "Wunder/Wundererzählung ist kein Gattungsbegriff, sondern moderne Beschreibung eines antiken Wirklichkeitsverständnisses." Cf. Zimmermann, "Frühchristliche Wundererzählungen," 23–24.

19 Berger, *Formgeschichte*, 306–7; idem, *Einführung*, 76–84.

20 Cf. G. Theißen, *Urchristliche Wundergeschichten: Ein Beitrag zur formgeschichtlichen Erforschung der synoptischen* Evangelien, 7th ed. (Gütersloh: Gütersloher Verlagshaus, 1998); idem, "Die Erforschung der synoptischen Tradition seit R. Bultmann: Ein Überblick über die formgeschichtliche Arbeit im 20. Jahrhundert," in Bultmann, *Geschichte* (10th ed.), 409–452 (435–439); M. Reiser, *Sprache und literarische Formen des Neuen Testaments*, 137–141; Zimmermann, "Frühchristliche Wundererzählungen," 22–25.

21 Zimmermann, "Frühchristliche Wundererzählungen," 23, adopts the term of a moderate nominalism of genres ("abgeschwächen Nominalismus").

22 In John 4:48, the evangelist also demonstrates an awareness of the term σημεῖα καὶ τέρατα used more frequently in the synoptic tradition and in Acts.

miracle stories have always been a *crux interpretum* in Johannine research. In the early period of modern research, with its strong interest in the historical value of the gospels for reconstructing the Jesus of history, scholars were particularly puzzled by the increased miraculous character and the historical incredibility of some Johannine episodes (e.g., the wine miracle [John 2:1–11] or the demonstration of Jesus' divine power in the resurrection of Lazarus [John 11:1–45]).[23] Thus, already in the early 19th century, critics suggested that the most implausible stories were secondary additions to an earlier apostolic work,[24] whereas others assumed a reverse development and considered the Johannine discourses later philosophical expansions of an earlier narrative work.[25] With the rise of a more subtle and methodologically reflective *Literarkritik*, the miracles were either attributed to an early "Grundschrift"[26] or to a pre-Johannine source.[27] The latter view, adopted by Rudolf Bultmann in his landmark commentary, became the most influential pattern of interpreting the Johannine miracle stories. Based on the observation of a tension between strongly miraculous episodes and other textual elements that represent a critical stance towards miracles, belief based on miracles (cf. John 4:48 etc.), or a more symbolic reading of the stories, this hypothesis enabled interpreters to separate the evangelist from his narrative material. Now, the evangelist himself could be considered a critical interpreter of his source and its miracle stories.[28] He could be "rescued" from the charge of a naïve belief in miracles, which were considered an incredible and unnecessary burden for the Christian kerygma. Bultmann's evangelist could thus serve as the

23 John stresses the large amount of wine, the leftovers of the bread, the healing in John 4 from a distance, the 38 years of illness of the man at the pool of Bethesda, the blind one as a man born blind, and Lazarus' smell of decay after four days.

24 Thus Ch. H. Weisse, *Die evangelische Geschichte kritisch und philosophisch bearbeitet* (Leipzig: Breitkopf & Härtel, 1838), and Alex. Schweizer, *Das Evangelium Johannis nach seinem inneren Wert und seiner Bedeutung für das Leben Jesu kritisch untersucht* (Leipzig: Weidmann, 1841); cf. G. van Belle, *The Signs Source in the Fourth Gospel: Historical Survey and Critical Evaluation of the Semeia Hypothesis*, BETL 116 (Leuven: Peeters, 1994), 1–4. The views were later adopted by Hans Hinrich Wendt in a number of publications. Cf. especially H.-H. Wendt, *Das Johannesevangelium: Eine Untersuchung seiner Entstehung und seines geschichtlichen Wertes* (Göttingen: Vandenhoeck & Ruprecht, 1900).

25 Thus Ernest Renan, *The Life of Jesus* (London: Trübner, 1891). On the predecessors of the later "Literarkritik" see Frey, *Die johanneische Eschatologie 1*, 51–53. More particularly with regard to the prehistory of the Signs Source hypothesis see van Belle, *Signs Source*, 1–24.

26 Cf. J. Wellhausen, *Das Evangelium Johannis* (Berlin: Reimer, 1908).

27 Cf. A. Faure, "Die alttestamentlichen Zitate im 4. Evangelium und die Quellenscheidungshypothese," *ZNW* 21 (1922), 99–121.

28 Cf. R. Bultmann, *Das Evangelium des Johannes*, KEK 2 (Göttingen: Vandenhoeck & Ruprecht, 1941). On the hermeneutical decisions of Bultmann's interpretation, see Frey, *Die johanneische Eschatologie 1*, 119–150; idem, "Johannine Christology and Eschatology," in *Beyond Bultmann. Reckoning a New Testament Theology*, ed. B. W. Longenecker and M. C. Parsons (Waco: Baylor University Press, 2014), 101–116.

herald of the critical view of miracles and a forerunner and biblical pattern of a modern Protestant theology of the Word. The idea of the Semeia Source was further developed by other exegetes[29] or modified toward a more comprehensive Signs Gospel in the works of Robert Fortna.[30] But the criteria and principles of reconstructing such a pre-Johannine source were also severely questioned.[31] At present, only a minority of Johannine scholars still maintain the assumption of a coherent source of John's signs or a narrative predecessor of the whole Gospel.[32] There is no need to enter the discussion here. Just two points must be noted: (1) Even for exegetes who methodologically accept the reconstruction of pre-Johannine strata of the miracle stories, their coherence in one common source has become questionable, and (2) if a certain knowledge of the synoptic tradition is accepted for the evangelist, the sources for the narratives in John 6 and some others (possibly 4:46–54 and 5:1–18) might be variations of the synoptic accounts or one of them. Most generally, the reductive method of stripping off all explanatory, metaphorical, or theological elements from the Johannine miracle narratives in order to arrive at a pure and simple form of the miracle story has become questionable since the "laws" of miracle stories developing from a pure form toward more developed forms cannot be applied to a literary work that is so thoughtfully designed by its author. More modern research, especially the new type of rhetorically inspired form criticism, has left the focus on John's sources behind and is more interested in the literary design of the Gospel and its impact on its implied readers. From the more recent works, I would like to highlight three contributions.

Michael Labahn, in his massive dissertation *Jesus als Lebensspender*, has re-established the form critical issues in his discussion of the Johannine miracle

29 Cf. especially J. Becker, "Wunder und Christologie," *NTS* 16 (1969/70): 130–148; idem, *Das Evangelium nach Johannes*, 3rd ed., ÖTK 4/1–2 (Gütersloh: Gütersloher; Würzburg: Echter, 1991), 134–142.

30 R. T. Fortna, *The Gospel of Signs. A Reconstruction of the Narrative Source Underlying the Fourth Gospel*, SNTSMS 11 (Cambridge: Cambridge University Press, 1970); idem, *The Fourth Gospel and its Predecessor* (Edinburgh: T&T Clark, 1988).

31 For criticism see most thoroughly G. van Belle, *The Signs Source* (originally idem, *De Semeia-Bron in het Vierde Evangelie. Ontstaan en groei van een hypothese*, SNTA 10 [Leuven: Peeters, 1975]; see also K. Berger, *Hellenistische Gattungen*, 1230–1; W. J. Bittner, *Jesu Zeichen im Johannesevangelium*, WUNT 2/26 (Tübingen: Mohr Siebeck, 1987), 4–14; U. Schnelle, *Antidoketische Christologie im Johannesevangelium* (Göttingen: Vandenhoeck & Ruprecht, 1987), 168–182; H. Thyen, "Liegt dem Johannesevangelium eine Semeia-Quelle zugrunde?" in idem, *Studien zum Corpus Iohanneum*, WUNT 214 (Tübingen: Mohr Siebeck, 2007), 443–452.

32 Among the exegetes still advocating for that theory are M. Theobald, *Das Evangelium nach Johannes. Kapitel 1–12*, RNT 4/1 (Regensburg: Pustet 2009), 32–42, and the two commentaries that try to renew a very idiosyncratic type of Literarkritik, F. Siegert, *Das Evangelium des Johannes in seiner ursprünglichen Gestalt: Wiederherstellung und Kommentar*, Schriften des Institutum Judaicum Delitzschianum 6 (Göttingen: Vandenhoeck & Ruprecht, 2007) and U. von Wahlde, *The Gospel and Letters of John*, 3 vols.; ECC (Grand Rapids: Eerdmans, 2010).

stories.[33] Although Labahn is still optimistic with regard to the identification of pre-Johannine sources, he could not maintain the idea of one coherent source of all the miracle stories. According to him, only the two Cana miracles in John 2 and 4 were linked before the composition of the Gospel as well as the two miracles from John 6 (cf. Mark 6–8), whereas the other three are single traditions.[34] In the seven episodes analyzed,[35] Labahn finds common characteristics that allow him to maintain the category of "Johannine miracle stories": In all of them, Jesus is sovereign and does not react to the need or request of others; in comparison with their synoptic parallels, the miracles are all increased, and there is always a particular focus on the discovery of the miracle (John 2:9–10; 4:51–53; 6:22–25a; 9:8–9, 18–23). In other aspects, there is more diversity, which may be due to the particular background and history of every single episode. Labahn generally confirms the view that the Johannine miracle stories represent a later stage of the early Christian literary development.[36] Although the analysis is still largely focused on their prehistory, Labahn finally highlights the interpreting insertions or dialogues by which the evangelist develops the "miracles" as "signs" that are transparent for the eschatological revelation and present Jesus as the "life-giver."[37]

In another work that has remained somewhat unnoticed in the English-speaking world, Christian Welck[38] has focused on the Johannine "miracle narratives" in their narrative design. Being more skeptical of the possibilities of reconstructing their prehistory, Welck demonstrates a literary structure of two levels in all seven narratives. First, there is the surface level, the level of the narrated story from the period of Jesus' ministry, a sequence of events from the

33 M. Labahn, *Jesus als Lebensspender: Untersuchungen zu einer Geschichte der johanneischen Tradition anhand ihrer Wundergeschichten*, BZNW 98 (Berlin and New York: de Gruyter, 1998), 78–113.

34 Cf. Labahn, *Jesus als Lebensspender*, 469–470.

35 Labahn does not include John 21:1–14. But for his later works see Michael Labahn, *Offenbarung in Zeichen und Wort: Untersuchungen zur Vorgeschichte von Joh 6,1–25a und seiner Rezeption in der Brotrede*, WUNT 2/117 (Tübingen: Mohr Siebeck, 2000); idem, "Fischen nach Bedeutung:—Sinnstiftung im Wechsel literarischer Kontexte: Der wunderbare Fischfang in Johannes 21 zwischen Inter- und Intratextualität," *SNTSU* 32 (2007), 115–140; idem, "'Blinded by the Light': Blindheit und Licht in Joh 9 im Spiel von Variation und Wiederholung zwischen Erzählung und Metapher," in *Repetitions and Variations in the Fourth Gospel: Style, Text, Interpretation*, ed. G. van Belle, M. Labahn, and P. Maritz, BETL 223 (Leuven: Peeters, 2009), 453–504; idem, "Beim Mahl am Kohlenfeuer trifft man sich wieder (Die Offenbarung beim wunderbaren Fang): Joh 21,1–14," in Zimmermann, *Kompendium der frühchristlichen Wundererzählungen I*, 764–780.

36 Cf. Labahn, *Jesus als Lebensspender*, 491.

37 Labahn, *Jesus als Lebensspender*, 501.

38 Ch. Welck, *Erzählte Zeichen: Die Wundergeschichten des Johannesevangeliums literarisch untersucht. Mit einem Ausblick auf Joh 21*, WUNT 2/69 (Tübingen: Mohr Siebeck, 1994).

narrated world.[39] Second, there is, embedded into the narrated story, a number of hints to other elements in the Gospel text, often related to Jesus' passion and resurrection or the salutary effects of those events for the Johannine readers. These references interrupt the flow of reading on the surface, create a certain symbolism, and constitute the meaning of the narrated event on a deeper level of the whole ministry of Jesus.[40] The title "Erzählte Zeichen" ("narrated signs") points to the view that, according to the concept of the evangelist, the signs are not the miracles as such on their surface level (i.e., not the events from Jesus' earthly period), but only those events in their narrative design and literary presentation. The Johannine narration creates the signs by presenting the past events for present readers. Their significance is presented by various literary elements, but it can be discovered only on the literary level through the lens of the evangelist (who is, in Welck's view, also the author of John 21).

This corresponds to the distinction in John 20:30–31 between the signs that Jesus merely did, and the signs that are written.[41] While many other "signs done" are omitted in the "book" of John, "these" (ταῦτα) are written so that the readers should believe. The signs merely done by Jesus, his deeds in his time, without the literary design created by the author may be unimportant. They do not lead to belief as they did not cause belief among Jesus' contemporaries. Only the "written signs" are designed to provoke belief in Jesus as the Messiah and Son of God. While the majority of Jesus' contemporaries did not (or could not) adequately react to the signs Jesus had done (cf. John 12:37–40), the readers of the Gospel are called to react by faith to the "narrated signs," the textual presentation of the gospel. Thus, the Johannine signs are paradigmatic and significant presentations of the whole of the gospel message.

In his 2003 Cambridge dissertation, Willis Hedley Salier focused on "The Rhetorical Impact of the Sēmeia in the Gospel of John."[42] The sign narratives are read in the context of the trial motif, a trial about the truth which is presented throughout the Gospel. These signs are "cumulative proofs in the trial conducted with respect to the reader."[43] The accompanying discourses or dialogues test and sift the response to Jesus' ministry.[44] But as the trial motif is present in the whole Gospel, Salier explicitly goes beyond the seven narratives usually linked with the

39 In his particular terminology, Welck characterizes that level as "vordergründig-dramatisch."

40 This level is, then, called "hintergründig-heilsdramatisch." Cf. Welck, *Erzählte Zeichen*, 132–133.

41 Welck, *Erzählte Zeichen*, 279–282.

42 W. H. Salier, *The Rhetorical Impact of the Sēmeia in the Gospel of John*, WUNT 2/186 (Tübingen: Mohr Siebeck, 2004).

43 Salier, *Rhetorical Impact*, 172.

44 Salier, *Rhetorical Impact*, 172.

term σημεῖον and considers even the death and resurrection of Jesus a sign. It is "the climactic sign in the Gospel"[45] or, rather, the "sign of signs."[46]

According to Salier, the sign narrative wants to engage the readers, thus serving the stated goal of the Gospel (cf. John 20:30–31): to bring the readers to a response of belief to the story of Jesus. The term thus negotiates "between the conceptual background" of the respective narrative and the "cultural foreground" of a "diversity of audience."[47]

The three works show the tendencies of current research: From the issue of sources to the issues of literary design and rhetoric, from mere issues of history to the exploration of the web of meaning created by the author and communicated by the text, and from the apologetic view that the evangelist did not believe naïvely in the narrated miracles to the acknowledgement that seeing and signs have a positive epistemological function.

3. Narrative Design Indicating Significance: The Making of *Sēmeia*

In the present context, I can only present two rather different sign narratives, the first sign of the wine miracle at Cana (John 2:1–11) and the healing of the man born blind with its extensive dialogical and dramatic expansion (John 9:1–41). Narrative elements point to the wider framework of the Gospel and demand a reading with regard to the whole of Jesus' ministry and its salvific effects.

3.1 The Prototypical Sign at Cana (John 2:1–11)[48]

The wine miracle at Cana is explicitly labelled the "beginning of the signs" (ἀρχὴ τῶν σημείων) or, as we might interpret, the "prototypical sign" of Jesus.[49] It is the evangelist's paradigm to discover the signifying structure of his *sēmeia* narra-

45 Salier, *Rhetorical Impact*, 172.
46 Cf. Salier, *Rhetorical Impact*, 142–171.
47 Salier, *Rhetorical Impact*, 175.
48 The literature is immense. Apart from the commentaries, cf. the early interpretation by the form critic K. L. Schmidt, "Der johanneische Charakter der Erzählung vom Hochzeitswunder in Kana," in *Harnack-Ehrung* (Leipzig: Hinrichs, 1921), 32–43; the pioneering interpretation of the symbolic dimensions in B. Olsson, *Structure and Meaning in the Fourth Gospel: A Text-Linguistic Analysis of John 2:1–11 and 4:1–42*, ConBNT 6 (Lund: Almquist & Wiksell, 1974), 18–114; M. Hengel, "The Interpretation of the Wine Miracle at Cana: John 2.1–11," in *The Glory of Christ in the New Testament*, Festschrift G. B. Caird; ed. L. D. Hurst and N. T. Wright (Oxford: Oxford University Press, 1987), 83–112; the extensive analysis in Labahn, *Jesus als Lebensspender*, 123–167; Welck, *Erzählte Zeichen*, 132–140; T. Nicklas, "Biblische Texte als

tives, although the significance is not inserted in a uniform manner.[50] On the surface level, the story has been classified as a typical miracle story.[51] It is not more extensive than some synoptic pericopes, but the brief text is full of riddles, puzzling textual elements, and suggestive allusions. Therefore, the Johannine technique of modifying the genre of miracle stories can be studied here.The basic structure of the narrative is simple: An exposition (vv. 1–2), the preparation of the miracle (vv. 3–5), its indirect description (vv. 6–8), its manifestation (vv. 9–10) and the concluding commentary (v. 11).[52] Or, with better reference to the pattern of "miracle stories," there is the description of the scene (vv. 1–2), the expression of the need (vv. 3a), and the mention of some (partly hindering) circumstances (vv. 3b–6). Then, the action of the miracle worker is narrated (vv. 7–8) without the event as such being described. Only indirectly (but much more efficiently), the miracle is uncovered. The brilliance of the miracle is stressed by the note about the massive amount of wine and its extraordinary quality (vv. 9–10).[53] The plot roughly matches the formal pattern of the synoptic miracle stories, and it is no coincidence that interpreters have tried to reduce the text to a simple form with only the most necessary elements and consider this the most original version (as part of the signs source or even as a tradition behind the signs source).[54] But such a procedure is not only speculative but also questionable

Texte der Bibel interpretiert: Die Hochzeit zu Kana (Joh 2,1–11) in 'biblischer Auslegung,' *ZKT* 126 (2004), 241–256; J. Zumstein, "Die Bibel als literarisches Kunstwerk—gezeigt am Beispiel der Hochzeit zu Kana (Joh 2,1–11)," in *Gott im Buchstaben? Neue Ansätze der Exegese*, ed. Th. Söding, QD 225 (Freiburg, Basel, and Wien: Herder, 2007), 68–82.

49 Welck, *Erzählte Zeichen*, 134. Cf. already Raymond F. Collins, "Cana (Jn. 2:1–12): The first of his Signs or the Key to his Signs?" *ITQ* 47 (1980): 79–95. H. Förster, "Die johanneischen Zeichen und Joh 2:11 als möglicher hermeneutischer Schlüssel," *NovT* 56 (2014), 1–23, stresses that the term not merely denotes "the first sign" but "the beginning of a dynamically structured sequence" (1).

50 The first two episodes are not interpreted by extensive discourses or dialogues, but only by textual elements within the narrative and brief concluding phrases, whereas the other miracles are followed and interpreted by lengthy discourses (John 5; 6) and dramatic dialogues (John 9; 11) with the particular feature in John 11 that the miracle is performed only after the interpretation.

51 Thus Bultmann, *Evangelium des Johannes*, 79: "typische Wundergeschichten"; so also Welck, *Erzählte Zeichen*, 132.

52 Cf. the analysis in J. Zumstein, *L'Évangile selon Saint Jean (1–12)*, CNT 4a (Genève: Labor et Fides, 2014), 94.

53 Thus the brief description of the plot (on the "dramatic" level) in Welck, *Erzählte Zeichen*, 132; cf. also A. Hentschel, "Umstrittene Wunder—mehrdeutige Zeichen im Johannesevangelium," in *Wunder in evangelischer und orthodoxer Perspektive*, ed. Stefan Alkier and Ioan Dumitru Popoiu, Kleine Schriften des Fachbereichs Evangelische Theologie der Goethe-Universität Frankfurt am Main 6 (Leipzig: Evangelische Verlagsanstalt, forthcoming)

54 Cf. Labahn, *Jesus als Lebensspender*, 134–145, Becker, *Evangelium*, 1:125–142; M. Theobald, *Das Evangelium nach Johannes. Kapitel 1–2*, RNT 4,1 (Regensburg: Pustet, 2009), 208–209; J. Zumstein, *L'évangile selon Saint Jean (1–12)*, 94–95.

regarding the composition of the text. It seems almost impossible to extract a pure and simple narrative from the present text and prove its former separate existence. It is hard to imagine how all those elements of double-entendre and symbolic overtones were added to an earlier pure narrative.

On the mere dramatic story level, the narrator presents Jesus performing an impressive miracle with the effect that his disciples "believe in him" (v. 11). But in view of the numerous interpretive elements, this reading cannot simply remain on the surface of the narrated story. These elements partly interrupt the flow of reading, distracting readers from the story to a wider context. This occurs by the author's allusion to particular motifs or reference to other parts of the Gospel (e.g., Jesus' passion and resurrection). Thus, in the reading of the text, a web of meaning is established which directs the reader beyond the story told on the dramatic level to an understanding within the context of the whole narrative or within the perspective of the Gospel as a whole. The narration, as it is, on its discourse level, is designed as an exemplary narration of the revelation in Jesus.[55] We can only very briefly mention those interpretive elements in the pericope:[56]

a) The mention of "third day" (v. 1) may simply point to the third day after the events narrated in John 1:43–51,[57] but for those acquainted with the Christian tradition or preaching, it clearly alludes to the Easter events.[58] So from its very beginning, the episode appears in the light of Jesus' resurrection.

b) The wedding motif also recalls several elements of the biblical tradition where wedding, feast, and wine[59] are related with messianic and eschatological motifs. In John, the symbolic dimension of the wedding motif is again strengthened when Jesus is called the bridegroom (John 3:29) and when he meets the Samaritan woman at a well in a setting that recalls several biblical wooing stories (e.g., with Moses, Isaac, and Jacob).[60]

---

55 This is also confirmed by the interpretive concluding phrase in v. 11: Jesus' "glory" is revealed.

56 Cf. especially Welck, *Erzählte Zeichen*, 132–140.

57 Cf. the debate on the "creation week" symbolism in John 1 in J. Frey, *Die johanneische Eschatologie 2: Das johanneische Zeitverständnis* (WUNT 110; Tübingen: Mohr Siebeck, 1998), 192–196; further suggestions in W. Lütgehetmann, *Die Hochzeit zu Kana (Joh 2,1–11): Zu Ursprung und Deutung einer Wundererzählung im Rahmen johanneischer Redaktionsgeschichte*, Biblische Untersuchungen 20 (Regensburg: Pustet, 1990), 28–38.

58 Admittedly, the wording in John 20:1 is different, but John 2:20 demonstrates that the evangelist and his readers knew the tradition (cf. 1 Cor 15:4; Matt 16:21; 17:23; 20:19; 27:64; Luke 9:22; 18:33; 24:7, 21, 446; Acts 10:40) and could see the link. Cf. Welck, *Erzählte Zeichen*, 137, and already C. H. Dodd, *The Interpretation of the Fourth Gospel* (Cambridge: Cambridge University Press, 1953), 300, and B. Lindars, *The Gospel of John*, NCB (London: HarperCollins, 1972), 128.

59 Cf. Gen 49:10–12; see especially M. Hengel, "Der dionysische Messias: Zur Auslegung des Weinwunders in Kana (Joh 2,1–11) in idem, *Jesus und die Evangelien*, WUNT 211 (Tübingen: Mohr Siebeck, 2007), 586–588.

60 See in particular M. Zimmermann and R. Zimmermann, "Brautwerbung in Samarien? Von

c) Particularly puzzling is the unexpectedly harsh rejection of Jesus' mother. Her hint at the shortage of wine implies the suggestion that Jesus should do something (and mirrors a certain confidence that Jesus might be able to do so). The rejection appears inappropriate and causes questions as to why Jesus treats his mother so harshly.[61] Interpreters suggest reading this as part of a narrative structure repeatedly used in the Gospel in order to demonstrate Jesus' independence from human suggestions or even to correct or deepen certain "christological" views considered insufficient by the Johannine author.[62] But Jesus' reply causes questions and stimulates further considerations in the reading of the story.

d) Very enigmatic is the explanation that his "hour" had not yet come. As the precise meaning of the term "Jesus' hour" is left unclear at this point and only clarified in later passages (John 7:30; 8:20; 12:23),[63] the readers are initially left with the riddle and then stimulated to link the initial sign to the events of Jesus' death and resurrection. As a confirmation, Jesus' mother is again present in the hour of Jesus' death (19:25–27).

e) The mention of the six water jars containing a massive amount of water, "according to the (custom of) purification of the Jews" (v. 6), also links the narrative with the motif of the conflict with the *Ioudaioi*. Although there is no open conflict yet at this point in the gospel narrative, the reader will also link the change from water (of purification) to wine (a sign of eschatological joy) with the motif of the eschatological change of times and thus with the issue of Jewish or other religious practice in contrast to the eschatological adoration in spirit and truth (cf. John 4:23).

f) An interesting narrative structure is constituted by the fact that the bridegroom does not know where the wine comes from (although he should know), whereas only the servants know. Although there is no reason to link the διάκονοι

---

der moralischen zur metaphorischen Interpretation in Joh 4," *ZNT* 1 (1998): 40–51, and L. Eslinger, "The Wooing of the Woman at the Well," *Journal of Literature and Theology* 1 (1987): 167–83.

61 Interestingly, he will show much more care for her when entrusting her to the Beloved Disciple in John 19:25–27.

62 Jesus' explanation in 2:4 can also be understood in the sense that the time for miracle working has not yet come. But such an understanding is then challenged by the fact that Jesus actually does a miracle, even though he had rejected his mother. This structure (suggestion–negative response–positive action) can be found in several Johannine passages (also John 4:46–54; 7:2–14 and 11:1–14) and seems to stress Jesus' independence from human suggestions and possibly to correct certain Christological attitudes. Cf. C. H. Giblin, "Suggestion, Negative Response, and Positive Action in St. John's Portrayal of Jesus (John 2,1–11; 4,46–54; 7,2–14; 11,1–44)," *NTS* 26 (1979/80), 197–211; A. Reinhartz, "Great Expectations: A Reader-Oriented Approach to Johannine Christology and Eschatology," *Journal of Literature and Theology* 3 (1989), 61–76; Frey, *Die Johanneische Eschatologie*, 2:198.

63 Cf. Frey, *Die johanneische Eschatologie*, 2:215–221.

mentioned here with a particular function in the church, the contrast establishes a distinction between those who understand and others who remain ignorant. Such a contrast may serve the didactic strategy of the Gospel, leading readers to a better understanding by means of ironically presenting the misunderstanding of some text-internal characters. The character ironically "victimized" here is the bridegroom of the wedding who finally appears in a rather ambivalent light.

g) The figure of the bridegroom is linked with further ambiguities: When the *architriklinos* rebukes him for having kept the good wine until now, the former has no idea who had really given the good wine but assumes that the wine is provided by the bridegroom. From that misunderstanding, the question arises whether the true giver of the wine might also be the true bridegroom, who invites individuals to the real feast, the eschatological wedding. This kind of symbolism is not made explicit in the present text, but when, in John 3:29, Jesus is again associated with "the bridegroom," this may further confirm such a symbolic reading.[64]

h) The saying in v. 10 seems even to contrast the bridegroom and "every man," suggesting that the (true) bridegroom is not like "every man." This can be read as a hint to the christological view that Jesus is different from any other human because, for example, he is from above and exists in unity with the Father. This is in some manner confirmed already in v. 11 when the evangelist comments that, by his signs, Jesus revealed his "glory," and his disciples believed "in him."

All these elements provide stumbling stones for a smooth reading of the story on its surface level. They insert additional references and contextualizations, especially links with the events of Jesus' death and resurrection. They also allude to various symbolic dimensions which may be considered when reading the story. None of those symbolic aspects is fully elaborated or developed to an unequivocal interpretation. Instead, they provide links and open spaces for reading the passage, opening up horizons and contexts for interpretation which may become more clearly defined upon a fuller or complete reading of the Gospel. One such context is the death and resurrection of Jesus, which is alluded to in the textual elements mentioned above. The "third day" and the enigmatic mention of Jesus' "hour" clearly point to that horizon. Additional confirmation of this horizon comes from the mention of Jesus' mother, possibly the aspect of purity or purification, and finally the mention of Jesus' "glory" in v. 11. Other textual elements such as a wedding, bridegroom, and wine allude to the context of messianic fulfilment. Not all of those symbolic references are compelling in themselves, but, on the basis of the clearly established links to Jesus' "hour," it is very likely that the other references are also deliberately considered as hints for reading the Cana pericope. Therefore, these textual elements strongly suggest

64 The scene in John 4 will then give additional confirmation, see the articles above note 60.

that the episode should be read within the framework of Jesus' death and resurrection (i.e., in the post-Easter perspective as prominent throughout the Gospel). In other words, the narrative urges its readers not to read it simply as an account of an episode at a certain point in the past ministry of Jesus but to perceive it in the framework of his whole ministry and its ultimate effects, as a representation of the eschatological salvation ultimately fulfilled in his death and resurrection (rather than by a single miracle before that time). Birger Olsson has already stated that all the features of the author's way of narrating the story are "in harmony with his post resurrection point of view."[65] As Welck phrases correctly, it is narrated as a significant, paradigmatic, and exemplary representation of the whole of Jesus' ministry. The narrative design of this first Johannine miracle story clearly shows that the narrated episode is not to be considered in itself but within a greater narrative and Christological framework.

In spite of the problems regarding the genre miracle story and the open question whether there ever existed a source or story behind the present text, we can see that the evangelist's treatment of the miracle story differs from the earlier Jesus tradition as presented in the Synoptics. There is a modification of the narrative technique towards a greater extent of symbolic references, and this modification is in accordance with the general perspective of the Fourth Gospel. Insofar as this is the case, one could use the term "genre bending" to describe that change in the way the evangelist narrates the miracle stories. We must observe, however, that the Johannine miracle stories are not designed according to a common scheme but utilize different techniques of interpretation. Whereas the interpretive elements in John 2:1–11 are given within the narrative, other miracle stories are interpreted by extensive discourses or dialogues. We have to consider this briefly with regard to the episode narrated in John 9:1–41.

3.2 The Healing of the Man Born Blind (John 9:1–41) as a Paradigm of God's Salvific Works

The healing of the man born blind (John 9:1–41) is the most complex miracle narrative in John.[66] Here, interpretive aspects are presented within the narrow context of the miracle (vv. 2–5) and in the subsequent dialogue scenes (vv. 8–41).

65 Olsson, *Structure and Meaning*, 101.

66 Comparable, also in its dramatic structure, is the Lazarus episode in John 11:1–45. Cf. my more extensive discussion in J. Frey, "Sehen oder Nicht-Sehen? (Die Heilung des blind Geborenen)—Joh 9,1–14," in Zimmermann, *Kompendium der frühchristlichen Wundererzählungen I*, 725–741; cf. further especially Ch. Welck, *Erzählte Zeichen*, 175–205; Labahn, *Jesus als Lebensspender*, 305–377; idem, "'Blinded by the Light'," 453–509; M. Rein, *Die Heilung des Blindgeborenen (Joh 9): Tradition und Redaktion*, WUNT 2/73 (Tübingen: Mohr

Unlike the discourses in John 5 and 6, which are only interrupted by a few interlocutions, these scenes present dialogues and actions, establishing a complex web of interaction between various groups who debate the reality and consequences of Jesus' miracle. Moreover, the testimony of the healed man gradually develops toward a clear confession of belief in Jesus, whereas the opponents become more and more hardened in their rejection. Thus, the whole story is a paradigm for the development of faith in Jesus and for the "trial" about its truth. Here, the narrative (including the dialogues until v. 41) is obviously transparent for later debates between the Jesus followers and their synagogal opponents. The episode is narrated from a post-Easter perspective and thus also requires a reading in that context.[67]

The performance and manifestation of the miracle, as such, is narrated already in v. 6–7 so that interpreters could consider parts of vv. 1–7 as an earlier source (vv. 1, 6–7 possibly even underlying the alleged Semeia Source).[68] But it is mere speculation whether there ever existed such a short form of the text from which the whole composition is said to have developed gradually.[69] Although the evangelist was probably aware of stories about the healings of blind men from the synoptic tradition, we cannot be sure that he drew on a particular *Vorlage* for the composition of John 9. Not only the interpretive dialogues but also the mere narration of the miracle itself shows elements of characteristically Johannine design: In contrast with the synoptic healings of the blind, this blind man is blind from birth, making this miracle greater than those in all the synoptic parallels. Jesus does not answer a request from the blind man or from others. Instead, he takes the initiative when, on his way from the temple precinct, he "sees" the man born blind and encounters him (v. 1). Finally the miracle is not performed immediately, nor observed directly. Only after the blind man follows Jesus' word by washing himself at the pool, he is healed. Thus, v. 7 can state, "he came back seeing." As in John 2:9–10 and in John 4:51–53, the miracle is only reported in an indirect manner and then repeatedly testified to by the healed person.

Siebeck, 1995); K. Scholtissek, "Mündiger Glaube. Zur Architektur und Pragmatik johanneischer Begegnungsgeschichten: Joh 5 und 9," in *Paulus und Johannes*, ed. D. Sänger and U. Mell, WUNT 198 (Tübingen: Mohr Siebeck, 2006), 107–158; J. Zumstein, "Crise du savoir et conflit des interpretations selon Jean 9: Un exemple du travail de l'école johannique," in *Early Christian Voices in Texts, Traditions and Symbols*, Festschrift F. Bovon; ed. D. H. Warren, A. G. Book, and D. W. Pao, BIS 66 (Leiden: Brill, 2003), 167–178.

67 This has been demonstrated prominently by J. L. Martyn, *History and Theology in the Fourth Gospel*, 2nd ed. (Nashville: Abingdon, 1979), 62 and 129, who interprets John 9 as a "two level drama" with corresponding events on the level of the ministry of Jesus and in the context of the later community.

68 Cf. Becker, *Evangelium I*, 370–372; Theobald, *Evangelium*, 630–631; see also Rein, *Die Heilung des Blindgeborenen*, 284–293.

69 Cf. J. Zumstein, *L'évangile selon Saint Jean (1–12)*, 315: "[L]e récit est, en premier lieu, l'oeuvre cohérente, aussi bien au niveau litteraire que théologique, de l'évangeliste."

The pericope can be structured in 7 scenes:[70] (1) the healing story (vv. 1–7), (2) which is followed by a discussion with the neighbours (vv. 8–12), (3) an initial questioning by the Pharisees (vv. 13–17), (4) an interlude with the Pharisees questioning his parents (vv. 18–23), (5) a subsequent questioning by the Pharisees/*Ioudaioi* (vv. 24–34), (6) the new encounter of the healed man with Jesus (vv. 35–38) and, finally, (7) a scene with Jesus and some of the Pharisees (vv. 39–41).

The interpretive dialogues contain various testimony by the healed one, who narrates his healing and points to his experience while the neighbours and then the Pharisees (described as synagogue authorities) react with doubt and unbelief. They ask him how the miracle happened (vv. 10, 13), question its reality, and discuss its legitimacy: Is the man really the same one who was known to be blind before (v. 8–9, 18–19)? Is the work a divine work, or is the miracle worker simply a sinner (v. 24, 30) because the healing was performed on Sabbath (v. 14)? The healed man comes to increasingly clear confessions of faith, calling Jesus a prophet, "from God," and finally he worships him as "the Son of Man" (v. 35–38). He presents himself as a disciple of Jesus, and is, therefore, distanced from the disciples of Moses, resulting in his expulsion from their community (v. 34). In the end, Jesus pronounces his verdict about the Pharisees who remain in sin (v. 41), and it becomes clear that they have been blinded by the light (v. 39), whereas the blind man had come to receive physical and spiritual light. It becomes implicitly clear that it is the Pharisees who are (still) blind or even made blind (v. 39) in their encounter with the light. So, the themes of the whole story are sin and belief and the works of Jesus who, as the "light of the world" (v. 4; cf. John 8:12), gives light to the blind and blinds those who claim to see or to know.

Both themes are already introduced in the interpretive elements in vv. 1–7 where the issue of sin and illness is brought up by Jesus' disciples (v. 2), the healing (physical or spiritual) is characterized as a "work of God" (v. 3), and Jesus' works are linked to the limited period of his mission (v. 4) by an explicit reference to Jesus' death (v. 5). Apart from these dialogical digressions within the miracle story, there is the puzzling interpretation of the name "Siloam" as a passive verbal adjective of the Hebrew שלח: ὃ ἑρμηνεύεται ἀπεσταλμένος ("that is translated: the one who is sent"). This enigmatic interpretation, which is unwarranted for understanding the healing story itself, suggests that the man born blind has to wash himself, not merely in a physical pool, but in the one who is sent (i.e., Jesus). With that interpretation, the story is clearly embedded in a wider symbolic framework in which blindness and healing are linked with unbelief and belief. Washing oneself in the pool, therefore, becomes an image of purification

70 Cf. Rein, *Heilung*, 170–172.

by Jesus, or the purification from sins. And seeing, or the healing from blindness, is a symbol of the spiritual process of coming to the light and coming to belief.

This demonstrates that the episode is deliberately designed as an exemplary and paradigmatic narrative that should not be read merely on the level of Jesus' past ministry, but as a paradigm of how the light of the world brings humans to the light of faith while others are hardened in opposition and unbelief. It is also a paradigm of separation processes caused by the Gospel message. The mention of the Pharisees and the expulsion from the synagogue (v. 22) explicitly refer to similar processes that took place later in history of the Johannine community. Symbolic and interpretive elements enrich the miracle story, including the reference in v. 4 to the earlier I-am-saying in John 8:12 and the hint to the end of Jesus' ministry in the "night." Thus, it is embedded into the Gospel as a whole. It is also extensively interpreted in terms of the consequences of Jesus' death and resurrection: Seeing and blindness, coming to the light and staying in the darkness, as well as life and death are presented as the consequences of Jesus' entire sending and ministry (v. 39).

Since we have to consider the whole chapter as a compositional unit, the miracle story is significantly extended and modified in order to become a paradigmatic example of God's salvific works through Jesus' ministry as a whole. As Welck rightly has shown, the sign is not (or not only) the healing as such, but the healing story in its Johannine narrative design. The interpretation provides the framework within which the episode should be perceived, and from the sign observed within the whole of Jesus' ministry, readers are called to belief. Again the story is significant for the whole of Jesus' ministry from a post-Easter perspective.

4. More *Sēmeia* and the Significance of the Narrative as a Whole

The observations made with regard to the miracles in John 2 and John 9 can be generalized in the analysis of all (seven) miracle stories in John 2–12. With the exception of the epiphany on the sea, every story is referred to as σημεῖον.[71] But if it is true that σημεῖον is not merely another word for "miracle" but that the signs can be primarily seen in the "written signs" (cf. John 20:30–31), i. e., the narratives including their interpretive elements that are composed to have an effect on the Johannine readers, we must ask whether the σημεῖα in the Johannine perspective are only and precisely the miracle stories or whether the character of a σημεῖον

71 For the miracle in John 5, it is striking that the term is not used in the context of the miracle, nor in the following Christological discourse, but only in John 6:2 and again (in a comment by Jerusalemites) in 7:31.

(or the epistemological structure of the σημεῖον narratives) can also be found in other textual elements of the Gospel. Here it is important to notice that the connection between the term σημεῖον/σημεῖα and the miracle stories is not so precise that its reference should be limited to those stories.[72] At least one miracle story (John 6:16–25) is not called a σημεῖον, and also the textual link between the other miracle narratives and the term is not in every case very close: The summary in John 2:23 (cf. 3:2) refers not only to one sign as narrated in John 2:1–11 but to many signs. Furthermore, the reference of John 6:2 is somewhat unclear so that it is even uncertain whether the miracle narrated in John 5 is precisely called a sign and where the idea of the signs is actually linked with that episode (cf. John 6:2; 7:31).

4.1 Signs in John 20: The Linen Wrappings and the Cloth in the Tomb

This is also important with regard to John 20:30–31 where the term is used for the last time in John. This first closure of the "book"[73] refers to "many other signs" done by Jesus in the presence of his disciples and "these signs" that have been written so that the readers may believe in Jesus as the Messiah and Son of God. But the question arises which signs are meant by "these signs"? Are they simply the six or seven miracle stories presented as signs in John 2–12 with the consequence that the reference in the closure skips or ignores the lengthy text between the Lazarus story and the end of John 20, including the foot washing, the farewell discourses, the trial and crucifixion, and the resurrection appearances? Some interpreters have veiled the difficulty by the suggestion that the phrase in John 20:30–31 was already the closure of a source of the Gospel, the Signs Source, which was then simply adopted to serve as the closure of the whole Gospel.[74] But the procedure assumed in such a hypothesis is problematic. Should the evangelist not have noticed the difference in the function of the saying at the end of a source presenting mostly miracles and of the present Gospel with its climax in the passion and resurrection narrative? Or should he have neglected the textual gap between the "written signs" in John 2–12 and the final mention of the signs in 20:31? As the Semeia Source hypothesis has lost its plausibility, this explanation

72 Thus also A. Hentschel, "Umstrittene Wunder", n.p. (forthcoming): "Die Gleichsetzung von σημεῖα mit den Wundertaten Jesu wird weder dem semantischen Befund noch den ausgeführten Erzählungen von Jesu Wirken im Johannesevangelium gerecht."

73 It should be noted that John 20:30 mentions "this book." Here we have a hint to the explicit literary character of the Fourth Gospel. It is a book and refers to that fact in a kind of self-referentiality. The second and final closure in John 21:25 again mentions "books" and thus integrates "this book" into a plurality of "books" in the world.

74 Thus Bultmann, *Evangelium*, 541; Becker, *Evangelium* 2.756; Fortna, *Gospel of Signs*, 197f.

has also become implausible, and the question about the reference of the σημεῖα in John 20:30 is open again. Hans-Christian Kammler has strongly suggested that in this passage the term σημεῖα can only refer to the appearances of the resurrected one.[75] His argument that σημεῖα in John 20:30 cannot refer to the miracles as they were not merely performed in the presence of his disciples but in a greater public is not compelling, but the argument is strong that the σημεῖα referred to in John 20:30 includes the episodes narrated in John 20.

We must, however, determine more precisely in which manner and for what reason those episodes can be characterized as σημεῖα. It is not the miraculous character of the resurrection or of the epiphanies narrated that constitutes a sign, but the internal structure of significance which demands the disciples to conclude from external perceptions to a dimension of meaning or to draw the consequence of belief from what they have perceived. This is most obvious in the first and paradigmatic episode about Peter and the Beloved Disciple at the tomb.[76] The story is probably designed on the basis of an earlier tradition about Peter at the tomb (Luke 24:12)[77] and expanded by insertion of the figure of the Beloved Disciple. This disciple arrives first at the tomb, but he only bows forward, looks inside, and sees the linen shroud lying there. As in the tradition, Peter is granted to step in first; it is quite accurately described that he can see the linen wrappings and, separately and folded in a place by itself, the cloth that had covered Jesus' head. But Peter does not draw any conclusions from that. He does not understand and does not (yet) believe, whereas the Beloved Disciple then enters, sees the same scenario, and believes. Although the term "sign" is not used in this context, the Beloved Disciple, as the paradigmatic believer, acts as a person who "sees the signs." He concludes from the position of the cloths, not only that Jesus is not there, but more precisely that he has actively risen and left his tomb in good order. The Beloved Disciple concludes that Jesus is the one who has the authority to lay down his life and take it again (John 10:18; cf. 5:26). When it is now said (for the first time in the Easter episodes) that someone "believes," this precisely implies that Jesus is now considered, as he is, the Son of God, who has (actively) risen from the tomb. And the Beloved Disciple comes to that belief as he

75 H.-Ch. Kammler, "Die ‚Zeichen' des Auferstandenen," in O. Hofius and H.-Ch. Kammler, *Johannesstudien*, WUNT 88 (Tübingen: Mohr Siebeck, 1996), 201.

76 Cf. more extensively J. Frey, "'Ich habe den Herrn gesehen' (Joh 20,18): Entstehung, Inhalt und Vermittlung des Osterglaubens nach Johannes 20," in *Studien zu Matthäus und Johannes / Études sur Matthieu et Jean*, Festschrift Jean Zumstein; ed. A. Dettwiler and U. Poplutz; ATANT 97 (Zürich: TVZ, 2009), 267–284 (274–276).

77 Cf. Schnelle, *Evangelium*, 324 and also Thyen, *Johanneseangelium*, 759–760.

draws the appropriate consequences from the well-arranged burial linen he perceives in the tomb. For him, the status of the tomb is a sign.[78]

The Beloved Disciple sees the sign, whereas Peter does not. But again, the sign is presented for the readers: The narrative design of the episode with the precise description of the linen cloths (ὀθόνια) and the cloth covering the face (σουδάριον) attracts attention and is reminiscent of the Lazarus episode where the resurrected one comes out of the tomb with his head still covered by a σουδάριον (John 11:44). So the reader is called to see the differences between Lazarus and Jesus and to draw the consequences—as the Beloved Disciple does. Thus, the narrative design of the story in John 20:6–7 is shaped by the similar epistemological structure that characterizes the miracle stories as signs. The readers are subtly directed to the sign of the linens and additionally pointed to "the Scripture" (John 20:9) as a testimony of Jesus' resurrection. But, while Peter still remains ignorant, the Beloved Disciple and the readers can come to belief. From external observations, they are called to discover the real significance and draw conclusions similar to those drawn by the figure of the Beloved Disciple, the paradigmatic believer. Thus, although the term σημεῖον is not used with regard to that episode, the narrative, in its literary design, can also be considered a sign since it is shaped by an epistemological structure quite similar to that of the σημεῖον narratives in John 2–12.

Perhaps we could also add the other episodes in John 20 where there is the call to conclude from an outward appearance the christological insight that Jesus has risen and that he is the Son of God or even God (John 20:28). Although the episodes of the encounter with Mary, the disciples, and Thomas are different, they too are shaped by the element of the recognition of Jesus.[79]

4.2 Other Signs in Johannine Narratives?

Narrative structures of creating significance can also be discovered in other Johannine narrative passages. More than the internal figures of the text, the readers are called to understand what is narrated. Likewise, the Gospel can state that the majority of Jesus' contemporaries did not believe despite having physically perceived the deeds of Jesus (John 12:37). Apparently, they did not see the signs performed in front of them. On the contrary, the readers are called to see the written signs and to understand, and so the numerous explaining remarks

78 J. Zumstein, *L'Évangile selon Saint Jean (13–21)*, CNT 4b (Genève: Labor et Fides, 2007), 272: "Pour lui, l'état du sépulcre est un signe."

79 Cf. K. B. Larsen, *Recognizing the Stranger: Recognition Scenes in the Gospel of John*, BIS 93 (Leiden: Brill, 2008), 196–211.

and hints create significance for readers. Ultimately, readers are able to understand significantly more than any of the characters in the text (perhaps with the exception of the Beloved Disciple). Such a structure is suggested when, in John 12:16, it is said that the disciples did not understand the episode of Jesus' entry into Jerusalem and the Scriptural quotation from Zech 9:9. It was only after his glorification that they remembered and understood (cf. similarly 2:22). Such a remembrance is, in the Johannine view, the work of the Spirit-Paraclete (John 14:25–26; 16:13–15), who is considered the author of the disciples' ability to rightly understand their remembrance after Easter and who is, in some manner, also the author of the christological understanding as presented in the written gospel.

Jesus' entry into Jerusalem on a donkey with the crowd hailing him as the messianic king (John 12:12–15) is narrated as an act that the disciples could not understand. The narrative design adds the quotation from Zech 9:9, and the term βασιλεύς (John 12:13–15) points to the episode with Pontius Pilate and to the crucifixion where Jesus is repeatedly presented as king. In view of the whole Gospel, with the Scriptural references provided by the evangelist (v. 15) and with the hint to the post-Easter understanding (v. 16), the story can be read in a wider context as a hint to Jesus' kingship despite the cross which might otherwise contradict and deny any royal aspirations. But for those who can see, the entry is already a sign of the coming kingship which is actually inaugurated in Jesus' death.

Other narratives, such as the foot washing, are similarly designed to hint at the climactic act of Jesus' ministry, his death, and are interpreted as an act of love (John 13:1, 3; 15:13). As such, they are not understandable within the episode, that is, in the time of Jesus' ministry. It is only in the post-Easter perspective (John 13:7) and under the instruction of the Spirit (or the narrated gospel) that their function becomes clear.

4.3 The Cross as a Sign?

From here, we can ask whether the cross should also be considered a "sign," even the "final and all-inclusive σημεῖον"[80] or "the sign of signs," as some authors have phrased it.[81] The problem is that all the other signs are linked with the events of

80 C. H. Dodd, *Interpretation*, 439. Cf. the considerations in J. Frey, "'Wie Mose die Schlange in der Wüste erhöht hat …': Zur frühjüdischen Deutung der 'ehernen Schlange' und ihrer christologischen Rezeption in Johannes 3:14f.'" in idem, *Die Herrlichkeit des Gekreuzigten*, ed. J. Schlegel, WUNT 307 (Tübingen: Mohr Siebeck, 2013), 130f.

81 Cf. Salier, *The Rhetorical Impact*, 143, with reference to the more structural than exegetical work by G. Østenstad, *Patterns of Redemption in the Fourth Gospel: An Experiment in*

Jesus' death and resurrection so that the signifying structure suggests viewing the cross and resurrection as the *sēmainomenon*, the element signified or referred to by the signifying textual elements. Unlike any other episode in Jesus' earthly ministry, the cross not only points to salvation, it *is* the act of salvation so that it cannot be labelled a "sign."[82]

On the other hand, the epistemological structure of the Johannine trial and crucifixion narrative deserves further consideration.[83] The Johannine design of the narration is full of hints that Jesus is not the victim of evil plans but goes deliberately into his death, that he is active or even the sovereign of his passion. Even more, he is presented as a king with a kingdom that is on a different level than that of Caesar (John 18:36–37) and as the judge who decides the guilt of his judge Pilate (John 19:11). He is lifted up on the cross, an act that has been called "exaltation" (John 3:14; 8:28) so that the reader may see, in his physical exaltation on the cross, a sign of his real exaltation to God the Father. The narrative design of Jesus' trial and crucifixion can be read as a parody on the enthronement of a king. Adopting the idea of the two levels of understanding as established in John 2:22 and 12:16 (where it is explicitly related to Jesus' messianic kingship), the whole narrative of his trial and crucifixion can be read on two levels. On the surface level, Jesus is accused, condemned, and finally crucified. But on a deeper level, he is crowned, enthroned, and proclaimed as the real king, and the humiliating acts of the soldiers reveal a deeper truth: Jesus presents himself as a king (18:37; βασιλεύς εἰμι); he is crowned, invested, and hailed (19:2) as king, although this is meant ironically. Twice, he appears and is presented (19.5, 13) to receive a (negative) acclamation (19:6–7, 15). He is exalted on the cross (19:18) and universally proclaimed (19:18) as king (19:20). And even in his death, Jesus is active in claiming "fulfillment," nodding, and actively giving away the spirit (John 19:30). So, his death can be considered the inauguration of his kingdom, and the narrative design of the trial and crucifixion story aims at directing the readers' eyes to that deeper level of truth which is in accord with the post-Easter perspective of the whole Gospel. As in the signs narratives of the Gospel, readers should not remain on the level of the story as such. Instead, readers should

---

Structural Analysis, Studies in the Bible and Early Christianity 38 (Lampeter: Edwin Mellen, 1988), 111. Both authors, however, use the term with reference to Christ's death *and* resurrection.

82 See Frey, "Wie Mose die Schlange in der Wüste erhöht hat …," 133: "Allein dieses Geschehen weist nicht nur auf das Heil hin, sondern ist im strengen Sinn das eschatologische Heilsgeschehen selbst."

83 On the following, cf. J. Frey, "Jesus und Pilatus. Der wahre König und der Repräsentant des Kaisers im Johannesevangelium," in *Christ and the Emperor*, ed. G. van Belle and J. Verheyden, BTS 20 (Leuven: Peeters, 2014), 337–393.

proceed to the meaning suggested by categories communicated in advance,[84] by particular terms used to interpret the episode (especially "exaltation" and "glorification"), by particularities of the narrative design, and by ambiguities and symbolic dimensions of the language. The Johannine text leads its readers to perceive the narrated events in the light of post-Easter faith, in the light of the insights communicated to the disciples by the Spirit (cf. John 16:13–15 etc.). Thus, the cross is not a sign as the other signs, but the passion and crucifixion narrative also point to a deeper level of meaning, and is thus in accord with the epistemological structure of the whole Gospel.

5. The Gospel as a Narrative of *Sēmeia* and as a Significant Narrative

From the wide range of observations collected, we can first conclude that, compared with the Synoptics, the Fourth Gospel strongly modifies the shape of miracle stories. They are all narrated in a manner that discloses their significance and presents them as exemplary narratives of the whole of Jesus' sending and ministry within the context of the whole Gospel. Thus, the genre of miracle stories is "bent" and modified according to the hermeneutical interests of the Gospel as explained in John 20:30–31.

But when the closure in John 20:30–31 draws on Jesus' "signs," the focus is not only on the six or seven miracle stories narrated in the first part of the Gospel. The narrative interest in the significance of the episodes of Jesus' earthly ministry shapes the whole Gospel. Such an interest should not be confused with a simple allegory: The evangelist's interest is not to get rid of the physical level of his narrative and to move on to a mere spiritual level. But he tells stories as significant stories, and they are significant in the light of the core event of Jesus' sending, his death, and resurrection. Therefore, the Gospel creates a web of meaning in which all the single narratives are linked to the final and climactic narrative of Jesus' death and resurrection. The whole Gospel, with its narrative and discursive parts, is shaped by the interest in an appropriate understanding of those events and, of course, in an appropriate understanding of Jesus himself as the Son of God and eschatological life-giver. As Jesus' death (i.e., his crucifixion) most openly contradicts such a belief, the Gospel's aim becomes, in particular, to present his death in a manner that helps readers understand and see Jesus' glory within the flesh, the truth of his kingdom within the narrative of his exaltation on the cross.

84 On those categories and interpretive hints see J. Frey, "Die '*theologia crucfixi*' des Johannesevangeliums," in idem, *Die Herrlichkeit des Gekreuzigten*, 507–535.

John's epistemology is comparable to a kaleidoscope which provides a different image when the item is turned a bit, or to a projection of two images where the one lies under the other so that each layer presents the other in a new light. Or, in narrative terms, John aims at creating a narrative language and design that leads its readers to christological insights. John's modification of the way miracle stories are told is a part of that overall structure, and the σημεῖα narratives, as significant narratives, are part of the literary strategy that shapes the Gospel in its entirety.

Tyler Smith

Characterization in John 4 and the Prototypical Type-Scene as a Generic Concept

1. Introduction

The past decade has seen a welcome surge of interest in literary-critical treatments of characterization in connection to the Fourth Gospel.[1] At the same time, work in genre theory has prompted readers of the Bible to reconsider assumptions about functions played by genre in their corpora.[2] Literary genre, no matter how conceptualized, has a bearing on characterization.[3] In particular, genre is an important generator of readerly expectations about characters in any given narrative. If we think of the hero in Homeric epic, the detective in a whodunit, or the villain in a Bond movie or Superman comic, familiarity with the genre in each case furnishes the reader with expectations for the as-yet-unknown characters to be met in future texts recognized as belonging to these genres. But how does this

1 Some notable recent examples include Cornelis Bennema, *Encountering Jesus: Character Studies in the Gospel of John* (Milton Keynes: Paternoster, 2009); Alicia D. Myers, *Characterizing Jesus: A Rhetorical Analysis on the Fourth Gospel's Use of Scripture in its Presentation of Jesus*, LNTS 458 (London: T&T Clark, 2012); Steven A. Hunt, D. Francois Tolmie, and Ruben Zimmermann, eds., *Character Studies in the Fourth Gospel*, WUNT 314 (Tübingen: Mohr Siebeck, 2013); Christopher W. Skinner, ed., *Characters and Characterization in the Gospel of John* (London: Bloomsbury, 2013).

2 Some important, early adoptions by biblical scholars of prototype theory to think about the genres of apocalyptic and wisdom literature have been made by Carol Newsom and Benjamin G. Wright III: Carol A. Newsom, "Spying Out the Land: A Report from Genology," in *Seeking Out the Wisdom of the Ancients: Essays Offered to Honor Michael V. Fox on the Occasion of His Sixty-Fifth Birthday*, ed. Ronald L. Troxel et al. (Winona Lake: Eisenbrauns, 2005), 437–50; Benjamin G. Wright, "Joining the Club: A Suggestion About Genre in Early Jewish Texts," *DSD* 17 (2010): 289–314.

3 This paper takes much of its impetus from an apt comment by Harold W. Attridge in his article on "genre bending" in the Fourth Gospel: "[I]n many cases where it is possible to identify significant generic parallels, and therefore to presume that the form in question generates regular expectations, the reader encounters something quite odd about the way in which the generic conventions seem to work" ("Genre Bending in the Fourth Gospel," *JBL* 121 [2002]: 11.). This paper takes up in particular the generic generation of expectations bearing on characters and characterization.

generation of expectations work? An answer demands inquiry into questions concerning how genres work on readers and how readers work with genres. Discussion in this chapter will focus in particular on the so-called patriarchal betrothal type-scene as a generic concept often connected by Johannine scholars to Jesus's encounter with the Samaritan woman at Jacob's well in John 4. The argument advanced is that thinking in terms of "prototypical" type-scenes instead of abstract, "list of features" type-scenes better approximates the use of category negotiation in real life and should encourage literary analysts to take stock of the relationships between Jesus and the figures in the prototypes upon which the scene draws. In the case of John 4, this means especially the patriarch Jacob.

2. Alter and "Type-Scenes" as a Literary Convention and Genre-Related Concept

In 1981 Robert Alter published the deservedly famous *The Art of Biblical Narrative*, in which he devoted a chapter to "type-scenes" in the Hebrew Bible.[4] Although he introduced the type-scene concept in connection to narratives in the Hebrew Bible, as a genre-related concept it quickly became important for thinking about certain New Testament texts also, perhaps none more so than Jesus's encounter with the woman of Samaria in John 4:3–42. Studies of Jesus and the Samaritan woman beginning from the mid-1980s cite Alter as a matter of course, but do not always pause to engage with him.[5] Here, after outlining some

4 References in this paper will be to the 2011 edition: Robert Alter, *The Art of Biblical Narrative*, rev. and updated ed. (New York: Basic Books, 2011). Alter takes the term "type-scene" from classical scholarship on Homer, where the term was introduced by Walter Arend, *Die typischen Scenen bei Homer* (Berlin: Weidmann, 1975). Here type-scenes include such items as the arrival, the message, the voyage, the assembly, the oracle, and the arming of the hero. Alter's introduction of the term to biblical studies is accompanied by "a couple of major modifications" predicated on his observation of differences between epic and the Bible in terms of descriptive detail and the narrative significance of the quotidian (Alter, *The Art of Biblical Narrative*, 59–60).

5 Two recent studies of John which do engage Alter are Michael W. Martin, "Betrothal Journey Narratives," *CBQ* 70 (2008): 505–23; and Andrew E. Arterbury, "Breaking the Betrothal Bonds: Hospitality in John 4," *CBQ* 72 (2010): 63–83. Among the many significant studies to adopt Alter's perspective in a fairly straightforward fashion, three important instances are R. Alan Culpepper, *Anatomy of the Fourth Gospel: A Study in Literary Design* (Philadelphia: Fortress, 1983), 136–37; Jeffrey Lloyd Staley, *The Print's First Kiss: A Rhetorical Investigation of the Implied Reader in the Fourth Gospel*, SBLDS 82 (Atlanta: Scholars, 1988), esp. 98–103; and Lyle Eslinger, "The Wooing of the Woman at the Well: Jesus, the Reader and Reader-Response Criticism," *Literature and Theology* 1 (1987): 167–83. Culpepper was one of the first to connect John 4 to Alter's type-scene, in his seminal work on John as literature. Staley draws on Alter's work in a sophisticated dissertation, where he concludes that John 4 constitutes a parody of the

challenges in the way type-scenes are currently conceptualized, I will suggest that "prototype theory" makes the type-scene concept a more useful tool for literary-critical approaches to Johannine characterization. The essay concludes with a brief look at the exegetical gains such an approach yields with respect to the cognitive dimension of characterization in John 4.[6]

Although he lists seven examples of type-scenes,[7] Alter offers a close analysis only of one: the encounter with a future betrothed at a well.[8] The three "full dress occurrences" of this literary phenomenon are found in Genesis 24 (Isaac and Rebekah), Genesis 29 (Jacob and Rachel), and Exodus 2 (Moses and Zipporah), and Alter mentions as narratives worth comparing the book of Ruth (Ruth and Boaz), Judges 14 (Samson and the woman of Timnah), 1 Samuel 9 (Saul and some anonymous maidens), and 1 Samuel 25 (David and two of his wives).[9] Of special interest for the present essay is his schema for the encounter-at-the-well scene, in which five "essential elements" are identified and listed.[10] They are:

- The future bridegroom or his surrogate travels to a foreign land.
- He encounters a girl or girls at a well.
- Someone, either the man or girl, draws water from the well.
- The girl(s) rush to bring home the news of the stranger's arrival.
- A betrothal is concluded between the stranger and the girl, generally only after he has been invited to a meal.[11]

---

type-scene. Eslinger invokes Alter's work to make his case that the evangelist deliberately deployed the type-scene as a "strategy designed to mislead the reader so that he may gain an actual experience of the gap between Jesus and his human auditors" (180).

6 By "cognitive dimension" here I mean the part of the narrative that concerns representations of cognition. I am thinking in particular of the creation and subversion of readerly expectations regarding the qualities, capacities, and inclinations of the fictional minds belonging to the Johannine Jesus and the Samaritan woman. For more on represented cognition as a central dimension of characterization, a good starting place is A. Palmer, *Fictional Minds* (Lincoln: University of Nebraska Press, 2004).

7 They are (a) the encounter with a future betrothed at a well, (b) the annunciation of the birth of a hero to his barren mother, (c) the epiphany in a field, (d) the initiatory trial, (e) danger in the desert, (f) discovery of a well or some other source of sustenance, and (g) the testament of the dying hero. Alter, *The Art of Biblical Narrative*, 60.

8 This may explain why John 4 has been the New Testament text scholars most often connect to Alter's work on the type-scene. The annunciation scenes in Matthew and Luke have also been discussed in dialogue with Alter's work, though Alter does not provide as full a discussion of the annunciation type-scene in the Hebrew Bible as he does the betrothal type-scene.

9 No wells are mentioned in Samson's and David's cases and wells are only incidentally mentioned in Saul's and Ruth's accounts (and in neither Saul's nor Ruth's case is the relationship between the protagonist and the person(s) drawing water developed).

10 This is the language used in Alter, *The Art of Biblical Narrative*, 58.

11 Ibid., 62.

Each of these five elements construed in these capacious terms is present in the three Penteteuchal scenes. As categorizing criteria, however, they present difficulties. Alter gestures towards at least two: "The key problem is not only the centuries elapsed since this body of literature was created," he writes, "but the small corpus of works that has survived." Alter accounts for the difficulties presented by the chronological gap and the small number of surviving works by introducing what seems more like a third difficulty than a solution to the two already named: The betrothal type-scene is a "macroscopic" aspect of stories, he says, not wedded to the more readily identifiable "microscopic" elements of the text such as formulae for beginning and ending narrative units. The literary analyst who would use the type-scene concept as a tool for understanding ancient literature must reckon with these challenges.[12]

Alter's chief and laudable goal in his work on type-scenes was to offer an alternative to the theretofore-unchecked hegemony of source criticism in the academy.[13] Alter's convincing point was that thinking about culturally-significant and recognizable conventions (in this case, especially generic conventions) offers a better perspective on a body of texts like Genesis 24, Genesis 29, and Exodus 2 than a form- and source-critical analysis that assumes a garbled genetic relationship among the three.[14] Not the least merit of his position is that (though it may seem counterintuitive at first) it takes into account the free play of storytellers, the people who produced later instances of type-scenes. Where the present account parts with Alter—or rather, where it develops his account—is in that part of the analysis where "essential elements" are catalogued. At least four considerations motivate this shift.

The first has to do with what Alter has already acknowledged: the data we have from which to reconstruct a type-scene are relatively paltry. He writes,

12 Ibid., 56–58.

13 His illustration with a modern type-scene familiar from Hollywood westerns is helpful: Future viewers, given a dozen examples of the genre, might notice that in eleven of the films the protagonist sheriff is armed with a six-shooter and is faster on the draw than his opponents. In the twelfth film, Alter asks us to imagine, the protagonist sheriff has a withered right arm but is able to achieve a comparable result ("fastest gun in the West!") using a rifle slung over his left shoulder. The imaginary, future, source-obsessed scholars unfamiliar with the convention would "divide between a majority that posits an original source-western (designated Q) that has been imitated or imperfectly reproduced in a whole series of later versions (Q_1, Q_2, etc. – the films we have been screening) and a more speculative minority that proposes an old California Indian myth concerning a sky-god with arms of lighting, of which all these films are scrambled and diluted secular adaptations. The twelfth film, in the view of both schools, must be ascribed to a different cinematic tradition" (ibid., 56). In his preface to the revised and updated edition of the book, he notes that toning down this polemic is one of the biggest changes introduced to the new text (ibid., xi).

14 Ibid., 76–77.

> Five or six examples . . . may seem a slender foundation on which to build a hypothesis of a literary convention. Not only would I concede the difficulty, I have presented type-scene as an important instance of how a literary understanding of the Bible works precisely because it poses the intrinsic difficulties and may show how by careful analysis they might be overcome.[15]

In due course, we shall see at least some of those difficulties removed by clarifying our conception of how readers work with type-scenes.

While retaining a critical perspective concerning source-critical assumptions about the ways later authors and redactors "used" traditional material (what was the nature of the "use"?), a second reason to adjust Alter's model is that—at least in the case of the Penteteuchal material—a genetic relationship demonstrably exists among the texts concerned. Producers of the later texts were aware of the stories told by their precursors. This does not mean that the later accounts must be understood as "alluding to" or "echoing" the earlier accounts, although (depending on how we define those relational terms) we ought not rule out such possibilities.

A third reason for developing Alter's model is its imprecision. At times Alter describe the type-scene in terms of "essential elements," as noted above. But elsewhere he speaks instead of "specific circumstances, according to a specific order," a "schema," a "fixed constellation of predetermined motifs," a "conventional constellation of motifs," "requirements of the type-scene," "requisite elements," or a "literary code."[16] It is not clear how uniformly *structured* type-scenes must be: Words like "essential" and "requisite elements" do not stress obligatory sequence in the same way as, for example, "specific circumstances, according to a specific order." There is slippage too in terms of how *intentional* type-scenes must be: A "code" suggests intention on the production side; a "constellation" does not.[17] The elements are sometimes described as "predetermined" (intentional language) and at other times as "conventional" (non-intentional language). Perceived aberrations in the presentation of a type-scene are sometimes described as a "deliberate strategy," again suggesting that we with Alter can peer into the minds of textual producers and work out their

15 Ibid., 75.

16 Ibid., 62, 63, 60, 64, 66–67, 68, 77, respectively.

17 Or at least it does not suggest intention in the same way. Constellations are "unintentional" in the sense the stars composing them were not laid out by human agency, but perhaps "intentional" in the sense that *Ursa Minor* is a human-generated and human-transmitted object (the conglomerate image) superimposed on a set of found objects (the individual stars). But constellations were not "intended" by humans in the sense that humans "intend" to drive under the speed limit or exercise regularly in the New Year or to produce a text in a given genre. A code, unlike a constellation, is prescriptive and almost inevitably "intended" to control behavior.

intentions.[18] Where there is less slippage is in terms of how *necessary* the elements are (it seems clear that all five are indispensible), but it is exactly this emphasis on necessity that makes the type-scene fail to hold in the cases of Ruth, Samson, Saul, and David.[19]

The lack of precision noted in connection to the structure of the five elements and the intentionality driving their deployment extends also to the level of the individual element. The careful reader will have noted already that each element is qualified in some way: Must the bridegroom be at the well in person? (No.) How many girls does he encounter at the well? (It varies.) Who draws water from the well? (It varies.) Must the girl(s) rush home? (Would "betrothal type-scene" no longer apply if the maiden walked?) Is the betrothal settled only after the stranger has been invited to a meal? (No, this is only generally the case.)

The fourth and most important reason to qualify Alter's model is finally the difficulties it encounters in *listing* exactly those features of the type-scene that are sufficient and necessary for the label to stick. Take the "elements" that show up in two out of the three primary examples. There is, for instance, the stress on endogamy in Genesis 24 and Genesis 29, not present in Exodus 2. Why say that the need to marry within one's larger kinship network is an added extra in Genesis 24 and Genesis 29 (as Alter suggests) rather than say that it is conspicuous for its absence in Exodus 2 (as he might well have done)?[20] Or what about the presence of an obstacle to drinking from the well—the stone lid in Genesis 29 and the bandits in Exodus 2? Who is to say that the obstacle was not a part of the convention, conspicuous for its absence in Genesis 24? After all, the obstacle is present in this small set with the same frequency as the meal or the presence of the groom-to-be.[21]

Alter is surely correct that type-scenes are useful categories for analyzing ancient texts. "Type-scene" is a modern signifier without an equivalent ancient signifier, but the phenomenon it signifies is as real in ancient literature as it is in

18 Alter, *The Art of Biblical Narrative*, "deliberate" on pp. 55, 57, 68, 73 and "conventional" on pp. 64, 65, 71, 75. Note especially the conclusion to the chapter: "In scrutinizing this vehicle, one is able to see . . . the workings of narrative convention as such. . . . As for the reading of the Bible itself, we may come not only to appreciate these ancient narratives better but, more important, to understand *what they intend to say*" (ibid., 77–78, emphasis added).

19 Ruth marries Boaz, not the young men who draw water from the well. There is no betrothal in Saul's case. There is no well in Samson's case or David's.

20 Commenting on idiosyncrasies of the scene in Gen 24: "All these features are merely elaborations of or accretions to the conventional constellation of motifs." Alter is somehow (without saying how he knows) able to distinguish these elaborations and accretions from the "pointed divergence from the convention" represented by the role played by bride and bridegroom in Gen 24 (i. e., that Isaac is replaced by a surrogate at the well; Alter, *The Art of Biblical Narrative*, 64).

21 Betrothal ensues after a meal in Rebekah and Zipporah's cases, but not in Rachel's. The groom-to-be is present in Jacob's and Moses's cases, but not in Isaac's.

modern texts. The task now is to clarify some means by which type-scenes function to communicate meaning to readers. The Johannine scholars who have adopted Alter's work on the type-scene as a concept have in general been quick to view the "betrothal type-scene" in terms of a list of features. While the list-of-features approach may possess value for a second-order audience of critics and analysts, it fails to capture the ways in which type-scenes function for primary audiences.

3. Altering Alter: Prototype Theory and Type-Scenes

One avenue for developing Alter's model of the type-scene and its narrative function may be found in prototype theory, a way of thinking about generic categories (including type-scenes) proceeding from the idea that we should theorize the creation of categories in literature with the help of research on how mental categories are formed in other domains. A classic example of how prototype theory makes a difference is with respect to the category "bird." Cognitive scientists have found that rather than consult a mental checklist of features (has feathers, flies, lays eggs, etc.) when asked if a given animal is a bird, people categorize new category candidates by comparing them to what they consider typical examples of the category (perhaps a sparrow or a robin).[22] It is important to note that what is "typical" of the category may vary by culture and by individual. One consequence of this is that the category betrothal type-scene could operate differently for different readers, depending on what each reader considers most prototypical of the genre. The other side of the coin concerns producers of new instances of the category: what the producer(s) of Ruth considered prototypical of the patriarchal betrothal scene is by no means necessarily the same as what the producer(s) of John 4 considered prototypical and, in each case,

22 Two classic studies that laid the groundwork for this approach to categorization were Eleanor Rosch, "Cognitive Representations of Semantic Categories," *Journal of Experimental Psychology: General* 104 (1975): 192–233; Eleanor Rosch and Carolyn B. Mervis, "Family Resemblances: Studies in the Internal Structure of Categories," *Cognitive Psychology* 7 (1975): 573–605. A note about the Wittgensteinian language of "family resemblances" since it has also been important for thinking about genre and related literary phenomena: As Newsom points out, following John Swales, "family resemblance theory can make anything resemble anything" (John M. Swales, *Genre Analysis: English in Academic and Research Settings*, Cambridge Applied Linguistics Series [Cambridge: Cambridge University Press, 1990], 51). This is because, as Newsom puts it, "texts in Group A might exhibit features a, b, c, Group B might exhibit features b, c, d, and group C might exhibit features c, d, e, and so forth. One is left with the uncomfortable conclusion that the family-resemblance model could produce a genre in which two exemplars in fact shared no traits in common!" (Newsom, "Spying Out the Land: A Report from Genology," 441).

the different prototypes can be expected to generate consequences for the production of meaning in those different texts.

The key difference between the classical approach to genre (assumed in Alter's list of essential elements in the type-scene) and the prototypical approach to genre is that where the latter compares the objects as wholes, the former compares abstracted lists of parts. Genre theorist Michael Sinding refers to the holistic perspective of a prototype approach as attending to the *Gestalt* structures familiar to students of schema theory.[23] The value added by this perspective to the "list of features" approach is twofold: first, a whole may be more than the sum of its parts; second, any given relationship among parts is potentially as important and interesting as a given part on its own.

Prototype theory, then, favors a folk-psychological classificatory approach over a "list-of-features" classificatory approach. In this folk-psychological classificatory framework, whole objects are compared to individually-variable idealized cognitive models for given categories.[24] This has several benefits. First, if we ask *what* type-scenes are for, we find that they are at a most basic level aids to conveying meaning in human communication, not tools for classification as an end in itself. If we ask *whom* type-scenes are for, we might conclude that the theorist and analyst have a vested interest, by virtue of their professions, in discerning a formal classificatory function, while for general readers formal classification is at most a second-order concern.[25] Approaching the "encounter

23 Michael Sinding, "After Definitions: Genre, Categories, and Cognitive Science," *Genre* 35 (2002): 196. Sinding credits Adena Rosmarin and Daniel Chandler with developing the equivalence of *genre* and *schema*. Cf. Adena Rosmarin, *The Power of Genre* (Minneapolis: University of Minnesota Press, 1985); Daniel Chandler, "Schema Theory and the Interpretation of Television Programmes," n.p. (cited 11 June, 2015). Online: http://visual-memory.co.uk/daniel/Documents/short/schematv.html.

24 The language of "idealized cognitive models" is from George Lakoff, *Women, Fire, and Dangerous Things: What Categories Reveal About the Mind* (Chicago: University of Chicago Press, 1987). Lakoff deserves most of the credit for first bringing Rosch's work into the study of language and literature.

25 In a related vein, Newsom notes: "[C]lassification continues to have its defenders in genre theory, but often in a way that quite changes the nature and purposes of classification from a descriptive enterprise to that of a critical category devised by the critic for the purposes of the critic. Thus Adena Rosmarin, in *The Power of Genre*, argues that genre can be seen as a kind of intentional category error in which two things that are not the same are brought together 'as if' they were the same. Drawing on art historian E. H. Gombrich's dictum that 'all thinking is sorting, classifying,' she argues that it is the critic who draws together different texts for productive purposes."

Newsom calls this practice neopragmatist genre criticism (eadem, "Spying Out the Land: A Report from Genology," 439–40. Cf. Rosmarin, *The Power of Genre*, 21–22). Alter also draws on Gombrich's work, but in connection to the dialectic between "the necessity to use established forms in order to be able to communicate coherently, and the necessity to break and remake those forms because they are arbitrary restrictions and because what is merely repeated automatically no longer conveys a message" (Alter, *The Art of Biblical Narrative*, 74).

with a future betrothed at a well" as a prototypical type-scene rather than a list-of-features type-scene permits us to make better sense of how meaning is made in what appear to be borderline or fringe cases on the list-of-features model: Ruth (Boaz and Ruth), 1 Samuel 9 (Saul and the young women), Judges 14 (Samson and his bride), and John 4 (Jesus and the Samaritan woman). A second, correlative benefit to a prototypical understanding of type-scenes is that it resists the binary logic of a list-of-features model, on which any given scene "counts" or "doesn't count" as an instance of the type-scene.[26] It allows for a spectrum of participation, from "more typical" examples to "less typical" where belonging to the category might be an issue for debate. This accounts for John 4's participation in what Alter calls the betrothal type-scene. Despite the fact that betrothal does not issue from Jesus's encounter with the Samaritan woman (at least not in any straightforward sense), it nevertheless participates in the general category. The nature of the participation is analogous to the participation of penguins and ostriches and dodos in our category "bird": They are just as much category participants as their flight-capable cousins, but they are "less typical" of the category (again, assuming that something like a sparrow or a robin is prototypical). John 4 is to "betrothal type-scene" as penguin is to "bird."

The example above suggests that "flight" and "betrothal" are default, but not necessary values for participation in the categories "bird" and the betrothal type-scene, respectively. This calls for clarification. Genre theorists advocating prototype theory have usefully extended to genres work done by visual semiotician Daniel Chandler on schemas.[27] Genres, accordingly, "can be envisaged as a kind of framework with 'slots' for 'variables', some of them filled-in and others empty." The filled slots can be "*either* filled in already with compulsory values (e.g., that a dog is an animal) or 'default values' (e.g., that a dog has four legs) *or* are empty (optional variables) until 'instantiated' with values from the current situation (e.g., that the dog's colour is black)."[28] At first glance, this looks like a tri-furcated version of the "list of features" approach to genres or type-scenes. But this model is an improvement insofar as it recognizes that values are weighted on a spectrum of the necessary to the optional in the context of *Gestalt* structures. Furthermore, it is important to stress that modeling in this way—identifying features of a type-scene as necessary, default, or optional—is only for the relatively weird task of criticism (none of the ancient texts we work with were written

26 These observations about the communication of meaning and resisting the binary logic are shared with Newsom, "Spying Out the Land: A Report from Genology," 26; Wright, "Joining the Club," 263.

27 Cf. note 23 above.

28 Chandler, "Schema Theory," n.p. Emphasis in the original. Cited also in Sinding, "After Definitions"; Newsom, "Spying Out the Land: A Report from Genology"; Wright, "Joining the Club."

for the modern critic). Prototype theorists are not suggesting that a sorting onto three lists is something that transpires consciously and/or physically in the brains of readers ancient or modern. With those caveats in mind, we return in the next section to our genre category "betrothal type-scene" and ask what necessary, default, and optional values might be operative in connection to John 4.

4. Genre, Prototype Theory, and John 4

In 1973, almost a decade before New Testament scholars adopted Alter's work for reading John 4, Normand R. Bonneau identified Genesis 24, Genesis 29, and Exodus 2 as formally resembling John 4 in two respects: (1) The focus of the action is the meeting of a woman and (2) the setting is at a well.[29] In my thinking about the genre category picked up by John 4, these two elements occupy the "necessary" slots. After all, there are plenty of scenes in the Hebrew Bible (and in other ancient literature) that unfold at or around a well.[30] But on arrival at John 4:7, where the narrator introduces the Samaritan woman, coming to draw water, the reader knows (even if not consciously or by this label) that she is looking at an instance of the betrothal type-scene just as much as the modern reader knows, on catching a glimpse of a spandex-clad, square-jawed strongman rescuing a distressed damsel from lumbering goons, that she is reading in the comicbook superhero genre. The necessary elements are accounted for. But now comes the

29 Normand R. Bonneau, "The Woman at the Well: John 4 and Genesis 24," *TBT* 67 (1973): 1252.

30 What would happen if we connected John 4 to the story of Hagar being met by the angel of the Lord by a spring (LXX: πηγή) of water, the well (LXX: φρέαρ) called Beer-lahai-roi (באר לחי ראי; LXX: Φρέαρ οὗ ἐνώπιον εἶδον; Gen 16:14)? Notice that both πηγή and φρέαρ are used in John 4, a point that has puzzled some interpreters. The translation choice for Beer-lahai-roi in the LXX is fascinating in light of Johannine motifs of physical and spiritual sight, ignorance and knowledge, and a moment of coming to see openly, motifs for which our passage in John 4 is a case in point. This could be connected to Hagar's later journey, where God opens her eyes to see a well of running/living water (LXX: καὶ ἀνέῳξεν ὁ θεὸς τοὺς ὀφθαλμοὺς αὐτῆς, καὶ εἶδεν φρέαρ ὕδατος ζῶντος). In fact, although not mentioned in Alter's treatment of Hebrew Bible well type-scenes, this story could be construed as participating in that genre, as it possesses both of the "necessary" elements we proposed are required for the category to obtain—the focus of the action on the meeting of a woman, and the setting at a well. And while betrothal does not follow from the encounter (just as it fails to follow from Saul's encounter with the maidens at a well in 1 Sam 9:11–12, and Ruth's interactions with the young men in Ruth 2), marriage and fecundity are evidently drivers of the larger plot of which this scene is a part. For other stories set around wells in the Hebrew Bible, we might point to the conflicts of Isaac's servants with the herders of Gerar in Gen 26, the φρέαρ mentioned in LXX Num 21:16, where the Lord says to Moses, "Gather the people together, and I will give them water" (cf. John 4:10), or the twelve springs (πηγαί) of water at Elim, at which the Israelites arrive after leaving behind the bitter waters of Marah and where they received bread from heaven (LXX Ex 15:27; cf. John 6 for "bread from heaven," and the two kinds of "water" in John 4).

interesting part. What "default" values does our reader of John 4 fill in, and what "optional" values lie as-yet unfilled? How one answers these questions—especially the question about the "default" values—provides an answer to our original question about what expectations the betrothal type-scene as a category can generate and what John 4 does with those expectations. How is meaning created in the coming together of a text like John 4 and a reader equipped with a prototype knowledge of the betrothal type-scene as a generic category?

We noted above that the textual producers responsible for John 4 might have had any number of exemplars of the betrothal type-scene on which to draw, while we are left only with the three texts Alter identified as "full dress occurrences" and a handful of other texts that appear to participate in the category in a (partially dressed?) manner. We saw that prototype theory allows us to speak of this assortment of texts as participating more or less fully in the category, and that the extent of category participation was determined by the extent to which a given text resembled the texts held to be most prototypical of the genre (i.e., the fullness of dress is in the eye of the beholder). While there is very little we can do to compare John 4 with lost exemplars of the category, it remains a valuable exercise to ask which—of the texts that have survived and which we can point to as known to the implied readers of the Fourth Gospel—might qualify as the most prototypical examples of the category for John 4. A case could be mounted for any of the three, but I think that the strongest case can be made for Genesis 29.[31]

In the first place, Genesis 29 allows for a simpler set of default values indicating participation in the category. Now there are no surrogates (as in the case of Isaac and Rebekah),[32] no sorority of maidens (as in Moses's experience), no prerequisite of a shared meal before the marriage discussion gets underway (as in Rebekah's and Zipporah's cases). When dealing with prototypes, simplicity is a virtue in itself (the fewer complicating features the better). Here, moreover, the

31 Bonneau finds the resemblances greatest between Gen 24 and John 4, largely on the strength of an observation that the "symbolic content of woman in the Bible certainly has an important role in both Genesis 24 and John 4" and an argument made by Aileen Guilding that the evangelist "wrote his Gospel according to the plan of the Palestinian synagogue lectionary system – the readings at the time of year when the Samaritan interlude takes place would be Exodus 2:15–22 and Genesis 24" (Bonneau, "The Woman at the Well," 1256–57; cf. Aileen Guilding, *The Fourth Gospel and Jewish Worship: A Study of the Relation of St. John's Gospel to the Ancient Jewish Lectionary System* [Oxford: Clarendon Press, 1960]). Bonneau also recognized, however, that there are compelling reasons for linking this text with Gen 29.

32 It would be interesting to imagine Jesus here as a surrogate for the Father, a task one might well attempt within the logic of the Johannine theological economy. If such an exercise of imagination were undertaken, however, it would be important to remember that in Gen 24 there are three parties on the sending side (Abraham the father, Isaac the son, and the servant as surrogate) but just two in John 4 (God the Father and Jesus the son). This discrepancy is not insuperable, and indeed might be made more interesting in light of the expectation-disrupting effects of the betrothal type-scene and John 4 discussed below.

more streamlined prototypical betrothal type-scene makes a better fit with what is actually found in John 4, where again there is no surrogate, no Samaritan sisterhood, no bandits, no meal with the Samaritan woman's father. As mentioned above, we might at least provisionally limit the "necessary" elements to those Bonneau observed about the four scenes: the focus of the action is on an encounter with a woman, and the setting is at a well.[33]

A second and perhaps more telling piece of the puzzle that falls into place if we accept Genesis 29 as more prototypical of the type-scene evoked in John 4 is that Jacob is mentioned by name both by the narrator (4:5–6) and in the conversation between Jesus and the woman: "Are you greater than our ancestor Jacob, who gave us the well, and with his sons and flocks drank from it?" (4:12). As Jerome Neyrey pointed out in an important 1979 article, both this question and the way it is answered belong to "a mode of discourse in the Gospel which both asserts the superiority of Jesus over Israel's patriarchs and makes an absolute claim on his behalf."[34] Whatever the relation of this type-scene to its Penteteuchal precedents, whatever its individual merits as a "masterpiece of narrative design" that "stands out as a sustained artistic accomplishment,"[35] it remains a piece of a larger narrative in which Jesus is made out to be superior to ancient Israel's founding figures, including especially Abraham (John 8:53) and Moses (1:17–18; 5:38; 6:32) in addition to Jacob.[36]

Above we noted that a case could be made for reading John 4 with other texts in the prototype position, but for the purposes of this paper Genesis 29 has been tentatively identified as a better prototype than the stories we find in Genesis 24 and Exodus 2.[37] The study at this point could turn to any number of domains

33 For this reason, to call the category a *betrothal* type-scene could be misleading. Betrothal, on the necessary-default-optional model presented here, is a default value. Shifting it from the necessary to the default allows for a better handling of John 4 as well as the cases Alter notes as marginal. To these, we could add the story of Hagar (mentioned above in note 30) and (with Martin, "Betrothal Journey Narratives") the story of Tobias in the Book of Tobit.

34 Jerome H. Neyrey, "Jacob Traditions and the Interpretation of John 4:10–26," *CBQ* 41 (1979): 421.

35 The accolades are from a lovely but short piece by P. Joseph Cahill, "Narrative Art in John IV," *Religious Studies Bulletin* 2 (1982): 41. In the same issue of the journal, Cahill provides a glowing review of Alter's *The Art of Biblical Narrative*. To my knowledge, Cahill offers the earliest reading of John 4 in light of Alter's book.

36 The Moses-Jesus relation in the Fourth Gospel more generally might suggest that we consider Ex 2 as the type-scene "more prototypical" for John 4, but the fact that Jacob is mentioned explicitly in the immediate context argues for Gen 29. On the Moses-Jesus relation, see especially Wayne A. Meeks, *The Prophet-King: Moses Traditions and the Johannine Christology*, NovTSup 14 (Leiden: Brill, 1967).
Note that I am not making in this paper any claims about the historical priority of Gen 29 to Ex 2 or Gen 24, nor any claims about which account was more prototypical for the author or audience (real or implied) of Ruth, 1 Sam 9:11–12, or the Samson cycle in Judges.

37 And in fact, if we are willing to restrict the "necessary" values to the two adapted from

where default values are created, but for the sake of economy in this paper and thematic centrality in the Fourth Gospel, we shall look at the subversion of three default values in the cognitive domain of characters in John 4. In each case, the expectations generated by the default values of the genre are met, but in each case with a surprising, superseding twist.[38]

The first default concerns prior knowledge. Like Jacob, Jesus is (from the woman's perspective) a stranger at the well in the middle of the day.[39] And like Jacob, Jesus the stranger nevertheless knows the identity of the approaching woman.[40] But there is a twist: Jacob's prior knowledge comes from questioning the men of Haran he first meets at the well; Jesus's prior knowledge comes from the Father. An important motif in the Fourth Gospel is that Jesus "knew all people and needed no one to testify about anyone; for he himself knew what was in everyone" (2:24b–25). Jesus's prior knowledge is greater than Jacob's.

A second default concerns recognition. The Jacob story puts in the default position the expectation that Jesus will produce water, as indeed he does, but again with a twist. It is not mundane well water for animals, but "living water" for people, and "a spring of water gushing up to eternal life" (4:10, 14).[41] This water is not only for the woman and eventually her townspeople in the sequel, but for the one "flock" that recognizes and responds to the voice of the shepherd sent by the Father to lay down his life and take it up again (10:16–18). In the Genesis account, the plot turns on Jacob's ability to recognize his mother's family. In John, that Jesus recognizes his Father's own is never in any doubt; what is more important is

---

Bonneau's work (the focus of the action as the meeting of a woman and the setting as at a well), we could look at other texts too. I would be especially interesting in considering John 4 with the Hagar narrative (Gen 16) in the prototype position (see above, note 30).

38 As Sune Auken pointed out to me, *that* the default values are met with a twist or a bend is not half as interesting as *how* they are taken up. On generic up-take, see Auken's contribution to this volume.

39 Cf. the motif of Jesus as the "heavenly stranger" in the Fourth Gospel. Wayne A. Meeks, "The Man from Heaven in Johannine Sectarianism," *JBL* 91 (1972): 44–72; Marinus de Jonge, *Jesus, Stranger from Heaven and Son of God: Jesus Christ and the Christians in Johannine Perspective*, trans. John E. Steely, SBLSBS 11 (Missoula: Scholars, 1977).

40 And in both cases the man remains a stranger until well past the time when things have become awkward! For Rachel, Jacob does not reveal his identity until after he has kissed her and wept on her (Gen 29:11). With the Samaritan woman, Jesus will not reveal his identity until she puts some of the pieces together for herself. A striking difference between the two accounts concerns the length of dialogue and the present degree of the woman's agency. Where Rachel receives Jacob's affections and self-identification passively, apparently without a word, the Samaritan woman shares a lengthy discussion with Jesus, which she directs at least as much as he does, raising questions about Jew-Samaritan relations, the proper place of worship, and the relative status of Jesus and Jacob.

41 The double entendre of τὸ ὕδωρ τὸ ζῶν is widely noted and appreciated. Ζῶν here can mean either "running" water (as opposed to the still water one might access from a well), or the water "of life," where life is understood in John's theological sense. Both (eternal) life and water in symbolic connection to the spirit are important themes in the Fourth Gospel.

that the woman, by means of "living water" as a token, recognize the one offering it to her.[42]

A third and striking default expectation subverted in John 4 is that the outcome of the encounter is betrothal and subsequent marital fidelity (πίστις).[43] Many commentators have noticed that the women in the Penteteuchal examples of this type-scene are maidens who wind up married to the men they meet at the well, while in John the marriage is revisioned as covenant and worship in the relationship between God and the world, drawing on and expanding a motif familiar from Israel's prophetic tradition.[44] Jesus does not "marry" the woman, at least not in a non-metaphorical sense of the word. But he does bring the woman, and with her many Samaritans, to πίστις, a point where they "believed in him because of the woman's testimony" (4:39) and confess, "We have heard for ourselves, and we know that this is truly the Savior of the world" (4:42). If Jacob labored 14 years to bring about his two troubled marriages, Jesus in the course of two days (4:40) brings about an eternal relationship between himself and many Samaritans (4:41; cf. 4:39).

5. Conclusion

In these briefly sketched facets of the cognitive dimension of the story in John 4, the evangelist answers "yes" to the question posed by the woman: "Are you greater than our ancestor Jacob?" That affirmation is brought out more remarkably if we reflect on the expectation-generating effects of the betrothal type-scene category best exemplified in John by Jacob's meeting with Rachel in Genesis 29. The default values of the scene proposed in these last few pages—expectations about prior knowledge, recognition, and πίστις, respectively—derive from the cognitive domain of characterization. By thinking about type-scenes as generic categories in the theoretical framework furnished by prototype theory rather than literary phenomena reducible to lists of features, we are

42 For a more nuanced analysis of the "reciprocal recognition" in this scene, see Kasper Bro Larsen contribution in this volume and, on recognition in John in general, see Kasper Bro Larsen, *Recognizing the Stranger: Recognition Scenes in the Gospel of John*, BIS 93 (Leiden: Brill, 2008).

43 For πίστις as a promise to one's spouse that can be set aside by remarrying, see for example 1 Tim 5:12.

44 Some support for this may be found in the woman's recognition of Jesus as a prophet in 4:19. Some scholars go further, and see in the woman's history of husbands a reference to Samaritan idolatry, "infidelity" with respect to the one God of Jacob/Israel. The case is put forward in, e.g., the article by Bonneau, who credits John Marsh's commentary for the formulation he finds persuasive. Bonneau, "The Woman at the Well," 1258–59; cf. John Marsh, *The Gospel of St. John*, PNTC (Philadelphia: Westminster, 1968), 214–21.

opening new opportunities for sophisticated and concretely intertextual analyses of meaning-making in the cognitive dimension of the Fourth Gospel's discourse of characterization.[45]

45 Earlier versions of this paper were presented at the Canadian Society of Biblical Studies Annual Meeting at Brock University (St. Catherines, Ontario, Canada) in May 2014 and at the "Gospel of John as Genre Mosaic" conference at Aarhus University (Aarhus, Denmark) in June 2014. I am grateful to the organizers and participants of both conferences for fruitful discussions. Harold Attridge, Sune Auken, Colleen Conway, Troels Engberg-Pedersen, Kasper Bro Larsen, David Miller, Hindy Najman, Jason Ripley, Ruth Sheridan, David Svärd, and Benjamin Wright provided encouragement and constructive feedback in conversations about the paper, for which I am especially grateful.

David Svärd

John 12:1–8 as a Royal Anointing Scene

1. Introduction[1]

In the Gospel of John, Jesus is described as the king of Israel and the king of the Jews.[2] Jesus' entry into Jerusalem, his trial, and his crucifixion also enhance his royal identity.[3] That Jesus is the Christ, the Anointed One, a notion that does not have to be exclusively royal, is further emphasized. If the fourth evangelist makes use of the conventions of ancient biography, the narration of not only his words but also of his deeds should be considered very important in order to understand John's characterization of Jesus as king and Messiah.[4] The episodes of the anointing of the most prominent Israelite kings are told in detail in the Old Testament (OT) and they create a connection between these anointed kings and the designation of them as "the Lord's anointed one." In a story inspired by the OT about Jesus as the ideal Israelite king and Messiah, as is present in John's Gospel, one would expect a description of his anointing to be included. Why does the evangelist not describe Jesus' anointing?[5]

Some scholars, however, have proposed that Jesus is, in fact, anointed king in the episode of the anointing of Jesus in Bethany,[6] while several others have rejected such an interpretation.[7] In this article I argue that there are good reasons

1 This article is part of a larger study and its topic will be further developed in my forthcoming dissertation at Lund University about John's episode of the anointing in Bethany.

2 See e.g., John 1:49; 12:13; 19:3, 19.

3 See e.g., Jocelyn McWhirter, *The Bridegroom Messiah and the People of God: Marriage in the Fourth Gospel*, SNTSMS 138 (Cambridge: Cambridge University Press, 2006), 39.

4 Cf. Richard A. Burridge, *Imitating Jesus: An Inclusive Approach to New Testament Ethics* (Grand Rapids: Eerdmans, 2007), 24–26, 30.

5 Alternative explanations could be that the historical Jesus never received such an anointing or that the descending of the Spirit in John 1:32–33 replaced any humanly performed anointing.

6 See e.g., C. K. Barrett, *The Gospel according to St. John: An Introduction with Commentary and Notes on the Greek Text*, 2nd ed. (Philadelphia: Westminster, 1978), 409; J. Edgar Bruns, "Note on Jn 12:3," *CBQ* 28 (1966): 219–22.

7 See e.g., Raymond E. Brown, *The Gospel according to John. i–xii*, AB 29, 2nd ed. (Garden City:

to understand the anointing in Bethany as a royal anointing. These reasons relate not only to the christology of the Gospel but also to literary genre. I propose that John 12:1–8 is a refashioned private royal anointing scene. That Jesus' entry into Jerusalem when he is acclaimed the king of Israel is told immediately after the anointing episode gives strong support to a royal interpretation of the anointing.[8] The refashioning and bending of the micro-genre of the royal anointing scene serves to support the bending of notions and motifs including royal messianic expectations.[9] To my knowledge, no scholar has yet described the royal anointing episodes mentioned above as a genre employed by early Christian authors.

In order to argue my case, I will present the analysis in three steps followed by a conclusion. First, I am going to introduce some important aspects of genre theory, followed by a short description of the social and cultural context of John 12:1–8. I will also briefly introduce the OT private royal anointing scene before my attention turns to the composition of the Johannine episode. Secondly, I will identify the generic elements of the private royal anointing scene of the OT and explore how John has treated each element. Note that when speaking of the OT private royal anointing scene as a genre, I do not refer to the individual OT episodes, but to a type of scene that is characterized by the common elements of these episodes.[10] Thirdly, I am going to analyze the effects that the changes of the generic scene have on John's composition. Finally, I will present my conclusions.

2. Reflections on Genre

At least for the study of literature, I find it fruitful to define genre as a major literary convention that an author uses to communicate the meaning of a text to an audience. The convention functions as a set of expectations that guide the

Doubleday, 1966), 454; cf. J. F. Coakley, "The Anointing at Bethany and the Priority of John," *JBL* 107 (1988): 241–56, esp. 243.

8 That Mark and Matthew do not narrate Jesus' entry in immediate relation to his anointing may further strengthen the notion that the fourth evangelist intended to describe the anointing as royal.

9 Harold W. Attridge brought to the fore the expression "genre bending" as a designation of modifications of genres in John in his article "Genre Bending in the Fourth Gospel," *JBL* 121 (2002): 3–21. I use the expression "micro-genre" to designate a genre that is employed merely for the composition of a limited part of a literary work.

10 This description resembles the concept of type-scene used by Robert Alter; see idem, *The Art of Biblical Narrative*, rev. ed. (New York: Basic Books, 2011). The concept of type-scene, however, seems to presuppose that the instances of the scene found in the Bible are only a portion of a more widespread convention that guided the composition of the texts. I find it more probable that the anointings of Saul, David, and Jehu are rather unique in the Israelite history and that the author chose to tell these specific episodes through a literary type that was not used for other Israelite kings.

interpretation and make it possible to reconstruct the author's intended meaning.[11] Thus, if one or more genres that the author of John used in composing the anointing episode are recognized, the meaning of the episode will be understood more clearly. The elements or features that make up a genre relate to both the form and content of a group of literary works, for instance, specific meter or structure, attitude, tone, and purpose.[12] Even if I do not touch upon all these kinds of elements in my analysis, I think that those I have focused on are sufficient in order to substantiate my proposal.

Genres need to be understood in their historical context.[13] If an author wants to successfully communicate meaning with the help of a certain genre, he or she needs to make the generic features clear enough to be recognized by the audience in mind, taking their social and cultural context into consideration. In the case of a micro-genre, the author has not only the extra-textual context to take into account but must also guide the audience to a certain genre by his/her composition of the intra-textual literary context. Thus, the historical situation and the literary context may indicate that a certain genre is used in John 12:1–8. It is not necessary that every generic element is reproduced when an existing genre is employed. Instead, one should expect that an author transforms and mixes genres in various ways when creating a literary work.[14] In general, some elements are more important than others for the constitution of a genre, but it is the overall picture created by the combination of unchanged, modified, removed, and added elements that will determine whether the author's communication will be successful or not.

Finally, it is worth emphasizing that genres often operate in implicit ways since generic conventions are frequently learned unconsciously by authors and readers.[15] Thus the OT private royal anointing scene (which I detail below) may have guided the composition and interpretation of John 12:1–8, even if that scene was never explicitly described as a certain type of episode or labeled in any specific way in antiquity.

11 Cf. Richard A. Burridge, *What are the Gospels? A Comparison with Graeco-Roman Biography*, BRS, 2nd ed. (Grand Rapids: Eerdmans, 2004), 33, 49.

12 Ibid., 40–41.

13 Ibid., 47.

14 Ibid., 42, 45–46.

15 Ibid., 42.

3. The Social and Cultural Context of John 12:1–8

The rhetorical situation of John is rather complex since it is likely that the fourth evangelist wrote his gospel with a broad audience in mind.[16] Most scholars would situate John and his primary addressees in a Jewish context towards the end of the first century CE. If so, at least the most knowledgeable among the Gospel's audience would be well-versed in the Scriptures whose interpretations would be bound up with views of the contemporary historical, political, and religious situation. The notion of the need for a messianic savior who would redeem the people of God from their enemies was deeply rooted in the culture, and the preaching about Jesus as the Messiah had contributed to a divided and sometimes polemic discourse. It is in this context that John presented a particular way to interpret the contemporary situation in view of the Scriptures. John's Gospel was intended to cause the addressees to believe that Jesus was the Christ, the Son of God, and that by believing they might have eternal life (John 20:31).

The evangelist could have made use of the presumably well-known convention of telling the life story of a prominent man, the *bios* ("life"). John is composed of a series of episodes containing events, discourses, and monologues. Each episode may contribute more or less directly to the overall purpose of the Gospel. In some episodes Jesus' identity is clearly revealed, while in other episodes it is revealed more implicitly, as is the case with the anointing in Bethany. The author of John presented Jesus in view of a multiplicity of scriptural motifs, concepts, and quotations, and therefore it is highly probable that he also made use of scriptural genres (e.g., betrothal scene and farewell discourse) that would fit his presentation.

The themes of Israelite kingship and messiahship are prominent in John, and the anointing episode (12:1–8) is surrounded with such references. For instance, the thought of a royal anointing of Jesus with oil may have been evoked earlier in the Gospel narrative when the people intended to take Jesus by force and make him king (6:15). In 11:1–2, the anointing in Bethany is anticipated and the characters Mary, Martha, and Lazarus, who will participate in the anointing scene, are introduced. The reference to Bethany may also allude to the first chapter of John where Jesus is declared to be the Messiah and the king of Israel. John 11:3–45 continues to tell the story about these characters, and contains, for

16 See Richard Bauckham, "For Whom Were the Gospels Written?" in *The Gospels for all Christians: Rethinking the Gospel Audiences*, ed. R. Bauckham (Edinburgh: T&T Clark, 1998), 9–49; Edward W. Klink, *The Sheep of the Fold: The Audience and Origin of the Gospel of John*, SNTSMS 141 (Cambridge: Cambridge University Press, 2007); contra, e.g., J. Louis Martyn, *History and Theology in the Fourth Gospel*, 2nd rev. ed. (Nashville: Abingdon, 1979); Raymond F. Brown, *The Community of the Beloved Disciple: The Life, Loves, and Hates of an Individual Church in New Testament Times* (New York: Paulist, 1979).

instance, Martha's confession of Jesus as "the Christ, the Son of God, he who is coming into the world" (v. 27). Immediately after the anointing episode, Jesus' entrance into Jerusalem and the people's celebration of him as the king of Israel are described. The literary context of the episode, as well as the socio-historical context, indicates what genres the author thought he would be able to communicate to his addressees at this point in his narrative.

4. The Old Testament Private Royal Anointing Scene and John 12:1–8

Some of the most detailed treatments of Israelite kingship are found in the books of Samuel and Kings. The anointing episodes which connect the notions of kingship and anointing, as well as the designation "the Lord's anointed one," have a significant place within these books. I propose that the fourth evangelist employed the patterns of the OT private royal anointing scene in John 12:1–8 in order to substantiate his presentation of Jesus as the royal Messiah. However, the generic scene has been refashioned in order to emphasize the differences and the richness of Jesus' messiahship in comparison to that of the kings Saul, David, and Jehu.

The stories of the anointings of Saul, David, and Jehu are told in ways that resemble each other in terms of style, form, and content.[17] Disregarding the question of how these stories were actually composed, their common literary pattern is likely to have been perceived by people of the first century CE who were well-versed in the Holy Scriptures. The conventional way of telling these royal anointings is what I call the royal anointing scene.

In his composition of John 12:1–8 as royal anointing scene, the fourth evangelist has probably also made use of traditions about a woman who anoints Jesus that are similar or identical to those told in the Synoptic Gospels. Mark seems to employ the micro-genre of the OT royal anointing scene in Mark 14:3–9 (par. Matt 26:6–13) where a woman pours oil on the head of Jesus while he is reclining in Bethany. One of Mark's major modifications to the generic OT scene is that a woman anoints Jesus rather than a man, but as in the OT accounts the oil is poured on his head. If the author of John knew this kind of tradition, his singling out of the feet in John 12:3 should be understood as one further way he modifies the scene, which carries christological significance. In this article,

17 Since these three kings are said to be anointed by God, Tryggve Mettinger calls these cases "divine" anointings. Tryggve N. D. Mettinger, *King and Messiah: The Civil and Sacral Legitimation of the Israelite Kings*, ConBOT 8 (Lund: CWK Gleerup, 1976), 203.

however, there is no room for an investigation of the synoptic episodes and their possible relations to John.[18]

5. The Generic Elements of the Scene

The generic elements that I have identified in the private royal anointing episodes that are included in 1 Samuel and 2 Kings can be roughly divided into the following aspects. The first generic element focuses upon the literary style and form of the episodes of the anointing of Saul, David, and Jehu, which are (1) relatively short narrative units of prose integrated into a larger narrative story. The following nine generic elements focus on aspects of the contents of the episodes. (2) The setting of the anointing scene is private, secret, dangerous, and in the vicinity of Jerusalem. (3) The scene is connected to table fellowship and a sacrifice. (4) A male prophet is commissioned to anoint (5) a divinely elected man. (6) One of them needs to travel in order to arrive at the scene. (7) The one who anoints takes a container and pours oil upon the head, (8) pronounces that the person is anointed to be king, and (9) adds a statement of commissioning. (10) Following the anointing act, the spirit of the Lord comes mightily upon the one who has been anointed. Allowing for the flexible nature of genres, I have included generic elements of the royal anointing scene that are present in only two of the three analyzed accounts.

5.1 An Integrated Narrative Unit of Prose

The episodes of the anointing of Saul, David, and Jehu are all narrative units of prose integrated into a larger narrative story. The story about the anointing of Saul (1 Sam 9:1–10:16), which includes a rather long introduction and ending, is made up of 1233 words in the LXX. This narration contains all the generic elements mentioned above. The story about the anointing of David (1 Sam 16:1–13) consists of 343 Greek words and has a rather short description of the anointing act itself. Jehu's anointing (2 Kgs 9:1–13) is told in 344 words in the LXX. The Johannine story about the anointing of Jesus is concentrated to John 12:1–8 and consists of 143 words of narrative prose. The anointing act, however, is mentioned in advance in 11:2 which is why the whole of chapter 11 functions as a type of introduction to the episode. In summary, the OT royal anointing epi-

18 Neither is there room to explore the retellings of the anointings of Israelite kings in Josephus' *Antiquitates judaicae* (*Ant.* 6.45–59; 6.157–164; 9.106–111) or Pseudo-Philo (*Liber antiquitatum biblicarum* 59.1–4).

sodes, as well as the Johannine anointing episode, are relatively short narrative units of prose integrated into a larger narrative story. The episode in John is rather short, however, which indicates that the present generic elements have not been given much space. The use of prose in the Johannine episode helps the reader or hearer to establish its relation to the royal anointing episodes of the books of Samuel and Kings, rather than the royal anointing mentioned in, for instance, the Psalms.

5.2 A Private, Secret, and Dangerous Setting in the Vicinity of Jerusalem

The above mentioned anointings of Saul, David, and Jehu all take place in a rather private setting in contrast to the public coronation and declaration of kingship. Saul is anointed early in the morning in the outskirts of the city after his servant has passed before him (1 Sam 9:26–10:1). Kyle McCarter characterizes this anointing as secret since Saul also conceals what happened from his family.[19] Later, Saul's kingship is declared in public (10:17–27; 11:12–15), and then he is anointed again according to the LXX (11:15).

David is anointed at a feast to which Jesse and his other seven sons, as well as the elders of the city, have been invited. The LXX text is not clear about whether the elders are invited or not. According to Graeme Auld, it is not a fully public sacrificial meal and is instead more of a family event where only David's brothers and father are present.[20] Walter Brueggemann, on the other hand, considers the elders to be present in the scene.[21] The relative privacy of the anointing act is emphasized in 16:13 which states that David was anointed "in the midst of his brothers." There is apparently a wish to keep the anointing secret since the appointment of a new king to replace Saul is dangerous (16:2). Public anointings of David are performed later when he is officially made king (2 Sam 2:4; 5:3). Privacy and secrecy also surrounds the anointing of Jehu who sits together with his brothers, the commanders of the army, but he is brought by Elisha's servant into the inner chamber of the house where he is anointed (2 Kgs 9:1–13). The danger of the occasion is partly revealed by the immediate flight of the servant once the anointing is completed. It is a dangerous thing to anoint a new king while the old one is still alive.

The anointing of Jesus in Bethany also takes place in a rather private setting in which at least five persons, Lazarus, Martha, Mary, Judas, and Jesus, are gathered

19 P. Kyle McCarter, Jr., *I Samuel: A New Translation with Introduction, Notes and Commentary*, AB 8 (Garden City: Doubleday, 1980), 187.

20 A. Graeme Auld, *I and II Samuel: A Commentary*, OTL (Louisville: Westminster John Knox, 2011), 96, 184.

21 Walter Brueggemann, *First and Second Samuel*, IBC (Louisville: John Knox, 1990), 122.

for a feast inside a house. Jesus has recently stopped walking openly and the people do not know where he is (John 11:54–57) which gives the occasion a sense of secrecy. Soon, however, his presence in Bethany becomes known and he will publicly be hailed as king (12:9, 12–19). The atmosphere of danger is present in the episode since the Jewish leaders want to arrest him and kill him (11:53, 57). One more trait that the Johannine episode has in common with the anointings of Saul and David, but not with the anointing of Jehu, is that Jesus is anointed in a city near Jerusalem. The nearness of Bethany to Jerusalem is emphasized in 11:18. Saul is anointed in Ramah and David is anointed in Bethlehem, cities located quite near Jerusalem, while Jehu is anointed in Ramoth-Gilead. To sum up, the settings of the royal anointings are private, secret, dangerous, and geographically in the vicinity of Jerusalem. This is true also for the setting of the episode of the anointing of Jesus in John.

5.3 Connection to Table Fellowship and Sacrifice

The anointings of Saul and David are both connected to a sacrifice and to reclining at a table. In the episode of the anointing of Saul, the people of Ramah shall have a sacrificial feast but the approximately thirty (LXX: seventy) invited men will not eat until Samuel comes and blesses the sacrifice (1 Sam 9:12–13, 19–24). Saul and his servant are invited and Saul is brought into the hall and given a place at the head of the guests. The anointing is performed early in the morning of the following day (9:26–10:1). When David is about to be anointed, Samuel brings a heifer and invites Jesse, his sons, and the elders to a sacrifice. The meal is delayed though because they will not recline until David comes (16:11). When he has arrived Samuel anoints him. In the case of Jehu, no meal is mentioned but when the young man sent by Elisha arrives, the commanders of the army (2 Kgs 9:2: "his brothers") are sitting outside the house (v. 3), indicating a rather static assembly similar to reclining at a table.

In John, a dinner is made for Jesus, and the guests recline at the table when he is anointed. The meal is connected in John 12:1 to the arrival of Jesus in Bethany six days before the Passover. The references to the high priest, the plans to kill Jesus, the Passover, and the temple (11:49–56) set the meal in a sacrificial context which recalls the characterization of Jesus as "the lamb of God who takes away the sin of the world" (1:29).[22] In summary, the anointings of Saul and David are

22 Several scholars have argued that Jesus is portrayed as a sacrificial Passover lamb in John. See e.g., Rudolf Schnackenburg, *The Gospel according to St John, Volume 1: Introduction and Commentary on Chapters 1–4*, trans. K. Smyth, Herder's Theological Commentary on the New Testament (London: Herder, 1980), 299–300; and Craig S. Keener, *The Gospel of John: A Commentary* (Peabody: Hendrickson, 2003), 454.

connected to a sacrificial meal where guests recline at a table. Likewise, the anointing of Jesus in John takes place at a meal with guests reclining at a table. The Johannine scene is set in the context of the sacrifice of the Passover lamb and the self-sacrifice of Jesus.

5.4 A Male Prophet Commissioned to Anoint

In the OT narratives, the anointing is performed by a male prophet who has been given this task. Both Saul and David are anointed by the prophet Samuel after he has been commissioned by the Lord. The Lord reveals to Samuel that the following day he would send him a man that he should anoint. As he sees Saul, the Lord tells Samuel that this is the man that he spoke of (1 Sam 9:15–17). A while after the Lord has rejected Saul as king, the Lord sends Samuel to Jesse, the Bethlehemite, with a horn of oil because he has provided for himself a king among Jesse's sons (16:1). When David has been fetched, the Lord tells Samuel to arise and anoint him (16:12).

The pattern is partly repeated in the episode of Jehu's anointing, where the anointer is called "one of the sons of the prophets" (2 Kgs 9:1) and in v. 4 of the Masoretic text (MT) "the young man, the servant of the prophet." However, in v. 4 of the LXX, the young man is also designated "prophet." Of greater significance is that the one who commissions the servant to anoint Jehu is not the Lord, but the prophet Elisha. As the Lord commissions the prophet Samuel to anoint Saul and David, respectively, the prophet Elisha likewise commissions the servant to anoint Jehu. The informed reader, however, knows from 1 Kgs 19:16 that the Lord ultimately has decided that Jehu should be anointed king.

In John it is not a man, but a woman who anoints Jesus. Even though Mary is never called "prophet" in the Gospel, commentators designate her action as prophetic.[23] The explanation of the anointing ascribed to Jesus in John 12:7–8 makes clear that the act anticipates Jesus' death, burial, and departure. Judas, who asks why the ointment was not sold and the money given to the poor (v. 5) is given the following answer by Jesus in v. 7: "Let her alone, [this ointment was not sold] so that [ἵνα] she might keep [τηρήσῃ] it for the day of my burial (preparation)." This is best understood in the context of John as a statement that indicates that this day in Bethany is Jesus' proleptic day of burial preparation.[24]

23 See e.g., Brown, *John*, 454, who characterizes Mary's action as unconsciously prophetic, while Colleen M. Conway speaks of Mary's "sensitivity to Jesus' impending death" (eadem, *Men and Women in the Fourth Gospel: Gender and Johannine Characterization*, SBLDS 167 [Atlanta: Society of Biblical Literature, 1999], 153).

24 Hartwig Thyen, *Das Johannesevangelium*, HNT 6 (Tübingen: Mohr Siebeck, 2005), 552;

The act is prophetic, at least as foretelling, and must therefore be considered divinely inspired, even though Mary is never known to be commissioned by God or anyone else to perform the anointing. To summarize, the male prophet commissioned by the Lord (or his representative) to anoint the next Israelite king in the OT stories is, in John, replaced by a woman who is implicitly characterized as divinely inspired to prophetically anoint Jesus in regards to his impending death, burial, and departure.

5.5 Anointing of a Divinely Elected Man

Saul, David, and Jehu, are all elected by the Lord to be kings over Israel. The Lord informs Samuel that he shall anoint Saul to be prince over Israel in 1 Sam 9:15–17. When Saul has been rejected, the Lord instructs Samuel that he has provided for himself one of Jesse's sons to be king. Seven of Jesse's sons pass in turn before Samuel, but the Lord indicates to him that it is none of them. When the eighth son, David, has arrived, the Lord tells Samuel that he is the one to be anointed (16:1, 6–12). In 1 Kgs 19:16 the Lord instructs the prophet Elijah to anoint Jehu, the son of Nimshi, king over Israel, but it is never related that Elijah carries out this command. In the anointing episode in 2 Kgs 9:1–13 the prophet Elisha, acting as a representative of Elijah and/or of the Lord, commands the son of the prophets to anoint Jehu the son of Jehoshaphat, son of Nimshi.

Thus, we have found that in these episodes divinely elected men are anointed kings. In the anointing episode in John 12:1–8, there is no explicit mentioning of Jesus being chosen by God to be anointed king, but Jesus' election by God to be his agent in an unparalleled way is emphasized throughout the Gospel.[25] That Jesus shall be king and Messiah is a pivotal aspect of this election (e.g., 12:15; 17:3). In summary, the men that are anointed in the royal anointing episodes are explicitly said to be elected by the Lord to be anointed kings. In John, Jesus is characterized to be God's chosen king and Messiah in the larger literary context.

5.6 A Journey

Recurrent in the anointing episodes of Saul, David, and Jehu is the motif of a journey occurring in order for the anointing to take place. The narrator informs the reader that Saul from the land of Benjamin is on a journey looking for some

Edwyn C. Hoskyns, *The Fourth Gospel*, ed. Francis N. Davey, 2nd rev. ed. (London: Faber and Faber, 1947), 416.

25 See e.g., John 1:18; 3:16; 5:22–23; 10:36; 11:27; 12:49; 14:10; 17:24–25.

lost donkeys. This seemingly casual journey is, however, guided by the divine providence so that it coincides with the Lord's sending of Saul to Samuel. Samuel is thus provided with the opportunity to anoint Saul (1 Sam 9:3–17).[26] When David is about to be anointed, the Lord tells Samuel that he will send him to Jesse in Bethlehem and Samuel obeys. In the case of Jehu, Elisha tells his servant to go to Ramoth-Gilead in order to anoint him, and the servant follows Elisha's instruction. In John 11:54 it is narrated that Jesus has left Bethany and the vicinity of Jerusalem and has gone "to the region near the wilderness, to a town called Ephraim," where he stays. The anointing episode begins with a temporal reference and the statement that Jesus came to Bethany. Thus, it is implied that Jesus has travelled in order to arrive at the location where he will be anointed. To sum up, the pattern in the OT royal anointing stories of a journey that is undertaken to the geographical location and social setting of the anointing is reproduced in John.

5.7 A Container Is Taken and Oil Is Poured upon the Head

The anointing act itself is narrated in a similar way in all three royal anointing episodes of the OT. The anointing of Saul is described in the following way: "And Samuel took [ἔλαβεν] the flask of oil [ἐλαίου] and poured upon [ἐπέχεεν ἐπί] his head [κεφαλήν]" (1 Sam 10:1). David's anointing is told with similar phrases: "And Samuel took [ἔλαβεν] the horn of oil [ἐλαίου] and anointed [ἔχρισεν] him" (1 Sam 16:13). Jehu's anointing is described with the words "And he poured [ἐπέχεεν] the oil [ἔλαιον] on [ἐπί] his head [κεφαλήν]" (2 Kgs 9:6), but the servant has been instructed by Elisha in advance (v. 3) to "take [λήμψῃ] the flask of oil and pour upon his head." Thus, all three anointing episodes contain the detail about *taking* (λαμβάνειν) the container with *oil* (ἔλαιον). In the cases of Saul and Jehu, the man that is commissioned to anoint is to *pour* oil *upon* (ἐπιχεῖν … ἐπί) the *head* (κεφαλή) of the elected man.

In John, it is said that Mary "took [λαβοῦσα] a pound of costly ointment of pure nard [μύρου νάρδου πιστικῆς] and anointed [ἤλειψεν] the feet of Jesus" (John 12:3). The detail about taking the ointment (λαμβάνειν) is thus present even if the container has been replaced by a weight measurement. Another difference is that the ointment is no longer designated as oil, but "costly ointment of pure nard [μύρου νάρδου πιστικῆς πολυτίμου]." Finally, the feet are said to be anointed (ἀλείφειν) and no pouring upon the head is described. The term ἀλείφειν "anoint" is sometimes used as a synonym for χρίειν, also in reference to

26 Cf. McCarter, *I Samuel*, 185.

theologically significant anointings.[27] To sum up, in all three private royal anointing episodes, as well as in the Johannine anointing episode, the one who anoints is described as taking the ointment or its container. In the OT royal anointing episodes, the ointment is oil which is poured upon the head of the one elected to be king. In John, pouring oil is not mentioned. Instead Mary is said to anoint the feet of Jesus with costly ointment of pure nard.

5.8 The Anoint-X-to-Be-King Formula

In connection to the OT royal anointing stories, the one who performs the anointing makes use of the formula "anoint [X] to be king/prince over Israel" (χρίειν … εἰς βασιλέα/ἄρχοντα ἐπὶ Ισραηλ; משח...למלך\נגיד על־ישׂראל) with minor variations. This generic element is of great importance since it explicates the meaning of the act. In the episode of the anointing of Saul, the Lord instructs Samuel to anoint Saul to be prince over his people Israel (1 Sam 9:16). When Samuel has poured oil upon Saul's head, Samuel says according to the LXX, "Has not the Lord anointed [κέχρικέν] you to be prince over [εἰς ἄρχοντα ἐπί] his people Israel?" (10:1).[28] After this statement the LXX, unlike the MT, adds the message that the Lord has anointed Saul to be prince over his inheritance.[29]

In the episode of David's anointing, it is mentioned that the Lord has provided a king for himself (16:1), but the formula "anoint [David] to be king/prince" is missing. However, that the Lord had anointed David to be king over Israel is told in 2 Sam 12:7. Furthermore, that David had been appointed to be prince and ruler over Israel is mentioned in 1 Sam 25:30 and 2 Sam 5:2; 7:8. Some ancient readers of these stories would probably connect the episode in 1 Sam 16 with these other passages which seem to provide complementary details about Samuel's anointing of David. When the anointing of Jehu is told, the son of the prophets is instructed to say to Jehu that the Lord has anointed him to be king over Israel (2 Kgs 9:3). As the young man fulfills this task, he says that the Lord has anointed Jehu to be king over the people of the Lord, over Israel (v. 6).

In the Johannine episode, the formula "anoint [Jesus] to be king" is not used of Mary's anointing of Jesus. The leaving out of this essential generic element may result in the royal anointing scene not being recognizable. However, this is compensated for in the following episode, in which Jesus enters Jerusalem and is

27 In reference to anointing of priests, see Exod 40:15; Num 3:3; Philo, *On the Life of Moses* 2.146, and for anointing of kings, see Josephus, *Ant.* 6.165.

28 The MT has "his inheritance" instead of "his people Israel."

29 Opinions concerning which text is the original differ among scholars. Auld explains for both alternatives how the textual variants may have arisen as the result of scribal errors (Auld, *I and II Samuel*, 110).

proclaimed to be the king of Israel (John 12:13, 15). This proclamation is more similar to the public declaration of the kingship of Saul (1 Sam 10:24) and Jehu (2 Kgs 9:13) that followed after their private anointings. In summary, the anoint-x-to-be-king formula is used in at least two of the OT private royal anointing episodes. It is not used in John, but in the scene which follows immediately after, Jesus is declared to be king of Israel.

5.9 A Statement of Commissioning

Following the anointing act and the formula mentioned above, a statement of commissioning is given to the one who has been anointed. In the episode of the anointing of Saul, immediately after the anointing act and the anoint-x-to-be-king formula, the LXX has in 1 Sam 10:1b a statement of commissioning that is lacking in the MT (see note 29). It reads, "And you shall reign over the people of the Lord and you will save them from the hand of their surrounding enemies." A similar statement about Saul is found earlier in the Lord's instruction to Samuel in both the Hebrew and the Greek text. "He shall save my people from the hand of the Philistines" (9:16). Similarly, right after Jehu has been anointed and the anoint-x-to-be-king formula has been pronounced, Jehu is commissioned by the prophet's servant with the following words, according to the MT, "And you shall strike down the house of Ahab your master" (2 Kgs 9:7). The servant of the prophet goes on to speak in the first person singular on how the Lord shall avenge the house of Ahab. In the LXX a greater portion of this speech, the whole of vv. 7–8, is given in the second person singular and thus is apprehended as part of the commission. In the episode of David's anointing, no statement of commissioning is given, but the ancient reader may infer from the literary context that a similar statement is spoken to David at some point. In 2 Sam 3:18, Abner claims that the Lord had spoken of David, saying, "By the hand of my servant David, I will save my people Israel from the hand of the Philistines, and from the hand of all their enemies."[30]

In the episode of the anointing in Bethany, Mary does not mention Jesus' commission in connection to the anointing, but Jesus himself gives a statement about the purpose of the anointing in John 12:7–8 that is bound up with his commission. Jesus implies that he has received a burial anointing and goes on to say to those assembled that he will not always be with them. In view of the Gospel narrative, these statements clearly refer to Jesus' death, burial, and departure, which are pivotal aspects of Jesus' salvific commission. Elsewhere in John, Jesus' divinely given commission to save the world is emphasized (3:17; 12:47). In

30 In the LXX the statement is a little shorter.

summary, a statement of commissioning is given by the one who anoints in at least two of the OT private royal anointing episodes. In the Johannine episode, Mary does not say anything, but Jesus suggests a purpose of the anointing that is closely connected with his commission stated elsewhere.

5.10 The Coming of the Spirit

In the anointing episodes of Saul and David, the spirit of the Lord comes upon each of them in connection to their anointings. This happens to Saul in a sign the day after he has been anointed by Samuel (1 Sam 10:6, 10). In the case of David, the Spirit comes upon him from the day of his anointing forward (16:13). The coming of the spirit is related by means of the Hebrew verb צלח and the Greek verbs ἐφάλλοσθαι and ἅλλοσθαι. The Hebrew term that may be translated "rush upon, leap on"[31] indicates a powerful, coercive, or aggressive movement. In the episode of the anointing of Jehu, the spirit is not mentioned. The anointing episode in John does not contain any explicit reference to the Spirit of God but, early in the Gospel narrative, the Spirit descends on Jesus as a dove from heaven and remains on him (John 1:32–33). On several occasions in John, Jesus is described as being endowed with the Spirit of God. To summarize, in the anointing episodes of Saul and David, the Spirit comes mightily upon them after their anointing. In the episode of the anointing of Jesus, the Spirit is not mentioned but, early in the Gospel narrative, the Spirit descends on Jesus.

6. The Generic Elements of the Scene: Summary

The analysis above has shown that several generic elements of the OT private royal anointing scene are present in the Johannine anointing episode, some of them have gone through minor or major changes, and some have been relocated to the context of the episode. John 12:1–8 is an integrated narrative unit of prose (element 1), describing an anointing in a private, secret, and dangerous setting in the vicinity of Jerusalem (element 2). There is a connection to table fellowship and sacrifice (element 3), and the motif of a journey is present (element 6). The "taking" section of element 7 is also found in the episode. The notion that Jesus is a divinely elected man (element 5) permeates the entire Gospel, even though it is only implied in the anointing episode. There is no explicit statement of commissioning (element 9) in the episode, but on several occasions in the Gospel it is made clear that Jesus has been given a commission by God. This commission is

31 Cf. McCarter, *I Samuel*, 276; Auld, *I and II Samuel*, 109.

also alluded to in the anointing episode. It is not a male prophet commissioned to anoint (element 4) that performs the anointing in John, but a "prophetic" woman. That such a different anointer performs the act is an obvious break with the genre convention. A break with the convention can also be spotted in the omission of several of the details of element 7 since "oil" has been replaced with "costly fragrant ointment of nard," "pouring" has been replaced with "anointing," and "the head" has been replaced with "feet."

Finally, there are two generic elements that appear to be missing from John's anointing scene. The anoint-x-to-be-king formula (element 8) is lacking from the episode, but a public declaration of kingship has been placed immediately after the episode. A similar pattern of a public declaration can be found in the OT texts, and therefore it works to confirm the royal aspect of the anointing of Jesus. The powerful coming of the Spirit (element 10) is not part of John's anointing episode, but a corresponding event has been incorporated in the beginning of the Gospel and thus contributes to the recognition of the private royal anointing scene in John 12:1–8.

Most of the generic elements of the royal anointing scene are present in John's anointing episode even though a few of them have been altered. When this result is combined with the description of the literary and cultural context, there is good reason to conclude that the evangelist employed the micro-genre of the OT royal anointing scene when he composed the story of the anointing of Jesus in Bethany. Consequently, the anointing of Jesus should be considered a royal anointing, which confirms Jesus as an Israelite king. In order to give more support to this conclusion, I will present a proposal in the next section for how John has refashioned the OT scene to fit his theological purposes.

7. John's Refashioning of the Generic Scene

I have argued that John has employed the micro-genre of the OT private royal anointing scene in order to present Jesus as an anointed king. Through the refashioning of the generic scene Jesus is depicted as a king that is in some ways similar to, and in other ways different from, Saul, David, and Jehu. By changing and relocating some of the generic elements, royal messianic expectations are modified in John's narration. For John, however, being king is not the only aspect of Jesus' messiahship. In John 3:28–29, Jesus' identity as Messiah is connected to him being the bridegroom. According to Brown, John 3:29 reflects "the well-known OT theme of the marriage between God and Israel" (Hos 1–2; Jer 2:2; Isa 61:10; Song of Songs).[32] The fourth evangelist develops a marriage metaphor in

32 Brown, *John*, 156.

John 2:1–11; 3:28–29; 4:4–42; 12:1–8; 20:1–18 that describes Jesus as the messianic bridegroom and the believing community as his bride.[33] When Mary of Bethany has anointed Jesus' feet with the expensive nard (νάρδος), 12:3c reports that "the house was filled with the fragrance [ὀσμῆς] of the ointment." This statement is likely to be an allusion to Song 1:12, "While the king was on his couch, my nard [νάρδος] gave forth its fragrance [ὀσμήν]," and thus depicts Jesus as a royal bridegroom.[34]

In John, Jesus is also described as a glory-filled tabernacle/temple (1:14; 2:21), the new locus of God's presence.[35] At the Feast of Dedication, when the re-sanctification of the temple is celebrated, Jesus declares himself to be the one sanctified by the Father (10:36).[36] At its inauguration, the Mosaic tabernacle was sanctified by its anointing with the fragrant holy anointing oil (Exod 30:23–29; 40:9). It is not unlikely that the evangelist, when he applied the tabernacle/temple imagery to Jesus' body, imagined him as the Anointed One also in this sense. Jesus as Messiah is the new anointed, sanctified, and glory-filled temple of God. Mary Coloe argues that, in Bethany, Jesus' body is anointed in this capacity of being God's temple.[37] In order to enhance the multiplicity of Jesus' messianic identity as king, bridegroom, and temple, I propose that the evangelist incorporated these three motifs into the episode of the anointing in Bethany.[38] However, this messianic imagery is made even more complex when it is connected to the idea of burial in John 12:7. This is in line with the evangelist's tendency "to make symbolism increasingly complex" and to interconnect "various sets of symbols while finding a single anchor for them" in "an allusive, narrative mode."[39]

---

33 See McWhirter, *Bridegroom Messiah*, 20–21.

34 The allusion has been suggested by e.g., McWhirter, *Bridegroom Messiah*, 82–88; Adeline Fehribach, *The Women in the Life of the Bridegroom: A Feminist Historical-Literary Analysis of the Female Characters in the Fourth Gospel* (Collegeville: Liturgical Press, 1998), 93; and Thyen, *Johannesevangelium*, 550.

35 E.g., Mary L. Coloe, *God Dwells with Us: Temple Symbolism in the Fourth Gospel* (Collegeville: Liturgical Press, 2001), and Alan R. Kerr, *The Temple of Jesus' Body: The Temple Theme in the Gospel of John*, JSNTSup 220 (London: Sheffield Academic Press, 2002). These examples demonstrate that temple christology is a pervasive theme in the Fourth Gospel.

36 Coloe, *God Dwells with Us*, 153.

37 Mary L. Coloe, *Dwelling in the Household of God: Johannine Ecclesiology and Spirituality* (Collegeville: Liturgical Press, 2007), 119–20.

38 The evangelist may also have wanted to include a prophetic or priestly dimension into Jesus' messiahship, but he does not seem to have incorporated any such references in the anointing episode.

39 Harold W. Attridge, "The Cubist Principle in Johannine Imagery: John and the Reading of Images in Contemporary Platonism," in *Imagery in the Gospel of John: Terms, Forms, Themes, and Theology of Johannine Figurative Language*, ed. J. Frey et al. (Tübingen: Mohr Siebeck, 2006), 47–60, esp., 53, 56.

The characterization of Jesus as king, bridegroom, and temple are all positive, indicating values such as power, joy, and glory. The motif of burial preparation, however, points to Jesus' death and departure and thus transforms the scene in a way that demonstrates the different messiahship of Jesus. As anointed king, Jesus is crowned with a crown of thorns (19:2), enthroned on a cross (19:19), and saves his people through his death (3:14–17; 12:32–33). The notion of Jesus as the messianic bridegroom is connected to the idea of the eschatological marriage between God and his people. The wedding feast was supposed to be a joyful occasion (cf. 3:29),[40] but Jesus' departure and death bring sorrow and pain (16:20–22) and Mary Magdalene will weep in her search for the lost body of the bridegroom-Messiah before he is reunited with his disciples and makes them rejoice (20:11–20). The anointed and sanctified temple of Jesus' body which is the locus of God's presence and contains the divine Spirit must be destroyed before it is raised anew to its proper function (2:19–21; cf. 4:21–23). Through the reference to burial in 12:7, all three motifs of Jesus Christ as king, bridegroom, and temple are modified by John's christology of servanthood, self-sacrifice, and death (e.g., 10:17–18). In order to be able to combine the different motifs and their re-interpretations in a comprehensible way, the evangelist needed to modify and relocate some of the elements of the micro-genre of the OT private royal anointing scene. I will now briefly explore how the modifications to the generic scene may support John's distinctive presentation of the anointed Jesus and his disciples.

7.1 A Prophetic Woman instead of a Male Prophet

That a woman anoints Jesus as king instead of a male prophet (element 4), as in the OT anointing episodes, contributes to the Johannine description of women as having important spiritual insights and tasks. Examples of this are the Samaritan woman, who through her words sows the fruit-bearing testimony about Jesus in her city (John 4:28–42); Mary Magdalene, who after having seen the risen Jesus is sent by him to tell his disciple "brothers" what he is about to do; (20:16–18); and Martha, who delivers the most insightful description of Jesus' messianic identity (11:27; cf. 20:31).[41] Likewise, the spiritual authority exercised by a woman is further emphasized when Mary's anointing act is seen as an anointing of the tabernacle of Jesus' body. In the OT, only the great prophet Moses anointed the tabernacle. This particular modification of the anointing scene's micro-genre contributes to the characterization of Jesus as a Messiah who provides and

40 Keener, *John*, 498.

41 See Raymond F. Brown, "Roles of Women in the Fourth Gospel," *TS* 36 (1975): 691–94.

acknowledges the spiritual gifts of women who, in general, had a lower social standing than men.

Having a woman anoint Jesus also facilitates John's incorporation of the bridegroom motif in the episode. Mary functions as a bride who anoints the messianic bridegroom[42] in an act of servitude and love. The change of the anointer in the generic scene works together with the change of the object of anointing, i.e., the feet instead of the head (element 7), to demonstrate John's theological principle of authority through service (John 13:13–15).

7.2 Fragrant Ointment on the Feet instead of Oil on the Head

Seen from the perspective of a royal anointing, it is fitting that very expensive ointment is used on Jesus, rather than simply oil, since he is a much greater king than Saul, David, and Jehu. That the feet of Jesus are singled out as the object of anointing instead of the head is an example of how John reverses messianic expectations. Oil was poured on the head of the Israelite kings when they were anointed to be elevated rulers of the people (element 7). The head was a widespread metaphor for a leader but Jesus is anointed to be a different king, one who acts as a servant as is demonstrated in the foot-washing scene (John 13:4–17). This is also signaled through anointing of the lowliest part of his body, the feet, in 12:3. Ancient sources show that feet were sometimes used as metaphors for servants and people of low social status.[43] The anointed king Jesus and his subjects are comparable to feet through their humble, loving service, even unto death (15:13).

The introduction of fragrant ointment of nard into the scene supports the incorporation of the bridegroom motif, and particularly the allusion to Song 1:12. The change from anointing of the head to anointing of the feet also works well with the messianic bridegroom motif. Washing of feet with water was an act of subordination and service (cf. John 13:13–17; 1 Sam 25:41) that could also be appropriate for a bride to carry out as an act of love (cf. Joseph and Aseneth 13.12; 20.2–5). To anoint the feet would not be unthinkable, at least not so in special circumstances.[44]

The change to fragrant ointment also supports the incorporation of the temple motif in the episode since the tabernacle is anointed with oil mixed with spices (Exod 30:23–26) and the holy anointing oil is called μύρον (Exod 30:25), as is the

42 See McWhirter, *Bridegroom Messiah*, 86, 132–34; Fehribach, *Women*, 20.

43 See e.g., Dio Chrysostom, *De administratione* 3; Artemidorus Daldianus, *Onirocritica* 1.2; cf. 1 Cor 12:21.

44 Cf. Coakley, "Anointing," 247–48.

ointment referenced in John 12:3. Furthermore, the anointing of "the feet" of the messianic temple may carry significance. In John, the temple as christological symbol is transferred from the temple building to the physical body of Jesus, and from Jesus to the community of believers,[45] and in antiquity, the body was often utilized as a hierarchal metaphor for a community.[46] By describing the anointing of the feet of Jesus' temple-body, the evangelist may have wished to convey the notion that, in the messianic age, even the lowly ones among God's people would be sanctified and would share in the messianic anointing.[47] All believers would be given the Spirit, not only an elite selection of kings, priests, and prophets (John 7:39; cf. 1 John 2:20, 27).

7.3 Other Significant Changes

The fourth evangelist has employed the OT private royal anointing scene in John 12:1–8, but has replaced the anoint-x-to-be-king formula (element 8) with a public declaration of Jesus' kingship in the following episode. This modification of the micro-genre serves to facilitate the incorporation of the bridegroom and temple motifs in the Johannine anointing episode. If the episode had contained the formula, it would probably have been difficult for the author to include these other aspects of Jesus' messiahship in the anointing episode. An explicit statement of commissioning, similar to those in the OT private royal anointing episodes (element 9), would have been intelligible if it was directed to the anointed king, but less so if it was directed to Jesus in his capacity of anointed bridegroom and temple, respectively. The implicit reference to Jesus' commission seems to suit the evangelist's theological purposes better. Furthermore, the powerful coming of the Spirit (element 10) in the generic private royal anointing scene has been relocated to the first chapter of the Gospel and has been transformed to a less aggressive descending of the Spirit as a dove. In doing this, the coming of the Spirit that suits Jesus' humble and peaceful kingship is still part of the Gospel narrative. The coming of the Spirit in such a way over the tabernacle/temple of Jesus' flesh would have been somewhat improper since the divine presence in the Israelite sanctuary was commonly depicted as a cloud of glory that filled the tent or house. The mention of the fragrant ointment that filled the house in Bethany fits better with the messianic temple motif, while it also works perfectly well with the bridegroom motif.

---

45 See Coloe, *Dwelling*, 106.

46 See Dale B. Martin, *The Corinthian Body* (New Haven: Yale University Press, 1995), 30–31.

47 Coloe argues that the community ("household") of believers is proleptically anointed, in John 12, in its capacity of the future temple (eadem, *Dwelling*, 122), but does not seem to give the detail about the feet sufficient explanation.

Through refashioning the micro-genre of the royal anointing scene, the evangelist has been able to incorporate several messianic motifs into the anointing episode. Jesus' anointing is given several dimensions that in part interact with each other, and in part work independently. That the evangelist would put so much consideration into his narration about Jesus' anointing is conceivable in the light of his conviction that those who believe that Jesus is the Anointed One (ὁ χριστός) would have eternal life (John 20:31).

8. Conclusion

I propose that the micro-genre of the OT private royal anointing scene is characterized by at least ten generic elements that I have identified. I also propose that the fourth evangelist employed this micro-genre when he composed the episode of the anointing of Jesus in John 12:1–8. This proposal is supported by the literary and cultural context of the episode in combination with my analysis, which shows that most of the generic elements are found in the episode in John. John's composition seems to be a refashioning of the private royal anointing scene, in which some of the generic elements have been changed in order to fit the theological purposes of the Gospel. The refashioning can mainly be explained as an adaptation of the scene to John's notion of Jesus as a serving and dying royal Messiah, as well as to his notions of Jesus as a missing bridegroom-Messiah and Jesus as an anointed temple-body about to be destroyed and rebuilt.

Eve-Marie Becker

John 13 as Counter-Memory: How the Fourth Gospel Revises Early Christian Historiography

1. John and History-Writing: The State of the Art

In recent years, an increasing amount of scholarly attention has been devoted to the rise of early Christian historiography and the role of the gospel narratives therein. This applies mainly to Mark and Luke-Acts,[1] since both these authors present the earliest narratives about the beginnings of the gospel proclamation. In these texts, history-writing appears to be "literary memory" by which the commemoration of the past is not only stored but also narrated and interpreted. In Luke-Acts, we even meet an author who reflects on his "historical" methods and his literary techniques—in his time, the genre of a gospel narrative was already well established.

But how does John—a contemporary, or rather one of the first recipients, of Luke—fit into this picture of early Christian literary history?[2] Does he continue the line of historiography-like writings? In recent scholarship, there have been various attempts to conceptualize the Fourth Gospel in the field of ancient history-writing. Such a contextualization is based on genre analysis of the macrotext,[3] but it can also take its point of departure in a narrative analysis of microelements; for example, Jürgen Becker has examined how, until chapter 12, John's

1 Cf. Adela Yarbro Collins, *Mark: A Commentary*, Hermeneia (Minneapolis: Fortress, 2007), 15–43; Eve-Marie Becker, *Das Markus-Evangelium im Rahmen antiker Historiographie*, WUNT 194 (Tübingen: Mohr Siebeck, 2006); eadem, ed., *Die antike Historiographie und die Anfänge der christlichen Geschichtsschreibung*, BZNW 129 (Berlin; New York: de Gruyter, 2005); Jörg Frey et al., eds., *Die Apostelgeschichte im Kontext antiker und frühjüdischer Historiographie*, BZNW 162 (Berlin; New York: de Gruyter, 2009).

2 In what follows, I will assume that John had literary access to Mark and Luke, cf. Udo Schnelle, *Einleitung in das Neue Testament*, 8th ed. (Göttingen: Vandenhoeck & Ruprecht, 2013), 579 with reference to similar models proposed by C. K. Barrett and M. Lang.

3 Cf., e.g., Richard Bauckham, "Historiographical Characteristics of the Gospel of John," *NTS* 53 (2007): 17–36.

narrative about Jesus' public activities is organized as an *itinerarium*.[4] Recognizing such a narrative element, which frequently forms part of ancient historiography,[5] initiates the discourse about John and history-writing, and this discourse has been further supported by two recent trends in Johannine studies. First, the fact that *genre studies* has become increasingly important within the field.[6] This means that, in terms of *literary criticism*, the Johannine Gospel is no longer analyzed in isolation from the Synoptic Gospels. This interest in the literary aspects of John manifests itself in narrative and literary analyses (e.g., Alan Culpepper)[7]—in a similar way, also interpretive paradigms used in synoptic studies can be transferred to John. Secondly, it has recently been argued that John's depiction of "historical facts" in and beyond the passion narrative is much more reliable than suggested during an earlier period of interpretation widely characterized by a gnostic or mystical reading of the Fourth Gospel (cf., e.g., Walter Bauer).[8] The following question therefore arises: Can John be understood as "historian," or does he rather present a competing gospel story: a counter-memory?

At first glance, both interpretive trends seem to imply a move away from a *Bultmannian* exegesis widely based on *Literarkritik* and *Traditionsgeschichte*. In contrast, more synchronic approaches to John argue for reconsidering the literary potential of the Fourth Gospel. Francis J. Moloney expresses this latter opinion. In his interpretation of John 13, he states: "[W]hatever the prehistory of the elements that form 13:1–38, there are a number of indications that the passage has been designed to read as a coherent, self-contained narrative."[9] Some years earlier, R. Alan Culpepper (1991) suggested a similar—literary—approach

4 Cf. Jürgen Becker, *Johanneisches Christentum: Seine Geschichte und Theologie im Überblick* (Tübingen: Mohr Siebeck, 2004), 123.

5 Cf. Claudius Sittig, "Reiseliteratur," in *Historisches Wörterbuch der Rhetorik*, ed. Gert Ueding (Berlin: de Gruyter, 2005), 7:1144–56, 1148.

6 Harold W. Attridge, "Genre Bending in the Fourth Gospel," *JBL* 121 (2002): 3–21, cf. Alastair Fowler, *Kinds of Literature: An Introduction to the Theory of Genres and Modes* (Oxford: Oxford University Press, 1982).

7 Cf. R. Alan Culpepper, *Anatomy of the Fourth Gospel: A Study in Literary Design* (Philadelphia: Fortress, 1983); idem, *The Gospel and Letters of John* (Nashville: Abingdon, 1998), 197ff.; idem and Fernando F. Segovia, eds., *The Fourth Gospel from a Literary Perspective* (*Semeia* 53 [1991]); Jörg Frey and Uta Poplutz, eds., *Narrativität und Theologie im Johannesevangelium*, BThS 130 (Neukirchen-Vluyn: Neukirchener Verlagshaus, 2012); cf. Jörg Frey and Uta Poplutz, "Narrativität und Theologie im Johannesevangelium," in ibid., 1–8.

8 For the discussions in the *John, Jesus, and History Group of the Society of Biblical Literature*, see for example Paul N. Anderson, Felix Just, and Tom Thatcher, eds., *John, Jesus, and History, Volume 1: Critical Appraisals of Critical Views*, SBLSymS 44 (Leiden; Boston: Brill, 2007); cf. Walter Bauer, *Das Johannesevangelium*, HNT 6, 2nd ed. (Tübingen: J. C. B. Mohr, 1925), 167 in his interpretation of John 13.

9 Francis J. Moloney, *The Gospel of John*, SP 4 (Collegeville: The Liturgical Press, 1998), 371.

to John 13.[10] However, even though such statements have clarified the limitations of *Literarkritik* and *Traditionsgeschichte*, John 13:1–20 remains a special case—especially if we consider Bultmann's impact on the exegesis of this passage.[11] This verdict is also inspired by reception-history and its various interpretations of the foot-washing (for example, sacramental, soteriological, or ritual).[12] By itself, the number of literary inconsistencies in John 13—particularly the interconnection between vv. 4–5 and vv. 6–11 and 12–20—raises ongoing questions about the origin of the text. Fernando F. Segovia (1982) has summarized the various *cruces interpretum* in the canonical version of John 13.[13] He attempts to solve these *cruces* by distinguishing between an "earlier layer - comprising vv. 1a.5.6–10a.10b–11" and "the latter layer - comprising vv. 1b–4, 12–17 and 18–20."[14] He also claims that the redaction "reflects the *Sitz im Leben*" of 1 John and is "construed as a part of further attack on the 'deviant group of believers' mentioned in the letter."[15] Thirty years later, Michael Theobald (2012) identifies a "vorgegebene Erzählung" and distinguishes between "Überlieferung" and "Bearbeitung."[16] In a similar way, Rudolf Schnackenburg,[17] Jürgen Becker[18]

---

10 R. Alan Culpepper, "The Johannine *Hypodeigma:* A Reading of John 13," *Semeia* 53 (1991): 133–52.

11 Cf. Christoph Niemand, *Die Fusswaschungserzählung des Johannesevangeliums: Untersuchungen zu ihrer Entstehung und Überlieferung im Urchristentum*, SA 114 (Rome: Pontificio Ateneo S. Anselmo, 1993).

12 Cf. Georg Richter, *Die Fusswaschung im Johannesevangelium: Geschichte ihrer Deutung*, Biblische Untersuchungen 1 (Regensburg: Friedrich Pustet, 1967); Wolfram Lohse, "Die Fußwaschung (Joh 13,1–20): Eine Geschichte ihrer Deutung," 2 vols. (Diss. Erlangen, 1967); Luise Abramowski, "Die Geschichte von der Fußwaschung (Joh 13)," *ZTK* 102 (2005): 176–203.

13 Fernando Segovia, "John 13:1–20: The Footwashing in the Johannine Tradition," *ZNW* 73 (1982): 31–51.

14 Segovia, "John 13," 48.

15 Segovia, "John 13," 50–51.

16 Michael Theobald, *Eucharistie als Quelle sozialen Handelns: Eine biblisch-frühkirchliche Besinnung*, BThS 77 (Neukirchen-Vluyn: Neukirchener Verlagshaus, 2012), 35–62 (58). Theobald relates 13:2a, 4f., 12a–d, 13f., 16, 20 to the "Überlieferung" and characterizes it as follows: It did not contain "die tiefe christologische Deutung …, wie sie das sekundär eingebrachte Gespräch zwischen Jesus und Petrus in Joh 13,6–11 entwickelte, sondern lediglich die Symbolhandlung von Joh 13,4f. samt anschließender paränetischer Deutung" (58). He interprets John 13 in affinity to Mark 10:45; Luke 12:37; 22:27: "Jesus als Tischdiener."

17 Cf. Rudolf Schnackenburg, *Das Johannesevangelium. III. Teil: Kommentar zu Kap. 13–21*, 2d ed., HThKNT 4 (Freiburg: Herder, 1976), 8–10 (depiction of the problems); 14–15 (his model). The model is: "Grundschicht (Evangelist)": v. 1f., 4, 5–10, 12a, 18b–19, 21–27, 30; "Größere Einfügung in die Grundschicht": v. 12b–17, 18a; "Kleinere Einfügungen der Redaktion": v. 2–3, 11, 20, 28f. "Eine gesonderte Quelle für die in Kap. 13 erzählten Vorgänge hatte der Evangelist sicher nicht zur Verfügung" (15).

18 Cf. Jürgen Becker, *Das Evangelium nach Johannes. Kapitel 11–21*, 3rd ed., ÖTK 4/2 (Gütersloh: Gütersloher Verlagshaus; Gerd Mohn; Echter Verlag, 1991). For reasons for and indications of *Literarkritik*, see 498–99.

and Udo Schnelle identify various inconsistencies in the text and re-construct the "literarische Genese" of John 13.[19] As it appears here, the foot-washing scene—in terms of *Traditionsgeschichte* or read against Luke 22:27—is interpreted as the Johannine method of dealing with the "community rule" (Mark 10:45 par.). In light of *Redaktionsgeschichte*, its final literary form is read against conflicts within the Johannine community. In neither case can John 13 be compared to Mark or Luke's narrative account of the last supper in Jerusalem (Mark 14:12ff. par.)[20].

So, does John 13 construct a totally different type of "literary memory"? Does the text—in its traditional elements as much as in its final literary version—encapsulate a memorial culture distinct from the synoptic (passion) narrative? I will argue that it does not. In this contribution, I will follow another line of interpretation. I will read John 13:1–20 in its present form as a narrative parallel to the last supper scene in Mark 14:12ff./Luke 22:3ff. In particular, I would like to discuss John's specific contribution to the early Christian *literary memorial culture.*[21] I will thus address the question of how John 13 reflects and transforms early Christian *literary memory* as presented in Mark and further developed in Luke. How does John 13 interplay with Mark 14 and Luke 22? In Mark and Luke's case, the narrative concept of gospel writing intentionally leaves the sphere of oral transmission.[22] In a similar way, John contributes to the shape of early Christian literary memory in and beyond the passion story. John's way of transforming literary memory can best be demonstrated by carefully analyzing ch. 13—which occupies a key position within the gospel narrative[23]—along the

19 Udo Schnelle, *Das Evangelium nach Johannes*, THKNT 4 (Leipzig: Evangelische Verlagsanstalt, 1998), 214. Schnelle distinguishes between a "ursprüngliche Fußwaschungserzählung" (v. 2a, 4, 5, 12ab, 16, 20, 17) that equals a "Gemeinderegel" on "Herrschen und Dienen," and a pre-redactional, ethical interpretation by the Johannine school (v. 12c, 13–15), and a Johannine interpretation with a focus on soteriology (v. 6–10ab), and finally an interpretation in regard to "Kreuzestheologie" (v. 1, 2bc, 3, 10c, 11, 18, 19).

20 Such an interpretive concept is supported by how the *Synopsis Quattuor Evangeliorum* programmatically moves John 13:1–20 away from the literary context of the last supper scene.

21 In this article, I am of course not interested in reading John 13 as a possible "historical source" for reconstructing the passion story.

22 For a renewed emphasis on *literary activity* in early Christian times, cf. Larry W. Hurtado, "Oral Fixation and New Testament Studies? 'Orality,' 'Performance,' and Reading Texts in Early Christianity," *NTS* 60 (2014): 321–40; Eve-Marie Becker, "Earliest Christian Literary Activity: Investigating Authors, Genres and Audiences in Paul and Mark," in *Mark and Paul: Comparative Essays Part II: For and Against Pauline Influence on Mark*, ed. E.-M. Becker, T. Engberg-Pedersen, and M. Müller, BZNW 199 (Berlin: de Gruyter, 2014), 87–105. Concerning the paradigm of orality in general, cf. various contributions in Annette Weissenrieder and Robert B. Coote, eds., *The Interface of Orality and Writing: Speaking, Seeing, Writing in the Shaping of New Genres*, WUNT 260 (Tübingen: Mohr Siebeck, 2010).

23 Cf. Schnelle, *Evangelium*, 212, who speaks of a "Schlüsselstellung."

lines of Mark 14 and Luke 22.[24] My thesis is to read John 13:1–20 as a "counter-memory" (Michel Foucault) which aims to intentionally transform and manipulate the literary memory designed by Mark and Luke.

2. John's Concept of "Literary Memory"

In his epilogue, John reveals his understanding of literary memory by providing some insights into his compositional technique. As he writes in 20:30–31, he has selected a *certain* number of narratives about Jesus' actions among his disciples (σημεῖα). This statement reflects an intentional choice and arrangement of narrative sections. For John, the purpose of selecting scenes and composing his narrative is to stimulate belief in Jesus as Christ (20:31). In this way, John must have considered yet disagreed with Luke's remarks about the purpose of gospel writing (Luke 1:1–4). For Luke, it is essential that his primary addressee—Theophilus—*understands* (ἐπιγινώσκειν) what "the things that have been accomplished among us" are about. He therefore explores the transmission of traditions meticulously in order to present the story in a reasonable order.[25] However, for John, the purpose of writing lies in shaping *belief* (πιστεύειν). This is how he defines *his* rationale for composing literary memory.

But how does this rationale influence John's composition of the last supper scene, in which he omits the Eucharist tradition, which, in his time, was already a well-established *ritual memory* (ἀνάμνησις: 1 Cor 11:24f.; Luke 22:19)?[26] The question about the origin of this tradition in Paul and Luke is not of central importance to us.[27] Instead, it is more important to see how the Eucharist tra-

24 This also applies to the outline of the entire book. Against the background of the Markan and Lukan account, it becomes evident how John revises crucial elements of the gospel concept, for example, the insertion of an extensive prologue and epilogue, the modification of a chronological setting, the presentation of various figures and protagonists, and the omission or inclusion of central semantic patterns (e.g., εὐαγγέλιον, ἀκολουθέω).

25 Cf. a recent contribution to the literary implications of this prescript: John Moles, "Luke's Preface: The Greek Decree, Classical Historiography and Christian Redefinitions," *NTS* 57 (2011): 461–82.

26 For Andreas Lindemann (*Der Erste Korintherbrief*; HNT 9/I [Tübingen: Mohr Siebeck, 2000], 257), the "Wiederholungsbefehl" (1 Cor 11:25b) is "traditionsgeschichtlich sekundär .... Gemeint ist, jüdischem Denken entsprechend, die 'Aktualisierung' des zurückliegenden geschichtlichen Ereignisses." On the variety of memorial forms and formulas, see Ulrike Mittmann-Richert, "Erinnerung und Heilserkenntnis im Lukasevangelium: Ein Beitrag zum neutestamentlichen Verständnis des Abendmahls," in *Memory in the Bible and Antiquity: The Fifth Durham-Tübingen Research Symposium*, ed. S. C. Barton et al., WUNT 212 (Tübingen: Mohr Siebeck, 2007), 243–76.

27 Cf., on the contrary, e.g., Lindemann, *Korintherbrief*, 258, who argues on the basis of *Traditionsgeschichte:* "Vieles spricht für die Vermutung, daß der Wortlaut der Mahlüberlieferung seinen Ursprung in der griechischsprechenden Gemeinde (Jerusalems?) gehabt hat, wo

dition is delivered as literary memory in Paul, Luke-Acts and Mark (even though Mark does not define it as ritual *memory*).[28] Despite varying valuations of its memorial status, the Eucharist tradition has become a well-established literary memory that is either affiliated to an epistolary setting (1 Cor 11) or to the pre-historiographical narrative about Jesus' ministry in Jerusalem and the commencing passion events (Mark 14; Luke 22). By being transformed into such a literary memory, the Eucharist also initiates a literary discourse. The rhetorical interaction between the Eucharist and its diverse literary framings in Paul and Luke (as *anamnesis*) and in Mark (as a narrative sequence) is very discursive. On the one hand, by placing the Eucharist in diverse literary settings, it is continually recalled and actualized as ritual memory (Paul and Luke); in this way, it serves the memorization of the ritual and its initiator: Jesus. On the other hand, by affiliating the Eucharist tradition to various epistolary or narrative literary discourses and thereby marking it as either *anamnesis* or not *anamnesis* (Mark), it provides authority to its current literary adaption.

Luke evidently makes use of such an authoritative adaption. In his narrative about the Emmaus disciples in ch. 24, he signifies that the purpose of the gospel narrative—which is designed to stimulate understanding (1:4: ἐπιγινώσκειν)—is reached when Jesus' followers recognize the risen Christ by remembering him; they can identify Jesus mnemonically by the way in which he prepares the meal (24:16, 31: ἐπιγινώσκειν). In Luke, the Eucharist functions as *the* crucial criterion for recognizing Jesus and consequently for understanding the purpose of the gospel narrative as such. The Eucharist is no less than an elementary part of Luke's literary strategy. It even serves to connect the passion and Easter stories in the Gospel with Acts (see below).

In John, the question of how to identify the risen Jesus also plays an important role (cf. John 20–21), but the Eucharist does not feature in this question—this even applies to John 21 (esp. v. 12–14).[29] Besides John 6 (v. 22–59), the Eucharist tradition does not seem to play any role in the Fourth Gospel. How do we explain this? It is unlikely that John did not know about the Eucharist; from certain passages in the Fourth Gospel—especially John 6:52–58—it is clear that John was familiar with it. So how can we explain the fact that John omitted the Eucharist from his depiction of the last supper? Why did John erase this particular memory and—at the same time—suggest the memorization of a different action: the foot-

möglicherweise die Erinnerung an Jesu letztes Mahl mit den Jüngern verbunden wurde mit einer soteriologischen Deutung seines Todes." Dieter Zeller relates the Lukan version to Antioch, the Markan version to the community in Jerusalem (idem, *Der erste Brief an die Korinther*, KEK 5 [Göttingen: Vandenhoeck & Ruprecht, 2010], 369).

28 Mark—instead—makes the anointing scene (14:9: μνημόσυνον) memorially significant.

29 Cf. Kasper Bro Larsen, *Recognizing the Stranger: Recognition Scenes in the Gospel of John*, BIS 93 (Leiden: Brill, 2008), 211–13.

washing (13:1–20)? Did he refer to another tradition, or did he intend to revise an existing literary memory which, in his opinion, had been misinterpreted? My claim is that, by omitting the narrative about the last supper, the Fourth Gospel manipulates memory.[30] John installs a counter-memory that is particularly oriented against Luke, and he does this in order to present a farewell scene (John 13 and 14–17) and passion narrative (John 18–19) that both "forget" the Eucharist and the narrative meaning it obtained in Luke.[31]

In light of this rationale, we can assume that John decided to compose literary memory (John 20:30f.) for reasons of Christology and gospel proclamation. For John, the Eucharist scene as part of a literary memory clearly represents an inappropriate way of stimulating belief in Jesus as the Christ. John also provides a different concept of how to recognize the risen Christ (John 20:16 etc.). The manipulation or suppression of memory which can be found in John 13 is not uncommon in antiquity or early Christianity.[32] Nor can it be seen as a "moral problem." It is rather a general and well-known element of ancient history-writing in a broader sense—including *bellum* literature (e.g., Caesar, Josephus) or biography.[33] However, in John 13, the author does not limit himself to suppression. Instead, he presents another—competing—memory that is only

30 Cf., in general, Martin Goodman, "Memory and Its Uses in Judaism and Christianity in the Early Roman Empire: The Portrayal of Abraham," in *Historical and Religious Memory in the Ancient World*, ed. B. Dignas and R. R. R. Smith (Oxford: Oxford University Press, 2012), 69–82.

31 For the social need of forgetting in antiquity, see Simon Price, "Memory and Ancient Greece," in B. Dignas and R. R. R. Smith, eds., *Historical and Religious Memory*, 15–36. For the tension between "collective memory" and amnesia, see Mark S. Smith, *The Memoirs of God: History, Memory, and the Experience of the Divine in Ancient Israel* (Minneapolis: Fortress Press, 2004), 126ff. and, in general (incl. theories about cultural memory), Eve-Marie Becker, *Writing History in New Testament Times: Memoria—Tempus—Historia* (New Haven: Yale University Press, forthcoming).

32 See, for instance, the varying accounts of the apostolic council in Jerusalem according to Paul (Gal 1–2) and Luke (Acts 15).

33 For the "manipulation of history," for instance in Herodotus, cf. Kurt Raaflaub, "Ulterior Motives in Ancient Historiography: What Exactly, and Why?" in *Intentional History: Spinning Time in Ancient Greece*, ed. L. Foxhall et al. (Stuttgart: Franz Steiner Verlag, 2010), 189–210. On manipulative strategies for commemorating people, see Mary R. McHugh, *Manipulating Memory: Remembering and Defaming Julio-Claudian Women* (Madison: University of Wisconsin, 2004). On Christian *damnatio memoriae* from the 4th century onwards, cf. E. Elm, "Memoriae damnatio," *RAC* 24:657–82; Charles W. Hedrick, *History and Silence: The Purge and Rehabilitation of Memory in Late Antiquity* (Austin: University of Texas Press, 2000), 92ff. Doron Mendels points to the fact that a manipulation "of any sort could be done … by *authority*" (idem, "How Was Antiquity Treated in Societies with a Hellenistic Heritage? And Why Did the Rabbis Avoid Writing History?" in *Antiquity in Antiquity: Jewish and Christian Pasts in the Greco-Roman World*, ed. G. Gardner and K. L. Osterloh, TSAJ 123 [Tübingen: Mohr Siebeck, 2008], 147).

loosely connected to the meal scene: the foot-washing.[34] Omission, suppression, and literary substitution go hand in hand. In ch. 13, John therefore does three things simultaneously: (a) He suppresses an existing ritual literary memory; (b) he opposes Luke's literary strategy to make the Eucharist a hermeneutical key to Luke-Acts; (c) he replaces the Eucharist with the foot-washing. John 13 appears to be a "counter-memory" which provides—especially in its interplay with Luke—a discursive practice "through which memories are continuously revised" and reshaped.[35]

3. John's Concept of "Counter-Memory"

3.1 A Foucauldian Approach

The concept of "counter-memory" occurs in a 1977 collection of Foucault's essays and interviews.[36] The general purpose of these essays is to analyze the evolution of modern literature, which can—to some degree—be understood as the shape of a counter-memory.[37] Even though counter-memory may "superficially appear to be a form of negation, it becomes … the affirmation of the particularities that attend any practice, and perhaps the activity that permits new practices to emerge."[38] As such, new steps in the development of literary history can appear as "counter-memories." According to Foucault, counter-memories

> … oppose and correspond to the three Platonic modalities of history. The first is parodic, directed against reality, and opposes the themes of history as reminiscence or recognition; the second is dissociative, directed against identity, and opposes history given as continuity or representative of a tradition; the third is sacrificial, directed against truth, and opposes history as knowledge.[39]

---

34 For this discussion, cf. Ernst Lohmeyer, "Die Fußwaschung," *ZNW* 38 (1939): 74–94. For Lohmeyer, however, the foot-washing functions as a "sacrament": "Diese Fußwaschung ist 'sakramental', denn sie erhebt die Jünger zu Priestern und Aposteln seiner Gemeinde" (89).

35 Cf. Barbara A. Misztal, *Theories of Social Remembering* (Maidenhead: Open University Press, 2003), 64f. with reference to Michel Foucault, *Language, Counter-Memory, Practice: Selected Essays and Interviews*, ed. D. F. Bouchard and S. Simon (Ithaca: Cornell University Press, 1977), 65.

36 Foucault, *Language, Counter-Memory, Practice.*

37 In particular, the various essays show how "the historical experience of language underwent a fundamental shift toward the end of the eighteenth century, when language took on a life of its own and became an 'objectivity' …. In developing a totally opposed relationship to language, literature has been transformed, since the nineteenth century, into a counter-memory" (D. F. Bouchard, "Preface," in Foucault, *Language, Counter-Memory, Practice*, 8).

38 D. F. Bouchard, "Preface," 9.

39 Michel Foucault, "Counter-Memory: The Philosophy of Difference," in idem, *Language, Counter-memory, Practice*, 160.

The various goals of construing counter-memory have something in common. Foucault explicates this by referring to Nietzsche's approach to genealogy:

> They imply a use of history that severs its connection to memory …, and constructs a counter-memory – a transformation of history into a totally different form of time."[40]

If we separate Foucault's description of counter-memory from its original setting in his analysis of 19th century literary discourse, and if we generalize it and apply it to our field of investigation, we can reach the following definition of counter-memory: *Counter-memory opposes a concept of history which serves the transmission of tradition and thereby the idea of continuity; in consequence, it conceptualizes history in opposition to memory and questions or deconstructs various types of identity (social, cultural, religious).*

3.2 John 13 as Counter-Memory

In what follows, I will attempt to demonstrate how Foucault's concept of counter-memory can be applied to John's manipulation of ritual, viz., literary memory in ch. 13. By shaping a counter-memory against Luke, John opposes tradition, marks a difference between memory and history, and ultimately deconstructs a narrative identity.

3.2.1 The Opposition of Tradition and Continuity

The transmission of the Eucharist was a well-established literary tradition in Paul, Mark, and Luke; and over a period of ca. 40 years (from Paul to Mark and Luke) as the commemoration of a ritual entered an epistolary and a narrative setting, *ritual* memory transformed into *literary* memory. To a large extent, the transmission of the Eucharist reflects a continuity of memory, even though Mark avoids defining it as *anamnesis.* At the same time, a literary memory gives literary authority to later literature: by displaying a well-established memory, current writing is authorized. Luke develops this literary strategy to a great extent; in his writing, the Eucharist tradition even connects the gospel story to the narrative intention of its author in (Luke 1 and 24) and beyond the Gospel (Acts 2). John's omission of the Eucharist is a literary attempt to refrain from *and* oppose a literary memory by counteracting its transmission from Paul and Mark to Luke. The Fourth Gospel places itself outside this literary tradition. At the same time, it rejects the way Luke used ritual memory as a literary strategy within his narrative account. However, John does not limit himself to omission; instead, by pre-

40 Foucault, "Counter-Memory," 160.

senting a different memory—the foot-washing—he reveals the actual meaning of a ritual memory that Jesus inaugurated among his disciples at the last supper (13:30). John 13 is as much a project of "replacing" as "omitting" memory. And both projects produce counter-memory.

The scope of this article does not allow us to examine all the aspects that distinguish the practice of foot-washing from the Eucharist.[41] For our purposes, it is more interesting to examine how both types of actions are contextualized in their literary settings. In Paul (1 Cor 11:23b), Mark and the synoptics, the Eucharist is attached to the narrative about Jesus' last supper with his disciples the evening before his betrayal and crucifixion (Mark 14:22–25 par.). The meal is characterized as a Passah meal (14:12, 16, 17–18; Luke 22:15) which is prepared by his disciples and takes place τῇ πρώτῃ ἡμέρᾳ τῶν ἀζύμων. In the context of this meal, Jesus introduces a ceremony in which he relates bread and wine to his body (14:22–24) and predicts—from an eschatological perspective—his imminent entrance into the βασιλείᾳ τοῦ θεοῦ (14:25).

In many respects, the Lukan account of the last supper and the Eucharist develops the Markan text.[42] Luke repeats and thus emphasizes the eschatological prediction (22:16, 18), which contrasts the notion that the historical hour has arrived and initiated the passion events (Luke 22:14: ἐγένετο ἡ ὥρα). Similar to Paul (1 Cor 11:23ff.) but in contrast to Mark, Luke emphasizes how Jesus himself defines the Eucharist as ritual memory (εἰς τὴν ἐμὴν ἀνάμνησιν, 22:19). It is precisely this motif that is taken up in Luke 24 (v. 13–35) when the Emmaus disciples recognize the risen Jesus by how he prepares the meal.[43] In Luke's view, the Eucharist scene serves the recognition of the risen Jesus. As a narrative strategy, it provides continuity between Jesus' ministry (Luke 22), the Easter epiphanies (Luke 24), and the subsequent ritual practice of the Jerusalem community (Acts 2:42). All synoptic versions connect the Eucharist scene with the prediction of Judas' betrayal, which—at the same time—initiates the commencing passion events. According to Luke, Jesus is in conflict with the Satanic power (Luke 22:3). At this point, the so-called "satansfreie Zeit" (Luke 4:13–22:3;

41 On the tradition, cf. J. C. Thomas, "Footwashing (Pedilavium)," *RPP* 5:163: "Evidence for the practice of footwashing can be found in every century of the church's history. The meaning of rite ranges from an expression of humble service to that of sacramental sign"; cf. also: B. Kötting and D. Halama, "Fußwaschung A. Nichtchristlich," *RAC* 8:743–59.

42 Lindemann, *Korintherbrief*, 257–58 specifies how Luke combines the Pauline and the Markan version. However, he thinks that Luke did not make direct use of First Corinthians but rather had access to a pre-Pauline tradition: "Ein traditionsgeschichtlich gemeinsamer Ausgangspunkt für die mk und die paulinische Textfassung im ganzen ist nicht identifizierbar" (258).

43 In Luke, the Eucharist tradition even serves the post-Easter recognition: 24:13–35; other types of recognition include the wish for peace (Luke 24:36) and Jesus' presentation of his body (Luke 24:39ff.)—both elements also occur in the Johannine Gospel (John 20:19; 20:24ff.).

Hans Conzelmann) comes to an end. By breaking the bread and offering his body and blood symbolically, Jesus prepares himself for crucifixion.

John's Gospel relates to the narrative concept designed by Mark and developed by Luke in that it both follows and departs from it. Like Mark and Luke, John also provides an account of Jesus' last supper with his disciples (13:2) in which the prediction of Judas' betrayal plays an important role (13:2, 21ff.). And, as in Luke, Judas is inhabited by Satanic power (13:2). However, instead of proceeding to describe the ritual meal that Jesus prepares for his disciples, John omits the Eucharist tradition. Instead, he depicts how Jesus—just *before* the Passah feast and aware of the time (εἰδὼς ... ὅτι ἦλθεν αὐτοῦ ἡ ὥρα = hour) to leave the *kosmos* and return to his Father (13:1, μεταβαίνω)—continued to love his disciples εἰς τέλος.[44] And even though the διάβολος entered Judas' heart and prepared him to betray and hand over Jesus (13:2), Jesus knew (εἰδὼς) that everything was given in his hands by his Father and that he both came from and was returning to God (13:3). At this point, when Jesus was certain of his divine origin, mission, and love for his disciples, Jesus began to wash his disciples' feet (13:4ff.). Later, Jesus defines this action as a ὑπόδειγμα (13:15) to be continued by his disciples—not only for his disciples to *know* about it (οἴδατε) or remember it, but rather for them to *perform* it (ἐὰν ποιῆτε, 13:17). Again, John invokes a Lukan idea (Luke 22:19: τοῦτο ποιεῖτε) by revising it. He provides an explanation for imitating the foot-washing in John 13:16. In this way, the foot-washing represents one of the few instances where John explicitly conceptualizes ethics.[45]

There are three ways in which John opposes the synoptic—and, in particular, the Lukan—"master narrative" of the Eucharist. Firstly, Jesus does not need to prepare for crucifixion. His mission is to be understood as a return to his Father. He himself knows about the "hour"—he does not await it. Secondly, Jesus is not in real conflict with the Satanic world. He has received all power from his Father. Finally, Jesus does not offer his body, thus preparing his disciples to remember his crucifixion. Instead, he teaches them how to strengthen community life after his return to God. For John, the symbolic action of the Eucharist has to be replaced with the paradigmatic action of foot-washing. John rejects the idea of Jesus instituting *anamnesis*. Instead, Jesus defines a *hypodeigma* which symbolizes *diakonia* (see Luke 22:24–27). This is how John contextualizes his version of the "community rule."

44 According to John, Jesus was crucified "zur Zeit der Schlachtung der Passalämmer" (18:28; 19:14, 36); John hereby is close to the Pauline depiction (1 Cor 5:7b), cf.: Zeller, *Brief*, 370.

45 Cf., e.g., Jan G. van der Watt, "Ethics and Ethos in the Gospel According to John," *ZNW* 97 (2006): 147–76, esp. 167ff.

3.2.2 The Difference between History and Memory

In his narrative account about the last supper, Luke proposes a close relation between history and memory (22:19). By doing so, he continues the Pauline view of the Eucharist as a ritual memory (*anamnesis*). At the same time, Luke follows a pattern typical of ancient historiography: "History" and "memory" are not viewed as opposing but co-operating modes of commemoration. The construction of history serves ancient memorial culture. Dionysius of Halicarnassus defines μνῆμαι κατὰ ἔθνη καὶ πόλεις as the elementary basis of history-writing (*De Thucydide* 5; 7). Early Christian authors also reflect on the interaction between history and memory. Augustine sees *historia* as the *memoria* of human action (*De Genesi ad litteram imperfectus liber* 2), and Eusebius classifies his work as μνήμη τῇσδε τῆς ἱστορίας (*Historia ecclesiastica* 4.15.1).[46] Therefore, from an ancient perspective, "history" and "history-writing" are elementary scripts for storing and performing "memory." History and memory are complementary. Accordingly, Luke inserts the ritual memory of the Eucharist in his narrative account of the passion events (Luke 22–23): The ritual memory is historicized, and the historiographical narrative serves a commemorative purpose.

By omitting the Eucharist tradition as *anamnesis*, John criticizes Luke's combination of a ritual memory and a historiographical account. John deconstructs the Lukan project of history-writing and instead proposes a counter-memory; he eliminates the tight connection between the passion story and the institution of memory. At the same time, John provides an alternative story—the foot-washing—and declares this to be an exemplary, viz., paradigmatic action (*hypodeigma*). By replacing *anamnesis* with *hypodeigma*, he shifts focus away from Jesus *institutionalizing a ritual* in front of his disciples towards Jesus *exemplifying ethical practice* among his disciples.[47] In other words, the author of the Fourth Gospel substitutes a ritual memory with exemplary memory.

4. Conclusion: John's Deconstruction of a Narrative Identity

From Paul to Mark and Luke, the Eucharist tradition functions as literary memory. It contributes to the shape of identity among Christ believers in various places around the Mediterranean (Jerusalem, Antioch, Corinth, etc.). As such, it

46 On Eusebius cf. Christoph Markschies, "Eusebius liest die Apostelgeschichte: Zur Stellung der Apostelgeschichte in der frühchristlichen Geschichtsschreibung," *Early Christianity* 4 (2013): 474–98.

47 Differently, Lohmeyer: "Es ist deshalb kaum richtig, die sakramentale Bedeutung unserer Erzählung in einen Gegensatz zu ihrer ethischen Vorbildlichkeit zu bringen." (idem, "Fußwaschung," 89).

defines ritual practice among Christian groupings (*ecclesiological function*) and—in a narrative sense—helps to interpret the Christ figure in light of the passion events (*christological function*). In Luke, the Eucharist scene is even used to illustrate how ἐπιγινώσκειν as the literary purpose behind gospel writing can be obtained (*historiographical function*). By omitting and replacing this literary memory, John deconstructs a crucial pattern of early Christian narrative identity. He refrains from a ritual practice that has institutional character and, instead, he provides an exemplary memory that has ethical significance (foot-washing).

In terms of ecclesiology, Christology, and historiography, John 13 differs significantly from Luke 22. Both types of narrative account prepare for a different literary and theological adaption of the passion narrative and its narrative prelude. Luke's construct of the last supper ultimately generates an *institutional* approach to history-writing,[48] while John depicts the commencing passion story as *exemplary* history.[49] Luke clearly focuses on the rise of missionary history in its global dimension, while John identifies how Jesus' cosmic presence has defined the paradigm of brotherly love and community.[50]

48 For a general discussion of this idea, cf. Hubert Cancik, "The History of Culture, Religion, and Institutions in Ancient Historiography: Philological Observations concerning Luke's History," *JBL* 116 (1997): 673–95; idem, "Das Geschichtswerk des Lukas als Institutionsgeschichte: Die Vorbereitung des Zweiten Logos im Ersten," in J. Frey et al., *Die Apostelgeschichte*, 519–38. For criticism of this, see Eve-Marie Becker, "Patterns of Early Christian Thinking and Writing of History: Paul–Mark–Acts," in *Thinking, Recording, and Writing History in the Ancient World*, ed. K. A. Raaflaub (Malden: Wiley-Blackwell, 2014), 276–96.

49 On the concept of "exemplary memory and history," see Ellen O'Gorman, "Repetition and Exemplarity in Historical Thought: Ancient Rome and the Ghosts of Modernity," in *The Western Time of Ancient History: Historiographical Encounters with the Greek and Roman Pasts*, ed. A. Lianeri (Cambridge: Cambridge University Press, 2011), 264–79.

50 I would like to thank Sarah Jennings (Aarhus) for her careful language revision.

Troels Engberg-Pedersen

A Question of Genre: John 13–17 as *Paraklēsis*

1. Genre Bending and Clarity

Harold Attridge opened up a new chapter in Johannine scholarship when in his 2001 Presidential Address to the Society of Biblical Literature he introduced the notion of Johannine "genre bending."[1] The idea is fruitful in a number of respects. First, it directs our attention to a place where it should constantly be directed: the text itself rather than any intriguing issues behind, beside or before it. Second, it implicitly addresses the text as a coherent whole instead of seeing it as a patchwork more or less professionally stitched together by a redactor on the basis of earlier traditions. Third, the idea seems to capture a feature of Johannine creativity that is actually there. Fourth, in the way the idea is handled in practice by Attridge it directs our attention not just to the text and its genres, but also to the even more fundamental issue of the meaning of the text: what understandings it is intended to convey through its use of genre. All of this is strongly to be applauded. It constitutes a healthy reaction to a whole number of impasses in Johannine scholarship.

Here I would particularly emphasize the fourth point: that attention to genre should not be seen as an end in itself.[2] Rather, *through* considerations of genre we should attempt to grasp the meaning that is expressed by the use of various genres in the text. This point is similar to one often made by Wayne A. Meeks in a comparable case. When Meeks studied the sociology of John and Paul, he always insisted that the aim was not to see how either author fitted into some pre-established social scientific category or box. Rather and conversely, the aim was to let the social scientific categories elucidate what was actually going on in all its complexity in the Johannine and Pauline texts themselves. *They* should be in

1 Harold W. Attridge, "Genre Bending in the Fourth Gospel," *JBL* 121 (2002): 3–21.

2 I am using "genre" in its traditional sense as employed in literary studies of highly wrought, fictional documents, not in the much broader sense employed in rhetorical genre studies since Carolyn R. Miller, "Genre as Social Action," *Quarterly Journal of Speech* 70 (1984): 151–167 (see Sune Auken's essay in this volume).

focus, not the social scientific tools. Similarly, our concern with genre in John should not be an end in itself, but a way of capturing the meaning of the text itself in all its complexity.

Having praised Attridge's intervention, I should also mention a point where I am somewhat more skeptical. After Attridge has convincingly established the fact of "genre bending" in John's text, he sensibly asks the question why it is there. One answer, he suggests, "lies in the intense reflection in the text on the process of transformation inaugurated by the Word's taking on flesh" (20). Allow me to cite a few more sentences from the end of the essay:

> If something quite spectacular happens to flesh when the Word hits it, something equally wondrous happens to ordinary words when they try to convey the Word itself. Revealing words reveal riddles; realistic similitudes become surreal; words of testimony undercut the validity of any ordinary act of testifying; words of farewell become words of powerful presence; words of prayer negate the distance between worshiper and God; words that signify shame, death on a cross, become words that enshrine value, allure disciples, give a command, and glorify God.

In the imagination of the fourth evangelist, genres are bent because words themselves are bent.[3]

And finally the concluding sentence:

> [T]he use of most of these forms suggests that none of them is adequate to speak of the Word incarnate. John's genre bending is an effort to force its audience away from words to an encounter with the Word himself.[4]

Here—and this has been presupposed all through Attridge's essay—the practice of genre bending is tied specifically to the strategy of the Fourth Gospel in contradistinction to the practice in other comparable texts. I agree completely, and this is where Attridge's general point does open up most fruitfully for a study of this particular text.[5] However, Attridge also suggests that the practice of bending is, as it were, required in order for the text to achieve its aim of removing its readers from the level of "mere words" (Attridge: "ordinary words") and the level of understanding to another level, which is one of "transformation" (of the readers)—Attridge even hints at the notion of "transubstantiation" (of the readers, 21), that is, of an actual physical change in their bodies. John's genre bending is an effort to force its audience away from words to an encounter with the Word "himself."

Here I detect a move that is not necessitated by the concept of genre bending. An alternative understanding is the following. John bends genres at the level of

3 Attridge, "Genre Bending," 21.
4 Ibid.
5 Thus, in my understanding, Attridge's notion of genre bending does not refer to the kind of bending or constant change that goes on in *any* use of a given genre, on which see more below.

ordinary words in order to bring across a message that is complex and calls for such a heightened literary practice. But the message itself remains one of understanding. John is striving for *clarity*, not aiming at producing riddles. Through his complex literary practice, John aims to generate a full *understanding* of a complex message. There is no move away from ordinary words, only a more concerted effort to bring the readers to understand the full message through a more varied and complex use of such words.

This point has wider implications for an understanding of the Fourth Gospel from the perspective of literary genre. The gospel genre as created by Mark should itself be seen as a macro-genre which allows for the inclusion of several micro-genres: speeches, parables, and many more. In John we may find even more micro-genres to be included and we may even find that the text implicitly raises and discusses questions of a distinctly philosophical kind (see more below). That move may make the text even denser and may add to its apparently riddling quality. And will that not fit the suggestion (also entertained by Attridge) that it was—among other things—intended for a "study group" in a "school" setting? I propose a somewhat different picture. John took up the gospel genre as established by Mark with an emphasis on its narrative shape.[6] And he wished to write a full story of Jesus aimed quite generally at Christians everywhere. But he also aimed to make clear to his readers his own take on the Jesus story. For this purpose he included a large number of micro-genres, a philosophical approach to basic issues raised by the story—and genre bending. But the point of it all was to generate as much clarity as was possible *within* the genre he had adopted: to bring his readers fully to understand what the story meant. Briefly put: Let us stop talking about "riddles," "enigmas," and the like in the Fourth Gospel. This text aims at achieving clarity for the benefit of its readers.

Attridge's fruitful concept of genre bending has been taken up more recently by Ruth Sheridan, who adds an important new dimension to the concept.[7] By drawing on modern genre theory, Sheridan shows that the phenomenon of bending of genres is endemic to a proper notion of genre itself.[8] Genres do not exist (as they were traditionally supposed to do in a "taxonomic" understanding of the concept) as fixed entities like Platonic ideas that a given literary text might then reflect more or less adequately. On the contrary, genres only exist *in* the

---

6 For the notion of an "uptake" of a given genre, see Anne Freadman, "Uptake," in *The Rhetoric and Ideology of Genre*, ed. R. M. Coe, L. Lingard, and T. Teslenko (Cresskill: Hampton, 2002), 39–53.

7 Ruth Sheridan, "John's Gospel and Modern Genre Theory: The Farewell Discourse (John 13–17) as a Test Case," *ITQ* 75 (2010): 287–299.

8 She thereby sides completely with the perspective adopted in so-called Rhetorical Genre Studies, as explained by Sune Auken elsewhere in this volume.

texts (or might we also say as *sets of expectations* in a reader?), where they are constantly being developed—or in other words "bent."

Seen in relation to John, this more dynamic concept of genre might seem helpful since it appears to match Attridge's insight. But then a question arises. Where Attridge was speaking only and specifically of the Fourth Gospel as exhibiting a case of genre bending, Sheridan understands "genre" *as such* along those same lines. This understanding of genre would therefore fit other texts too, e.g., the Synoptic Gospels, as it in fact does. But in that case, one seems to lose the actual force of Attridge's insight, which captures something that is specifically true about the Fourth Gospel and not, for instance, the other Gospels. Another problem I find in Sheridan's approach is that she in effect ends up celebrating genre bending in John (in particular!) along the same lines as Attridge did towards the end of his essay, that is, by pointing to the "ineffable" character of John's message. Sheridan concludes by stating that she has argued with regard to genre bending in the farewell discourse that

> allowing the paradox of Jesus' presence-in-absence through the Paraclete to simply "speak" relieves the burden of trying to "resolve" the text's tensions as though it were an algebraic puzzle. There is no need to excise the Paraclete texts from the discourse, nor is there a need to reassign John 13–17 to another generic category. One can appreciate [of] the legitimacy of "genre-stretching" as heralded by modern genre theorists. And so, one can also appreciate that the incomprehensible mystery of the presence of Jesus through the Paraclete in the Johannine "farewell discourse" is necessarily reflected in the "tension" between the content and genre of chapters 13–17.[9]

This is commendably outspoken. "Paradox," "tension," "the incomprehensible mystery": once again we should insist that genre bending in John does not *necessitate* such an understanding of what is going on in the text. Quite to the contrary, it may well be that John bends genres and writes the way he does in order to achieve *clarity* in his readers' minds on what it all means, thereby trying to bring them to a full understanding of the Christ event and its meaning for human beings. Off-hand one might be tempted to say that that is the aim of all human communication.

One more point on Sheridan's preference for a dynamic understanding of genre as against the traditional, "taxonomic" one: If Sheridan is right in her account of the modern understanding of genre, does she mean to imply that no matter what the ancients themselves may have thought about genre, the modern understanding should in fact also be applied to them? That seems a stark claim, which it would be very difficult to sustain. Even Bakhtin, whom Sheridan helpfully introduces (295) to suggest that in John's hand "gospel" may have been a "secondary" or "complex" genre like the novel in Bakhtin's view, probably did

9 See Sheridan, "Genre Theory," 299.

not have "the" modern understanding of genre.[10] The upshot is that we should be careful about theorizing too rigidly about genre. The concept may actually have been theorized differently at different times and places.

In what follows, I will consider some genre bending that occurs in Jesus' so-called farewell speech in John 13:31–17:26 and attempt to show how it serves an aim of clarity that can in fact be spelled out on the basis of the text's "algebraic puzzle." To show this I will further draw on a so-called "narrative philosophical approach" to the Fourth Gospel that I am developing, which claims that the text often begins a major stretch of narrative by implicitly raising a philosophical question, which it then goes on to answer, though still by exclusively narrative means.[11] With these tools we should be able to dispel some of the mists that scholars are otherwise accustomed to both finding and celebrating in John.

Basically, I am claiming that Attridge's concept of genre bending raises the analysis of the Johannine text to a new level where it becomes possible to see a literary *unity* of the text that is achieved in and through its shifts of genre and all sorts of conceptual motifs. This also pertains to the chosen text, which we should definitely see, not as a conglomerate of speeches, but as a single speech, *the* farewell speech in John.[12]

2. Three Problems in the Scholarly Understanding of John 13:31–17:26

Critical scholarship has been wrestling with at least three connected problems in trying to reach a satisfactory understanding of this text.[13] There is general agreement about its overall shape. Once John's account of Jesus' activity in Galilee and Jerusalem is over (end of chapter 12), he clearly embarks on the passion story with a splendid single sentence in 13:1–4. However, that story

10 See Sheridan, "Genre Theory," 295.

11 Compare my analysis of John 9–10 in Engberg-Pedersen, "Philosophy and Ideology in John 9–10 Read as a Single Literary Unit," *Histos* 7 (2013): 181–204.

12 Attridge speaks of the "farewell discourses" ("Genre Bending," 17–18), whereas Sheridan prefers the singular (passim) without discussion. Here I think her intuition was exactly right. George Parsenios' understanding is more complex. On the one hand, he goes on talking about "the Johannine Farewell Discourses." On the other hand, he also argues for "narrative unity" and "narrative coherence": "The discourses are a composite of various literary forms .... On another level, however, this generic variety supports narrative unity," see George L. Parsenios, *Departure and Consolation: The Johannine Farewell Discourses in Light of Greco-Roman Literature*, NovTSup 117 (Leiden: Brill, 2005), 7.

13 For a good discussion of scholarship on the compositional difficulties of the text, see Fernando F. Segovia, *The Farewell of the Word: The Johannine Call to Abide* (Minneapolis: Fortress, 1991), 20–47.

proper does not begin until at 18:1. In between Jesus shares a meal with his disciples before Passover (13:1–3), from where the text moves, first, into the so-called "footwashing scene" (13:4–17), next, into a scene in which Jesus almost forces Judas to undertake his treachery (13:18–30)—and finally into the scene of our text, in which Jesus speaks of his own departure and how the disciples should and will overcome that. Problems begin in that final, long stretch of text, 13:31–17:26.

The most fundamental problem is that of unity. Is 13:31–17:26 a single, coherent piece that gives the whole of Jesus' final speech, as it were *the* farewell speech? Or is it a conglomerate of several farewell speeches? Chapter 14 looks like a single speech of its own in which John is primarily concerned to show (*a*) that the disciples do not understand Jesus' talk about his departure (13:36–38, 14:4–7, 8–11; 14:22), (*b*) that Jesus promises them a substitute for himself which he calls "another Paraclete" (14:16) and characterizes as "the *pneuma* of truth" (14:17), and (*c*) that he also promises his own return, either in the distant future (14:1–3) or as something about to happen very soon when Jesus and God (!) will "come to" Jesus' followers "and make our home with them" (14:23).[14] Already here one meets the problem of how to understand the precise relationship between the "Paraclete" and Jesus and also the precise relationship between Jesus' distant and more immediate return. Is the text then coherent even within chapter 14? The question of unity is further raised by the end of the chapter (14:27–31), which looks distinctly valedictory (cf. 14:27: "Peace I leave with you …") and in any case ends with a famous interpretative crux when Jesus says "Rise, let us be on our way" (14:31)—and then continues speaking for three more chapters.

The question of unity becomes even more acute in what follows. Chapter 15 consists of (*x*) a parable of Jesus as a vine (15:1–8), (*y*) an elaboration of the love command that was very briefly introduced in 13:34–35 (15:9–17), and (*z*) a section on the world's hatred for Jesus and the disciples (15:18–25). These are basically new topics. By contrast, chapter 16 appears to repeat the content of chapter 14. Once again, (*a*) there is the question of the disciples' lack of understanding (16:16–33). Once again (*b*) Jesus speaks of the "Paraclete" (16:7–15, cf. 15:26–27). And once again (*c*) there is the question of understanding the

14 Scholars regularly point to certain ideas that connect the beginning and end of chapter 14, e.g. "Do not let your hearts be troubled" in 14:1 and 27 and the repeated insistence on the need for faith in 14:1 and 29, see, e.g., John Ashton, *Understanding the Fourth Gospel*, 2nd ed. (Oxford: Oxford University Press, 2007), 427. I need hardly say that the summary of ch. 14 just given relies on a number of exegetical decisions on points that have been endlessly disputed among scholars. I do believe, though, that my summary has quite general support. For instance, for a traditional "apocalyptic" understanding of 14:1–3, see the extensive, persuasive defence in Jörg Frey, *Die johanneische Eschatologie*, WUNT 96, 110, 117 (Tübingen: Mohr Siebeck, 1997–2000), e.g., 3:119.

meaning of Jesus' claim that he will return: In "a little while ... you will see me" (16:16–19). So, if chapter 15 brings in something new and chapter 16 is basically mere repetition, how do the three chapters 14–16 *together* constitute a unity? It is easier with chapter 17, which consists of a prayer by Jesus to God on behalf of the disciples. This looks like a conclusion to the whole scene. But here too there are difficulties. For instance, Jesus explicitly states that the disciples do know and understand everything (17:6–8), as they precisely did not in chapters 14 and 16. This confidence about the disciples parallels the picture given of them in chapter 15, where Jesus at one point says this: "I have called you friends, because I have made known (ἐγνώρισα) to you everything that I have heard from my Father" (15:15). In sum, do chapters 14–17 constitute a unity across these difficulties?

The second and third problems to be noted focus on two of the issues that gave rise to the sense of disunity. The second problem: Do the disciples actually understand or do they not? *If* the text is a unity, then why does it describe their understanding in such a complicated manner? And the third problem: How should one understand (*m*) the relationship between Jesus and the Paraclete and (*n*) the time frame for Jesus' return? And why are the two issues described in such a complex way? In chapter 14, Jesus speaks of the coming of the Paraclete in 14:15–17 and again in 14:25–26. In between (14:18–24) he speaks of *his own* return to the disciples (14:23). In 15:26–16:11 the text again speaks of the coming of the Paraclete, but in 16:12–15 Jesus affirms that everything the Paraclete will say is something that "he will take from me and declare to you" (16:14, my trans.). Chapter 14 contains a reference to Jesus' return both in the more distant and in the immediate future, as we saw. Similarly, in chapter 16 (16:16–19) he tells the disciples that they will see him again "in a little while," but 17:24 seems to rely on the more traditional idea of Jesus' return in the more distant future. What is the relationship between Jesus and the Paraclete and how does that relationship match with the time frame for Jesus' return?

3. Unity: The Structure of 13:31–17:26 as a Piece of *Paraklēsis* in the Pauline Sense

Scholars agree that the literary genre of our text is that of the "farewell speech," of which there were several examples in antiquity.[15] As a general characterization this fits.[16] But through the work of Harold Attridge we have also come to see that

15 The classic account of the genre is Johannes Munck, "Discours d'adieu dans le Nouveau Testament et dans la littérature biblique," in *Aux sources de la tradition chrétienne: Mélanges offerts à M. Maurice Goguel à l'occasion de son soixante-dizième anniversaire*, ed. O. Cullmann and P. Menoud (Neuchâtel: Delachaux & Niestlé, 1950), 155–170.

John is a genre bender and through the work of Ruth Sheridan that the concept of genre itself invites bending. We may therefore see the practice of categorizing our text as a farewell speech as an invitation to note any ways in which John may have creatively added his special foci to that genre. This is how the consideration of genre may lead to real insights into the text's meaning.

One such feature of the text—and still viewed as a farewell speech—has not been given the emphasis it deserves. At the very beginning (13:31–35) Jesus makes two announcements that may in a precise way be taken to structure the text as a whole.[17] He first (13:31–33) states that he is about to depart from his disciples. Next (13:34–35), he gives them a "new commandment": "that you love one another" (13:34). Together, these two announcements may be seen as constituting a rhetorical *propositio* for the whole ensuing speech, stating its overall theme.

Compare also Raymond E. Brown, *The Gospel According to John*, AB 29a (New York: Doubleday, 1970), 2:597–601, and more recently Christian Dietzfelbinger, *Das Evangelium nach Johannes*, 2nd ed., ZBK (Zürich: Theologischer Verlag, 2004), 2:26–31. Segovia has a good discussion with the relevant *Forschungsgeschichte* in idem, *Farewell*, 5–20.

16 There is one caveat, though. Whereas in a traditional farewell speech like those contained in the *Testaments of the Twelve Patriarchs* the speaker may tell about his own life as it were on its own and for its own sake and then also more or less loosely add various kinds of exhortations, in John everything Jesus says about himself, namely, primarily his future whereabouts, is exceedingly closely connected with his exhortations of the disciples. Compare below on the Johannine farewell speech as also a piece of *paraklēsis*. In producing such a tight inner logic among otherwise somewhat disparate genre elements John does bend the genre of the farewell speech in a specific direction. Following Attridge, Kasper Bro Larsen has suggested that John's bending of the farewell speech should rather be found in the fact that Jesus' death (or absence) also means his presence, see "At sige ret farvel: Jesus' afskedstale i genrehistorisk belysning (Joh 13–17)," in *Hvad er sandhed: Nye læsninger af Johannesevangeliet*, ed. G. Buch-Hansen and C. Petterson (Frederiksberg: Alfa, 2009), 85–102, espec. 93. I agree that the point about Jesus' continued presence is extremely important, but propose that John's use of a "Pauline" genre of *paraklēsis* fits better into the picture of *genre* bending.

17 Brown, *Gospel*, 586, "along with Dodd" takes "xiii 31–38 as the introductory part of Division 1 [13:31–14:31] rather than as an introduction to the whole Discourse (xiv–xvii)." See his discussion in idem, *Gospel*, 608–609, which presupposes the "composite" approach to the Gospel. Personally, I find it exceedingly difficult to imagine that a text that would have contained the love command as given in 13:34–35 might ever have been part of an "overture" (*Gospel*, 608) to ch. 14 *alone*. Normally, a major theme that is presented in an overture will be taken up later in the piece to which it is the overture. But there is no trace of the love command in ch. 14. If, then, 13:34–35 should be taken as pointing towards ch. 15, one may either say that ch. 15 was part of the writer's original design (as I am proposing) or else that a "redactor" later "inserted" both 13:34–35 and ch. 15 (and 16), a position that very many scholars adopt. (Compare Jean Zumstein in the next note). In the latter case, is not the "redactor" an even more consummate thinker than the original writer? And would he have left in place the famous verse 14:31 (on the Markan reading of that, see below) if he had been such a skilled writer? It is interesting to note that in Raymond Brown's latest discussion of the relationship between the "evangelist" and the "redactor" the distinction between the two almost vanishes (idem, *An Introduction to the Gospel of John*, ed. Francis J. Moloney [New Haven: Yale, 2003], 82).

Jesus' departure is treated in chapters 14 and 16, the love command in chapter 15. Chapter 17 has a special function, but we saw that it belongs with chapter 15 with regard to the disciples' understanding: Whereas in chapters 14 and 16 the disciples do not understand Jesus' statements about his departure, in chapters 15 *and* 17 they are explicitly taken by Jesus to understand. This suggests that the text as a whole has an ABAB structure which matches the two themes announced in 13:31–35. This idea will be spelled out in what follows.[18]

If 13:31–35 constitutes a *propositio* for the rest of the speech, the question arises whether there is any special connection between the two parts of the *propositio*, Jesus' departure and the love command. At its deepest level that is a philosophical question. If the sequence of the two themes is not just accidental but intentional, is there anything about Jesus' departure (which the disciples do not yet fully understand, according to chapters 14 and 16) that *explains* that they should love one another as Jesus' friends—and will come to do so *once* they have obtained the required knowledge (as stated in chapters 15 and 17)? I insist on calling this a philosophical question since it turns on the issue of a deeper understanding. Jesus apparently aims to tell his disciples something that turns on their understanding both of *what* is going to happen (his departure etc.) and also of what this *means* for them (the love command). So, what is the logical connection between the two themes? Similarly, we may say that the text itself aims to make its *readers understand* that logical connection. What we see here is a central feature of my proposed narrative philosophical approach to the Fourth Gospel: the *propositio* (13:31–35) of Jesus' farewell speech implicitly raises a question of understanding, and the remainder of the text is then intent on spelling out the answer to that question.

To further clarify the question of the logical connection between the two themes, we may bring in the notion of *paraklēsis*, which is of course central in Paul. As is well known, Paul uses the term and its verbal counterpart, παρακαλεῖν, in two senses. In the more common sense, it means "moral exhortation" and

18 It is instructive to compare the proposed reading of 13:31–35 with Jean Zumstein's treatment in *L'Évangile selon Saint Jean (13–21)*, CNT 4b (Genève: Labor et fides, 2007), 44–50. On the one hand, Zumstein claims (44) that "[l]es v. 31–38 forment … un introduction qui esquisse de façon programmatique la thématique du premier discours d'adieu" (which Zumstein takes to be 13:31–14:31). On the other hand, he also claims (48) that "notre passage [13:31–38] peut être considéré à la fois comme introduction du premier discours d'adieu et plus largement comme introduction aux chs. 14–17." Similarly, he both finds (48 n. 9) the "motif fondamental" of ἀγαπᾶν in chs. 14 (14:15, 21, 23, 24, 28 and 31), 15 and 17—and also claims (49, rightly to my mind) that "[l]a thématique ecclésiologique du commandement d'amour [13:34–35] fait figure de bloc erratique; absente du chap. 14, elle ne sera reprise que dans le second discourse d'adieu (Jn 15–16 …)." This position appears to me too complicated. It seems dictated by Zumstein's—in itself fascinating—notion of "relecture." (Incidentally, Zumstein notes [49 n. 16] that Frey, Schnelle, Barrett, Blank, Brown and Wilckens think that 13:34–35 are in their proper, original place—"et sont donc de la plume de l'évangeliste.")

"exhort." Here it refers to the Pauline practice of *paraenesis.*[19] In another use, παράκλησις means "comfort."[20] But the term remains the same. We may bring out this fact by translating παράκλησις and παρακαλεῖν as "encouragement" and "encourage."[21] In his "exhortation encouragement" (*paraenesis*) Paul "encourages" his addressees to do what they already know should be done. In his "comfort encouragement" he rather "comforts" them by appealing to what they already know has happened in the Christ event and spelling out how that should make them "rejoice" (Greek: χαίρειν and χαρά) vis-à-vis the suffering and tribulation (θλίψις) that they encounter in their relations with the world.[22] In both cases they are being encouraged. But the focus differs. Paul's "comfort" focuses on what his addressees know has happened in the Christ event. His "exhortation" focuses on how they, as they also already know, should behave *in the light of* that event. But a tight logical connection is implied by Paul's use of the same term for both. We shall gradually spell out the connection and show its importance for John.

Drawing on the Pauline distinction, we may understand Jesus' first announcement in John (13:31–33) as spelled out in chapter 14 and parts of chapter 16 (in particular 16:16–33) as "comfort encouragement." Here Jesus encourages his disciples against the background of his departure, not least by telling them of his return and the coming of the Paraclete. "Do not let your hearts be troubled" (14:1 and 14:27). "[P]ain (λύπη) has filled your hearts" (16:6, my trans.) and "you have pain (λύπη) now; *but* I will see you again, and your hearts will rejoice (χαίρειν), and no one will take your joy (χαρά) from you" (16:22). This is closely similar to the "comfort encouragement" that Paul gives to his addressees.

By contrast, Jesus' second announcement in the *propositio* (13:34–35) as spelled out in chapter 15 is clearly "exhortation encouragement" (*paraenesis*). The parable of the vine and the exhortation to love one another are permeated with imperatives that have the same logical form as the imperatives in Paul's *paraenesis.* They presuppose that the addressees are already where they are exhorted to be, and the imperatives are intended to make them stick to that. As

19 For one account of the relationship between *paraklēsis* and *paraenesis* in Paul, see Troels Engberg-Pedersen, "The Concept of Paraenesis," in *Early Christian Paraenesis in Context*, ed. James M. Starr and T. Engberg-Pedersen, BZNW 125 (Berlin: de Gruyter, 2004), 47–72.

20 A striking example is 2 Corinthians 1 and 7 where Paul repeatedly contrasts his own and his addressees' "suffering" (θλίψις) with the "comfort" provided by God (2 Cor 1:3–8 and 7:4–6).

21 The point of this translation is that it may cover both senses of παράκλησις and παρακαλεῖν under a single term. It thereby hints at an inner connection between the two senses which may make speaking of two different "senses" obsolete. I am specifically wary about translating παράκλησις as "consolation" in Paul since that translation removes the concept fairly drastically from that of "exhortation." And we do not know beforehand that Paul saw the two postulated "senses" as different.

22 For χαρά in Paul in connection with θλίψις and παράκλησις, see 2 Cor 7:4 and 7:5–7.

Jesus says in John 15:4 and 15:9: "Abide in me," "abide in my love." Similarly, in chapter 17 we hear that the disciples "have kept your *logos*" (17:6) and then Jesus goes on to ask (17:9, ἐρωτῶ) the Father to "keep them in your name" (17:11).[23] Superficially, of course, this is not directed to the disciples, but to God. In an intriguing way, however, which would deserve further exploration, it is definitely also paraenetically directed to the disciples: *they* should abide in the *logos* they have kept.

We may provisionally conclude that 13:31–35 constitutes a *propositio* for the whole text that leads directly into the basic question of content: What is the logical connection between Jesus' "comfort encouragement" and his "exhortation encouragement"? In doing this, 13:31–35 suggests that the text as a whole has a very high degree of unity. We may also note, in connection with the question of genre, that on this reading the Johannine farewell speech incorporates a central element from another genre that was available to the earliest Christians: that of *paraklēsis* in the precise way this had (also) been developed by Paul.[24] What John has done is to tighten the various traditional elements in the genre of a farewell speech so as to make them all have a single focus: *paraklēsis* of the disciples, which they on their side will achieve and realize when they manage to see the inner connection in the present case between those different elements.

4. The Dynamic Movement in Time in 13:36–17:26

Suppose that Jesus is engaged in "comfort encouragement" in chapters 14 and 16, where it is also stated that the disciples do *not yet* understand, and in "exhortation encouragement" in chapter 15 (and cf. chapter 17), where they are explicitly stated to know. Then he will address the disciples in two distinct ways in the concrete narrative situation just before his death.[25] In chapters 14 and 16 he addresses them in "the fictional present." They feel pain now (hearing of Jesus'

23 Incidentally, the punctuation of 17:11 in Nestle-Aland appears very unsatisfactory. The full stop after ἔρχομαι should be a colon. Jesus' prayer (in πάτερ ἅγιε, etc.) is directly *introduced* by ἐρωτῶ at the beginning (the fourth word) of 17:9. All the rest is parenthetical.

24 It is immaterial here whether one takes John to have drawn directly on Paul or not. In accordance with more recent genre theory, I am only asking whether seeing the Johannine text in this light *works*.

25 I am here taking up a question about time that has been extensively discussed, not only in German scholarship (see Frey, *Eschatologie*, espec. vol. 2: *Das johanneische Zeitverständnis*), but also in the American tradition that began with J. Louis Martyn's highly influential book on the "two levels" that are present in the discourses of the Johannine Jesus, see Martyn, *History and Theology in the Fourth Gospel*, 2nd ed. (Nashville: Abingdon, 1979). My own attempt remains strongly focused on the immediate narrative situation in which Jesus is speaking (what I call "the fictional present") and aims to be as simple as possible.

imminent departure), but should also be comforted by the fact that certain good things will happen to them immediately upon Jesus' death. In chapters 15 and 17, by contrast, Jesus addresses the disciples (in the fictional present) in the way they are *going* to be once he *has* departed and once those good things have happened that will turn their present pain into joy. Then they will no longer need any comfort, but rather exhortation that they *remain* where they have now come to be.

This reading introduces an element of dynamic movement into the text. In chapter 14 (beginning at 13:36) Jesus gives comfort to his disciples in the fictional present in the way we have seen. By contrast, in chapter 15 (and in fact up until 16:15) he looks into the future and describes them as they will be once they have received the Paraclete (15:1–17). This dynamic movement from (*i*) 13:36–14:31 (comfort in the fictional present) into (*ii*) 15:1–16:15 (exhortation in the fictional future) is reflected in the way Jesus speaks of the world. In section *i*, the world only makes a few brief appearances (14:17, 14:19 and 14:22). At the end of chapter 14, however, it plays a much more important role when Jesus states that "the ruler of this world is coming" (14:30). Jesus first reacts by saying that this "ruler" (Satan, one suspects) "has no share in me" (14:30, my trans.) and then utters the famous words: "Rise, let us be on our way" (14:31). Whither? Certainly not to meet Satan.[26] On the contrary, when Jesus goes immediately on to say that "I am ('Εγώ εἰμι) the true vine" etc. (15:1), he is developing the image of the group of Jesus himself and his followers that will turn their back on the world and its ruler. Where chapter 14 gradually brings in the world until it ends up speaking of its ruler, Jesus reacts by bringing in himself (contrastively matching the world's ruler) and the disciples as full members of the Jesus group (contrastively

26 This is unfortunately the way it is almost invariably understood by commentators, who recall the somewhat similar expression in the Gospel of Mark (14:42). Against this, I am suggesting that Jesus is calling upon his disciples, as it were, to leave the world *behind*. Dodd's discussion is interesting (C.H. Dodd, *The Interpretation of the Fourth Gospel* [Cambridge: Cambridge University Press, 1953], 406–409). On the one hand, he connects John's ἐγείρεσθε, ἄγωμεν ἐντεῦθεν closely with Mark 14:42 and hence translates the phrase as a "stirring battle-cry" (408, n. 1) meaning march "to meet the approaching enemy" (406 n. 1) and "let us go to meet the advancing enemy" (408). That must be wrong. First, we should at least attempt initially to make sense of John's sentence without thinking of Mark. Second, Dodd pays no attention whatever to ἐντεῦθεν (which is not in Mark). This suggests that John's Jesus is not inviting the disciples to go and *meet* Satan, but rather—since Satan is approaching and since he has no share in Jesus—to go away (with Jesus) from Satan's world. On the other hand, Dodd attempts a kind of "spiritual" reading of the sentence (408–409), which Brown rejected as "farfetched and unnecessary" (*Gospel*, 656–657). However, if we link the "spiritual" reading directly with the Jesus-vine of 15:1–17, it makes a lot of sense: *that* is the goal towards which they should be going. (Incidentally, Dodd got the syntax of 14:31 exactly right [409], as Brown did not [651–652]—or for that matter Nestle Aland: a full stop before v. 31 and no full stop, but a comma after ποιῶ in v. 31.) For a different attempt at removing the supposed "aporia" of 14:31, see Parsenios, *Departure and Consolation*, 49–76.

matching the world at large). To *them* he may precisely say: "*Remain in* me or my love." And *them* he may call his "friends" because he has made everything known to them (15:15). By now, that is, *after* Jesus' departure, they constitute a group of their own that is directly attacked by the world. This is then further spelled out in 15:18–16:15. Here they are first explicitly contrasted, and precisely as the group of Jesus' friends, with the world (15:18–25). Next, the point is taken into chapter 16, now focusing on the role that the Paraclete will play in their relations with the world (15:26–27 and 16:7–15). And here their future trouble with the world is spelled out most explicitly (16:1–4) when Jesus says that "[t]hey will put you out of the synagogues" etc. In sum, the dynamic movement from section *i* (13:31–14:31) to *ii* (15:1–16:15) turns on a change from the fictional present to the fictional future when the "disciples" will have received the Paraclete and then stand united as the group of Jesus' friends in direct confrontation with the world.

Why, then, does John's Jesus go back—in section *iii:* 16:16–33—to provide "comfort encouragement" in the fictional present?[27] Apparently, John aims to focus on the crucial issue of the disciples' understanding. Here they are again very explicitly described in the fictional present as lacking the understanding which we know they will eventually obtain. This is spelled out in 16:16–19. And it lies behind the fact that "[v]ery truly, I tell you, you will weep and mourn, but the world will rejoice ..." (16:20). It is true that Jesus goes on to declare that "[t]he

27 Scholars regularly discuss how far the section that begins with 15:1 should be taken to go. One popular suggestion is: until 16:4a. See, e. g., the careful discussion in Frey, *Eschatologie*, 3:111–113. The question hangs on how one should understand 16:4b–7. Here 4b–5a go together to identify the new situation of Jesus (he is on his way to the Father) that was introduced in 13:33 and discussed from 13:36 onwards and will be taken up again in 16:16 onwards. Verses 5b–7, however, focus on the disciples. Apparently, they *no longer* ask where Jesus is going (note καὶ in 5b; this contrasts with the usual understanding, cf. NRSV: "... yet none of you asks me, 'Where are you going?'"). Instead (v. 6, ἀλλ'), they are (now) filled with pain. Yet (v. 7, ἀλλ') it is all to their benefit since the Paraclete will be coming. We may paraphrase these verses freely in the following way. "I did not tell you about these future events when I was with you (for good reason: ...), only now that I am going away. You on your side are now no longer asking where I am going. Instead, you are filled with pain at the prospect. But I tell you: It is all to your benefit since otherwise the Paraclete would not be coming. And he will help you in that future situation." It seems, then, that 16:4b–7 as a whole is a kind of run-up to Jesus' insistence on the beneficial effect of his departure: that it makes possible the arrival of the Paraclete. Thus, the focus remains on the Paraclete and its importance in the future. It is worth noting that a nineteenth century commentator on John, the excellent F. Godet, divided the text in the way I am also doing: (*i*) 13:31–14:31; (*ii*) 15:1–16:15; (*iii*) 16:16–33—and of course (*iv*) 17:1–26, (idem, *Commentar zu dem Evangelium Johannis* [Hannover: Carl Meyer, 1869], 508–9). Godet's title for 15:1–16:15 is particularly apt: "The Position of the Disciples in the World after the Infusion of the Holy Spirit" (idem, *Commentar*, 529). The equally admirable twentieth century commentator, Dodd (*Interpretation*, 410–416), took the whole of chapters 15 and 16 together, but also in fact saw the special place of 16:16–33: "With xvi. 16 we seem to be brought back to the theme of the dialogue in xiii. 31–xiv. 31" (415). Exactly—which is what raises the question I am addressing: why?

hour is coming when I will no longer speak to you in figures" (16:25), to which the disciples happily reply: "Yes, now you are speaking plainly, not in any figure of speech!" (16:29). But this is immediately rejected by Jesus (16:31–33); they will all soon be scattered and leave him alone. Clearly, in all this John is out to emphasize the role of the disciples' lack of understanding. Apparently, they *could* not understand fully until after Jesus had departed. At the same time he also intimates that even though they do not yet fully understand, they are perhaps somewhat further on the road towards understanding than they were in section *i*. At least, Jesus does say that "you ... have believed (πεπιστεύκατε) that I came from God" (16:27). But he then also adds—and this is actually one version of the required *full* knowledge of Jesus—that "I came from the Father and have come into the world [this the disciples do understand, cf. 16:30]; again, I am leaving the world *and going to the Father* [this they have not yet understood]" (16:28). With this degree of knowledge among the disciples, Jesus may then go on in chapter 17 (section *iv*) to pray to God on their behalf *as if* they had the required knowledge (cf. 17:6–8). In that way Jesus' prayer provides a sort of bridge from the fictional present into the fictional future when they will fully know.

We may conclude that corresponding to the fact (on my hypothesis) that Jesus is moving back and forth in the whole text between "comfort encouragement" and "exhortation encouragement," there is a dynamic movement from section *i* (13:36–14:31) into section *ii* (15:1–16:15) and again from section *iii* (16:16–33) into section *iv* (17:1–26). Here section *ii* is in a way the most important one since it describes both positively and negatively (with regard to the world) the state that the disciples will be in in the future once they have received the Paraclete.[28] We have also seen that this interpretation makes particularly good sense of the one rift in the text that has for more than a hundred years led scholars to question its unity: the transition from 14:31 into 15:1. This is another place—like at 10:1—

28 This is perhaps the best place to register a disagreement with Attridge's understanding of ch. 15 ("Genre Bending," 17–18): "The language of abiding presence reaches its climax in the second of the Gospels 'parables,' the vine and the branches of John 15. Here, as dialogue shifts to monologue, the future temporal perspective of the testament modulates into the present of relationship between the Father, Jesus, and his disciples. And, as the testamentary perspective recedes, the language becomes that of moral philosophy. The lapidary formulation of the superlative love of friends (John 15:13) finds its closest parallels in literature on true friendship, such as the *De amicitia* of Cicero!"

Wonderful as this reference to moral philosophy is (I could not agree more), I do not see any straightforward "modulation into the present" in the chapter. It is all about the future, relative to the narrative starting point, which is the "fictional present" and Jesus' addressing the disciples *then*. In ch. 15 Jesus addresses the disciples in a kind of "*projected* future" *as if* it were already a present reality. That this future is also the *readers'* present is true enough. But we should not let that fact destabilize our grasp of the time frame of 15:1–16:15, which is the kind of projected future vis-à-vis the fictional present that is quite well known in apocalyptic speeches (e.g., Mark 13).

where the transmitted chapter division (and a too bookish reference to Mark 14:42) seems to have led scholars astray.[29] With the proposed reading, the transition is strikingly smooth. In terms of genre bending, however, we may note that John apparently presupposes an ability in his readers to move rapidly from one type of genre to another without, as it were, losing the thread. Not all of his readers have been able to follow him in this.

5. Answering the Philosophical Question

We asked whether there is something in the motif of Jesus' departure that explains that the disciples should love one another as Jesus' friends—and indeed will come to do so once they have obtained the required knowledge. In other words, how may one explain the dynamic movement from section *i* into section *ii* and again from section *iii* into section *iv?* How will the disciples obtain full knowledge? What is its content? How will it make them "friends" of Jesus? And how will it make them do what they should do as Jesus' friends, namely, act on the love command?

In a way we already know the answer: The disciples will receive the Paraclete. When that has happened, they will understand everything: that Jesus has died on their own behalf, as their friend (cf. 15:13); that he has been resurrected and gone to his Father; and that the appropriate response on their own part to Jesus' love for them is that they *similarly* love one another (cf. 15:12) whereby they will fully be Jesus' friends (cf. 15:14).[30] All of this, which constitutes the content of the Christ event, they will fully understand once they have received the Paraclete. And so they will also apply it in practice.

However, this answer may be made clearer if we remember that the Paraclete is explicitly identified by John as *pneuma*—and if we then bring in the Stoic notion of *pneuma* to elucidate the logic of the Paraclete's identity and function.[31] In

29 It is interesting to note that Dodd (*Interpretation*, 411) does see the similarity between the transitions at 15:1 and 10:1: "The closest parallel [to the transition from 14:31 to 15:1] is the transition from ix. 41 to x. 1." Unfortunately, he does not make anything of this insight. But he should have done that: The sudden shift to a parable that is in fact about the fictional future ties these two transitions exceedingly closely together; and so, if chapters 9 and 10 are internally coherent, so are chapters 14 and 15.

30 Note John's exceptional care in bringing out the crucial connections in 15:12–14: "This is my commandment, that you love *one another* as *I* have loved you. No one has greater love than this, to *lay down one's life* [as Jesus evidently does] for one's friends. *You* are my *friends* if you do what I command you." Jesus' love for the disciples as shown in his dying for them generates their coming to love one another, which in turn is a sign that they are friends of Jesus.

31 I am drawing here on Gitte Buch-Hansen's analysis of the Fourth Gospel (see eadem, '*It is the*

Stoicism, the *pneuma* is both a material and a cognitive entity. It may be infused into human bodies and it may in this way generate knowledge in human beings. In John the same thing happened initially to Jesus himself. In the baptism scene of chapter 1, John the Baptist bore witness that God had sent his *pneuma* down upon Jesus (1:29–34). In this way Jesus of Nazareth became the bearer in his own body of the divine *pneuma*. But this event also had a cognitive side to it. For the material *pneuma* is also the divine, cognitive *logos* of which the Prologue speaks, the one that "became flesh" (1:14) precisely when the *pneuma* descended upon Jesus.[32] So, even Jesus came to know. Now this is exactly what will also come to pass for the disciples when they will receive the Paraclete, which is also called "the *pneuma* of truth" (14:17; 15:26; 16:13). Then they will come to know "Jesus' *logos*" (as opposed to merely having faith in him: *pisteuein*): who he is, that he came from and went back to heaven, and what the purpose of that was. But in addition to this cognitive side of the disciples' experience there is a material one. The disciples will receive the *pneuma* within their bodies (thereby being able to remain in the "Jesus-vine" just as he remains in them, 15:4), which explains that they will by then "bear much fruit" and act on the love command.[33]

We should conclude that underlying the whole text of John 13:31–17:26 there is a philosophical question of what explains the logical connection between the two statements in Jesus' *propositio* for the whole speech: his telling them of his departure and his instructing them to love one another. With the help of the Pauline distinction between two senses of παράκλησις, we reformulated that question as asking what explains the dynamic movement or change from the situation of the disciples in the fictional present (sections *i* and *iii*), when they receive "comfort encouragement," to their situation in the fictional future (sections *ii* and *iv*), for which they receive "exhortation encouragement." In the light of our discussion we may now also conclude that the text itself provides a simple and clear answer to that question. What accounts for the change is the fact that upon Jesus' departure the disciples will receive the Paraclete—*and that the Paraclete is pneuma with the features that we know from Stoicism.* When the disciples have received a Paraclete of that kind, they will both fully know the

---

Spirit That Gives Life' (John 6:63): A Stoic Understanding of Pneuma in John, BZNW 173 [Berlin, de Gruyter, 2010]) and my own analysis of the function of the *pneuma* in Paul (Troels Engberg-Pedersen, *Cosmology and Self in the Apostle Paul: The Material Spirit* [Oxford: Oxford University Press, 2010]). Again, there is no claim that John drew directly on Paul.

32 I have argued for this—unorthodox—understanding of the "incarnation" in Troels Engberg-Pedersen, "*Logos* and *Pneuma* in the Fourth Gospel," in *Greco-Roman Culture and the New Testament: Studies Commemorating the Centennial of the Pontifical Biblical Institute*, ed. D. E. Aune and F. Brenk, NovTSup 143 (Leiden: Brill, 2012), 27–48.

33 We moderns may have problems about taking the "in"-relation so literally. It is a virtue of Stoicism—and one that helps strikingly to understand both Paul and John—to insist that it should be so taken.

complete Jesus story and also understand what it means for their own lives and how they should behave in that light.[34]

6. Jesus and the Paraclete; the Immediate and the Distant Future

Then we may also solve the second and third problems we identified to begin with, on the relationship between Jesus and the Paraclete and between the immediate and the more distant future. Jesus and the Paraclete are one and the same figure in a very precise way. The Jesus who is speaking and acting in John's Gospel is a (possibly Stoically conceived) "amalgam" of two entities: Jesus of Nazareth and the *pneuma* that he received in the baptism scene.[35] The Jesus who dies and is raised to heaven is the same composite figure. But that figure may come to be present on earth again, but now within the disciples and in "dis-amalgamated" form, *as pneuma.* That *pneuma is* the Paraclete. Though Jesus departs in one form, he also immediately returns in a slightly different form, namely, as nothing but *pneuma*, which is nevertheless the form that makes him what he both was and is: Jesus *Christ.* There is absolutely no reason, therefore, to be surprised that Jesus speaks rather indiscriminately in chapter 14 of the coming of the Paraclete and of his own return: He is referring to the same event.

Then we can also understand the relationship between the immediate and the more distant future in Jesus' statements about his own return. Jesus will return in

34 It would be worth considering here in more detail all the issues that surround the figure of the Paraclete in John. That cannot be done, of course. The classic, and still generally persuasive, discussion is Brown, "The Paraclete in the Fourth Gospel," *NTS* 13 (1967): 113–132. One basic conclusion, with which we should agree, is this: "If there remains something unique in John' understanding of the Paraclete, so that the Christian concept goes beyond the mere sum of all the elements in the Jewish background, and no one translation of the Greek word can capture all its aspects, then the last approach to what is unique must be sought in John's own description of the Paraclete (126)."

Here Brown in effect leaves the tradition historical analysis behind and focuses instead on what the text itself says about the παράκλητος. Earlier, he has identified its functions according to the text as follows: "[T]he basic functions … are twofold: the Paraclete comes to the disciples and dwells within them, guiding and teaching them about Jesus; but the Paraclete is hostile to the world and puts the world on trial" (114). One might be tempted to take a different track. If the Paraclete will in the future come to the disciples and basically do to them what Jesus has in the present been doing to them in his speech (cf. 16:12–15), and if that content is captured by the *propositio* of the speech which fits Paul's double use of παράκλησις, then the dual function of the Paraclete will be this: to provide "comfort encouragement" by reminding the disciples of the Christ event and what it means for their relationship with the world and "exhortation encouragement" by reminding them of how they should behave to one another. No wonder, then, that this figure is also *called* a παράκλητος.

35 The Stoic amalgam would be a case of proper, Stoic κρᾶσις (mixture), cf. Hans von Arnim, *Stoicorum Veterum Fragmenta* (Stuttgart: Teubner, 1903–1924), 2:463–481 (*De mixtione*) with the subtitle σῶμα διὰ σώματος χωρεῖ ("a body penetrates a body").

the immediate future *as pneuma* (the Paraclete). But Jesus (possibly the whole package of Jesus' human body as transformed by the *pneuma*) will also return in the more distant future when human beings too will be resurrected according to the traditional picture. There is no need to choose here. Both events may equally well take place as two distinct events as soon as one sees how to differentiate between them.[36]

7. The Johannine Vision

Imagine a group of men standing in a circle in the middle of a stage holding one another's hands and turning their faces inward towards one another. The stage itself is dark, but right in the middle there is a pyramid of warm light of *pneuma* coming down from above that illuminates the men's faces while also contrasting that light with the darkness behind their backs. This is the group of men that John was trying to depict and also bring into existence by means of the farewell speech he attributed to Jesus as he was leaving his disciples behind. The vision expresses the two main features of the whole speech, as these are articulated in its initial *propositio:* what will happen "cosmologically" at Jesus' departure and what this will mean "ethically" for the lives of the disciples. The vision pinpoints the connection between the two features, which is the arrival of the *pneuma* that turns the men into Jesus' friends and makes them love one another. The aim of the text is, then, to make its readers grasp this vision by coming to see the connection between its two parts which is generated by the *pneuma.* By grasping that, they may also themselves come to realize the vision.

How, then, did John manage to present this vision to his readers? By working creatively with a large number of genre elements—a farewell speech, παράκλησις, a "parable," a prayer and more—but also with a set of philosophical strategies and motifs: asking for the logical connection between certain distinctive items; drawing on the moral philosophical language of friendship; drawing on a certain philosophical understanding of *pneuma* that gives immediate, bodily meaning to talk of being "in" one another; and much more. There is not one genre here or any single philosophical idea. It is all, as it were, bent and fractured—or perhaps rather enriched by all those additional layers of meaning that are generated by the fractures. But it is bent and fractured in order to generate complete clarity in its

36 This claim is in close agreement with the main result reached in Frey, *Eschatologie*, vol. 3. The route and ontological underpinning differ widely.

readers. If they follow the text in its numerous meanderings and allow themselves to think—then they will end up knowing and understanding.[37]

37 In Attridge's term in his essay in this volume, think of the Fourth Gospel as an "arabesque." But it is a "maze" that leads to a single goal.

Ruben Zimmermann

The Woman in Labor (John 16:21) and the Parables in the Fourth Gospel*

1. Introduction: The Woman in Labor—Disregarded

Among several studies on women and gender in the Fourth Gospel,[1] very little attention has been given to the woman in John 16:21.[2] The reason cannot be found in the woman being unnamed, because there are many other women (e.g., the Samaritan woman in John 4; the mother of Jesus in John 2 and 19) who are also unnamed, but often considered in the scholarly literature. Nor can it be for

* For Mirjam, who bore our four children and has done much more – with gratefulness, admiration, and love.

1 See Robert G. Maccini, *Her Testimony is True: Women as Witnesses according to John*, JSNTSup 125 (Sheffield: Sheffield Academic Press, 1996); Adeline Fehribach, *The Women in the Life of the Bridegroom: A Feminist Historical-Literary Analysis of the Female Characters in the Fourth Gospel* (Collegeville: Liturgical Press, 1998); Colleen M. Conway, *Men and Women in the Fourth Gospel: Gender and Johannine Characterization*, SBLDS 167 (Atlanta: Society of Biblical Literature, 1999); Margaret M. Beirne, *Women and Men in the Fourth Gospel: A Genuine Discipleship of Equals*, JSNTSup 242 (London: Sheffield Academic Press, 2003). See my overview in Steven A. Hunt, D. Francois Tolmie, and Ruben Zimmermann, "An Introduction to Character and Characterization in John and Related New Testament Literature," in *Character Studies in the Fourth Gospel: Narrative Approaches to Seventy Figures in John*, ed. iidem, WUNT 314 (Tübingen: Mohr Siebeck, 2013), 1–33 (27–30).

2 The only monograph is one by Kathleen P. Rushton, *The Parable of the Woman in Childbirth of John 16:21: A Metaphor for the Death and Glorification of Jesus* (Lewiston: Edwin Mellen, 2010). A handful of articles have also been published (chronologically): Andre Feuillet, "L'heure de la femme (Jn 16,21) et l'heure de la Mère de Jesus (Jn 19,25–27)," *Bib* 47 (1966): 169–84, 361–80, 557–73; Judith M. Lieu, "The Mother of the Son in the Fourth Gospel," *JBL* 117 (1998): 61–77; Kathleen P. Rushton, "The (Pro)creative Parables of Labour and Childbirth (Jn 3.1–10 and 16.21–22)," in *The Lost Coin: Parables of Woman, Work and Wisdom*, ed. M. A. Beavis, (London et al.: Sheffield Academic Press, 2002), 206–29; Mira Stare, "Gibt es Gleichnisse im Johannesevangelium?" in *Hermeneutik der Gleichnisse Jesu: Methodische Neuansätze zum Verstehen urchristlicher Parabeltexte*, ed. R. Zimmermann, 2nd ed. WUNT 238, (Tübingen: Mohr Siebeck, 2011), 321–64 (358–62); Judith Hartenstein, "Aus Schmerz wird Freude (Die gebärende Frau) – Joh 16,21 f.," in *Kompendium der Gleichnisse Jesu*, ed. R. Zimmermann et al., 2nd ed. (Gütersloh: Gütersloher Verlag, 2015), 840–847. Furthermore, concerning the metaphor, see Jan van der Watt, *Family of the King: Dynamics of Metaphor in the Gospel according to John*, BIS 47 (Leiden: Brill, 2000), 109–10.

the lack of interest in motifs like childhood/childlikeness or child-bearing; indeed, the semantic field of children or the child/parent relationship plays an important role in the Fourth Gospel. It also cannot be due to the location of the verse within the Gospel, for the farewell discourse has been the focus of many studies over the past several years.[3] Why then is this text disregarded within Johannine scholarship? Why is the woman so often neglected in studies on characters and characterization within the Fourth Gospel?[4]

The woman in John 16:21 is not a figure of the narrative on the primary level of the plot. Jesus is the one speaking during the whole farewell discourse and he recounts a brief story about this woman. In essence, this passage is a "fictitious story which narrates a particular event,"[5] which just happens to be the definition of a "parable" suggested by Klyne Snodgrass. At the same time, however, Snodgrass himself disregards this text in his *opus magnum* on the parables of Jesus. But he does not stand alone in not treating this text. In parable scholarship, John 16:21 and the Gospel of John in general are usually excluded because there seems to be a consensus in New Testament scholarship that there are no parables in John.[6]

I have challenged this consensus in several publications and the following article follows this line of thinking. Therefore, I will first briefly summarize my arguments on rethinking the genre of parables within the Fourth Gospel including some remarks on genre theory (2). In the following part (3), I will give attention to the interpretation of the parable of the "Woman in labor" (John 16:21) applying the method of parable interpretation used in the *Kompendium der Gleichnisse Jesu* and recently explored in my book *Puzzling the Parables of Jesus*.[7]

3 See the survey of research by Hans-Josef Klauck, "Der Weggang Jesu: Neue Arbeiten zu Joh 13–17," *BZ* 40 (1996): 236–50.

4 See Cornelis Bennema, *Encountering Jesus: Character Studies in the Gospel of John*, 2nd ed. (Minneapolis: Fortress Press, 2014); Alicia D. Myers, *Characterizing Jesus: A Rhetorical Analysis on the Fourth Gospel's Use of Scripture in Its Presentation of Jesus*, LNTS 458 (London: T & T Clark, 2012); Hunt et al., *Character Studies*; Christopher W. Skinner, ed., *Characters and Characterization in the Gospel of John* (London: Bloomsbury, 2013).

5 Klyne R. Snodgrass, *Stories with Intent: A Comprehensive Guide to the Parables of Jesus* (Grand Rapids: Eerdmans, 2008), 13. Snodgrass distinguishes six designations for parables, and the given definition matches the third one, which is called "Double Indirect Narrative Parables" (ibid., 13).

6 See the recent works of Amy-Jill Levine, *Short Stories by Jesus: The Enigmatic Parables of a Controversial Rabbi* (New York: HarperOne, 2014), 1–23; Richard Lischer, *Reading the Parables* (Louisville: Westminster John Knox, 2014), 69–74.

7 See Ruben Zimmermann, *Puzzling the Parables of Jesus: Methods and Interpretation* (Minneapolis: Augsburg Fortress, forthcoming).

2. Parables in the Gospel of John

2.1 Are there Parables in John?[8]

2.1.1 The Disregard of Johannine Parables in Scholarship

Both parable and Johannine scholarship seem to agree that there are no parables of Jesus to be found in the Fourth Gospel. The origin of the exclusion of the Gospel of John in parable research in the twentieth century was the work of Adolf Jülicher. Jülicher categorically denigrated the "parables" in John and summarily excluded them from his discussion and analysis. He contended: "Was die Synoptiker παραβολή nennen, ist eine Gattung von Bildreden, die im vierten Evangelium fast gänzlich mangelt."[9] Jülicher admitted that John also offered figurative speech, but it had been allegorically transformed and it lacked the narrativity of an example story or the strict form of a parable. Only "thoughtless allegorists" could miss the difference between the synoptic parables and the Johannine *paroimiai.*[10] Jülicher's search for the original, oral form of Jesus' words foundered at the text of John.

The path taken by Jülicher determined the direction of parable scholarship for the entirety of the twentieth century. Even when major and deep-reaching methodological changes entered the world of parables study, the exclusion of John from the discussion was not questioned. Instead, more arguments, mostly from the perspective of Historical Jesus research, strengthened the point. (1) The Gospel of John was considered to be composed very late and contained no old historical material. (2) The genre term παραβολή does not appear in John. Furthermore, (3) the form of the Johannine sayings are not historical. Jesus could not have spoken in such a complex manner. The figurative speeches in John are wild allegories that immediately depart from the realm of the actual image and are pervaded by theological "deeper meanings." In addition (4), the high christology of the Fourth Gospel is opposed to the parabolic discourse. Whereas the Jesus of the Synoptic Gospels speaks about the kingdom of God in parables, the Johannine Jesus speaks about himself in the first person, dressing this speech in the garb of "I am" sayings.

---

8 The following section is taken, at points verbatim, from my article Ruben Zimmermann, "Are there Parables in John? It is Time to Revisit the Question," *Journal for the Study of the Historical Jesus* 9 (2011): 243–76.

9 "What the Synoptics call παραβολή is a genre of figurative speech that is almost entirely lacking in the Fourth Gospel." Adolf Jülicher, *Die Gleichnisreden Jesu*, 2nd ed. (Tübingen: Mohr Siebeck, 1910), 117.

10 Jülicher, *Gleichnisreden,* 201: "rücksichtslose Allegoristen." Jülicher goes so far as to speak of a mistreatment of Jesus' parabolic speech (see ibid.: "Misshandlung von Jesu Gleichnisreden").

I have challenged these arguments in detail elsewhere,[11] so a brief summary must be sufficient in this contribution. (1) Even without entering into the discussion concerning the dating of the Gospel of John,[12] in present scholarship it can hardly be denied that even in the Fourth Gospel one finds some memory of historical material.[13] In fact, James Charlesworth is already referring to a "paradigm shift" in which the Gospel of John has been given greater significance for historical Jesus research.[14] (2) With regard to terminology, it can be stated, that the technical term for figurative language utilized in John, namely παροιμία,[15] is traditionally very similar to the term παραβολή—in some instances the terms are used synonymously.[16] In John 10:6 the term is used retrospectively in reference to the shepherd-παροιμία of John 10:1–5, a brief narrative text.[17]

11 See Zimmermann, "Are there Parables in John?" 245–60.

12 See, for instance, Peter Hofrichter, *Für und wider die Priorität des Johannesevangeliums: Symposion in Salzburg am 10. März 2000*, Theologische Texte und Studien 9 (Hildesheim: Olms, 2002) and Klaus Berger, *Im Anfang war Johannes: Datierung und Theologie des vierten Evangeliums* (3rd ed.; Gütersloh: Gütersloher Verlagshaus, 2004).

13 Different areas of research have, in their own way, added support to the historicity of at least some elements in John. See, for one approach, the publications arising out of the "John, Jesus, and History" project (Paul N. Anderson, Felix Just, and Tom Thatcher, eds., *John, Jesus, and History, Vol. 1: Critical Appraisals of Critical Views*, SBLSymS 44 [Atlanta: Society of Biblical Literature, 2007] and *John, Jesus, and History, Vol. 2: Aspects of Historicity in the Fourth Gospel*, SBLSymS 44 [Atlanta: Society of Biblical Literature, 2009]) or Paul Anderson, *The Fourth Gospel and the Quest for Jesus: Modern Foundations Reconsidered*, LNTS 321 (London: T&T Clark, 2007). See also Francis J. Moloney, "The Fourth Gospel and the Jesus of History," *NTS* 46 (2000): 42–58; John P. Meier, *A Marginal Jew: Rethinking the Historical Jesus, I: The Roots of the Problem and the Person* (New York: Doubleday, 1991), 44, 174–175; another approach is the "eyewitness thesis" of Richard Bauckham, *The Testimony of the Beloved Disciple: Narrative, History, and Theology in the Gospel of John* (Grand Rapids: Baker Academic, 2008).

14 James H. Charlesworth, "The Historical Jesus in the Fourth Gospel: A Paradigm Shift?" *Journal for the Study of the Historical Jesus* 8 (2010): 3–46.

15 Cf. Ruben Zimmermann, *Christologie der Bilder im Johannesevangelium: Die Christopoetik des vierten Evangeliums unter besonderer Berücksichtigung von Joh 10*, WUNT 1/171 (Tübingen: Mohr Siebeck, 2004), 30–45 and Ruben Zimmermann, "Imagery in John: Opening up Paths into the Tangled Thicket of John's Figurative World," in *Imagery in the Gospel of John: Terms, Forms, Themes, and Theology of Johannine Figurative Language*, ed. J. Frey, J. G. van der Watt, and R. Zimmermann, WUNT 200 (Tübingen: Mohr Siebeck, 2006), 1–43, (9–15). On παροιμία see van der Watt, *Family*, 158–60.

16 The terms παροιμία and παραβολή are used, for example, to translate the same Hebrew term *mashal* and are put synonymously in *parallelismus membrorum* (Sir 39:3; 47:17). In addition, in ancient rhetoric both terms are linked together (Quintilian, *Institutio oratoria* 5.11), see Ruben Zimmermann, "Jesus' Parables and Ancient Rhetoric: The Contribution of Aristotle and Quintilian to the Form Criticism of the Parables," in Zimmermann, *Hermeneutik der Gleichnisse*, 238–58 (250–55).

17 The use of παροιμία in John has to be examined more closely. I have argued elsewhere, that there are indeed slight differences in the use of παραβολή among the Synoptics. For instance, παροιμία is used in John sparingly (a total of four times: John 10:6; 16:25 [two times], 29), only one time referring directly to a saying. However, when using it as a heading that is to be

(3) Although it is not to be denied that there are allegories within the synoptic parable tradition (see Mark 4:11–20; Matt 13:36–42), we find simple, realistic sayings in John concerning "fields, which are ripe for harvesting" (John 4:35–39), a "grain of wheat" being sown (John 12:24), or the "walking by day and by night," (John 11:9–10) to mention only a few examples. (4) Conversely, the conception of "non-theological" parables in the Synoptics must be questioned, since key terms and themes such as vineyard, shepherd, and harvest had already been imbued with theological meanings in previous Jewish traditions. Even more, some scholars are convinced that there is a christological meaning of the parables from the beginning.[18] The idea of a low Christology at the birth of Christianity already fails with regard to the Pauline letters, which can be dated to the 50s CE. Equally problematic is the thesis that the parables primarily concerned the kingdom of God since in the Mark and Q parables this connection is rarely directly attested, and it is only in Matthew that the "kingdom of God parable" becomes dominant.[19] Finally, the form of the "I am" sayings can in no way be characterized as exclusively Johannine since the Synoptic Gospels utilize precisely this form of speech at key points in their narratives as can be seen, for example, in Mark 6:50 (Jesus' walking on the sea) or 14:62 (Jesus' response to the High Priest in the trial).[20]

In sum, it is rather evident that the decisions and perspectives of past scholarship, though in some points problematic, are interwoven with broader, more contemporary trends in New Testament scholarship. Even as, e.g., Historical Jesus and parables scholarship have changed, certain viewpoints, like the widespread disregard of Johannine parables, are still alive and well. Moreover, in light of the above-noted findings, one legitimately might ask if one should rather speak of "*paroimiai*" and not of "parables" in the Gospel of John. If the language of analysis is strictly tied to the language of the sources, then παροιμία would indeed be the correct term. Yet, in this way the narratival figurative texts of John would terminologically be carried back into an inappropriate isolation. For this reason, I consider it not only valid, but also prudent to utilize the term "parable,"

applied to the entire speech of Jesus: "I have said these things to you in figures of speech (ἐν παροιμίαις)" (John 16:25), there is still similarity with the Synoptics. See, for instance, Mark 4:33–34: "With many such parables he spoke the word to them, as they were able to hear it; he did not speak to them except in parables."

18 See, for instance, Craig L. Blomberg, *Interpreting the Parables*, 2nd ed. (Downers Grove: IVP Academic, 2012), 434–47.

19 See, e.g., Q 13:18, 20 and Mark 4:26, 30 among many other parables in both texts; in contrast, the *basileia*-reference is dominant in Matthew (cf. Matt 13:24–30; 13:44–46; 13:52; 18:23–35; 20:1–16; 21:28–32; 22:1–14; 25:1–13).

20 See already Charlesworth, "The Historical Jesus," 28–29 and especially the article by Paul N. Anderson, "The Origin and Development of the Johannine Ego Eimi Sayings in Cognitive-Critical Perspective," in *Journal for the Study of the Historical Jesus* 9 (2011): 139–206.

as an established genre term within New Testament scholarship, and even within modern genre theory when referring to the narratival figurative texts in John.

2.1.2 Parables in John in Research

A few exegetes have already contended that there are, in fact, parables in John and have offered analyses of these texts.[21] Among these scholars, however, no consensus has developed concerning precisely which pericopes or passages are to be identified as parables. Charles H. Dodd classified seven passages in John as parables and examined John 12:24; 16:21; 11:9–10; 8:35; 10:1–5; 3:29 and 5:19–20a, in this order.[22] Dodd was of the opinion that these passages diverged from the typical Johannine figures of speech in that they were genuinely parabolic, not allegorical, and revealed an affinity in form and content with the parables handed down in the Synoptic Gospels. Archibald M. Hunter, in a commentary geared more towards a lay audience, compiled a list of twelve Johannine parables: John 3:8; 4:35–38; 5:19–20a; 8:35; 10:1–5; 11:9–10; 12:24; 12:35–36; 14:2; 15:1–2 and 16:21.[23] Beyond these, in his doctoral dissertation, Simon Kaipuram also included John 3:29; 10:11b–13; and 15:1–17 in the list of *paroimiai* in John.[24] In his comprehensive volume, Michael Theobald examined John 5:19b–20c; 10:1–5; 10:11–13; 12:24, and 15:1–8 in a chapter entitled "Gleichnisse und weitere Bildworte."[25] He explicitly indicates that in considering these texts he wishes to offer a "repräsentative Auswahl" (representative selection) of the Johannine parables,[26] and subsequently offers a table with fifteen passages that Theobald classifies as "im eigentlichen Sinne parabolischen Redeformen"[27]: John 3:8; 3:29; 4:35–36; 4:37b; 5:19–20; 5:35; 8:35; 9:4; 10:3–5; 10:11–12; 11:9–10; 12:24; 12:35–36; 15:1–2, 5–6; 16:21. In the *Kompendium der Gleichnisse Jesu,* eighteen passages have been classified as Johannine parables of Jesus.[28] Taking up the literary genre definition of the *Kompendium* (see below), several passages in John can be brought together

21 For a history of research, see Stare, "Gleichnisse," 325–33.

22 Charles H. Dodd, *Historical Tradition in the Fourth Gospel* (Cambridge: Cambridge University Press, 1963), 366–87.

23 Archibald M. Hunter, *The Gospel according to John*, CBC (Cambridge: Cambridge University Press, 1965), 78–89.

24 Kaipuram's more extensive analysis of John 12:24–25 in his dissertation was published separately. See Simon Kaipuram, *Paroimiai in the Fourth Gospel and the Johannine Parables of Jesus' Self-Revelation (with special Reference to John 12:24: the Grain of Wheat)* (Rome: Pontificia Universitas Gregoriana, 1993), 9–68.

25 I.e., "Parables and other figurative Sayings", see Michael Theobald, *Herrenworte im Johannesevangelium,* HbS 34 (Freiburg: Herder, 2002), 334–423.

26 Theobald, *Herrenworte,* 334.

27 "Parabolic speech as such", see Theobald, *Herrenworte,* 419–20.

28 See the table in Zimmermann, *Kompendium,* 709 and (with English titles) in Zimmermann, "Are there Parables in John?" 269.

as a special group of texts within the figurative world of the Fourth Gospel. These passages demonstrate similar literary criteria as fictional, realistic, narratival, and metaphorical texts.

The divergence in number found in various works is the result of different methods and definitions. Often, and especially in the works by Dodd and Theobald, a diachronic perspective comes to the fore, where one seeks to find older traditions in the selected passages. Taking up the old classification by Jülicher, Theobald concludes that "das vierte Ev *Parabeln* oder *Gleichniserzählungen*, wie sie für Jesus selbst so typisch sind, überhaupt nicht kennt bzw. nicht rezipiert hat. Dafür zeigt es eine ausgeprägte Vorliebe für *Gleichnisse im engeren Sinn*."[29] At the same time, however, the passages listed in Theobald's above-mentioned table reveal the range of variation in the forms, which, incidentally, corresponds with the various passages that the Synoptics bring together and characterize as belonging to the genre of παραβολή.[30] The range of variation leads to the conclusion, that the classification and examination of parables in John must be rooted in a more sophisticated reflection on genre in general and the parable genre in particular.

2.2 Genre Theory: Some General Considerations

First, it is necessary to make a few preliminary and foundational observations concerning the existence of genres and the possibility of defining them.[31] One major question concerning the definition of a genre can be expressed as follows: Are we to offer a "realist definition" that *describes* extant genres or are we only pursuing a "nominalist definition" allowing for various *constructions* of a genre?[32] Within more recent theories on genres there is a

29 "... the Fourth Gospel does not know, or at least has not passed on, *Parabeln* or *Gleichniserzählungen*, which are so typical for Jesus. On the other hand, though, it reveals a distinct penchant for *Gleichnisse im engeren Sinn*." See Theobald, *Herrenworte*, 420.

30 See, for instance, the variety of forms in Luke 5:36; 6:39; 8:4, 9, 11; 8:1; 12:16; 14:7; 18:9; and 21:29, all of which are introduced by the author of Luke as παραβολή. For details, see Ruben Zimmermann, "Parabeln – sonst nichts! Gattungsbestimmung jenseits der Klassifikation in 'Bildwort', 'Gleichnis', 'Parabel' und 'Beispielerzählung'," in idem, *Hermeneutik der Gleichnisse*, 395–97.

31 See my recent discussion of this issue in Ruben Zimmermann, "Gattung 'Wundererzählung': Eine literaturwissenschaftliche Definition," in *Hermeneutik der frühchristlichen Wundererzählungen: Geschichtliche, literarische und rezeptionsorientierte Perspektiven*, ed. B. Kollmann and Ruben Zimmermann, WUNT 339 (Tübingen: Mohr Siebeck, 2014), 311–43 (313–20). For the following passage in the present contribution, see also Zimmermann, *Puzzling Parables*, ch. 4.

32 Harald Fricke, "Definieren von Gattungen," in *Handbuch Gattungstheorie*, ed. R. Zymner (Stuttgart: Metzler, 2010), 10–12 (10). On the problem more generally, see Rüdiger Zymner,

relatively broad consensus inclined toward the constructivist position. Genres do not exist to be discovered, but rather they are created. They are invented by people and exist only in the terms created for them. At the same time, however, these constructions are not arbitrary. They are based on that which is at hand, insofar as reflecting on language always presupposes language and communication. I, therefore, find the approach of Klaus W. Hempfer and Rüdiger Zymner, and their presentation of a "weak nominalism," helpful.[33] Hempfer refers to "virtually normative facts" (*faits normatifs*), which scholarly analysis can identify and describe, leading to an interaction between the subject and the object of cognition out of which the construction of a genre arises.[34] In other words, even though referring to genres is ultimately governed by a construction, these constructions are not free-floating and gratuitous, at least not when they are intended to serve intersubjective communication. The construction of genre already presupposes a communicative process involving genres, a certain discourse concerning genre, and often even a history of genre.

Thus, we can affirm that the question concerning the existence of genres hints at an essentialist misunderstanding that does not do justice to linguistic artifacts and communication. Instead of asking whether genres exist or not, one should rather, along the lines of a "critical nominalism," query in what regard we can speak of genres or the extent to which a particular genre construction does justice to the text being described so that meaningful communication is made possible.

With a view towards ancient texts, it is also significant to consider whether we can recognize a consciousness of genre among early Christian authors that can be taken up in the definition of a genre, particularly if one is intent on offering a definition that does justice to the material at hand. Therefore, I have raised doubts concerning the postulated subgenres of parables[35] precisely in this regard, for in the creation of subgenres, constructs were imposed upon the texts that are

Gattungstheorie: Probleme und Positionen der Literaturwissenschaft (Paderborn: Mentis, 2003), ch. 2: "Gibt es Gattungen überhaupt?" 37–60.

33 See Zymner, *Gattungstheorie*, 59; Klaus W. Hempfer, *Gattungstheorie: Information und Synthese* (München: Fink, 1973), 124–25.

34 See Hempfer, *Gattungstheorie*, 125.

35 In German scholarship there is a dominant tradition since Adolf Jülicher at the beginning of 20th century concerning the subgenres "Gleichnis im engeren Sinn," "Parabel," and "Beispielerzählung" (see my critique in Zimmermann, *Puzzling the Parables*, ch. 4). In American scholarship Snodgrass has more recently once again set forth subgenres, in this instance naming five: 1. aphoristic sayings; 2. similitudes (double indirect); 3. interrogative parables (double indirect) ; 4. narrative parables, of which there are three further distinctions: 4.1. Double indirect narrative parables; 4.2. juridical parables, a particular type of double indirect narrative parables; 4.3. single indirect narrative parables; 5. "how much more" parables (a logic used with other categories) (Snodgrass, *Stories with Intent*, 11–13).

not reflected by the authors in their broad use of the term παραβολή.[36] The specific question concerning the definition of the "parable" genre can thus be formulated as follows: Is there a group of texts that share certain, recognizable characteristics and that were recognized and received by early Christian authors as comprising an overarching form?

Genre terms and definitions are constructions of meta-communication. When we offer a definition, we combine the basic classification of a "story proper" with one or more distinctive features (short, fictional, metaphorical, etc.). A text can then be attributed to a genre when it contains these distinctive features. Though the structure of a definition appears simple at first glance, it is quite challenging to apply it to the interaction with actual texts. Either the list of features is reduced to a bare minimum or expanded to an extensive catalogue of precise characteristics. In the former case, the definition is diffuse and permits the inclusion of many texts that could be distinguished from each other in a more precise manner. In the latter case the problem arises that hardly any text actually ends up fulfilling all the identified features. For this reason, genre theory has appropriated the term *Familienähnlichkeit* ("family resemblance") from Ludwig Wittgenstein in order both to express a "belonging to" on the basis of similarities and at the same time to create a space for certain differences. Genres can be defined on the basis of a certain cluster of features where some of the features are essential, but not every single feature must necessarily be present.

A definition along these lines does not list a fixed set of "necessary" features (e.g., feature 1 and feature 2 and feature 3), but rather includes "optional" features identified by the idea of "and/or" (e.g., feature 1 and/or feature 2 and/or feature 3). In this way, one or more features may be applicable resulting in greater flexibility for discussing a variety of individual texts. Such a definition, however, suffers from a certain imprecision in that it does not reveal the features that must actually be present. That is to say, it does not indicate which features are constitutive for the genre and which remain at the periphery. For this reason, Fricke has suggested a combination of "necessary" and "optional" features for a definition that is both precise and flexible (i.e., containing both "and" and "and/or" elements).[37] In this way, we may clearly identify the features that texts must have

36 See, for instance, Luke, who in the introductions to so-called "figurative sayings" simply refers to all of these as παραβολή; See, e.g., "proverb" ("the physician who is to heal himself," Luke 4:23), "similitudes" (e.g., "humility and hospitality," Luke 14:7), "parables" (e.g., "the widow and the judge," Luke 18:1), and "example stories" ("the Pharisee and the tax collector," Luke 18:9). For details concerning the issue of parable subgenres, see Zimmermann, *Puzzling the Parables*, ch. 4.1 ("The Classic Genre Distinctions and Their Critics").

37 See Fricke, "Definitionen," 9: "Am angemessensten also bestimmt man einen Gattungsbegriff weder zu stark durch eine ‚einfache Addition' notwendiger Merkmale noch zu weich durch eine ‚offene Reihe' alternativer Merkmale, sondern durch eine Verbindung aus beiden: durch

in common while at the same time allowing room for concrete variation and historical developments and changes.

2.3 The Parable Genre: A Definition

Following the New Testament authors regardless of some disparity in linguistic form, the texts that in the New Testament are called παραβολή do demonstrate unifying characteristics that would justify the notion of a common "genre." "Narrativity" and "metaphoricity" are often named as the most striking criteria,[38] and some consider "brevity" to be an additional criterion.[39] These characteristics, however, are closely connected to other criteria that for the purposes of accuracy must also be mentioned.[40] Drawing on literary parable theories,[41] the following genre definition is offered in order to take the most significant criteria into account:

A *parable* is a short narratival (1) fictional (2) text that is related in the narrated world to known reality (3) but, by way of implicit or explicit transfer signals, makes it understood that the meaning of the narration must be differentiated from the literal words of the text (4). In its appeal structure (5) it

---

eine *flexible Definition.*" See also idem, *Norm und Abweichung: Eine Philosophie der Literatur*, Beck'sche Elementarbücher (München: Beck, 1981), 144–54.

38 See, for instance, Bernhard Heininger, *Metaphorik, Erzählstruktur und szenisch-dramatische Gestaltung in den Sondergutgleichnissen bei Lukas*, NTAbh 24 (Münster: Aschendorff, 1991), 21–30; Thomas Söding, "Die Gleichnisse Jesu als metaphorische Erzählungen: Hermeneutische und exegetische Überlegungen," in *Die Sichtbarkeit des Unsichtbaren: Zur Korrelation von Text und Bild im Wirkungskreis der Bibel*, ed. B. Janowski and N. Zchomelidse, AGWB 3 (Stuttgart: Deutsche Bibelgesellschaft, 2003), 81–118; Detlev Dormeyer, "Gleichnisse als narrative und metaphorische Konstrukte – sprachliche und handlungsorientierte Aspekte," in Zimmermann, *Hermeneutik der Gleichnisse*, 420–37.

39 John D. Crossan, *Cliffs of Fall: Paradox and Polyvalence in the Parables of Jesus* (New York: Seabury Press, 1980), 2–5; Eckhard Rau, *Reden in Vollmacht: Hintergrund, Form und Anliegen der Gleichnisse Jesu*, FRLANT 149 (Göttingen: Vandenhoeck & Ruprecht, 1990), 73–83; Bernhard B. Scott, *Hear then the Parable: A Commentary on the Parables of Jesus* (Minneapolis: Fortress Press, 1989), 35: "a short narrative fiction."

40 Kurt Erlemann names 12 common traits that, for him, are true for all parable texts (idem, *Gleichnisauslegung: Ein Lehr- und Arbeitsbuch*, Uni-Taschenbücher 2093 [Tübingen et al.: Francke, 1999], 75–76).

41 Rüdiger Zymner, "Parabel," *Historisches Wörterbuch der Rhetorik* 6:502–514 (502): "The parable is an (1) epic-fictional text with (2) at least one *implicit* or *explicit transfer signal* that calls attention to the fact that the meaning of the narration must be distinguished from the wording of the text and that thereby challenges one to search for a meaning that is different from the wording of the text; to undertake a 'change of course of meaning'. This change of course is (3) steered either by co-text or context information .... In no case should (4) there be an anthropomorphized figure that is familiar from well-known reality (such as 'the speaking oak')."

challenges the reader to carry out a metaphoric transfer of meaning that is steered by contextual information (6).

Concentrating on attributes, we can name a bundle of six characteristics of a parable that will be examined more closely below. Four of them are core criteria (AND), which means that whenever one is missing, the genre of the text in question is not a "parable." Two of them are supplemental criteria, which are relevant for most parable texts (AND/OR); however, they are not necessarily required.

The "parable" is
1) narratival,
AND 2) fictional,
AND 3) realistic,
AND 4) metaphoric,
AND/OR 5) active in appeal and interpretation,
AND/OR 6) contextually related.

It is the presence of the first four criteria that characterizes a text as parable. Each criterion individually could be met by many other texts. There are many "narrative" text types. A text, which is, for instance, "fictional" could belong to a fantasy genre or to a fairy tale; however, it is only the conjunction of "fictional" and "realistic" at the same time that makes the text a parable. To define not only determines, but also limits. Thus, as will be seen in the ensuing discussion, the characteristics mentioned above also serve to demarcate the parable from other genres in an ideal-typical way. To take an example: Due to their relationship to reality, parables clearly differ from science fiction or apocalyptic visions. They also differ from fables (e.g. the Jotham fable in Judges 9), in which animals or plants are able to speak or act anthropomorphically, or from myths in which the general world of experience is eclipsed.[42] It is helpful to be strict in retaining the element of realism so as not only to achieve the greatest possible precision for the definition of a parable but also to recognize the clear points of distinction between the parable and other genres. The mentioned criteria will be explained when applying them to John 16:21.

42 In this regard I disagree with Levine, *Short Stories*, 4–5 who considers the Jotham fable (Judg 9:8–15) to be a "parable," thus intermingling the genres "parable" and "fable." In Judg 9 trees are behaving like human beings; they talk to each other and want to elect a king. Hence, the realistic realm is abandoned in this text and we are no longer dealing with a parable.

3. John 16:21 as a Parable

3.1 Does John 16:21 Fulfill the Criteria for Being a Parable?

There is consensus among several scholars in John that John 16:21 is to be classified as a figurative text. However, most of them label this text more generally as simply an "image" ("Bild"[43]), a figurative saying ("Bildwort"),[44] or a "comparative illustration"[45] and avoid entering into a more detailed genre discussion. Nevertheless, there are some scholars, who already have identified John 16:21 as a "parable," even apart from those scholars mentioned above, who generally accept the existence of parables in John.[46]

Hence, is John 16:21 a "parable" or not? As we have seen, each classification depends on the definition of a genre, which is to a certain extent the construction of scholarship. Along the lines of the definition set forth above, I will first consider whether the text of John 16:21 fulfills the criteria that I have noted to be essential for a text to be identified as a "parable."

Parables are short narratives, meaning *narrative texts* in which at least one plot sequence or one change of status is reported or introduced. There is no need for a complex story with several sequences including many characters. Even the so-called long parables are miniature narratives that concentrate on the essence of meaning and are narrated in a rather concise style. In the context of literary scholarship, they are clearly to be distinguished from "short stories" or "novels."[47]

Narratival elements in John 16:21 can be identified clearly. The reader is presented with two characters, namely, a woman and her child. The woman is the major character, who is characterized with different traits (e.g. she is in labor, has pain and joy). Furthermore, there is a sequence of action, as the woman is in labor first and then, in the second sentence, her status has changed and the child is born. Now her feelings also change from pain to joy. Although the plot is limited

43 See Jürgen Becker *Das Evangelium des Johannes: Kapitel 11–21*, 3rd ed., ÖTK 4/2 (Gütersloh: Mohn, 1991), 601.

44 See Konrad Haldimann, *Rekonstruktion und Entfaltung: Exegetische Untersuchungen zu Joh 15 und 16*, BZNW 104 (Berlin/New York: De Gruyter, 2000), 362.

45 See Van der Watt, *Family*, 109.

46 All of these scholars (Dodd, Archibald, Hunter, Theobald) agree in including John 16:21 in their differing lists of parables in John. Furthermore, see Rudolf Schnackenburg, *Das Johannesevangelium*, HTKNT 4/3 (Freiburg im Breisgau: Herder, 1975), 177: "Gleichnis von der gebärenden Frau"; Lieu, "Mother," 71 entitled John 16:21 as a "mini-parable."

47 It seems to me that the title used by Levine, *Short Stories*, should be understood as a metaphor and not with scholarly precision as a reference to literary genre terminology. Nevertheless, with this title Levine at least formally intermingles genres similar to what she does with "fable" and "parable."

to a bare minimum, there is development and change. The brief story also reveals a clear structure with regard to time (hour, first–then) and space (into the world). Hence, there can be little doubt that this text is a narratival text.

A *fictional text* is one that from the outset indicates that it is "invented." On the level of the narrated world it is Jesus who is the speaker throughout the farewell discourse. Within the so-called third speech, Jesus talks about the sorrow of his disciples after he goes to the Father (John 16:17). Jesus wants to console his disciples by proclaiming that there will be a shift from grief to happiness. We read in John 20:20: "You will be sorrowful, but your sorrow will turn into joy." To explain this promise and give a direct example from daily life illustrating how such a sudden change could occur, Jesus refers to the woman in labor. He is not referring to a particular woman whom he or the disciples actually know. There is no introductory sentence, like "As you remember, some time ago in Galilee we saw that woman from Magdala in labor ...," which would indicate a historical story about an event in the past by using local and temporal deictic elements. Quite the contrary; the example starts in a general mode with an indefinite temporal clause referring to woman ("When a woman ..."). The following sentence addresses the disciples once again: "So you have sorrow now, but I will see you again and your hearts will rejoice, and no one will take your joy from you" (John 20:22). Hence, this contextual embedding demonstrates two other criteria of the parable: first the *context relatedness* of the parables. Parables are embedded in larger narrative contexts as well as in speeches and arguments. They are not isolated wisdom aphorisms, but fulfill a function in a communicative context. And second, the so called "*appeal structure*" of the parables. The parable demands a response as it is directed to someone and creates an impact. On the level of the narrative of the Gospel, the speech is addressed to the disciples who are invited to come to a fuller understanding of Jesus' absence and *parousia*. However, due to the two-level-drama of the Fourth Gospel, the disciples within the plot on the textual level serve as a model for the addressees of the Gospel within the Johannine Community. We can also open this perspective towards the current reader. The finding of meaning in the parable must be carried out in each act of reading. It is not finished in the text itself.

Parables are related to daily life and reality. Although they are fictional they do not recount abnormal or fantastic events. What is told within the parable, could have happened. The parables gain their power from the world as experienced. In John 16:21 the story of the woman in labor is *realistic*, it contains no extraordinary elements. This particular, sudden change of emotions was part of the normal experience of daily life, even more so in a world in which childbirth took place at home, since every member of the household, adults and children alike, observed and experienced the entire process of childbirth and the emotions attendant to it. Nevertheless our text can also be identified as *metaphoric*. The realistic story is not told for its own sake. The domain from daily life is transferred to a second semantic domain in that the reader is invited to find a meaning on a secondary, mostly theological level. With regard to John 16:21 in the context of the farewell discourse, the sorrow of the disciples and the relationship to Jesus are obviously a second level located outside the meaning of childbirth. There are also transfer signals within the brief story of the parable itself. The formulation that a child is "born into the world" is linked to similar theological expressions in the Fourth Gospel. These multiple levels of meaning will be examined in further detail below.

To sum up: It is obvious that all six criteria of the parable genre can be identified in the text John 16:21. There is no reason to exclude this text from the parable genre.[48]

3.2 Text: Analyzing Narrative Elements and Context

John 16:21 (according to NA[28])		English Translation by Ruben Zimmermann
ἡ γυνὴ		A woman
1a	ὅταν τίκτῃ λύπην ἔχει,	when she is in labor, she has pain,
1b	ὅτι ἦλθεν ἡ ὥρα αὐτῆς·	because her hour has come.
2a	ὅταν δὲ γεννήσῃ τὸ παιδίον, οὐκέτι μνημονεύει τῆς θλίψεως διὰ τὴν χαρὰν	when, however, she has borne the child, she no longer remembers the anguish due to the joy
2b	ὅτι ἐγεννήθη ἄνθρωπος εἰς τὸν κόσμον.	because a human being is born into the world.

3.2.1 Discourse (Narrative Elements and Semantics)

The parable tells the story of a woman bearing a child. After mentioning the woman first, the following verse is structured as a parallelism consisting of two temporal sub-clauses (1a and 2a: ὅταν), each of which leads to a ὅτι-clause (1b and 2b). Hence, the causal clause presents the reason for the proposition, which is stated in the temporal clause. In the *protasis* the concrete event of childbearing is described (ὅταν τίκτῃ … ὅταν δὲ γεννήσῃ τὸ παιδίον), while in the *apodosis* the semantic domain is opened to more general temporal (ἡ ὥρα) and spatial (εἰς τὸν κόσμον) aspects. However, it is part of the literary device employed by the text that the *apodosis* is still linked to the domain of childbirth. The hour (of birth) and bringing a child into the world are expressions used when referring to a birth;

48 See the same conclusion with even more details in Stare, "Gleichnisse," 358–362.

however, they include a certain ambiguity allowing for additional or deeper meanings.

The two parts are set in contrast. This is most obvious in the reference to emotions, where in the first phrase "pain" (λύπη) is mentioned, in the second the reader is told about "joy" (χαρά). The emotions experienced are related to the particular moment in the process of giving birth. During the prenatal period there is pain in the onset of labor; in the postnatal phase there is joy over the newborn baby.

This structure is intensified by the use of tenses. Within the ὅταν-clause the leading verbs are in the present tense (τίκτῃ … ἔχει … μνημονεύει), within the ὅτι-clauses we find the aorist tense (ἦλθεν … ἐγεννήθη). Though the *Aktionsart* of these tenses are primarily in view, they also indicate that the reason for the pain or joy lies in a singular event that has already occurred.

Apart from this clear structure there are other components of note along with elements revealing an inner coherence. The end of the first part fulfills a hinge function within the plot. The hour marks the starting point of the birth process when the birth pangs begin, it also refers to the moment of the baby's delivery.

The second part of the parable is augmented, which departs from the minimalistic, brief style of the other parts. The shortest formulations presenting the same oppositional propositions could have been written like this:

1a	ὅταν τίκτῃ	λύπην ἔχει,	when she is in labor,	she has pain,
2a	ὅταν δὲ γεννήσῃ,	χαρὰν ἔχει.	when, however, she has given birth,	she has joy.

The second part of the verse, in contrast, extends both sections. First, a direct object is mentioned (1a: γεννήσῃ τὸ παιδίον) and secondly, there is not only the statement of joy, but the negation of pain. This negation is expressed with terminological variation: οὐκέτι μνημονεύει τῆς θλίψεως, and it concludes with διὰ τὴν χαράν, which provides an additional reason to the one stated in the causal clause (ὅτι ἐγεννήθη ἄνθρωπος). It would have been sufficient to say: "There is no more pain because a human being was born." The manner in which the second part of the verse is formulated, however, allows different aspects to come to the fore.

In using the verb μνημονεύω, the link between the first and the second part of the verse is made obvious. It is not a radical shift without any memory of the time before. The pain of the past is still in the consciousness on the level of the text and in the reader's mind. However, the woman herself does not remember the period of grief anymore due to her present joy.

Furthermore, the emotional impact of the second part is strengthened by means of the pleonastic combination of the negation (no anguish) and the position (due to the joy). Finally, the most important event, the reversal point of the story, is mentioned twice, thus framing the second part of the verse: 2a) she has borne a child – 2b) the human being is born. Hence, the focus changes and with this also the subject. In 2a it is the woman who delivers the child and in 2b the human being is born (passive), which evokes the impression of a more general statement.

3.2.2 Character and Characterization

Right from the outset the central focus is on the woman. The text begins with the introduction of the main character in the initial position: ἡ γυνή. In the following account, this woman is characterized by direct and indirect description.[49] She is expecting a child, but the reader encounters her only in the final stage of her pregnancy. When entering the plot, the reader sees her already in labor (τίκτῃ) and she is in pain (λύπην ἔχει). No further information is provided concerning why the woman is suffering, so obviously her pain is caused by the birth pangs. Evidently the moment of birth has come right now, which is indicated by "her hour." The possessive pronoun demonstrates that it must be the time for her to deliver the baby. Furthermore, in the second part, the focus is on the postnatal stage. The woman does not remember the anguish, for she feels joy at the birth of the child. Only now, the second character enters the scene. It was already logically assumed that there must be a baby in the womb of the pregnant woman. However, the little child (τὸ παιδίον; diminutive of child, ὁ παῖς) is mentioned only after being born and the focalization moves from the woman's point of view to a more open perspective. Although we notice a narrow, interior focus at first (she has pain, her hour, she has born), the joy is not linked as closely to the woman (not "her" joy; not "she has joy") but mentioned more generally (διὰ τὴν χαράν). In the same way, there is no longer any reference to the woman in the final subordinate clause.[50] Like a concluding statement, the reader is told that a "human being" is born into the world (ἐγεννήθη ἄνθρωπος εἰς τὸν κόσμον). The individual instance of this woman giving birth is widened to an abstract anthropological and worldwide perspective. The minor character of the child at the end seems to be the one to influence the whole world.

49 Four verbs are used with the woman as subject: τίκτω (bear), ἔχω (have), γεννάω (bear) and μνημονεύω (remember).

50 The translation of the NRSV is misleading in this regard in that it changes the voice of the Greek text. Whereas in the middle phrase the woman is the subject of childbearing, the NRSV translates with a passive construction ("her child is born"). At the end, however, when the passive mode is used in the Greek text, the translation employs a gerund phrase, assuming that the woman remains active ("having brought a human being into the world").

3.2.3 Semantics and Metaphorical Transfer Signals

The semantics of the brief story is clearly located within the perinatal domain: woman, bear, pain (of birth), hour (of birth), joy, human being. Indeed, the scene from daily life recounted in this text is the foundational and most elementary event in a human life. Therefore, the event which is described within this parable not only relates the story of a particular childbirth in Galilee in the first century but also recounts a fundamental story about humans throughout the ages.

The language is reduced to only the most necessary expressions; however, one notices that despite this economy of words, some synonyms are used. The central semanteme is "to give birth," which is used three times with two different Greek words: at the beginning τίκτω (bear), in the second part of the verse γεννάω (bear), which appears twice, once in the active voice in 2a, and once in passive voice at the end (2b). Furthermore the text employs different words for the pain (λύπη … θλῖψις) and the child who has been born (παιδίον … ἄνθρωπος).

Beyond the contextual embedding, it is as a result of this semantic variations that the reader starts to think about a secondary meaning of the text. The little scene of the childbirth does not only serve as an illustration for the sudden change of feelings. It has a deeper meaning, which has to be discovered by the reader. The careful reader of the Fourth Gospel notices signal words, which have already been introduced and used in theological considerations in the Gospel. To mention two examples: The motif of the "hour" (ἡ ὥρα) is well established, especially in the first part of the Gospel (John 1–12).[51] In the same way, the term "into the world" (εἰς τὸν κόσμον) reminds the reader of the frequent use of this expression throughout the macro-text.[52] Both terms have christological implications. Hence, the realistic scene of childbirth is transferred to theology. In other words, what we have here is a metaphoric text, a text that evokes meaning on a secondary level.

3.3 Reality: Mapping the Socio-Historical Background

The basic domain for the metaphor in John 16:21 is natural birth. Many aspects of birth remain constant throughout different temporal and cultural contexts. The process of birth is basic to humanity, independently of where and when the delivery takes place. So, there are elements of a natural birth that can be observed in childbirth in all cultures. Concerning John 16:21, one of these aspects is the pain of labor. This experience is also reflected in Isa 66:7–8:

51 See the occurrences in John 2:4; 4:21, 23; 5:25, 28; 7:30; 8:20; 12:23, 37; 13:1; 16:2, 4, 21, 25, 32; 17:1.

52 See John 1:9; 3:17, 19; 6:14; 8:26; 9:39; 10:36; 11:27; 12:46; 16:21, 28; 17:28 (two times); 18:27.

"Before she was in labor she gave birth; before her pain came upon her she delivered a son. Who has heard of such a thing? Who has seen such things"? Giving birth without pain is impossible. The rhetorical questions indicate that the prophetic vision announced something which is beyond ordinary human experience. There is no birth without a woman's pain.

A second aspect is the sudden and extreme change of feelings. In the current medical worldview, one can explain this affective dimension during childbirth along the lines of a biological phenomenon brought about by hormones. Most important in this regard is the hormone oxytocin, which is released in large amounts during and after childbirth. There is a consensus, that this hormone has direct impact on the feelings of the mother though it may enhance some fear and anxiety,[53] it facilitates maternal bonding and stimulates lactation. Childbirth would not work without this hormone. Therefore, the sudden change from anxiety and sorrow to feelings of happiness and joy is something which is evoked by hormones, as a regular process within every birth.[54]

However, many aspects around birth can also be distinguished and are interpreted differently depending on the cultural context. Accordingly Rushton states: "[P]eople become mother in particular historical and social circumstances. A birthgiver engages in a social, adoptive act when she commits herself to sustain an infant in the world."[55] Childbirth is indeed "a culturally produced event."[56] Therefore, it is important to take a closer look at childbirth in antiquity, especially in the Jewish and biblical tradition.

Ancient medical texts as they are preserved in the Corpus Hippocraticum or works from outstanding doctors like Galen provide insights into how childbirth was experienced and interpreted in Greco-Roman antiquity.[57] Most important for our topic is the writing Περὶ γυναικείων from the physician Soranus of

53 See, for instance, Y. F. Guzmán, N. C. Tronson, V. Jovasevic et al., "Fear-Enhancing Effects of Septal Oxytocin Receptors," *Nature Neuroscience* 16 (2013): 1185–1187.

54 Therefore, I think Rushton is too negative in her critical deconstruction of the maternal feelings. She states: "Even the birth of a longed-for child may be fraught with ambivalence. For an alarming number of women, childbirth is dangerous for both themselves and the infant. 'Joy' does not necessarily follow." See Rushton, "Parables of Labour," 208. I myself have experienced the joy of birth during my time in the población La Victoria, Santagio de Chile (1992–1993) even by women in very poor and difficult circumstances.

55 Rushton, "Parables of Labour," 208. With such statements Rushton is referring to the work of S. de Beauvoir and S. Ruddick.

56 See Adrienne Rich, *Of Woman Born: Motherhood as Experience and Institution* (New York: Norton, 1976), 177–179.

57 For an overview, see Fridolf Kudlien, "Geburt I (medizinisch)," *RAC* 9:36–43; Nancy H. Demand, *Birth, Death, and Motherhood in Classical Greece*, ASH (Baltimore et al.: Johns Hopkins University Press, 1994); Valerie French, "Birth Control, Childbirth and Early Childhood," in *Civilization of the Ancient Mediteranean*, ed. M. Grant and R. Kitzinger (New York: Scribner, 1988), 3:1355–1362.

Ephesus (ca. 98–138 CE).[58] An interesting note concerning anxiety and pain is the following in the context of explaining the midwife's duty during labor:

> [T]he midwife … should sit down opposite and below the labouring woman; for the extraction of the fetus must take place from a higher towards a lower plane. … Furthermore it is proper that the face of the gravida should be visible to the midwife who shall allay her anxiety, assuring her that there is nothing to fear and that delivery will be easy … Thus one must advise the women to compress their breath and not to give in to the pains, but to strain themselves most when they are present. (Soranus, *Gynecology* 2.70a–b [Tempkin])

Soranus's account clearly confirms that there is pain and anxiety during the labor. The midwife, however, should seek to comfort and reassure the women so that the pain and anxiety does not cause negative consequences for the process of giving birth.

Biblical texts also provide information about the process of giving birth.[59] Different than in ancient medical texts in which the "medical" procedures and stages are reported, in the biblical texts one must draw conclusions concerning the reality of childbirth from the religious and image-filled texts. Birth is depicted as a strenuous exertion: childbirth commences with labor (Isa 13:8; 21:3; 26:17; Jer 13:21; Mic 4:9; John 16:21; 1 Thess 5:3, etc.), which is described as "pangs"/ "quaking of the loins" (Isa 21:3; Nah 2:10) or "agony" (Isa 13:8). The process of giving birth is perceived as robbing one of strength (2 Kgs 19:3; Isa 37:3), as difficult (Gen 35:17), and as painful (Isa 66:7; Jer 22:23; John 16:21; Rev 12:2) and described in vivid terms (e.g., "I will cry out like a woman in labor, I will gasp and pant" in Isa 42:14; "Like a woman with child, who writhes and cries out in her pangs when she is near her time" in Isa 26:17). The "cry" (Jer 4:31; see Rev 12:2) or "groan" (Mic 4:10) of a woman in childbirth even entered the traditional language of the Hebrew Bible.

As in all cultures, the treatment of women delivering or just having delivered a baby is carefully regulated. The woman gave birth with the help of neighbors (1 Sam 4:20; Ruth 4:13–17) or professional midwives (Exod 1:15–21) in her home. After clipping the umbilical cord, the child was washed, rubbed with salt, swaddled (Ezek 16:4; Wis 7:4; Luke 2:7), and laid at the breast of the mother or a wet nurse. The father was not present during the birth. Originally, it was the mother who named the child, though several OT texts already give this right to the

58 See Soranus von Ephesus, *Περὶ γυναικείων*, trans. H. Lüneburg (München: Lehmann, 1894); Soranus, *Gynecology*, trans. O. Tempkin (Baltimore: The Johns Hopkins Press, 1956); and for a brief summary Peter M. Dunn, "Soranus of Ephesus (circa AD 98–138) and Perinatal Care in Roman Times," *Archives of Disease in Childhood* 73 (1995), F51–F52.

59 The following is a translation and adaptation of the discussion found in Silvia Schroer and Ruben Zimmermann, "Geburt," in *Sozialgeschichtliches Wörterbuch zur Bibel*, ed. Frank Crüsemann et al. (Gütersloh: Gütersloher Verlag, 2009), 186–190.

father, a right also attested in the NT (see Matt 1:20–21; Luke 1:62–63). After the biological birth, the giving of a name entailed the first step of the "social birth." A next step for boys entailed circumcision on the eighth day (Lev 12:3). If he was also the firstborn, after forty days an animal sacrifice was to be brought to the temple in his place in order to redeem the child (Exod 13:2, 13; 22:28–29; Luke 2:22–23, cf. Gen 22:2, 10–14). The weaning of the child after about three years entailed a further stage of development (cf. Gen 21:8). The woman having delivered the child became unclean through the birth for an extended period of time, the length of which was determined by the sex of the child (cf. the valuation of people in Lev 27:2–7; a boy rendered the woman unclean for 7 + 33 days, and a girl twice as long). A sacrificial offering at the conclusion of this time was required before the woman could return to the routine of normal, daily life (Lev 12:1–8; Luke 2:22–24).

Undoubtedly, there are significant differences between birthing a child in antiquity and in the modern world, in particular in that childbirth was far more dangerous in the ancient world than in the developed world today. For this reason, before the advent of modern medicine, fear for the life of the mother and the child was also present in addition to the birth pains.[60] Insight into this reality can be gained in particular through dedicatory epigrams written prior or subsequent to the birth of a child,[61] as well as inscriptions at the graves of women who died during childbirth.[62] One can also postulate that since the birth of a child took place in the home, the birthing process was part of the experience of men, women, and children. From childhood one was a witness to the sounds and sights of childbirth.[63]

Returning to John 16:21, one recognizes that only a small excerpt of the birthing process is explicitly mentioned. It is the emotional state of the woman (pain/joy) that is thematized and apart from this, many details are missing. Whether one can therefore posit intentional narrative "gaps," is a question that must be answered by each individual interpreter. One may also find it curious that no other person is mentioned (e.g., a midwife), which is rather striking given the socially embedded nature of the birth process. It is also notable that the naming of the child, which elsewhere plays a significant role in the Gospel (e.g.,

60 It is not, however, easy to ascertain percentages concerning the mortality rate of women in child birth from the sources. See Helen King, "Geburt," *DNP* 4:835–842 (836).

61 See Sigmar W. Wittke, "Wöchnerinnen in griechischen Weiheepigrammen: Eine Studie auf der Grundlage der Anthologia Palatina" (diss., Erlangen-Nürnberg, 1973).

62 See Werner Peek, *Griechische Grabgedichte*, SQAW 7 (Berlin: Akademischer Verlag, 1960). See the selection of examples in Luiza Sutter Rehmann, *Geh – Frage die Gebärerin: Feministisch-befreiungstheologische Untersuchungen zum Gebärmotiv in der Apokalyptik* (Gütersloh: Gütersloher Verlagshaus, 1995), 175–178.

63 See Hartenstein, "Aus Schmerz wird Freude," 843.

John 1:12; 2:23; 10:3; 20:16), is not mentioned. Finally, questions concerning the cleanliness of the woman or other cultic concerns are excluded from the account.

3.4 Tradition: Exploring Stock Metaphors and Symbols

Parables are figurative texts which gain meaning by transferring the experiences of daily life to the theological domain. There is a broad consensus in parable scholarship concerning this metaphorical character in general. Scholars differ, however, in their conceptions of where this symbolic meaning begins and where it ends. Since Adolf Jülicher's *opus magnum*, arguments have often been made against the so-called allegorical reshaping of parables. Most recently Lauri Thurén suggested reading the parables "unplugged."[64] For him, this entails "detaching the parables from all other perspectives,"[65] in particular theological overtones.

However, language does not start from scratch since it is always already culturally conditioned. The meaning of a word or text is, in fact, closely bound to the use of a word in a historical and cultural context.[66] So-called "historical lexicology" or more precisely "historical semantics" has investigated, in particular, how the meaning of a word is shaped by the cultural context, formed within traditional use, and transformed in the process of tradition.[67] This is not only true for single words, or more precisely "semantemes," which reveal their meaning only within a cultural context. It is also true for metaphors, which are quintessential examples of the transformation of meaning.[68] There are metaphorical concepts with *longue durée* found in the bedrock of cultural communication or even in the roots of basic human experiences (like light and darkness, altitude, etc.).[69] Some metaphors have become fixed in the socio-linguistic repertoire of a cultural group, as when Christians speak of fellow believers as "brothers" and "sisters," even though they are not blood-relatives.

64 See Lauri Thurén, *Parables Unplugged: Reading the Lukan Parables in Their Rhetorical Context* (Minneapolis: Fortress, 2014).

65 Thurén, *Parables Unplugged*, 4.

66 For details see Zimmermann, *Puzzling Parables*, chapter 6.

67 See Dirk Geeraerts, *Diachronic Prototype Semantics: A Contribution to Historical Lexicology* (Oxford: Clarendon Press, 1997); Rudi Keller and Ilja Kirschbaum, *Bedeutungswandel: Eine Einführung* (Berlin et al.: de Gruyter, 2003); Gerd Fritz, *Historische Semantik*, Sammlung Metzler 313, 2nd ed. (Stuttgart et al.: Metzler, 2006).

68 See, for instance, Fritz, *Historische Semantik*, 42–44. Fritz takes the metaphor as the first example for "innovative kommunikative Verfahren," by which the transformation of meaning can be demonstrated only against the well-known and fixed tradition of meaning.

69 See, most prominently, George Lakoff and Marc Johnson, *Metaphors We Live By* (Chicago: University of Chicago Press, 1980).

These cultural metaphorical concepts can be called "stock metaphors," "symbols" or "Bildfelder," which are the basic building blocks of religious language and communication. Applying these insights to parables, we can analyze the metaphoric structure of the parable as a whole against the background of cultural stock metaphors as well as symbolic overtones of certain words, characters, and motifs used within the discourse of the story itself. Symbols and stock metaphors may lead to allegorical interpretation. However, they can be distinguished from arbitrary, wild allegorization as long as there are signals in the text or context that indicate a link to the metaphoric tradition.[70]

For the analysis of John 16:21, then, it is important to take notice of certain, traditional stock metaphors. Since *Bildfelder* involve the joining of two semantic fields that has become conventional, it is necessary to ask where and how the birth motif was utilized in religious language prior to and in the context of the NT or how it is used in other NT texts.[71] Though somewhat simplified, two basic conceptions can be recognized and distinguished.

On the one hand, there is a birth symbolism connected to and largely drawn from Gen 3. On the other hand, there is the prophetic-apocalyptic proclamation that has made use, in particular, of the emotional experiences of childbirth in the proclamation of salvation or judgment.[72]

3.4.1 Birth and Creation Symbolism and Gen 3

In John 16:21, birth is basically interpreted as an expression of becoming human (see above). In addition, with the term λύπη, anyone with knowledge of the OT would immediately be reminded of the creation account or, more precisely, of Adam and Eve being cast out of the garden. This is all the more the case since λύπη, is not a *terminus technicus* for labor pains but can also be used to refer to hardships of men: "To the woman he said, 'I will greatly increase your pain [λύπας] and your groaning in pain [λύπαις] when you will bear children'" (LXX Gen 3:16).

Adam and Eve's expulsion from the Garden of Eden is a consequence of their sin. For this reason, birth brings a fundamental ambivalence to expression in that

70 I have suggested a two-criteria approach that combines conventional plausibility and textual plausibility as "controls" for metaphorical interpretation. See Zimmermann, *Puzzling the Parables*, chapter 3.

71 See in general Margaret L. Hammer, *Giving Birth: Reclaiming Biblical Metaphor for Pastoral Practice* (Louisville: John Knox, 1994), 17–83 ("Birthing Metaphors in Biblical Perspective"); Sutter Rehmann, *Geh – Frage die Gebärerin*, passim; more recently Anna Rebecca Solevåg, *Birthing Salvation: Gender and Class in Early Christian Childbearing Discourse*, BIS 121 (Leiden: Brill, 2013), 43–84 ("Greco-Roman Childbearing Discourse").

72 Rushton, however, argues for a slightly different focus on two major fields: "the barren woman tradition" and the "birth image tradition." See Rushton, "Parables of Labour," 217.

it is both blessing and curse. Giving birth must take place in pain as a reminder of humanity's transgression. Yet, it remains a sign of hope in that life continues. The humans are not put to death, instead, according to Gen 2:4b–3:24 procreation begins after the exclusion from the garden.

In several biblical texts, YHWH functions as a divine midwife, taking over the responsibilities assigned to one assisting in the birth process. He already participated, in a mysterious way, in the creation of the embryo in the mother's womb (Ps 139:13–16), and it is he who brings the child into the world and lays the infant at the mother's breast (Ps 22:10–12). It is likely, however, that in the everyday reality of biblical times a central role was also played by female birthing gods, as was the case in Egypt with the gods Bes and Thoeris.[73]

Traces of such mythological conceptions can be found in the OT in instances where death is imagined and depicted as a return to the mythical womb or the earth (Job 1:21; Sir 40:1; Isa 26:19). In the NT, the connection between birth and astrology (Matt 2:1–12; Rev 12:1–2) could also attest reminiscences of this myth. In the Johannine prologue, there are several instances where such mythological elements appear, such as the mention of birth from God (John 1:13: ἐκ θεοῦ ἐγεννήθησαν)[74] and of origin in the "motherly" bosom of God (see John 1:18: μονογενὴς θεὸς ὁ ὢν εἰς τὸν κόλπον τοῦ πατρός; see also John 13:23).[75]

It was Kathleen Rushton, in particular, who highlighted the close connection between John 16 and the birth symbolism of Gen 3:

> When the metaphor of the woman of Jn 16.21 is read intertextually with the woman of Gen. 3.16, the latter's symbolic "bundles" are evoked. For the γυνή of the Genesis parable has, multiple relatedness to the other elements of the myth. … The Johannine text itself echoes this multiple relatedness.[76]

Rushton rightly emphasizes that the creation account in Gen 1–3 plays an important role throughout the Gospel of John, from the prologue to the breathing on the disciples in John 20:22.[77] For this reason, the broader context of the Fourth Gospel presses for the connection between John 16:21 and Gen 3:17. At the same time, the "birth" theme also plays an important metaphorical role in the Gospel,

73 See Schroer and Zimmermann, "Geburt," 188–89.

74 Γεννάω is semantically ambivalent in that it can mean both "to beget" and "to give birth." Here I am intentionally foregrounding the feminine aspect.

75 According to Seim there is a close connection between gender categories in the Fourth Gospel. Birth from a mother needs to be complemented by divine paternity, see Turid Karlsen Seim, "Descent and Divine Paternity in the Gospel of John: Does the Mother Matter?" *NTS* 51 (2005): 361–75.

76 Rusthton, "Parables of Labour," 215–16.

77 See in general Mary L. Coloe, "Creation in the Gospel of John," in *Creation is Groaning: Biblical and Theological Perspectives*, ed. eadem (Collegeville: Liturgical Press, 2013), 71–90.

as demonstrated by Jan van der Watt, among others.[78] A central passage in this regard is the dialogue with Nicodemus. Entering into the kingdom of God is here depicted as a "birth." More explicitly than in John 16:21, the birth in John 3 is immediately identified as symbolic in that it is a "birth from above (ἄνωθεν, John 3:3)," a birth "of water and Spirit (ἐξ ὕδατος καὶ πνεύματος, John 3:5)." Birth continues to be employed symbolically in John as illustrated, for example, in formulations such as "born of the spirit" (ὁ γεγεννημένος ἐκ τοῦ πνεύματος, John 3:8), "born of porneia" (ἐκ πορνείας, John 8:41) or "born blind" (τυφλὸς γεννηθῇ, John 9:2, 19, 20, 32). In this way "birth" is interpreted as and illustrative of faith or the lack thereof.

3.4.2 The Stock Metaphors of the Pangs of Birth in the Prophetic and Apocalyptic Tradition

The experience of childbirth often appears in prophetic and apocalyptic proclamations, at times also in the wisdom tradition, as images are drawn from this experience in order to make theological pronouncements.[79] The expressions are so prevalent and varied that restricting the meaning to "the daughter of Zion" seems not to do justice to that which we find in the sources.[80] In most instances, the birth process is used to illustrate and consider theologically the issues of need, pain, and danger (of losing one's life) along with personal or historical catastrophes. Often particular focus and emphasis falls upon "labor" (the "pangs of birth") where in addition to the "birth pangs of a woman in labor" (ὠδῖνες ὡς τικτούσης; Hos 13:13; Jer 6:24; etc.) one also finds the metaphorically intensified "birth pangs of death" (ὠδῖνες θανάτου, LXX Ps 17:5).[81] Two specific examples will be considered here in which the exile in Babylon is depicted with images of birth:

> For I heard a cry as of a woman in labor, anguish as of one bringing forth her first child, the cry of daughter Zion gasping for breath, stretching out her hands, "Woe is me! I am fainting before killers!" (Jer 4:31)

> Now why do you cry aloud? Is there no king in you? Has your counselor perished, that pangs have seized you like a woman in labor (LXX: ὅτι κατεκράτησάν σου ὠδῖνες ὡς τικτούσης)? Writhe and groan, O daughter Zion, like a woman in labor; for now you shall go forth from the city and camp in the open country; you shall go to Babylon. There

78 Van der Watt, *Family*, 109–110.

79 See Hos 13:13; Mic 4:9–10; Isa 13:8; 21:2–4; 26:16–19; 37:3 (= 2 Kgs 19:3); 42:14; 66:7–17; Jer 4:31; 6:24; 8:21; 13:21; 22:23; 27:43LXX (= 50:43); 30:6–7; Ps 47/48:6–8; Sir 7:27; 19:11; 48:19–20; Exod 15:14; Deut 2:25; 2 Kgs 19:34; 4 Macc 15:7; 16:8; *Ps. Sol.* 3:9.

80 Contra Rushton, "Parables of Labour," 216.

81 See "birth pangs of death" (ὠδῖνες θανάτου) in the Septuagint in 2 Sam 22:6; Ps 17:5–6; Ps 114:3, in each instance differing from the Hebrew Text. See also Acts 2:24.

you shall be rescued, there the LORD will redeem you from the hands of your enemies. (Mic 4:9–10)

The metaphor is usually employed to depict the dramatic fate of Israel, though it can also be transferred to Israel's enemies and thus function as a comfort for Israel. This phenomenon is particularly evident in Jeremiah where in nearly verbatim formulations, the metaphor is applied to the people of Israel (Jer 6:24) and then to the king of Babylon (Jer 27:43).

Greek Text	English Translation (Ruben Zimmermann)
ἠκούσαμεν τὴν ἀκοὴν αὐτῶν παρελύθησαν αἱ χεῖρες ἡμῶν θλῖψις κατέσχεν ἡμᾶς ὠδῖνες ὡς τικτούσης	We have heard news of them, our hands fall helpless; anguish has taken hold of us, pain as of a woman in labor. (Jer 6:24)
ἤκουσεν βασιλεὺς Βαβυλῶνος τὴν ἀκοὴν αὐτῶν καὶ παρελύθησαν αἱ χεῖρες αὐτοῦ θλῖψις κατεκράτησεν αὐτοῦ ὠδῖνες ὡς τικτούσης	The king of Babylon heard news of them, and his hands fell helpless; anguish seized him, pain as of a woman in labor. (LXX Jer 27:43)

A notable example of how a helpless situation can be described with reference to a hollow birth can be found in Isa 26:17–19:

> Like a woman with child, who writhes and cries out in her pangs when she is near her time (LXX: ἐγγίζει τοῦ τεκεῖν), so were we because of you, O LORD; 18 we were with child, we writhed, but we gave birth only to wind. We have won no victories on earth, and no one is born to inhabit the world (LXX: ἐπὶ τῆς γῆς). Your dead shall live, their corpses shall rise. O dwellers in the dust, awake and sing for joy! For your dew is a radiant dew, and the earth will give birth to those long dead. (Isa 26:17–19)

A proximity to the depiction in John 16:21 occurs not only in the pain, but also in the mentioning of the element of time and the cosmic dimension, even as, of course, one must be cognizant of the terminological differences between the LXX and John.

The sudden shift from pangs to joy in the Hebrew text (v. 18 to v. 19) is preempted in the LXX where the "spirit/breath of salvation" (πνεῦμα σωτηρίας) is birthed, promising and pointing to the proclamation of resurrection:

> ἐν γαστρὶ ἐλάβομεν καὶ ὠδινήσαμεν καὶ ἐτέκομεν πνεῦμα σωτηρίας σου ἐποιήσαμεν ἐπὶ τῆς γῆς ἀλλὰ πεσοῦνται οἱ ἐνοικοῦντες ἐπὶ τῆς γῆς. ἀναστήσονται οἱ νεκροί καὶ ἐγερθήσονται οἱ ἐν τοῖς μνημείοις καὶ εὐφρανθήσονται οἱ ἐν τῇ γῇ (LXX Isa 26:17–19)

As already in Mic 4:9–10, in Isa 26 the experience of birth brings to expression not only fear of death and pain but also future hope and even joy. For this reason, it is not surprising that this emotional bipolarity in the birth process, the experience of extreme danger and extreme joy, is also taken up in later pronouncements and promises of judgment and salvation.

This is also the case for Isa 66:7–17, a passage often referenced in the commentaries as part of the background of John 16:21, with some even positing an allusion to the verses.[82] The specific terms utilized in John 16, however, are so general and stereotypical that an allusion remains speculative.

In the Jewish apocalyptic traditions of the Second Temple era the *Bildfeld* is advanced (e.g., *1 En.* 62:4; LAB 12:5), be it as a metaphor of personal distress (see "birth pangs of death" in LXX Ps 17:5) or as a metaphor of the end times. "Birth pangs came to illustrate the period of intense suffering immediately preceding the end, as the final sufferings giving birth to a new world."[83] As an example of this, one can consider a psalm found in the Qumran *Hodayot* text (1QH XI, 7–12).[84] Finally, there is one more specific use of the metaphor that is also interesting for the NT. In rabbinic literature we read of the "birth pang [singular] of the Messiah" or the "messianic travail" (חבלו של משיח).[85] Rabbi Eliezer (ca. 90 CE) is reported to have said:

> If you observe the Sabbath (properly), you will be protected from three punishments: the birth pangs of the Messiah, the day of Gog, and the day of the great judgement" (*Mek. Exod.* 16:29).

Though the text is attributed to Rabbi Eliezer, and thus placed in the first century, the tradition is transmitted in much later documents. Nevertheless, "birth pangs of the Messiah" appear to be a traditional expression associated with the eschatological judgment and punishment. In the NT one also finds "birth pangs of the end times," for example, in the Markan apocalypse:

> For nation will rise against nation, and kingdom against kingdom; there will be earthquakes in various places; there will be famines. This is but the beginning of the birth pangs (ἀρχὴ ὠδίνων ταῦτα; Mark 13:8, see Matt 24:8)

82 See Barnabas Lindars, *The Gospel of John,* NCB (London: Oliphants, 1970), 509: "There is probably a literary allusion to Isa. 66.14: You shall see, and your heart shall rejoice." See also Raymond E. Brown, *The Gospel according to John,* AB 29 A (Garden City: Doubleday, 1970), 2:618; Craig S. Keener, *The Gospel of John: A Commentary* (Peabody: Hendrickson, 2003), 2:1045; Hartwig Thyen, *Das Johannesevangelium,* HNT 6 (Tübingen: Mohr Siebeck, 2005), 673.

83 Keener, *John,* 2:1045.

84 "I was in distress like a woman giving birth the first time when her labour-pains come on her and a pang racks the mouth of her womb to begin the birth in the "crucible" of the pregnant woman." The translation is that of Florentino García Martínez and Eibert J.C. Tigchelaar, eds., *The Dead Sea Scrolls Study Edition,* 2 vols. (Leiden: Brill, 2000).

85 See *b. Ketub.* 111a; *Mek. Exod.* 16:29; *b. Sanh.* 98b; *b. Pesaḥ.* 118a. See also the occurences listed in Paul Billerbeck and Hermann L. Strack, *Das Evangelium nach Matthäus erläutert aus Talmud und Midrasch,* 2nd ed. (München: Beck, 1926), 950.

Within this apocalyptic discourse the motif of birth pangs of the end are explicitly associated with the envisioned coming of the eschatological Son of Man, that is, within the context of the Gospels, the *parousia* of Jesus.

3.5 Meaning: Opening up Horizons of Interpretation

There is growing agreement among parable scholars that no one single meaning of a parable exists, but that there are a variety of possible interpretations. In her pioneering work, Mary Ann Tolbert stated that "multiple interpretations are intrinsic to the very form of the parable."[86] Nevertheless, it remains a challenge for many scholars to explore different lines of interpretation and accept them as equally valuable or at least possible. In the following I want to follow my methodological guideline and argue for a polyvalent, but still defensible interpretation.[87]

3.5.1 Christological Interpretation

The parable in John 16:21 includes some terms which are well established within the theological network of the Fourth Gospel. All of them are closely linked to Johannine Christology. Therefore, the first interpretation to be explored is the christological one.

Introduced at the first σημεῖα-story, the "hour" (ἡ ὥρα) is developed as a motif that links different parts of the Gospel's narrative.[88] The "hour" is bound to Jesus, in that he refers to "my hour [ἡ ὥρα μου]" (John 2:4; see 7:30; 8:20: ἡ ὥρα αὐτοῦ), though first in an enigmatic manner: his hour has "not yet come."[89] Only in chapter 12 is the hour said to have arrived: "Jesus answered them: The hour has come for the Son of Man to be glorified" (John 12:23). Here, the "hour" is connected to the christological title "Son of Man." Furthermore, it reveals its deeper meaning as the moment of "glorification." However, this glorification of Jesus takes place by means of his death on the cross (John 12:32–33). Therefore, one can conclude that the "hour" of Jesus is nothing else than the hour of his

86 See Mary Ann Tolbert, *Perspectives on the Parables: An Approach to Multiple Interpretations* (Philadelphia: Fortress Press, 1979), 50. More recently Levine, *Short Stories*, 1 and 4. Levine has contended that "reducing parables to a single meaning destroys their aesthetic as well as ethical potential. … When we … look for a single meaning in a form that opens to multiple interpretations, we are necessarily limiting the parables and, so, ourselves." Similarily Lischer, *Reading Parables*, 43–68 ("Parables Teach Many Truths").

87 See Zimmermann, *Puzzling Parables*, chs. 5 and 6.

88 See the occurrences in John 2:4; 4:21, 23; 5:25, 28; 7:30; 8:20; 12:23, 37; 13:1; 16:2, 4, 25, 32; 17:1.

89 See Francis J. Moloney, *Love in the Gospel of John: An Exegetical, Theological, and Literary Study* (Grand Rapids: Baker, 2013), 71–98 ("The Hour Has Not Yet Come").

crucifixion. That the hour is linked to Jesus' passion can also be seen in comparison with the Synoptic Gospels. It has been argued that the whole motif of the hour has been developed out of the "hour" which is mentioned in the account of Jesus' wrestling in prayer in the Garden of Gethsemane (Mark 14:41: ἦλθεν ἡ ὥρα).[90] Following Frey, the hour is not limited to the actual moment of Jesus' death since it refers to the passion event as a whole.[91] The "hour" of birth, therefore, may be interpreted as the hour of Jesus' death. Some scholars have argued that John uses birthing categories also in his crucifixion scene. Water and blood, which came out after the piercing of the side (John 19:34), are the liquids of parturition to describe Jesus' death as an act of giving birth.[92] This argument is supported by another New Testament text, which explicitly applies the traditional idea of the deathly "birth pangs" (see above) to Jesus' death. Acts 2:24 proclaims that God freed Jesus from the "birth pangs of death" by resurrection (ὃν ὁ θεὸς ἀνέστησεν λύσας τὰς ὠδῖνας τοῦ θανάτου). This intertextual reading reveals that it was at least possible to interpret Jesus' death with the tradition of birth imagery.

The christological dimension of the parable is most transparent in the last line of the second part: ἐγεννήθη ἄνθρωπος εἰς τὸν κόσμον. The change to the passive voice moves the focus from the woman to the child. The woman is no longer mentioned. The child, however, is not named παιδίον, παῖς, nor τέκνον. Instead, it is entitled ἄνθρωπος. This term is frequently used for human characters like John the Baptist (John 1:6), Nicodemus (John 3:1) or the man born blind (John 9:1) within the Fourth Gospel. Yet, it is also taken to classify Jesus, mostly by Jesus' opponents (e.g. the high priest in John 11:47, 50) or ambiguous characters (e.g. the man born blind in 9:11; the gatekeeper in 18:17; Pilate in 18:29). In John 10:33 the appellation of Jesus as "human being" is set in direct contrast to his origin from God. Though here there is a rejection on the part of "the Jews" of Jesus making himself God, it is not denied that Jesus is human within the Fourth Gospel.[93] Furthermore, the presentation of Jesus wearing the purple robe in Pilate's trial (John 19:5: ἰδοὺ ὁ ἄνθρωπος) is not only to be meant ironically. It is

90 See Jörg Frey, *Die Herrlichkeit des Gekreuzigten: Studien zu den Johanneischen Schriften I*, ed. Juliane Schlegel, WUNT 307 (Tübingen: Mohr Siebeck, 2013), 266–268, 510–515.

91 Frey, *Herrlichkeit des Gekreuzigten*, 511: "Der Begriff der ‚Stunde' bildet somit ein *Integral* für die Gesamtheit der Ereignisse um Jesu Tod und Auferstehung. Als solche bildet diese ‚Stunde' den *Fluchtpunkt* der johanneischen Erzählung …."

92 See Dorothy A. Lee, *Flesh and Glory: Symbolism, Gender and Theology in the Gospel of John* (New York: Crossroad, 2002), 152–59; Deborah Sawyer, "John 19.34: From Crucifixion to Birth, or Creation?" in *A Feminist Companion to John, Volume II*, ed. Amy-Jill Levine (Sheffield: Sheffield Academic Press, 2003), 134; Turid Karlsen Seim, "Motherhood and the Making of Fathers in Antiquity: Contextualizing Genetics in the Gospel of John," in *Woman and Gender in Ancient Religions: Interdisciplinary Approaches*, ed. Stephen P. Ahearne-Kroll et al., WUNT 263 (Tübingen: Mohr Siebeck, 2010), 99–124 (118).

93 See Udo Schnelle, *Antidocetic Christology in the Gospel of John* (Minneapolis: Fortress Press, 1992).

the last time when the term ἄνθρωπος appears in the Gospel and it occurs shortly before the crucifixion. Hence, one might conclude that this scene wants to depict this moment as the lowest point of Jesus' career: In anticipation of the "King of the Jews" at the cross (see John 19:19), it is the tortured Jesus who is presented as the "human being" in his weakness and vulnerability. Therefore, in this final scene ἄνθρωπος can be understood as a christological title within the context of a specific Johannine Christology as already announced in the prologue. The word became flesh. In other words, the logos entered the visible and mortal essence of a human being. This declaration must be balanced with the high christological confession that Jesus is with God (John 1:1) and even God himself (John 20:28). This tension is one that the Christology of the Fourth Gospel explicitly seeks to express. Jesus Christ is not the "über die Erde schreitender Gott" (Käsemann),[94] he is a "human being," the son of Joseph from Nazareth (John 1:45; 6:42) and born from an ordinary Jewish mother (John 6:42; see also Gal 4:4). This aspect is underscored in John 16:21 before Jesus' prayer in chapter 17 offers "a privileged insight into the inner relationship between Jesus and God."[95]

Finally, the term "into the world" (εἰς τὸν κόσμον) reminds the reader of the frequent use of this expression throughout the macro-text.[96] Once again, it is Jesus (Son of Man, Son of God, etc.) who is the one who is sent into the world: "Indeed, God did not send the Son *into the world* to condemn the world, but in order that the world might be saved through him" (John 3:17, see 6:14; 10:36; 11:27). A close parallel to our parable can be seen in the undoubtedly christological Ἐγώ-Saying in John 18:37, which also combines γεννάω with the phrase εἰς τὸν κόσμον:

> For this I was born, and for this I came into the world, to testify to the truth (ἐγὼ εἰς τοῦτο γεγέννημαι καὶ εἰς τοῦτο ἐλήλυθα εἰς τὸν κόσμον, ἵνα μαρτυρήσω τῇ ἀληθείᾳ). (John 18:37)

The "world" is developed as a theological concept in John, though it can also be interpreted as a "character."[97] In a significant number of occurrences (78 times) it can be seen that the κόσμος is opposed to the space of Jesus and God (see John 8:23: ἐγὼ οὐκ εἰμὶ ἐκ τοῦ κόσμου τούτου); however, it is not a counter-world to be overcome as later Gnosticism has interpreted it. The world is "the physical realm into which Jesus has entered, and the object of God's affection and salvific

94 Ernst Käsemann, *Jesu letzter Wille nach Johannes 17*, 3rd ed. (Tübingen: Mohr Siebeck, 1971), 154.

95 See Francis J. Moloney, *Glory not Dishonor: Reading John 13–21* (Minneapolis: Augsburg Fortress, 1998), 103.

96 See John 1:9; 3:17, 19; 6:14; 8:26; 9:39; 10:36; 11:27; 12:46; 16:21, 28; 17:28 (two times); 18:27.

97 See Christopher W. Skinner, "The World: Promise and Unfulfilled Hope," in S. A. Hunt et al., *Character Studies*, 61–70; Lars Kierspel, *The Jews and the World in the Fourth Gospel: Parallelism, Function, and Context*, WUNT 2/220 (Tübingen: Mohr Siebeck, 2006).

intention."[98] Jesus was in the world (John 1:9), he is the "light of the world" (John 8:12; 9:9; 11:9), and he was sent into the world in order to illuminate the darkness and ultimately to give himself as "bread" for the "life of the world" (John 6:51: ὑπὲρ τῆς τοῦ κόσμου ζωῆς). Hence, the term εἰς τὸν κόσμον is an outworking of an incarnational Christology. The spatial concept implied in the preposition (εἰς) indicates that there must be a different realm, something outside, from where Jesus has come, was sent, and was born. Apart from the term "world" itself, there is very little awareness of this salvific meaning of the child born into the world within the parable of John 16:21. Yet, it is the "joy" of the mother, which can also be transferred metaphorically to the theological domain. The reason for the happiness is not only a little baby, but the arrival of the "human being into the world." Within the semantic network of this expression, the term χαρά may be read against the theological usage within the Fourth Gospel. It was first John (the Baptist) in his parable of the friend of the bridegroom, whose joy arose out of the recognition of Christ (John 3:29).[99] According to Keener the motif of "joy" could also be linked to the joy of resurrection, which is prepared in the Jewish apocalyptic motif of the "joy of the righteous."[100] In the following, the joy of Jesus himself is to be transferred to the disciples (John 15:11; 17:13). Especially in John 16:20–24, the everlasting relationship to Jesus and faith may be seen as the source of joy (see below). Christology in John never results solely in text-internal confession and admiration. It is reader-orientated Christology,[101] which affects the believers emotionally as also seen in the parable of the joy of birth. In summary, there is little doubt that the verbal material used in the parable of John 16:21 offers avenues for christological meaning. Nevertheless, this is not the only way in which this parable can be understood.

3.5.2 Eschatological Interpretation

The parable also reflects "time," as I have already pointed out in the narrative analysis of the text. There is a time structure within the temporal clauses (when …), the function of the tenses, and the use of key words like ὥρα, θλῖψις, all contributing to an opening up of an apocalyptic horizon in the text. This horizon becomes even more obvious when one takes into account the context of the farewell discourse, which includes many eschatological aspects (e.g., sending of the Paraclete, parousia of Jesus, see John 14:3).

98 Skinner, "The World," 61.

99 See Mirjam Zimmermann and Ruben Zimmermann, "Der Freund des Bräutigams: Deflorations- oder Christuszeuge?" *ZNW* 90 (1999): 123–30.

100 See Keener, *John*, 1044. Keener refers to *T. Jud.* 25:4 and *Apoc. Mos.* 39:1–2, where God announces that he will turn Adam's sorrow into joy.

101 See Zimmermann, *Christologie*, 425–46.

The most striking signal word within John 16:21 is the apocalyptic term θλῖψις. The term was used with reference to Israel's suffering within history.[102] It is not used within ancient medical text for the natural birth pain, though in the metaphorical tradition it was already combined with birth imagery (2 Kgs 19:3; Ps 114:3; Jer 6:24; 27:43). The term not only serves as a transfer signal in that the pain at this birth is far more than pain of a natural birth, it also takes up a stock metaphor of the prophets. The metaphors of birth are frequently used in prophetic-apocalyptic speech, and the "woes of the end time," in particular, are part of the apocalyptic repertoire (see above).

The meaning of the "hour" cannot be limited simply to Johannine use and interpretation. The hour is a more narrow version of the traditional motif of the "day of the Lord" (Hebr. *yom YHWH*, e.g., Amos 5:18–20; Isa 2:12), which is largely transposed from the historical to the eschatological dimension in later OT texts and Second Temple Judaism (Joel 1:15; 2:1; Zech 14:1–5; Mal 3:23). The idea of the eschatological day is also used from the earliest New Testament texts onward as a reference to the parousia of Christ.[103] In 1 Thess 5:2–4 the eschatological "day of the Lord" is even connected with the motif of the birth pains of the pregnant women. In Matt 25:13 "day and hour" of the coming of the Lord[104] are combined: "Keep awake therefore, for you know neither the day nor the hour."

In the Johannine context, it is in particular the combination of "hour" with "coming" that alludes to the eschatological tradition. At the same time, there is a tension between the hour which has "not yet come" (John 2:4; 7:30; 8:20) and the hour which "has come" now (John 12:32; cf. 13:1; 17:1), a tension that functions as a motif at the center of Johannine eschatology. Eschatological statements of the present and future are closely intertwined and cannot and should not be separated in John (e.g., John 5:25: "the hour is coming, and is now here").[105] Within this horizon, let us examine John 16:21 more closely. In the parable it is declared that "the hour has come" (ἦλθεν ἡ ὥρα). Within the indefinite temporal clause (ὅταν), in the context of the farewell speech, and even more within the realm of figurative speech, this statement still includes future aspects. The reader should imagine the hour of birth. It is not said within the parable itself, if this hour has already come or is yet to come. Within the plot of the broader Johannine

102 See Isa 26:16: 37:3; 63:6; 65:16, cf. Heinrich Schlier, "θλῖψις/θλίβεω," *TDNT* 3:140–43.

103 See Q 17:23, 24; 1 Cor 1:8; 5:5; 2 Cor 1:14; Phil 1:6, 10; 2:16.

104 In Matt 25:13 the coming one is not explicitly identified. The parallel structure, however, reveals the connection to Matt 24:42, where it is stated that it is the "Coming of the Lord" that is in view.

105 See Jörg Frey, "Die Gegenwart von Vergangenheit und Zukunft Christi: Zur ‚Verschmelzung' der Zeithorizonte im Johannesevangelium," in *Zeit*, ed. D. Sattler and M. Wolter, Jahrbuch für Biblische Theologie 28 (Neukirchen-Vluyn: Neukirchener, 2013), 129–158.

story, this hour (of death) *will* come, and on the level of the post-Easter reader, it *has* come already. However, the "birth pangs" could also indicate the parousia, the second coming of Jesus into the world, which is also mentioned in John. In John 14:28 Jesus said: "You heard me say to you, 'I am going away, and I am coming to you'," which includes a future sense.[106]

One of the most obvious sections of the Gospel to study this intermingled eschatology is the farewell discourse itself. Scholarship has often explored the manner in which the farewell discourse as a whole wants to address the reader of the Gospel by projecting the community's current situation into Jesus' lifetime. Hence, from a narratological or hermeneutical point of view, the addressees of the speech on the level of the text coincide with the addressees, and the readers, of the Gospel.[107] In this way a "fusion of time horizons" takes place.[108]

The current situation is, on a literary level, projected into the past. On the level of the plot, Jesus announces a future situation, which after his death will have taken place. In that situation it is not only Jesus' fate, but the fate of the disciples, which is to be reflected.

Hence, the concept of the "hour" is not limited to Jesus' death or the parousia. It is also applied to an hour of difficulties within the Johannine community. According to John 16:2–4, Jesus said: "They will put you out of the synagogues. Indeed, *an hour is coming* when those who kill you will think that by doing so they are offering worship to God. … But I have said these things to you so that when their hour comes you may *remember* that I told you about them" (my italics).

"Remembering" is one of the major issues within the farewell discourse and in the Gospel of John in general.[109] It is Jesus himself who prompted his disciples: "Remember the word that I said to you" (John 15:20), and the Paraclete will be sent and "remind you of all that I have said to you" (John 14:26). Once again the idea of memory is also present in John 16:21. In the middle section there was a slightly longer phrase recounting that the woman does not remember: "[T]he woman will not remember the pain … ." It is noteworthy that here the concept differs from most of the others. Regularly remembering is connotated positively, it is required from Jesus

106 Past, future, and present dimensions are also consciously combined in chapter 16 in particular. In John 16:32 we read: "The hour is coming, indeed it has come."

107 See D. Francois Tolmie, *Jesus' Farewell to the Disciples: John 13:1–17:26 in Narratological Perspective*, BIS 12 (Leiden: Brill, 1995); Christina Hoegen-Rohls, *Der nachösterliche Johannes: Die Abschiedsreden als hermeneutischer Schlüssel zum vierten Evangelium*, WUNT 2/84 (Tübingen: Mohr Siebeck, 1996).

108 Gadamer's metaphor of the "fusion of horizons" is frequently applied to John. See Frey, "Gegenwart"; cf. Hans-Georg Gadamer, *Truth and Method* (New York: Continuum, 1997), 302.

109 See Michael Theobald, "'Erinnert euch der Worte, die ich euch gesagt habe …' (Joh 15,20)," in *Die Macht der Erinnerung*, ed. O. Fuchs and B. Janowski, Jahrbuch für Biblische Theologie 22 (Neukirchen-Vluyn: Neukirchener, 2008), 105–130.

and should be done. In the parable, by contrast, it is exactly the non-remembering of the pain which enables the woman to rejoice. What does that mean?

It is still the potential of the image of birth which helps the disciples cope with the situation after Jesus' death. Normally, the death of a loved one is such a painfully moving experience that it cannot be forgotten. It is only the birth metaphor that offers an idea of how joy can return. Whereas painful experiences otherwise take deep root in our memories, childbirth is able—not least because of the release of hormones (see above)—to make the most horrific events become almost irrelevant only a few hours later. Women who have given birth report that on the one hand there is no pain more intense and overwhelming than the pain of labor. On the other hand, the memory of this pain is completely transformed as soon as the woman holds the child in her arms. Through the actual birth the memory of pain is bathed in new light. The painful experience is not simply counter-balanced, the positive far exceeds the negative. Only along these lines is it possible to explain how women, despite traumatic pain and experiences (e.g., perineal tear), are repeatedly willing to have another child. The process of remembering becomes part of the process of a new evaluation. On the level of the reader of John 16:21, remembering is not suppressed, but repeated through negation. When the "no longer remembers" is mentioned, this does not drive the memory of the pain of birth from the mind of the reader, but rather draws them to the surface so as to reinforce them.

The birth motif also refers the reader back to John 3, a passage dealing with "birth from above" and "being born of water and spirit." Whereas in John 3 the spatial dimension is prominent (birth from above) and used to focus upon faith, in John 16:21 the temporal dimension is of primary significance. Yet, just as being born again must not be misunderstood as returning to the mother's womb, seeing Jesus again must not be transposed solely to the afterlife. It takes place in the here and now through the Paraclete, the Comforter, and for the one who believes, even if she or he does not (yet) see (John 20:29). This aspect becomes even more apparent and central in the following interpretation.

3.5.3 Feminist Interpretation

The parable tells a story about a woman. More than this, the woman becomes a mother and therefore represents one of the most fundamental characteristics which distinguishes women from men. For this reason it is all the more astonishing, that this woman has attracted relatively minimal attention, even in feminist Johannine scholarship. As Rushton proclaims: "There is a surprising lack of acknowledgement of the γυνή. The woman and her body all but disappear."[110]

110 Rushton, "Parables of Labour," 211.

This lack of acknowledgement is most striking with regard to the "hour." The motif of the "hour" evokes associations of the "hour of Jesus," which is a motif found throughout the Gospel (see above). However, a close examination of the text reveals that in John 16:21 the possessive pronoun relates the "hour" not to the child, but to the mother: *Her* hour has come (ἦλθεν ἡ ὥρα *αὐτῆς*). Yet, what is obvious with regard to the time dimension, namely that the future and the present aspect coincide, also happens with regard to the social dimension. The hour of the mother giving birth is at the same time the hour of the child being born. Therefore, though "the hour" in John is usually that of the Son, in childbirth, a son's hour is also the hour of his mother. For this reason, there is no need to play the feminist position against a christological reading of the "hour" motif. At the same time, this dual nature of the hour reveals that it should be noted and taken seriously that the "hour" is not an image solely reserved for Jesus, but includes others.

In this way the hour is taken up again in John 16:32: "The hour is coming, indeed it has come, when you will be scattered, each one to his home, and you will leave me alone." In this verse it is primarily the hour of the disciples, though still with reference to the hour of Jesus' death. The crucifixion is the reason why the disciples will be scattered. Once again, similar to the woman and the child in the parable, the "hour" has an "interrelational" function. It connects different persons, a reality which is demonstrated most clearly on the narrative level beneath the cross itself: it was in the hour of crucifixion when the beloved disciple was declared to be the "new son" of Jesus' mother and vice versa.[111]

From there, one recognizes even more obviously the allusions of the parable in John 16:21 to the *mother of Jesus.*[112] Along the lines of the manner in which we have read this parable christologically we may also read it with a view towards Mary. If the child coming into the world can be identified with Jesus, then evidently the laboring mother of this child must be the "mother of Jesus." It was in the controversy between Jesus and his mother at the wedding in Cana that the hour-motif was first introduced (John 2:4). Interestingly, Jesus, in his dialogue, does not address his mother by name "Mary" nor by her role as "mother." He simply states: τί ἐμοὶ καὶ σοί, *γύναι*; οὔπω ἥκει ἡ ὥρα μου (Joh 2:4). In the context of John 2, this surprising phrase might be explained as an expression creating greater distance between the son and his mother. However, in the light of John 16:21 it may also be a signal which bridges the opening scene in John 2 with the parable in the farewell discourse.

111 See Jean Zumstein, "The Mother of Jesus and the Beloved Disciple: How a New Family is Established Under the Cross," in S. A. Hunt et al., *Character Studies*, 641–45.

112 See Lieu, "Mother"; Mary L. Coloe, "The Mother of Jesus: A Woman Possessed," in S. A. Hunt et al., *Character Studies*, 202–213.

The birth motif, just like the mother motif, is located within a noticeable appreciation of women and their sphere of life in the Gospel of John.[113] On the one hand, numerous women appear in dialogue with Jesus, including the Samaritan woman (John 4), Martha (John 11), and Mary Magdalene (John 20), all of whom, in their encounters with Jesus, are of profound significance for the unfolding of Johannine Christology. On the other hand, the sphere of a woman's life often provides images for theological metaphors.[114] Drawing water (John 4:7–15; 7:37–38) was the task of women; baking bread (John 6) or washing feet can be conceived as the work of women; agricultural metaphors such as a grain of wheat (John 12:24), a vine (John 15:1–8), or a gate (John 10:7) are also borrowed from realms in which women played a significant role. Within this general attention to women and the female body "birthing imagery is important for the overall theology of the Fourth Gospel."[115]

4. Conclusion

Ultimately, the Fourth Gospel is not particularly interested in exploring feminist theology. Women, like men, are addressed as human beings, all of whom should be touched through the incarnational theology. This theology cannot be limited to the past or to sophisticated dogmatic confessions. It must be experienced emotionally and existentially in every aspect of life. The parable of the woman within the farewell discourse therefore reveals one other aspect of the narrative ethics in John. Characters invite the reader to follow their example and may serve as role models for the reader's own behavior.[116]

113 See the various aspects in Amy-Jill Levine and Marianne Blickenstaff, eds., *A Feminist Companion to John*, FCNTECW 2 (London: Sheffield Academic Press, 2003).

114 In the conversation with the Samaritan woman a multi-staged process of christological recognition takes places in that she refers to Jesus as a "Jewish man" (John 4:7–9), "husband/bridegroom" (John 4:16–18; see John 3:29), "prophet" (John 4:19), "Messiah" (John 4:25–26), and finally "Savior of the world" (John 4:42). For discussion, see Ruben Zimmermann, "From a Jewish Man to the Savior of the World. Narrative and Symbols Forming a Step by Step Christology in John 4,1–42," in *Studies in the Gospel of John and its Christology*, ed. Joseph Verheyden et al., BETL 265 (Leuven et al.: Peeters, 2014), 99–118. Martha's confession (John 11:27) is on a level with Peter's confession (John 6:69). Mary Magdalene is the first witness to the resurrection in the Fourth Gospel (John 20:11–18). Concerning these encounters, see Ruth Habermann, "Das Evangelium nach Johannes: Orte der Frauen," in *Kompendium feministische Bibelauslegung*, ed. L. Schottroff and M.-Th. Wacker, 2nd ed. (Gütersloh: Gütersloher Verlagshaus, 1999), 527–541.

115 Solevåg, *Birthing Salvation*, 81.

116 See Ruben Zimmermann, "Narrative Ethik im Johannesevangelium am Beispiel der Lazarus-Perikope Joh 11," in *Narrativität und Theologie im Johannesevangelium*, ed. J. Frey and U. Poplutz, BThS 130 (Neukirchen-Vluyn: Neukirchener Theologie, 2012), 133–170; and now

One important aspect in this regard can be identified as the following: The process of coping with pain and crises, even when confronting death. The reader should be consoled, and it makes some sense to read the whole farewell discourse within the context of contemporary consolation literature.[117] This functions on different levels of the text, as already mentioned above. The disciples are to be consoled regarding the death and absence of Jesus; the addressees of the Gospel are to be consoled after being thrown out of the synagogue and experiencing persecution (John 16:2); the reader may be consoled in her or his different, yet similar situation.

Having this wide hermeneutical horizon in mind, the parable can be interpreted on the level of the narrow context and plot. In the verses surrounding John 16:21 one notes a parallelism which includes a contrast between grief and joy, and in particular the sudden shift from one extreme to the other.

Grief	Joy
20b ὑμεῖς *λυπη* θήσεσθε,	ἀλλ᾽ ἡ λύπη ὑμῶν εἰς *χαρὰν* γενήσεται.
21 ἡ γυνὴ ὅταν τίκτῃ *λύπην* ἔχει, ὅτι ἦλθεν ἡ ὥρα αὐτῆς·	ὅταν δὲ γεννήσῃ τὸ παιδίον, οὐκέτι μνημονεύει τῆς θλίψεως διὰ τὴν *χαρὰν* ὅτι ἐγεννήθη ἄνθρωπος εἰς τὸν κόσμον.
22 καὶ ὑμεῖς οὖν νῦν μὲν *λύπην* ἔχετε·	πάλιν δὲ ὄψομαι ὑμᾶς, καὶ χαρήσεται ὑμῶν ἡ καρδία, καὶ τὴν *χαρὰν* ὑμῶν οὐδεὶς αἴρει ἀφ᾽ ὑμῶν.

In v. 20b and v. 22 it is the disciples who are addressed, allowing and even inviting a metaphoric interaction between the disciples and the woman giving birth. The woman serves as a role-model for the addressees. The present grief of the disciples can and should be turned into joy, in the same manner as the woman's emotions change during the process of giving birth.

Within the broader context one can also state that just as the birth is the physical separation between woman and infant, the pain of the disciples described in John 16 is the pain of separation at the departure of Jesus. The depth of the comparison is striking: whereas the physical connection between mother and child is more intense prior to the birth, the child ultimately is a stranger within one's own body. The mother feels the child's presence but can ultimately only vaguely perceive who is living in her body. Despite the closest proximity, the true shape and form of her child remains hidden. Only through, or rather after, the

Fredrik Wagener, "Figuren als Handlungsmodelle" (Diss. Johannes Gutenberg-Universität Mainz 2015).

117 See Manfred Lang, "Johanneische Abschiedsreden und Senecas Konsolationsliteratur. Wie konnte ein Römer Joh 13,31–17,26 lesen?" in *Kontexte des Johannesevangeliums: Das vierte Evangelium in religions- und traditionsgeschichtlicher Perspektive*, ed. J. Frey and U. Schnelle, WUNT 175 (Tübingen: Mohr Siebeck, 2004), 365–412.

birth can the child be recognized, that is, be seen by the mother. Only now can a social relationship emerge and be formed in which two individuals are brought into contact face to face. The disciples are confronted with the same reality. Jesus has always been with them, but they have not seen him as he truly is (John 14:9: "Have I been with you all this time and you still do not know me?"). Only in the departure and only in the pain of the separation at the hour of the cross can the disciples truly come to know and recognize Jesus. Cutting the "cord" of the physical symbiosis opens their eyes to see the Christ. Only now can a new, believing relationship with Jesus come into existence and grow. In this way one arrives at the specific, Johannine mode of vision: the christological "seeing as …".[118]

One is reminded of the encounter between Mary Magdalene and the risen Jesus. Mary is not to cling to him (John 20:17). The physical dimension thus recedes to the background, but she recognizes him and can tell the disciples: "I have seen the Lord" (John 20:18). Though birth creates distance, this crisis is in this way transformed into a new beginning in faith and even more fundamentally, in life itself.[119]

In this way the christological, eschatological, and feminist dimensions can be integrated after all. The christological birth parable reveals, once again, how becoming truly human according to the theology of John is possible. He who has come into the world makes it possible for every man or woman to come into the world. This, after all, is already found in the equivocal statement of the prologue about "[t]he true light, which enlightens everyone, [who] is coming into the world" (John 1:9).

118 Franz Mussner, *Die Johanneische Sehweise und die Frage nach dem historischen Jesus*, QD 28 (Freiburg im Breisgau: Herder, 1965); see also Zimmermann, *Christologie der Bilder*, 45–60 ("Verstehen im Sehen").

119 See Lee, *Flesh and Glory*, 80, in particular with regard to „the significance of the crucifixion as life-giving." More generally and concerning a "birthing Theology and Ministry" in pastoral practice see Hammer, *Giving Birth*, 153–214.

Kasper Bro Larsen

The Recognition Scenes and Epistemological Reciprocity in the Fourth Gospel

... a lover's eyes are so quick to recognize the object of their love (ὀξὺ γάρ τι πρὸς ἐπίγνωσιν ἐρωτικῶν ὄψις) (Heliodorus, *Aethiopica* 7.7 [Morgan])

1. Introduction: Reciprocity in the Gospel of John[1]

Commentators, ancient and modern, have seldom failed to notice how reciprocity language permeates the Fourth Gospel. In modern exegetical scholarship, interest has focused on understanding the historical background and the theological significance of the so-called immanence formulae (e.g., "Abide in me as I abide in you" [John 15:4, NRSV]).[2] Whatever the solution to these historical and theological problems, the Johannine language of reciprocity describes a mutual *ontological* indwelling of different entities (e.g., 10:30; 14:20; 15:4; 17:11, 22) as well as an *ethical* practice of exchange and redistribution (e.g., 13:34; 15:4–5, 10, 12). It includes the Father in relation to the Son (the horizontal divine–divine relation), the Father or Son in relation to the disciples (the vertical divine–human relation), and the individual disciples in relation to each other (the horizontal human–human relation). Thus Jesus prays, "As you, Father, are in me and I am in you, may they also be in us" (John 17:21).

The ontological and ethical aspects of Johannine reciprocity language are obvious. In scholarly literature, however, less attention has been paid to the *epistemological* aspect concerning the exchange of mutual knowledge between

1 Parts of this article have been presented at the following conferences: *The Gospel of John as Genre Mosaic* (June 26, 2014; Aarhus University), *The Society of Biblical Literature Annual Meeting* (November 22, 2014; San Diego), and *The Nordic New Testament Conference* (May 29, 2015; Aarhus University). I wish to thank the participants for valuable questions and comments, especially Ole Jakob Filtvedt, Geurt Henk van Kooten, and Tyler Smith.

2 Rudolf Schnackenburg, "Zu den joh. Immanenzformeln," in idem, *Die Johannesbriefe*, HThKNT (Freiburg: Herder, 1963), 105–110; Fernando F. Segovia, *The Farewell of the Word: The Johannine Call to Abide* (Minneapolis: Fortress, 1991); Klaus Scholtissek, *In ihm sein un bleiben: Die Sprache der Immanenz in den johanneischen Schriften*, HbS 21 (Freiburg: Herder, 2000).

God/the Son and "his own."[3] It is the purpose of this paper to show (1) that reciprocity language is a key to understanding the theological epistemology of the Gospel, and (2) that this key is found in both the Gospel's prologue, its discourses and in the recognition type-scenes where the Johannine principle of reciprocity is illustrated and dramatized.[4] The Gospel bends the ancient micro-genre of the recognition type-scene in order for it to serve as a vehicle of the theological epistemology of the Gospel. We shall begin with a brief survey of the recognition type-scene.

2. Reciprocal Recognition Scenes in Ancient Literature

The Gospel of John is, like other ancient literary works such as Homer's *Odyssey* and Heliodorus' *Aethiopica*, a narrative that progresses in a series of recognition type-scenes focusing on the disclosure of the identity of one or more characters. Often the recognition scene is an encounter between a main character with a secret identity and other characters who are put to the test by this epistemological challenge.[5] Whereas some characters fail to identify the main character in disguise, others experience a sudden or gradual anagnorisis (ἀναγνώρισις/ἀναγνωρισμός, i.e., recognition, identification, or discovery). In Aristotle's *Poetics*, anagnorisis was one of the key concepts, defined as motion from ignorance to knowledge (ἐξ ἀγνοίας εἰς γνῶσιν μεταβολή; *Poet.* 11 [1452a29–30]). According to Aristotle, anagnorisis is the storyteller's most effective means of moving the audience (ψυχαγωγεῖ; *Poet.* 6 [1450a31–34]). Suspense is unbearable when the audience watches the story characters acting in blindness and then finally real-

3 Influential exegetes of the 20th century, however, did of course notice this aspect. Rudolf Bultmann, for example, drew attention to "die Formeln, in denen das Verhältnis zwischen Jesus und den Seinen als ein gegenseitiges *γινώσκειν* beschrieben wird (10,2f.14f.27)," idem, *Theologie des Neuen Testaments*, NTGr (Tübingen: J. C. B. Mohr [Paul Siebeck], 1953), 431. C. H. Dodd concurred: "It is to be observed that there is an obviously intentional parallelism between expressions used regarding the mutual indwelling, and the mutual knowledge, of God (Christ) and men." (Idem, *The Interpretation of the Fourth Gospel* [Cambridge: Cambridge University Press, 1953], 187 with a clarifying illustrative chart on the same page). See also, Scholtissek, *In ihm sein und bleiben*, 166–169.

4 In my book on Johannine recognition scenes, I briefly touched upon the reciprocity motif in Johannine epistemology, the subject that I am trying to develop here. See Kasper Bro Larsen, *Recognizing the Stranger: Recognition Scenes in the Gospel of John*, BIS 93 (Leiden: Brill, 2008), 109, 223.

5 This is the main argument in Larsen, *Recognizing the Stranger*. In terms of genre theory, I am not analyzing Johannine encounter episodes with the purpose of identifying them as recognition type-scenes once and for all; rather, the aim is, by means of comparative genre criticism, to understand how John's Gospel—at the same time a unique and a conventional text—would communicate in an ancient literary context where recognition scenes were both a common type-scene and an object of discussion in literary theory.

izing what they did not know, whether this vital knowledge is of a positive kind (e.g., in Homer's *Odyssey*) or of a negative kind (e.g., in Sophocles, *Oedipus tyrannus* or Euripides, *Bacchae*). No wonder that recognition scenes became part of the storyteller's standard repertory in ancient Greco-Roman narrative and drama, especially in epic, novel, tragedy, and comedy.[6]

In the *Poetics*, Aristotle conceived of genres as categories by analogy with the species of nature, thus also dividing anagnorisis into various forms and subcategories. One interesting distinction in terms of reciprocity is his differentiation between unilateral and bilateral or double recognitions.

> Now, because recognition is recognition between people, some cases involve only the relation of one party to the other (when the other's identity is clear), while in others there is need for double recognition [ἀμφοτέρους δεῖ ἀναγνωρίσαι]." (Aristotle, *Poetics* 11 [1452b3–5; Halliwell])

As regards "double recognition," Aristotle mentions one example: the mutual recognition between two of King Agamemnon's children, Orestes and Iphigenia (*Poet.* 11 [1452b5–8]; Euripides, *Iphigenia in Tauris* 727–841). Iphigenia, having survived her fate as human sacrifice to the goddess Artemis, is serving as a local priestess in Tauris when Orestes appears on stage. Unwittingly she gives her identity away so that Orestes is free to reveal his, leading to reunion between the siblings. However, examples abound. In the dramas about Orestes and his other sister Electra, he returns from exile in order to find Electra in a state of despair. Orestes nevertheless recognizes her as she mourns their father's death at his tomb. Orestes seeks to convince his sister of his identity by means of different recognition tokens—and eventually succeeds, yet in quite different ways depending on which playwright one consults (Aeschylus, *Choephori* 212–45; Sophocles, *Electra* 1126–1231; Euripides, *Electra* 487–595). In Chariton's novel *Chaereas and Callirhoe* from around the turn of the Common Era, the hero's voice is the token that facilitates a short and touching reciprocal recognition: "Before he had finished speaking, Callirhoe recognized his voice and threw the covering from her face. They both cried out at the same time: 'Chaereas!' 'Callirhoe!'" (Chariton, *Chaer.* 8.1.7 [Reardon]).[7] These examples suggest that in ancient narrative and drama, mutual recognition is a device used to expose the mutual love of the characters. It intensifies the moment of reunion for characters

6 For further examples of anagnorisis and the recognition type-scene in ancient (and modern) literary theory and practice, see Larsen, *Recognizing*, 25–72 and Terence Cave, *Recognitions: A Study in Poetics* (Oxford: Clarendon, 1988). Recognition scenes, of course, also appear in the Hebrew Bible and the Septuagint (see, e.g., Gen 27; 42–45; Tob 12).

7 Other examples of mutual recognitions (with some modification) are Homer, *Od.* 13.187–351; Euripides, *Ion* 1369–1605; Xenophon Ephesius, *Ephesiaca*, 5.13; Heliodorus, *Aeth.* 2.5–6; 5.11; 7.7.

with particularly strong mutual emotional attachment. In anagnorisis of this kind, recognition is not only *reflective* self-recognition (as in the *Oedipus tyrannus*, for instance), or unilaterally *transitive* recognition of another character (as in most recognitions in the *Odyssey*, for instance), but a *reciprocal* event where the characters embrace each other as subject/object and object/subject, recognizer and recognized.

3. Reciprocal Recognition Scenes in the Gospel of John

When turning to the Gospel of John, one might expect the recognition scenes of this text to be unilateral and transitive since Jesus is the primary object of belief and recognition in the Gospel. He is the main character whose divine identity (δόξα or λόγος) is disguised by his human appearance (σάρξ; 1:14). However, as we shall see in the following paragraphs, a considerable number of Johannine recognition scenes have a reciprocal structure. Not only Jesus's identity, but also the identities of the secondary characters are revealed when they encounter Jesus. We shall first discuss the three main examples (3.1–3 below) before we turn to additional recognition scenes in John (3.4 below). The first main example is Jesus's calling of his disciples in John 1.

3.1 The Recognition Catena of John 1:35–51

In John 1:35–51, the call narratives known from the synoptic tradition have transformed into a chain of recognition scenes. Whereas the Synoptics thematize obedience and willingness to leave mundane life behind and follow Jesus (Mark 1:16–20 par.), John concentrates on processes of identification. As regards identification, John 1:35–51 contains clear reciprocal elements. The text is a sequence of four meetings between Jesus and his first disciples, and it can be divided into two parallel sections, each beginning with a temporal marker (τῇ ἐπάυριον; "the next day"; 1:35, 43), in the following manner:

Section One (1:35–42)	Section Two (1:43–51)
1.a. Jesus's arrival "the next day." Jesus meets John the Baptist with two of his disciples. John the Baptist recognizes Jesus (vv. 35–36)	2.a. Jesus's arrival "the next day." Jesus goes to Galilee and meets Philip (v. 43a)[8]

8 In light of the close parallelism between the two sections, I assume that Jesus, not Simon Peter/Cephas is the subject of the first two finite verbs in v. 43 before Jesus is explicitly mentioned as the subject of the third finit verb.

(Continued)

Section One (1:35–42)	Section Two (1:43–51)
1.b. The first meeting. Jesus with John the Baptist's two disciples (vv. 37–40)	2.b. The third meeting. Jesus with Philip (vv. 43b–44)
1.c. The disciple's departure. Andrew, one of the two disciples, informs his brother Simon (v. 41)	2.c. The disciple's departure. Philip informs Nathanael (vv. 45–46)
1.d. The return. Andrew brings Simon Peter to Jesus (v. 42a)	2.d. The return. Nathanael goes to Jesus (v. 47a)
1.e. The second meeting. Jesus with Simon Peter/Cephas (v. 42b–e)	2.e. The fourth meeting. Jesus with Nathanael (vv. 47b–51)

Reciprocal recognition can be said to take place in all four meetings, but the final climactic meetings with Nathanael (2.e.; vv. 47b–51) is the clearest example. Though Jesus is the primary character in focus, the meeting begins by turning the roles around so that Jesus in the first instance acts as the observer recognizing the disciple. Nathanael is instantly identified by Jesus as "an Israelite in whom there is no deceit" (v. 47). In other words, before Nathanael gets the opportunity to recognize Jesus, he identifies him. This also applies, albeit in a less explicit fashion, to the first three meetings in the two sections, i. e., the meeting with John the Baptist's two disciples (1.b.; vv. 37–40), the meeting with Simon (1.e.; v. 42b–e), and the meeting with Philip (2.c.; vv. 45–46). When John the Baptist's disciples turn to follow Jesus, his first words to them are, "What are you looking for [τί ζητεῖτε]?" (1:38)—which is in fact the first statement by Jesus in the whole Gospel. The question is not one of surprise or ignorance, but is a rhetorical question indicating how Jesus diagnoses the conditions of the human heart.[9] As such it is comparable to Jesus's question to the sick man at the pool of Bethzatha, "Do you want to be made well?" (5:7) and his words to Mary Magdalene, "Whom are you looking for [τίνα ζητεῖς]?" (20:15; see also 21:5).

The meeting with Simon displays a similar structure. Jesus lays his eyes on Simon (ἐμβλέψας; 1:42) and instantaneously recognizes him: "You are [σὺ εἶ] Simon son of John. You are to be called Cephas" (v. 42). Jesus knows of Simon's old identity and origin and creates a new identity for him. In Jesus's subsequent meeting with Philip there may also be a first move of recognition by Jesus since the text does not only report that the two meet but states that Jesus "finds [εὑρίσκει]" Philip (1:43a). In John, εὑρίσκω sometimes carries cognitive connotations so that "finding" also becomes "spiritual finding" (1:41b, 45b; 18:38;

9 The introduction of τίνα ζητεῖτε in 18:4 accentuates that Jesus is not asking out of ignorance: "Jesus, knowing all that was to happen to him, came forward and asked them: 'Whom are you looking for [τίνα ζητεῖτε]?'" (cf. 18:7).

19:4, 6 in contrast to 1:41a, 43b).[10] When interpreted in this manner, even the meeting with Philip begins with Jesus's recognition of the disciple—not the other way around.

As we have seen, Jesus is the first to recognize during the encounters in 1:35–51: He addresses John the Baptist's disciples with a maieutic question, he identifies Simon by name and gives him a new identity, he "finds" Philip, and he knows Nathanael even before they meet. These recognitions by Jesus, however, are not examples of anagnorisis in exactly the same manner as in the abovementioned examples from Greco-Roman literature. Jesus obviously does not move from ignorance to knowledge, suddenly realizing whom he has met, but his words and actions rather represent his insightful identification of the disciples as well as his social recognition and calling of them. He confers upon them a new identity of discipleship.[11] Jesus's omniscience—one of his most projected characteristics in John (see, e.g., 2:24; 16:30; 18:4)—changes the conditions of the mutual recognition.[12] It creates an asymmetry that we do not find in the bilateral recognitions of Greco-Roman literature, where the two actors are equally ignorant to begin with. Jesus, though participating in a mutual recognition scene, does not experience a process of coming-to-know in the manner of the disciples since Jesus's omniscience precludes further realization. His recognition of others is an act of acknowledgment—which at the same time serves as a revelation and a token of his own divine identity.

This becomes clear when we look at the recognitions in 1:35–51 from the disciples' point of view. How do they recognize Jesus? Again, the final meeting with Nathanael's recognition of Jesus is the most developed example. Nathanael recognizes Jesus when realizing that Jesus, in spite of never having met Nathanael before in person, is able to identify Nathanael on the basis of extraordinary knowledge. This prompts Nathanael to ask: "Where did you get to know me [πόθεν με γινώσκεις]?" (v. 48). Judging from Nathanael's reaction, he is soon convinced that Jesus (by knowing that he was "under the fig tree") possesses knowledge that is not accessible to any man. Nathanael confesses his new insight with a "you are" formula (σὺ εἶ; v. 49), well-known from other ancient recognition scenes (see John 1:42; 4:19; Homer, *Od.* 3.122; 19.474), and he takes the

---

10 This is a common feature in the language of the Jewish wisdom tradition (see, e.g., Job 11:7; 28:12; Prov 8:17; Eccl 3:11; 8:17; Sir 6:18; Wisd 13:6, 9). The related verb ζητέω ("to search") may evoke similar connotations (e.g., John 1:38; 16:19; 20:15).

11 Anagnorisis in ancient Greek contains both a cognitive and a social dimension; it is both *Wiedererkennung* (identification) and *Anerkennung* (social acknowledgment/honor).

12 On Jesus's omniscience in John, see R. Alan Culpepper, *Anatomy of the Fourth Gospel: A Study in Literary Design* (Philadelphia: Fortress, 1983), 22, 108–10 and Kasper Bro Larsen, "Narrative Docetism: Christology and Storytelling in the Gospel of John," in *The Gospel of John and Christian Theology*, ed. Richard Bauckham and Carl Mosser (Grand Rapids: Eerdmans 2008), 346–355.

Rabbi title given to Jesus by John the Baptist's disciples in v. 38 to a higher level: "Rabbi, you are [σὺ εἶ] the Son of God! You are [σὺ … εἶ] the King of Israel!" (1:49). We shall return to Jesus's knowledge as a recognition token below.

The recognition scenes appearing before the Nathanael episode in John 1:35–51 narrate reciprocal recognition in a similar manner. Jesus acts; the disciples react. Andrew, one of John the Baptist's disciples, proclaims that Jesus is the Messiah (v. 41) after Jesus has revealed what he knows of Andrew. And Philip regards Jesus as the one who has been promised by Moses and the prophets (v. 45) after having been found by Jesus himself. In the episode featuring Peter (1.e. in the chart above; v. 42), however, only Jesus's unilateral recognition of Peter is mentioned explicitly. Considering the parallelism illustrated in the chart above, the scene appears as a torso implying a reverse recognition. In the present context, Peter is not said to have confessed his belief the way the other disciples do; but the fact that Peter in the course of the narrative follows Jesus, confesses his faith and love (6:69; 21:15–19), and becomes a key figure among the disciples even in the Fourth Gospel with its preference for the Beloved Disciple shows that Peter's process of recognition started at this point. Thus, Jesus's meeting with Peter, which concludes the first section in the recognition catena (1.e.), seems to imply a reciprocal recognition like the one between Jesus and the other disciples.

The chain of recognitions in John 1:35–51 is a quite peculiar example of Johannine genre bending. The synoptic call narratives have become recognition scenes of the reciprocal kind. However, they are not quite conventional. John's Christology creates an important asymmetry between the two recognizers: an asymmetry with a particular message to which we shall return. Now it is important to notice that in the first encounter between Jesus and his own, his recognition of them precedes their recognition of him.

3.2 The Samaritan Woman: Betrothal Scene and Reciprocal Recognition Scene (4:4–42)

In the course of John's narrative, Jesus's meeting with the Samaritan woman at the well in Sychar is the next main example of a reciprocal recognition scene. In Johannine studies, there has been a tendency to read the meeting as a scene evoking betrothal or courtship type-scenes from the Hebrew Bible. However, the pericope with its interest in hidden identities certainly also participates in the game played by ancient recognition type-scenes.[13] The woman apparently never

13 Identity comes to the fore in, for example, the following remarks in the dialogue: "If you knew … who it is that is saying to you, 'Give me a drink'" (v. 10) and "Are you greater than our ancestor Jacob?" (v. 12). For more examples, see Larsen, *Recognizing the Stranger*, 124–41.

reaches full recognition—in contrast to the Samaritans in vv. 39–42—but she gives voice to identifications of Jesus that climb toward a climax: Jewish man (v. 9), prophet (v. 19), and Messiah (v. 29). Her recognition of him as a prophet in v. 19 belongs to a reciprocal event of recognition because it is instigated by Jesus's preceding disclosure of his special knowledge of her: "You are right in saying, 'I have no husband'; for you have had five husbands, and the one you have now is not your husband. What you have said is true!" (4:17–18). Scholars who understand the pericope as a betrothal scene often see this place in the dialogue as the point where erotic innuendo between Jesus and the woman is left behind,[14] but from an anagnorisis perspective this is a romantic motif from contemporary reciprocal recognition scenes, once again bent in the fashion we have seen in, for example, the Nathanael episode. This is confirmed by the content of the woman's testimony to the Samaritans: "Many Samaritans from the city believed in him because of [διὰ] the woman's testimony, 'He told me everything I have ever done'." (v. 39; see also v. 29). Jesus's recognition of the woman prompts her—and the other Samaritans'—nascent understanding of his identity.

3.3 Jesus and Mary Magdalene—and Vice Versa (20:11–18)

Mary Magdalene's meeting with the risen Lord is the third main example of a reciprocal recognition scene in the Fourth Gospel. Before Mary understands that the apparent gardener is her rabbi, he identifies her. As in the meeting with John the Baptist's disciples (1:38), Jesus first approaches Mary with a telling question that expresses his compassion and understanding of her distress: "Woman, why are you weeping? Whom are you looking for?" (20:15). However, the question does not lead to instant recognition of Jesus on Mary's behalf. Instead, Jesus now further pins down her identity. His identification of Mary is narrated in a very compact manner, simply by mention of her proper name: "Jesus said to her, 'Mary!'" (20:16).[15] The name is a token of Jesus's knowledge, even though it is not extraordinary knowledge in this case since Jesus has in fact met Mary before (19:25). By telling her name, Jesus reveals his close knowledge of her, and *that* is the recognition token in the story. As in the previous examples, Jesus's recognition of the other character is the way to human recognition of Jesus.[16]

14 Lyle Eslinger, "The Wooing of the Woman at the Well: Jesus, the Reader and Reader-Response Criticism," *Literature and Theology* 1 (1987): 179.

15 The exclamation of the proper name at the moment of recognition is a regular feature in recognition scenes. See, e.g., Homer, *Od.* 23.209; Euripides, *Hel.* 625; Chariton, *Chaer.* 8.1.8.

16 On John 20:11–18 as recognition scene, see Larsen, *Recognizing the Stranger*, 196–205.

3.4 Other Recognition Scenes, Potentially Reciprocal

Jesus's encounters with disciples (1:35–51), with the Samaritan woman (4:4–42), and with Mary Magdalene (20:11–18) all reveal an obvious pattern of reciprocity in Johannine recognition scenes. In light of these scenes, I shall argue that this pattern is a relatively consistent feature in the Johannine recognition scenes as such, even where it is not as explicit as in the above-mentioned examples.

If we turn back to the Gospel's first chapter, Jesus's appearance to John the Baptist by the Jordan displays recognition scene features (1:29–34).[17] In John, Jesus's baptism is not recounted per se, and the Spirit's primary function thus becomes not to equip Jesus with divine powers that he as the *Logos* already possesses, but to serve as a recognition token that enables John the Baptist to identify the Lamb of God among the people gathered at the river. This recognition, at first sight, is unilateral (John the Baptist identifies Jesus), but in the Baptist's explanatory words concerning the Spirit, we hear of events that took place before his recognition of Jesus: "I myself did not know him [οὐκ ᾔδειν], but the one who sent me to baptize with water said to me, 'He on whom you see the Spirit descend and remain is the one who baptizes with the Holy Spirit'" (1:33). Before John the Baptist even knew Jesus, he was appointed by God and received a revelation giving him the necessary competence to recognize Jesus. The Father appointed John the Baptist; John the Baptist pointed out the Son.

Jesus's second sign, the healing of the official's son (4:46–54), is a miracle story that can reasonably be held up against the recognition type-scene since it contains some of its recurrent features, not least a final coming-to-know (vv. 50, 53). What brings about the belief of the officer and his household is obviously the healing, the *sēmeion*—which is in fact the technical term that Aristotle used for recognition tokens (*Poet.* 16 [1454b20]). But Jesus's preceding comment may also play a role in light of our previous observations: "Unless you see signs and wonders you will not believe" (John 4:48). Scholars have discussed with great intensity whether one should understand this statement as a negative reproach or a neutral ascertainment, but perhaps the most important message of the words is that they reveal Jesus's insight into the hearts and minds of the officer and his entourage, thus once again depicting Jesus as the proactive recognizer. Human recognition of Jesus presupposes his recognition of humans.

The healing of the man born blind in John 9 is perhaps the most artistic and playful of the Johannine recognition scenes. The major part of the chapter deals with the true identity of the healed man (9:8–34), and only secondarily with the identity of Jesus, until Jesus re-enters the stage in v. 35.[18] The *Ioudaioi*, who

17 Larsen, *Recognizing the Stranger*, 96–103.
18 Larsen, *Recognizing the Stranger*, 150–63.

investigate the healed man's identity, are not able to understand who he is without the parents' testimony. Jesus, on the other hand, "sees" the man (cf. εἶδεν in 9:1) and knows of his past and his blindness ("Neither this man nor his parents sinned; he was born blind so that God's work might be revealed in him," 9:3) And when Jesus reappears after the healing, he recognizes the man right away: "Jesus heard that they had driven him out, and when he found him [εὑρὼν αὐτὸν], he said, 'Do you believe in the Son of Man?'" (9:35). As in the encounter with Philip in 1:43, εὑρίσκω probably conveys the deeper meaning of spiritual or intellectual unification. This "finding" of the healed man by Jesus, along with Jesus's self-proclamation in v. 37, brings the healed man to his confession of faith in v. 38. Jesus, the light of the world, "saw" (v. 1) the blind man, and the blind man "came back able to see" (v. 7).[19]

Finally, Jesus's appearances to the disciples in chs. 20–21, besides the encounter with Mary Magdalene in 20:11–18, also contain reciprocal elements. In 20:19–23 Jesus appears to the disciples, who hide behind locked doors "for fear of the Jews" (20:19a). Jesus apparently knows of their fear since he comforts them by his greeting: "Peace be with you" (20:19b). These words of divine insight, together with other signs, prompt their joyful recognition of him (20:20). Next, the climactic recognition scene of the Gospel, where Thomas is confronted with Jesus's wound marks and confesses him to be Lord and God (20:28), begins when Jesus reveals his insightful knowledge of Thomas. Jesus knows that Thomas wishes to touch the risen Lord and instructs him not to doubt but to believe (20:27). The wound marks are not the only tokens enabling Thomas's belief; Jesus's recognition of Thomas is itself a complementary token prompting anagnorisis.

The meeting at Lake Tiberias in ch. 21 is the final recognition scene of the Gospel in its canonical shape. As in "the race to the tomb" between the Beloved Disciple and Simon Peter in 20:1–10, the anonymous disciple is the first to understand also in this scene: "It is the Lord!" (21:7). What causes the Beloved Disciple to recognize Jesus is of course the miraculous catch of fish, but as in the healing of the official's son in 4:46–54, a word of recognition by Jesus precedes the sign. In John 21, the word of recognition is the following remark: "Children [παιδία], you have no fish, have you?" (21:5). Jesus not only knows of the disciples' night of futile fishing, but also recognizes them by evoking paternal, familial language as he has previously done in the Farewell Discourse: "Little children [τεκνία], I am with you only a little longer (13:33; cf., 1:12; 11:52; 1 John 2:1, 12, 28; 3:7, 18; 4:4; 5:21; 2 John 1:1, 4). Thus, Jesus's final encounters with the disciples, as well as the first ones in 1:35–51, are recognition scenes that contain

19 According to text witnesses like Papyrus 75 and Codex Sinaiticus* which do not contain John 9:38–39a, the man born blind apparently never confesses or demonstrates his faith. For the man's view of Jesus, see also 9:17, 33.

reciprocal elements. The scenes more or less explicitly show that Jesus is recognized on the basis of his recognition of others.[20]

4. The Shepherd Discourse: A Johannine Poetics of Epistemological Reciprocity

As we have now seen, Johannine recognition scenes show remarkable consistency in terms of epistemological reciprocity. Secondary characters recognize Jesus when he recognizes them. However, this structure is not only a recurrent narrative phenomenon played out in scene after scene. It also appears as an epistemological programme in Johannine discourses, especially in the Shepherd Discourse: "I am the good shepherd. I know my own and my own know me, just as the Father knows me and I know the Father" (10:14–15a). Since there is no trace of interruption between chs. 9 and 10 in the text, the Shepherd Discourse appears in direct continuation with a recognition scene, i. e., the healing of the man born blind (ch. 9). The Shepherd Discourse is, in other words, an interpretation of that scene, just as we may find "theoretical" reflections (concerning the truth status of knowledge obtained) in conjunction with recognition scenes proper in, e. g., Euripides' *Electra* (487–595) and Heliodorus' *Aethiopica* (10.10–17).

According to the above quotation from the Shepherd Discourse, there is an intimate connection between the shepherd's knowledge of the sheep and vice versa. However, modern translations like the NRSV do not translate this difficult passage, loaded with instances of καί, with necessary sensitivity. In light of what we have seen above concerning reciprocity in Johannine recognition scenes, some of these instances of καί would benefit from being interpreted as examples of *καί consecutivum* (see also John 2:19; 7:34, 36; 8:59; 12:40; 3 John 14).[21] That would render the following translation:

> I am the good shepherd; and I know my own, *so* my own know me, just as the Father knows me, *so* I know the Father [Ἐγώ εἰμι ὁ ποιμὴν ὁ καλὸς καὶ γινώσκω τὰ ἐμὰ καὶ γινώσκουσί με τὰ ἐμά, καθὼς γινώσκει με ὁ πατὴρ κἀγὼ γινώσκω τὸν πατέρα] (John 10:14–15a, my emphasis)

20 There are, of course, exceptions to this tendency in the Gospel. In some of the encounters between Jesus and other characters in the story-world, Jesus recognizes them without it prompting an equivalent response on their behalf (3:10; 5:6, 14 [in spite of 5:15]; 6:26). And some human characters apparently recognize Jesus without it being preceded by his explicit recognition of them (6:16–21; 11:27).

21 On *καί consecutivum*, see Friedrich Blass, Albert Debrunner, and Friedrich Rehkopf, *Grammatik des neutestamentlichen Griechisch*, 16. ed. (Göttingen: Vandenhoeck & Ruprecht, 1984), § 442.2, p. 367.

The suggested translation highlights that epistemological reciprocity in John is established in a specific order, i. e., through divine initiative, just as the recognition scenes in the narrative illustrate, one by one. Such reciprocity seems to represent a Johannine development of a phenomenon that we may coin "covenantal epistemology," i. e., the Jewish theological idea that God knows human beings before they know him. Covenantal epistemology is virtually omnipresent in the Hebrew Bible (e. g., Num 16:5; Pss 44:22; 69:6; 139:1–6)[22] and also a recurrent element in the texts of the Christ movement (e. g., Matt 6:4, 6, 18; Luke 16:15; Acts 1:24; 15:8; Gal 4:9; 2 Tim 2:19; 1 John 3:20; *Odes Sol.* 9:12–14).[23] John's narrative of divine-human encounter seems to narrativize the idea by means of recognition scenes. In the Shepherd Discourse, the καθώς formula shows that the covenantal epistemological structure even appears in the relation between the Father and the Son, so that the epistemological relationship between the master and his disciples imitates the relation between the Father and the Son. Even in terms of knowledge, the disciples come to participate in the divine circumincession.

According to the Shepherd Discourse—and the recognition scenes that we have examined—the disciples (the sheep) know their master (the shepherd) through his knowledge of them. Interestingly, a similar mode of recognition (i. e., recognition prompted by the other person's knowledge) is discussed by Aristotle in his anagnorisis typology in *Poet.* 16 (1454b18–1455a12). There it is called recognition "through memory" (διὰ μνήμης; *Poet.* 1454b37), which is when a person's identity is revealed by his or her memory of things or facts that are only known by that particular person and by the recognizer.[24] One example, albeit a late one from the 3rd or 4th century CE, is the mutual recognition between the heroine Charikleia and her beloved Theagenes in Heliodorus's *Aethiopica*. At first, Theagenes does not recognize Charikleia in dirty and ragged clothes but believes she is a vagabond and even hits her to stop her from embracing him. But then she reveals her knowledge to Theagenes:

> "O Pythian," she whispered, "have you forgotten [οὐδε … μέμνησαι] the torch?" Her words pierced Theagenes' heart like an arrow, for he recognized [γνωρίσας] the torch as one of the signs [συμβόλων] that they had agreed upon. He gazed hard at Charikleia and

22 Scholtissek, *In ihm sein und bleiben*, 167–68.

23 "Covenantal epistemology" is epitomized in Paul's eschatological hope: "[T]hen I will know fully, even as I have been fully known [τότε δὲ ἐπιγνώσομαι καθὼς καὶ ἐπεγνώσθην]" (1 Cor 13:12b). The Gospel of Thomas apparently presents an alternative: "When you come to know yourselves, then you will become known" (*Gos. Thom.* 3; NHC II,*2* 32,26 [Lambdin]).

24 In his typology, Aristotle locates recognition "through memory" at the upper end of the scale, taking it to be one of the more artistic modes of anagnorisis. As examples, he refers to an unknown work (*Cyprians*) by the late 5th century tragedian Dicaeogenes and the recognition of Odysseus by Alcinous in Homer, *Od.* 8.521–22. However, a more famous example is Penelope's recognition of Odysseus by his knowledge of details concerning the wedding bed that he once crafted from an olive tree (Homer, *Od.* 23.172–208).

> was dazzled by the brilliance of her eyes, as if by a shaft of sunlight shining out between the clouds. He took her in his arms and held her tight. (Heliodorus, *Aeth.* 7.7 [Morgan])

It seems that recognition "through memory" is also an important aspect of Johannine epistemology, of course with the important addition that Jesus's special knowledge does not concern an arbitrary object or fact but is divine knowledge of the *identity* of his personal counterparts: "[H]e knew all people and needed no one to testify about anyone; for he himself knew what was in everyone" (2:24–25). Not only do the Shepherd Discourse and the recognition scenes confirm this, but Jesus's knowledge is also seen as his primary identity token by the disciples in the Farewell Discourse: "Now we know that you know all things, and do not need to have anyone question you; by this [ἐν τούτῳ] we believe that you came from God" (16:30). In other words, the disciples' belief is not merely an abstract theological affirmation of Jesus's paradoxical claims to divinity (*das Dass*), but is a response to their experience of "being seen." This recognition is sometimes gradual on the part of the human characters (for example, the Samaritan woman and the man born blind), but instantaneous with regard to Jesus. This ability of his to instantly recognize other characters is of course a divine attribute, but it also portrays him as a loving parent or a passionate lover vis-à-vis the recognition scenes, especially in the Greek romances. Notice how affection and recognition intertwine:

> When they saw each other [ἀλλήλους], they recognized each other at once [εὐθὺς ἀνεγνώρισαν], for that was their fervent desire [τοῦτο γὰρ αὐτοῖς ἐβούλοντο αἱ ψυχαί] (Xenophon Ephesius, *Eph.* 5.13.3 [Anderson])

> She was following hard on Kalasiris's heels and had recognized Theagenes from afar [πόρρωθεν ἀναγνωρίσασα]—for a lover's eyes are so quick to recognize the object of their love that often the mere movement of gesture, even if seen from a great distance or from behind, is enough to suggest an imaginary resemblance (Heliodorus, *Aeth.* 7.7 [Morgan])

> The one incontrovertible token of recognition … is maternal instinct, which, by the workings of an unspoken affinity [ἀπορρήτῳ συμπαθείᾳ], disposes the parent to feel affection [πάθος] for her child the instant she sets eye on it. Let us not deprive ourselves of the one thing that would make all the other tokens convincing [πιστὰ] (*Aeth.* 9.24 [Morgan])[25]

In these texts, mutual recognition happens rapidly between characters who share a mutual affection. Silvia Montiglio states that in some of the romances, "the couple's direct recognition of each other unfolds quickly and simply because

25 For earlier examples of instant recognition as illustration of close relationship see, e.g., Homer, *Od.* 17.300–304 (Odysseus' dog, Argos); Chariton, *Chaer.* 8.1.7–8 (Callirhoe); Luke 15:20 (the prodigal son's father).

lovers need no other proof of identity than their love."[26] Also in John, knowledge is not only a question of cognition, but also connotes an intimate relationship (see 17:3; 1 John 4:7–8).[27] Mutual recognition is a highly emotional motif, exploited by the Greek romances, and in John it illustrates the intimate relation between Jesus and his own. The shepherd calls his sheep "by name [κατ' ὄνομα]" (10:3; cf. 20:16) and thus acknowledges them, as in the naming of Simon Peter (Cephas) in 1:42 and of Mary Magdalene in 20:16. And as if by instinct, the sheep who are his own know his voice (10:3–5, 16, 27). Thus, God first "so loved the world" (3:16), and the *Beloved* Disciple is the first to recognize Jesus in chs. 20 and 21 (20:8; 21:7).

5. The Reader as Recognized Recognizer

In John's Gospel, covenantal epistemology is thematized in speeches and recognition scenes in the story-world. According to the famous purpose statement in 20:30, the reader is to adopt the same stance as the believers of the story-world, and thus story characters function as epistemological "orientation points" with which the reader may identify. The reader is supposed to see herself or himself as object and subject of recognition vis-à-vis Christ, as did story characters. But does the text, in a more direct manner, invite its implied reader to participate in the reciprocal recognition between God and human beings? At the discursive level of the Gospel (i. e., the direct communication between implied author and reader), the prologue is of special interest to us. From the very starting point, the prologue orchestrates an eureka moment for the reader by means of its riddle structure: The reader is introduced to a series of undefined roles (λόγος, θεός, ζωή, etc.) and pronouns (οὗτος; vv. 1–5) and is kept in suspense until the final exposure of the proper name (Jesus Christ) in v. 17. The reader's anagnorisis takes place in the prologue. The act of reading the whole gospel narrative thus becomes a processual confirmation and calibration of the initial recognition performed by the reader in the prologue.

26 Silvia Montiglio, *Love and Providence: Recognition in the Ancient Novel* (Oxford: Oxford University Press, 2012), 58.

27 Scholtissek rightly states, "Im JohEv bezeichnet γινώσκειν ‚ein zur Gemeinschaft führendes Kennen'. ‚Erkennen' meint das Gemeinschaft-Finden mit einer Person'. Im JohEv wird ‚erkennen' komplementär und teilweise auch isotop mit den Verben des … ‚lieben' verwendet"; idem, *In ihm sein un bleiben*, 169. Scholtissek quotes B. Kowalski, *Die Hirtenrede (Joh 10,1–18) im Kontext des Johannesevangeliums*, SBB 31 (Stuttgart: Katholisches Bibelwerk, 1996), 46 and R. Schnackenburg, *Das Johannesevangelium. III. Teil: Kommentar zu Kap. 13–21*, 2nd ed., HThKNT 4 (Freiburg: Herder, 1976), 76.

Recognition in the prologue, however, is not only about the reader as subject recognizing Jesus Christ as the *Logos.* It also communicates God's prior recognition of the reader as object. One of the prologue's many conundrums relates to the interpretation of the statement concerning the *Logos* as "the true light, which enlightens everyone [ὃ φωτίζει πάντα ἄνθρωπον]" (1:9; see also 3:20–21; 12:46). Considering the general dominance of covenantal epistemology in John, this may very well be the Gospel's first declaration of Jesus's ability to reveal the true identity of all humans, including the reader of the prologue. The prologue is, in other words, inviting the reader to see Jesus not only as a medium that enables humans to see God, but also the medium through which God looks upon human beings. And, as we have seen multiple times, the latter leads to the former. It is when human beings through Jesus's recognition realize who they are, that they may see the Father's light in Jesus's eyes. In 1:7, the prologue claims that John the Baptist came as a witness to the light, "so that all might believe by it [ἵνα πάντες πιστεύσωσιν δι' αὐτοῦ]" (my translation). Again, the light shines on everyone so that everyone may see the light. Thus in the prologue, the Gospel prepares its reader to be included (see 1:7: πάντες; 1:9: πάντα ἄνθρωπον) in the reciprocal recognition narrative of God and man that the story-world subsequently unfolds.

6. Conclusion

It has been the aim of this article to show how the Johannine language of reciprocity and mutual indwelling contains not only an ontological and an ethical aspect but also appears in John's theological epistemology ("covenantal epistemology"). In this respect, the Shepherd Discourse offers a principle—"I know my own, so my own know me (10:14, my translation)—which the Gospel elaborates upon and elucidates in a considerable number of recognition scenes. These recognition scenes have a reciprocal structure since secondary characters come to recognize Jesus on the basis of his knowledge and recognition of them (cf. Aristotle's concept of anagnorisis "through memory"). Even though Jesus does not move from ignorance to knowledge as characters normally do in recognition scenes, he initiates and participates in such scenes as the true recognizer. The recognition type-scene is not a straitjacket but a literary micro-genre by means of which John presents his vision of divine–human interaction. In John's Gospel, the reciprocity motif from contemporary recognition scenes serves to illustrate the fact that the relationship between Jesus and his own is one of mutual acknowledgment and love, a relationship that also, according to the prologue, may include the reader. The close affinity between mutual recognition, knowledge, and love in the Fourth Gospel thus permits a slight modification of a well-known Johannine maxim: "We recognize because he first recognized us" (cf. 1 John 4:19 and 1 John 3:16; 4:9–11).

Bibliography

Ancient Texts

Achilles Tatius. *Leucippe and Clitophon.* Translated by John J. Winkler. Pages 170–284 in *Collected Ancient Greek Novels.* Edited by B. P. Reardon. Berkeley: University of California Press, 1989.

Antiphon and Andocides. *Minor Attic Orators.* Translated by K. J. Maidment. Vol. 1. LCL 308. Cambridge: Harvard University Press, 1960.

Aristotle. *Athenian Constitution, Eudemian Ethics,* and *Virtues and Vices.* Translated by H. Rackham. LCL 285. Cambridge: Harvard University Press, 1935.

—. *Nicomachean Ethics.* Translated by H. Rackam. LCL 73. Cambridge: Harvard University Press, 1926.

—. *On Rhetoric: A Theory of Civic Discourse.* Translated by George A. Kennedy. 2nd ed. Oxford: Oxford University Press, 2007.

—. *On Sophistical Refutations, On Coming-to-Be and Passing-Away,* and *On the Cosmos.* Translated by E. S. Forster and D. J. Furley. LCL 400. Cambridge: Harvard University Press, 1955.

—. *Poetics.* Edited and translated by Stephen Halliwell. LCL 199. Cambridge: Harvard University Press, 1999.

—. *Poetics.* Translated by Anthony Kenny. Oxford: Oxford University Press, 2013.

—. *Poetics: Editio Maior of the Greek Text with Historical Introductions and Philological Commentaries.* Edited by Leonardo Tarán and Dimitri Gutas. Mnemosyne Supplements 338. Leiden: Brill, 2012.

—. *The Complete Works of Aristotle: The Revised Oxford Translation.* Edited by Jonathan Barnes. Bollingen Series 71/1–2. Princeton: Princeton University Press, 1984.

Augustine. *Tractates on the Gospel of John.* Translated by John W. Rettig. 5 vols. FC 78, 79, 88, 90, 92. Washington, D.C.: Catholic University of America Press, 1988–1994.

Callimachus. *Aetia: Volume 1: Introduction, Text, and Translation.* Edited by Annette Harder. Oxford: Oxford University Press, 2012.

Chariton. *Callirhoe.* Edited and Translated by G. P. Goold. LCL 481. Cambridge: Harvard University Press, 1995.

—. *Chaereas and Callirhoe.* Translated by B. P. Reardon. Pages 17–124 in *Collected Ancient Greek Novels.* Edited by B. P. Reardon. Berkeley: University of California Press, 1989.

Cicero. *On Invention, The Best Kind of Orator, Topics.* Translated by H. M. Hubbell. LCL 386. Cambridge: Harvard University Press, 1949.

Dead Sea Scrolls Study Edition, The. Edited by Florentino García Martínez and Eibert J.C. Tigchelaar. 2 vols. Leiden: Brill, 2000.

Demosthenes. *Speeches 60 and 61, Prologues, Letters.* Translated by Ian Worthington. Oratory of Classical Greece 10. Austin: University of Texas Press, 2006.

Dionysius of Halicarnassus. *On the Character of Thucydides.* Translated by S. Usher. LCL. Cambridge: Harvard University Press, 1974.

Dionysius of Halicarnassus. *Roman Antiquities.* Translated by Earnest Cary. 7 vols. LCL. Cambridge: Harvard University Press, 1960.

Gospel of Thomas. Translated by Thomas O. Lambdin. Pages 53–93 in *Nag Hammadi Codex* II, *2–7.* Edited by Bentley Layton. Nag Hammadi Studies 20. Leiden: Brill, 1989.

Heliodorus. *An Ethiopian Story.* Translated by J. R. Morgan. Pages 349–592 in *Collected Ancient Greek Novels.* Edited by B. P. Reardon. Berkeley: University of California Press, 1989.

—. *Les Éthiopiques (Théagène et Chariclée).* Edited by R. M. Rattenbury and T. W. Lumb. Translated by J. Maillon. 3 vols. 2nd ed. Collection des universités de France. Paris: "Les belles lettres," 1960.

Hermetica: The Corpus Hermeticum and the Latin Asclepius in a New English Translation. Translated by Brian Copenhaver. Cambridge: Cambridge University Press, 1992.

Herodotus. *The Persian Wars.* Translated by A. D. Godley. 4 vols. LCL 117–120. Cambridge: Harvard University Press, 1920–1925.

Homer. *Iliad 1.* Translated by Simon Pulleyn. Oxford: Oxford University Press, 2000.

Horace. *Satires, Epistles, Art of Poetry.* Translated by H. R. Fairclough. LCL. Cambridge: Harvard University Press, 1942.

Josephus. *The Jewish War: Books 1–3.* Translated by H. St. J. Thackeray. LCL. Cambridge: Harvard University Press, 1956.

Longinus. *On the Sublime.* Translated by W. Hamilon Fyfe. Revised by Donald A. Russell. LCL 199. Cambridge: Harvard University Press, 1995.

Midrash Rabbah: Exodus. Translated by S. M. Lehrman. Edited by Harry Freedman and Maurice Simon. 3 vols. London: Soncino, 1939.

Ovid. *Tristia* and *Ex Ponto.* Translated by Arthur Leslie Wheeler. LCL. Cambridge: Harvard University Press, 1939.

Philo, *Works.* Translated by F. H. Colson. 10 vols. LCL. Cambridge: Harvard University Press, 1935.

Philostratus, *The Life of Apollonius of Tyana.* Translated by Christopher Jones. LCL. Cambridge: Harvard University Press, 2005.

Plato. *The Republic.* Translated by Chris Emlyn Jones and William Preddy. LCL. Cambridge: Harvard University Press, 2013.

—. *The Republic.* Translated by Paul Shorey. 2 vols. LCL 237, 276. Cambridge: Harvard University Press, 1937, 1942.

Polybius, *Histories.* Translated by W. R. Paton. Revised by Frank W. Walbank and Christian Habicht. LCL 128. 6 vols. Cambridge: Harvard University Press, 2010–12.

Progymnasmata: Greek Textbooks of Prose Composition and Rhetoric. Translated by George A. Kennedy. WGRW 10. Atlanta: Society of Biblical Literature, 2003.

Pseudo-Augustine. "On Rhetoric: Additional Material." Pages 6–24 in *Readings in Medieval Rhetoric.* Edited by Joseph M. Miller, Michael H. Prosser, and Thomas W. Benson. Translated by Joseph M. Miller. Bloomington: Indiana University Press, 1973.

Scholia Graeca in Aeschylum quae exstant omnia. Edited by O. L. Smith. 2 vols. Leipzig: Teubner, 1976–82.

Soranus. *Gynecology.* Translated by O. Tempkin. Baltimore: The Johns Hopkins Press, 1956.

—. *Περ γυναικείων.* Translated by H. Lüneburg. München: Lehmann, 1894.

Stoicorum Veterum Fragmenta. Edited by Hans von Arnim. Stuttgart: Teubner, 1903–1924.

Thucydides. *History of the Peloponnesian War.* 4 vols. Translated by C. F. Smith. LCL 108–110, 169. Cambridge: Harvard University Press, 1919–1923.

Xenophon Ephesius. *An Ephesian Tale.* Translated by Graham Anderson. Pages 125–69 in *Collected Ancient Greek Novels.* Edited by B. P. Reardon. Berkeley: University of California Press, 1989.

—. *Les Éphésiaques ou le roman d'Habrocomès et d'Anthia.* Edited and Translated by Georges Dalmeyda. 2nd ed. Collection des universités de France. Paris: "Les belles lettres," 1962.

—. *Xenophon: Scriptora Minora.* Translated by E. C. Marchant and G. W. Bowersock. Revised ed. LCL 183. Cambridge: Harvard University Press, 1968.

Modern Works

Abramowski, Luise. "Die Geschichte von der Fußwaschung (Joh 13)." *ZTK* 102 (2005): 176–203.

Adams, Sean A. *The Genre of Acts and Collected Biography.* SNTSMS 156. Cambridge: Cambridge University Press, 2013.

Adrados, Francisco R. "The 'Life of Aesop' and the Origins of the Novel in Antiquity." *Quaderni urbinati di cultura classica* 1 (1979): 93–112.

Agrell, Beata. "Genre and Working Class Fiction." Pages 286–327 in *Genre and … .* Edited by S. Auken, P. S. Lauridsen, and A. J. Rasmussen. Copenhagen Studies in Genre 2. Copenhagen: Ekbátana, 2015.

Alexander, Loveday C. A. *Acts in its Literary Context: A Classicist Looks at the Acts of the Apostles.* LNTS 289. London: T&T Clark, 2005.

—. *The Preface to Luke's Gospel: Literary Convention and Social Context in Luke 1.1–4 and Acts 1.1.* SNTSMS 78. Cambridge: Cambridge University Press, 1993.

—. "What is a Gospel?" Pages 13–33 in *The Cambridge Companion to the Gospels.* Edited by Stephen Barton. Cambridge: Cambridge University Press, 2006.

Alter, Robert. *The Art of Biblical Narrative.* Rev. & updated ed. New York: Basic Books, 2011.

Andersen, Jack. "Re-Describing Knowledge Organization: A Genre and Activity-Based View." Pages 13–42 in *Genre Theory in Information Studies.* Edited by J. Andersen. Bingley: Emerald Group, 2015.

Anderson, Paul N. "Bakhtin's Dialogism and the Corrective Rhetoric of the Johannine Misunderstanding Dialogue: Exposing Seven Crises in the Johannine Situation." Pages

133–59 in *Bakhtin and Genre Theory in Biblical Studies.* Edited by Roland Boer, SemeiaSt 63. Leiden: Brill, 2008.

—. *The Fourth Gospel and the Quest for Jesus: Modern Foundations Reconsidered.* LNTS 321. London: T&T Clark, 2007.

—. "The Origin and Development of the Johannine Ego Eimi Sayings in Cognitive-Critical Perspective." *Journal for the Study of the Historical Jesus* 9 (2011): 139–206.

—. *The Riddles of the Fourth Gospel.* Minneapolis: Fortress, 2011.

Anderson, Paul N., Felix Just, and Tom Thatcher, eds. *John, Jesus, and History. Vol. 1: Critical Appraisals of Critical Views.* SBLSymS 44. Atlanta: Society of Biblical Literature, 2007.

—. *John, Jesus, and History. Vol. 2: Aspects of Historicity in the Fourth Gospel.* SBLSymS 44. Atlanta: Society of Biblical Literature, 2009.

Annas, Julia, and Jonathan Barnes. *The Modes of Scepticism: Ancient Texts and Modern Interpretations.* Cambridge: Cambridge University Press, 1985.

Arend, Walter. *Die typischen Scenen bei Homer.* Berlin: Weidmann, 1975.

Artemeva, Natasha. "Approaches to Learning Genres: A Bibliographical Essay." Pages 9–99 in *Rhetorical Genre Studies and Beyond.* Edited by N. Artemeva and A. Freedman. Winnipeg: Inkshed, 2008.

Arterbury, Andrew E. "Breaking the Betrothal Bonds: Hospitality in John 4." *CBQ* 72 (2010): 63–83.

Ashton, John. "The Transformation of Wisdom: A Study of the Prologue of John's Gospel." *NTS* 32 (1986): 161–186.

—. *Understanding the Fourth Gospel*, 2nd ed. Oxford: Oxford University Press, 2007.

Askehave, Inger and John Swales. "Genre Identification and Communicative Purpose." *Applied Linguistics* 2 (2001): 195–212.

Attridge, H. W. "An Emotional Jesus and Stoic Traditions." Pages 77–92 in *Stoicism in Early Christianity.* Edited by Tuomas Rasimus, Troels Engberg-Pedersen, and Ismo Dunderberg. Peabody: Hendrickson, 2010.

—. "Argumentation in John 5." Pages 188–99 in *Rhetorical Argumentation in Biblical Texts: Essays from the Lund 2000 Conference.* Edited by A. Eriksson, Th. H. Olbricht, and W. Übelacker. Emory Studies in Early Christianity 8. Harrisburg: Trinity, 2002.

—. "Divine Sovereignty and Human Responsibility in the Fourth Gospel." Pages 183–199 in *Revealed Wisdom: Studies in Apocalyptic in Honour of Christopher Rowland.* Edited by John Ashton. Leiden: Brill, 2014.

—. *Essays on John and Hebrews.* WUNT 264. Tübingen: Mohr Siebeck, 2010.

—. "Genre Bending in the Fourth Gospel." *JBL* 121 (2002): 3–21. Repr. pages 31–45 in idem, *Essays on John and Hebrews.* WUNT 264. Tübingen: Mohr Siebeck, 2010.

—. "Historiography" and "Josephus and His Works." Pages 157–232 in *Jewish Writings of the Second Temple.* Edited by Michael E. Stone. CRINT 2.2. Philadelphia: Fortress, 1984.

—. "Plato, Plutarch, and John: Three Symposia about Love." Pages 367–78 in *Beyond the Gnostic Gospels: Studies Building on the Work of Elaine Pagels.* Edited by Edward Iricinschi, Lance Jenott, Nicola Denzey Lewis, and Philippa Townsendal. STAC 82. Tübingen: Mohr Siebeck, 2013.

—. "'Seeking' and 'Asking' in Q, Thomas and John." Pages 295–302 in *From Quest to Q: Festschrift James M. Robinson.* Edited by Jon Ma. Asgeirsson, Kristin de Troyer, and Marvin W. Meyer. Leuven: University Press; Peeters, 2000.

—. "The Cubist Principle in Johannine Imagery: John and the Reading of Images in Contemporary Platonism." Pages 47–60 in *Imagery in the Gospel of John*. Edited by Jörg Frey, Jan G. van der Watt, and Ruben Zimmermann. WUNT 200. Tübingen: Mohr Siebeck, 2006.

—. *The Interpretation of Biblical History in the* Antiquitates Judaicae *of Flavius Josephus*. HDR 7. Missoula: Scholars, 1976.

—. "The Restless Quest for the Beloved Disciple." Pages 71–80 in *Early Christian Voices: In Texts, Traditions, and Symbols: Essays in Honor of François Bovon*. Edited by David H. Warren, Ann Graham Brock, and David W. Pao. BIS 66. Leiden: Brill, 2003.

Auken, Sune. "Genre and Interpretation." Pages 154–183 in *Genre and …* . Edited by S. Auken, P. S. Lauridsen, and A. J. Rasmussen. Copenhagen Studies in Genre 2. Copenhagen: Ekbátana, 2015.

—. "Genre as Fictional Action." *Nordisk Tidsskrift for Informationsvidenskab og Kulturformidling*, 2/3 (2013): 19–28.

—. "Utterance and Function in Genre Studies: A Literary Perspective." Pages 155–178 in *Genre Theory in Information Studies*. Edited by J. Andersen. Studies in Information 11. Bingley: Emerald Group, 2015.

Auld, A. Graeme. *I and II Samuel: A Commentary*. OTL. Louisville: Westminster John Knox, 2011.

Aune, David E. *The New Testament in its Literary Environment*. LEC. Philadelphia: Westminster, 1987.

Austin, John L. *How To Do Things With Words*. Oxford: Oxford University Press, 1976.

Baird, William. *History of New Testament Research. Volume Two: From Jonathan Edwards to Rudolf Bultmann*. Minneapolis: Fortress, 2003.

Bakhtin, Mikhail M. *The Dialogic Imagination: Four Essays by M. M. Bakhtin*. Edited by Michael Holquist. Translated by Caryl Emerson and Michael Holquist. Austin: University of Texas Press, 1981.

—. *Problems of Dostoyevsky's Poetics*. Edited and translated by Caryl Emerson. Theory and History of Literature 8. Minneapolis: University of Minnesota Press, 1984.

—. *Rabelais and his World*. Translated by Hélène Iswolsky. Bloomington: Indiana University Press, 1984.

—. *Speech Genres and Other Late Essays*. Edited by Caryl Emerson and Michael Holquist. Translated by Vern W. McGee. Austin: University of Texas Press, 1990.

—. "The *Bildungsroman* and Its Significance in the History of Realism (Toward a Historical Typology of the Novel)." Pages 10–59 in *Speech Genres and Other Late Essays*. Edited by Caryl Emerson and Michael Holquist. Translated by Vern W. McGee. Austin: University of Texas Press, 1986.

—. "The Problem of Speech Genres." Pages 60–102 in *Speech Genres and Other Late Essays*. Edited by Caryl Emerson and Michael Holquist. Translated by Vern W. McGee. Austin: University of Texas Press, 1986.

Ballengee, Jennifer R. "Below the Belt: Looking into the Matter of Adventure Time." Pages 130–63 in *The Bakhtin Circle and Ancient Narrative*. Edited by Robert Bracht Branham. Groningen: Barkhuis, 2005.

Bandstra, Barry. *Genesis 1–11: A Handbook on the Hebrew Text*. BHHB. Waco: Baylor University Press, 2008.

Barrett, C. K. *The Gospel according to St. John: An Introduction with Commentary and Notes on the Greek Text.* London: SPCK, 1956. 2nd. ed., 1978.

Basser, Herbert W. *The Gospel of Matthew and Judaic Traditions: A Relevance-Based Commentary.* With Marsha B. Cohen. BRLJ 46. Leiden: Brill, 2015.

Bastian, Heather: "Capturing Individual Uptake: Toward a Disruptive Research Methodology." Composition Forum 31 (2015): n.p.

Bauckham, Richard. "For Whom Were the Gospels Written?" Pages 9–49 in *The Gospels for all Christians: Rethinking the Gospel Audiences.* Edited by R. Bauckham. Edinburgh: T&T Clark, 1998.

—. "Historiographical Characteristics of the Gospel of John." *NTS* 53 (2007): 17–36.

—. *The Testimony of the Beloved Disciple: Narrative, History, and Theology in the Gospel of John.* Grand Rapids: Baker Academic, 2008.

Bauer, Walter. *Das Johannesevangelium.* 2nd ed. HNT 6. Tübingen: J. C. B. Mohr, 1925.

Bawarshi, Anis. *Genre and the Invention of the Writer.* Logan: Utah State University Press, 2003.

Bawarshi, Anis, and Mary Jo Reiff. *Genre: An Introduction to History, Theory, Research, and Pedagogy.* Fort Collins: Parlor, 2010.

Bazerman, Charles. "The Life of Genre, the Life in the Classroom." Pages 19–26 in *Genre and Writing: Issues, Arguments, Alternatives.* Edited by Wendy Bishop and Hans Ostrom. Portsmouth: Boynton; Cook, 1997.

—. *Shaping Written Knowledge.* Madison: The University of Wisconsin Press, 1988.

—. "Systems of Genres." Pages 79–101 in *Genre and the New Rhetoric.* Edited by A. Freedman and P. Medway. London: Taylor & Francis, 1994.

Beasley-Murray, George. *John.* WBC 36. Waco: Word Books, 1987.

Beck, David R. *The Discipleship Paradigm: Readers and Anonymous Characters in the Fourth Gospel.* BIS 27. Leiden: Brill, 1997.

—. "The Narrative Function of Anonymity in Fourth Gospel Characterization." *Semeia* 53 (1993): 143–58.

Becker, Adam H. and Annette Yoshiko Reed, eds. *The Ways that Never Parted: Jews and Christians in Late Antiquity and the Early Middle Ages.* TSAJ 95. Tübingen: Mohr Siebeck, 2003.

Becker, Eve-Marie, *Das Markus-Evangelium im Rahmen antiker Historiographie.* WUNT 194. Tübingen: Mohr Siebeck, 2006.

—. "Earliest Christian Literary Activity: Investigating Authors, Genres and Audiences in Paul and Mark." Pages 87–105 in *Mark and Paul. Comparative Essays Part II: For and Against Pauline Influence on Mark.* Edited by Eve-Marie Becker, Troels Engberg-Pedersen, and Mogens Müller. BZNW 199. Berlin: de Gruyter, 2014.

—. "Patterns of Early Christian Thinking and Writing of History: Paul–Mark–Acts." Pages 276–298 in *Thinking, Recording, and Writing History in the Ancient World.* Edited by K. A. Raaflaub. Malden: Wiley-Blackwell, 2014.

—. *Writing History in New Testament Times: Memoria–Tempus–Historia.* New Haven: Yale University Press, forthcoming.

Becker, Eve-Marie, ed. *Die antike Historiographie und die Anfänge der christlichen Geschichtsschreibung.* BZNW 129. Berlin: de Gruyter, 2005.

Becker, Jürgen. *Das Evangelium nach Johannes.* 3rd ed. ÖTK 4/1–2. Gütersloh: Gütersloher Verlagshaus; Würzburg: Echter, 1991.

—. *Johanneisches Christentum: Seine Geschichte und Theologie im Überblick.* Tübingen: Mohr Siebeck, 2004.

—. "Wunder und Christologie." *NT* 16 (1969/70): 130–148.

Beirne, Margaret M. *Women and Men in the Fourth Gospel: A Genuine Discipleship of Equals.* JSNTSup 242. London: Sheffield Academic Press, 2003.

Belle, Gilbert van. *The Signs Source.* SNTA 10. Leuven: Peeters, 1975.

—. *The Signs Source in the Fourth Gospel: Historical Survey and Critical Evaluation of the Semeia Hypothesis.* BETL 116. Leuven: Peeters, 1994.

Bennema, Cornelis. *Encountering Jesus: Character Studies in the Gospel of John.* 2nd ed. Minneapolis: Fortress Press, 2014.

Berger, Klaus. *Einführung in die Formgeschichte.* UTB 1444. Tübingen: Francke, 1987.

—. *Formen und Gattungen im Neuen Testament.* UTB 2532. Tübingen: Francke, 2005.

—. *Formgeschichte des Neuen Testaments.* Heidelberg: Quelle & Meyer, 1984.

—. "Hellenistische Gattungen im Neuen Testament." *Aufstieg und Niedergang der Römischen Welt.* Vol. II 25,2. Berlin: de Gruyter, 1985: 1031–1432.

—. *Im Anfang war Johannes: Datierung und Theologie des vierten Evangeliums.* 3rd ed. Gütersloh: Gütersloher Verlagshaus, 2004.

Bergmeier, Roland. "Die Bedeutung der Synoptiker für das johanneische Zeugnisthema: Mit einem Anhang zum Perfekt-Gebrauch im vierten Evangelium." *NTS* 52 (2006): 458–83.

Betz, Hans Dieter, et al., eds. *Religion Past and Present: Encyclopedia of Theology and Religion.* 14 vols. Leiden: Brill, 2007–2013.

Beutler, Johannes. *Do not be Afraid: The First Farewell Discourse in John's Gospel.* New Testament Studies in Contextual Exegesis 6. Frankfurt am Main: Peter Lang, 2011.

—. *Habt Keine Angst: Die erste Johanneische Abschiedsrede (Joh 14).* SBS 116. Stuttgart: Katholisches Bibelwerk, 1984.

—. "Literarische Gattungen im Johannesevangelium: Ein Forschungsbericht 1919–1980." *ANRW*, II 25.3: 2506–2568.

Bhatia, Vijay K. *Worlds of Written Discourse.* London: Continuum, 2004.

Bittner, Wolfgang J. *Jesu Zeichen im Johannesevangelium.* WUNT 2/26. Tübingen: Mohr Siebeck, 1987.

Blank, Josef. *Krisis: Untersuchungen zur johanneischen Christologie und Eschatologie.* Freiburg im Breisgau: Lambertus, 1964.

Blass, Friedrich, Albert Debrunner, and Friedrich Rehkopf. *Grammatik des neutestamentlichen Griechisch.* 16. ed. Göttingen: Vandenhoeck & Ruprecht, 1984.

Blomberg, Craig L. *Interpreting the Parables.* 2nd ed. Downers Grove: IVP Academic, 2012.

Boismard, M.-Emile. *Le prologue de saint Jean.* Paris: du Cerf, 1953.

Bonneau, Normand R. "The Woman at the Well: John 4 and Genesis 24." *TBT* 67 (1973): 1252–59.

Borgen, Peder. *Bread from Heaven: An Exegetical Study of the Concept of Manna in the Gospel of John and the Writings of Philo.* NovTSup 10. Leiden: Brill, 1965.

—. "Observations on the Targumic Character of the Prologue of John." *NTS* 16 (1969/70): 288–295.

Boring, M. Eugene, Klaus Berger, and Carsten Colpe, eds. *Hellenistic Commentary to the New Testament.* Nashville: Abingdon, 1995.

Bouchard, D. F. “Preface.” Pages 7–9 in *Language, Counter-Memory, Practice: Selected Essays and Interviews.* By Michel Foucault. Edited by D. F. Bouchard and S. Simon. Ithaca: Cornell University Press, 1977.

Bowie, Ewen. “Literary Milieux.” Pages 17–38 in *The Cambridge Companion to the Greek and Roman Novel.* Edited by Tim Whitmarsh. Cambridge: Cambridge University Press, 2008.

Boyarin, Daniel. “The Gospel of the *Memra:* Jewish Binitarianism and the Prologue to John.” *HTR* 94 (2001): 243–84.

Brant, Jo-Ann A. *Dialogue and Drama: Elements of Greek Tragedy in the Fourth Gospel.* Peabody: Hendrickson, 2004.

—. “Divine Birth and Apparent Parents: The Plot of the Fourth Gospel.” Pages 199–211 in *Ancient Fiction and Early Christian Narrative.* Edited by Ronald F. Hock, J. Bradley Chance, and Judith Perkins. SBLSymS 6. Atlanta: Scholars, 1998.

—. “Husband Hunting: Characterization and Narrative Art in the Gospel of John.” *BibInt* 4 (1996): 205–23.

Brant, Jo-Ann A., Charles W. Hedrick, and Chris Shea, eds. *Ancient Fiction: The Matrix of Early Christian and Jewish Narrative.* SBLSymS 32. Leiden: Brill, 2005.

Bremond, Claude. *Logique du récit.* Paris: Éditions du Seuil, 1973.

Brooke, George J. “Genre Theory, Rewritten Bible and Pesher.” *DSD* 17 (2010): 361–386.

—. “Reading. Searching and Blessing: A Functional Approach to the Genres of Scriptural Interpretation in the יחד.” Pages 140–56 in *The Temple in Text and Tradition: A Festschrift in Honour of Robert Hayward.* Edited by R. Timothy McLay. London: Bloomsbury, 2015.

Brown, Raymond E. *An Introduction to the Gospel of John.* Edited by Francis J. Moloney. New Haven: Yale University Press, 2003.

—. “Roles of Women in the Fourth Gospel.” *TS* 36 (1975): 691–94.

—. *The Community of the Beloved Disciple: The Life, Loves, and Hates of an Individual Church in New Testament Times.* New York: Paulist, 1979.

—. *The Gospel according to John.* 2 vols. AB 29. Garden City: Doubleday, 1966–1970.

—. “The Paraclete in the Fourth Gospel.” *NTS* 13 (1967): 113–132.

Bruce, F. F. *The Gospel of John: Introduction, Exposition, Notes.* Grand Rapids: Eerdmans, 1994.

Brueggemann, Walter. *First and Second Samuel.* IBC. Louisville: John Knox, 1990.

Bruns, J. Edgar. “Note on Jn 12:3.” *CBQ* 28 (1966): 219–22.

Buch-Hansen, Gitte. *‘It is the Spirit That Gives Life’ (John 6:63): A Stoic Understanding of Pneuma in John.* BZNW 173; Berlin: de Gruyter, 2010.

Buell, Denise Kimber. *Why this New Race? Ethnic Reasoning in Early Christianity.* New York: Columbia University Press, 2005.

Bultmann, Rudolf. *Das Evangelium des Johannes.* KEK 2. Göttingen: Vandenhoeck & Ruprecht, 1941. 21st ed., 1986.

—. *Die Geschichte der synoptischen Tradition.* FRLANT 29. Göttingen: Vandenhoeck & Ruprecht, 1921. 10th ed., with a postscript by G. Theißen, 1995.

—. *The Gospel of John: A Commentary.* Translated by G. R. Beasley Murray et al. Oxford: Blackwell, 1971.

—. “The Gospels (Form).” Pages 1:86–92 in *Twentieth Century Theology in the Making.* Edited by Jaroslav Pelikan. Translated by R. A. Wilson. London: Collins, 1969.

—. *The History of the Synoptic Tradition.* Translated by John Marsh. New York: Harper & Row, 1963.

—. *Theologie des Neuen Testaments.* Neue Theologische Grundrisse. Tübingen: J. C. B. Mohr (Paul Siebeck), 1953.

Burridge, Richard A. "The Genre of Acts—Revisited." Pages 3–28 in *Reading Acts Today: Essays in Honour of Loveday C. A. Alexander.* Edited by Steve Walton, Thomas E. Phillips, Lloyd Keith Pietersen, and F. Scott Spencer. LNTS 427. London: T&T Clark, 2011.

—. *What are the Gospels? A Comparison with Graeco-Roman Biography.* 2nd ed. Grand Rapids: Eerdmans, 2004.

—. *Imitating Jesus: An Inclusive Approach to New Testament Ethics.* Grand Rapids: Eerdmans, 2007.

—. "Genres of the Old and New Testaments: Gospels." Pages 432–444 in *The Oxford Handbook of Biblical Studies.* Edited by John Rogerson and Judith M. Lieu. Oxford: Oxford University Press, 2006.

Buss, Martin J. *Biblical Form Criticism in its Context.* JSOTSup 274. Sheffield: Sheffield Academic Press, 1999.

Byrskog, Samuel. *Story as History—History as Story: The Gospel Tradition in the Context of Ancient Oral History.* WUNT 2/106. Tübingen: Mohr Siebeck, 2000.

Cahill, P. Joseph. "Narrative Art in John IV." *Religious Studies Bulletin* 2 (1982): 41–48.

Cancik, Hubert. "Das Geschichtswerk des Lukas als Institutionsgeschichte: Die Vorbereitung des Zweiten Logos im Ersten." Pages 519–538 in *Die Apostelgeschichte im Kontext antiker und frühchristlicher Historiographie.* Edited by Jörg Frey, Clare K. Rothschild, and Jens Schröter. BZNW 162. Berlin: de Gruyter, 2009.

—. "The History of Culture, Religion, and Institutions in Ancient Historiography: Philological Observations concerning Luke's History." *JBL* 116 (1997): 673–95.

Carmicheal, Calum M. *The Story of Creation: Its Origin and Interpretation in Philo and the Fourth Gospel.* Ithaca: Cornell University Press, 1996.

Carson, Donald A. *The Gospel According to John.* Grand Rapids: Eerdmans, 1991.

Cave, Terence. *Recognitions: A Study in Poetics.* Oxford: Clarendon, 1988.

Chandler, Daniel. "Schema Theory and the Interpretation of Television Programmes." No pages. Cited 11 June 2015. Online: http://visual-memory.co.uk/daniel/Documents/short/schematv. html.

Charlesworth, James H. "The Historical Jesus in the Fourth Gospel: A Paradigm Shift?" *Journal for the Study of the Historical Jesus* 8 (2010): 3–46.

Chibici-Revneanu, Nicole. *Die Herrlichkeit des Verherrlichten.* WUNT 2/231. Tübingen: Mohr Siebeck, 2007.

Clark, Elizabeth A. *History, Theory, Text: Historians and the Linguistic Turn.* Cambridge: Harvard University Press, 2004.

Classen, C. J. "Melanchthon's Rhetorical Interpretation of Biblical and Non-Biblical Texts." Pages 99–177 in idem, *Rhetorical Criticism of the New Testament.* WUNT 128. Tübingen: Mohr Siebeck, 2000.

Claussen, Carsten. "Das Gebet in Joh 17 im Kontext von Gebeten aus zeitgenössischen Pseudepigraphen." Pages 205–232 in *Kontexte des Johannesevangeliums: Das vierte Evangelium in religions- und traditionsgeschichtlicher Perspektive.* Edited by Jörg Frey and Udo Schnelle. WUNT 175. Tübingen: Mohr Siebeck, 2004.

Coakley, J. F. "The Anointing at Bethany and the Priority of John." *JBL* 107 (1988): 241–56.

Collins, Raymond F. "Cana (Jn. 2:1–12): The First of His Signs or the Key to His Signs?" *ITQ* 47 (1980): 79–95.

—. *Studies on the Fourth Gospel.* Louvain: Peeters; Grand Rapids: Eerdmans, 1990.

Coloe, Mary L. "Creation in the Gospel of John." Pages 71–90 in *Creation is Groaning: Biblical and Theological Perspectives.* Edited by Mary L. Coloe. Collegeville: Liturgical Press, 2013.

—. "The Mother of Jesus: A Woman Possessed." Pages 202–213 in *Character Studies in the Fourth Gospel: Narrative Approaches to Seventy Figures in John.* Edited by S. A. Hunt, D. F. Tolmie, and R. Zimmermann. WUNT 314. Tübingen: Mohr Siebeck, 2013.

—. *God Dwells with Us: Temple Symbolism in the Fourth Gospel.* Collegeville: Liturgical Press, 2001.

—. *Dwelling in the Household of God: Johannine Ecclesiology and Spirituality.* Collegeville: Liturgical Press, 2007.

Conway, Colleen M. *Behold the Man: Jesus and Greco-Roman Masculinity.* Oxford: Oxford University Press, 2008.

—. "'Behold the Man!' Masculine Christology and the Fourth Gospel." Pages 163–80 in *New Testament Masculinities.* Edited by Stephen D. Moore and Janice Capel Anderson. Atlanta: Society of Biblical Literature, 2003.

—. *Men and Women in the Fourth Gospel: Gender and Johannine Characterization.* SBLDS 167. Atlanta: Society of Biblical Literature, 1999.

Copeland, Rita. *Rhetoric, Hermeneutics, and Translation in the Middle Ages: Academic Traditions and Vernacular Texts.* Cambridge: Cambridge University Press, 1991.

Cory, Catherine. "Wisdom's Rescue: A New Reading of the Tabernacles Discourse (John 7:1–8:59)." *JBL* 116 (1997): 95–116.

Crawford, Sidnie White. *Rewriting Scripture in Second Temple Times.* SDSS. Grand Rapids: Eerdmans, 2008.

Crossan, John D. *Cliffs of Fall: Paradox and Polyvalence in the Parables of Jesus.* New York: Seabury Press, 1980.

—. *The Historical Jesus: The Life of a Mediterranean Jewish Peasant.* New York: Harper-Collins, 1992.

Culpepper, R. Alan. *Anatomy of the Fourth Gospel: A Study in Literary Design.* Philadelphia: Fortress, 1983.

—. "Cognition in John: The Johannine Signs as Recognition Scenes." *PRSt* 35 (2008): 251–60.

—. *The Gospel and Letters of John.* Nashville: Abingdon, 1998.

—. "The Pivot of John's Prologue." *NTS* 27 (1981): 1–31.

—. "The Johannine *Hypodeigma:* A Reading of John 13." *Semeia* 53 (1991): 133–52.

Culpepper, R. Alan, and Fernando F. Segovia, eds. *The Fourth Gospel from a Literary Perspective: Semeia* 53 (1991).

Davenport, Anthony. *Medieval Narrative: An Introduction.* Oxford: Oxford University Press, 2004.

Davidsen, Ole. "Adam–Christ Typology in Paul and Mark: Reflections on a *Tertium Comparationis.*" Pages 243–272 in *Mark and Paul. Comparative Essays Part II: For and Against Pauline Influence on Mark.* Edited by Eve-Marie Becker, Troels Engberg-Pedersen, and Mogens Müller. BZNW 199. Berlin: de Gruyter, 2014.

—. *The Narrative Jesus: A Semiotic Reading of Mark's Gospel.* Aarhus: Aarhus University Press, 1993.

Demand, Nancy H. *Birth, Death, and Motherhood in Classical Greece.* ASH. Baltimore: Johns Hopkins University Press, 1994.

Demke, C. "Der sogenannte Logos-Hymnus im Johannes-Prolog." *ZNW* 58 (1967): 45–68.

Denaux, Adelbert, ed. *John and the Synoptics.* Leuven: Leuven University Press; Peeters, 1992.

Denniston, J. D. *Greek Prose Style.* Oxford: Clarendon, 1952.

Denzey, Nicola Frances. "Genesis Traditions in Conflict? The Use of Some Exegetical Traditions in the *Trimorphic Protennoia* and the Johannine Prologue." *VC* 55 (2001): 20–44.

Derrida, Jacques. "La loi du genre / The Law of Genre." *Glyph* 7 (1980): 176–232.

—. "The Law of Genre." *Critical Inquiry* 7 (1980): 55–81.

Devitt, Amy J. "Intertextuality in Tax Accounting: Generic, Referential, and Functional." Pages 291–303 in *Dynamics of the Professions: Historical and Contemporary Studies in Writing in Professional Communities.* Edited by C. Bazerman and J. Paradis. Madison: University of Wisconsin Press, 1991.

—. "Re-Fusing Form in Genre Study." Pages 27–48 in *Genres in the Internet.* Edited by J. Giltrow and D. Stein. Philadelphia: John Benjamins, 2009.

—. "Teaching Critical Genre Awareness." Pages 337–351 in *Genre in a Changing World.* Edited by C. Bazerman, A. Bonini, and D. Figueiredo. Fort Collins: Parlor, 2009.

—. *Writing Genres.* Rhetorical Philosophy and Theory. Carbondale: Southern Illinois University Press, 2004.

Dibelius, Martin. *Die Formgeschichte des Evangeliums.* Tübingen: Mohr Siebeck, 1919. 6th ed., with additions by G. Iber, 1971.

—. *From Tradition to Gospel.* Translated by Bertram Lee Woolf. Scribner Library. New York: Charles Scribner's Sons, n. d.

Dietzfelbinger, Christian. *Das Evangelium nach Johannes.* 2nd ed. 2 vols. ZBK. Zürich: Theologischer Verlag, 2004.

Dodd, C. H. "The Dialogue Form in the Gospels." *BJRL* 37 (1954): 54–67.

—. *Historical Tradition in the Fourth Gospel.* Cambridge: Cambridge University Press, 1963.

—. *The Interpretation of the Fourth Gospel.* Cambridge: Cambridge University Press, 1953.

Doležel, Lubomír. *Heterocosmica: Fiction and Possible Worlds.* Baltimore: Johns Hopkins University Press, 1998.

Dormeyer, Detlev. "Gleichnisse als narrative und metaphorische Konstrukte: Sprachliche und handlungsorientierte Aspekte." Pages 420–37 in *Hermeneutik der Gleichnisse Jesu: Methodische Neuansätze zum Verstehen urchristlicher Parabeltexte.* Edited by R. Zimmermann. 2nd ed. WUNT 238. Tübingen: Mohr Siebeck, 2011.

Doulamis, Konstantin. "Rhetoric and Irony in Chariton: A Case Study from *Callirhoe.*" *Ancient Narrative* 1 (2000–2001): 55–72.

Duke, Paul D. *Irony in the Fourth Gospel.* Atlanta: John Knox Press, 1985.

Dunn, Francis M. and Thomas Cole, eds. *Beginnings in Classical Literature.* Yale Classical Studies 29. Cambridge: Cambridge University Press, 1992.

Dunn, James D. G. "John and the Synoptics as a Theological Question." Pages 301–313 in *Exploring the Gospel of John: In Honor of D. Moody Smith.* Edited by R. Alan Culpepper and C. Clifton Black. Louisville: Westminster John Knox, 1996.

—. "Let John Be John: A Gospel for Its Time." Pages 293–322 in *The Gospel and the Gospels.* Edited by Peter Stuhlmacher. Grand Rapids: Eerdmans, 1991.

Dunn, Peter M. "Soranus of Ephesus (circa AD 98–138) and Perinatal Care in Roman Times." *Archives of Disease in Childhood* 73 (1995): F51–F52.

Edwards, Ruth. "ΧΑΡΙΝ ΑΝΤΙ ΧΑΡΙΤΟΣ (John 1:16): Grace and Law in the Johannine Prologue." *JSNT* 32 (1988): 3–15.

Emmons, Kimberly K. "Uptake and the Biomedical Subject." Pages 134–157 in *Genre in a Changing World.* Edited by C. Bazerman, A. Bonini, and D. Figueiredo. Lafayette: Parlor, 2009.

Engberg-Pedersen, Troels. *Cosmology and Self in the Apostle Paul: The Material Spirit.* Oxford: Oxford University Press, 2010.

—. "*Logos* and *Pneuma* in the Fourth Gospel." Pages 27–48 in *Greco-Roman Culture and the New Testament: Studies Commemorating the Centennial of the Pontifical Biblical Institute.* Edited by D. E. Aune and F. Brenk. NovTSup 143. Leiden: Brill, 2012.

—. "Philosophy and Ideology in John 9–10 Read as a Single Literary Unit." *Histos* 7 (2013): 181–204.

—. "The Concept of Paraenesis." Pages 47–72 in *Early Christian Paraenesis in Context.* Edited by James M. Starr and Troels Engberg-Pedersen. BZNW 125. Berlin: de Gruyter, 2004.

Erlemann, Kurt. *Gleichnisauslegung: Ein Lehr- und Arbeitsbuch.* Uni-Taschenbücher 2093. Tübingen: Francke, 1999.

Eslinger, Lyle. "The Wooing of the Woman at the Well: Jesus, the Reader and Reader-Response Criticism." *Literature and Theology* 1 (1987): 167–183. Reprint in *The Gospel of John as Literature: An Anthology of Twentieth-Century Perspectives.* Edited by Mark W. G. Stibbe. NTTS 17. Leiden: Brill, 1993, 165–182.

Estes, Douglas. *The Questions of Jesus in John: Logic, Rhetoric and Persuasive Discourse.* BIS 115. Leiden: Brill, 2013.

—. *The Temporal Mechanics of the Fourth Gospel: A Theory of Hermeneutical Relativity in the Gospel of John.* BIS 92. Leiden: Brill, 2008.

Evans, Craig A. "'The Book of the Genesis of Jesus Christ': The Purpose of Matthew in Light of the Incipit." Pages 61–72 in *Biblical Interpretation in Early Christian Gospels, vol. 2: The Gospel of Matthew.* Edited by Thomas R. Hatina. LNTS 310. London: T&T Clark, 2008.

—. "Peter Warming Himself: The Problem of an Editorial Seam." *JBL* 101 (1982): 245–49.

—. *Word and Glory: On the Exegetical and Theological Background of John's Prologue.* JSNTSup 89. Sheffield: JSOT Press, 1993.

Farrell, Joseph. "Classical Genre in Theory and Practice." *New Literary History* 34 (2003): 383–408.

Faure, A. "Die alttestamentlichen Zitate im 4. Evangelium und die Quellenscheidungshypothese." *ZNW* 21 (1922): 99–121.

Fehribach, Adeline. *The Women in the Life of the Bridegroom: A Feminist Historical-Literary Analysis of the Female Characters in the Fourth Gospel.* Collegeville: Liturgical Press, 1998.

Feuillet, Andre. "L'heure de la femme (Jn 16,21) et l'heure de la Mère de Jesus (Jn 19,25–27)." *Bib* 47 (1966): 169–84, 361–80, 557–73.

Foley, Helene P. *Female Acts in Greek Tragedy*. Princeton: Princeton University Press, 2001.

Förster, Hans. "Die johanneischen Zeichen und Joh 2:11 als möglicher hermeneutischer Schlüssel." *NovT* 56 (2014): 1–23.

Fortna, R. T. *The Fourth Gospel and its Predecessor*. Edinburgh: T&T Clark, 1988.

—. *The Gospel of Signs: A Reconstruction of the Narrative Source Underlying the Fourth Gospel*. SNTSMS 11. Cambridge: Cambridge University Press, 1970.

Foucault, Michel. "Counter-Memory: The Philosophy of Difference." Pages 113–196 in *Language, Counter-Memory, Practice: Selected Essays and Interviews*. By Michel Foucault. Edited by D. F. Bouchard and S. Simon. Ithaca: Cornell University Press, 1977.

—. *Language, Counter-Memory, Practice: Selected Essays and Interviews*. Edited by D. F. Bouchard and S. Simon. Ithaca: Cornell University Press, 1977.

Fowler, Alastair. *Kinds of Literature: An Introduction to the Theory of Genres and Modes*. Oxford: Oxford University Press, 1982.

Fraade, Steven. "Interpretive Authority in the Studying Community at Qumran." *JJS* 44 (1993): 46–69.

Freadman, Anne. "Anyone for Tennis?" Pages 43–66 in *Genre and the New Rhetoric*. Edited by A. Freedman and P. Medway. London: Taylor & Francis, 1994.

—. "Uptake." Pages 39–53 in *The Rhetoric and Ideology of Genre*. Edited by R. Coe, L. Lingard, and T. Teslenko. Cresskill: Hampton, 2002.

French, Valerie. "Birth Control, Childbirth and Early Childhood." Pages 3:1355–62 in *Civilization of the Ancient Mediteranean*. Edited by M. Grant and R. Kitzinger. 3 vols. New York: Scribner, 1988.

Freud, Sigmund. "Massenpsychologie und Ich-Analyse." Pages 61–134 in idem, *Fragen der Gesellschaft: Ursprunge der Religion*. Studienausgabe 9. Frankfurt: S. Fischer, 1974.

Frey, Jörg. "Die Gegenwart von Vergangenheit und Zukunft Christi: Zur ‚Verschmelzung' der Zeithorizonte im Johannesevangelium." Pages 129–158 in *Zeit*. Edited by D. Sattler and M. Wolter. Jahrbuch für Biblische Theologie 28. Neukirchen-Vluyn: Neukirchener Verlag, 2013.

—. *Die Herrlichkeit des Gekreuzigten: Studien zu den Johanneischen Schriften I*. Edited by Juliane Schlegel. WUNT 307. Tübingen: Mohr Siebeck, 2013.

—. *Die johanneische Eschatologie*. WUNT 96, 110, 117. 3 vols. Tübingen: Mohr Siebeck, 1997–2000.

—. *Die johanneische Eschatologie 1: Ihre Probleme im Spiegel der Forschung seit Reimarus*. WUNT 96. Tübingen: Mohr, 1997.

—. *Die johanneische Eschatologie 2: Das johanneische Zeitverständnis*. WUNT 110. Tübingen: Mohr Siebeck, 1998.

—. *Die johanneische Eschatologie 3: Die eschatologische Verkündigung in den johanneischen Texten*. WUNT 117. Tübingen: Mohr Siebeck, 2000.

—. "Die '*theologia crucfixi*' des Johannesevangeliums." Pages 485–554 in idem, *Die Herrlichkeit des Gekreuzigten*. Edited by J. Schlegel. WUNT 307. Tübingen: Mohr Siebeck, 2013.

—. "'Ich habe den Herrn gesehen' (Joh 20,18): Entstehung, Inhalt und Vermittlung des Osterglaubens nach Johannes 20." Pages 267–284 in *Studien zu Matthäus und Johannes /*

Études sur Matthieu et Jean. Festschrift Jean Zumstein. Edited by A. Dettwiler and U. Poplutz. AThANT 97. Zürich: TVZ, 2009.

—. "Jesus und Pilatus: Der wahre König und der Repräsentant des Kaisers im Johannesevangelium." Pages 337–93 in *Christ and the Emperor.* Edited by G. van Belle and J. Verheyden. BTS 20. Leuven: Peeters, 2014.

—. "Johannine Christology and Eschatology." Pages 101–32 in *Beyond Bultmann: Reckoning a New Testament Theology.* Edited by B. W. Longenecker and M. C. Parsons. Waco: Baylor University Press, 2014.

—. "Love-Relations in the Fourth Gospel: Establishing a Semantic Network." Pages 171–98 in *Repetitions and Variations in the Fourth Gospel: Style, Text, Interpretation.* Edited by Gilbert van Belle, Michael Labahn, and Petrus Maritz. BETL 223. Leuven: Peeters, 2009.

—. "Sehen oder Nicht-Sehen? (Die Heilung des blind Geborenen)—Joh 9,1–41." Pages 725–741 in *Kompendium der frühchristlichen Wundererzählungen. Vol. 1: Die Wunder Jesu.* Edited by R. Zimmermann. Gütersloh: Gütersloher Verlagshaus, 2013.

—. "'Wie Mose die Schlange in der Wüste erhöht hat …': Zur frühjüdischen Deutung der 'ehernen Schlange' und ihrer christologischen Rezeption in Johannes 3:14 f." Pages 89–145 in *Die Herrlichkeit des Gekreuzigten.* Edited by J. Schlegel. WUNT 307. Tübingen: Mohr Siebeck, 2013.

Frey, Jörg and Uta Poplutz, eds. *Narrativität und Theologie im Johannesevangelium.* BThS 130. Neukirchen-Vluyn: Neukirchener Verlagshaus, 2012.

Frey, Jörg and Uta Poplutz. "Narrativität und Theologie im Johannesevangelium." Pages 1–8 in *Narrativität und Theologie im Johannesevangelium.* Edited by Jörg Frey and Uta Poplutz. BThS 130. Neukirchen-Vluyn: Neukirchener Verlagshaus, 2012.

Frey, Jörg, Clare K. Rothschild, and Jens Schröter, eds. *Die Apostelgeschichte im Kontext antiker und frühjüdischer Historiographie.* BZNW 162. Berlin: de Gruyter, 2009.

Frey, Jörg, Jan G. Van der Watt, and Ruben Zimmermann, eds. *Imagery in the Gospel of John: Terms, Forms, Themes and Theology of Figurative Language.* WUNT 200. Tübingen: Mohr Siebeck, 2006.

Fricke, Harald. *Norm und Abweichung: Eine Philosophie der Literatur.* Beck'sche Elementarbücher. München: Beck, 1981.

Fritz, Gerd. *Historische Semantik.* Sammlung Metzler 313. 2nd ed. Stuttgart: Metzler, 2006.

Frow, John. *Genre.* The New Critical Idiom. New York: Routledge, 2005.

Frye, Northrop. *Anatomy of Criticism: Four Essays.* Princeton: Princeton University Press, 1957.

Fusillo, Massimo. "Modern Critical Theories and the Ancient Novel." Page 277–305 in *The Novel in the Ancient World.* Edited by Gareth Schmelling. Leiden: Brill, 1996.

Futre Pinheiro, Marilia P. "The Genre of the Novel: A Theoretical Approach." Pages 201–16 in *A Companion to the Ancient Novel.* Edited by Edmund P. Cueva and Shannon N. Byrne. London: Routledge, 2014.

Gadamer, Hans-Georg. *Truth and Method.* New York: Continuum, 1997.

Gagarin, Michael. *Antiphon the Athenian: Oratory, Law, and Justice in the Age of the Sophists.* Austin: University of Texas Press, 2002.

Gardner-Smith, Percival. *Saint John and the Synoptic Gospels.* Cambridge: Cambridge University Press, 1938.

Geeraerts, Dirk. *Diachronic Prototype Semantics: A Contribution to Historical Lexicology.* Oxford: Clarendon Press, 1997.

Genette, Gérard. *Narrative Discourse Revisited.* Ithaca: Cornell University Press, 1988.
—. *Palimpsests: Literature in the Second Degree.* Translated by Channa Newman and Claude Doubinsky. Stages 8. Lincoln: University of Nebraska Press, 1997.
—. *Paratexts: Thresholds of Interpretation.* Translated by Jane E. Lewin. Literature, Culture, Theory 20. Cambridge: Cambridge University Press, 1997.
Giblin, C. H. "Suggestion, Negative Response, and Positive Action in St. John's Portrayal of Jesus (John 2,1–11; 4,46–54; 7,2–14; 11,1–44)." *NTS* 26 (1979/80): 197–211.
—. "Two Complementary Literary Structures in John 1:1–18." *JBL* 104 (1985): 87–103.
Glad, Clarence. *Paul and Philodemus: Adaptability in Epicurean and Early Christian Psychagogy.* Leiden: Brill, 1995.
Godet, Frédéric. *Commentar zu dem Evangelium Johannis.* Hannover: Carl Meyer, 1869.
Goldhill, Simon "Genre." Pages 185–200 in *The Cambridge Companion to the Greek and Roman Novel.* Edited by Tim Whitmarsh. Cambridge: Cambridge University Press, 2008.
—. *The Invention of Prose.* Greece & Rome: New Surveys in the Classics 32. Oxford: Oxford University Press, 2002.
Goodman, Martin. "Memory and Its Uses in Judaism and Christianity in the Early Roman Empire: The Portrayal of Abraham." Pages 69–82 in *Historical and Religious Memory in the Ancient World.* Edited by B. Dignas and R. R. R. Smith. Oxford: Oxford University Press, 2012.
Gordley, Matthew. "The Johannine Prologue and Jewish Didactic Hymn Traditions: A New Case for Reading the Prologue as a Hymn." *JBL* 128 (2009): 781–802.
Gourgues, Michel. "Le Paraclet, l'esprit de vérité: Deux désignations, deux functions." Pages 83–108 in *Theology and Christology in the Fourth Gospel: Essays by the Members of the SNTS Johannine Writings Seminar.* Edited by Gilbert van Belle, Jan G. van der Watt, and P. Maritz. BETL 184. Leuven: Leuven University Press, 2005.
Gregory, Andrew F. and C. Kavin Rowe. *Rethinking the Unity and the Reception of Luke and Acts.* Columbia, SC: University of Columbia Press, 2010.
Greimas, Algirdas Julien and Joseph Courtés. "Débrayage." *Sémiotique* 79–82.
—. "Embrayage." *Sémiotique* 119–121.
—. " Énonciation." *Sémiotique* 125–128.
—. "Narrativité." *Sémiotique* 247–250.
—. *Sémiotique: Dictionnaire raisonné de la théorie du langage.* Paris: Hachette, 1979.
Grimaldi, William M. A. "The Sources of Rhetorical Argumentation by Enthymeme." Pages 115–59 in *Landmark Essays on Aristotelian Rhetoric.* Edited by Richard Leo Enos and Lois Peters Agnew. Mahwah: Lawrence Erlbaum Associates, 1998.
Guilding, Aileen. *The Fourth Gospel and Jewish Worship: A Study of the Relation of St. John's Gospel to the Ancient Jewish Lectionary System.* Oxford: Clarendon Press, 1960.
Guzmán, Y. F., N. C. Tronson, V. Jovasevic et al. "Fear-Enhancing Effects of Septal Oxytocin Receptors." *Nature Neuroscience* 16 (2013): 1185–87.
Habermann, Ruth. "Das Evangelium nach Johannes: Orte der Frauen." Pages 527–41 in *Kompendium feministische Bibelauslegung.* Edited by L. Schottroff and M.-Th. Wacker. 2nd ed. Gütersloh: Gütersloher Verlagshaus, 1999.
Hägerland, Tobias. "John's Gospel: A Two-Level Drama?" *JSNT* 25 (2003): 309–22.
Hägg, Thomas. *The Art of Biography in Antiquity.* Cambridge: Cambridge University Press, 2012.

Hahn, F. "Die Formgeschichte des Evangeliums: Voraussetzungen, Ausbau und Tragweite." Pages 427–477 in idem, *Zur Formgeschichte des Evangeliums.* Wege der Forschung 81. Darmstadt: Wissenschaftliche Buchgesellschaft, 1985.

Haldimann, Konrad. *Rekonstruktion und Entfaltung: Exegetische Untersuchungen zu Joh 15 und 16.* BZNW 104. Berlin: de Gruyter, 2000.

Hallbäck, Geert. *Det Nye Testamente: En lærebog.* Copenhagen: Anis, 2010.

—. "The Gospel of John as Literature: Literary Readings of the Fourth Gospel." Pages 31–46 in *New Readings in John. Literary and Theological Perspective: Essays from the Scandinavian Conference on the Fourth Gospel in Århus 1997.* Edited by Johannes Nissen and Sigfred Pedersen. JSNTSup 182. Sheffield: Sheffield Academic Press, 1999.

Hammer, Margaret L. *Giving Birth: Reclaiming Biblical Metaphor for Pastoral Practice.* Louisville: John Knox, 1994.

Harris, Elizabeth. *Prologue and Gospel: The Theology of the Fourth Evangelist.* JSNTSup 107. Sheffield: Sheffield Academic Press, 1994.

Harrison, Stephen. "Epic Extremities: The Openings and Closures of Books in Apuleius' *Metamorphoses.*" Pages 239–254 in *The Ancient Novel and Beyond.* Edited by Stelios Panayotakis, Maaike Zimmerman, and Wytse Keulen. Mnemosyne Supplements 241. Leiden: Brill, 2003.

Hartenstein, Judith. "Aus Schmerz wird Freude (Die gebärende Frau) – Joh 16,21 f." Pages 840–47 in *Kompendium der Gleichnisse Jesu.* Edited by R. Zimmermann et al. 2nd ed. Gütersloh: Gütersloher Verlag, 2015.

Heath, Stephen. "The Politics of Genre." Pages 163–74 in *Debating World Literature.* Edited by Christopher Prendergast. London: Verso, 2004.

Hedrick Charles W. "Authorial Presence and Narrator in John." Pages 74–93 in *Gospel Origins and Christian Beginnings.* Edited by James E. Goehring, Charles W. Hedrick, and Jack Thomas Sanders. Sonoma: Polebridge, 1990.

—. *History and Silence: The Purge and Rehabilitation of Memory in Late Antiquity.* Austin: University of Texas Press, 2000.

Heininger, Bernhard. *Metaphorik, Erzählstruktur und szenisch-dramatische Gestaltung in den Sondergutgleichnissen bei Lukas.* NTAbh 24. Münster: Aschendorff, 1991.

Hemer, Colin. *The Book of Acts in the Setting of Hellenistic History.* WUNT 49. Tübingen: Mohr, 1989.

Hempfer, Klaus W. *Gattungstheorie: Information und Synthese.* München: Fink, 1973.

Hengel, Martin. "Der dionysische Messias: Zur Auslegung des Weinwunders in Kana (Joh 2,1–11)." Pages 568–600 in idem, *Jesus und die Evangelien.* WUNT 211. Tübingen: Mohr Siebeck, 2007.

—. "The Interpretation of the Wine Miracle at Cana: John 2.1–11." Pages 83–112 in *The Glory of Christ in the New Testament.* Festschrift G. B. Caird. Edited by L. D. Hurst and N. T. Wright. Oxford: Oxford University Press, 1987.

Hentschel, Anni. "Umstrittene Wunder—mehrdeutige Zeichen im Johannesevangelium." In *Wunder in evangelischer und orthodoxer Perspektive.* Edited by Stefan Alkier and Ioan Dumitru Popoiu. Kleine Schriften des Fachbereichs Evangelische Theologie der Goethe-Universität Frankfurt am Main 6. Leipzig: Evangelische Verlagsanstalt, 2015 (forthcoming).

Hock, Ronald F. "The Greek Novel." Pages 127–46 in *Greco-Roman Literature and the New Testament.* Edited by David E. Aune. SBLSBS 21. Atlanta: Scholars, 1988.

Hock, Ronald F., J. Bradley Chance, and Judith Perkins, eds. *Ancient Fiction and Early Christian Narrative*. SBLSymS 6. Atlanta: Scholars, 1998.

Hoegen-Rohls, Christina. *Der nachösterliche Johannes: Die Abschiedsreden als hermeneutischer Schlüssel zum vierten Evangelium*. WUNT 2/84. Tübingen: Mohr Siebeck, 1996.

Hofrichter, Peter. *Für und wider die Priorität des Johannesevangeliums: Symposion in Salzburg am 10. März 2000*. Theologische Texte und Studien 9. Hildesheim: Olms, 2002.

Hogan, Patrick Colm. *Affective Narratology: The Emotional Structure of Stories*. Lincoln: University of Nebraska Press, 2011.

—. *Philosophical Approaches to the Study of Literature*. Gainesville: University of Florida Press, 2000.

—. *The Mind and Its Stories: Narrative Universals and Human Emotion*. Cambridge: Cambridge University Press, 2003.

Hornblower, Simon. *Commentary on Thucydides*. 3 vols. Oxford: Oxford University Press, 1991–2008.

—. *Thucydides and Pindar: Historical Narrative and the World of Epinikian Poetry*. Oxford: Oxford University Press, 2006.

Hoskyns, Edwyn C. *The Fourth Gospel*. Edited by Francis N. Davey. 2nd rev. ed. London: Faber and Faber, 1947.

Hunt, Steven A., D. Francois Tolmie, and Ruben Zimmermann, eds. *Character Studies in the Fourth Gospel*. WUNT 314. Tübingen: Mohr Siebeck, 2013.

Hunter, Archibald M. *The Gospel according to John*. CBC. Cambridge: Cambridge University Press, 1965.

Hurtado, Larry W. "Oral Fixation and New Testament Studies? 'Orality', 'Performance,' and Reading Texts in Early Christianity." *NTS* 60 (2014): 321–40.

Hyon, Sunny. "Genre in Three Traditions: Implications for ESL." *TESOL Quarterly* 4 (1996): 693–722.

Iser, Wolfgang. *Prospecting: From Reader Response to Literary Anthropology*. Baltimore: Johns Hopkins University Press, 1989.

Jackson, Howard M. "Ancient Self-Referential Conventions and Their Implications for the Authorship and Integrity of the Gospel of John." *JTS* 50 (1999): 1–34.

Jamieson, Kathleen M. "Antecedent Genre as Rhetorical Constraint." *Quarterly Journal of Speech* 61 (1975): 406–415.

Jauss, Hans Robert. "Theory of Genre and Medieval Literature." Pages 76–109 in *Toward an Aesthetic of Reception*. Translated by Timothy Bahti. Brighton: The Harvester Press, 1982.

Johnson Hodge, Caroline. *If Sons, Then Heirs: A Study of Kinship and Ethnicity in the Letters of Paul*. Oxford: Oxford University Press, 2007.

Jonge, Marinus de. *Jesus, Stranger from Heaven and Son of God: Jesus Christ and the Christians in Johannine Perspective*. Translated by John E. Steely. Sources for Biblical Study 11. Missoula: Scholars, 1977.

Jonsen, Albert R. and Stephen Toulmin. *The Abuse of Casuistry: A History of Moral Reasoning*. Berkeley: University of California Press, 1988.

Jülicher, Adolf. *Einleitung in das Neue Testament*. 5/6th ed. Tübingen: Mohr Siebeck, 1906.

—. *Die Gleichnisreden Jesu*. 2nd ed. Tübingen: Mohr Siebeck, 1910.

Kaipuram, Simon. *Paroimiai in the Fourth Gospel and the Johannine Parables of Jesus' Self-Revelation (with special Reference to John 12:24: the Grain of Wheat)*. Rome: Pontificia Universitas Gregoriana, 1993.

Kammler, Hans-Christian. "Die ‚Zeichen' des Auferstandenen." Pages 191–211 in O. Hofius and H.-Chr. Kammler, *Johannesstudien*. WUNT 88. Tübingen: Mohr Siebeck, 1996.

Käsemann, Ernst. *Jesu letzter Wille nach Johannes 17*. 3rd ed. Tübingen: Mohr Siebeck, 1971.

—. "The Structure and Purpose of the Prologue to John's Gospel." Pages 138–67 in idem, *New Testament Questions of Today*. London: SCM, 1968.

Keener, Craig S. *Acts: An Exegetical Commentary: Introduction and 1:1–2:47*. Grand Rapids: Baker, 2012.

—. *The Gospel of John: A Commentary*. 2 vols. Peabody: Hendrickson, 2003.

Kelber, Werner H. *The Oral and the Written Gospel: The Hermeneutics of Speaking and Writing in the Synoptic Tradition, Mark, Paul, and Q*. 2nd ed. Minneapolis: Fortress, 1997.

Keller, Rudi and Ilja Kirschbaum. *Bedeutungswandel: Eine Einführung*. Berlin: de Gruyter, 2003.

Kennedy, George A. *Invention and Method: Two Rhetorical Treatises from the Hermogenic Corpus*. WGRW 15. Atlanta: Society of Biblical Literature, 2005.

Kerr, Alan R. *The Temple of Jesus' Body: The Temple Theme in the Gospel of John*. JSNTSup 220. London: Sheffield Academic Press, 2002.

Kierspel, Lars. *The Jews and the World in the Fourth Gospel: Parallelism, Function, and Context*. WUNT 2/220. Tübingen: Mohr Siebeck, 2006.

Kim, Lawrence. "Time." Pages 145–61 in *The Cambridge Companion to the Greek and Roman Novel*. Edited by Tim Whitmarsh. Cambridge: Cambridge University Press, 2008.

Klauck, Hans-Josef. "Der Weggang Jesu: Neue Arbeiten zu Joh 13–17." *BZ* 40 (1996): 236–50.

Klauser, Theodor et al., eds. *Reallexikon für Antike und Christentum*. Stuttgart: Hiersemann, 1950–.

Klein, Michael L. *The Fragment-Targums of the Pentateuch according to Their Extant Sources*. 2 vols. AnBib 76. Rome: Biblical Institute Press, 1980.

Klink, Edward W. *The Sheep of the Fold: The Audience and Origin of the Gospel of John*. SNTSMS 141. Cambridge: Cambridge University Press, 2007.

Koch, Klaus. *The Growth of the Biblical Tradition: The Form-Critical Method*. London: Adam & Charles Black, 1969.

Koester, Craig. *Symbolism in the Fourth Gospel: Meaning, Mystery, Community*. 2nd ed. Minneapolis: Augsburg Fortress, 2003.

Konstan, David. *Sexual Symmetry: Love in the Ancient Novel and Related Genres*. Princeton: Princeton University Press, 1994.

Konstan, David and Ilaria Rameli. "The Novel and Christian Narrative." Pages 180–97 in *A Companion to the Ancient Novel*. Edited by Edmund P. Cueva and Shannon N. Byrne. London: Routledge, 2014.

Kowalski, B. *Die Hirtenrede (Joh 10,1–18) im Kontext des Johannesevangeliums*. SBB 31. Stuttgart: Katholisches Bibelwerk, 1996.

Kudlien, Fridolf. "Geburt I (medizinisch)." *RAC* 9:36–43.

Labahn, Michael. "Beim Mahl am Kohlenfeuer trifft man sich wieder (Die Offenbarung beim wunderbaren Fang): Joh 21,1–14." Pages 764–780 in *Kompendium der frühchristlichen Wundererzählungen I: Die Wunder Jesu.* Edited by Ruben Zimmermann. Gütersloh, Gütersloher Verlagshaus, 2013.

—. "'Blinded by the Light': Blindheit und Licht in Joh 9 im Spiel von Variation und Wiederholung zwischen Erzählung und Metapher." Pages 453–504 in *Repetitions and Variations in the Fourth Gospel: Style, Text, Interpretation.* Edited by Gilbert van Belle, Michael Labahn and Petrus Maritz. BETL 223. Leuven: Peeters, 2009.

—. "Fischen nach Bedeutung—Sinnstiftung im Wechsel literarischer Kontexte: Der wunderbare Fischfang in Johannes 21 zwischen Inter- und Intratextualität." *SNTU* 32 (2007): 115–40.

—. *Jesus als Lebensspender: Untersuchungen zu einer Geschichte der johanneischen Tradition anhand ihrer Wundergeschichten.* BZNW 98. Berlin: de Gruyter, 1998.

—. *Offenbarung in Zeichen und Wort: Untersuchungen zur Vorgeschichte von Joh 6,1–25a und seiner Rezeption in der Brotrede.* WUNT 2/117. Tübingen: Mohr Siebeck, 2000.

Labahn, Michael and Manfred Lang. "Johannes und die Synoptiker: Positionen und Impulse seit 1990." Pages 443–516 in *Kontexte des Johannesevangeliums: Das vierte Evangelium in religions- und traditionsgeschichtlicher Perspektive.* Edited by Jörg Frey and Udo Schnelle. WUNT 175. Tübingen: Mohr Siebeck, 2004.

Lakoff, George and Marc Johnson. *Metaphors We Live By.* Chicago: University of Chicago Press, 1980.

—. *Women, Fire, and Dangerous Things: What Categories Reveal About the Mind.* Chicago: University of Chicago Press, 1987.

Lang, Manfred. "Johanneische Abschiedsreden und Senecas Konsolationsliteratur: Wie konnte ein Römer Joh 13,31–17,26 lesen?" Pages 365–412 in *Kontexte des Johannesevangeliums: Das vierte Evangelium in religions- und traditionsgeschichtlicher Perspektive.* Edited by J. Frey and U. Schnelle. WUNT 175. Tübingen: Mohr Siebeck, 2004.

—. *Johannes und die Synoptiker: Eine redaktionsgeschichtliche Analyse von Joh 18–20 vor dem markinischen und lukanischen Hintergrund.* FRLANT 182. Göttingen: Vandenhoeck & Ruprecht, 1999.

Larsen, Kasper Bro. "At sige ret farvel: Jesus' afskedstale i genrehistorisk belysning (Joh 13–17)." Pages 85–102 in *Hvad er sandhed? Nye læsninger af Johannesevangeliet.* Edited by G. Buch-Hansen and C. Petterson. Frederiksberg: Alfa, 2009.

—. "*Famous Last Words:* Jesu ord på korset i evangeliernes sammenhæng." *Kritisk Forum for Praktisk Teologi* 111 (2008): 3–11.

—. "Narrative Docetism: Christology and Storytelling in the Gospel of John." Pages 346–55 in *The Gospel of John and Christian Theology.* Edited by Richard Bauckham and Carl Mosser. Grand Rapids: Eerdmans, 2008.

—. *Recognizing the Stranger: Recognition Scenes in the Gospel of John.* BIS 93. Leiden: Brill, 2008.

Lateiner, Donald. "Heralds and Corpses in Thucydides." *Classical World* 71 (1977): 97–106.

Layton, Bentley. *The Gnostic Scriptures.* Garden City: Doubleday, 1983.

Lee, Dorothy A. *Flesh and Glory: Symbolism, Gender and Theology in the Gospel of John.* New York: Crossroad, 2002.

Leroy, Herbert. *Rätsel und Missverständnis: Ein Beitrag zur Formgeschichte des Johannesevangeliums.* BBB 30. Bonn: Hanstein, 1968.

Leung, Mavis M. "The Narrative Function and Verbal Aspect of the Historical Present in the Fourth Gospel." *JETS* 51 (2008): 703–20.

Levine, Amy-Jill. *Short Stories by Jesus: The Enigmatic Parables of a Controversial Rabbi.* New York: HarperOne, 2014.

Levine, Amy-Jill and Marianne Blickenstaff, eds. *A Feminist Companion to John.* FCNTECW 2. London: Sheffield Academic Press, 2003.

Levinson, Joshua. "Dialogical Reading in the Rabbinic Exegetical Narrative." *Poetics Today* 25 (2004): 497–528.

Lieu, Judith M. "The Mother of the Son in the Fourth Gospel." *JBL* 117 (1998): 61–77.

Lim, Timothy. "The Origins and Emergence of Midrash in Relation to the Hebrew Scriptures." Pages 595–612 in *The Midrash: An Encyclopedia of Biblical Interpretation in Formative Judaism.* Edited by Jacob Neusner and Alan J. Avery-Peck. Leiden: Brill, 2004.

Lincoln, Andrew T. *Truth on Trial: The Lawsuit Motif in the Fourth Gospel.* Peabody: Hendrickson, 2000.

Lindars, Barnabas. *The Gospel of John*, New Century Bible. London: Oliphants, 1972.

Lindemann, Andreas. *Der Erste Korintherbrief.* HNT 9/I. Tübingen: Mohr Siebeck, 2000.

Lischer, Richard. *Reading the Parables.* Louisville: Westminster John Knox, 2014.

Littman, Robert J. *Tobit: The Book of Tobit in Codex Sinaiticus.* Septuagint Commentary Series. Leiden: Brill, 2008.

Lohmeyer, Ernst. "Die Fußwaschung." *ZNW* 38 (1939): 74–94.

Lohse, Wolfram. "Die Fußwaschung (Joh 13,1–20): Eine Geschichte ihrer Deutung." 2 vols. Erlangen: Univ. Dissertation, 1967.

Loisy, A. *Le quatrième évangile.* 2nd ed. Paris: Picard, 1921.

Lundhaug, Hugo. *Images of Rebirth: Cognitive Poetics and Transformational Psychology in the Gospel of Philip and the Exegesis on the Soul.* NHS 73. Leiden: Brill, 2010.

Lütgehetmann, W. *Die Hochzeit zu Kana (Joh 2,1–11): Zu Ursprung und Deutung einer Wundererzählung im Rahmen johanneischer Redaktionsgeschichte.* Biblische Untersuchungen 20. Regensburg: Pustet, 1990.

Lyotard, Jean-François. *La Differend: Phrases in Dispute.* Translated by G. van den Abeele. Manchester: Manchester University Press, 1988.

Maccini, Robert G. *Her Testimony is True: Women as Witnesses according to John.* JSNTSup 125. Sheffield: Sheffield Academic Press, 1996.

MacNeil, Heather. "What Finding Aids Do: Archival Description as Rhetorical Genre in Traditional and Web-Based Environments." *Archival Sciences* 12 (2012): 485–500.

MacRae, George W. "Theology and Irony in the Fourth Gospel." Pages 83–96 in *The Word in the World: Essays in Honour of F. L. Moriarty.* Edited by Richard J. Clifford and George W. MacRae. Cambridge: Weston College, 1973. Reprint in *The Gospel of John as Literature: An Anthology of Twentieth-Century Perspectives.* Edited by Mark G. W. Stibbe. NTTS 17. Leiden: Brill, 1993, 103–113.

Margolin, Uri. "Telling in the Plural: From Grammar to Ideology." *Poetics Today* 21 (2000): 591–618.

Marincola, John. *Authority and Tradition in Ancient Historiography.* Cambridge: Cambridge University Press, 1997.

Markschies, Christoph. "Eusebius liest die Apostelgeschichte: Zur Stellung der Apostelgeschichte in der frühchristlichen Geschichtsschreibung." *Early Christianity* 4 (2013): 474–98.

Marsh, John. *The Gospel of St. John.* PNTC. Philadelphia: Westminster, 1968.
Martin, Dale B. *The Corinthian Body.* New Haven: Yale University Press, 1995.
Martin, Michael W. "Betrothal Journey Narratives." *CBQ* 70 (2008): 505–23.
Martyn, J. Louis. *History and Theology in the Fourth Gospel.* 2nd rev. ed. Nashville: Abingdon, 1979.
McCarter Jr., P. Kyle. *I Samuel: A New Translation with Introduction, Notes and Commentary.* AB 8. Garden City: Doubleday, 1980.
McDonough, Sean. *Christ as Creator: Origins of a New Testament Doctrine.* Oxford: Oxford University Press, 2010.
McHugh, John. *John 1–4.* ICC. London: T&T Clark, 2009.
McHugh, Mary R. *Manipulating Memory: Remembering and Defaming Julio-Claudian Women.* Madison: University of Wisconsin, 2004.
McNamara, Martin. "Logos of the Fourth Gospel and *Memra* of the Palestinian Targum: Ex 12:42." *ExpTim* 79 (1986): 115–117.
McWhirter, Jocelyn. *The Bridegroom Messiah and the People of God: Marriage in the Fourth Gospel.* SNTSMS 138. Cambridge: Cambridge University Press, 2006.
Meeks, Wayne A. *In Search of the Early Christians.* New Haven: Yale University Press, 2002.
—. "The Man From Heaven in Johannine Sectarianism." *JBL* 91 (1972): 44–72. Repr. in *Interpretations of the Fourth Gospel.* Edited by John Ashton. London: SPCK; Philadelphia: Fortress, 1986, 141–73.
—. *The Prophet-King: Moses Traditions and the Johannine Christology.* NovTSup 14. Leiden: Brill, 1967.
Meier, John P. *A Marginal Jew: Rethinking the Historical Jesus, I: The Roots of the Problem and the Person.* New York: Doubleday, 1991.
Mendels, Doron. "How Was Antiquity Treated in Societies with a Hellenistic Heritage? And Why Did the Rabbis Avoid Writing History?" Pages 131–151 in *Antiquity in Antiquity: Jewish and Christian Pasts in the Greco-Roman World.* Edited by G. Gardner and K. L. Osterloh. TSAJ 123. Tübingen: Mohr Siebeck, 2008.
Mettinger, Tryggve N. D. *King and Messiah: The Civil and Sacral Legitimation of the Israelite Kings.* ConBOT 8. Lund: CWK Gleerup, 1976.
Miller, Carolyn R. "Genre as Social Action." *Quarterly Journal of Speech* 70 (1984): 151–167.
Miller, Ed L. *Salvation-History in the Prologue of John: The Significance of John 1:3–4.* NovTSup 60. Leiden: Brill, 1989.
—. "The Johannine Origins of the Johannine Logos." *JBL* 112 (1993): 445–57.
Misztal, Barbara A. *Theories of Social Remembering.* Maidenhead: Open University Press, 2003.
Mittmann-Richert, Ulrike. "Erinnerung und Heilserkenntnis im Lukasevangelium: Ein Beitrag zum neutestamentlichen Verständnis des Abendmahls." Pages 243–76 in *Memory in the Bible and Antiquity: The Fifth Durham-Tübingen Research Symposium.* Edited Stephen C. Barton, Loren T. Stuckenbruck, and Benjamin G. Wold. WUNT 212. Tübingen: Mohr Siebeck, 2007.
Moles, John. "Luke's Preface: The Greek Decree, Classical Historiography and Christian Redefinitions." *NTS* 57 (2011): 461–82.
Moloney, Francis J. *Glory not Dishonor: Reading John 13–21.* Minneapolis: Augsburg Fortress, 1998.
—. *John.* SP 4. Collegeville: Liturgical Press, 1998.

—. *Love in the Gospel of John: An Exegetical, Theological, and Literary Study*. Grand Rapids: Baker, 2013.

—. "The Fourth Gospel and the Jesus of History." *NTS* 46 (2000): 42–58.

Montiglio, Silvia. *Love and Providence: Recognition in the Ancient Novel*. London: Oxford University Press, 2012.

Moody Smith, Dwight. *John Among the Gospels: The Relationship in Twentieth-Century Research*. Minneapolis: Fortress, 1992.

Muilenburg, James. "Form Criticism and Beyond." *JBL* 88 (1969): 1–18.

Munck, Johannes. "Discours d'adieu dans le Nouveau Testament et dans la littérature biblique." Pages 155–170 in *Aux sources de la tradition chrétienne: Mélanges offerts à M. Maurice Goguel à l'occasion de son soixante-dizième anniversaire*. Edited by O. Cullmann and P. Menoud. Neuchâtel: Delachaux & Niestlé, 1950.

Mussner, Franz. *Die Johanneische Sehweise und die Frage nach dem historischen Jesus*. QD 28. Freiburg im Breisgau: Herder, 1965.

Myers, Alicia D. *Characterizing Jesus: A Rhetorical Analysis on the Fourth Gospel's Use of Scripture in Its Presentation of Jesus*. LNTS 458. London: T&T Clark, 2012.

Najman, Hindy. "The Idea of Biblical Genre: From Discourse to Constellation." Pages 307–22 in *Prayer and Poetry in the Dead Sea Scrolls and Related Literature: Essays in Honor of Eileen Schuller on the Occasion of Her 65th Birthday*. Edited by Jeremy Penner, Ken M. Penner, and Cecilia Wassen. Leiden: Brill, 2012.

Newsom, Carol A. "Pairing Research Questions and Theories of Genre: A Case Study of the Hodayot." *DSD* 17 (2010): 437–50.

—. "Spying Out the Land: A Report from Genology." Pages 437–50 in *Seeking Out the Wisdom of the Ancients: Essays Offered to Honor Michael V. Fox on the Occasion of His Sixty-Fifth Birthday*. Edited by Ronald L. Troxel, Kelvin G. Friebel, and Dennis Robert Magary. Winona Lake: Eisenbrauns, 2005. Reprint in *Bakhtin and Genre Theory in Biblical Studies*. Edited by Roland Boer. SemeiaSt 63. Leiden: Brill, 2008, 19–30.

Neyrey, Jerome H. "Jacob Traditions and the Interpretation of John 4:10–26." *CBQ* 41 (1979): 419–37.

Nicklas, Tobias. "Biblische Texte als Texte der Bibel interpretiert: Die Hochzeit zu Kana (Joh 2,1–11) in 'biblischer Auslegung'." *ZKT* 126 (2004): 241–56.

Nicolai, Roberto. *La storiografia nell' educazione antica*. Biblioteca di materiali e discussioni per l'analisi dei testi classici 10. Pisa: Giardini, 1992.

Nielsen, Jesper Tang. *Die kognitive Dimension des Kreuzes: Zur Deutung des Todes Jesu im Johannesevangelium*. WUNT 2/263. Tübingen: Mohr Siebeck, 2009.

Niemand, Christoph. *Die Fusswaschungserzählung des Johannesevangeliums: Untersuchungen zu ihrer Entstehung und Überlieferung im Urchristentum*. SA 114. Roma: Pontificio Ateneo S. Anselmo, 1993.

Nolan, Brian M. *The Royal Son of God: The Christology of Matthew 1–2 in the Setting of the Gospel*. OBO 23. Göttingen: Vandenhoeck & Ruprecht, 1979.

Norden, Eduard. *Agnostos Theos: Untersuchungen zur Formengeschichte religiöser Rede*. Leipzig: Teubner, 1913.

Nunlist, Rene. *The Ancient Critic at Work: Terms and Concepts of Literary Criticism in Greek Scholia*. Cambridge: Cambridge University Press, 2009.

Nussbaum, Martha. *Love's Knowledge: Essays on Philosophy and Literature*. London: Oxford University Press, 1992.

O'Day, Gail. *Revelation in the Fourth Gospel: Narrative Mode and Theological Claim.* Philadelphia: Fortress, 1986.

O'Gorman, Ellen. "Repetition and Exemplarity in Historical Thought: Ancient Rome and the Ghosts of Modernity." Pages 264–79 in *The Western Time of Ancient History: Historiographical Encounters with the Greek and Roman Pasts.* Edited by A. Lianeri. Cambridge: Cambridge University Press, 2011.

Olsson, Birger. *Structure and Meaning in the Fourth Gospel: A Text-Linguistic Analysis of John 2:1–11 and 4:1–42.* ConBNT 6. Lund: Almquist & Wiksell, 1974.

Orlikowski, Wanda J. and JoAnne Yates. "Genre Repertoire: The Structure of Communicative Practices in Organizations." *Administrative Science Quarterly* 39 (1994): 541–574.

Østenstad, G. *Patterns of Redemption in the Fourth Gospel: An Experiment in Structural Analysis.* Studies in the Bible and Early Christianity 38. Lampeter: Edwin Mellen, 1988.

Palmer, A. *Fictional Minds.* Lincoln: University of Nebraska Press. 2004

Paré, Anthony. "Genre and Identity: Individuals, Institutions, and Ideology." Pages 57–71 in *The Rhetoric and Ideology of Genre.* Edited by R. Coe, L. Lingard, and T. Teslenko. Cresskill: Hampton, 2002.

Paré, Anthony, Doreen Starke-Meyerring, and Lynn McAlpine. "The Dissertation as Multi-Genre: Many Readers, Many Readings." Pages 179–193 in *Genre in a Changing World.* Edited by C. Bazerman, A. Bonini, and D. Figueiredo. Fort Collins: Parlor, 2009.

Parente, Faosto. "The Impotence of Titus, or Flavius Josephus's *Bellum Judaicum* as an Example of 'Pathetic' Historiography." Pages 45–69 in *Josephus and Jewish History in Flavian Rome and Beyond.* Edited by Joseph Sievers and Gaia Lembi. JSJSup 104. Leiden: Brill, 2005.

Parsenios, George L. *Departure and Consolation: The Johannine Farewell Discourses in Light of Greco-Roman Literature.* NovTSup 117. Leiden: Brill, 2005.

—. "'No Longer in the World' (John 17:11): The Transformation of the Tragic in the Fourth Gospel." *HTR* 98 (2005): 1–18.

—. *Rhetoric and Drama in the Johannine Lawsuit Motif.* WUNT 258. Tübingen: Mohr Siebeck, 2010.

Parsons, Mikael and Richard I. Pervo. *Rethinking the Unity of Luke and Acts.* Minneapolis: Fortress, 1993.

Pastorelli, David. *Le Paraclet dans le corpus johannique.* BZNW 142. Berlin: de Gruyter, 2006.

Peek, Werner. *Griechische Grabgedichte.* SQAW 7. Berlin: Akademischer Verlag, 1960.

Pepe, Cristina. *The Genres of Rhetorical Speeches in Greek and Roman Antiquity.* International Studies in the History of Rhetoric 5. Leiden: Brill, 2013.

Perkins, Pheme. *Gnosticism and the New Testament.* Minneapolis: Fortress, 1993.

Pervo, Richard I. *Acts.* Hermeneia. Minneapolis: Fortress, 2009.

—. *Profit with Delight: The Literary Genre of the Acts of the Apostles.* Philadelphia: Fortress, 1987.

Petersen, Anders Klostergaard. "At the End of the Road: Reflections on a Popular Scholarly Metaphor." Pages 45–72 in *The Formation of the Early Church.* Edited by Jostein Ådna. Tübingen: Mohr Siebeck, 2005.

—. "The Diversity of Apologetics: From Genre to a Mode of Thinking." Pages 15–41 in *Critique and Apologetics: Jews, Christians, and Pagans in Antiquity.* Edited by Anders-Christian Jakobsen, Jörg Ulrich, and David Brakke. Frankfurt am Main: Peter Lang 2009.

—."Wisdom as Cognition: Creating the Others in the Book of Mysteries and in 1 Cor 1 and 2." Pages 405–32 in *The Wisdom Texts from Qumran and the Development of Sapiential Thought*. Edited by Charlotte Hempel, Armin Lange, and Hermann Lichtenberger. BETL 159. Leuven: Leuven University Press; Peeters, 2002.

Platter, Charles. *Aristophanes and the Carnival of Genres*. Arethusa. Baltimore: Johns Hopkins University Press, 2007.

Plepelits, Karl. "Achilles Tatius." Pages 387–414 in *The Novel in the Ancient World*. Edited by Gareth Schmelling. Leiden: Brill, 1996.

Price, Simon. "Memory and Ancient Greece." Pages 15–36 in *Historical and Religious Memory in the Ancient World*. Edited by B. Dignas and R. R. R. Smith. Oxford: Oxford University Press, 2012.

Pryor, John. "Jesus and Israel in the Fourth Gospel: John 1:11." *NovT* 32 (1990): 201–18.

Raaflaub, Kurt. "Ulterior Motives in Ancient Historiography: What Exactly, and Why?" Pages 189–210 in *Intentional History: Spinning Time in Ancient Greece*. Edited by Lin Foxhall, Hans-Joachim Gehrke, and Nino Luraghi. Stuttgart: Franz Steiner Verlag, 2010.

Rau, Eckhard. *Reden in Vollmacht: Hintergrund, Form und Anliegen der Gleichnisse Jesu*. FRLANT 149. Göttingen: Vandenhoeck & Ruprecht, 1990.

Reardon, Bryan P. *The Form of Greek Romance*. Princeton: Princeton University Press, 1995.

Reardon, Bryan P., ed. *Collected Ancient Greek Novels*. Berkeley: University of California Press, 1989.

Rehm, Rush. *Greek Tragic Theatre*. New York: Routledge, 1994.

Rehmann, Luiza Sutter. *Geh - Frage die Gebärerin: Feministisch-befreiungstheologische Untersuchungen zum Gebärmotiv in der Apokalyptik*. Gütersloh: Gütersloher Verlagshaus, 1995.

Rein, Matthias. *Die Heilung des Blindgeborenen (Joh 9): Tradition und Redaktion*. WUNT 2/73. Tübingen: Mohr Siebeck, 1995.

Reinhartz, Adele. "Anonymity and Character in the Books of Samuel." *Semeia* 63 (1993): 117–42.

—. "Great Expectations: A Reader-Oriented Approach to Johannine Christology and Eschatology." *Journal of Literature and Theology* 3 (1989): 61–76.

—. *Why Ask My Name? Anonymity and Identity in Biblical Narrative*. New York: Oxford University Press, 1998.

Reiser, Marius. *Sprache und literarische Formen des Neuen Testaments*. UTB 2197. Paderborn: Schöningh, 2001.

Renan, Ernest. *The Life of Jesus*. London: Trübner, 1891.

Rich, Adrienne. *Of Woman Born: Motherhood as Experience and Institution*. New York: Norton, 1976.

Richardson, Brian, ed. *Narrative Beginnings: Theories and Practices*. Lincoln: University of Nebraska Press, 2008.

Richter, Georg. *Die Fusswaschung im Johannesevangelium: Geschichte ihrer Deutung*. Biblische Untersuchungen 1. Regensburg: Pustet, 1967.

Roberts, Celia and Sirkant Sarangi. "Uptake of Discourse Research in Interprofessional Settings: Reporting from Medical Consultancy." *Applied Linguistics* 24 (2003): 338–59.

Rochais, G. "Jean 7: Une construction littéraire dramatique, à la manière d'un scenario." *NTS* 39 (1993): 355–78.

—. "La Formation du Prologue (Jn. 1:1–18)." *SE* 37 (1985): 7–9.

Rosch, Eleanor. "Cognitive Representations of Semantic Categories." *Journal of Experimental Psychology: General* 104 (1975): 192–233.

Rosch, Eleanor and Carolyn B. Mervis. "Family Resemblances: Studies in the Internal Structure of Categories." *Cognitive Psychology* 7 (1975): 573–605.

Rosmarin, Adena. *The Power of Genre.* Minneapolis: University of Minnesota Press, 1985.

Rossi, Andreola. *Contexts of War: Manipulation of Genre in Virgilian Battle Narrative.* Ann Arbor: University of Michigan Press, 2004.

Rushton, Kathleen P. *The Parable of the Woman in Childbirth of John 16:21: A Metaphor for the Death and Glorification of Jesus.* Lewiston: Edwin Mellen, 2010.

—. "The (Pro)creative Parables of Labour and Childbirth (Jn 3.1–10 and 16.21–22)." Pages 206–29 in *The Lost Coin: Parables of Woman, Work and Wisdom.* Edited by M. A. Beavis. London: Sheffield Academic Press, 2002.

Russel, David R. "Rethinking Genre in School and Society: An Activity Theory Analysis." *Written Communication* 4 (1997): 504–54.

Salier, Willis Hedley. *The Rhetorical Impact of the Sēmeia in the Gospel of John.* WUNT 2/186. Tübingen: Mohr Siebeck, 2004.

Sawyer, Deborah. "John 19.34: From Crucifixion to Birth, or Creation?" Pages 130–39 in *A Feminist Companion to John.* Edited by Amy-Jill Levine and Marianne Blickenstaff. FCNTECW 2. Sheffield: Sheffield Academic Press, 2003.

Schelfer, Lochlan. "The Legal Precision of the Term 'παράκλητος'." *JSNT* 32 (2009): 131–50.

Schmidt, Karl Ludwig. "Der johanneische Charakter der Erzählung vom Hochzeitswunder in Kana." Pages 32–43 in *Harnack-Ehrung.* Leipzig, 1921.

—. *Der Rahmen der Geschichte Jesu: Literarkritische Untersuchungen zur ältesten Jesusüberlieferung.* Berlin: Trowitzsch & Sohn, 1919.

—. "Formgeschichte." Pages 2:638–40 in *Die Religion in Geschichte und Gegenwart.* Edited by Herman Gunkel. 2nd ed. Tübingen: Mohr, 1928.

Schnackenburg, Rudolf. *Das Johannesevangelium. III. Teil: Kommentar zu Kap. 13–21.* 2nd ed. HThKNT 4. Freiburg: Herder, 1976.

—. "Logos-hymnus und johanneischer Prolog." *BZ* 1 (1957): 69–109.

—. *The Gospel According to St. John.* 3 vols. Translated by K. Smyth et al. London: Burns & Oates, 1968–82.

—. "Zu den joh. Immanenzformeln." Pages 105–110 in idem, *Die Johannesbriefe,* HThKNT. Freiburg: Herder, 1963.

Schnelle, Udo. *Antidocetic Christology in the Gospel of John: An Investigation of the Place of the Fourth Gospel in the Johannine School.* Translated by Linda M. Maloney. Minneapolis: Fortress, 1992.

—. *Antidoketische Christologie im Johannesevangelium.* Göttingen: Vandenhoeck & Ruprecht, 1987.

—. *Das Evangelium nach Johannes.* THKNT 4. Leipzig: Evangelische Verlagsanstalt, 1998.

—. *Einleitung in das Neue Testament.* 8th ed. Göttingen: Vandenhoeck & Ruprecht, 2013.

Scholtissek, Klaus. *In ihm sein und bleiben: Die Sprache der Immanenz in den johanneischen Schriften.* HBS 21. Freiburg: Herder, 2000.

—. "Mündiger Glaube. Zur Architektur und Pragmatik johanneischer Begegnungsgeschichten: Joh 5 und 9." Pages 107–158 in *Paulus und Johannes.* Edited by D. Sänger and U. Mell. WUNT 198. Tübingen: Mohr Siebeck, 2006.

Schroer, Silvia and Ruben Zimmermann. "Geburt." Pages 186–190 in *Sozialgeschichtliches Wörterbuch zur Bibel.* Edited by Frank Crüsemann et al. Gütersloh: Gütersloher Verlag, 2009.

Schryer, Catherine. "Genre and Power: A Cronotopic Analysis." Pages 73–102 in *The Rhetoric and Ideology of Genre.* Edited by R. Coe, L. Lingard, and T. Teslenko. Cresskill: Hampton Press, 2002.

—. "Records as Genre." *Written Communication* 10 (1993): 200–34.

—. "The Lab vs the Clinic." Pages 105–124 in *Genre and the New Rhetoric.* Edited by A. Freedman and P. Medway. London: Taylor & Francis, 1994.

Schulz, Siegfried. *Untersuchungen zur Menschensohn-Christologie im Johannesevangelium: Zugleich ein Beitrag zur Methodengeschichte der Auslegung des 4. Evangeliums.* Göttingen: Vandenhoeck & Ruprecht, 1957.

Schwartz, Daniel R. *Reading the First Century: On Reading Josephus and Studying Jewish History of the First Century.* WUNT 300. Tübingen: Mohr Siebeck, 2013.

Schwartz, Saundra. "Clitophon the *Moichos:* Achilles Tatius and the Trial Scene in the Greek Novel." *Ancient Narrative* 1 (2000–2001): 93–113.

Schweizer, Alexander. *Das Evangelium Johannis nach seinem inneren Wert und seiner Bedeutung für das Leben Jesu kritisch untersucht.* Leipzig: Weidmann, 1841.

Scott, Bernhard B. *Hear then the Parable: A Commentary on the Parables of Jesus.* Minneapolis: Fortress Press, 1989.

Seeman, Don. "'Where is Sarah Your Wife?' Cultural Poetics of Gender and Nationhood in the Hebrew Bible." *HTR* 91 (1998): 103–25.

Segal, Judy Z. "Breast Cancer Narratives as Public Rhetoric: Genre itself and the Maintainance of Ignorance." *Linguistics and the Human Sciences* 3 (2007): 3–23.

Segovia, Fernando. *The Farewell of the Word: The Johannine Call to Abide.* Minneapolis: Fortress, 1991.

Seim, Turid Karlsen. "Descent and Divine Paternity in the Gospel of John: Does the Mother Matter?" *NTS* 51 (2005): 361–75.

—. "Motherhood and the Making of Fathers in Antiquity: Contextualizing Genetics in the Gospel of John," Pages 99–124 in *Woman and Gender in Ancient Religions: Interdisciplinary Approaches.* Edited by Stephen P. Ahearne-Kroll, Paul A. Holloway and James A. Kelhoffer. WUNT 263. Tübingen: Mohr Siebeck, 2010.

Seitel, Peter. "Theorizing Genres—Interpreting Works," *New Literary History* 34 (2003): 275–97.

Sellin, Gerhard. "'Gattung' und 'Sitz im Leben' auf dem Hintergrund der Problematik von Mündlichkeit und Schriftlichkeit synoptischer Erzählungen." *EvT* 50 (1990): 311–331.

Sheridan, Ruth. "Identity, Alterity, and the Gospel of John." *BibInt* 22 (2014): 188–209.

—. "Issues in the Translation of *Hoi Ioudaioi* in the Fourth Gospel." *JBL* 132 (2013): 671–95.

—. "John's Gospel and Modern Genre Theory: The Farewell Discourse (John 13–17) as a Test Case." *ITQ* 75 (2010): 287–99.

—. *Retelling Scripture: 'The Jews' and the Scriptural Citations in John 1:19–12:15.* BIS 110. Leiden: Brill, 2012.

Shutt, R. J. H. *Studies in Josephus.* London: SPCK, 1961.

Siegert, Folker. *Das Evangelium des Johannes in seiner ursprünglichen Gestalt: Wiederherstellung und Kommentar.* Schriften des Institutum Judaicum Delitzschianum 6. Göttingen: Vandenhoeck & Ruprecht, 2007.

Sievers, Joseph and Gaia Lembi, eds. *Josephus and Jewish History in Flavian Rome and Beyond.* JSJSup 104. Leiden: Brill, 2005.

Sinding, Michael. "After Definitions: Genre, Categories, and Cognitive Science." *Genre* 35 (2002): 181–219.

Sittig, Claudius. "Reiseliteratur." Pages 7:1144–56 in *Historisches Wörterbuch der Rhetorik.* Edited by Gerd Ueding. Tübingen: Max Niemeyer, 1992–2014.

Skinner, Christopher W. "The World: Promise and Unfulfilled Hope." Pages 61–70 in *Character Studies in the Fourth Gospel: Narrative Approaches to Seventy Figures in John.* Edited by S. A. Hunt, D. F. Tolmie, and R. Zimmermann. WUNT 314. Tübingen: Mohr Siebeck, 2013.

Skinner, Christopher W., ed. *Characters and Characterization in the Gospel of John.* London: Bloomsbury, 2013.

Skouvig, Laura. "Genres of War: Informing a City." Pages 133–154 in *Genre Theory in Information Studies.* Edited by J. Andersen. Bingley: Emerald Group, 2015.

Sloan, Michael C. "Aristotle's *Nicomachean Ethics* as the Original *Locus* for the *Septem Circumstantiae.*" *Classical Philology* 105 (2010): 236–51.

Smart, Graham. "A Central Bank's 'Communications Strategy': The Interplay of Activity, Discourse Genres, and Technology in a Time of Organizational Change." Pages 9–61 in *Writing Selves/Writing Societies.* Edited by C. Bazerman and D. R. Russel. Fort Collins: The WAC Clearinghouse, 2003.

Smedegaard, Anne. "Genre and Writing Pedagogy." Pages 21–55 in *Genre and ….* Edited by S. Auken, P. S. Lauridsen, and A. J. Rasmussen. Copenhagen Studies in Genre 2. Copenhagen: Ekbátana, 2015.

Smith, Justin Marc. *Why βίος? On the Relationship between Gospel Genre and Implied Audience.* LNTS 518. London: Bloomsbury T&T Clark, 2015.

Smith, Mark S. *The Memoirs of God: History, Memory, and the Experience of the Divine in Ancient Israel.* Minneapolis: Fortress Press, 2004.

Snodgrass, Klyne R. *Stories with Intent: A Comprehensive Guide to the Parables of Jesus.* Grand Rapids: Eerdmans, 2008.

Söding, Thomas. "Die Gleichnisse Jesu als metaphorische Erzählungen: Hermeneutische und exegetische Überlegungen." Pages 81–118 in *Die Sichtbarkeit des Unsichtbaren: Zur Korrelation von Text und Bild im Wirkungskreis der Bibel.* Edited by B. Janowski and N. Zchomelidse. AGWB 3. Stuttgart: Deutsche Bibelgesellschaft, 2003.

Solevåg, Anna R. *Birthing Salvation: Gender and Class in Early Christian Childbearing Discourse.* BIS 121. Leiden: Brill, 2013.

Spinuzzi, Clay and Mark Zachry. "Genre Ecologies: An Open-System Approach to Understanding and Constructing Documentation." *Journal of Computer Documentation* 24 (2000): 169–181.

Staley, Jeffrey Lloyd. *The Print's First Kiss: A Rhetorical Investigation of the Implied Reader in the Fourth Gospel.* SBLDS 82. Atlanta: Scholars Press, 1988.

Stare, Mira. "Gibt es Gleichnisse im Johannesevangelium?" Pages 321–64 in *Hermeneutik der Gleichnisse Jesu: Methodische Neuansätze zum Verstehen urchristlicher Parabeltexte.* Edited by R. Zimmermann. 2nd ed. WUNT 238. Tübingen: Mohr Siebeck, 2011.

Stibbe, Mark W. G. *John.* Sheffield: Sheffield Academic Press, 1994.
—. *John as Storyteller: Narrative Criticism and the Fourth Gospel.* SNTSMS 73. Cambridge: Cambridge University Press, 1990.
—. *John's Gospel*, London: Routledge, 1994.
Stibbe, Mark W. G., ed. *The Gospel of John as Literature: An Anthology of Twentieth-Century Perspectives.* NTTS 17. Leiden: Brill, 1993.
Stock, Brian. *Listening for the Text: On the Uses of the Past.* Baltimore: Johns Hopkins University Press, 1990.
Stroumsa, Gedalyahu A. *Esoteric Traditions and the Roots of Christian Mysticism.* Leiden: Brill, 2005.
Stube, John Carlson. *A Graeco-Roman Rhetorical Reading of the Farewell Discourse.* LNTS 309. London: T&T Clark, 2006.
Swales, John. *Research Genres.* Cambridge: Cambridge University Press, 2004.
Sweeney, Marwin A. "Form Criticism." Pages 58–89 in *To Each its Own Meaning: Biblical Criticisms and Their Application.* Edited by S. L. McKenzie and S. R. Haynes. Louisville: Westminster John Knox, 1999.
Tachino, Tosh. "Theorizing Uptake and Knowledge Mobilization: A Case for Intermediary Genre." *Written Communication* 29 (2012): 455–76.
Talbert, Charles. *What is a Gospel? The Genre of the Canonical Gospels.* Philadelphia: Fortress, 1977.
Tentler, Thomas N. *Sin and Confession on the Eve of the Reformation.* Princeton: Princeton University Press, 1977.
Thatcher, Tom. "Riddles, Repetitions, and the Literary Unity of the Johannine Discourses." Pages 357–77 in *Repetitions and Variations in the Fourth Gospel: Style, Text, Interpretation.* Edited by Gilbert van Belle, Michael Labahn, and Petrus Maritz. BETL 223. Leuven: Peeters, 2009.
—. *The Riddles of Jesus in John: A Study in Tradition and Folklore.* SBLMS 53. Atlanta: SBL, 2000.
Theißen, Gerd. *A Theory of Primitive Christian Religion.* London: SCM Press, 1999.
—. "Die Erforschung der synoptischen Tradition seit R. Bultmann: Ein Überblick über die formgeschichtliche Arbeit im 20. Jahrhundert." Pages 409–52 in Rudolf Bultmann, *Die Geschichte der synoptischen Tradition.* 10th ed. with a postscript by G. Theißen. FRLANT 29. Göttingen: Vandenhoeck & Ruprecht, 1995.
—. *Urchristliche Wundergeschichten: Ein Beitrag zur formgeschichtlichen Erforschung der synoptischen Evangelien.* 7th ed. Gütersloh: Gütersloher Verlagshaus, 1998.
Theißen, Gerd and Annette Merz. *Der historische Jesus: Ein Lehrbuch.* Göttingen: Vandenhoeck & Ruprecht, 1997.
Theobald, Michael. *Das Evangelium nach Johannes: Kapitel 1–12.* Regensburger Neues Testament 4/1. Regensburg: Pustet, 2009.
—. "Der Tod Jesu im Spiegel seiner 'letzten Worte' vom Kreuz." *TQ* 190 (2010): 1–31.
—. "'Erinnert euch der Worte, die ich euch gesagt habe …' (Joh 15,20)." Pages 105–130 in *Die Macht der Erinnerung.* Edited by O. Fuchs and B. Janowski. Jahrbuch für Biblische Theologie 22. Neukirchen-Vluyn: Neukirchener Verlag, 2008.
—. *Eucharistie als Quelle sozialen Handelns: Eine biblisch-frühkirchliche Besinnung.* BThS 77. Neukirchen-Vluyn: Neukirchener Verlagshaus, 2012.
—. *Herrenworte im Johannesevangelium.* HbS 34. Freiburg: Herder, 2002.

Thieme, Katja. "Uptake and Genre: The Canadian Reception of Suffrage Militancy." *Women's Studies International Forum* 29 (2006): 279–88.

Thomas, Christine M. *The Acts of Peter, Gospel Literature, and the Ancient Novel: Rewriting the Past.* Oxford: Oxford University Press, 2003.

Thomaskutty, Johnson. *Dialogue in the Book of Signs: A Polyvalent Analysis of John 1:19–12:50.* BIS 136. Leiden: Brill, 2015.

Thurén, Lauri. *Parables Unplugged: Reading the Lukan Parables in Their Rhetorical Context.* Minneapolis: Fortress, 2014.

Thurman, Eric. "Novel Men: Masculinity and Empire in Mark's Gospel and Xenophon's *An Ephesian Tale.*" Pages 185–229 in *Mapping Gender in Ancient Religious Discourses.* Edited by Caroline Vander Stichele and Todd Penner. Leiden: Brill, 2007.

Thyen, H. *Das Johannesevangelium.* HNT 6. Tübingen: Mohr Siebeck, 2005.

—. "Johannes und die Synoptiker: Auf der Suche nach einem neuen Paradigma zur Beschreibung ihrer Beziehungen anhand von Beobachtungen an Passions- und Ostererzählungen." Pages 81–108 in *John and the Synoptics.* Edited by Adelbert Denaux. BETL 101. Leuven: Leuven University Press, 1992.

—. "Liegt dem Johannesevangelium eine Semeia-Quelle zugrunde?" Pages 443–52 in idem, *Studien zum Corpus Iohanneum.* WUNT 214. Tübingen: Mohr Siebeck, 2007.

Thyssen, Henrik Pontoppidan. "Philosophical Christology in the New Testament." *Numen* 53 (2006): 133–176.

Tierno, Michael. *Aristotle's* Poetics *for Screenwriters: Storytelling Secrets from the Greatest Mind in Western Civilization.* New York: Hyperion, 2002.

Tilborg, Sjef van. *Imaginative Love in John.* BIS 2. Leiden: Brill, 1993.

Tilg, Stefan. *Chariton of Aphrodisias and the Invention of the Greek Love Novel.* Oxford: Oxford University, 2010.

Todorov, Tzvetan. "The Origin of Genres." *New Literary History* 8 (1976): 159–70.

—. *The Fantastic: A Structural Approach to a Literary Genre.* Translated by R. Howard. Ithaca: Cornell University Press, 1975.

Tolbert, Mary Ann. *Perspectives on the Parables: An Approach to Multiple Interpretations.* Philadelphia: Fortress Press, 1979.

Tolmie, D. Francois. *Jesus' Farewell to the Disciples: John 13:1–17:26 in Narratological Perspective.* BIS 12. Leiden: Brill, 1995.

Troxel, Ronald L., Kelvin G. Friebel, and Dennis R. Magary, eds. *Seeking out the Wisdom of the Ancients: Essays Offered to Honor Michael V. Fox on the Occasion of His Sixty-Fifth Birthday.* Winona Lake: Eisenbrauns, 2005.

Via, Dan O. *Kerygma and Comedy in the New Testament: A Structuralist Approach to Hermeneutic.* Philadelphia: Fortress Press, 1975.

Vines, Michael E. *The Problem of Markan Genre: The Gospel of Mark and the Jewish Novel.* AcBib 3. Leiden: Brill, 2002.

Von Wahlde, Urban. *The Gospel and Letters of John.* 3 vols. ECC. Grand Rapids: Eerdmans, 2010.

Votaw, Clyde Weber. *The Gospels and Contemporary Biographies in the Greco-Roman World.* Philadelphia: Fortress, 1970.

Wagener, Fredrik. "Figuren als Handlungsmodelle." Diss. Johannes Gutenberg-Universität. Mainz, 2015.

Warren, Meredith. "Equal to God: Divine (Mis)Identification in the Greek Novels and the Gospel of John." Paper presented at the International Meeting of the Society of Biblical Literature, London 2011.

—. *My Flesh Is Meat Indeed: A Nonsacramental Reading of John 6:51–58*. Minneapolis: Fortress, 2015.

Wasyl, Anna Marie. *Genres Rediscovered: Studies in Latin Miniature Epic, Love Elegy, and Epigram of the Romano-Barbaric Age*. Kraków: Jagiellonian University Press, 2011.

Watt, Jan G. van der. "Ethics and Ethos in the Gospel According to John." *ZNW* 97 (2006): 147–76.

—. *Family of the King: Dynamics of Metaphor in the Gospel according to John*. BIS 47. Leiden: Brill, 2000.

Webb, Ruth. *Ekphrasis, Imagination and Persuasion in Ancient Rhetorical Theory and Practice*. Surrey: Ashgate, 2009.

Weisse, Christian Hermann. *Die evangelische Geschichte kritisch und philosophisch bearbeitet*. Leipzig: Breitkopf & Härtel, 1838.

Weissenrieder, Annette and Robert B. Coote, eds. *The Interface of Orality and Writing: Speaking, Seeing, Writing in the Shaping of New Genres*. WUNT 260. Tübingen: Mohr Siebeck, 2010.

Welck, Christian. *Erzählte Zeichen: Die Wundergeschichten des Johannesevangeliums literarisch untersucht. Mit einem Ausblick auf Joh 21*. WUNT 2/69. Tübingen: Mohr Siebeck, 1994.

Wellhausen, Julius. *Das Evangelium Johannis*. Berlin: Reimer, 1908.

Wendt, Hans-Hinrich. *Das Johannesevangelium: Eine Untersuchung seiner Entstehung und seines geschichtlichen Wertes*. Göttingen: Vandenhoeck & Ruprecht, 1900.

Westermann, Claus. *Genesis 1–11*. Translated by John J. Scullion. CC. Minneapolis: Fortress, 1994.

Whitmarsh, Tim. "Philostratus." Pages 413–33 in *Time in Ancient Greek Literature*. Vol. 2 of *Ancient Greek Literature Studies in Ancient Greek Narrative*. Edited by Irene J. F. de Jong and René Nünlist. Leiden: Brill, 2007.

Williams, P. J. "Not the Prologue of John." *JSNT* 33 (2011): 375–86.

Williamson, R. "Pesher: A Cognitive Model of the Genre." *DSD* 17 (2010): 307–31.

Wills, Lawrence M. *Quest of the Historical Gospel: Mark, John and the Origins of the Gospel Genre*. London: Routledge, 1997.

Winsor, Ann Roberts. *A King Is Bound in the Tresses: Allusions to the Song of Songs in the Fourth Gospel*. New York: Peter Lang, 1999.

Winsor, Dorothy A. "Ordering Work: Blue-Collar Literacy and the Political Nature of Genre." *Written Communication* 17 (2000): 155–84.

Wise, Jennifer. *Dionysus Writes: The Invention of Theatre in Ancient Greece*. Ithaca: Cornell University Press, 2000.

Witherington III, Ben. *John's Wisdom: A Commentary on the Fourth Gospel*. Louisville: Westminster John Knox, 1995.

Wittke, Sigmar W. "Wöchnerinnen in griechischen Weiheepigrammen: Eine Studie auf der Grundlage der Anthologia Palatina." Diss. Erlangen-Nürnberg, 1973.

Wohl, Victoria. *Intimate Commerce: Exchange, Gender, and Subjectivity in Greek Tragedy*. Austin: University of Texas Press, 1998.

Wright, Benjamin. "Joining the Club: A Suggestion about Genre in Jewish Texts." *DSD* 17 (2010): 288–313.

Yarbro Collins, Adela. *Is Mark's Gospel a Life of Jesus? The Question of Genre.* Milwaukee: Marquette University Press, 1990.

—. *Mark: A Commentary.* Hermeneia. Minneapolis: Fortress, 2007.

Zeitlin, Froma I. *Playing the Other: Gender and Society in Classical Greek Literature.* Chicago: University of Chicago Press, 1996.

Zeller, Dieter. *Der erste Brief an die Korinther.* KEK 5. Göttingen: Vandenhoeck & Ruprecht, 2010.

Zimmermann, Mirjam and Ruben Zimmermann. "Brautwerbung in Samarien? Von der moralischen zur metaphorischen Interpretation in Joh 4." *ZNT* 1 (1998): 40–51.

—. "Der Freund des Bräutigams: Deflorations- oder Christuszeuge?" *ZNW* 90 (1999): 123–30.

Zimmermann, Ruben. "Are there Parables in John? It is Time to Revisit the Question." *Journal for the Study of the Historical Jesus* 9 (2011): 243–76.

—. *Christologie der Bilder im Johannesevangelium: Die Christopoetik des vierten Evangeliums unter besonderer Berücksichtigung von Joh 10.* WUNT 171. Tübingen: Mohr Siebeck, 2004.

—. "From a Jewish Man to the Savior of the World: Narrative and Symbols Forming a Step by Step Christology in John 4,1–42." Pages 99–118 in *Studies in the Gospel of John and its Christology.* Edited by Joseph Verheyden et al. BETL 265. Leuven: Peeters, 2014.

—. "Frühchristliche Wundererzählungen: Eine Hinführung." Pages 5–67 in *Kompendium der frühchristlichen Wundererzählungen: Band 1: Die Wunder Jesu.* Edited by R. Zimmermann. Gütersloh: Gütersloher Verlagshaus, 2013.

—. "Gattung 'Wundererzählung': Eine literaturwissenschaftliche Definition." Pages 311–43 in *Hermeneutik der frühchristlichen Wundererzählungen: Geschichtliche, literarische und rezeptionsorientierte Perspektiven.* Edited by B. Kollmann and R. Zimmermann. WUNT 339. Tübingen: Mohr Siebeck, 2014.

—. "Imagery in John: Opening up Paths into the Tangled Thicket of John's Figurative World." Pages 1–43 in *Imagery in the Gospel of John: Terms, Forms, Themes, and Theology of Johannine Figurative Language.* Edited by J. Frey, J. G. van der Watt, and R. Zimmermann. WUNT 200. Tübingen: Mohr Siebeck, 2006.

—. "Jesus' Parables and Ancient Rhetoric: The Contribution of Aristotle and Quintilian to the Form Criticism of the Parables." Pages 238–58 in *Hermeneutik der Gleichnisse Jesu: Methodische Neuansätze zum Verstehen urchristlicher Parabeltexte.* Edited by R. Zimmermann. 2nd ed. WUNT 238. Tübingen: Mohr Siebeck, 2011.

—. "Metaphoric Networks as Hermeneutic Keys in the Gospel of John: Using the Example of the Mission Imagery." Pages 381–402 in *Repetitions and Variations in the Fourth Gospel: Style, Text, Interpretation.* Edited by Gilbert van Belle, Michael Labahn, and Petrus Maritz. BETL 223. Leuven: Peeters, 2009.

—. "Narrative Ethik im Johannesevangelium am Beispiel der Lazarus-Perikope Joh 11." Pages 133–70 in *Narrativität und Theologie im Johannesevangelium.* Edited by J. Frey and U. Poplutz. BThS 130. Neukirchen-Vluyn: Neukirchener Theologie, 2012.

—. "Parabeln – sonst nichts! Gattungsbestimmung jenseits der Klassifikation in 'Bildwort', 'Gleichnis', 'Parabel' und 'Beispielerzählung'." Pages 383–419 in *Hermeneutik der*

Gleichnisse Jesu: Methodische Neuansätze zum Verstehen urchristlicher Parabeltexte. Edited by R. Zimmermann. 2nd ed. WUNT 238. Tübingen: Mohr Siebeck, 2011.

—. *Puzzling the Parables of Jesus: Methods and Interpretation.* Minneapolis: Augsburg Fortress, forthcoming.

Zimmermann, Ruben, ed. *Kompendium der frühchristlichen Wundererzählungen: Band 1. Die Wunder Jesu.* Gütersloh: Gütersloher Verlagshaus, 2013.

Zipes, Jack. *Why Fairy Tales Stick: The Evolution and Relevance of a Genre.* New York: Routledge, 2006.

Zumstein, Jean. "Crise du savoir et conflit des interpretations selon Jean 9: Un exemple du travail de l'école johannique." Pages 167–78 in *Early Christian Voices in Texts, Traditions and Symbols.* Festschrift F. Bovon. Edited by D. H. Warren, A. G. Book, and D. W. Pao. BIS 66. Leiden: Brill, 2003.

—. "Die Bibel als literarisches Kunstwerk—gezeigt am Beispiel der Hochzeit zu Kana (Joh 2,1–11)." Pages 68–82 in *Gott im Buchstaben? Neue Ansätze der Exegese.* Edited by Th. Söding. QD 225. Freiburg: Herder, 2007.

—. *L'Évangile selon Saint Jean (1–12).* CNT 4a. Genève: Labor et Fides, 2014.

—. *L'Évangile selon Saint Jean (13–21).* CNT 4b. Genève : Labor et Fides, 2007.

—. "The Mother of Jesus and the Beloved Disciple: How a New Family is Established Under the Cross." Pages 641–45 in *Character Studies in the Fourth Gospel: Narrative Approaches to Seventy Figures in John.* Edited by S. A. Hunt, D. F. Tolmie, and R. Zimmermann. WUNT 314. Tübingen: Mohr Siebeck, 2013.

Zymner, Rüdiger. *Gattungstheorie: Probleme und Positionen der Literaturwissenschaft.* Paderborn: Mentis, 2003.

—. "Parabel." Pages 6:502–14 in *Historisches Wörterbuch der Rhetorik.* Edited by Gerd Ueding. Tübingen: Max Niemeyer, 1992–2014.

Subject Index

Index of Ancient Texts

1. Hebrew Bible

2. Deuterocanonical Books and Septuagint

3. Old Testament Pseudepigrapha

4. Dead Sea Scrolls

5. Ancient Jewish Writers

6. New Testament

7. Rabbinic Works

8. Early Christian Writings

9. Greco-Roman Literature